PRAISE FOR DR. REISMAN'S SCHOLARSHIP

The sexual revol[ution...]
Reisman has spe[nt...]

— **National Review**

Dr. Judith Reisman is one of the world's foremost experts on Alfred Kinsey and the harmful effects of pornography, particularly with respect to children. Dr. Reisman's research has opened my eyes to the root cause of many of the societal ills we deal with today. Stolen Honor is a book unlike others you may have read. This book will not be one you read and put on a shelf. It will stay with you and affect how you view the world, the family, human sexuality, and the culture wars.

Mathew D. Staver, Founder and Chairman of Liberty Counsel

Dr. Reisman has produced a scholarly and devastating study revealing the ugly and frighteningly dangerous pseudo-scientific assault on our children's innocence.

Dr. Laura Schlessinger

When I first came across Judith Reisman's work, my view of Alfred Kinsey was unquestioningly benign. Dr. Reisman's allegations—that Kinsey had collaborated with paedophiles to obtain so-called 'scientific data' on children's reactions to sexual activity with adults—were so serious that they clearly warranted much deeper examination than they had received.

In the course of producing my documentary—Kinsey's Paedophiles—it became clear that every substantive allegation Reisman made was not only true but thoroughly sourced with documentary evidence—despite the Kinsey Institute's reluctance to open its files.

My film built on the foundations laid by Dr. Reisman. Those foundations—and the additional evidence we uncovered about Kinsey's involvement with paedophiles who were actively abusing children—make it imperative that his successors at the Kinsey Institute today allow a rigorous and independent investigation of this dark corner of human study.

Tim Tate, UNESCO and Amnesty International Award-winning Producer-Director of "Kinsey's Paedophiles," Yorkshire Television, Great Britain

Judith Reisman explodes, once and for all, the myth that Alfred Kinsey's sex research is scientific. This book will shock you with the little-known facts about a man who has left us with a legacy of misinformation and whose legacy haunts society with a broad array of social disorders and pathologies.

Joseph Farrah, Editor in Chief, WorldNetDaily.com

Dr. Reisman's *Kinsey: Crimes & Consequences** is "must reading" for every American who wants to understand the "demoralization" of our nation. She is a scholar of international renown who brings courage, integrity, tenacity and profound insight to her world-class research and writing, which is sorely needed in America where powerful special interests often distort the truth for financial gain or unconstitutional political ends. Her important work has been successfully presented to Congress, the U.S. Supreme Court, a Presidential Commission, many Executive Branch Departments and to members of the Joint Chiefs of Staff.

Admiral Thomas H. Moorer, USN
Former Chairman, Joint Chiefs of Staff, now deceased

Dr. Reisman's scholarship is sound, accurate and has proven very useful for political and military leaders, private-sector decision-makers or any American. Because her research is so useful, she has taken a lot of fire from powerful special interests. But Reisman marshals historical facts meaningfully, and she is brilliant in her content analysis. Reisman always presents those facts well before Congress, high-level commissions and the highest courts in the land. I strongly recommend that every American read this book and respond to Dr. Reisman's call for citizens and public officials to demand that the Kinsey files be opened and that those responsible for any wrongdoing be held publicly accountable.

Rear Admiral C. A. "Mark" Hill, USN (RET.)
Director, Naval Aviation Foundation

Dr. Reisman: Your manuscript does an impressive and important job of exposing how heavily Kinsey's data relate to criminals and sex deviates…. Kinsey does, to be sure, scatter bits of information about this… no one previously has done the painstaking detective work of pulling the bits and pieces together and estimating the proportion of respondents who were in these categories… your figure of "roughly 86 percent" does appear to be in the right ballpark; but even if the correct figure were only a quarter of that, the effect on Kinsey's validity would be devastating. Overall, your manuscript strongly reinforces my 1949 conclusion that "…it is impossible to say that the book has much value…."

W. Allen Wallis, Past President of The American Statistical
Association and Past Editor of *The Journal of the American*
Statistical Association, **now deceased**

Dr. Reisman's study supports the conclusion that Alfred Kinsey's research was contrived, ideologically driven and misleading. Any judge, legislator or other public official who gives credence to that research is guilty of malpractice and dereliction of duty.

Charles E. Rice, Professor of Law, Notre Dame Law School

***NOTE:** *Stolen Honor Stolen Innocence* was previously published under the title *Kinsey: Crimes & Consequences*

America has undergone a sexual revolution from which it has yet to recover. But if it is to recover from that revolution and restore the moorings we have lost — the protection of children and the reservation of sexuality to marriage — books like Judith Reisman's *Kinsey: Crimes & Consequences** must reach the widest possible audience.

**Charles Donovan, Executive Vice President and
Acting CEO Family Research Council, Washington, D.C.**

*Kinsey: Crimes & Consequences** is an original and comprehensive expose of Alfred C. Kinsey's fraudulent and influential sex 'research.' As Dr. Reisman shows, the Kinsey legacy touches virtually every area of life. It may take years to reverse the damage. But the place to begin is by learning the truth. This book shines a very bright light on a dark topic. It's an eye-opener from the first to the last page.

—**Robert H. Knight, who wrote and directed the video documentary about
Alfred Kinsey entitled** *The Children of Table 34*, **is Senior Director of Cultural
Studies for the Family Research Council, a former** *Los Angeles Times* **news editor
and writer and former Hoover Institution Media Fellow**

We should probably call her Detective Reisman for finding the hidden clue to Kinsey's crimes against children and families. She alone noticed that babies were molested in the name of Kinsey's macabre science, and her book is the victims' grand jury indictment of perhaps the most destructive sexual revolutionary since Caligula. *Kinsey: Crimes & Consequences** is a blueprint for justice for victims of sexual exploitation and abuse. In the face of Kinsey's handbook for perpetrators, Dr. Reisman is the victims' amicus curiae.

**Bruce A. Taylor, President & Chief Counsel, National Law
Center for Children and Families**

This book, *Kinsey: Crimes & Consequences**, is one of the most important works of our times. I have found Dr. Reisman's research to be absolutely invaluable to me as an author, a parent, a social scientist and a college professor. Based on the information in *Kinsey: Crimes & Consequences**, I now use the Kinsey studies as an example of tragically flawed research methodology when I teach college psychology classes. Kinsey was a key step down into the depths of cultural depravity; and now, thanks to Dr. Judith Reisman, we can revisit this "step," but this time on the way back up.

Lt. Col. Dave Grossman, author: *On Killing* **and**
Stop Teaching Our Kids to Kill.

The medical model of human sexuality has been greatly influenced by the teachings of Dr. Alfred Kinsey, a zoologist. Over the last decade, the scientific merit of the *Kinsey Reports* has been found to be completely absent as exposed by the work of Dr. Judith Reisman.

Dr. John R. Diggs, Jr., M.D.

*****NOTE:** *Stolen Honor Stolen Innocence* was previously published under the title *Kinsey: Crimes & Consequences*

STOLEN HONOR STOLEN INNOCENCE

This book was previously published under the title *KINSEY: Crimes & Consequences*

© Judith A. Reisman, PhD — Institute for Media Education
Graphic Design by Heather Kirk, GraphicsForSuccess.com
and by Alfred Moreschi

All rights reserved, including those under International and Pan-American Copyright Conventions. No portion or part of this book may be used or reproduced in any manner whatsoever without written permission, except in the case of brief quotations embodied in critical articles and reviews. For more information, to report any typos or corrections, or to contact Dr. Reisman at the Institute for Media Education, please visit:

www.DrJudithReisman.com

Published by
New Revolution™ Publishers

PO Box 540774
Orlando, Florida 32854
(800) 671-1776
Email: liberty@LC.org
http://www.LC.org

First Edition, print, published by the Institute for Media Education, 1998,
Library of Congress Control Number: 99170286.
Second Edition, print, published by the Institute for Media Education, 2000.
Third Edition, print, published by the Institute for Media Education, 2003.
Previous editions were titled *KINSEY: Crimes & Consequences*
Fourth Edition, print & digital, published by New Revolution Publishers, 2013.

ISBN 978-1-937102-02-9

STOLEN HONOR
STOLEN INNOCENCE

How America was Betrayed by the Lies and Sexual Crimes of a Mad "Scientist"

Judith Reisman, PhD

NEW AUTHOR'S INTRODUCTION

New Revolution Publishers

Previously published under the title *KINSEY: Crimes & Consequences*

What is liberty without wisdom and without virtue? It is the greatest of all possible evils; for it is folly, vice, and madness, without restraint. Men are qualified for civil liberty in exact proportion to their disposition to put moral chains upon their own appetites.... Society cannot exist, unless a controlling power upon will and appetite be placed somewhere; and the less of it there is within, the more there must be without. It is ordained in the eternal constitution of things, that men of intemperate minds cannot be free. Their passions forge their fetters.

> **The Right Honorable Edmund Burke,**
> "Letter to a Member of the National Assembly,"
> 1791, in *The Works of the Right Honorable Edmund Burke*, Volume 4 (1899).

No one man, however brilliant or well-informed, can come in one lifetime to such fullness of understanding as to safely judge and dismiss the customs or institutions of his society, for these are the wisdom of generations after centuries of experiment in the laboratory of history. A youth boiling with hormones will wonder why he should not give full freedom to his sexual desires; and if he is unchecked by custom, morals or laws, he may ruin his life before he matures sufficiently to understand that sex is a river of fire that must be banked and cooled by a hundred restraints if it is not to consume in chaos both the individual and the group.

> **Will and Ariel Durant**
> *The Lessons of History*
> New York: Simon & Schuster (1968, pp. 35-36).

Also by Judith A. Reisman, Ph.D.

"Soft" Porn Plays Hardball: Its Tragic Effects on Women and Children

Images of Children, Crime and Violence in Playboy, Penthouse and Hustler
Project No. 84-JN-AX-K007 the U.S. Department of Justice,
Juvenile Justice and Delinquency Prevention

Partner Solicitation Language as Reflection of Male Sexual Orientation
Reisman & Johnson

Kinsey, Sex and Fraud: The Indoctrination of a People
Reisman et al.

Kinsey, Crimes & Consequences (1st, 2nd and 3rd edition)

Sexual Sabotage: How One Mad Scientist Unleashed a Plague of Corruption and Contagion on America

Stolen Honor Stolen Innocence
(4th edition, title change & new author's introduction)

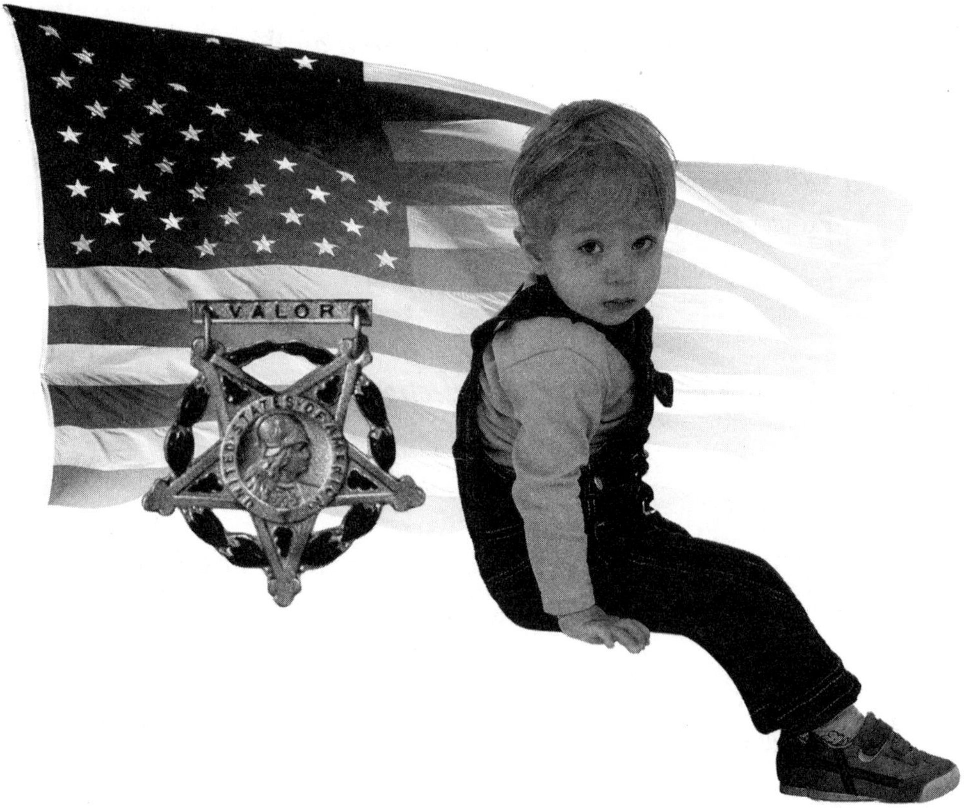
VALOR

TABLE OF CONTENTS

PART I: KINSEY

CHAPTER 1 1
KINSEY'S YOUTH TO FAMILY MAN
- BOYHOOD AND EDUCATION 3
- PREFERENCE FOR BOYS 6
- "MIDNIGHT" COWBOYS 9
- "FAMILY MAN" 11
- MILITANT ATHEIST 13
- CHAPTER 1 NOTES 14

CHAPTER 2 17
THE INDIANA UNIVERSITY SEXOLOGIST
- "MR. MAN" 18
- BERLIN TO BLOOMINGTON 22
- LAYING THE GROUNDWORK 26
- ROCKEFELLER FUNDING 29
- CHOOSING AND CONDITIONING HIS TEAM 30
- SECRETS AS POWER 36
- ROCKEFELLER'S MASS COMMUNICATIONS MACHINE TAKES KINSEY PUBLIC 38
- THE PRETEND STATISTICIAN 41
- DISMISSING THE CRITICS 41
- CHAPTER 2 NOTES 43

PART II: CRIMES

CHAPTER 3 49
RATIONALIZATION OR SCIENCE?
- IS IT SCIENCE? 49
- THE SAMPLE 50
- STATISTICAL CONFUSION OR DECEPTION? 51
- "SCIENTOMANIA" 53
- MASLOW'S "VOLUNTEERS" AND KINSEY'S COERCION 55
- GRAND INQUISITOR OR SCIENTIFIC INTERVIEWING? 56
- "MASSAGING" THE DATA 59
- CHILD-RESEARCH "METHODS" OR SYSTEMATIC SEX ABUSE? 60
- PERPETUAL DAMAGE CONTROL 63
- THE RED QUEEN: WORDS MEAN WHAT I SAY THEY MEAN 65
- CHAPTER 3 NOTES 68

CHAPTER 4 71
STAG FILMS AS SEX RESEARCH
- SEX FILMS AT IU, IN KINSEY'S ATTIC 74
- SEX-TORTURE EXPERIMENTS 76
- WIVES AS SUBJECTS 78
- INSTITUTE FOR THE ADVANCED STUDY OF HUMAN SEXUALITY 82
- CHAPTER 4 NOTES 85

CHAPTER 5 87
AMERICAN MEN: ELIMINATING FATHERS
- WHOM DID KINSEY ACTUALLY INTERVIEW? 88
- KNOWN SUBJECTS 90
- SEX CRIMINALS NOT IN KINSEY'S "UNDERWORLD" CATEGORY 92
- MISSION IN CHICAGO: COLLECT "HOMOSEXUAL HISTORIES" 93
- "NORMAL" REMAINDER 97
- WHY "COLLEGE LEVEL," NOT "COLLEGE"? 97
- WERE ONE PERCENT NORMAL? 99
- THE KRONHAUSENS' FINDINGS 100
- CHAPTER 5 NOTES 103

CHAPTER 6 .... **107**
AMERICAN WOMEN: ELIMINATING MOTHERS
- THE FEMALE DATA 109
- DEFINING "MARRIED" 110
- CENSORING MASLOW 113
- WHY EXCLUDE FEMALE PRISONERS? 116
- WHY EXCLUDE "NONWHITE" WOMEN? 116
- HIDING CHILD SEXUAL ABUSE 118
- NOTHING ABOUT ABORTION OR NARCOTICS 118
- MARITAL ORGASM DATA 120
- PEAK EXPERIENCES 121
- KINSEY ON CAMPUS 123
- THE LOVELESS, CHILDLESS PAJAMA GAME 124
- VENEREAL DISEASE 126
- "EROTICA" IN THE FEMALE VOLUME 128
- CHAPTER 6 NOTES 130

CHAPTER 7 .... **133**
THE CHILD EXPERIMENTS
PART I: THE LITTLE BOY EXPERIMENTS **135**
- TABLE 30: "PRE-ADOLESCENT EROTICISM AND ORGASM" 139
- TABLE 31: "PRE-ADOLESCENT EXPERIENCE IN ORGASM" 140
- TABLE 32: "SPEED OF PRE-ADOLESCENT ORGASM" 142
- TABLE 33: "MULTIPLE ORGASM IN PRE-ADOLESCENT MALES" 144
- TABLE 34: "EXAMPLES OF MULTIPLE ORGASM IN PRE-ADOLESCENT MALES" 144
- DARWIN VERSUS KINSEY: INTERPRETING PHYSIOLOGICAL RESPONSES 146
- SOME CHILDREN STRAPPED OR "HELD DOWN" 148
- "SCIENTIFICALLY TRAINED OBSERVERS" 150

PART II: THE LITTLE GIRL EXPERIMENTS **151**
- "ESTHER," INCEST SURVIVOR INTERVIEW FOR "KINSEY'S PAEDOPHILES" 152
- RECORDS OF 23 YOUNG GIRLS IN "ORGASM" 153
- KINSEY'S ALLEGED GIRL "ORGASM" DATA (FEMALE, P. 127) 154
- GIRL "MASTURBATION" DATA (FEMALE, PP. 177 & 180) 154
- GIRL'S SEXUALLY VICTIMIZED BY MEN AND OLDER BOYS (FEMALE, P. 118] 156
- INCEST OFFENDERS DEFINED AS CHILDREN'S SEXUAL "PARTNERS" 157
- RELATIONSHIP OF ADULT TO GIRL INCEST "VICTIMS" ADDED TO KINSEY'S ORIGINAL UNNAMED TABLE [FEMALE, P. 118] 158
- SEXUALIZED IMAGES OF CHILDREN 160
- WHO CONDUCTED, TIMED, AND FILMED THE EXPERIMENTS? 162

PART III: KINSEY'S NAZI PEDOPHILE **166**
- "THE MOST IMPORTANT PEDOPHILE IN THE CRIMINAL HISTORY OF BERLIN" ... 166
- "KINSEY…ASKED THE PAEDOPHILE SPECIFICALLY FOR MATERIAL OF HIS PERVERSE ACTIONS" 168

PART IV: THE "NEW BIOLOGY" AND "THE KINSEY MODEL" **170**
- THE RESEARCHERS 171
- THE FUNDERS 171
- THREE PIONEERING CENTERS 171
- SEXUAL ATTITUDE RESTRUCTURING (SAR) 173
- SAR AS SEX EDUCATION IN "THE DECADE OF THE BRAIN" 174
- THE PROFESSIONAL SEX FIELD ACCREDITING AGENCIES AND SOCIETIES 175
- SIECUS 177
- IS THE SIECUS/PLAYBOY PARTNERSHIP A RICO CASE IN THE MAKING? 177
- PLANNED PARENTHOOD, BRIEFLY 180
- CHAPTER 7 NOTES 181

PART III: CONSEQUENCES

CHAPTER 8 .... **187**
KINSEY'S IMPACT ON AMERICAN LAW
PART I: "THE AMERICAN LAW INSTITUTE'S MODEL PENAL CODE OF 1955 IS VIRTUALLY A KINSEY DOCUMENT" **187**
- THE AMERICAN LAW INSTITUTE (ALI) MODEL PENAL CODE (MPC) 188

FOUR KINSEY BOOKS CALL FOR "SCIENCE-BASED" SEX-LAW REFORM IN 1948 189
"A BOOK CAN END AN ERA"... 193
DID ERNST AND/OR GUYON WRITE KINSEY'S "LAW" ARGUMENTS? 194
IN 1948 ERNST & LOTH TARGET 52 SEX CRIME LAWS 195

PART II: THE HISTORY OF AMERICA'S "FIXED" LAW ORDER: THE PURITY CRUSADE & COMSTOCK ERA 196

THE HISTORY OF AMERICA'S "FIXED" LAW ORDER:
    ORIGINS OF THE EVOLUTIONARY "STREAM OF THE LAW" AT HARVARD 198
THE HARVARD LAW REVIEW HERALDS THE CALL FOR THE MODEL PENAL CODE............ 199
THE CODE MUST BE CHANGED--IT RELIES UPON THE "COMMON LAW" 200
COMMON LAW SEX OFFENSES YEILD TO KINSEY'S "SOCIAL SCIENCE" DATA 201

PART III: THE ROCKEFELLER FOUNDATION: "WITHIN THE STATE A STATE SO POWERFUL" 202

THE ROCKEFELLER FOUNDATION'S SUPPORT OF
    THE SEXUAL REVOLUTION IN THE NAME OF CODIFICATION 203
KINSEY'S THIRD VOLUME WAS TO BE A LEGAL REPORT 203
"VIRTUALLY EVERY PAGE OF THE KINSEY REPORT TOUCHES ON THE LEGAL CODE" 204

PART IV: APPROXIMATELY 650 CITATIONS TO KINSEY IN LAW REVIEW ARTICLES 1982-2000; 90 MORE BY 2011 205

NONCOMPREHENSIVE "KINSEY" WESTLAW CITES, 1982-2011 205

PART V: "PENALTIES SHOULD BE LIGHTENED" FOR SEX OFFENDERS AND VIOLENT FELONS 211

KINSEY TESTIFIES TO THE CALIFORNIA LEGISLATURE 212
WHAT RIGHTS SHOULD THE PAROLEE HAVE? 213
WHAT RIGHTS SHOULD VICTIMS HAVE? 214
THE ALI-MPC NORMALIZING FORNICATION AND ADULTERY 215
FORNICATION AND ADULTERY LAWS 216
ADULTERER'S "RIPPLE EFFECT" 217
KINSEY: ONE-HALF MARRIED MALES, ONE-FOURTH FEMALES, COMMIT ADULTERY 218
PROFOUND SOCIETAL CONSEQUENCES FROM DECRIMINALIZING ADULTERY,
    COHABITATION AND FORNICATION 219
"DEADBEAT DADS OR FLEECED FATHERS?" THE STRANGE POLITICS OF CHILD SUPPORT 220
NORMALIZING RAPE 221
THE FRESH COMPLAINT AND FORCIBLE RAPE 221
CONSEQUENCES: A "RAPE EPIDEMIC" 223
NEW YORK RAPE DATA PRE- AND POST-KINSEY ERA 223
NORMALIZING STATUTORY RAPE AND INCEST 224
"YOUNG PERSONS ARE PLACED IN PENITENTIARIES
    MERELY BECAUSE THEY INDULGED THEIR SEXUAL FEELINGS" 225
NORMALIZING SEXUAL ASSAULTS AS "VICTIMLESS CRIME" 226
THE NATIONAL SURVEY OF CRIME SEVERITY 227
A "MODEST SEX OFFENDER" IMAGE 228
THE "PEER SEX PLAY" DEFENSE 229
GUYON, A PHILOSOPHER, AND KINSEY, AN EMPIRICIST 231
LEGISLATIVE AND JUDICIAL CLOUT 232
THE ALI-MPC URGED AGE OF CONSENT AT TEN-YEARS-OLD 233
KINSEY'S HOMOSEXUAL INCEST DATA CONCEALED FROM THE LAW 235
NORMALIZING ALL ADULT-CHILD SEX 235

PART VI: NORMALIZING PEDOPHELIA AND PORNOGRAPHY 236

OBSCENITY: BOOKLEGGERS AND SMUTHOUNDS 237
LAW DICTIONARY DEFINES OBSCENITY PRIOR TO 1957 239
PORNOGRAPHY AND THE REPEAL OF RETICENCE 239
"LOCAL DRIVES AGAINST SO-CALLED OBSCENE MATERIALS" 242
U.S. SUPREME COURT HEEDS ALI-MPC'S "PRURIENT INTEREST" STANDARD 242
"HARD CORE" INJURY FELT BY THE JURIST 243
LAW CLERKS DISAPPOINTED 244
NORMALIZING OBSCENITY IN THE CASE LAW
    JUSTICE DOUGLAS: THINGS "STIMULATE SEXUAL DESIRE" MORE THAN READING 244
NORMALIZING BESTIALITY 245

PART VII: HOW DID WE COME TO PARTIAL-BIRTH ABORTION? 246

WHERE DID KINSEY'S 90 PERCENT (UNMARRIED)
    AND 22 PERCENT (MARRIED) ABORTIONS COME FROM? 247
KINSEY'S SUDDEN ABORTION DATA 248

xi

- PREGNANCY, BIRTH AND ABORTION 249
- "PLANNED PARENTHOOD: A PRACTICAL HANDBOOK OF BIRTH-CONTROL METHODS" 249
- THE NATIONAL COMMITTEE ON MATERNAL HEALTH (NCMH) 250
- PREGNANCY, BIRTH AND ABORTION 250
- NORMALIZING PROSTITUTION AND NARCOTICS 251
- **PART VIII: NORMALIZING SODOMY AND MASTURBATION** 253
- KINSEY SCALE #1 253
- THE APA YIELDS TO KINSEY AND THE LAW TO THE APA 254
- KINSEY SCALE #2 254
- NORMALIZING SODOMY/HOMOSEXUALITY IN THE MILITARY 256
- SUMMING UP 258
- UPDATE 2011 259
- CHAPTER 8 NOTES 260
- 261

CHAPTER 9 269
ELITE AMERICAN EUGENICISTS
- POWERFUL POLITICAL INTERVENTION AND THE KINSEY FILE "NEVER SAW THE LIGHT OF DAY" 273
- STATISTICAL STUFF, NONSENSE, AND CONTROL 275
- THE VICTORY TOUR: KINSEY TO THE LAND OF GUYON, HIRSCHFELD AND CROWLEY 276
- ROMAN HOLIDAY 279
- ITALY 281
- THE TURIN GIRL 282
- SPAIN AND PORTUGAL 285
- LAST DAYS 285
- THE COLD, DEADLY HANDS OF KINSEY 288
- AFTER WORLD WAR II 288
- CHAPTER 9 NOTES 289

CHAPTER 10 293
FROM BERLIN TO BLOOMINGTON
KINSEY'S "SCIENTIFICALLY TRAINED OBSERVERS"
- BANCROFT'S "LONE PEDOPHILE THEORY" 294
- DIARIES OF "OLDER ADULTS" 295
- COLLABORATION WITH "SCIENTIFICALLY TRAINED OBSERVERS" 296
- "COORDINATING" THE WORK 297
- SCIENTIFIC CONNECTIONS: 298
- ROCKEFELLER, MULLER, GERMANY, AND RUSSIA WHO WAS HERMANN MULLER? 299
- BERLIN WELCOMES MUELLER 301
- DACHAU, 1933: 8,000 SLAVE LABORERS 306
- MULLER IN STALINIST RUSSIA 307
- FURTHER KINSEY/MULLER NETWORK CONNECTIONS 307
- BUSCHMANNSHOF: KRUPP'S CHILD CONCENTRATION CAMP 309
- CONCLUSION 311
- CHAPTER 10 NOTES 317
- 323

ADDENDUM 329
- FROM DER MORGENPOST, MAY 19, 1957 329
- FROM DER MORGENPOST, MAY 15, 1957 330
- FROM DER AUSSCHNITT, MAY 5, 1957 331
- FROM DER MORGENPOST, MAY 16, 1957 331
- FROM DER AUSSCHNITT, MAY 15, 1957 332
- FROM NEUSS DEUTSCHLAND, (EAST BERLIN), MAY 17, 1957 332
- FROM DER TAGESPIEGEL, OCTOBER 1, 1957 333
- FROM DER TAGESPIEGEL, MAY 16, 1957 334
- FROM THE MEDICAL TRIBUNE, JULY 19, 1991 334

INDEX 337

DEDICATION

I am honored to dedicate this book to my daughter Jennie, and my parents, Ada and Matthew Gelernter who, as virtuous Americans, lovingly instilled in me the desire to leave this Earth a little better than I found it.

I also dedicate this effort to the little children used as subjects in Kinsey's sex experiments, the children sacrificed to satisfy the perverse lust for money and power.

Finally, in an era in which cynicism and self-importance grow daily, I give thanks for the privilege of serving God in this "One Nation Under God." I am also grateful for the opportunity to work with His people, without whom I could never have delivered this book to "We The People."

ACKNOWLEDGMENTS

It is impossible to thank everyone who gave me support, encouragement and help in researching and writing this history of Alfred C. Kinsey and his era. First and foremost I am eternally grateful to my children for supporting my investigative research into the crimes and consequences of Kinsey.

Next, this book is about two problems with the Kinsey research. One is a problem of Kinsey's moral violations regarding human experimentation in the name of science, and the other hinges on his bad methodology and fraudulent statistics. Each reader will judge Kinsey's moral integrity for himself, but grappling with Kinsey's indecipherable statistics is more difficult. Thus, my deepest gratitude goes to W. Allen Wallis, past president of the American Statistical Association and past editor of the journal of the American Statistical Association for his critical approval of my work on Kinsey's statistical maze. Wallis' skilled review and professional insight confirmed that Kinsey's report was not as was stated by W. B. Saunders "Publishers Forward;" "an objective, factual study of sexual behavior in the human male… female." My commentary and criticism focused on what Kinsey called his "Historical Introduction, Interviewing, Statistical Problems and Validity of the Data." Wallis' informed conclusions—supported in part by documents obtained only after deposing the Kinsey Institute director in 1993—gives the lay reader confidence that a statistician of his stature has validated this author's criticism, commentary and analysis of Kinsey's seriously flawed methodology and skewed data.

I am grateful indeed for the freedom in this country which permits the scholar to "set the record straight" via fair use of images and textual references for visual and textual commentary. This work of research and scholarship, intended primarily for public benefit as commentary and criticism, has employed a number of photographs and other images drawn from works about Kinsey and the Kinsey era. The scholarly importance of reproducing these images is grounded directly in their decades of wide public use to promote, popularize, propagandize, indeed to market, Kinsey as a "sexpert" and his false data worldwide. The majority of the visuals in this study have been selected from the biographies of Alfred Kinsey cited in the chapter notes, from the 1948 Indiana University yearbook, and from sexological and historical sources relevant to Kinsey and his era, also cited in the chapter notes.

As an independent researcher and scholar, I am dependent on those with a wider reach into the public arena. I owe a special debt of gratitude to former Congressman Steve Stockman (R-Texas) and his 41 congressional cosponsors who introduced HR. 2749 in December 1995, calling for a public investigation of Kinsey's research. It was this federal outreach which caused the Kinsey Institute and its supporters to protest that "otherwise reasonable people" were questioning the legality and integrity of the Kinsey reports. Following on the heels of that first mass media challenge to the hegemony of the Kinsey influence, the national Concerned Women for America stepped up, 500,000 women strong, to lend their voices to the call for an end to the Kinsey era.

Special thanks to the Naval Aviation Foundation, Page Lee Hufty, Tom and Ann Cummings, Jr., Jim Wootton, Alex Magnus, Cis Ohrstrom, David J. Stouvenel, and Barbara Christian, to Joan Veon, Margaret and Dan Maddox, Beverly LaHaye, Jim Woodall, Tim Wildmon, Bob Knight, Gladys Dickleman, Michelle Moore, Barbara Whitacre, Beth Trotto, Cindy Weatherly, Neil Markva, Mike Engler, Jack Richardson, Quentin R. Ray, Dr. Jack D. Amis, Stan Reedy and Thomas Riner. My sincerest thanks to the hundreds of women and men who have called and written to me over the years to encourage and aid me in my efforts to bring the facts of this case to one of the last honest tribunals, the American court of public opinion, and especially to you, the friend who in the rush of getting this to print, I have not thanked!

I am indebted to the research staff at the Guggenheim Foundation, the National Research Council, the Rockefeller Archives, The American Law Institute, and the Eli Lilly Foundation for their professionalism and aid in providing me with my requested materials.

Because of the Kinsey Institute's close association with the powerful pornography industry and the well-entrenched sexology lobby, I look forward to the day when it will be possible for me to publicly thank the many public officials, psychologists, lawyers, doctors, teachers and scholars whose sense of honor as American citizens drove them, despite their legitimate concerns about the harm to their careers and livelihoods, to aid me in myriad ways. Thank you also to those who provided me with information, verification and confirmation of details about the gradual but widespread implementation of the Kinsey findings and philosophy throughout public institutions.

On point, most important, in this revised edition I am especially grateful to Robert H. Knight of the Family Research Council for his shepherding through the powerful 1994 doucmentary on the Kinsey team's child sexual abuse, "*The Children of Table 34*," and to the generous narration by film actor Efraim Zimbalist, Jr. Four years later, the distinquished investigative journalism of the prestigious British Yorkshire Television research team, headed by Tim Tate, the award winning (UNESCO, Amnesty International) documentary producer-director, produced, "*Secret Histories: Kinsey's Paedophiles,*" broadcast throughout Great Britain August 10, 1998. This major English television studio put its credibility on the line in setting the record straight. They located one of Kinsey's many "trained" serial pedophile aides in Frankfurt, Germany--Dr. Fritz von Balluseck, a Nazi child molester--another serial pedophile aide, Rex King, in Arizona and five pedophile headmasters in Princeton, New Jersey, among others. Yorkshire's costly and diligent investigations confirmed my child abuse charges against the Kinsey team and the Kinsey Institute's past and current culpability.

I earnestly hope that similarly "credible" *American* media will eventually show the nerve exhibited by the British, whose citizens were given full access to the truth of Kinsey's crimes against children and society. I am deeply grateful to Dr. James Dobson for his stalwart expose of Kinsey's pedophile science and especially for allowing me to reach his radio constituency of millions of Americans. I am additionally beholden to Dr. Laura Schlessinger and her staff, led by Cornelia Koehl. "Dr. Laura" has unflinchingly exposed Kinsey and the connections between these false sexual beliefs and the toxic sex education inflicted upon our children. Dr. Stanley Monteith also has opened his "Radio Liberty" to me as have hundreds of smaller broadcasters across the country. Without access to the alternative media we would have little chance to alert the nation to the sex science assault upon our nation.

On the production end of this book, special recognition goes to Alfred Moreschi, a skilled graphic artist and a generous gentleman and to his able, creative and chivalrous associate, Duncan Barlow. My gratitude certainly to the editorial assistance of William Lee while words cannot express my appreciation for the editorial aid of Barbara Elliot, a devoted and faithful woman who voluntarily and painstakingly reviewed this manuscript and who passed away just after completing her final corrections.

To Randal Shaheen a sterling young attorney made of the stuff of legend, I owe more than I could ever repay. Mr. Shaheen validated and rectified much of the datum in the massive Chapter 8, "Kinsey's Impact on American Law," a chapter that had been rushed headlong into print in time for the first 1998 edition. All who read and use this critical chapter which establishes Kinsey's toxic role in changing American law and public policy will similarly be in his debt, as is our nation. For, this chapter may be used diligently and creatively to revisit the fraudulent basis for scores of laws, law book citations, history book allegations, journal articles and public statutes.

To Shelby and Kelley Frances Sears, my deepest appreciation for your assistance and many sacrifices. Lastly, there is no possible way to express my love and appreciation for Colonel Ronald D. Ray and Eunice Ray, whose friendship, dedication, broad knowledge, humor and grit, Christian principles, style and eclectic library helped pound, shape and stretch this document. To them, my eternal thankfulness and devotion for their willingness to reveal their truth to me. Without this honorable couple, this book would doubtless have remained a collection of facts and documents, a mere shadow of the final book you hold in your hands.

This revised edition is a work in progress. New documents are emerging from the dust all the time. As for any flaw or criticism, I accept responsibility for it all, and look forward to receiving your comments, additions, corrections and information for the next edition.

NEW AUTHOR'S INTRODUCTION

How a (Truly) Mad Scientist Secretly Took America from Purity to Promiscuity, from Devotion to Deviance
By Judith A. Reisman, Ph.D.

You might have heard the bit of folk wisdom that says if a farmer sees a turtle sitting on top of a fence post, he can be sure it did not get there by itself. My behind-the-scenes research into America's moral decline have confirmed the farmer's astuteness: this disaster did not just happen, it was planned. The sexual revolution was based on an academic fraud so breathtaking, on a hidden agenda so sinister, and on sex crimes so unspeakable, that I've devoted my life to exposing them and to undoing the devastation they caused.

The (truly) mad scientist who secretly spawned this revolution was Prof. Alfred Kinsey, pervert extraordinaire and author of the famous *Kinsey Reports* on human sexuality of 1948 and 1953. Crammed with shocking statistics, these purportedly "scientific" volumes seemed to prove that most Americans were committing immoral, perverted and even illegal sex acts on a regular basis. Later, Prof. Kinsey and his fellow revolutionaries would inaugurate the stealth fields of "sexology" and "sex education," using their alleged "scientific findings" to overthrow Judeo-Christian sexual morality and millennia of human experience.

Actress Laura Linney played Mrs. Kinsey in Fox's feature film "Kinsey," which starred Liam Neeson as Prof. Kinsey. In 2004 Linney accurately said, "Any sort of sexual education that anybody has had in the past 50 years came right from the [Kinsey] Institute.... So his impact is enormous, and in ways that it's probably impossible for us to completely grasp.... When Kinsey published that information, he changed our culture completely." (ABC News's "Primetime Live" show, "Kinsey," October 14, 2004.)

You and your loved ones are now living in the "post-Kinsey era" that was launched in 1948. Every hour of every day, you are affected by radically sexualized education, laws, healthcare, politics, media, entertainment, fashions and behavior, all institutionalized by Prof. Kinsey's disciples. If you are like most Americans, you probably wonder how we went from the America that the Greatest Generation knew to a place where…

- God and the Ten Commandments are purged from our public schools
- Soon after the Commandments came down from schoolhouse walls, AIDS posters took their place
- Doctors and major pharmaceutical companies criminally experiment on infants[1]
- "Assisted suicide" and euthanasia threaten the lives of sick and elderly people
- Countless Web sites make every conceivable form of pornography instantly available to everyone
- So many adults and youths are addicted to pornography that treating them is now a growth industry for sex therapists
- 65 million Americans have a venereal disease (now euphemized as "STDs")
- 19 million more are infected each year, many incurable and some fatal
- Increasing numbers of university presidents, administrators, professors, coaches, doctors, clergy, teachers and school counselors have been convicted of child pornography use and sex crimes against children

- Respected universities sponsor courses for credit in which vulnerable students "study" pornographic films
- Sexually deviant professors require terrified students to view pornography and to report their states of "arousal"
- More than 2,000 Pentagon personnel who paid for online child pornography remain uninvestigated by authorities
- A famous Johns Hopkins University psychiatrist "destigmatizes" pedophiles as mere "minor-attracted persons"
- Pedophiles seek to end age-of-consent laws—a horror that they euphemize as "intergenerational male intimacy"
- Smiling politicians march in "gay pride" parades alongside the "North American Man-Boy Love Association"
- Homosexuals who arrange to couple together can legally adopt helpless children
- Police officers do nothing as nude men and women commit perverted sex acts illegally at public "gay" events
- Violating the will of the voters, judges and lawmakers impose homosexual "marriage" on entire states
- United Nations sex radicals pressure abortion "rights," "gay rights" and children's "sexual rights" on the entire world
- Abortionists killed more than 50 million unborn babies, creating a lucrative traffic in these babies' body parts
- Philanthropic foundations like Ford and Rockefeller, and scores of corporations like PepsiCo, Sears Roebuck, J.C. Penny, Office Depot, Barnes & Noble, Safeway, Target, Office Max, Home Depot, Costco, Walgreens, Hallmark Cards and Google, pour millions into marketing "gay," "transgender," bisexual, homosexual, etc., "rights"[2]
- In 2003, 60% of American Academy of Matrimonial Lawyers reported pornography increases divorce[3]
- Rapes and even rape-murders, often serial in nature, are increasingly common occurrences
- The careers of one politician after another implode in sex scandals involving adultery, even child abuse
- Movies and TV shows insert hetero and homosexual nudity, sex, rapes, gutter language and ridicule of sexual morality
- Major hotel chains make barely legal "teen" pornography and other obscene videos available to their guests
- "Sexology" institutes train many thousands of "sexperts" and "sex educators" who impart anything-goes sex lessons to countless couples, educators, college students and schoolchildren
- Millions of children are force-fed heterosexual and homosexual sex "ed" assertions that children are "born that way"
- Classics such as *Tom Sawyer* are forgotten as publishers market award-winning "kiddie-lit" pornography featuring rape, incest, sodomy, homosexuality, suicide, masturbation and family nudity
- Schoolgirls think it harmless to post naked photos of themselves on the Internet or "sexting" them to current boyfriends

- The "news" media censor evidence that teachers commit more child sex abuse than do priests and other clergymen
- As was done earlier to American Indian and Australian Aborigine children, "over one million North American" children (circa 2002), ripped from innocent parents, are sent to shelters, jails and "foster" homes by "social workers"[4]
- Both child and woman "sex trafficking" is a massive and growing industry
- The State markets "same-sex marriage" as normal, thus covers up early sex abuse as largely causal in bi/homosexuality
- Legalizing "same-sex marriage" equates injurious, formerly criminal sodomy with the God-ordained conjugal act designed to cement the institution of matrimony for the dedicated rearing of children
- Over half of all children birthed by American women under 30 are born out of wedlock[5]
- In 1950, 96 percent of children overall had married parents; now 63 percent have married parents (resulting in 1.5 million fatherless children born each year)[6]
- In 1950, 85 percent of black children had married parents; now 35 percent have married parents[7]
- Fatherlessness costs $99 billion a year for basic care, plus homeless, criminal, rapist, suicidal, etc., youth[8]
- We have gone from two major venereal diseases in the 1960s to now having over 25, some incurable, even fatal[9]
- Thousands of pulpits remain silent about these horrors, and some religious leaders even condone them

These are just a few of the "bleeding indicators" of modern society's systemic sex sickness. I am sure you could add a few of your own. Yet irrational, cowardly, in-denial people will tell you that Americans have always done these things, and that today we are just more honest about reporting "normal" sexual conduct.

After you read this book, you will confirm that what you always knew in the deepest recesses of your mind, heart and soul is really true. You will also understand why, despite decades of financial, verbal and physical harassment, the Boy Scouts of America still deny admission of homosexual leaders or scouts who say they are "gay."[10]

Stolen Honor, Stolen Innocence will prove to you the obvious: that what you perceive around you is not "just better reporting," but a deliberate destruction of our God-given right to normal, loving, conjugal living, and to living civilly and honorably, with a noble, healthy and sober character.

You will discover how a cadre of sexual psychopaths, like Kinsey, deliberately, deviously and deceitfully stole our national honor, as well as our children's and our own right to innocence, and to our historic, common-sense values of virtue in sex and in life. You will learn about our virtuous laws that had raised the age of consent to 16, 18 and even 21, had outlawed seduction, abortion, pornography, sodomy, adultery, etc., and often provided death or life in prison for rape—and how these laws were systematically dismantled by a cult whose malicious leader's own twisted sexuality drove him to assault the sexual morals and laws that had long protected and prospered our Judeo-Christian nation.

In the earlier editions of this book, I introduced myself at length so that you, kind reader, would know something about my life and about how I came to discover Prof. Kinsey's crimes against children, his falsified data on Americans' sex lives and his deviant design to corrupt the "faithful city"—the United States. I will not do that this time, but let me tell you about one horrific incident that changed my life forever.

With my daughter.

I lived a very happy life until 1966, when my 10-year-old daughter was raped by a 13-year-old friend of the family. She had told him to stop, but he persisted. She would like it, he said; he learned this from his father's *Playboy* magazines. The boy left the country before we learned of his crime, and the fact that my daughter was just one of several neighborhood children he had raped, including his own little brother. My heart broke for all the families involved. This appalling atrocity, I would later learn, fit a pattern that was typical among juvenile sex offenders. Over the years, that pattern would spread throughout society; it was an infectious environmental disease.

I might never have known about my daughter's victimization if she had not slipped into a deep depression. Only after I promised not to call the police would she talk about what happened. After assuring her it was not her fault, I called my dependable, staid aunt who listened sympathetically and who then declared, "Well, Judy, she may have been looking for this herself. Children are sexual from birth." Stunned, I replied that my child was *not* seeking sex.

Next, I dialed my Berkeley school chum, Carole, still seeking confirmation of my righteous indignation at my daughter's violation, which I badly needed to hear. Instead, Carole counseled, "Well, Judy, she may have been looking for this herself. You know, children are sexual from birth." I wondered why I was hearing this same locution from two such different people who were so widely separated geographically. I did not realize I had just entered the world according to Kinsey. I would hear that "children are sexual from birth" again, but at that later date, I would learn the covered-up truth about its source.

Years after my daughter's trauma, following the trail of Prof. Kinsey's crimes led me to become involved with international scholarly conferences, federally funded investigations, the FBI, the Pentagon's Joint Chiefs of Staff and national and international governmental hearings on science fraud, sexual abuse and trafficking of children, juvenile delinquency, rape and other sex crimes, pornography, drugs, abortion and the other critical social and moral issues of our time. You can now find this information on my Web site, www.DrJudithReisman.com.

In this new Introduction, though, I will give you a peek into some of the information that had to be left on "the cutting-room floor" in earlier editions.

For now, let us fast-forward to 1976. Based on my professional writing and work in public television, at NBC, at ABC, on CBS's "Captain Kangaroo" show, and at a score of art and history museums, Case Western University admitted me, pending a 4.0 grade average. After I received my doctorate in Communications in 1977, I did a research report on children, women and pornography that was accepted by the British Psychological Association's International Conference on "Love and Attraction" at Swansea University, Wales. As I was leaving London for Wales, news headlines announced that the leader of the "Pedophile Information Exchange" (PIE), Tom O'Carroll, was touring the UK en route to promoting pedophilia at the Swansea conference. PIE listed sites and addresses where pedophiles could seduce and rape vulnerable children. But when Swansea University's housekeeping staff learned that O'Carroll was to speak on their campus, they went on strike. If he speaks, they declared, we'll walk—he won't promote sex with *our* children!

Earlier, I had clashed with a Tufts University professor, Larry Constantine, a *Penthouse* magazine board member who endorsed child pornography and pedophilia in his paper on "The Sexual Rights of Children." At an emergency meeting of the conference's speakers, he urged the international attendees to sign his "free speech" petition that insisted the strikers work and O'Carroll speak. I argued that as guests of Swansea, we had no right to threaten the staff and leave behind a community traumatized by a university-sponsored advocate of child molestation. I was the only speaker who did not sign Constantine's petition. Eventually the president of the university ruled that O'Carroll was not credentialed to speak, and housekeeping services resumed.

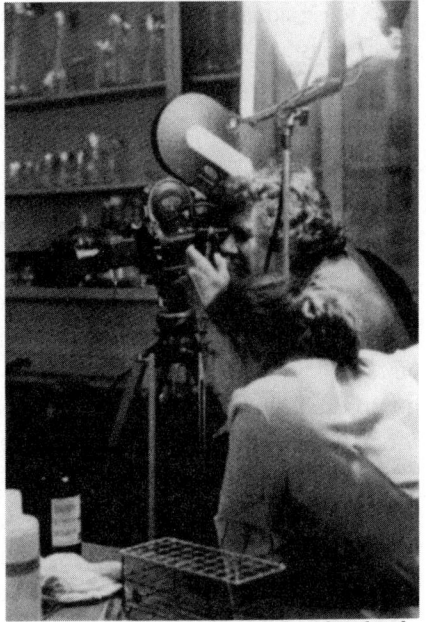

To introduce children to fine art, I produced and directed a music video segment on sculpture for the Cleveland Museum of Art, broadcast on CBS Television's "Captain Kangaroo."

Why, I wondered, would academics support an advocate of child abuse, while the university's workers aggressively protected their children? I thought this showed callous contempt for the housekeeping staff's concerns about protecting children, and it increased my disappointment with the morality and integrity of the university community at large.

After O'Carroll fled the Swansea conference, I presented 80 slides depicting child pornography in *Playboy* magazine (and some in *Penthouse*). Later, as I left for London, a Canadian psychologist whispered to me that I was right, that images of child abuse in *Playboy* and *Penthouse* would trigger copycat sex crimes against children. But, he said, if I wanted to learn where *Playboy* publisher Hugh Hefner and this sexual abuse of children were stemming from, I should read about Prof. Alfred Kinsey in Edward Brecher's book, *The Sex Researchers*. "Why?" I asked. "I worked with Kinsey and Pomeroy," he answered. "One is a pedophile and the other a homosexual." Which is which, I asked? "Read and discover," he replied.

Flying back to the States, I realized I had just been witness to a growing, international, academic pedophile movement—people who were dependent on pornography, even at the conference, and who now sought sex with children. I had stumbled right into their midst. What kind of academic training, I wondered, was producing such a degraded and predatory intelligentsia?

Reading *The Sex Researchers*, I could not decide which was worse—the depictions of Prof. Kinsey's cold, criminal, experimental sexual abuse of infants and toddlers at The Kinsey Institute at Indiana University, or Brecher's eager celebration of Prof. Kinsey's methods of studying "child sex." This was madness! Incredulous, I checked Prof. Kinsey's book to verify Brecher's quotes. Yes! Brecher quoted Prof. Kinsey accurately—infants were genitally "tested" for their ability to have what he called orgasms, as were hundreds of other children. Prof. Kinsey was the world's "scientific" authority on "child sexuality." So both my aunt and my chum who had told me years ago that "children are sexual from birth" were just parroting Prof. Kinsey and his disciples.

xxi

After graduation from Case Western, doctorate in hand, I left America with my family to do research in Israel. In 1981 I sat in my mountaintop office at Haifa University, staring at Prof. Kinsey's world-famous book, *Sexual Behavior in the Human Male*. I was re-reading page 180, which contained something called Table 34. Had I missed or misunderstood something? I had read biographies of Prof. Kinsey, hundreds of positive articles and chapters about him and his work, and the few scathing reviews, but nowhere had anyone mentioned these tables and graphs of "child orgasms." The thousands of international scientists who quoted and cited Prof. Kinsey were blind to what he put right before their eyes.

After Prof. Kinsey's death in 1956, Paul Gebhard his co-author succeeded him as director of The Kinsey Institute. In February, 1981, I wrote to the Institute, asking several questions, including where they got their child orgasm data for Tables 30-34. On March 11, 1981, Gebhard stunned me when he replied, saying the child orgasm figures came from "parents...nursery school owners or teachers... homosexual males," some of whom used "manual or oral techniques" to record the number of alleged "orgasms" that infants and other children had while being timed with stopwatches by adults.

Four months later, on July 23, 1981, my paper, "The Scientist As a Contributing Agent to Child Sexual Abuse; a Preliminary Consideration of Possible Ethics Violations," spotlighted Prof. Kinsey in the Abstracts of the Fifth World Congress of Sexology in Jerusalem. It was no surprise that my talk was standing room only. "Human sexuality" leaders from around the world attended: England, the USA, France, Denmark, Israel, Norway, Canada, Scotland, the Netherlands, Sweden and scores of other nations were represented by their top sex researchers, curriculum writers, therapists, counselors, etc. The entire conference was abuzz. My talk on Prof. Kinsey was bigger than the one by Xaviera Hollander ("the Happy Hooker") on "Out of Touch with Sex."

Armed with Gebhard's confessions, I projected Tables 30-34 and pages 160 and 161, including Prof. Kinsey's rates and speeds of "orgasms" of at least 317 infants and children (the youngest being two months old). I quoted his statement that many of a group of 196 children and infants "fainted," "screamed," "wept" and "convulsed!" Though he said these reactions represented sexual pleasure, I said, "No, this was evidence of children's terror and pain, and it was criminal." Only a sadomasochistic pedophile, I thought to myself, would call a child's convulsions "pleasure." The revered Prof. Kinsey was a sexual psychopath.

The crowd was silent. No questions. No challenges. Black silence. Finally, a tall, blond Nordic type who had been standing near the podium stepped forward and barked:

> I am a Swedish reporter, and I never have spoken out at a conference. That is not my role. But what is the matter with all of you? This woman has just dropped an atomic bomb in this very room, and you have nothing to ask? Nothing to say?

Hands shot up. The Kinsey Institute's chief librarian stood and said, "Let's have tea. This is not true." I simply quoted pages in Prof. Kinsey's own book and pointed to plainly visible tables of child torture. My angry moderator shut down the debate, but many people tacitly agreed an investigation was needed. Later, Sweden's director of sex education told me she was shocked that children were used without consent. However, *with* consent, she assured me, children could be sexually stimulated by adults, even parents—for their own good, of course. Late that afternoon my young Haifa University assistant, visibly shaken, joined me. She had just dined with the leaders of the international conference. My lecture was hotly condemned. Her 12 dinner companions all agreed that children could take part in "loving" (not angry) sex with adults.

It turned out that *millions* of dollars in grants that such "experts" received for sex "education," research and "therapy," and even future profits in sex, drugs, films, "toys," etc., hinged on Prof. Kinsey's human sexuality "data." (Millions of dollars still do, with more than $20 million in "health" grants showered on Kinsey Institute researchers even from 1986 to today.[11]) At this conference, I had just proven that the world's "sexperts" were following a child molesting, psychopathic, criminal con man. Little did I know then, that with the funding and reputations of universities and agencies worldwide riding on Prof. Kinsey's data, no investigation could—or would—ever be allowed.

But then things seemed to change. In 1982, not long after my exposé in Jerusalem of Prof. Kinsey's frauds, the U.S. Department of Justice's Office of Juvenile Justice and Delinquency Prevention (OJJDP) flew me back from Israel. I received an appointment as a Full Research Professor at American University (AU), to serve as the principal investigator for an $800,000 grant to investigate Prof. Kinsey's role in sex crimes against children and his link to images of children in mainstream pornography—specifically, *Playboy, Penthouse* and *Hustler* magazines.

The commercial sex industry, however, soon joined The Kinsey Institute and academic sexologists to keep Prof. Kinsey's crimes hidden. Years later I obtained copies of classified letters and packages secretly sent worldwide by The Kinsey Institute to discredit my findings about Prof. Kinsey and about child exploitation in *Playboy, Penthouse* and *Hustler*. As soon as the news media revealed my appointment at AU, The Kinsey Institute threatened to sue the school if I studied Prof. Kinsey, and it helped launch the first attempt in the U.S. Congress to kill my study. Violating both academic freedom and the public's right to know, AU killed my investigation of Prof. Kinsey—but it "allowed" me to continue researching child sexploitation in the media.

Ever since 1984, The Kinsey Institute and its pro-pornography co-conspirators have maintained a constant vigil, lobbying legislators to suppress my findings and to hide the truth from the news media, professional conferences, journals, book publishers, etc.

My key opponents knew my researchers would find child sexploitation to be a raging, systemic theme in *Playboy*, et al., as well as finding advocacy of other crimes—e.g., gang rape of women and girls, seducing and then abandoning the women whom men impregnate, voyeurism ("peeping"), exhibitionism (exposing oneself), adultery, using prostituted women and girls, harming women who refused sex, etc. So Sen. Arlen Specter (then a Republican, now a Democrat) was chosen to lead two of three (yes *three*) congressional hearings to bushwhack my study. Failing that, he and his team would discredit me and the data in a news media barrage before we released our study.

Hence, my Department of Justice grant, signed in February, 1984, was followed by a major congressional investigation on April 11, 1984, led by Congressman Ike Andrews (D-NC) aide, Gordon Raley, who later wrote for *Penthouse* magazine. After this failed to kill the work, the Senate picked up the "no credibility" line for a hearing of its own on May 7, 1985, and yet another one on August 1, 1985. The national news media were lined up to report that our investigation of sexual abuse of children in mainstream pornography was a worthless boondoggle, and its investigator was equally worthless. My three key accusers were Sen. Ted (Chappaquiddick) Kennedy and two other senators, Senator Arlen Specter and Senator Howard Metzenbaum, who carefully hid their own conflicts of interest. Years later, the *Washington Times* (March 18, 1992) reported that Specter was funded by a pornography profiteer. We also turned up an awkwardly glowing *Penthouse* interview with Sen. Howard Metzenbaum in November, 1982.

On August 1, 1984, I testified before the Senate committee that "present in the content of all three magazines is a documentable evolution of children portrayed as viable sex targets." Portrayals of children, I noted, became "more sexually explicit and more violent over time" (p. 67). Obviously, Metzenbaum and the other senators didn't want the public to know that.

In November 1985, although my study was not yet complete, AU administrators locked me out of my files, refused to give me copies of my computer disks, held my report "in editing" for nearly two years (more on that in another book). Then, while denying me a copy, AU sent my "edited" report to OJJDP. Things became clearer when, during the AU "editing process," the chairman of AU's department of psychology, Dr. Elliot McGinnies, a key foe of my child pornography research was arrested for sex crimes

Princeton University, November 20, 1985. Following my lecture to the students, I returned to the podium to refute–with pictorial documentation–the denials by Larry Flynt (upper right) that his Hustler publication did not illegally portray children sexually.

against a child in his trailer at a nudist colony (*Washington Post*, September 19, 1986). In 1990 AU president, Dr. Richard Berendzen, with unspeakable child pornography magazines tucked away in his presidential desk, was arrested for child-sex-related offenses (*Washington Post*, September 23, 1990). The reasons for AU's efforts to stop my investigation of child sex abuse in mainstream pornography were glaringly obvious, even to the most naïve observer.

The plot thickens. In November 1985 I was forced to leave my research with AU for "editing." I had no idea that AU would deliberately bowdlerize my two-year study and send their bogus document to OJJDP on September 2, 1986. Regrettably, I possessed only one original hard copy to compare to the AU brutally gutted document. What to do? After spending almost a year to find and correct the frauds, reenter the missing data and get approvals for the final work from my academic peers, I received an offer from Heaven, as it were. Dr. Jerry Falwell, founder of Liberty University, had somehow heard of my plight. He flew me to Lynchburg, Virginia, and provided a hotel, meals and his entire secretarial and publishing facility to reconstruct my 2,500 pages of research, stipulating only that his aid be anonymous. I agreed.

My report was re-typed and all the graphs, charts and statistics were being re-entered when I received a curt, gratuitous deadline from OJJDP to deliver my corrected, complete report tomorrow or they would announce the rejection of my study. The next day! When Dr. Falwell learned of this sudden mandated OJJDP zero hour he organized an assembly line of kind ladies who stoically worked through the night, printing and collating the documents by hand. Six copies of each three-hole punched, quasi-leather-bound report in three-parts were ready in the morning. Charlie Judd, then executive director of Liberty Federation and Moral Majority accompanied me on the Falwell jet as we spun off to Washington, D.C. A taxi waited at the National airport to drive us to the OJJDP office. November 1986, Mr. Judd and I delivered multiple copies of my tome, on deadline, to a very sour faced and upset Robert Speirs, the OJJDP Administrator, and his even more peeved program monitor, Ms. Pamela Swain! We were unaware that as Mr. Judd and I left the unhappy couple, Speirs and Swain were busy couriering the peer-approved study out of their building in order to reject its' scientific findings. In another book, I will go into what happened after that—indeed, the battle had just begun.[12]

It was June 1, 1988 when I arrived again in Lynchburg for a TV interview with Dr. Falwell on the "Pastor's Study." After going into detail about what our research uncovered, Dr. Falwell smiled at me and said, in his easy, friendly voice…

> DR. FALWELL: You did this for the Department of Justice. It was delivered to the Department of Justice, and I will assume that the wonderful Department of Justice would, by now, have done something wonderful about it.
>
> DR. REISMAN: Well, that's what I would have assumed…but first of all, they blocked the publication of the report consistently. They claimed our academic peers didn't approve it. We proved

that the academic peers did approve it. All of their statements and critiques were included, so that we thought that problem was solved. Just recently, this last month, a memo went out....

DR. FALWELL: I have it. Let me read this memo. It is unbelievable! It's on the screen there, but I'm going to read it to you. It was a memo distributed to the various divisional managers in the Justice Department responsible for reviewing this study. "Please be advised that I have received a memo from Charles A. Lauer, General Counsel, regarding the report 'Images of Children, Crime and Violence in Playboy, Penthouse and Hustler Magazines, Executive Summary' that was recently received in the office." That's your study. "Please review the following relevant portions of the memo from the office of General Counsel and notify all of your staff immediately." Then there is a writing of the law that says this is all illegal stuff and here's the bottom line, the last paragraph, "Please advise all staff that this report should not be duplicated or sent through the mails" because the law says "to print or distribute this is a crime." Now if it's a crime for the Justice Department managers to distribute this, why is it not a crime for Guccione, Hefner, and Flynt to distribute this?

DR. REISMAN: That's a very good question. Because they are referring specifically to the fact that we found child pornography, young people, under the age of 18....

DR. FALWELL: [Speaking about then-Attorney General Ed Meese] It would seem like there are forces beneath him that are very powerful.

DR. REISMAN: Very powerful. Incredibly powerful. Because what we see here is a federal report that identifies child pornography, and its researcher, identified as having done something illegal, while those who produce the material, make the profit on the material, continue to do what they've been doing and are not prosecuted. Playboy, Penthouse, these people are not prosecuted.

Dr. Jerry Falwell interviews Dr. Judith Reisman

DR. FALWELL: Why would the Justice Department be attempting to squelch this report and refusing to act upon it?

DR. REISMAN: Well, it is my opinion that there is a very strong, a very powerful, sex-industry lobby that is having its way in the Department of Justice.

Indeed, after years of defamation of my work (and me), a new head of the OJJDP, Robert Sweet, investigated the whole shameful, dirty business and wrote, "While the massive, affluent sex industry has employed nearly every technique in their arsenal, short of violence, to stop Dr. Reisman's work, they have not shown her findings to be incorrect or methodologically flawed—in even the smallest detail" (August 25, 1994).

And, as I have documented in *Stolen Honor, Stolen Innocence*, Kinsey's "pamphleteer," Hugh Hefner, had joined forces with The Kinsey Institute to threaten anyone who would let me investigate Prof. Kinsey.

In 1990, my first book, *Kinsey, Sex and Fraud* was released by a small Christian publisher, and in 1991, the same publisher released my book *"Soft" Porn Plays Hardball*. Phil Donahue, a popular TV talk-show host and Kinsey disciple, thinking to expose my work as bogus, put me on his show—and assessed Kinsey's worldwide importance:

> "Kinsey was to sexuality what Freud was to psychiatry, what Madame Curie was to radiation, what Einstein was to physics. Comes along this woman [Reisman]

saying, 'Holy cow! E doesn't equal mc². *We've based an entire generation of education of sexologists on Kinsey, and Kinsey was a dirty old man.*'"

I agreed, but Donahue argued forcefully that Kinsey was really a conservative family man, a myth now fully disproven by his own laudatory biographers. The public has a right to know what has been covered up, and why. The nation has a responsibility to know *what happened to the children of Table 34* and how a demonic, Faustian sexual psychopath sold all of us his deviant, demented sexual revolution via colossal lies and trickery.

It is time to connect Prof. Kinsey, the father of the sexual revolution, sexology and "sex education," to our massive, growing, global addiction to pornography. Since 1948, public health report data have confirmed the staggering social costs and consequences of this sea change in the way America and the rest of the Western world have come to view human sexuality. As America's founding moral order has been jettisoned and the standard of judgment has shifted radically over the last 50 years, the statistical evidence proves that our country's present direction deserves review, and on an urgent basis. The crisis is far worse and more menacing to our children and our nation's survival than even Mr. Donahue said. For what will become of a society that has based *three* "generations of education of sexologists on Kinsey, when Kinsey was a dirty old man?"

Since Americans left the "pre-Kinsey era" behind and plunged headlong into the "post-Kinsey era," what has this meant for all of us? *Stolen Honor, Stolen Innocence* will, I believe, give you enlightening—and motivating—answers. Today The Kinsey Institute at Indiana University still receives millions of dollars in grants and, through the world's "sex educators," trains millions of young people in utterly amoral Kinseyan sexuality. As a citizen, a scholar, a mother, grandmother, and a great-grandmother, it is my fondest hope that the facts you discover here will help you understand the pervasive effects that Prof. Kinsey and Hefner, his personal "pamphleteer," have had on everyone's lives, and inspire you to end their demonic influence on your children and grandchildren. Thank you for caring—and, I pray, rising up and taking action.

AUTHOR'S INTRODUCTION NOTES

1. http://www.infowars.com/glaxosmithkline-fined-over-illegal-vaccine-experiments-killing-14-babies. See also the Guatemala expose as well as those I have written on elsewhere.
2. "Human Rights Campaign Foundation," Buying Guide: http://www.hrc.org/files/assets/resources/2012_BuyersGuide.pdf
3. http://www.huffingtonpost.com/vicki-larson/porn-and-divorce_b_861987.html
4. http://groups.yahoo.com/group/FathersRightsNetwork-International/message/1254
5. http://articles.businessinsider.com/2012-02-21/home/31081751_1_illegitimacy-black-children-unmarried-women#ixzz215ffHhme
6. http://futureofchildren.org/publications/journals/article/index.xml?journalid=37&articleid=105&sectionid=674 and http://www.msnbc.msn.com/id/15835429/ns/health-pregnancy/t/nearly-us-babies-born-out-wedlock/#.UAbWGvUnC8U
7. http://www.ewtnnews.com/catholic-news/US.php?id=358
8. http://chastity.com/chastity-qa/stds/infections/how-many-stds-are-there/how-many
9. http://thefatherlessgeneration.wordpress.com/statistics
10. http://www.infowars.com/boy-scouts-were-keeping-policy-banning-gays
11. See Liberty Counsel Researcher Donna Gallagher for documentation of Kinsey Institute funding, www.LC.org.
12. See, Howard Kurtz, "$743,371 Later," *Washington Post*, Sept. 12, 1986.

STOLEN HONOR
STOLEN INNOCENCE

PART I:
Kinsey

CHAPTER 1

KINSEY'S YOUTH TO FAMILY MAN

How was it possible for a sickly, religious boy who grew up to be a serious college student with an obvious talent for biology and an abysmal ignorance of sex—how did this young man evolve into a world authority on sexual behavior who could be mentioned in the same breath with Freud?[1]

Wardell Pomeroy, Kinsey coauthor, 1972

Alfred C. Kinsey's 1912 high school senior photo.

Alfred Charles Kinsey was born in Hoboken, New Jersey, on June 23, 1894. He grew up in South Orange, and was 16 when Congress halted the traffic in young girls ("White Slave Trade") in 1910. It was largely to oppose such forced prostitution that religious women and feminists joined forces to encourage a return to virtue, temperance and chastity that would safeguard the institutions of marriage and family.

The erosion of the family was obvious everywhere as economically powerful saloon and brothel franchises, and their organized crime associates corrupted politics and society. Many families were impelled to leave independent family farms and move to industrialized, impersonal cities.

Targets of the "virtuous women's coalition," which was also dubbed the "Purity Movement," included (in addition to the White Slave Trade) prostitution in general, promiscuity, poverty, child labor, drug and alcohol abuse, deleterious food and diet, disrespect for women, unsanitary conditions, and obscene literature. The movement, bolstered by many male proponents, harangued law enforcement officials, and state and federal legislatures, but to little avail. Eventually, however, the persistence of this relatively small band of "restoration agents" helped secure the franchise for women, which in turn generated increasing support for the enforcement of existing laws, and the enactment of new legislation, to protect marriage and improve the lives of women, children and families. The so-called "Victorian repression and prudery" took the form of a public appeal to male chivalry by women anxious to restore personal and civic virtue.

The White Slave trade. Kidnapped or destitute girls were often imprisoned in window-barred brothels as in photos like this Chicago "disorderly" house. The first accomplishment of the Purity Crusade was the removal of such window bars. (Bell)

In 1910, Dr. Winfried Scott Hall, Professor of Physiology at the Northwestern University Medical School, catalogued some of the deleterious results of public toleration of adultery and prostitution:

> Statistics show that of the operations on women in the hospitals of New York City... for the removal of one or both ovaries, sixty-five per cent of those operations were brought about and necessitated because of gonorrheal infection [largely contracted by wives infected by their] lawfully wedded husbands.[2]

Commenting on the growing influence of organized vice and crime in the merchandising of sex, the police chief of Des Moines, Iowa, reported that neighborhood "segregation" of brothel "cribs" created such a sex market that "Landladies... by reason of competition [put] red lights over the doors... displaying the charms of [girls] in the windows."[3]

In 1908, Edward Bok, editor of *The Ladies Home Journal*, implored parents to speak frankly to their children about sex, and to stress that "There can be but one standard: that of moral equity," which requires that "the young man" be "physically clean" before being granted the privilege of matrimony.

The famed Helen Keller, blind and deaf after a bout with scarlet fever in infancy, warned in the same magazine of the perils of "free love." Her article, "I Must Speak," candidly addressed marriage and family life issues:

> The most common cause of blindness is ophthalmia of the newborn. One pupil in every three at the institution for the blind in New York City was blinded by this disease. What is the cause[?]... [Her husband]... has contracted the infection in licentious relations before or since marriage. "The cruelest link in the chain of consequences," says Dr. Prince Morrow," is the mother's innocent agency. She is made a passive, unconscious medium of instilling into the eyes of her newborn babe a virulent poison which extinguishes its sight." ...It is part of the bitter harvest of the wild oats he has sown.[4]

Helen Keller

Miss Keller noted that blindness was by no means the most terrible result of this "pestilent sin."[5] Diseased children reared in poorhouses, and scores of young, once-healthy women, died in great pain and misery as a direct result of their husbands' sexual irresponsibility. Discussions of the effects of venereal disease were sorely needed, since "some surgeons attribute three-fourths of the surgical operations on women to this disease: one-fourth is a very conservative reckoning."[6]

Motivated by the Purity Movement, *all* states eventually required would-be brides and grooms to be "clean" of venereal diseases before marrying. Prior to publication of Kinsey's *Sexual Behavior in the Human Male* volume, (hereafter *Male*) in 1948, and *Sexual Behavior in the Human Female* volume, (hereafter *Female*) in 1953, America witnessed a successful "Women's War" against alcoholism and vice, as thousands of "women marched from church meetings to saloons where, with prayer and song, they demanded an end [to alcohol sales]." (During Prohibition, the *per capita* annual consumption of hard liquor plummeted from 2.6 to 0.97 gallons.[7]) While traffic in sex slaves, drugs, alcohol, obscenity, and child labor escalated in Europe, there were significant inroads against such vices in the U.S. Not until mid-century, with Kinsey's help, would they flourish once again.

Kinsey blamed "sexual repression" for everything from the "high" rate of divorce to rape and homosexuality. Yet he was in his own mid-20s at the start of the "Roaring 20s," which was hardly a decade of sexual repression. Rather, it was a time when girls bobbed their hair, donned shorts, shortened their skirts, and rolled up their stockings, sometimes to attend risqué collegiate alcohol, drug, and sex parties. By 1930, at age 36, Kinsey would have been aware of the considerable success of ordinary citizens in overcoming state-sanctioned (or state-ignored) "commercial vice."

Cover Illustration for *Fighting the Traffic in Young Girls* (1910)

Fighting the Traffic in Young Girls urged restoration of social virtue and purity after an era of incivility.

BOYHOOD AND EDUCATION

Alfred Kinsey's father, though not himself a college graduate, taught engineering at Stevens Institute of Technology, a small college in Hoboken. He is said to have reared his son in a strict, churchgoing Methodist household where dancing, tobacco, alcohol, and dating were forbidden. Alfred's animosity toward his parents would surface over the most trivial slights. His eventual break with his father, writes Kinsey biographer Wardell Pomeroy, "had been a deep hurt even though Kinsey had little feeling for his family, and seldom talked about them at all in later years."[8] After establishing a family of his own, Kinsey explained why he had severed all contact with his parents, blaming his father's domineering personality and his mother's thrift. His biographers suggest that he especially despised his father for cutting off financial support after he transferred from engineering at Stevens Tech to zoology at the more prestigious Bowdoin College.[9] Pomeroy recalls that a "single suit of clothes costing $25.00 was the only help he received from home from this point on."[10]

Kinsey was sickly, "frail and not by nature or experience a toughie." Cornelia Christenson continues in *Kinsey: A Biography* that he was not "an able bodied man" and was ineligible to serve in World War I "due to his physical condition, a double curvature of the spine and a possibly defective heart …caused by rickets in his childhood… bouts of rheumatic fever and even typhoid."[11] He felt "physically inferior to other boys" and was the "shyest guy around girls you could think of."[12] Christenson and others have noted that Kinsey inscribed a line from Shakespeare's *Hamlet* under his high school yearbook photograph: "Man delights me not; no, nor woman either." Pomeroy asks (without answering):

> How was it possible for a sickly, religious boy who grew up to be a serious college student with an obvious talent for biology and an abysmal ignorance of sex—how did this young man evolve into a world authority on sexual behavior who could be mentioned in the same breath with Freud?[13]

Pomeroy, Christenson, and Indiana University (where Kinsey's sex-research operations were based) claim that Kinsey was asexual, disinterested in sex, and celibate prior to marrying in 1921. But in 1997, James H. Jones, another pro-Kinsey biographer who had also received support from the University, revealed startling new details about Kinsey's sexual obsessions in his book, *Alfred C. Kinsey: A Public/Private Life* (hereafter *Alfred C. Kinsey*). Interviewed for a 1998 British television program entitled "Kinsey's Paedophiles," Jones asserted:

Kinsey in 1927

> There is no way that the American public in the 1940s and the 1950s would have sanctioned any form of behavior that violated middle class morality on the part of the scientist who was telling the public that he was disinterested and giving them the simple truth.... Any disclosure of any feature of this private life that violated middle class morality would have been catastrophic for his career.... For Kinsey, life in the closet came complete with a wife, children, a public image... that again he preserved at all costs. Kinsey's reputation still in large measure rests upon an image of him that he cultivated during his lifetime... the official mystique. (Yorkshire Television (Channel 4), United Kingdom, August 10, 1998.)

Scrutiny of Kinsey's formative years is imperative to understand how and why he became motivated to conduct his later research, especially his study of sexual responses in children. Pomeroy reports that Kinsey himself argued that early life experiences largely shape one's adult behavior:

> The inside story that lies back of the journal and newspaper articles is, in many instances, much more important than the material that was actually published. The backgrounds of the individuals who have done the writing very often supply the key to the attitude in the published article.[14]

According to Christenson and Pomeroy, as a 22-year-old college student Kinsey showed no interest in women or sex, opting instead for such activities as playing the piano at fraternity parties while the others danced.[15] Yet he was handsome, educated, and athletic. Some have said that he resembled the late President John F. Kennedy. Pomeroy writes, "Young Al Kinsey was also known in South Orange High School as the boy who never had a girl,"[16] and as a young man he "was ignored by or ignored women."[17] Christenson describes one occasion when he played the "Moonlight Sonata":

> The image of his striking figure at the piano, with his curly blond hair, clean-cut face, swaying slightly as he felt the rhythm of his music [held great appeal for women].... [But] He was the shyest guy around girls you could think of... [Claimed Pomeroy] he was still unbelievably innocent.[18]

Kinsey with his family circa 1917. (Christenson)

Kinsey reportedly secured a scholarship,[19] and money from an "elderly widow," [20] to finance his final two years at Bowdoin College (1914-1916). According to Christenson, he devoted most of his time to zoology (16 credit hours the first year) and biology (four hours), while "[s]ociology and psychology courses rounded out the year's work."[21] He was primarily interested in insects and animals.

During his last year at Bowdoin he added "fifteen hours more of zoology" and began to collect wasps. His courses in psychology, especially those dealing with Pavlovian concepts of control through conditioned reflex, would serve him well in later years.[22] In *Female*, Kinsey cites Russian physiologist Ivan Petrovich Pavlov's use of dogs as "subjects"[23] to detect the "conditioned reflex, a physiological reaction to environmental stimuli" that shaped the development of behaviorism.[24]

Charles Darwin

Another major influence on Kinsey was Charles Darwin, the English naturalist who is credited with formulating the theory of evolution in such works as *The Origin of Species* (1859).[25] Kinsey was so impressed with Darwin's scientific acumen that, upon graduating *magna cum laude* from Bowdoin in 1916, he quoted him in his commencement address.[26]

Following graduation, Kinsey continued his studies at Harvard's Bussey Institution, which was a hotbed of Darwinism and the "New Biology" that led scientists to envision improving the human species through "eugenics." Jones identifies Kinsey as one of the scholarly pre-World War II eugenicists who issued a "terrifying" call for the *mass* sterilization of *"lower level"* Americans and a breeding plan for superior classes.[27]

Sir Thomas Huxley (1825-1895), the foremost proponent of Darwinism in England, was credited by Kinsey with crafting a scientific "declaration of independence."[28] Kinsey claimed to agree with Huxley's dogged determination to accept only those "facts" which could be confirmed via the scientific method. No other authority (including church and state) was accepted.

Sir Thomas Huxley

Kinsey would also play in the same elite eugenic league as Sir Thomas Huxley's grandsons, Aldous and Julian. Sir Julian Huxley, a geneticist and first director-general of UNESCO (United Nations Educational, Scientific, and Cultural Organization) became acquainted with Kinsey's work through Indiana University President Herman Wells. In 1932, Aldous Huxley wrote *Brave New World*, which became required reading in many American schools. It is often misunderstood as "science fiction," but was actually an exposé of the cosmopolitan eugenic vision of state-controlled free love and selective breeding.

Others undoubtedly influenced Kinsey's personal life and professional career, but with the Kinsey Institute archives closed to non-admiring scholars,[29] critics seeking background information relating to the development of Kinsey's "attitude," the early experiences that permeate his research findings and conclusions, are compelled to look elsewhere.

Cover of Aldous Huxley's 1932 book prophesying science's eugenic utopian future.

PREFERENCE FOR BOYS

As "shy" as he was around women, Kinsey was much at home with young boys. He preferred their company in both outdoor and indoor settings. He joined the Boy Scouts at about age 17, and later as a married man continued to wear his Scout uniform, take boys on nature hikes and the like, and sleep alongside them in tents. The Boy Scout movement, which was founded in Great Britain in 1907, has helped to instill such character traits as honesty, courage, tenacity, cooperation, and devotion to God and country in tens of millions of boys worldwide. Additional millions of devoted men have served as leaders in the Boy Scouts of America (hereafter BSA), founded in 1910, providing young Scouts with positive role models and rewarding experiences. Sadly, however, Scouting has too often been exploited by deviates with less honorable objectives in mind.

Claiming that Kinsey's obsession with boys was entirely platonic, Pomeroy and Christenson insist that he led a largely sexless life. Evidence from Kinsey's own writings, however, raised serious questions about his sexual orientation long before publication of Jones' *Alfred C. Kinsey* confirmed his deviancy. Even in college he opted for the companionship of youths and boys. A fellow counselor describes Kinsey (then age 21) at the Newark YMCA:

> His tent, with his nature "library" of a dozen volumes, was a rendezvous for dozens of campers during the day and well into the night, even after taps had sounded and we were supposedly tucked in.... The boys loved "Al" and couldn't get enough of him. He had a merry eye, a wide smile and a hearty laugh.... Always ready for the latest camp prank, he was just as ready to pitch in and help any kid in trouble...

> Unlike most of us, Kinsey had experience at several other camps also; was an active leader in Boy Scout work, often wore his Scout uniform. A camp history refers to war games in 1914... "under... Field Marshal Alfred Kinsey." [While Kinsey was a student at Bowdoin] he was by far the greatest specialist in that group of young men... [H]e was thoroughly enjoyed as a companion by everyone.[30]

Pictured above is an older Kinsey as a "Boys Club leader" circa 1920s. (Christenson)

Note that Pomeroy places nature "library" in quotation marks. People in the 1920's would have understood this to mean that Kinsey collected nature (nudist) magazines, with drawings and photographs of nude youths and adults. Commenting on the 1920s nudist movement, including the "Manifesto of Nudism," Christopher Stevens writes in *Secret and Forbidden* (1966):

> The most important document in the first years of nudism is the manifesto published by Professor Georg Herrmann.... It read: "The problem of nudity, nude social life, was always the battleground of prudish Pharisees and the honest children of nature, the subject of constant quarrels between senile hypocrites and the fresh, young joy of beauty."[31]

Kinsey with young charges as a "Counselor at Camp Wyanoake." (Christenson)

The founder of the nudist or "physical culture" movement was Dr. Heinrich Pudor. He published the pamphlet *Naked Humanity, Jubilant Future* in 1893, followed by a monthly nudist journal entitled *Strength and Beauty*. Critics of the movement feared that it would ultimately weaken nations by promoting the "Greek vice." Nevertheless, fully one-third of German youth, prior to Hitler, were staunch supporters.[32] Advocates of nudism perceived it to be a "physical expression of the modern spirit, free of the dark influences which cause the human body to be called ugly or immoral." They advocated the "viewing of the opposite sex with clear eyes and no shameful or hidden thoughts."[33] (Some psychologists would argue that this may reveal the origin of Kinsey's nudist, nature, pornography collection at Indiana University, discussed further on). Biographer James H. Jones confirms that Kinsey received nudist magazines at the family home-certainly an interest in conflict with his public "conservative" persona.[34]

Years later, Kinsey would write a curious letter to an old Scouting friend, perhaps one of the boys with whom he had shared his "nature library," or to whom he devoted so much attention during his adolescent, college, postgraduate, and even married years.[35] Kinsey wrote, "We did have good times together, and you must understand from that Scout troop I began to learn some of the things that made it possible for me to do some of the research that we are now engaged in."[36] Clearly, Kinsey was not referring to wasp collecting, but to the sexual research and experimentation that would eventually result in publication of *Male*.

According to Pomeroy, "Kinsey began to leave Scouting and the sexually sterile world of his boyhood behind him when he graduated from high school."[37] Not mentioned is Kinsey's continuing close association with boys through his leadership activities, as above, during his college years at Bowdoin and in the Bethany Boys' Club. According to Christenson:

> A major activity during his three years of postgraduate studies was the Bethany Boys' Club at the local Bethany Methodist Episcopal Church. [There were] Saturday hikes and weekend overnight camping trips with Kinsey.[38]

Indeed, Kinsey so enjoyed the Scouting atmosphere that he continued to lead a summer camp program after he was married. He and his wife, Clara, once examined property with the thought of "establishing a boys' camp of their own."[39] Though nothing came of it, Kinsey did spend a "month at Camp Winona in Maine, alone… since Clara now had two children."

In *Male*, Kinsey claims that children are sexual from birth. He argued that most American boys engage in some form of sexual activity with other boys, that adolescent homosexuality is "a common phenomenon," and that males reach their sexual "peak" as teenagers. True or false, it is not unreasonable to speculate that Kinsey observed at least *some* sexual activity among the many boys with whom he had been closely associated in Scouting and boys clubs. But, was Kinsey himself a participant-a pederast (a man who desires sex with boys)? Neither he nor his friendly biographers ever broached the matter.

Kinsey (upper right) with Bethany Boys Club "Sunday School Class." (Christenson)

A report by Patrick Boyle, author of *Scout's Honor: Sexual Abuse in America's Most Trusted Institution*, describes Kinsey's role in removing a warning about masturbation from the Scout handbook. According to Boyle, an early edition of the handbook advised Scoutmasters:

> Because boys of Scouting age are naturally curious about sex, you may... discover or hear about incidents of sexual experimentation among troop members.... Incidents of sexual experimentation call for a private and thorough investigation, and frank discussion with those involved.[40]

Boyle recalls Kinsey's response when the BSA sought his advice for updating the manual in 1947:

> Our years of research have failed to disclose any clear cut cases of harm resulting from masturbation, although we have thousands of cases of boys who have had years of their lives ruined by worry over masturbation.... We should be glad to serve wherever the Boy Scouts can use factual material," he wrote. The BSA later dropped the discussion of masturbation from its handbook.[41]

This Kinsey-backed move increased the vulnerability of young Scouts to sexual abuse by older peers and adult pederasts.

Some accounts claim that Kinsey attended church regularly as a child, and remained devout until he entered college, but an incident involving masturbation was apparently a turning point in his life. He often described to others how a college classmate obsessed with masturbation had sought his help. Kinsey claimed that he accompanied the fellow to his room, knelt, and prayed that the lad would receive strength to stop masturbating.[42] However, after reviewing Kinsey's personal diaries and letters at the Kinsey Institute, Jones concluded that it was not a *friend* who was plagued by the impulse to masturbate, but Kinsey himself:

> Kinsey prayed, asking God to forgive him and to give him the strength not to sin again. The Boy Scout manual... (along with many doctors and moral instructors)... advised boys to take cold showers to improve their health and to take their minds off sex. Kinsey took a cold shower every morning, a practice he continued for life. But neither prayer nor cold showers enabled him to stop masturbating. As a result, Kinsey was consumed by guilt.[43]

Kinsey's interest in Scouting appears to have been similar to that of the movement's founder, Sir Robert Baden-Powell. Like Baden-Powell, Kinsey married relatively late for his time (age 26) and seemed obsessed with nude males. These and other similarities to Baden-Powell, who is known to have collected "nature" photographs of young boys engaged in such activities as skinny-dipping, is both noteworthy and disturbing.

"MIDNIGHT" COWBOYS

Kinsey's interest in camping with young boys continued after college. His professorship at Indiana University, as well as his field research in zoology, placed him in close contact with young male students. One was Ralph Voris, a friend whom Kinsey nicknamed "Mr. Man." From as early as 1926 the two shared intimate correspondence. Sex historian and friendly Kinsey biographer Paul Robinson depicts Voris as Kinsey's most intimate, though possibly latent, homosexual companion. Robinson recalls Kinsey's low regard for effeminate, "citified" homosexuals and his apparent admiration for so-called "cowboy homosexuals":

Patrick Boyle's exposé of pederast sex abuse in the Boy Scouts.

> Elsewhere Kinsey argued that the affections associated with homosexuality were in fact the exclusive property of certain urban homosexual groups, which, he maintained, represented only "a small fraction" of the males with homosexual experience. He contrasted these citified homosexuals with a type that he apparently considered no less prevalent: what might be called cowboy homosexuals: "hard-riding, hard-hitting, assertive males," who enjoyed sexual relations with women (when they were available), but who turned to other males when "outdoor routines" brought them together in exclusively male society.[44]

Photographs portray Kinsey living the rugged life of an outdoorsman. We see him camping in the wild, away from his family, for months at a time, suntanned and stripped to the waist while visiting cowhands in Mexico accompanied by young male students and staffers on gall-wasp trapping expeditions. Although research by others has found relatively high rates of homosexuality among hoboes and so-called "feminine" professions, Kinsey seemed disinterested in those potential subjects. Instead, in the Male, he focused on the,

> fair amount of sexual contact among the older males in Western rural areas. It is a type of homosexuality, which was probably common among pioneers and outdoor men in general. Today it is found among ranchmen, cattlemen, prospectors, lumbermen, and farming groups in general—among groups that are virile, physically active. These are men who have faced the rigors of nature in the wild. They live on realities and on a minimum of theory. Such a background breeds the attitude that sex is sex, irrespective of the nature of the partner with whom the relation is had. Sexual relations are had with women when they are available or with other males when outdoor routines bring men together into exclusively male groups. Such a pattern is not at all uncommon among preadolescent and early adolescent males in such rural areas, and it continues in a number of histories into the adult years and through marriage.[45]

Kinsey had no actual data on the sexual proclivities of "pioneers," yet implied that homosexuality was common among them. And if he had data on American "ranchmen, cattlemen, prospectors, lumbermen, and farming groups in general," it was so sparse that he failed to include it in his 1948 *Male* volume.

On the other hand, "dressing-up" as a virile male ("cowboy," "lumberman," etc.) is common in homosexual circles, where males in such "manly" occupations are viewed as highly attractive.[46] This attitude has been evident in such cultural landmarks as the Oscar-winning movie "Midnight Cowboy," and many hits by the Village People, beginning with their chart-topping recording "YMCA."

Kinsey is pictured here "Asking directions" during his trip to Mexico in 1935. (Christenson)

Credible accounts of Kinsey's contact with such men are limited to his gall-wasp trapping trips to Mexico. He did not speak Spanish and did not claim to have witnessed sex acts during those ventures. In short, his sensational claims about alleged homosexuality among pioneers, cattlemen, lumbermen, and other rugged outdoorsmen lacked objective evidence. Interviewed for the 1996 Yorkshire program, "Kinsey's Paedophiles," Jones described how,

> [T]wo male students, Brayland and Coons, worked under Kinsey's supervision in 1934/35. There were numerous episodes, nude and whatnot nude. [There is an explicit] photograph of Kinsey in the buff. On that trip [they engaged in] masturbation sessions, group masturbation. Both of the young men were trying to keep Kinsey at arm's length.

Asked what Brayland's wife thought about it, Jones recalled: "I can tell you that she didn't like Alfred Kinsey. [She responded] that they were just kids from Mississippi and that Alfred Kinsey hurt them." And in his recent biography, Jones notes,

> Kinsey bathed with his students… striding about camp naked… [Confided one student] "You'd see him… going to the bathroom, and all that sort of thing… He'd just take a leak right there in front of us…" Professors simply did not engage in that sort of behavior with their graduate students. Yet Kinsey seemed totally oblivious to sexual taboos… as though he was determined to flaunt them… Kinsey had become a sexual rebel… manipulative and aggressive, a man who abused his professional authority and betrayed his trust as a teacher… [O]nly… a compulsive man would have taken such risks.[47]

"FAMILY MAN"

It was Kinsey's interest in gall wasps that brought him together with the only woman he is known to have dated. Clara Braken McMillen, whom Kinsey called "Mac," was a chemistry major at Ohio State University and also an insect enthusiast. After seeing each other casually at several events, in 1921 Kinsey, at age 26, took "Mac" for a walk and proposed marriage.[48]

Clara was reportedly considering another suitor, and did not immediately accept. Pomeroy notes that Kinsey was "profoundly disappointed and surprised when she did not say yes immediately to his offer of marriage."[49]

According to Christenson, Clara was a talented woman who garnered national honors for a chemistry paper and was elected to an honorary science club. Her father was a Fort Wayne high school teacher, while her mother graduated from the Cincinnati College of Music. At a university picnic, unsatisfied with the campfire built by a colleague, Kinsey made his own fire elsewhere. Clara joined him and their courtship began.

Clara Braken McMillen

Christenson notes that "Alfred described in detail to Clara his church work with the Bethany Boys' Club while he was at Harvard,"[50] which suggested to Clara that Kinsey was "too churchy" for her.[51] Pomeroy insists, to the contrary, that by age 26 Kinsey was a committed atheist. If so, he apparently hid that fact from Clara.

Christenson describes how Alfred Kinsey used the couple's honeymoon to "test" his wife's courage and stamina. Though his bride was allegedly an outdoor girl, she had never climbed a mountain. Kinsey, who worked for years to overcome his sickly youth, had acquired mountain-climbing skills and commonly utilized them to establish his superiority over other men. Christenson writes,

> They climbed Mount Washington in a blizzard. Since Clara had never seen a mountain before, this was a real initiation into rugged climbing and all-weather camping. On the first stiff ascent Alfred selected a fire-warden's trail, which was the shortest feasible route and, in Clara's words, "straight up." Alfred, in good trim, led the way, with his new bride lagging somewhat behind.[52]

Kinsey and Clara at their wedding. (Christenson)

As the honeymoon trek continued, Kinsey would forge ahead, then wait for his bride to catch up. Christenson notes: "It was clearly a test of her mettle, and she was equal to it."[53]

Christenson does not ask why Dr. Kinsey did not opt for a traditional honeymoon of blissful togetherness. Instead of wine and roses, he brought pitted prunes and prepackaged trail foods. Instead of a cozy cottage with a warm fire, the future sex authority chose wind, rain, and frigid nights outdoors—conditions virtually guaranteed to preclude consummation of their marriage: "When necessary they built a lean-to for shelter from the wind and rain. The evening routine was to take off their boots and belts and to put on clean socks, plus all the extra clothing available, before climbing into their blankets."[54]

Biographer Jones confirmed that the Kinseys did not, in fact, consummate their marriage during the honeymoon. "Kinsey later confided to a friend that the problem was the result of both inexperience and physiology," Jones writes.[55] He claimed that Clara required minor surgery, and that "Victorian prudery" was to blame for their sexual failure and the delay in seeking medical help.

Until Jones described Clara's complicity in Kinsey's homosexual life, as well as his secret sex productions, Kinsey's biographers told us little else about Clara. She smiles with her children in the family publicity photograph reproduced in Pomeroy's book. Her short hair is combed straight to one side. She is plain, wears no earrings or jewelry, no makeup. In her dark suit she could be mistaken for a man.

Clara and Alfred. (Christenson)

Alfred and Clara were married on June 3, 1921. She gave birth to their first son, Donald, in mid 1922. A diabetic, he died at a young age. They had three other children: daughters Anne (1924) and Joan (1925), and son Bruce (1928). Little is known about the Kinsey children, other than that one took piano lessons, they were forbidden to receive confirmation despite attending church and that they eventually gave their sex histories to Pomeroy and their father. Jones reports that Kinsey led his family on nudist vacations to the Smoky Mountains, and that nudist magazines were perused in the home. Kinsey himself would often shave in the nude in the presence of the children.[56] We are not told at what age this practice ended, or if it ended.

Appearing on the 1996 BBC program "Reputations," Kinsey's two (by then elderly) daughters claimed that their father was a typical middle-class dad who was thoughtful in all things. Surviving son Bruce has repeatedly refused interviews with anyone writing about his father.

All of the young Kinseys attended church. "Both parents," Pomeroy explains, "felt it was a cultural experience they should have." It is conceivable that Dr. Kinsey attended primarily to enhance an aura of respectability. Years earlier, Jones reports, he had joined with leaders of the eugenics movement, whose devotees disdained the Judeo Christian belief system. But a churchgoing image would provide useful cover for his secret life and unorthodox research.

Son Bruce on friend's shoulders. Kinsey, daughters Anne and Joan, and wife Clara.

MILITANT ATHEIST

One day when he was about five years of age, Kinsey's son, Bruce, saw a flower and exclaimed, "Look at the pretty flower, Daddy. God made it." Kinsey could not let it pass. "Now Bruce," he said, "where did the flower really come from?" "From a seed," Bruce dutifully replied, apparently aware of the answer that would please his father.[57] There was the implication that if one believes in God, one cannot believe in seeds.

A later incident, while Kinsey was mentoring his sexology disciples, further underscored his atheism. He and Pomeroy were talking about theological matters. Pomeroy, puzzled by the impression "that [Kinsey] still entertained religious feelings," interjected, "I've known you a long time and I've never heard you talk this way. Do you really believe in God?" Kinsey was irate and "surprised" that Pomeroy could have thought for an instant that he was a believer. "Don't be ridiculous. Of course not," he snapped.[58]

According to Pomeroy, Kinsey became an atheist shortly after he prayed for divine intervention for the college "friend" (who was, you will recall, Kinsey himself) who could not stop masturbating:

Kinsey (center) with two unnamed graduate students in Mexico, early 1930s. (Pomeroy)

> Kinsey began to lose his beliefs as a college student, when his study of science disclosed to him what he saw as a basic incongruity between it and religion. Having so decided for himself, he could not understand why every other scientist did not think as he did.[59]

Kinsey sought thereafter to avoid those who believed in God. Members of his carefully selected staff were disbelievers. Years later, his *Male* and *Female* volumes would blame religious-based "ancient taboos" for America's supposedly repressive sexual attitudes and resulting social disorder:

> Our particular systems certainly go back to the Old Testament philosophy on which the Talmud is based, and which was the philosophy of those Jews who first followed the Christian faith. In many details, the prescriptions of the Talmud are nearly identical with those of our present-day legal codes governing sexual behavior.[60]

Kinsey was fond of telling audiences that his Institute's collection of obscenity was the largest in the world, "except for the Vatican's." Following his death on August 25, 1956, that apocryphal attempt at humor became part of the Kinsey Institute's official propaganda and was thereafter passed along by gullible academicians and journalists who neglected to confirm it. E. Michael Jones, editor of *Fidelity* magazine, recalls Associated Press news feature writer John Barbour's claim that the story was true. "It's in some basement somewhere. I can't tell you exactly," Barbour told Jones, adding that he was certain that AP's Rome bureau had confirmed its existence. But when Jones called the Vatican, he was told in no uncertain terms that the alleged collection did not exist. "It's absolute nonsense. Absolute nonsense," a Vatican spokesman declared.[61]

Jones then spoke to Stephanie Sanders, a representative of the Kinsey Institute, who claimed that the Vatican had "been in the business of restricting those materials for Catholics for years, and so they have archived those materials." Finally, Jones turned to Paul Gebhard, one of Kinsey's early research assistants and later director of the Kinsey Institute. Gebhard himself had wondered about the collection as a potential source of information. He, too, had been told by the Vatican that there was no such accumulation of pornography. Gebhard then turned to the American Library Association, which merely repeated Kinsey's anti-Vatican line. Eventually, he reported:

> Many years before I joined the staff, somewhere about 1940 or so, old Dr. Robert Dickinson had just been at the Vatican and had visited Kinsey. At that time Kinsey had a bookcase about half full of porn, and Dickinson looked at it and said, "Gosh, you've got quite a collection. You've got almost as much as the Vatican." At that point Kinsey started making this remark.[62]

Kinsey's publicity photos imply his trip to Peru was to locate Peruvian erotica. However, Gebhard had quietly whisked the sexologist thence for repairs after Kinsey contracted "orchitis" apparently due to gonorrhea and/or his obsessive sadomasochistic phallic abuse.

It was a memorable line, which Kinsey employed for entertainment and propaganda purposes. It bolstered one of his favorite themes: that people who preach morality are hypocrites secretly obsessed with sex. It was a fabrication, and Kinsey knew it to be such, but no one in academia or the pro-Kinsey press ever pressed him for proof, just as they rarely, if ever, questioned his many other outlandish assertions. And though Gebhard admitted to E. Michael Jones that the story was a myth, he took no steps to set the record straight.

CHAPTER 1 NOTES

[1]. Dr. Wardell Pomeroy, *Kinsey and The Institute for Sex Research,* Harper & Row, New York, 1972, p. 21.
[2]. Ernest Bell, Ed. *Fighting the Traffic in Young Girls*, Chicago, The Illinois Vigilance Association, 1910, p. 292.
[3]. Bell, p. 292.
[4]. Bell, p. 459.
[5]. Bell, pp. 284-285.
[6]. Bell, p. 287.
[7]. "Prohibition" *Encarta*, Funk & Wagnalls Corporation, 1995.
[8]. Pomeroy, p. 88.
[9]. Pomeroy, p. 24.
[10]. Pomeroy, p. 24.
[11]. Cornelia Christenson, *Kinsey: A Biography*, Indiana University, Bloomington, 1971, p. 16.
[12]. Christenson, p. 19.
[13]. Pomeroy, p. 21.
[14]. Pomeroy, p. 343.
[15]. Christenson, pp. 26-30.
[16]. Pomeroy, p. 25.
[17]. Pomeroy, p. 31.
[18]. Christenson, p. 26 and p. 19; Pomeroy, p. 33.

[19]. Pomeroy, p. 34.
[20]. Christenson, p. 24.
[21]. Christenson, p. 25.
[22]. I. P. Pavlov, *Conditioned Reflexes, A Physiological Activity of the Cerebral Cortex,* Dover Publications, Inc., New York, 1926.
[23]. Kinsey, Pomeroy, Martin and Gebhard, *Sexual Behavior in the Human Female*, W.B. Saunders Co., Philadelphia, 1948, p. 647.
[24]. *The Concise Columbia Encyclopedia*, Columbia University Press, 1991.
[25]. *Concise*.
[26]. Christenson, p. 30.
[27]. James H. Jones, *Alfred C. Kinsey: A Public/Private Life,* W. W. Norton, New York, 1997, p. 194, 809 f. 78.
[28]. Jones, p. 190.
[29]. See letters in the author's archive, including those from Andrea Dworkin and Dr. E. Michael Jones.
[30]. Pomeroy, p. 27.
[31]. Christopher Stevens, *Secret and Forbidden,* Living Books, New York, 1966, p. 202.
[32]. Stevens, Ibid. p. 216.
[33]. Stevens, Ibid, p. 210.
[34]. Jones, p. 395.
[35]. Christenson, p. 23.
[36]. Pomeroy, p. 26.
[37]. Pomeroy, p. 32.
[38]. Christenson, p. 35.
[39]. Christenson, p. 54.
[40]. Patrick Boyle, *Scout's Honor: Sexual Abuse in America's Most Trusted Institution*, Prima Publishing, Rocklin, California, 1994, p. 22.
[41]. Pomeroy, p. 12.
[42]. Pomeroy, p. 33.
[43]. Jones, p. 75.
[44]. Paul Robinson, *The Modernization of Sex*, Harper & Row, New York, 1976, pp. 42-119.
[45]. *Male*, p. 457.
[46]. See the Reisman & Johnson report, "Partner Solicitation Language as a Reflection of Male Sexual Orientation," 1995, *Collected Papers from the NARTH Annual Conference*, July 29, 1995.
[47]. Jones, pp. 273-283.
[48]. Pomeroy, p. 38.
[49]. Pomeroy, p. 38.
[50]. Christenson, p. 45.
[51]. Christenson, p. 45.
[52]. Christenson, p. 49.
[53]. Christenson, p. 49.
[54]. Christenson, p. 49.
[55]. James H. Jones, "Dr. Yes," *The New Yorker*, September 1, 1997, p. 103.
[56]. Jones, "Dr. Yes," p. 103.
[57]. Pomeroy, p. 29.
[58]. Pomeroy, p. 29.
[59]. Pomeroy, p. 29.
[60]. *Male*, p. 465.
[61]. E. Michael Jones, "The Case Against Kinsey," *Fidelity*, April 1989, pp. 22-35.
[62]. E. Michael Jones, pp. 22-35.

CHAPTER 2

THE INDIANA UNIVERSITY SEXOLOGIST

Alfred Kinsey asked questions and analyzed their answers statistically in ways which implicitly assumed that all forms of "sexual outlets" are the same in meaning, value, emotional power, consequences and everything else... Kinsey literally reduced all human sexuality to the single dimension of orgasmic "outlet." In his behaviorist metaphysics, the number of "outlets" alone has any meaning. His revolutionary zeal knew no bounds. His casual pronouncement on animalism shows the monomaniacal zealot at work.[1]

Jack Douglas, The Rockford Institute, 1987

Alfred Kinsey's close friend Ralph ("Mr. Man") Voris died on May 9, 1940. Despite repeated requests by Voris' wife for a bedside visit, Kinsey was too deeply involved in sex interviews to see him. He and Clara did, however, drive immediately to Springfield, Missouri, to comfort the widow and attend the funeral service. Then,

[U]nder the cover of darkness, he [Kinsey] entered Voris' office and removed certain items, including copies and originals of their private correspondence. This accomplished, Kinsey and Clara returned to Bloomington, without staying for the interment two days later. Until he joined his beloved friend in death, Kinsey kept a photograph of Voris on his desk.[2]

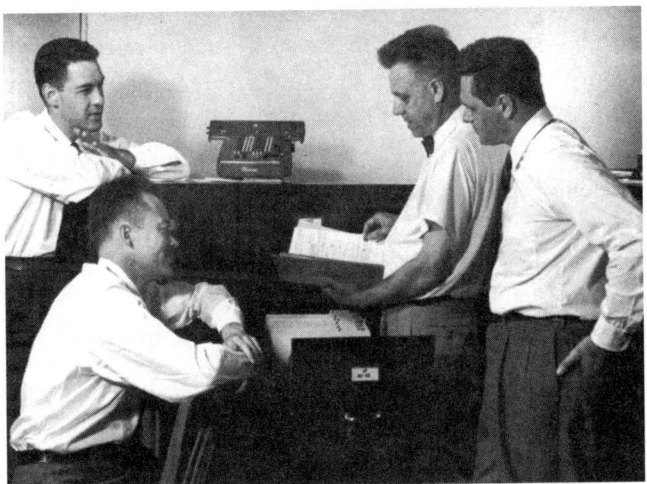

Kinsey and his draft-deferred team. Jones identifies Martin (far left), Pomeroy (far right), Kinsey's coauthors and his young sexual partners. The "amoral" Gebhard (seated) was a coauthor of the Female Volume.

At the time, America and most of the world were embroiled in World War II. Most able-bodied young men anticipated military service. After the U.S. entered the war in 1941, Kinsey arranged draft deferments for himself and members of his staff, claiming that they could best serve the nation by continuing their research. The groundwork was laid for their eventual report on male sexuality.

In 1938, Kinsey's marriage course at Indiana University was "officially" approved. To this day, despite the substantial body of evidence to the contrary, both the Kinsey Institute and University administrators claim that he had no early unusual interest in sex; knew little about the subject before being "asked" to teach the marriage course; and found little usable information in the library when his students asked questions he was unable to answer. Former Institute Director June Reinisch, in her book *The Kinsey Institute New Report on Sex,* states:

> Students at Indiana University petitioned the administration for a course in human sexuality for students who were either engaged, married, or considering marriage.... The university asked a well-respected professor of zoology to coordinate the [marriage course] and felt that Dr. Alfred C. Kinsey, a Harvard-trained scientist known for his... exhaustive research on gall wasps, would provide a scholarly perspective to this sensitive subject.[3]
>
> As he set out to gather materials for his curriculum, Kinsey soon discovered that few scientific data were available on human sexual behavior. The little that did exist was in general either distorted by personal bias or based on studies of small numbers of clinical patients.[4]

Indiana University's 1948 year book illustrates the "married" couples who were--initially--the only students permitted to attend Kinsey's "Marriage Course."

Kinsey's formal sex research, under cover of the "marriage course," began in 1938. According to the University's official account, he was asked by the Association of Women Students to create the course. Surprised by the alleged dearth of source materials, he set out to fill the void with his own research. John Bancroft, current director of the Kinsey Institute, continues to promote the myth of Kinsey as a disinterested, serendipitous sex researcher. In his Introductions to the 1998 editions of the *Male* and *Female* volumes, Bancroft states that "Kinsey's Mission" was to "striv[e] for a greater understanding of the varieties of sexual expression and a resulting greater tolerance of such variability." (*Female* volume, p. 9.)

"MR. MAN"

Kinsey included an update about the course in a letter to Ralph Voris:

> In the first four semesters, we have had 100, 200, 230, 260, 290 students. A few flurries with unfavorable criticisms from older faculty who had no firsthand knowledge-but even that is gone. The students would do anything to defend us, their appreciation is so great. We have their written comments at the end of each semester. Several have written personal letters to express their appreciation for their personal benefit... The Gridiron banquet brought only one reference to it-a reprimand to a couple of the boys for having engaged in biologic activities "without benefit of Kinsey's course in connubial calisthenics." The personal conferences totaled 280 for me alone to which, Mr. Man, I hope to prove to the world some day that any subject may be a profitable field for scientific research if zealously pursued and handled with objective scholarship. We have over 350 histories now-I will have my 1,000 within another year and a half. Gosh, I wish I could discuss with you these data, the summaries, etc. I have presented a progress report to our faculty discussion club, nearly bowled some of them over, but they were game and objective, and most encouraging in their approval of further investigation. Wish you were here to see this material.[5]

"Presentation photograph of Ralph Voris. The photograph of Voris that Kinsey kept on his desk all his life--a less formal picture—seems to have vanished." (Caption and photo taken from Gathorne-Hardy's *Sex, the Measure of All Things*.)

That it was already being called "Kinsey's course" annoyed other faculty members, who complained that Kinsey's "biology" sex segment was disproportionately lengthy and that he should be saying considerably less on the subject. James Jones, in his doctoral dissertation on Kinsey, reveals that while an overwhelming number of faculty members strenuously objected to the course, Kinsey gave only glowing reports about its reception to the Rockefeller Foundation when requesting-and receiving—funds earmarked for sex "research." The Foundation's stated policy at the time was that "[n]othing was more highly valued in the Rockefeller camp than fact finding pursued without conscious bias. Only after all the facts were known could the proper action be taken."[6]

During the first semester, only married, engaged, or special "serious" students were allowed to take the course, but the acceptance protocol was broadened beginning with the second term. Jones reports that the University's Board of Trustees again approved the course, along with Kinsey's list of 350 intimate sexual questions to be asked students behind closed doors.[7] He cites evidence that plans were prepared and approved long before Kinsey was supposedly requested to initiate the course:

> [Kinsey] merely substituted people for gall wasps. There can be no doubt that Kinsey intended to use the Marriage Course to launch a major study of human sexual behavior. The interview he used... had taken many months, and quite possibly more than a year to structure.[8]

Students seemed more interested in the type of "biological" information they received than in Kinsey's moral, legal, and ethical instruction. Predictably, he was elated. Reprising his early camping pattern with the Boy Scouts, he often accompanied his young charges on field excursions. There are no photographs identifying young Voris as a Kinsey camper, but in a rather unusual letter to "Mr. Man" Kinsey wrote:

> Following your lead, I have adopted shorts and nothing more as the garden costume, and have the best tan ever, more than I ever thought a bleached blond could have, and the most glorious live feeling that my skin has ever known. Incidentally, I weigh just 20 pounds less than I did in February, from 162 to 142, and practically all that came off the waistline. Had all my trousers let out last February and now every pair is in folds at the waist.[9]

The tone of Kinsey's letters to Voris did not resemble customary man-to-man correspondence. Considering the sensitive nature of Kinsey's unusual research, and its inherent risk to the University, it is remarkable that after Herman Wells became University president Kinsey behaved as if he had thrown caution to the wind:

> Kinsey's neighbors were shocked to see him work the garden clad only in a brief loin cloth that covered the bare essentials, but nothing more... Kinsey's "male bikini"... Joan Reid, Kinsey's younger daughter, also discusses her father's scant gardening attire and its impact on neighbors.[10]

THE INDIANA UNIVERSITY SEXOLOGIST

Jones reports that Clyde Martin, Kinsey's coauthor and erstwhile lawn boy, occasionally joined Kinsey in similarly scanty garden attire.[11] And the latter became even more unconventional when hunting gall wasps. Jones quotes a student with whom Kinsey worked in the field:

> "He would go naked if we were in a campground," Homer T. Rainwater recalls. "He just didn't give a damn. Nor did he show any inhibitions about his bodily functions." Kinsey's eagerness to talk about sex was more disconcerting. After several nights, Rainwater discerned a pattern. Kinsey would begin by sharing intimate details about his own private life. "He'd talk about his wife, and what a good sex partner she was, and then he'd go from there. He had a pretty wife, and apparently she was very accommodating, and he talked about that to us, I thought, more than was appropriate." Much to Rainwater's embarrassment, Kinsey would then ask about *his* sex life.[12]

Kinsey (center) on Mexican trip, apparently with Voris (foreground). (Christenson)

It is instructive to compare a segment of Kinsey's letter to Voris, describing his (Kinsey's) slim waist, "bleached blond" hair, tan, short shorts, and "glorious" feeling on his skin, with a fragment of another letter revealed by Pomeroy, in which Kinsey wrote (regarding Greek pederasty),

> Knowing what I do of the human animal, I cannot believe that the love and affection which the older males bestowed upon Greek boys, and their aesthetic admiration for the bodies of Greek youth, could have failed to arouse specific sexual response [sic] which found their outlet in overt sexual relations.[13]

Regarding "aesthetic admiration for the bodies of Greek youth," Kinsey wrote to Voris about his collection of "gorgeous" male homosexual photographs[14] in a manner somewhat reminiscent of Scouting founder Sir Robert Baden Powell's remarks about young male nudes:[15]

> What I would have done without your earlier help, I do not know.... I have whole albums of photographs of their friends, or from commercial sources-fine art to putrid. Some of the art model material is gorgeous. I want you to see it....[16]

Moreover, Kinsey felt "love and affection" for Voris. According to Pomeroy, "Voris became the closest friend Kinsey ever had; their friendship probably meant more to him than any other."[17] Kinsey wrote often to Voris:

> And would you believe it, when hot weather came on, I [Kinsey] went to the city swimming pool (which my family patronizes every day) and finding it hot as soup, I turned to

the University pool and swam at the end of every day until school closed. The first time I have been in University pool since you deserted me here.[18]

By 1935 we find Kinsey writing to Voris about the enforcement of hygiene standards among male students during field trips. Earlier, young campers loved "Al," the camp leader with the merry eye, wide smile, and hearty laugh. But now he seems to be a rigid, controlling taskmaster unusually interested in the bathing habits of his young charges:

> You [Voris] helped me establish certain traditions in our field work which I have had to fight to maintain. For instance the daily bath conditions permitting. You may know of the scrap I had with [name deleted] and [name deleted] one day in West Virginia. When I discovered they had sidestepped the bath, I sent them back to their room, and like good boys they disrobed and took to the water. Well, I had a scrap with [name deleted] on this Alabama trip. I reckon he missed 3 baths out of 5 days. Discipline, man! What with our difficulties in keeping decent in field work anyway. We kept sweet enough in the subsequent arguments but he calmly insisted that he wouldn't bathe. After all due warnings, I left him in Southern Tennessee at Columbia... where the old colored woman came out with a big stick for us, some years ago. He beat his way back, of course, O.K. He hasn't come around yet to promise any reformed behavior, so I'm not quite certain he goes to Mexico with us. But perhaps we can teach him some hygiene and discipline before we are done trying to make a taxonomist of him.[19]

Kinsey was apparently interested in more than hygiene. Jones reveals that he not only watched the reluctant nude bathers, but joined in. In another letter Kinsey wrote,

> If there is any chance of our getting into the field together, I would very much like to. It was a glorious day we spent together last fall... God, how I needed you that week, to show them that someone besides myself considered our field technique worth working for![20] It will always be one of my regrets that your bugs and mine do not always live in exactly the same place.[21]

> Wish so much that you could go over this material with me. You are among the very few individuals to whom I can ever tell all of the story and the part that has too much dynamite to get into even the most objective, scientific print. Your reactions would mean much to me as your common sense advice has so often before.[22]

Moreover, Kinsey marked some of the letters sent to Voris' home "Personal," to discourage scrutiny of their contents by others, including Mrs. Voris. Pomeroy writes,

> At this point a singular thing happens. The letter concludes with the usual signature, but then it is followed by four more pages, on which Kinsey has printed in block letters "PERSONAL" at the top of each page. Here he explodes some of the "dynamite" he has just talked about, and apparently he has concealed it in this way because he thinks it may offend Voris' wife, Geraldine, or else believes it would be discreet not to let anyone but Voris read it. Voris will be able to show the first part of the letter to his wife, and read the last four pages privately.[23]

Pomeroy does not expound upon the "dynamite" that Kinsey exploded. Ralph Voris died tragically at age 38 on May 9, 1940.[24]

Despite the "dynamite" with which he was playing, and the open secret that his attitudes and behavior around students were highly irregular, Kinsey continued to benefit from the veneer of respectability, and continuing financial support, provided by Indiana University.

BERLIN TO BLOOMINGTON

The Kinsey Institute and the University contend to this day that Kinsey began gathering sexuality data after 1938 so that he could accurately answer questions posed by students about marriage and family life. Yet he was well aware of the wealth of available information on the subject. He was, for instance, familiar with the work of Dr. Magnus Hirschfeld. Kinsey's friend, Dr. Harry Benjamin,[25] had brought Hirschfeld to America to speak against the social reform accomplishments of the Purity Movement.[26] In 1919, Hirschfeld established the world's first Institute for Sexology in Berlin, organizing it into four departments: Sexual Biology, Sexual Medicine, Sexual Sociology, and Sexual Ethnology.[27] Englishman Christopher Isherwood wrote three novels about life in Berlin at the time, from which the stage production and movie *Caberet* was drawn. Isherwood, a pederast, summarized his view of Germany as "Berlin is for boys."[28]

This photograph of Hirschfeld's pioneering Institute for Sexology, established in Berlin in 1919, is taken from a catalogue celebrating the 75th anniversary of "sexology" (1908-1983). Hirschfeld's Institute was the prototype for Kinsey's Bloomington, Indiana, sex center. The sexology seminar project was partly supported by the Kinsey Institute.

In his autobiography, *Christopher and His Kind, 1929-1939,* Isherwood describes the activities and events at Hirschfeld's Institute, including the incongruity of respectable elegance in the dining hall while another chamber featured "live exhibits… whips, chains and other sexual torture instruments" routinely used in "therapy" by Hirschfeld's "patients," Nazis, and others. Isherwood notes that Hirschfeld publicly advocated sex between consenting individuals, including adult sex with older children.[29] He urged "tolerance" and called Americans sexual "hypocrites"-terms later popularized by Kinsey in a similar U.S. context. Hans Blueher, an early leader in the Wandervogel [organized German youth], records his visit to Hirschfeld and the Berlin Institute:

Kinsey colleague Harry Benjamin (left), with Magnus Hirschfeld, in 1929. Benjamin wrote a glowing introduction to pedophile Rene Guyan's 1948 book, *The Ethics of Sexual Acts*. (1983 commemorative brochure).

> **CHICAGO HERALD AND EXAMINER...**
>
> **cans Incomes of 55 La**
>
> ## Hirschfeld Asks Scientific Sex View, Not Theological
>
> **German Expert Likes Magistrates' Attitude in U. S. Courts**
>
> By Dr. Magnus Hirschfeld, World-Famous Advocate of Sex Reform, Eminent German Authority on the Manifestations of Love, Who Has Often Been Called "The Einstein of Sex." In a Dialogue With George Sylvester Viereck.
>
> PRESENT—Dr. Magnus Hirschfeld and the Interviewer.
> PLACE—The library of the Interviewer on Riverside drive, New York. On the wall, pictures of many celebrities, including Roosevelt, Marconi, the Kaiser, Einstein, Conan Doyle, Mussolini, Foch, Joffre, Clemenceau, Steinach, Voronoff and Dr. Hirschfeld.
> Dr. Magnus Hirschfeld, whose benignant smile redeems the ferocity of his bushy mustache, rests in an easy chair after prolonged visits to the Women's Court, the Night Court and other metropolitan institutions where magistrates mete out justice.
>
> **Liberal Spirit Amazing**
>
> HIRSCHFELD: I am pleased and astonished by the liberal spirit which prevails in your magistrates courts. I have "sat in" with a number of judges. I have talked to them and closely watched the cases that come up before them. Their decisions and their attitude toward the defendants appearing before them demonstrate an extraordinary understanding of the vagaries of the human heart. The judges seem to me more humane than the law. They are certainly more humane than the police.
> I: You cannot expect policemen to be familiar with the mysteries of sex expounded by Krafft-Ebing, Havelock Ellis and yourself.
> HIRSCHFELD (smiling gently): Of course not. The entire science of sex is comparatively young. Sex science was the last of the sci-
>
> *Dr. Magnus Hirschfeld.*
>
> I: Surely the law must be enforced?
> HIRSCHFELD (shrugging his shoulders): Our moral code is largely the product of climate and chance. It is not always possible to draw a line where the permissible ends. A historical survey of the laws prevailing at different times in one society and a geographical survey of the laws prevailing in different societies at any one time reveal surprising variations.
>
> **Moral Code Varies**
>
> No objective principles have yet been established in matters governing the love life of the world. Until the age of enlightenment at the end of the eighteenth century set in, many minor sex offenses were punishable with death. After the French revolution they ceased to be regarded as crimes or misdemeanors.
> The attitude of society toward
>
> **Moral Code Largely Result of Fate and Climate, He Declares**
>
> No oath should be required from the defendant.
> I: What do you think of our penal system and our prisons?
> HIRSCHFELD: On my tour of inspection of Welfare Island and the Tombs I was struck by the kindliness of some of the guards to their prisoners. But I was shocked by the physical condition of the cells, which hardly allow one-third of the space necessary for the decencies of life to the prisoners. You should throw open your prisons to the modern spirit. In Russia the prison authorities experiment with "week-end vacations" for convicts. These vacations enable the prisoners to attend to urgent business and to visit their families. There is no reason why wives should suffer by being deprived for a long term of their husbands. Morality in the home and the prison profits from the Russian innovation. Revolutionary as it may seem, it works.
>
> **Disease Breeds Crime**
>
> I: Is crime not always the product of disease?
> HIRSCHFELD: Most habitual criminals are physically and psychically defective.
> Your judges are as lenient as possible with the wayward girl and other offenders of this description. But leniency should not depend upon the whim of the intelligence or the good humor of the magistrate.
> I: How would you remedy the situation?
> HIRSCHFELD: Your courts need medical experts thoroughly familiar with all the physical and psychic factors involved, to whom the judge can turn for advice. If a medical expert of wide experience had the opportunity to examine offenders, he would be able to determine whether their condition is amenable to medical treatment.

Hirschfeld's 1931 trip across the USA was arranged by Dr. Harry Benjamin, who aided Kinsey and their collaborator, world famous pedophile judge, Rene Guyon, (1993 Commemorative Brochure)

I was led into the study of the "Wise Man of Berlin" (as he was called). Sitting on a silk covered fauteuil, legs under him like a Turk, was an individual with bloated lips and cunning, dimly coveting eyes who offered me a fleshy hand and introduced himself as Dr. Hirschfeld... [Later in a meeting of the Scientific Humanitarian Committee, the most influential homosexual organization in the German "gay rights" movement] the first to greet me was a corporal with a deep bass voice; he was however, wearing women's clothes... "A so-called transvestite!" commented Dr. Hirschfeld, whose nickname was "Aunt Magnesia," and introduced us... Then a most beautiful youth appeared... "A hermaphrodite!" said Hirschfeld. "Why don't you come to me during my office hours tomorrow, you can see him naked then"... An older gentleman in his sixties... recited a poem... to a sixteen year old youth, full of yearning... I [suddenly realized] I was in the middle of a brothel.[30]

Hirschfeld complained that U.S. attitudes toward sex were not "scientific." Dr. Benjamin hoped to have Hirschfeld lead an American sexual reform movement, but apparently the publicly-acknowledged homosexual German sexologist did not fit the profile that U.S. society would trust. Midwestern "family man" Kinsey would eventually fill the void.

In "The Sexual Modernists," University of California-San Diego sociologist Jack Douglas describes the pervasive European sexuality movement:

> The standard picture presented by sexual modernists today depicts a few lonely culture heroes, especially Havelock Ellis and Sigmund Freud, suddenly launching a revolution against massive Victorian sexual repression. This picture is completely false. Havelock Ellis'[31] work was built on a mass of earlier scholarly and scientific work, all carefully footnoted, and Freud drew almost all of his major ideas from Ellis and other sex researchers and from literature and philosophy. There were specialized journals of sexual research, case studies of every conceivable form of sexual activity, and for every article or book proposing repression there was generally another proposing

Havelock Ellis

Sigmund Freud

the opposite and several proposing something in between. What is striking, by contrast with our own day in which there is a reigning dogmatism of sexual modernism, is how lively and undogmatic the massive controversies over sexuality were.[32]

Public documents confirm that Kinsey's "sex research" actually began much earlier than 1938. Former Kinsey Institute librarian Cornelia Christenson, writing in *Kinsey: A Biography*, recalls a sexuality lecture delivered by Kinsey in April, 1935, three years before "the call" to become a marriage/sexuality instructor. As summarized by Christenson:

> This is a strongly worded but thoughtful exposition of the influence of social institutions on sexual and reproductive behavior. It predated the marriage course by three years, and it provides convincing evidence of his early interest in and concern for the problems arising from the social restrictions on man's biological nature. On page ten he cites "the ignorance of sexual structure and physiology, of the technique fundamental in the normal course of

Leaders of the global sexology movement at the 1929 Berlin sex conference, demanding worldwide elimination of prudish sex laws and sexual "repression." (1983 commemorative brochure)

sexual activities and the prudish aversion to adequate participation in the one physiologic activity on which society is most dependent, as the chief sources of psychic conflict and resulting broken marriages."[33]

Warren Weaver, head of the natural science division of the Rockefeller Foundation, pointed out that his American Statistical Association colleagues had conducted a standard literature search and were stunned by the amount of sexological writings, books, articles, and conferences spawned by the academic European sexual freedom movement:

> First, my friends of the American Statistical Association committee who have been studying the Kinsey project, have told me that they were completely surprised at the volume and value of other work done in this field. When I talked with them they were not ready to say whether Dr. Kinsey's work actually exceeded other work. *The only thing they were sure of was that Dr. Kinsey had a large edge with respect to publicity.* Thus there is at least reasonable question as to [his] pioneering character.[34] [Emphasis added.]

There are other early indications of Kinsey's interest in sex, and familiarity with the available research. Consider, for example, his acquaintance with one of America's first sex researchers, Dr. Robert Dickinson, a gynecologist and author of *A Thousand Marriages* (1931). Kinsey arranged to have Dickinson visit Indiana University to lecture on his work. According to Pomeroy,

> Dickinson was to talk about a massive study he had made of the physiologic effects of masturbation on the sexual organs of women to be illustrated with slides showing shots of the vulvas of his subjects. Quite naturally the lecture hall was jammed to the doors... Dickinson's work was one of the original sources of inspiration for his [Kinsey's] own study.[35]

Clarence Tripp, Kinsey's early sex photographer and colleague, explained during his 1998 (British) Yorkshire television interview that Dickinson, Kinsey's inspirational "mentor in sex research," had "collaborated with [a] pedophile for several years, and taught him how to record his child abuse in scientific detail."

Writing to Dickinson in 1941, Kinsey claimed that he had abandoned his interest in wasps by around 1930. "It was your own work which turned my attention to the purposes of research in this field some 10 or 12 years ago," he recalled, although "circumstances were not propitious for starting the work until three years ago."[36]

In his 1973 doctoral dissertation, James Jones records Kinsey's assertion that he had been working on sexual studies since 1912-1913, while a teenager. That would have been during Kinsey's Scouting, camping, and early masturbation-counseling days. Jones further reports that in 1938, in response to complaints about the marriage course, Kinsey stated: "My first contact with sex instruction came twenty-six

Kinsey shifted from gathering data about the structure of gall wasps to gathering data about the sexuality of human beings.

years ago. I have watched it critically and contributed something to it in the secondary schools ever since." And, in 1935, Kinsey had claimed that men and women were not having sex early enough or often enough: "Most of the social problems and the sexual conflicts of youth are the result of the long frustration of the normal sexual activities," he contended. "Biologically, delayed marriage is all wrong."[37]

Indiana University marketed Kinsey, the free-sex crusader, as a disinterested scholar in an attempt to pacify Kinsey's colleagues and the public. Kinsey did not reluctantly respond to a plea from sexually ignorant students for sex information. He *created* the call through his lectures, earlier research, and long-standing plan to win approval for "the work." In the early 1920s he had cultivated influential faculty members as a base of support for his sex research. Pomeroy tells us,

> In these early days, Kinsey also laid the foundations for his survival when sex and sex research became an issue on the campus. As it proved, one of his best investments of time was his membership in a faculty discussion group which he joined soon after he came to the University [1920], long before there was any controversy about him. It was a valuable association for Kinsey. He was able to try out some of his early data on them, and because of his long association with the group and their friendship with him, they could discuss the work freely, without prejudice. It was also a way of letting a limited number of influential faculty members know about what he was up to in a project filled with potential academic dangers.[38]

LAYING THE GROUNDWORK

Atop Kinsey's list of influential officials was Indiana University President Herman Wells. Wells, unmarried and still living with his mother, enthusiastically approved Kinsey's proposals for everything from wasps to sex. In his letter to Wells accepting the "marriage course" offer, Kinsey wrote: "Thanks for all the support which you have lent to the consummation of this program. I trust that history will justify its existence." Friendly Kinsey biographer Cornelia Christenson recounts,

> A petition to institute such a course for college seniors had been presented to the Board of Trustees that spring. The committee from the Association of Women Students evidently *had worked out these stipulations in meetings in Kinsey's office the preceding spring. Thus*, Kinsey's appointment to chair the committee *could have come as no surprise* to him.[39] [Emphasis added.]

Shifting responsibility for the marriage course to the coeds insulated Kinsey from "potential academic dangers." Jones interviewed Cecilia Wahl, a member of the Association of Women Students, who did not recall if the women or Kinsey had first proposed the course. She was, however, "inclined to think it was the latter."[40] Careful scrutiny of pertinent segments of the three major Kinsey biographies confirms that he maneuvered to secure the marriage course as a bridge to legitimizing university-supported sex travels, "surveys," and experiments.

Indiana University's bachelor president, Herman Wells.

Kinsey's often abrasive treatment of his wife, female members of the IU faculty, and female students attests to his misogynistic view of women. Summarizing his interview with IU Dean of Women Kate Mueller, Jones writes,

> For her part, Mueller had been worried about Kinsey's behavior for some time. In addition to fretting over the information and permissive attitudes he conveyed during interviews, she was concerned about the persistence with which he pursued female histories on campus. She had heard complaints on this score in the past, and she had no reason to doubt that the future would bring more... The basic problem, she maintained, was that Kinsey put too much pressure on students.... If he got some members of a complete group, he wanted all of them."

Dean of Women Students, Kate Mueller, was stunned by Kinsey's wrath after she refused to compel IU college girls to answer his intimate sexual questions.

In her judgment, Kinsey crossed the line between soliciting and badgering when he attempted to draw in girls who were either reluctant or simply did not wish to give their histories. When he pursued them, Mueller declared, "[He] ran into difficulties with parents and girls who objected, girls who were really scandalized, you see"... "So, this was the conflict, quite simply, which Mr. Kinsey and I found each other facing," she sighed.

"I felt very strongly that I could not ever ask the girls to give him interviews when they did not voluntarily want to do so," she explained. "As we discussed this a little further," she continued, "Mr. Kinsey became very angry with me, emotionally angry, and he shouted. Perhaps I shouted too," she allowed, "but he did shout at me." As their conversation became more heated, Kinsey underwent a physical transformation: "His face changed; he became more pale," she declared. "He was really shaken by my refusal, because I think that the one thing that he could not endure was to be thwarted in his need for getting more cases."

"I was quite frightened by this, and I remember feeling that I was glad he could be overheard by Mrs. (Lottie) Kirby, associate dean, who was in the next office, because I thought if I can't get him out quietly at least she can rescue me." After a brief silence in which Kinsey appeared to be struggling to regain his composure, another outburst ensued. Kinsey, however, was not done. As nastily as he had treated her, he could not resist the temptation to add insult to fear before leaving. "He did tell me I was unsuited for the job I had; he thought I ought to give him my own history," she said with a grimace. Choking back tears, she added, "He went so far as to say I should have some treatment by a psychiatrist to correct my bad attitudes and so forth." [41]

Moreover, in his Indiana University dissertation, Jones confirms the fact that both prior biographers misled the public about Kinsey's motivation for teaching the marriage course:

> The contention that Kinsey just happened to be selected to head the Marriage Course cannot be supported by fact. Moreover, the assertion that the Marriage Course raised questions in

Kinsey's mind which led him to study human sexual behavior ignores the fact that Kinsey planned from the beginning to use the Marriage Course to launch an investigation of human sexual behavior.[42]

In his 1973 dissertation, Jones revealed further that the University board of trustees had approved the sex survey questions and Kinsey's lectures *prior* to his supposed initial involvement in 1938. That is, the board was informed that Kinsey would be questioning students for his marriage course despite the abundance of sexual information in the existing professional literature.

Kinsey states in the *Male* volume, "In July of 1938, we undertook to take the first histories,"[43] and the marriage course was approved that same month. But he would likely have required considerable lead-time to plan his research agenda and prepare his lengthy, meticulous interview protocol. Jones writes,

> The interview he used on students at Indiana University during the summer of 1938 could not have been improvised. Undoubtedly, it had taken many months, and quite possibly more than a year, to structure. It seems certain that Kinsey invested years of reading in sex education to obtain the familiarity with human sexual behavior reflected by such a sophisticated interview... Kinsey had defined the approach and scope of his research before he took his first history! That he had committed to memory the interview's 350 questions offers additional evidence of careful preparation.[44]

Due to the nature of his research, securing a truly "random sample" was virtually impossible. He circumvented that obstacle by questioning entire groups. He would accept speaking engagements for organizations only if allowed to take histories of their members. Kinsey called this highly irregular technique a "100% sample" and implied that the equivalent of a "random sample" was self-contained within each organization's membership. On its face it was scientific fancy.

Jones reports that Kinsey, as a taxonomist, "proposed to measure variations among specimens that might explain differences within the species. He had, in effect, merely substituted people for gall wasps."[45] His chief intramural opposition was an Indiana University medical school professor, Thurman Rice, who had been one of Kinsey's early supporters. Prior to Kinsey, Rice had taught the

The 1948 Indiana University Board of Trustees. (*Arbutus*, school yearbook, 1948)

Kinsey (left) with patron, IU President Wells (center). George Comer (far right) was director of the National Research Council, the agency that credentialed and brokered Kinsey's Rockefeller grant for sex research.

required sex hygiene class, providing (according to Pomeroy) "the customary bumbling array of misinformation typical of such lectures in 1932." Kinsey's closed-door interviews with coeds for the marriage course changed Dr. Rice's mind. "Rice charged that Kinsey had even asked them about the length of their clitorises, which indeed he had,"[46] writes Pomeroy, adding that "measuring a clitoris is an extremely technical matter, as Kinsey pointed out, a woman could certainly get no clear estimate of her own clitoris without technical training."[47]

Even in the 1990s this humiliating invasion of privacy would qualify as sexual harassment or worse, a stunning example of public exploitation of intimate private concerns in the name of "science."

ROCKEFELLER FUNDING

According to the *International Encyclopedia of the Social Sciences* (1968), Kinsey "began his sex research, unassisted, in 1938.... Support first came from the National Research Council and the Medical Division of The Rockefeller Foundation."[48] Writing in *Twenty-Five Years of Sex Research, History of the National Research Council Committee for Research in Problems of Sex, 1922-1947*,[49] Sophie D. Aberle and George W. Corner report that the Foundation helped organize and fund the American Social Hygiene Association in 1913 "for reconsideration of public attitudes toward prostitution," and to work for birth control and other social reforms. European and English sex studies were fashionable, and a number of major treatises had been published by men (and a few by women) between 1885 and 1912.

The Scientific Humanitarian Committee, established in the United States in 1897, focused on "scientific" sex and held annual conferences for some years. The Institute for Sexual Science, formed in Berlin in 1911, was well known throughout Europe, where "investigations of this type had begun to attain respectability in the eyes of European medicine and jurisprudence."[50]

Social anthropology entailed the study of sexual habits amongst "primitive" peoples, and "by the 1920s [American and European] field workers were documenting the sexual behavior and mores of the peoples they were studying."[51] Like Margaret Mead, many of them produced faulty research which pleased their benefactors while misleading the West with effusive claims about the supposedly positive, happy nature of wildly promiscuous "primitive" sexuality.

Studies on reproduction and sexual hormones were well underway by 1921. It was into this milieu of sexual activity that Kinsey stepped, with enthusiastic backing from the National Research Council. Robert M. Yerkes, Yale zoologist/psychologist and specialist in primate behavior (for whom the Yerkes Primate Center at Emory University in Atlanta was named), chaired the Council's Committee for Research in Problems of Sex. Kinsey became its key problem-finder.

In the "Historical Introduction" to his 1948 *Male* volume, Kinsey wrote:

> The present volume is a progress report from a case history study on human sex behavior. The study has been underway during the past nine years. Throughout these years, it has had the sponsorship and support of Indiana University, and during the past six years the support of the *National Research Council's Committee for Research on Problems of Sex, with funds granted by the Medical Division of The Rockefeller Foundation*. It is a fact-finding survey in which an attempt is being made to discover what people do sexually, and what factors account for differences in sexual behavior among individuals, and among various segments of the population.[52] [Emphasis added.]

Robert M. Yerkes, primatologist and Kinsey's chief Rockefeller supporter.

Kinsey's claims about the alleged dearth of information about sex in the 1930s were largely accepted at face value by the American public. Despite the increasing acceptance of behaviorist psychology (as espoused by such luminaries as Ivan Pavlov, Edward Lee Thorndike, Robert Yerkes, J.B. Watson, and B.F. Skinner), few Americans had paid serious attention to the massive sex reform movement that had metastasized throughout Europe since the turn of the century:

> The Rockefeller Foundation's statement filed with the Committee explained... [funding] the Kinsey studies. In 1931 it "became interested in systematic support for studies in sexual physiology and behavior." Its work in these areas was chiefly in connection with the "committee for research in problems of sex of The National Research Council," to which, by 1954, the Foundation had granted $1,755,000 in annual grants running from $75,000 to $240,000. Beginning about 1941, a considerable portion of these funds was supplied to Dr. Kinsey's studies, and one grant was made direct to Dr. Kinsey. The work of the NRC produced some results of truly noteworthy importance. [However] the much-publicized "best-seller" Kinsey studies base an advocacy of criminal and social reform on the very *un*scientific material which Dr. Kinsey had collected and permitted to be widely disseminated.[53]

CHOOSING AND CONDITIONING HIS TEAM

Kinsey's research objectives determined the makeup of the research staff he selected. Loyal workers, sympathetic to the director of a project, are crucial to the endeavor's success. It is also vital that staff members be sufficiently knowledgeable and skilled in their fields so that they can help direct and critique the developing studies. James Jones writes in his doctoral dissertation that Kinsey selected young, insecure students as his assistants, but only after they had given him their own personal sexual histories. Even his coauthors had to agree to be filmed in intimate sexual situations on the Indiana campus and in Kinsey's attic.[54] Jones stated in his Yorkshire interview that "Kinsey wants [his staff] to understand that as scientists they are not bound, okay, by bourgeois morality... [H]e builds a staff where there is some wife-swapping... gay contacts... [for] both professional and private [needs]."

Kinsey's principal assistants and coauthors of the *Male* volume-Wardell Pomeroy and Clyde Martin-were both young, inexperienced, and without doctorates or published academic work. Their lack of professional standing was unusual for such a controversial and high profile research study. For Kinsey, their loyalty would be reinforced by their lack of academic achievement. The team was entirely dependent on Kinsey for professional advancement. In 1937, Martin was "so lonely," writes Jones, that he was about to drop out of school before Kinsey brought him into his sex research. "I never thought of myself as a particularly professional person... [not] very competitive. I kind of happily stepped aside because I didn't want to compete," he said.[55] Jones continues,

Kinsey, Martin, Pomeroy circa 1947. This photograph by Dallenbeck would have been taken during the period when Kinsey was engaged in sexual liaisons with his young coauthors. (Weinberg)

> The power relationship between Kinsey and then unmarried Martin... was not exactly equal. Kinsey was older, well established professionally, and Martin's employer. Kinsey worked hard at seducing this insecure, anxious, and financially strapped young man.[56]

With no professional or practical statistical background or training, Martin was entrusted with statistical analysis of data for the nationally significant project fraught with "potential academic dangers." Those responsible for oversight of the Kinsey grant at the Rockefeller Foundation would complain that,

> [T]here has never been, in this group, any trained mathematical statistician who comes within gunshot of having the competence, training, and experience which are required. In Dr. Kinsey's own listing of his staff (Progress Report, April 1, 1950) he says that Mr. Clyde E. Martin 'continues in charge of the statistical handling our data (sic).' His scientific stature has not as yet caused him even to be listed in *American Men of Science*, the latest edition of which contains about 50,000 names. Dr. Kinsey must approve highly of him, for in 1951, he raised his salary by 36 per cent. In his own diary record of a visit to Kinsey in July 1950, Dr. Gregg said, under the heading of personnel: 'Past and present needs remain unsatisfied in point of... statistics." This fault - this admittedly absolutely basic fault - existed in the project in 1942, it has existed ever since, there is no promise whatsoever that it will cease to exist - and we do nothing about it.[57]

Clyde Martin, Kinsey's young aide, statistician, and coauthor.

The publicity photographs of Kinsey and his team, staff, and family continue to portray them all as typical Americans. While Pomeroy states that Kinsey insisted on having only married men on the team, Jones found that claim to be less than candid. Several of Kinsey's student research associates were unmarried. Presumably, if Kinsey claimed that his aides were all married, it was not because he believed the emotional health of husbands superior to that of bachelors, but because "people who had never married were suspect to a good many Americans."[58] Inclusion of single men could jeopardize the team's public image.

Project secrecy was essential, since Kinsey was interviewing not only homosexuals, but rapists, pedophiles, pederasts, and other criminal types. Pomeroy writes:

> His requirements for interviewers, in fact, were so narrowly defined that only a few people could hope to qualify. Even for the less highly skilled jobs on the staff he took particular pains to secure people who were completely trustworthy, mature, and stable, and especially would not be offended by the kind of material with which we dealt. Even janitorial service was a problem because of security restrictions.[59]

Mass distributed publicly photograph of Kinsey's group as orthodox middle-American scholars. Note: second woman standing on the left, wearing horn-rimmed glasses, who poses as Kinsey's "typical female interviewee" for *Sexual Behavior in the Human Female*.

Kinsey selected men who were not "prone to moral evaluations"[60] in the area of human sexuality. He hired no "prudes," Jews, Blacks, or committed Christians. Pomeroy explains:

> As usual, when we considered anyone we might hire, we took his [sexual] history first. Kinsey and I did this one together. When we were finished, Kinsey put down his pen and said, "I don't think you want to work for us."
>
> "But I do," the researcher insisted.
>
> "Well," Kinsey observed, "you have just said that premarital intercourse might lead to later difficulties in marriage, that extramarital relations would break up a marriage, that homosexuality is abnormal and intercourse with animals ludicrous. Apparently you already have all the answers. Why do you want to do research?"[61]

Kinsey hired only men to interview women about their intimate sexual feelings and private experiences. So few women were willing to reveal their sexual histories that Kinsey resorted to reclassifying prostitutes as "married women." In a letter to sociologist David Reisman,[62] Kinsey accused his critics of envy.

It is to be remembered that both Pomeroy and Martin were, reports Jones, Kinsey's "lovers" from time to time. So, as expected, Kinsey's "tightly knit little group"[63] appears to have been tightly wound as well:

> Kinsey, myself, Paul Gebhard and Clyde Martin-were quite unlike as human beings. To begin with, we differed physically. Kinsey dominated us in that respect, as he did in every other. He hated beards. Only a senior member such as Paul Gebhard could have survived Kinsey's

displeasure over mustaches... He could be extremely gentle with others if the issue was important. It was only among people he really trusted, such as the staff members, that he permitted himself to let go with sharp words, exaggerations and harsh language. He meant every word he said. He was a stubborn man, so determined to win arguments that occasionally he found himself defending positions and opinions he had previously attacked.[64]

Pomeroy and Christenson reveal that Kinsey controlled his staff through fear and shame, alternating warm fatherly acceptance with cold, contemptuous disapproval. The technique is basic to Pavlov's conditioned response/positive reinforcement, rat-and-dog training, which helps create passive and obedient creatures and populations. When he wrote the following in 1972, Pomeroy had held his doctorate in psychology for more than a decade. He would soon become Academic Dean of the Institute for the Advanced Study of Human Sexuality (IASHS) in San Francisco, the key training and accrediting agency for America's sexologists, sex therapists, and sex educators worldwide:[65]

Carefully staged photographs suggest Kinsey's sensitive interviewing techniques. However, his treatment of those opposing his moral views is exemplified by his description of one woman doctor as "an inhibited old maid" for cautioning her patients that masturbation could become compulsive and injurious.

> That was Kinsey, the mother superior keeping us within the strict boundaries of his schedule, yet we did not often resent it.... Kinsey was in fact an aggressive individual, and I think it was because of his hidden fear of failure.... He was aggressive, too, when someone attempted to "get something" on him. Sometimes I might feel hurt by a remark he had made to me and after licking my wounds for two or three weeks I would make an attempt at revenge by trying to trap him in some inconsistency.[66]

Kinsey, the zoologist, had learned Pavlovian conditioned-response techniques and apparently applied them effectively. As he explained in *Female*,

> An animal may become conditioned to respond not only to particular stimuli, but to objects and other phenomena which were associated with the original experience. Pavlov's classic experiment with the dog which was so conditioned that it salivated upon hearing a dinner bell, as well as when it came in contact with the food with which the bell was originally associated, stands as the prototype of such associative conditioning.[67]

The staff was impotent in the face of Kinsey's abrasive verbal assaults. Pomeroy reports that Kinsey once directed Gebhard, who was suffering from diarrhea, to eat only citrus fruits. The diarrhea predictably worsened in the wake of that faulty medical advice. When the patient finally ordered a hamburger, Kinsey (nicknamed "Prok") denounced him for going off the prescribed diet:

> Thinking to pass it off with a little levity (always a mistake with Kinsey), Gebhard said, "Prok, those bacteria are always eating on me, so I thought I'd give them something to eat on."

Prok's reaction astonished even me. He turned on Paul, and said very seriously, "Gebhard, sometimes I despair of you as a scientist."[68]

Pomeroy reprises Kinsey's shower obsession:

[O]ne had to deal with Kinsey on his terms, such as his irritating insistence on cleanliness at prescribed times. He demanded, for example, that on trips everyone must take a shower every morning. I grumbled about it for a while, because my routine was to take a shower in the evening, but I gave in and fell into the morning habit, and retain it to this day. Gebhard was not so easy to conquer, however. He pretended compliance, but he was not above going into the bathroom, turning on the shower and letting it run for the proper time while he did something else.[69]

Pomeroy hints that Kinsey used field trips and cleanliness demands, developed years before with young Ralph Voris, as an excuse for watching and controlling the younger men in their bathing and other intimate activities. This is confirmed in Jones' biography. We also know from Jones' biography that Kinsey initiated "field" sexual activity, at which his students balked at great risk to themselves and their careers.

Key members of the Kinsey team were intimidated, and occasionally infuriated, by their aging associate's authoritarian bent:

From the beginning, it can be admitted now, Gebhard felt some hostility toward Kinsey, although a large part of it was due to a misunderstanding. I shared Paul's feeling that Kinsey did not want or intend to give either of us any autonomy. We were in the position of workhorses, harnessed to the project under Kinsey's direction, and we resented it, Paul perhaps more than I. There were many evidences of Prok's suppression. For example, Gebhard had been on the staff for two years before Kinsey permitted him to give a lecture. Again, when letters came from those who had given histories asking questions of Paul or me, Kinsey took them over and answered them himself, the habitual "we" in his correspondence could almost always be translated as "I."[70]

Yet, earlier in his biography Pomeroy states that the team "did not often resent" Kinsey. Typical of victims of the conditioning process, these men began behaving as jealous siblings seeking parental affection. Pomeroy claims that Gebhard resented Kinsey because, although Gebhard was by then a Ph.D., Kinsey preferred Pomeroy: "[Gebhard] expected to be treated as a colleague, according to academic usage. And, it was true that Kinsey did treat me as a colleague, which I found extremely satisfying."[71]

Kept in a vacillating state of confusion about their "value" in Kinsey's eyes—competing for his favor, condemned one moment and lauded the next—the staff became increasingly pliable and conditioned for obedience and loyalty. It is apparent that Kinsey's entire "team" had to have malleable personalities, and that such traits as amorality and lack of conviction were key elements of Kinsey's litmus test.

Kinsey would appear to soften and Paul would respond instantly. This alteration, blowing hot and cold, left Gebhard a little groggy. Actually, he and I and Martin could have united and outvoted Kinsey . . . but... [t]he sense of hierarchy was always there, and

Gebhard found it difficult to adjust to, as well as to Prok's quick switches in attitude toward him.[72]

Like a classic cult leader, Kinsey dominated his team by erratic rewards and punishments. George Mandler, psychologist and Guggenheim Fellow, explains:

> Behavior theory derives generally from I.P. Pavlov and J.B. Watson. The role of anxiety for learning theory is to explain the nature and consequences of punishment. In the case of punishment, a previously neutral event or stimulus (the conditioned stimulus, or CS), when paired with an unconditioned stimulus (U.S.), which produces a noxious state such as pain, will elicit a conditioned response (CR) after a suitable number of pairings. This conditioned response is commonly called fear... Fear-or anxiety-is viewed as a secondary or acquired drive established by classical conditioning. Fear is a psychological warning of impending discomfort.[73]

Gathorne-Hardy revealed the nature of the film being watched by the excited, grinning Kinsey and the somewhat confused children in this popular IU press photo. The children are being shown a film of porcupines copulating. Reports Hardy,

> Kinsey loved these films and often watched and showed them. And the porcupines were ingenious enough: the foreplay - standing on hind legs... the male pressing the female down, at which she dramatically and completely opened up all her quills and the male descended over her, entered with a number of rapid strokes, jackknifed over to suck his penis clean, and relaxed.... "[M]ore human than monkeys - slower, moodier, soberer... only their shining eyes and occasionally bared teeth showing through."[74]

This may be said to be the first of many such films shown to children nationwide as part of the desensitization process used in many sex or AIDS "prevention" curricula. Psychologist Pomeroy knew that Kinsey's "hot-and-cold" technique, disdain for "casual" conversation, and seemingly random selection of victims for hit-or-miss outbursts, all served to keep his staff insecure, anxious, fearful, and conditioned to follow Kinsey's lead with minimal resistance. In addition to the "hot-and-cold" tactic, Kinsey (who also majored in zoology and psychology) could also use economic, sexual, and employment leverage to solidify his control. Pomeroy suggests that the crew could have "outvoted" Kinsey, but each was dependent on the pro-Kinsey University system for their livelihood. On the positive side, from their perspective, was the prospect of eventually becoming leaders in the emerging field of sexology, and the sex education movement that Kinsey's research would fuel.

Now that we know the violent porcupine copulation scenes these children were required to view, the reactions of each child and each adult take on some significance. Even Gathorne-Hardy wonders: "The expressions on the faces of Kinsey [and "Mac" in the rear] and some of the children bear examination."

Another of Kinsey's control devices entailed stripping staff members of their sexual privacy. He required *all* staff, including janitors, to "volunteer" their sex histories. Spouses and other family members were also subject to scrutiny. Few Americans, even today, would submit to intimate, probing questions about the size and shape of their genital organs in sundry states of arousal, and their masturbatory and other sexual habits (or non-habits). Nor would they allow themselves to be filmed in intimate sexual situations.

Pomeroy states that his wife "had been a little in awe of [Kinsey], as might be expected of the young wife of a young psychologist, [but] it was another thing to give him her history, and Martha had qualms about it."[75] Understandably so, since she had not yet shared some of that history with her own husband. Nevertheless, bullied by both Pomeroy and Kinsey, and with her husband's job and career at stake, Martha "gave her sex data" as required. In turn, Pomeroy admits, he was able to access "Kinsey's own history, his wife's and his daughter's. . . ."[76] Indeed, during the BBC's 1996 television biography of Kinsey, Gebhard claimed that he, too, had perused Kinsey's sex history.

"In the old days," Pomeroy asserts, "no one could have come to work for Kinsey without giving his history first. It was a condition of employment, which a few employees in the lower echelons [sic] resented."[77] But today, he assures us, the Institute no longer forces staff members to disclose such intimate personal matters. As for his Institute for the Advanced Study of Human Sexuality, Pomeroy continues to obtain sex histories from those receiving degrees.

The only known "straight" member of Kinsey's team, Vincent Nowlis, was hired due to his friendship with Robert Yerkes, Kinsey's Rockefeller Foundation mentor. In his Kinsey biography, Jones quotes Nowlis' observation that, "Martin was really senile and Kinsey demanded that he be." Nowlis left abruptly. During an interview with Yorkshire TV, he confirmed that his departure was the result of Kinsey's efforts to recruit him into the "homosexual experience." And, in the 1998 Yorkshire television documentary, "Kinsey's Paedophiles," Jones recalls that "Kinsey and other [male] members of the Institute staff show[ed] up in Vincent Nowlis' room, inviting him to disrobe with the clear understanding that sexual activity would follow." Nowlis resigned quietly. Until the Jones interview, he never revealed the tainted research team, or the child sex abuse underpinning Kinsey's chapters on child sexuality.

SECRETS AS POWER

Kinsey's aggressive, intrusive, and arguably illegal conduct was protected by Indiana University's public relations apparatus. We now know that some of the women and children in publicity photographs may have paid a high price to maintain the carefully honed Kinsey image. In October 1997, syndicated columnist Mona Charen, commenting on James Jones' biography, noted that "according to one wife of another employee, there was 'sickening pressure' to agree to have sex on film."[78]

Many officials and scholars covered up Kinsey's highly improper activities during his lifetime, and continue to do so at the Kinsey Institute and Indiana University today. Pomeroy adds some perspective to what was foisted onto the public and misrepresented as an objective scientific quest for human betterment:

> I think he liked secrets, that their possession gave him a sense of power. And there was no question that *the histories did give him unique potential power. On* the Indiana campus alone, there were at least twenty professors with homosexual histories unknown to anyone else,

not to mention the numerous extramarital experiences recorded.... With his intimate knowledge of the sexual lives of important people, Kinsey could have figuratively blown up the United States socially and politically. [P]erhaps he liked to feel sometimes that he was putting something over on the world.[79] [Emphasis added.]

Kinsey's possession of such sex secrets amounted to a subtle form of coercion bordering on blackmail. There was always the possibility that he might reveal the information whenever he deemed it in his best interest. This could partially explain his obsession with collecting sexual histories. "One of the things he dreaded most was to be turned down if he asked someone, or a group, for a history (or histories)," writes Pomeroy.[80] Kinsey reportedly "often remarked that he found most irksome the fact that social mores made it so difficult to witness human sexual behavior."[81]

In his landmark *Male* volume, Kinsey stated:

> Nothing has done more to block the free investigation of sexual behavior than the almost universal acceptance, even among scientists, of certain aspects of that behavior as normal and of other aspects of that behavior as abnormal.... As scientific explorers, we in the present study, have been *unlimited* in our search to find out what people do sexually.[82] [Emphasis added.]

According to Pomeroy, Kinsey (above) controlled all photos taken of him and his staff. He threatened to sue one photographer whose picture of the zoologist, said Kinsey, could destroy his sex research.

And Christenson cites this excerpt from a Kinsey lecture:

> The resolution of erotic arousal, the relation of erotic stimulation and response to physical health, and the possibility of ignoring, suppressing, resolving, or sublimating such arousal are first of all questions of physical and mental hygiene, and their solution must lie in the laboratory and science classroom, and not in the chair of the philosophers... or moralists.... *[S]cientists must have the right to decide*.[83] [Emphasis added.]

Kinsey often expressed an elitist right to unlimited, uncontrolled "scientific research" into everyone's sexuality, including that of children from birth. It should hardly surprise us, then, that in the chapter on child sexuality in the *Male* volume he writes wistfully of the great things that science might accomplish with absolute freedom to conduct human experiments: "Erotic arousal [of children] could be subjected to precise instrumental measurement if objectivity among scientists and public respect for scientific research allowed such laboratory investigation."[84] This noxious attitude caused Ashley Montagu to accuse Kinsey of "scientomania:"

> The analyst must first and foremost be human, must be responsive to the emotions which motivate human beings. Kinsey doesn't appear to be very interested in emotions. The passion to know has in many cases

THE INDIANA UNIVERSITY SEXOLOGIST

produced a scientific character that is out of balance. The desire to know can become like dipsomania, a "scientomania" in which the victim loses control of himself and becomes controlled by the intoxicating potions of knowledge to which he has become addicted. I am afraid this has happened to many scientists, with results that are at this stage in the history of humanity, almost too frightening to contemplate.[85]

Most amazing, however, is Montagu's participation in the carefully planned "critique" *About the Kinsey Reports*, (A Signet Special, New York), published in May and July 1948, five months after the release of Kinsey's tome. Here, alongside ten other renowned academicians (Fromm, Ford, Llewellyn, Dickinson, etc.), Montagu glows with appreciation for the Kinsey Reports.

ROCKEFELLER'S MASS COMMUNICATIONS MACHINE TAKES KINSEY PUBLIC

The immense amount of public interest in Kinsey's first book, *Sexual Behavior in the Human Male*, supposedly came as a surprise to its authors and publisher. That is doubtful, however, considering the enormous advance effort to promote it, including efforts of the Rockefeller-connected mass media to effusively hype the book and its culturally corrosive message.

Kinsey and his benefactors set in motion massive publicity campaigns preceding release of both the *Male* volume in 1948 and the *Female* volume in 1953.[86] Journalists were briefed and courted, and as publication date approached, wined and dined (occasionally at taxpayers' expense). In addition to print advertisements, an unprecedented number of gratis copies of the first book (primarily targeting the medical profession) were distributed nationally. Allen Wallis, past president of the American Statistical Association, recalls, "Yes, the book was promoted commercially in a big way and they were taking sort of a holier-than-thou attitude, saying we're not promoting it at all, it's just that the public is naturally interested in the subject."[87]

This carefully contrived publicity effort was designed to create an international media sensation that would appear to be spontaneous. Clamor for the book could then be portrayed as "proof" that Kinsey's claims about America's sexual hypocrisy were valid. After all, it was the first "racy" U.S. scholarship in print, and supposedly moral and monogamous men and women would be standing in line to buy it. Parading the book under the "respectable" cover of "science" further enhanced the scheme. However, this too was a media crafted and controlled fantasy.

In his 1971 doctoral dissertation on Kinsey, Paul Brinkman recalled that "One of the first meetings between Kinsey and journalists came in 1946 [when] Kinsey spoke on his preliminary findings."[88] According to Johnson, reports of Kinsey's press plans,[89] advertising schedule, and "promotional timetable" began surfacing as early as 1935, *three years before he was named to conduct the study.* In a letter dated February 2, 1946, the editor of *Harper's Magazine* complained to the Rockefeller Foundation that she was merely one of many on the "list of magazines" vying for an opportunity to write about Kinsey's forthcoming book.[90] Journalists who accepted invitations to visit Bloomington and review proofs of the pending volume were required to sign a contract stipulating, among other things, that no articles about it would be published prior to a prearranged November date. And, according to *Editor and Publisher,* more than 70 percent of a cross section of daily newspapers carried stories about the "Female" book on August 20, 1953. Such advance publicity efforts were unprecedented for an academic study.

The first Kinsey-approved articles began appearing in November, 1947, one month before the formal publication date.[91] Robert Cecil Johnson writes:

Kinsey lectures to future leaders at the University of California at Berkeley, a site of massive cynicism and revolution in the late '60s.

> Much of the credit (or blame) for [the book's success] can be attributed to the public relations efforts of Kinsey himself. Far from attempting to confine his studies to professional channels, Kinsey actively participated in providing the widest possible circulation of his data.[92]

But how did this bow-tied, Midwestern biology professor become a savvy public relations wizard capable of conducting a book promotion rivaling that of a Madison Avenue ad agency? An indication of the answer is found in the record of the Rockefeller Foundation's extensive influence on mass communication. During the late 1930s, writes Christopher Simpson in *Science of Coercion*, the Foundation "believed mass media... constituted a uniquely powerful force in modern society" for imposing the will of the elite "on the masses."[93] According to Simpson, "secret psychological war projects" to control public opinion were supported by America's tax-exempt foundations. For example, campaigns were developed to induce Americans to support U.S. entry into World War II. The Rockefeller Foundation funded communications experts from the field of social science to shape pre- and postwar public attitudes. In the postwar era, this experienced group of operatives turned its attention to our domestic population. Simpson continues:

Kinsey lectured en masse to students who would become our future authorities as well as medical doctors and other professionals. "Typical of the packed, totally absorbed meetings Kinsey addressed for sixteen years, all over America. Here a gathering of GPs in San Diego (Hotel Coronado) in October 1953." (Caption and photo taken from Gathorne-Hardy's *Sex, the Measure of All Things*.)

> [There was] a remarkably tight circle of men and women who shared several important conceptions about mass communication research. They regarded mass communication as a tool for social management and as a weapon in social conflict, and they expressed common assumptions concerning the usefulness of quantitative research-particularly experimental and quasi-experimental effects research, opinion surveys,

THE INDIANA UNIVERSITY SEXOLOGIST

and quantitative content analysis as a means of illuminating what communication "is" and improving its application to social management. [94]

Kinsey's quantitative research and numbers were a perfect fit with the Rockefeller plan to manipulate the mass media to "shape public attitudes and conduct." Such "social management" meant nothing less than changing America's way of life by altering what Kinsey called "breeding patterns" to conform to an animalistic, (pseudo-evolutionary) view of human sexual conduct as gall-wasps.

Simpson describes how agents trained in psychological warfare by the American intelligence and espionage apparatus (i.e., the Office of Strategic Services (OSS), forerunner of the Central Intelligence Agency (CIA), and the Office of War Information (OWI)) were infiltrated, with assistance from tax-exempt foundations, into influential positions in journalism, politics, university communications departments, and other powerful mass-media positions. There they could work to "engineer mass consent" as described by Christopher Simpson (addressed further in Chapter 10), and Simpson further states:

> In 1939 the [Rockefeller] Foundation organized a series of secret seminars with men it regarded as leading communication scholars, to enlist them in an effort to consolidate public opinion in the United States in favor of war against Nazi Germany-opposed by many conservatives, religious leaders, and liberals at the time.[95]

> [These secret psychological warfare projects] helped define U.S. social science and mass communication studies long after the war had drawn to a close. Virtually all of the scientific community that was to emerge during the 1950s as leaders in the field of mass communication research spent the war years performing applied studies on U.S. and foreign propaganda public opinion (both domestically and internationally), clandestine OSS operations.

Among OWI alumni-in 1953, are,

> The publishers of *Time, Look, Fortune* and several dailies; editors of such magazines as *Holiday, Coronet, Parade,* and the *Saturday Review,* editors of The *Denver Post,* New Orleans' The *Times-Picayune,* and others; the heads of the Viking Press, Harper & Brothers, and Farrar, Straus and Young; two Hollywood Oscar winners; a two-time Pulitzer Prize winner; the board chairman of CBS and a dozen key network executives; President Eisenhower's chief speech writer; the editor of *Reader's Digest* international editions; at least six partners of large advertising agencies; and a dozen noted social scientists; chief of the U.S. government's covert psychological warfare effort from 1950 to 1952 and later dean of the Columbia Graduate School of Journalism and founder of the *Columbia Journalism Review.*

> World War II psychological warfare work established social networks that opened doors to crucial postwar contacts inside the government, funding agencies, and professional circles [and] *unprecedented access to human research subjects.*[96] [Emphasis added.]

With connections to the mass media via the Rockefeller organization, Kinsey was able to generate widespread public curiosity and interest in his book prior to publication. And selection of the prestigious medical publisher W.B. Saunders served to further enhance the impression that the book was an authentic scientific endeavour.

Kinsey with members of the press. Such briefings were financed by the Rockefeller Foundation and Indiana University's public funds.

THE PRETEND STATISTICIAN

Hagiographer, Gathorne-Hardy, revealed that Kinsey *never* hired a statistician. "Frank Edmondson, a young astronomer" who had had "some rather superficial statistical training" was Kinsey's fake statistician.[97] Clyde Martin "'was no scholar'" and had no such knowledge. [98] Said Edmondson, Kinsey "'wasn't a mathematician,'" in fact Kinsey "often got muddled between mean (average) and median,"[99] elementary statistical concepts.

Rockefeller's Warren Weaver's objections meant that "If Kinsey just ignored the criticisms (which he did and was to continue to do) and repeated the mistakes - the grant would end. Why didn't he take on new (statistical) staff?"[100] He did, but no statistician. As "a sop to Corner, Kinsey gave $500 to his old friend the astronomer Frank Edmondson and pretended he was active on the staff in this capacity."[101] When the three American Statistical Association representatives arrived, Edmondson, Kinsey's 'statistician,' remarked that the committee had no idea "of what Kinsey was up to."[102] Gathorne-Hardy notes these statisticians never heard of Kinsey's "100 per cent groups." After all the "committee had given their sex histories (one of Kinsey's conditions)" they were more agreeable [103]

DISMISSING THE CRITICS

Predictably, criticism of the *Male* volume surfaced from many quarters soon after publication. Kinsey and his staff largely dismissed the detractors. Pomeroy placed the "unfair and jealous" critics in five categories: "(1) Moralists; (2) Attention Seekers; (3) Conservatives; (4) Uninformed Perfectionists," and (5):

> Finally, there were those who pointed to the real mistakes we had made, but sometimes did not allow for the fact that the *Male* volume was really a progress report. Even *where the statistics erred the conclusions we drew from them were correct.*[104] [Emphasis added.]

Pomeroy insinuated that those who disagreed with Kinsey in any way had dark, sexual secrets. Pomeroy projected onto any Kinsey opponents the Kinsey team's own clinically defined sexual psychopathology. The *opponents* were now the sexual psychopaths:

THE INDIANA UNIVERSITY SEXOLOGIST

"I think we are objective and fair when we say that the animus of the whole review is jealousy and a considerable prudery." Kinsey remained convinced that Terman [a well-known psychologist and early friend] had betrayed him, through jealousy and a basic prudery. Gorer [a well-known sociologist and not a friend] was either incapable of understanding the differences between proportionate and stratified sampling, or else he had ulterior motives.[105]

It is likely that Kinsey welcomed the opportunity to defend attacks on the *mechanics* of his methodology to academicians and the public. This deflected attention from other, more controversial, aspects of the study, not the least of which was his potentially volatile child "orgasm" data. Kinsey wrote to a close friend,

> You ask about the percentage of our histories who were sex offenders and other low characters. I will tell you as a good friend exactly why we did not publish the exact figures of the constitution of our population. We anticipated that there would be a good many people like Terman, who would have their own ideas as to the exact percentage of barbers and college professors of one rank and another who should be included. We anticipated that we would spend the rest of our lives arguing exactly who should be accepted as a normal individual, and who should be ruled out as a low character. Psychologists of Terman's generation [suggest] we confine ourselves to a good, normal, middle-class group.[106]

Again, had the public *known* that Kinsey, his team and his male population were sexually aberrant, the popular use of their data to change American law, education, culture, and public policy would likely have come to the proverbial screeching halt. As Jones noted during the 1998 Yorkshire documentary,

> The Kinsey myth... the official version that Kinsey was prevailed upon by students to offer a sex education class [was] part of a larger [mythology] of the disinterested scientist, the person with no ax to grind, no vested interest, no desire to influence policy one way or the other, a kind of simple 19th century empiricist who is just collecting, assembling, and presenting data, a Victorian metric minded, morally neutral, totally dispassionate investigator who simply sees a hole in the literature... to just serve his students and science.[107]

Kinsey's self-serving "low-class" population could hardly have been selected by chance. He knew that scientific privilege would not allow him to commit crimes or protect others who had done so.

> I know perfectly well that some people would suggest that all persons who have ever been convicted and done jail sentence [sic] should be ruled out. By the same token, one would have to rule out anyone who ever will do a jail sentence. For our part we have felt that a man who has lived sixty or seventy or eighty years without going to jail and then is arrested on a drunk charge after his wife has divorced him, or some other similar thing, is a normal individual, the same as a thirty year old who has not lived long enough to prove that he will never be caught by the law.[108]

Kinsey in prison, while interviewing "typical" subjects for his 1948 *Male* **volume. This photograph was not widely distributed.**

Kinsey was understandably anxious to downplay the extent to which his "research" had been based on the experiences of deviants, prisoners, homosexuals in bars and baths, and child molesters. Much of Kinsey's animosity was directed at critics within the scientific community. Scientists, he claimed,

> have proved as likely as anyone else to become emotionally disturbed at the very notion of research in the area of human sexual behavior in facing facts ...with anything like objectivity. A prominent scientist, a leader in science at a great university, and ultimately an important figure in scientific political organization in the national capital, began his review of our first volume by saying: "I do not like Kinsey, I do not like the Kinsey project, I do not like anything about the Kinsey study of sexual behavior."[109]

> The persons who have been most vociferous, both verbally and in their writing against our undertaking [ellipses in original] would include some who honestly believe that ignorance is safer than knowledge in this, and presumably many other areas. But the prime objectors have been persons who are most disturbed in their own sexual lives. *This we know specifically because we have case histories on some of these individuals.*[110] [Emphasis added.]

Once again, as noted earlier, there was the veiled threat that he could, and perhaps would, reveal such information should a critic go too far.

There were so few scholarly critics of Kinsey at the time that when one raised his head (as did Gorer and Terman), this raised questions about the critic's own sexual life, whether justified or not. Christenson quotes Kinsey, hinting at the "strain" of protecting the critic's sex history:

> We have guaranteed to keep confidence on each individual history which we have taken in this study, but it must be admitted that it has imposed a terrific strain upon us at times to know the sexual history of some of the persons who have been the bitterest opponents of our sex research, as they would be of any other sex research.[111]

Such was the mindset of the man widely credited with triggering a destructive "sexual revolution" that has radically altered our nation's morals, culture, and politics.

CHAPTER 2 NOTES

1. Jack Douglas, *The Family in America,* The Rockford Institute, Mount Morris, Illinois, May 1987, pp. 1-8.
2. James H. Jones, *Alfred C. Kinsey, A Public/Private Life,* W. W. Norton & Company, New York, 1997, p. 390.
3. June Reinisch, *The Kinsey Institute New Report On Sex: What You Must Know To Be Sexually Literate,* St. Martin's Press, New York, 1991, Introduction, p. xvi.
4. Reinisch, p. xvi.
5. Dr. Wardell Pomeroy, *Kinsey and The Institute for Sex Research,* Harper & Row, New York, 1972, p. 53.
6. Gerald Jonas, *The Circuit Riders,* W. W. Norton, New York, p. 135.
7. James H. Jones, *The Origins of the Institute for Sex Research,* UMI Dissertation Services, Ann Arbor, Michigan, 1973, pp. 96-99.
8. Jones, p. 98.
9. Pomeroy, p. 48.
10. Jones, p. 103, f. 43.
11. Jones, pp. 391-93.
12. James Jones, *The New Yorker,* "Annals of Sexology, Dr. Yes", August 25 & September 1, 1997, pp. 103-104.
13. Pomeroy, p. 322.
14. George Platt Lynes, *Photographs from the Kinsey Institute,* Little, Brown and Company, Inc., Boston. 1993.
15. T. Jeal, *Baden-Powell,* Pimlco, London, 1995.

16. Pomeroy, p. 64.
17. Pomeroy, p. 46.
18. Pomeroy, p. 48.
19. Pomeroy, p. 150.
20. Pomeroy, p. 48.
21. Pomeroy, p. 49.
22. Pomeroy, p. 62.
23. Pomeroy, p. 62.
24. Pomeroy, p. 64.
25. Jones, p. 741 and Christenson pp. 154, 156 and 215.
26. *San Francisco Examiner*, February 25, 1931, p. 1.
27. Erwin Haeberle, *The Birth of Sexology: A Brief History in Documents, Science and Research*, Berlin, 1983, p. 25. The citation for this publication states: "Research for this project has been supported by The Kinsey Institute for Research in Sex, Gender and Reproduction, Indiana University, Bloomington, Indiana."
28. Christopher Isherwood, *Christopher and His Kind*: 1929-1939, Farrar, Straus, & Giroux, New York, 1976.
29. Isherwood, pp. 17-19.
30. Scott Lively & Kevin Abrams, *The Pink Swastika: Homosexuality in the Nazi Party*, Founder's Publishers: Keizer, Oregon, 1995, p. 13. See also Blueher in Richard Mills, *The German Youth Movement*, in Winston Leyland, Ed., *Gay Roots: Twenty Years of Gay Sunshine: An Anthology of Gay History, Sex, Politics, and Culture*, Gay Sunshine Press: San Francisco, 1989.
31. Havelock Ellis was an early British sexologist whose own sexual life was seriously disordered. The tone of Kinsey's books is akin to that of Ellis' *Studies in the Psychology of Sex*, Parts I and II, first published in English in 1905 and republished often thereafter. Kinsey's contempt for Ellis, according to Pomeroy, stemmed mainly from the latter's timidity and the tendency to craft his sexual theory largely from correspondence (Pomeroy, p. 69). Ellis, whose use of mescaline (a hallucinogenic) may have contributed to his dysfunctions, argued for euthanasia. According to biographer Arthur Calder-Marshall in *The Sage of Sex* (Putnam's, New York, 1959, (pp. 275, 88)), Ellis believed that all sexual conduct is normal if it does not result in physical harm, engaged in urinary "sex" acts, married a lesbian, and was one of Margaret Sanger's lovers.
32. Douglas, p. 2.
33. Cornelia V. Christenson, *Kinsey: A Biography*, Indiana University Press, Bloomington, 1971, p. 97.
34. Warren Weaver to CIB, *Subject: Kinsey*, May 7, 1951, p. 7, The Rockefeller Archive Center.
35. Pomeroy, p. 156-157.
36. Christenson, pp. 96-97.
37. Christenson, p. 98.
38. Pomeroy, pp. 42-43.
39. Christenson, pp. 99, 100.
40. Jones, *The Origins of the Institute for Sex Research*, p. 106, f 70.
41. Jones, *Kinsey: A Public/Private Life*, pp. 514-515.
42. Jones, *The Origins of the Institute for Sex Research*, p. 109, f. 107.
43. Kinsey, Pomeroy and Martin, *Sexual Behavior in the Human Male*, W. B. Saunders Co., 1948, Philadelphia, p. 10.
44. Jones, *The Origins of the Institute for Sex Research*, pp. 98-99.
45. Jones, p. 98.
46. Pomeroy, p. 58.
47. Pomeroy, p. 317.
48. *International Encyclopedia of the Social Sciences*, 1968, p. 389.
49. Sophie D. Aberle and George W. Corner, *Twenty-Five Years of Sex Research, History of the National Research Council Committee for Research in Problems of Sex, 1922-1947*, W. B. Saunders, Philadelphia, 1953.
50. Aberle, p. 7
51. Aberle, pp. 4-7.
52. *Male*, p. 3.
53. Rene A. Wormser, *Foundations: Their Power and their Influence*, Covenant house Books, Sevierville, TN, 1958;1993, pp. 100-101.
54. Jones, *Alfred C. Kinsey, A Public/Private Life*, pp. 605-614, 669-684, 755.
55. Jones, p. 208.
56. Jones, p. 393.
57. Warren Weaver, Desk Diary, May 7, 1951, pp. 4-5, Rockefeller Archive Center.
58. Pomeroy, p. 101.
59. Pomeroy, p. 103.
60. Pomeroy, p. 101.
61. Pomeroy, p. 71.
62. Pomeroy, p. 102
63. Pomeroy, p. 155.
64. Pomeroy, pp. 5-10.

65. Indeed, IASHS students designed much of the sex education curricula for the nation as part of their training in human sexuality. See the IASHS curriculum schedule outlined in their annual brochures.
66. Pomeroy, pp. 9-10.
67. Kinsey, Pomeroy, Martin and Gebhard, *Sexual Behavior in the Human Female*, W.B. Saunders Co., Philadelphia, 1953, p. 647
68. Pomeroy, pp. 236-237.
69. Pomeroy, p. 149.
70. Pomeroy, p. 235.
71. Pomeroy p. 235.
72. Pomeroy, p. 236.
73. George Mandler, *Mind and Body*, W.W. Norton, New York, 1984, p. 225.
74. Jonathan Gathorne-Hardy, *Sex, the Measure of All Things: A life of Alfred C. Kinsey*, 1998, Chatto & Windus, London, p. 347.
75. Pomeroy, p. 106.
76. Pomeroy, p. 107.
77. Pomeroy, p. 461.
78. Mona Charen, "Unmasking Kinsey," *The Courier-Journal*, October 20, 1997.
79. Pomeroy, pp. 107, 108.
80. Pomeroy, p. 9.
81. Pomeroy, p. 25.
82. *Male*, pp. 7, 51.
83. Christenson, p. 211.
84. *Male*, p. 157.
85. Donald Porter Geddes, Ed., *An Analysis of the Kinsey Reports*, Mentor, New York, 1954, pp. 123-5.
86. Robert Cecil Johnson, *Kinsey, Christianity, and Sex: A Critical Study of Reaction In American Christianity to the Kinsey Reports on Human Sexual Behavior*, UMI Dissertations Services, Ann Arbor, Michigan 1973, pp. 12-13.
87. Author's conversation with Wallis in Washington, D.C., September 1, 1997, following his review of the authors' methodology chapter addressing the male sample.
88. Paul Dilbert Brinkman, *Dr. Alfred C. Kinsey and the Press: Historical Case Study of the Relationship of the Mass Media and a Pioneering Behavioral Scientist*, UMI Dissertation Services, 1971. This laudatory Indiana University dissertation is similar to virtually all dissertations on Kinsey, with little or no critical evaluation. It is therefore important to compare what the author wrote to what he ignored; what he perceived to what he avoided. For example, Brinkman, when focusing on the mass media, overlooked Johnson's report regarding the placement of advertisements in major press avenues, and especially the claim that the media blitz began gearing-up three years prior to the instigation of Kinsey's research.
89. L. Allen, Editor, *Harper's Magazine*, February 2, 1946, Letter to George W. Gray, Rockefeller Archive Center, New York.
90. L. Allen, Editor, ibid.
91. Johnson, pp. 12-13.
92. Johnson, pp. 12-13.
93. Christopher Simpson, *Science of Coercion: Communication Research & Psychological Warfare*, 1945-1960, Oxford University Press, New York, 1994, p. 29.
94. Simpson, pp. 20-22 and 29.
95. Simpson, pp. 22-23.
96. Simpson, pp. 28-30.
97. Johnathan Gathorne-Hardy, *Alfred C. Kinsey: Sex the Measure of All Things*, Chatto & Windus, London, 1998, p. 130.
98. Hardy, p. 144.
99. Hardy, pp. 130-131
100. Hardy, p. 330.
101. Hardy, p. 330.
102. Hardy, p. 341.
103. Hardy, p. 341
104. Pomeroy, p. 286.
105. Lewis Terman was a highly reputed Stanford psychologist and Geoffrey Gorer was a British cultural anthropologist.
106. Pomeroy, p. 286.
107. See other chapters in this book on prisoners and other "low" members of the sample.
108. Pomeroy, p. 292.
109. Pomeroy, p. 223
110. Pomeroy, p. 223
111. Christenson, p. 224.

STOLEN HONOR
STOLEN INNOCENCE

PART II:
Crimes

CHAPTER 3

RATIONALIZATION OR SCIENCE?

The worst thing about the report was not Kinsey's facts, if they were indeed trustworthy.... The most disturbing thing is the inability of the readers to put their fingers on the falsity of its premises.

David Halberstam, *American Heritage,*
May/June 1993

Looking back fifty years with the benefit of hindsight, it seems astonishing that so many Americans were swayed by Kinsey's revolutionary findings. His conclusions not only conflicted with public health data, but with virtually everything everyone knew about their personal circle of friends and loved ones.

IS IT SCIENCE?

When Hirschfeld addressed the First International Conference for Sexual Reform held in Berlin in 1921, he reminded his audience that the term "sexual science" derived from Charles Darwin's *The Descent of Man* and Ernst Haeckel's *Natuerliche Schofungsgeschicte.* (E. Michael Jones, *Culture Wars,* "Magnus Hirschfeld and the Gay Science," September 1997, Vol. 16, #9, pages 30-43.)

Publicity photo of Kinsey as scholar.

The Kinsey team understood and portrayed human sexual behavior as a closed Darwinian system of simple mammalian behavior: a stimulus provided, followed by a genital response, produces an orgasmic "outlet." Kinsey applied Pavlovian conditioning to sex, contending that *all* sex is conditioned by environment, and that love, jealously, fear, anger, shame, and similar emotions have no operational meaning independent of sex. From the start, Kinsey denied explanations for human behavior that conflicted with his evolutionary assumptions. He enthusiastically utilized research techniques appropriate for the study of insects for his evaluation of human sexual behavior.[1]

> The techniques of this research [have been] born out of the senior author's longtime experience with a problem in insect taxonomy. The transfer from insect to human material is not illogical, for it has been a transfer of a method that may be applied to the study of any variable population, in any field. The sex studies were on a very different scale from the insect studies where we had 150,000 individuals available for the study of a single species of gall wasp.[2]

In a review of **my** earlier book, *Kinsey, Sex and Fraud* (Reisman, *et al*), the respected British medical journal *The Lancet* summarized Kinsey's *qualitative* and *quantitative* research findings as follows: (1) "any questionnaire survey in a normally private area is subject to bias from differences in those who respond and those who refuse, and there is no ready means of checking the information"; and (2) Kinsey *et al* "questioned an unrepresentative proportion of prison inmates and sex offenders in a survey of 'normal' sexual behavior." In its March 1991 issue, *The Lancet* also noted that Kinsey's "methodology" involved "unethical, possibly criminal, observations of children."[3]

THE SAMPLE

For his database, Kinsey classified more than 1,400 criminals and sex offenders as "normal,"[4] on grounds that such miscreants are essentially the same as normal men. By doing so, he bolstered the belief that reported increases in sex crimes are spurious; the result of sexually disturbed police or repressive "reform groups." In his *Female* volume, he wrote,

> Preliminary analyses of our data indicate that only a minute fraction of one per cent of the persons who are involved in sexual behavior which is contrary to the law are ever apprehended, prosecuted, or convicted, and that there are many other factors besides the behavior of the apprehended individual which are responsible for the prosecution of the particular persons who are brought to court. The prodding of some reform group, a newspaper-generated hysteria over some local sex crime, a vice drive which is put on by the local authorities to distract attention from defects in their administration of the city government, or the addition to the law-enforcement group of a *sadistic officer who is disturbed over his own sexual problems*, may result in a doubling-a hundred percent increase-in the number of arrests on sex charges, even though there may have been no change in the actual behavior of the community, and even though the illicit sex acts that are apprehended and prosecuted may still represent no more than a fantastically minute part of the illicit activity which takes place every day in the community.[5] [Emphasis added.]

Kinsey associate Paul Gebhard explained that even the prison sample was heavily weighted toward sexual disorder, since the Kinsey team specifically sought the worst sex offenders:

> At the Indiana State Farm we had no plan of sampling-we simply sought out sex offenders and, after a time, avoided the more common types of offense (e.g. statutory rape) and directed our efforts toward the rarer types. In the early stages of the research, when much interviewing was being done at Indiana correctional institutions, Dr. Kinsey did not view the inmates as a discrete group that should be differentiated from people outside; instead, he looked upon the institutions as reservoirs of potential interviewees, **literally captive subjects**. *This viewpoint resulted in there being no differentiation in our 1948 volume between persons with and without prison experience.* . . . the great majority of the prison group was collected omnivorously without any sampling plan-we simply interviewed all who volunteered and when this supply of subjects was exhausted we solicited other inmates essentially at random.... Kinsey... never... [kept] a record of refusal rates-the proportion of those who were asked for an interview but who refused.[6] [Emphasis added.].

STATISTICAL CONFUSION OR DECEPTION?

It is unclear how many subjects-prisoners or otherwise-the Kinsey team surveyed. The map legend on page 5 of the 1948 *Male* volume claims that each of 427 dots represents 50 or more interviewees, which would total 21,350 persons.[7] Yet on page 10, Kinsey asserts that the final sum of his subjects is 12,214. This leaves 9,136 (43 percent) of his "subjects" unaccounted for.

In his summary of "Published Studies on Sex" (*Male* volume, page 29), Kinsey associate and statistician Clyde Martin states that Kinsey gathered "6,200 male" histories. But in his 1949 review of the *Male* volume, W. Allen Wallis, University of Chicago statistician and past-president of the American Statistical Association, concluded that Kinsey interviewed a total of 4,120 men at most. According to Wallis, whom Kinsey biographer James Jones describes as "one of the nation's most distinguished statisticians,"[8]

That 5,300 is the number of "white males who have provided the data for the present publication" (p. 6) is not confirmed by any of the statistical tables in the book. The largest total I have noticed (often the totals are not shown, but have to be computed) in any of the tables that appear to cover all of the white males is the 4,120 shown distributed by religion in Table 41, p. 208. This same table shows 4,940 males distributed by occupation, but since the adjacent column which is said to distribute 179 males by occupation totals 237, it may be that some individuals are classified under more than one occupation. Indeed, it may be that the 4,120 included some classified under more than one religion, for 4,120 is the number in the same table classified by education and 4,069 is the number classified by age at onset of adolescence. The number for whom information is not available on a given item is never shown. In general, very little is revealed in the statistical data about the number of males covered in the volume.[9]

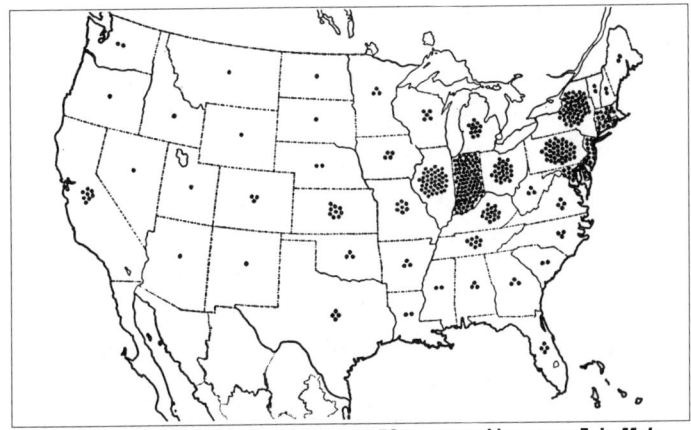

Kinsey claims 21,350 subjects (427 dots at 50 cases each) on page 5, in *Male*, while listing 12,214 subjects on page 10, leaving roughly 9,036 "missing" subjects in his Male/Female data base. [A. Wallis, ASA Journal, 12/49, p. 474.]

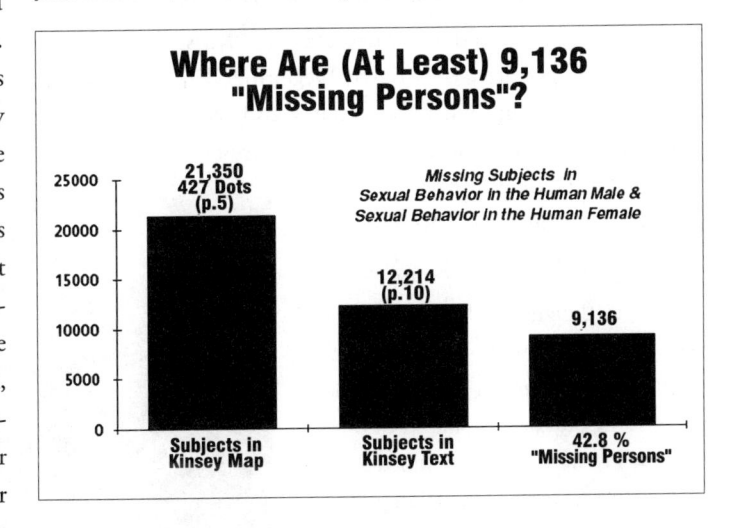

Where Are (At Least) 9,136 "Missing Persons"?

Missing Subjects in *Sexual Behavior in the Human Male* & *Sexual Behavior in the Human Female*

- Subjects in Kinsey Map: 21,350 / 427 Dots (p.5)
- Subjects in Kinsey Text: 12,214 (p.10)
- 42.8 % "Missing Persons": 9,136

Wallis' best estimate is 4,120. This approximation is supported by former senior Kinsey team member William Simon, who had, with a colleague, sought (with little success) to clean up the Kinsey data for the Russell Sage Foundation. Simon told psychiatrist Arno Karlen that data from only about 4,500 total males *and* females were actually used for the Kinsey studies. Karlen quotes Simon:

> Kinsey interviewed 18,000 people and used only a quarter of the cases in his two reports. Some of the data are still on file, but haven't ever been coded on the IBM cards for statistical study yet.[10]

The Kinsey team (left to right): Christenson, Gebhard, Gagnon and Simon (1969). Two years later, Simon admits that three-fourths of Kinsey's subjects were eliminated from the data (*Sex Research Studies from the Kinsey Institute*, 1971). (Weinberg)

Apparently, the Kinsey team used only 4,500 or so (25 percent) of the 18,000 persons interviewed. And more than one-third of the male subjects (1,400 of the 4,120 men identified by Wallis) could have been criminal sex offenders.

Simon's interview with Karlen occurred several years after Simon, Gagnon, and another senior Kinsey Institute researcher abandoned their Russell Sage Foundation-funded effort to "clean" the Kinsey data. The Foundation was yet another philanthropy interested in "sex science." The cleanup crew attempted to correct "the biases resulting from sampling and interview techniques," and produce a "comparison of the variances reported in the original [Kinsey] volumes with those computed on the complete set of data."[11] Since there were no codes to establish who was or was not a prisoner, or a member of some other "special" population, the task proved to be impossible. A decade later, Kinseyans Gebhard and Johnson prepared a report on the project which acknowledged: "To have done a thorough comparison would have involved the equivalent of rewriting both Kinsey Reports."[12]

Simon's admission that three-quarters of Kinsey's data were dumped dovetails with Clyde Martin's assertion, in a private letter (dated December 13, 1990) to Kinsey Institute Director June Reinisch, that data were computed helter-skelter and with little attempt at scientific precision or objectivity. Martin admitted that there was no precise way to "clean" the data due to the lack of identifying codes for the criminal or abnormal men who permeated the sample.

> I am certain there wasn't a code to designate which of the case histories were included in the male volume or used in computing prevalence data. [N]ew case histories were being added during preparation of the 1948 publication, and some cases were included in some calculations which were not included in prevalence calculations. It is confusing even now since the basic sample is nowhere well described.[13]

Publicity photograph of Kinsey (left), pseudo-statistician Martin (right), and Pomeroy, with their IBM data processing equipment. Such photos were widely distributed to suggest that the excellence of the equipment meant that their own statistical efforts were of similar quality.

The accompanying chart visualizes the wide-ranging estimates of Kinsey's universal sample size for the *Male* volume. Statistician Wallis asserts:

> Actually, it isn't quite clear that the total number of histories is 12,214, as stated on p. 10.... The total number of males is given at least once as "about 6,300" (p. 5) and at least once as "6,200" (p. 29). However, 12,214 is the total number shown both in the table contributing histories by year of collection (p. 10) and in the one distributing them by interviewers (p. 11).[14]

Although Wallis was one of the most perceptive and thorough critics of the Kinsey statistics, he was not alone in noting the methodological nonsense involved. It bears repeating here again that Warren Weaver, head of the Natural Science Division of the Rockefeller Foundation, registered his concern in a letter to the Foundation dated May 7, 1951:

Life Magazine cameos "statistician" Clyde Martin. "[T]he completed questionnaire goes on IBM cards to be computed with all the others." (*Life Magazine*, August 24, 1953, "The Kinsey Report on Women", p. 54)

> In his own diary record of a visit to Kinsey in July 1950, Dr. Gregg said, under the heading of personnel: 'Past and present needs remain unsatisfied in point of statistics. This fault-this admittedly absolutely basic fault-existed in the project in 1942, it has existed ever since, there is no promise whatsoever that it will cease to exist-and we do nothing about it.'[15]

That the fundamental flaws in Kinsey's statistical analyses were allowed to stand despite such criticism points to willful deception, rather than mere confusion or negligence, as the likely explanation.

"SCIENTOMANIA"

Warren Weaver

As noted earlier, anthropologist Ashley Montagu accused Kinsey of "scientomania," while world-renowned scholar and literary critic Lionel Trilling complained that the Kinseyans viewed sex as merely "anatomical and physiological" and were "resistant to the possibility of making any connection between the sexual life and the psychic structure." Furthermore, Trilling noted, the Kinsey Report,

> does not conduct itself the way it says it does. I have already suggested that the Report overrates its own objectivity. The authors, who are enthusiastically committed to their method and to their principles, make the mistake of believing that, being scientists, they do not deal in assumptions, preferences, and conclusions. Nothing comes more easily to their pens than the criticism of the subjectivity of earlier writers on sex, yet their own subjectivity is sometimes extreme.[16]

Dr. Alan Gregg

RATIONALIZATION OR SCIENCE: THE MYTH OF KINSEY'S "SCIENTIFIC" METHODOLOGY

Dr. Albert H. Hobbs, a respected sociologist and author at the University of Pennsylvania, has also noted the Kinsey team's departure from sound scientific methods, asserting that it violated elementary statistical rules to create nonexistent data by using a manipulative statistical device ("accumulative incidence") to conjure up illusionary American men. In the same year that the *Male* volume was published, Dr. Hobbs wrote,

> The [accumulative incidence] technique used for expansion of the data is, briefly, to treat each case as if it were an additional case falling within each previous age group or previous experience category. Thus, a man who was 45 at the time of the interview would provide a case for each age group previous to that, and if he was married at the time of interview would constitute a case for the single tabulations in the years before he was married. With this technique one could demonstrate that well over 50% of the adult male white population is "exclusively unemployed" (have been unemployed for at least three years) and that over 90% is "exclusively employed," according to the same criteria. Since the data from one age category are included in others, the age categories are not independent and cannot be designated as random samples. Comparison of one age group with another necessitates a degree of representativeness which is not present.[17]

In a subsequent unpublished manuscript, Hobbs further summarized the inconsistent and unscientific nature of the Kinsey team's methodology:

> Kinsey, in his studies of sexual behavior, violated all three of the precepts necessary to scientific procedure. He denied, flatly and repeatedly, that he had any hypothesis, insisting that he merely, in his words, "presented the facts." Yet to any observant reader, Kinsey obviously had a two-pronged hypothesis. He vigorously promoted, juggling his figures to do so, a hedonistic, animalistic conception of sexual behavior, while at the same time he consistently denounced all biblical and conventional conceptions of sexual behavior. He refused to publish his basic data. He kept secret not only his hypotheses, but also refused to present the basic facts on which his conclusions rested. He also refused to reveal the questionnaire which was the basis for all of his facts. In addition, it is possible to derive conclusions opposite to Kinsey's from his own data.[18]

Hobbs would later testify before a congressional committee regarding the shortcomings of the Kinsey statistics, asserting that these were pseudo-statistics in the service of ideology:

> Note how impressive is the word "scientific." And how false. How dangerous to society if foundations support the theory that social problems can be scientifically solved by mere interviewing techniques. Apart from the doubtful veracity of the samples of men and women questioned by Kinsey, his statistical methods have been seriously criticized by organs of the American Statistical Association and several scholarly reviewers. But even if the sampling had been representative of American attitudes on sex, and even if all the persons interviewed had been willing to give truthful answers and were psychologically capable of doing so, it seems preposterous to propose that social change should be justified upon empirical inquiry alone.[19]

Kinsey's *Female* volume generated additional criticism. Marital-adjustment consultant Harriet R. Mowrer warned of the danger of accepting Kinsey's "findings" at face value. She wrote:

> To accept the Kinsey findings without exacting scrutiny and numerous qualifications would be to perpetuate the error, which Kinsey implies has characterized the work of many, if not all, of the others in the field-both researchers and clinicians-namely, the acceptance and application of unsubstantiated findings, sometimes with harmful results to society. The possible methodological fallacies in the collection and analysis of the data of the sexual activities of the 5,940 white females are numerous and can only be briefly mentioned here. There is no assurance that Kinsey's findings are representative and can be extended to the general population.[20]

In 1954, the American Statistical Association (ASA) published *Statistical Problems of the Kinsey Report: A Report of the American Statistical Association Committee to Advise the National Research Council Committee for Research in Problems of Sex*, by Cochran, Mosteller, Tukey and Jenkins. Jones documents the fact that the ASA yielded to unrelenting pressure from the Rockefeller Foundation and the National Research Council to alter their original conclusion that Kinsey's statistics were meaningless.[21] Nevertheless, Cochran and his colleagues noted three key flaws in the *Male* volume:

- [T]he present results must be regarded as subject to systematic errors of unknown magnitude due to selective sampling (via volunteering, etc.).
- [T]he 'sampled populations' are startlingly different from the composition of the U.S. white male population. The inference from [Kinsey's] sample to the (reported) behavior of all U.S. white males contains a large gap which can be spanned only by expert judgment.
- "[T]here was 'substantial discussion' of social and legal attitudes about sexual behavior 'not based on evidence presented.'[22]

The statisticians criticized the Kinsey group's use of the "so-called U.S. Corrections calculations I have made with them do not check with Kinsey's," and their "assumption that everyone has engaged in all types of [sexual] activity [which] seems likely to encourage exaggeration by the respondents."[23] The ASA team also wondered why there had been no effort to measure the effect of self-selection (volunteers), apparently unaware that Kinsey had opted to ignore Abraham Maslow's warning about the bias of sex studies based on volunteers rather than subjects selected at random.

MASLOW'S "VOLUNTEERS" AND KINSEY'S COERCION

The Kinsey-Maslow scandal is a fascinating account of how Kinsey, a largely unknown gall wasp zoologist, became the world's most famous sexologist, and a mover and shaker in the scientific world. He was able to craft an American sexual revolution, while Abraham Maslow, a psychologist of global acclaim in the 1940s, appears as a mere footnote in American scientific history.

In the *Male* volume, Kinsey claimed to be "indebted" to Maslow for the latter's efforts to preclude volunteer bias. Maslow, a libertarian member of the Humanist Society and an early fan of Kinsey's research, had scrutinized "volunteerism" in studies of human sexuality. In 1942, he had reported that "any study in which data are obtained from volunteers will always have a preponderance of [aggressive] high dominance people and therefore will show a *falsely high percentage of non-virginity, masturbation, promiscuity, homosexuality, etc.*, in the population."[24] [Emphasis added.]

Maslow's student recruits at Brooklyn College revealed that people offering themselves for *any* sex study would likely generate "volunteer error." For Kinsey, it meant that he would undoubtedly end up with sexually "unconventional" women and men with high rates of unhealthy and disapproved sexual activity. Once he understood how Maslow's data and analysis could compromise his efforts, Kinsey terminated their collaboration. In a letter to a colleague, Maslow wrote,

> [W]hen I warned him [Kinsey] about "volunteer error" he disagreed with me and was sure that his random selection would be okay. So what we did was to cook up a joint crucial test. I put the heat on all my five classes at Brooklyn College and made a real effort to get them all to sign up to be interviewed by Kinsey. We had my dominance test scores for all of them, and then Kinsey gave me the names of the students who actually showed up for the interviews. As I expected, the volunteer error was proven and the whole basis for Kinsey's statistics was proven to be shaky. But then he refused to publish it and refused even to mention it in his books, or to mention anything else that I had written. All my work was excluded from his bibliography. So after a couple of years I just went ahead and published it myself. Whatever contacts I had with him in his last years were not cordial. He seemed to have changed in character.[25]

Maslow, not at odds with Kinsey ideologically, was limited by the rigors of honest scientific method. Kinsey pressed reluctant students to "volunteer" their sex histories with results that can best be described as a statistical flop. He began downplaying the issue of volunteer error, telling his readers that it was minor and that "how these [results] affect a sexual history is not yet clear."[26]

The extent to which Kinsey dismissed volunteer error as a pertinent factor in his research surfaced during his vigorous challenge of data presented by a group of Harvard medical researchers who were anxious to determine if homosexuality is caused by hormonal factors. In a 1940 paper presented to the Psychology Session of the American Association for the Advancement of Science, he seriously questioned the Harvard medical argument, speculating that it was not "likely that any hormonal factors" caused homosexuality. His "evidence" included an extrapolation of his heavily biased inmate and sex offender data to the entire American male population.

In 1941, another paper by Kinsey on the subject was published in a prestigious professional journal.[27] Entitled, "Criteria for a Hormonal Explanation of the Homosexual," it, too, was based on interviews with allegedly "normal" male "volunteers" (in this instance, 1,058).[28]

GRAND INQUISITOR OR SCIENTIFIC INTERVIEWING?

Even if Kinsey's subjects had constituted a valid sample of the American citizenry at the time, interview techniques would have assured questionable results. He had written, "A scientist studying sex should be able to accept any type of sexual behavior objectively without adverse reaction, and record without social or moral evaluation."[29]

The face-to-face, one-on-one interview was employed for his larger research effort. In *Taking a Sex History* (1982), Pomeroy and his so-authors gave his readers a glimpse of some of the explicit questions. The blanks are inserted here by the author. *This use of blanks is designed to enable full access to this information for the many persons who are extremely vulnerable due to past experiences as well as those who wish to have information, but who seek to preserve an ethical and moral standard this language would violate:*

After puberty, how young were you the first time you had a homosexual experience? Was there any payment? How young were you the first time you were m_____ by another male? another male put his _____ in your _____? his _____ in your _____? his _____ between your legs? penetrated your _____?[30]

Pomery and company, ask about very violent, sadistic acts. Then they query, "How much did you enjoy your first experience," not, "Was your experience, a) enjoyable, b) unimpressive, c) painful, d) humiliating," or other queries likely to obtain a more negative response.

It is pertinent to note that the authors also maintain that pedophilia is a natural act because "sex play among young animals and between adults and the young is commonplace. This would lead us to conclude that a 'natural' sex act is whatever people do sexually."[31] They suggest that sex with children is a problem only because we have laws against it in this country.

Kinsey claimed his intrusive list of 350 sexual questions had been approved by the Indiana University Board of Trustees.[32] He also insisted that his interview technique elicited "detailed and accurate information from an enormous variety of subjects regarding their most intimate experiences-experiences that many of them had never before verbalized to another person."[33] But he and his team largely rejected normal sexual behavior, exhibiting disbelief, contempt, and other negative reactions toward subjects who refused to participate in perverted acts. Note, for example, interview protocol #13 in the *Male* volume:

> **13. Placing the burden of denial on the subject.** The interviewer should not make it easy for a subject to deny his participation in any form of sexual activity. It is too easy to say no if he is simply asked whether he has ever engaged in a particular activity. *We always assume that everyone has engaged in every type of activity.* Consequently we always begin by asking *when* they first engaged in such activity . . . . It might be thought that this

"'The Kinsey Report on Women' Long-awaited study shows they are not very interested in sex.... One of the 5,940 [women] is questioned (left) by Pomeroy." (Life Magazine, August 24, 1953, pp. 41, 54) A staff member re-appears in this carefully staged photo shoot as the Kinsey team's prototypical "average" 1940s housewife, interviewed now by Pomeroy.

Widely circulated posed publicity photo of Kinsey with a supposedly typical subject. However, this staged photo, of a staff member, posed here as an "average" 1940s housewife (see pgs. 33 and 36 in Chapter 2). Note: that she is wears horn-rimmed glasses in this picture, and that the dress and hairstyle is identical with the Pomeroy interview photo at left.

approach would bias the answer, but there is no indication that we get false admissions.³⁴ [Emphasis added.]

Regarding coercion, interview protocol #18 states:

> **18. Forcing a subject.** There are some persons who offer to contribute histories in order to satisfy their curiosity, although they have no intentions of giving an honest record of their sexual activities. As soon as one recognizes such a case, *he should denounce the subject with considerable severity, and the interviewer should refuse to proceed with the interview.* Such an attack on a dishonest subject is quite contrary to the usual rules for interviewing, and a procedure which we at first hesitated to employ in the present study. We have, however, decided that it is a necessary technique in dealing with some individuals, particularly some older teenage males and some females in underworld groups. Failure to command the situation in these cases would lower the community's respect for the investigator and make it impossible for him to secure honest answers from others.³⁵ [Emphasis added.]

This ominous photograph in shadow was not seen until December 1990 when it appeared in The Village Voice *alongside a flattering article about Kinsey by Philip Nobile, a Kinsey disciple.*

Kinsey's resort to "forcing a subject" conflicted with the claim that the slightest suggestion of annoyance or disbelief could prejudice the interview and render the information useless. For most subjects:

> The sympathetic interviewer records his reactions in ways that may not involve spoken words but which are nonetheless readily comprehended by most people. A minute change of a facial expression, a slight tensing of a muscle, the flick of an eye [one can judge] the true nature of another person's reactions.... *If the interviewer's manner spells surprise, disapproval, condemnation, or even cold disinterest, he will not get the whole of the record.*³⁶ [Emphasis added.]

By urging that some subjects be denounced "with considerable severity," Kinsey was assuring that he would "not get the whole of the record."

Did he obtain the answers he wanted? If a subject was uncooperative, the interview could be terminated and the data discarded. Even Lewis Terman was moved to comment on the nature of the questions and the admissions they elicited:

> Unfortunately, the author [Kinsey] tells us nothing about the wording of the questions asked, a matter which the professional pollsters have found to be extremely important. The reason given for this omission is lack of space in this 800 page book. What the author does say about the questions is not always reassuring. In the first place we are told that they have never been standardized; instead, the manner of wording them varies according to the age, intelligence, and personality of the subject being interviewed. The necessity of alternative forms of wording will be granted, but no other investigator can repeat the Kinsey experiment with any assurance that he is getting comparable results.³⁷

Terman continues,

> The validity of a self-selected sample is always questionable and usually absent. The level of psychological sophistication of the investigators appears to be very low. Although there is much talk of Freud and psychoanalysis, there seems to be little comprehension of psycho-sexuality and unconscious desires. Everything in the Kinsey report takes place on the level of the obvious and overt, but in sexuality the obvious and overt are not reliable indexes of human sexual behavior.[38]

As another example of Kinsey's desperate effort to conjure up seemingly credible statistics, he included in his sample an unidentified number of feebleminded[39] subjects (possibly all males) from the Michigan State Training School at Coldwater. This captive population was part of the Kinsey Institute's "100%" group, an unscientific selection devised by Kinsey to offset his team's inability to recruit a cross section of the population. He refers to the "100% sample," and to his "feebleminded" group, on several occasions, though he carefully avoids reporting how many simpletons he included among his samples of normal males and females:

> [F]eebleminded individuals vary considerably in their capacities to remember. It is possible to get a fair record from most feebleminded individuals whose IQs are not below 50, although interviewing any person with a rating below 70 becomes slow. Each idea must penetrate endless repetition, a vocabulary confined to the simplest of words.

> With uneducated persons, and particularly with feebleminded individuals, it is sometimes effective to expose the truth by answering as though he had never given a negative reply. "Yes, I know you have never done that, but how old were you the *first* time that you did it?" [Such questioning] may break down the cover-up of a feebleminded individual.[40]

It is unlikely that a feebleminded person, after being wooed and flattered into participating, then pressured to respond, could withstand the artifice of the interrogator. Such an interview is tailor-made to yield data fitting an inquisitor's preconceived position.

"MASSAGING" THE DATA

Despite "placing the burden of denial" on his subjects, and using degrees of coercion when deemed appropriate, Kinsey was concerned that he might miss sex acts that some subjects might conceal. His advance planning took that problem into account:

> Nevertheless, in spite of all that may be done, a certain amount of deliberate cover-up may slip by, and the investigator must find some means of measuring the extent of that cover-up in each part of his data.[41]

Members of the Kinsey team have yet to publicly reveal their "scientific" method for "measuring" how to change a subject's answers. Some college students who were interviewed recall telling Kinsey the wildest stories they could think of, since they were what he wanted to hear. Friendly Kinsey critic Terman writes:

> Cover-up, the author says, is harder to catch. On p. 54 it is said that cover-up is combated by "the use of a considerable list of interlocking questions which provide cross-checks throughout the history, and particularly in regard to socially taboo items." However, the

author is not very explicit about the exact nature of these cross-checks, and the examples given do not impress this reviewer as altogether convincing. Moreover, as the author admits (p. 125), the retakes do not test the validity of the data, but rather the constancy of memory and of tendency to cover up.[42]

Kinsey's figure of 10 percent homosexuality, for example, mirrors what is called the statistical "fudge factor." It can also be applied to his data on adultery, sodomy, etc. If a subject stubbornly refuses to admit committing acts recited by the interviewer, the latter simply speculates about what *really* happened. Among scientists, such manipulation is euphemistically termed "massaging the data."

Each cell (a set of answers to a particular question) in Kinsey's data collection could have received corrective treatment. For example, since Kinsey was sure that his subjects denied their homosexual activities, he could "correct" the answers to reflect what he felt were more "honest" responses. And he utilized a ploy that he called "proving the answer:" "If it becomes apparent that the subject's *first* answer is not correct, [one should] make him prove his answer or expose the falsity of his reply."[43]

Another friendly Kinsey critic, sex historian Paul Robinson, has observed that Kinsey "normally sought to minimize the importance of exaggeration and inflate that of cover-up." Writing in *The Modernization of Sex*, Robinson explains that "because he inclined to an ethic of abundance in sexual matters, he suggested that many sexual activities were even more common than his figures indicated."[44] On the evidence, Kinsey's methodology was designed to portray as "average" documentably "unconventional" men, women, and children. This was accomplished and concealed in such ways as,

- Secret interviews which precluded scientific verification of answers by independent examination.
- Courting and otherwise giving positive reinforcement to subjects deemed to be answering questions "correctly."
- Coercing and "forcing" those who answered "incorrectly" by expressing disbelief and threatening to terminate the interviews unless the subjects relented.
- "Massaging the data" by altering answers thought to be incorrect or misleading.
- Purging three-fourths of the total sample, including all black women and female prisoners.

CHILD-RESEARCH "METHODS" OR SYSTEMATIC SEX ABUSE?

Kinsey described three child-research "methods": recalling childhood, interviewing children, and direct observation. Substantial amounts of his data were based on adolescent and adult recall of experiences long past, but he was unsatisfied with the results, so sought more direct sources.[46] Pomeroy explains:

> In taking a sexual history, we asked people about their sexual behavior from earliest memory- four, five and six-and realized how fragmentary these memories were, and how much we were missing. At some point, Kinsey wondered what would happen if he went to children themselves and asked them about their sex play.
>
> Although it was possible to find a few liberal parents who would be willing to have a sex researcher question their children on this subject, we doubted that we could get an adequate sample unless we got the parents to act. It would also be difficult and time-consuming to establish rapport with young children, without the parents involved. Consequently

Kinsey began to create situations with children with the parents present [unless they were] interviewees in ghetto areas.⁴⁷

According to Gebhard and Johnson, some prepubescent children qualified as one of the "special groups" in the Kinsey samples.⁴⁸ They write that most of them "were too young to have received our standard interview and were given a variant of it."⁴⁹ And in *Male* volume (p. 180), Kinsey commented on the selection of children found in the notorious Table 34:

> 317 preadolescents who were either observed in self-masturbation or who were observed in contacts with other boys or older adults. [T]his is a record of a somewhat select group of younger males and not a statistical representation for any larger group.⁵⁰

The young "subject" with "Uncle Kinsey" in publicity photos was Clyde Martin's daughter. (As cited in Gathorne-Hardy's biography.)

It is not clear whether the "somewhat select" group of 317 young boys was subjected to Kinsey's force-and-threaten, measure-and-change interview "variant," but a supposedly socially acceptable protocol was described in the *Male* volume. It is often publicized with photographs of Kinsey playing with a little girl of perhaps six years of age. With at least one parent present, the "technique is one in which the interviewer looks at dolls, at toys of other sorts, joins in games, builds picture puzzles, romps, shares candies and cookies, and withal makes himself an agreeable guest."⁵¹

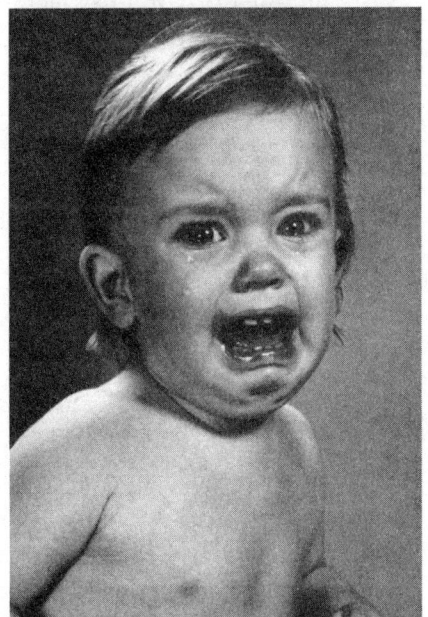

Pomeroy describes the fondness children felt for their "Uncle Kinsey" and "Uncle Pomeroy."⁵² He also indicates the actual purpose of the sessions:

> Tucked into these activities are questions that give information on the child's sexual background. If the picture book shows kittens putting on nightgowns for bed, the child may be asked whether she wears nightgowns when she goes to bed. When the interviewer tussles with the four-year-old boy, he may ask him whether he similarly tussles with the other boys in the neighborhood, and rapidly follows up with questions concerning tussling with girls, whether he plays with any girls, whether he likes girls, whether he kisses girls.⁵³

From a popular book, *Oh! Dr. Kinsey! A Photographic Reaction to the Kinsey Report* (1953), this baby's photograph is captioned, "ARE YOU GLAD YOU'RE STILL A VIRGIN?"

One is struck with the vision of Kinsey as he "tussles" with the "four-year-old boy." One may fairly wonder just whose sexuality is being discerned.

RATIONALIZATION OR SCIENCE: THE MYTH OF KINSEY'S "SCIENTIFIC" METHODOLOGY

> He [the four-year-old] may or may not so freely admit that there are girls in the neighborhood with whom he also plays, and his embarrassment, his hesitancy, his disturbed giggling or his calm acceptance of the fact, are important things for the student of sexual behavior to note. Many of the adult attitudes toward various items of sex are already discernible in the three- or four-year-old's history. A later volume will cover this aspect of the study. [54]

That "later volume" is as yet unpublished, but we understand that "research" in sex, gender, and reproduction, is on going at the Kinsey Institute today.

Pomeroy's definition of preadolescent sex play *excluded* hugging, kissing, or fondling, which would have ruled out such childhood activities, as well as "romping" and "tussling." Kinsey disagreed, stating:

> Adult [sexual] behavior is more obviously a product of the specifically genital play which is found among children, and on which we can now provide a statistical record. Our own interviews with children younger than five, and observations made by parents and others who have been subjects in this study, indicate that hugging and kissing are usual in the activity of the very young child, and that self-manipulation of genitalia, the exhibition of genitalia, the exploration of the genitalia of other children, and some manual and occasionally oral manipulation of the genitalia of other children occur in the two- to five-year-olds more frequently than older persons ordinarily remember from their own histories.[55]

Who would associate children's hugging and kissing with "genital play?" Pomeroy claimed:

> Kinsey tried to train me to help with interviewing the children, but I found that I wasn't good at it. For that matter, none of the other staff members was any more successful at this delicate job, and Kinsey had to do nearly all of it alone.[56]

Although Kinsey claimed that the child interviews were innocuous, at least one critic noticed the potentially traumatic impact they may have had. George A. Baitsell, writing in *Yale News*, is quoted by Pomeroy:

> I don't like Kinsey! I don't like his report; I don't like anything about it. Kinsey is not trained to do work in this field.... In his interviews, Kinsey employed a thoroughly objectionable technique. The interviews often have a serious effect on the subject's nerves. Children, reluctant to be questioned, have been virtually forced to submit because of the possibility of being labeled "deficient." The Kinsey Report might well be called the "Kinsey Inquisition."[57]

Yale zoologist Baitsell's suspicions about the abuse inherent in the Kinsey team's methodology have gone largely unheeded by the academic elite, and by the thousands of world-famous analysts, psychiatrists, psychologists, sociologists, anthropologists, criminologists, educators, ministers, and others whose careers have largely been built around Kinsey.

Pomeroy explains how critics were lulled into a false sense of security about the sources of the child samples by Kinsey's euphemistic description of the interview process:

> He concentrated at first on the three-, four- and five-year-old levels, working primarily in nursery schools, and always getting parents' histories first. He also took a scattering of older

children, and found that after age eight it was better to exclude parents. There were a few nine-and ten-year-olds that gave histories, but this aspect of the project never really developed. Kinsey had hopes and dreams of exploring in depth such a relatively untouched field, but that part of the investigation died with him.[58]

Note Pomeroy's admission that post-eight-year-old children were left alone with "Uncle Kinsey." Kinsey told Dr. Frank K. Shuttleworth of the Institute of Child Welfare, University of California at Berkeley, "that students in the field had all been 'too prudish' to make an actual investigation of sperm count in early adolescent males." Pomeroy stated that Kinsey himself collected "some material" in the "first ejaculate," but "he did not yet have any actual counts."[59]

The third research method employed by the Kinsey team entailed genital experiments; observing, recording, and filming not only adults, but children and infants as well. This technique primarily underpins Chapter 5 of the *Male* volume and Chapter 4 of the *Female* volume. Data about the sexual response of children could not be obtained by interview, and the precise details on how the data *were* obtained may never be fully revealed. It will likely require intense public pressure to force full disclosure. As noted, however, comments about the process have occasionally surfaced from Kinsey Institute team members. In *Human Sexualities* (1997), John Gagnon, a Kinsey Institute associate, offhandedly acknowledges the illegality of the experiments:

> A less neutral observer than Kinsey would have described these events as sex crimes, since they involved sexual contact between adults and children. Whether or not these observers were "scientifically trained" [as Kinsey claimed] it seems advisable to use caution in interpreting their findings.[60]

Gagnon did not demand that the adults who committed the "sex crimes" be arrested and prosecuted, or that the public be fully informed about the ghastly project.

PERPETUAL DAMAGE CONTROL

Kinsey and his team knew that they were undertaking research with "potential academic dangers."[61] Initially, the threat was circumvented by a mix of caution, discretion, occasional secrecy, and a loyal staff. As the work progressed, however, it moved beyond *potential* dangers into the realm of criminal and civil infractions.

During the past half-century, enormous changes in law, medicine, science, and education have been wrought by Kinsey's data. Were Kinsey alive, he would be pleased. That was the intent of his "grand scheme" from the beginning. The immense legal, educational, and political effort to continue the deception and to suppress efforts to expose the truth, is largely carried out by the pornography and multi-disciplinary sexology movement, metastasizing throughout the United Nations. This movement is energized in large part by Alfred Kinsey's fraudulent sex science data which has justified the billions of tax dollars expended annually on grants for government programs dealing with sex, gender, and human reproduction. Such expenditures would doubtless violate the Federal False Claims Act, (31 USC 3729-3733, 3729).

A confidential 1990 letter from erstwhile Kinsey Institute Director Paul Gebhard, to then-director June Reinisch, focused on your author's challenge to Kinsey's data and techniques. Gebhard asserted:

> In your recent letter of December 3, which I gather was sent to a number of individuals as well as to me, you refuted Judith Reisman's allegations about Kinsey and the Institute. However, I fear that your final paragraph on page 1 may embarrass you and the university if it comes to Reisman's attention. Hence, I want to warn you and relevant university officials so that some damage control might be devised. The paragraph ends with the sentence: "He never used data from the special samples, derived from such populations as the gay community or prisons, to generalize to the general public."
>
> This statement is incorrect. *Kinsey did mix male prison inmates in with his sample used in Sexual Behavior in the Human Male.* I describe this defect at the bottom of page 28 of *The Kinsey Data* and add that Kinsey later recognized this error and hence did not use prison inmates in *Sexual Behavior in the Human Female*. This inclusion of prison inmates was a major reason why on page 35 of *The Kinsey Data* I state the sample " was misleading with respect to the lower socioeconomic class." As to generalizing to a wider population, *in his first volume Kinsey did generalize to the entire U.S. population.* See, for one example, the tables on page 188 and 220 where he clearly extrapolates to the U.S. Subsequently he realized this error and no such extrapolation is found in his second volume.
>
> I am distressed that neither you nor your staff seem to be familiar with Kinsey's first book nor with *The Kinsey Data* and consequently produced the erroneous statement in your letter.[62] [Other than book titles, emphasis added.]

Gebhard could have added that Kinsey once claimed that he and his team had earned the rights of "a priest or of a physician"[63] to keep confidential the information provided by rapists, murderers, child-molesters, and pedophile murderers.

During a 1982 interview with Eric Trimmer of the *British Journal of Sexual Medicine*, Wardell Pomeroy was asked about the methodological bias of the Kinsey reports. A National Research Council report on AIDS had charged that the Kinsey Institute's sexuality data were indeed biased, but toward Midwestern white, upper class, college men and women. Pomeroy denied it:

Publicity photo of Kinsey (center, holding baby) and staff at picnic. Clara stands toward upper-right in a dark sundress.

TRIMMER: I've also heard it said that selection of subjects in the two reports was in some way biased towards the middle class, the easy talkers about sex. Critics allege that this bias makes the books less valid than was originally suggested. Would you go along with that?

POMEROY: Definitely not! We spread our net widely and indiscriminately. Kinsey was an excellent organizer and a wise researcher. He would not allow his studies to be slanted. He was a scientist primarily.[64]

Here was yet another member of the Kinsey team either engaging in deception or seriously confused. Pomeroy himself once claimed that the Kinsey reports were the most often-cited, but *least-read*, books of all time.[65] The reports continue to negatively impact our lives, despite their colossal flaws, but that can change as more Americans begin to realize the ominous implications of their content.

THE RED QUEEN: WORDS MEAN WHAT I SAY THEY MEAN

"Let the jury consider their verdict," the King said for about the twentieth time that day.

"No, no," said the Queen. "Sentence first-verdict afterwards."

"Stuff and Nonsense," said Alice loudly. "The idea of having the sentence first."

"Hold your tongue!" said the Queen, turning purple.[66]

Like the Red Queen in Lewis Carroll's *Alice's Adventures in Wonderland,* Kinsey's contention that in the late 1940s and early 1950s the U.S. was steeped in promiscuous sex was heavily dependent on his use of self-serving semantics. For example, he defined a "married woman" as one who had lived with a man for "at least a year, which could include working prostitutes."[67] In an especially slick semantic sleight-of-hand, he modified the standard litmus test for those who have been to "college" (13-plus years of school), so that folks who merely travel or read a lot and might "ultimately go to college" could qualify for his "college-level" category.[68]

For Kinsey, "normal" was a non-word, as were "criminal" and "crime." His definition of "underworld" eliminated sex crimes, unless they had a monetary motive. A child molester was simply a "partner," since the word "rape" is excluded from his study. And in his lengthy studies of human sexuality, such terms as "love" and "childbirth" do not appear in the indices.

In Chapter 5 of the *Male* volume, Kinsey defines as "contacts" what most Americans would likely describe as sexual assault, rape, and sodomy. He mixes the experiences of "older subjects" with those of "older boys" and "adult men," as though the categories are interchangeable. He also combines "younger boys" with "preadolescent boys," which camouflages the rape of children under age 13.

Pomeroy explains that Kinsey,

> was constantly working with language, trying to put the proper word in the proper place, and in the course of doing so he developed a fine sense of the use of the vernacular... [Kinsey's dictum was] "Evasive terms invite dishonest answers." Unlike previous researchers, we did not say "touching yourself" when we meant masturbation or "relations with other persons" when "sexual intercourse" was intended.[69]

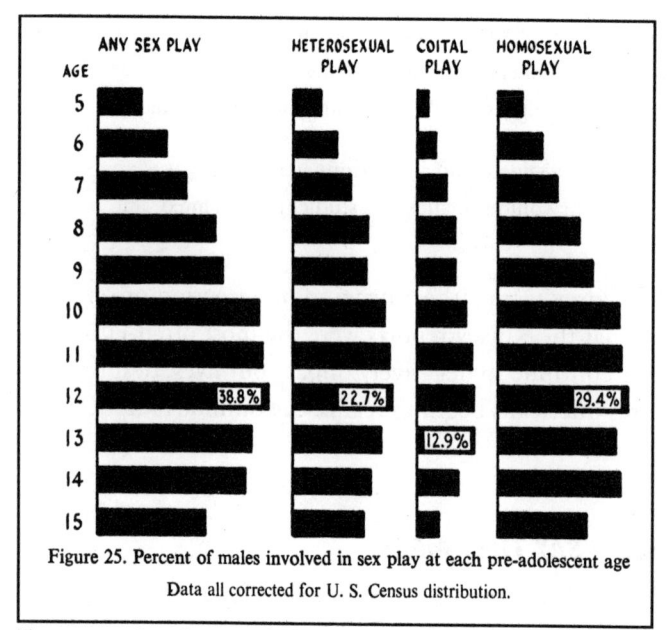

Figure 25. Percent of males involved in sex play at each pre-adolescent age
Data all corrected for U. S. Census distribution.

AGE	ANY SEX PLAY	HETEROSEXUAL PLAY	COITAL PLAY	HOMOSEXUAL PLAY
12	38.8%	22.7%		29.4%
13			12.9%	

Kinsey grouped sundry sex activities involving young children as sex "play," including sex abuse by adults. By reclassifying all sex abuse of children as "play," Kinsey logically had reported no data on child "rape."

Kinsey, according to Pomeroy, was successful because he used "the same simple language his audience employed:"

> People were never "ill," for example; they were "sick." They were not "injured," but "hurt." If the subject of a history knew the word "prick" but not "penis," Kinsey used it too [He used] "sex organ," not "vagina"... Kinsey never used jargon or euphemisms, and he insisted on precise definitions. He avoided technical words such as "cunnilingus" or "fellatio," even though "mouth-genital" used as a substitute might not be quite accurate in some cases. Jargon covered up meanings and was not a proper way to communicate.[70]

Despite such claims, it is apparent that Kinsey's peculiar definitions of such terms as "college," "married," "rape," "contacts," and "partner" were precisely designed to bolster his team's bizarre views of rape, crime, marriage, and child molestation.

Pomeroy states that "as scientific prose [Kinsey's writing] was wholly admirable and has often been cited as a model of clear, scholarly writing in science."[71] Yet in *Sexual Behavior in the Human Male*, such terms as "contacts," "partners," and "sex play" were utilized by Kinsey and his associates as euphemisms to cover what was in fact grown men forcibly sodomizing infants and children. Kinsey and his team went to great lengths to imply that such sex was consensual for all parties.

British anthropologist Geoffrey Gorer described as "ludicrous" Kinsey's ploy of extrapolating from his largely deviant male sample to the entire U.S. population. Charging that Kinsey's philosophy was "antireligious humanism," Gorer wrote in the mid-Fifties,

> As can be seen, Dr. Kinsey is not really either dispassionate or neutral (probably nobody dealing with human emotions and values could be); behind the "scientific" smoke-screen of statistical tables, graphs, codes, and rebarbative language there is a continuous propaganda for more, and more varied, sexual "out lets" as physiologically good in themselves. There is even the stupendous claim that taxonomic studies of behavior should be the basis for laws.[72]

Just as "love" does not exist for Kinsey, "motherhood" as a legitimate, differentiating enterprise does not exist. Kinsey offers some data about the number of women who have out-of-wedlock babies, but is silent regarding the percentage of the 5,000 to 7,000 female "sample" who were *lawful* mothers.

Jordan Hall on the Indiana University campus, where the Kinsey Institute was housed. Circa 1956 (Weinberg)

Scientists who questioned Kinsey's scientific "purity" were brutally attacked. Kinsey launched one such personal offensive against a world-famous scholar who had critiqued his conclusions about female orgasm. And Pomeroy reprinted a letter from Kinsey to a scholar who dared express concern about their research. Kinsey stated at one point: "Your suggestion [of our understanding of coitus]... is a travesty which you have invented for your own ulterior purpose.... Your article contains other similar misinterpretations and distortions of our position."[73]

Taking the offensive, Kinsey insisted that his own scientific credentials were pristine as he challenged those of others. "Your treatment smacks more of a dogmatic effort to win a point than a scientist's effort to discover the fact,"[74] he declared in one missive.

Neither Kinsey nor members of his team can properly be termed "scientists." Replication and validation are two key attributes of authentic scientific investigation, but Kinsey's data has yet to be validated, and his methodology has not been replicated. One wonders how it could be. Would the abusive treatment of infants and children that became a sordid hallmark of the Kinsey investigation be tolerated today, even in the name of "science"? Subjects of all ages were anonymous, some coerced, and data were clandestinely altered and destroyed at whim.

As with the discredited turn-of-the-century "science" of phrenology, which entailed measuring bumps on the head to estimate intelligence and other traits, the "new academic discipline"[76] of sexology is a shaman's trade; its claim of sound "methodology" is hokum. No sensitive-or sensible-person, including a scientist, who understands the dynamics of marriage, real human love, and the absolute trust and commitment they require, would propose or participate in perverse studies such as those conducted by Alfred Kinsey and his team.

CHAPTER 3 NOTES

1. Kinsey, Pomeroy and Martin, *Sexual Behavior in the Human Male*, W.B. Saunders, Philadelphia, 1948. Among other citations, Kinsey says here that he used the same techniques for the study of wasps as he did for humans. "The techniques of this research [were] born out of the senior author's longtime experience with [i]nsect[s]. The transfer from insect to human material is not illogical and can be applied to all population studies." (p. 9). This statement is repeated by Hermann Muller about fruit flies. Muller, also a Rockefeller grantee, joined Kinsey's zoology department at IU in 1946.

2. *Male*, 1948, p. 9.

3. *The Lancet*, "Really, Dr. Kinsey?" March 2, 1991, p. 547.

4. Kinsey, Pomeroy, Martin and Gebhard, *Sexual Behavior in the Human Female*, W.B. Saunders, Philadelphia, 1953. "Satisfactory increases of figures on the homosexual cannot be obtained by any technique short of a carefully planned population survey... every segment of the total population," p. 618. Kinsey states that they have data in the *Male* volume on "1200 persons who have been convicted of sex offenses," p. 392. Elsewhere the figure is 1,400, etc.

5. *Male*, p. 18.

6. Gebhard, Gagnon, Pomeroy, and Christenson, *Sex Offenders*, Bantam Books, New York, 1965, pp. 33, 32, 31.

7. Alfred C. Kinsey, *The Origins of Higher Categories*, UMI, Books on Demand, Ann Arbor Michigan, 1936, pp. 18 and 68. In his 1936 book on wasps, Kinsey included the same map of "wasps" as he does the map of humans in the *Male* volume. There is some documentation, however, for the nature of his wasp collection, but none for the nature and number of his human collection.

8. James H. Jones, *Alfred C. Kinsey, A Public/Private Life*, W. W. Norton, New York, 1997, p. 636.

9. W. Allen Wallis, "Statistics of the Kinsey Report," *Journal of the American Statistical Association*, December 1949, No. 248, Vol. 44, p. 463-484. Also see, Paul Wallin, "An Appraisal of some Methodological Aspects of the Kinsey Report," in *The American Sociological Review*, April 1949, pp. 197-210.

10. Arno Karlen, *Sexuality and Homosexuality*, W. W. Norton, Inc., New York, 1971, p. 456.

11. Reisman *et al*, *Kinsey, Sex and Fraud*, Huntington House, Lafayette, LA, 1990, pp. 189-192, "Re-analysis of the Kinsey Data on Sexual Behavior" (grant description), Russell Sage Foundation Annual Report, 1968-1969, pp. 46-7. Russell Sage Foundation, 230 Park Avenue, New York, New York, 10017.

12. Paul Gebhard and A. Johnson, *The Kinsey Data: Marginal Tabulations of the 1938-1963 Interviews Conducted by the Institute for Sex Research*, W.B. Saunders Co., Philadelphia, 1979, pp. 31 and 8. Beginning in 1963, Gebhard and Johnson spent three years on a National Institute of Mental Health grant in an unsuccessful attempt to "clean," code, and store the Kinsey data.

13. Private letter from Clyde Martin to June Reinisch, December 31, 1990, included in the body of deposition papers legally released to Judith Reisman in 1993. In the Author's archive.

14. Wallis, p. 474.

15. Warren Weaver, Head of the Natural Science Division of the Rockefeller Foundation, letter, May 7, 1951, Rockefeller Archive Center.

16. Lionel Trilling, "The Kinsey Report," in Donald Porter Geddes, Ed. *Analysis of the Kinsey Report*, Mentor, New York, 1954, p. 218.

17. Albert H. Hobbs and R. D. Lambert, "An Evaluation of 'Sexual Behavior in the Human Male," reprinted from *The American Journal of Psychiatry*, Vol. 104, No. 12, June 1948, pp. 758-764.

18. Albert H. Hobbs, unpublished manuscript, in the author's archive.

19. Albert Hobbs testimony in Rene Wormser, Ed, *Foundations,* Covenant House Books, Sevierville, Tennessee, 1993, p. 104.

20. Harriet Mowrer, on Kinsey's "Methodological Inadequacies," in [Eds.], J. Himelhoch and S. Fava, *Sexual Behavior in American Society: An Appraisal of the First Two Kinsey Reports*, W.W. Norton & Co., Inc, New York, 1955, p. 146.

21. Cochran, Mosteller, Tukey and Jenkins, *Statistical Problems of the Kinsey Report; A Report of the American Statistical Association Committee to Advise the National Research Council Committee for Research in Problems of Sex*, The American Statistical Association, Washington, DC, 1954.

22. Jones, pp. 638-648, 653-665, 683.

23. Cochran, Mosteller, Tukey and Jenkins, pp. 18, 28-29, 122.

24. Abraham Maslow, "Test for Dominance-Feeling (Self-Esteem) in College Women," 1940, pp. 255-270, and Maslow, "Self-Esteem, Dominance...and Sexuality In Women," *The Journal of Social Psychology*, 1942, 16: 259-294.

25. Letter from Maslow to Amram Scheinfeld, April 29, 1970. On file in the Archives of the *History of American Psychology*, University of Akron, Ohio. See reprint in Reisman, *et al, Kinsey, Sex and Fraud*, p. 221.

26. *Male*, p. 103.

27. Alfred C. Kinsey, "Criteria for a Hormonal Explanation of the Homosexual," *Journal of Clinical Endocrinology*, Vol. 1, 1941, pp. 424-428.

28. Cornelia Christenson, *Kinsey: A Biography*, Indiana University Press, Bloomington, 1971, p. 118,

29. *Male*, p. 41.

30. Pomeroy, Flax and Wheeler, *Taking a Sex History*, The Free Press, New York, 1982, pp. 259-261.

31. Pomeroy, *et al*, p. 7.

32. James H. Jones, *The Origins of the Institute for Sex Research*, UMI Dissertation Services, Ann Arbor, Michigan, 1973, pp. 96-99.

33. Pomeroy, *et al.*, p. 1.

34. *Male*, p. 53.

35. *Male*, pp. 55-56.
36. *Male*, p. 42.
37. Lewis Terman, "Kinsey's Sexual Behavior in the Human Male: Some Comments and Criticisms," *Psychological Bulletin* 45, 1948, pp. 443-459.
38. Terman, pp. 443-459.
39. *Male*, p. 15.
40. *Male*, pp. 49-50, 55.
41. *Male*, pp. 55.
42. Terman, p. 445.
43. *Male*, p. 55.
44. Paul Robinson, *The Modernization of Sex*, Harper and Row, New York, 1976, pp. 42-119.
45. See discussion of "Forcing the Subject," etc.
46. John Gagnon, *Human Sexualities*, Scott Foresman & Co., Glenview, Illinois, 1977, p. 84, and Paul Robinson, The *Modernization of Sex*, p. 45.
47. Wardell Pomeroy, *Dr. Kinsey and the Institute for Sex Research*, Harper & Row, New York, 1972, pp. 218-219.
48. Gebhard and Johnson, p. 6.
49. Gebhard and Johnson, p. 6.
50. *Male*, p. 177.
51. Pomeroy, p. 114-115.
52. Pomeroy, pp. 221.
53. Pomeroy, pp. 114-115.
54. *Male*, pp. 58-9.
55. *Male*, p. 163.
56. Pomeroy, p. 219.
57. Pomeroy, p. 287.
58. Pomeroy, p. 219.
59. Pomeroy, p. 315.
60. Gagnon, p. 84.
61. Pomeroy, pp. 42-43.
62. Private letter from Gebhard to Reinisch, December 6, 1990, obtained during Reisman deposition. In the author's archive.
63. *Male*, p. 47.
64. Eric Trimmer interview with Wardell Pomeroy in the *British Journal of Sexual Medicine*, January 1982, pp. 37-38.
65. Pomeroy, pp. 3-4.
66. Lewis Carroll, *Alice's Adventures in Wonderland*, Smithmark, New York, 1995, p. 155.
67. *Female*, p. 53.
68. *Male*, p. 689.
69. Pomeroy, pp. 200-201, and 112.
70. Pomeroy, pp. 200-201.
71. Pomeroy, pp. 338, 261.
72. Geoffrey Gorer, "Nature Science & Dr. Kinsey," in Jerome Himelhock and Sylvia Fava, *(Eds.) Sexual Behavior in American Society: An Appraisal of the First Two Kinsey Reports*, W.W. Norton, New York, 1955.
72. Himeloch and Fava, p.57.
73. Pomeroy, p. 305
74. Pomeroy, p. 305
75. *The New York Times* Letters, "Kinsey's Numbers," December 28, 1997.
76. Ethan Bronner, "Study of Sex Experiencing 2nd Revolution," *The New York Times*, December 28, 1997, p. 1.

CHAPTER 4

STAG FILMS AS SEX RESEARCH

[The Kinsey Institute] already moved Kinsey's notorious sex-films to a secret location. And they have vowed to destroy painstakingly accumulated material (including a $40 million erotic art collection almost never seen) if the police arrive with warrants—as the Tate documentary suggests is desirable... I am afraid a lot of material has probably already been destroyed. I think it's inevitable that things will be got rid of. They are under siege... Tate ...marks Kinsey down as a fifth-columnist... the very image of deceit and lies. [1]

Jonathan Gathorne-Hardy, Kinsey biographer, 1998

[The] public would have been astounded and disbelieving to know the names of the eminent scientists who appeared at the Institute from time to time to examine our work and talk with Kinsey, and who volunteered before they left to be photographed in some kind of sexual activity. [2]

Wardell Pomeroy, 1972

Kinsey decided to film people having sex, using the attic of his own house as a location. I was in some, having some sexual contact, and many of us were. And, it was all done in secrecy of course.... At that time we would have lost our funding. [3]

Earl Marsch (Kinsey friend) and Paul Gebhard (Kinsey coauthor), 1996

Indiana University publicity photograph of a thoughtful Kinsey and his ostensibly conventional teammates, mainstreamed to Americans for more than half a century.

Kinsey was openly disdainful of other famous sex researchers, whom he viewed as too conventional. Pomeroy tells us that he was "appalled" to read that Freud treated masturbation as a sign of immaturity and sickness. Freud also acknowledged the social value of sexual morality and taught that children have a "latency" period during which sexual disturbance or stimuli is harmful. For these reasons, among others, Kinsey had contempt for Freud.

He likewise scorned Havelock Ellis as "timid" for his mail-in sex surveys; Kinsey believed that one had to "see" one's subjects to determine the truth. A famed English "sex researcher," Ellis was an adulterer and a sex partner of eugenicist Margaret Sanger, founder of Planned Parenthood. He was afflicted with premature ejaculation and "urolaglia," and also had problems with his wife's lesbian affairs, suggesting an abnormal marital and psychosexual life.[4] Such "problems" were irrelevant for Kinsey, however. His complaint was that Ellis did not have the courage to interview subjects face-to-face.[5]

Kinsey similarly dismissed Magnus Hirschfeld, the notorious German sexologist and admitted homosexual, as "unobjective" because he was, according to Kinsey, a "special pleader." And he found Karl Augustus Menninger, the psychiatrist who founded the Menninger Clinic in Topeka, Kansas, to be "invalid."

Even anthropologists Bronislow Malinowski and Margaret Mead were too moral for Kinsey: Malinowski was, in Kinsey's view, "afraid of sex," while Mead was a woman and, according to Kinsey, "one of the worst examples of feminism."[6]

Margaret Sanger, founder of Planned Parenthood and early eugenicist advocate believed, like Kinsey, in sterilizing the lower classes.

Kinsey tried to position himself at the vanguard of a new breed of American sexual revolutionaries who favored experimentation and direct observation rather than the distance and abstraction of psychological analysis. Social researcher and trends analyst Jack Douglas explains:

> The sexual revolutionaries who came after Freud were even more keenly aware of the tremendous power of the rhetoric of "hard science" in our society, presumably because the power of this rhetoric was growing. They made use of ever more rigidly experimental methods and progressively eliminated everything but the physiology of genital sex and other "erotogenic" zones from their studies.[7]

Kinsey's fixation on direct participation in, and observation of, sex acts led eventually to the construction of a soundproof laboratory at Indiana University's Wiley Hall, where Kinsey, his staff, their wives, and invited guests could engage in all sorts of sexual antics. Some were documented on film. Kinsey believed that sexual experiments on humans should not differ measurably from those on "other animals." Wrapped in the protective aura of "scientific research," he sought to access and study human subjects. Film, he argued, was a way to capture the ephemeral features of sexual interaction. Pomeroy writes:

> [We] were eager in the 1940's and early 1950's to supplement our interview studies with controlled laboratory observations.... At an early point in the development of our research, Kinsey began to feel a certain impatience with the fact that the data we were collecting was necessarily secondhand. Like any scholar, [Kinsey] yearned for original sources.... [I]t occurred

Above is a recent photograph of the "typically mainstream American" house in Bloomington, Indiana where Alfred Kinsey was said to have lived. Kinsey, his staff and faculty produced illegal pornography in his attic.

to him that we ought to observe at firsthand some of the behavior we were recording.... Kinsey began looking for opportunities to observe. He was acutely aware of the serious dangers implicit in such work and proceeded cautiously, knowing that he could expect little understanding of what he was doing if it was ever disclosed.... [N]ot even many scientists could be expected to condone it. Few people would believe in the scientific purity of his motives [Emphasis added].

William Masters   **Virginia Johnson**

Masters and Johnson claimed that they could not have accomplished their own laboratory sex research without Kinsey. Pomeroy states that M&J knew of Kinsey's illegal sex films.

With the idea of recording what he hoped to observe, Kinsey hired Bill Dallenback, who was Clarence Tripp's partner in a photographic studio in New York.... The University authorities, who had to approve our budget, quite naturally wanted to know why we needed a photographer. Kinsey told them, truthfully, that we wanted to photograph animal behavior, but he did not add that he included humans in this category.[9]

He set aside space for a laboratory after he returned from the initial photographic session in New York and began looking for subjects. As Masters and Johnson have since demonstrated, it is no trick at all, in spite of what the public believes, to obtain people for sexual observation, nor are they prostitutes, exhibitionists, or any other kind of variant from the conventional norm, as is popularly supposed.... The folk belief that no "decent" person will allow himself to be observed is only one more illustration of the vast distance between what Americans say they believe and what they do.[10]

Pomeroy adds:

> For the benefit of skeptics, let me say that Kinsey possessed the ability to observe actual sexual behavior with the same objectivity he maintained during interviews.[11]

To the contrary, common sense and evidence made public by others indicate that Kinsey found his interviews to be highly libidinal. James Jones documents such in his reports on Kinsey's personal sexual obsessions, including his sexual involvement with subjects and with young coauthors Pomeroy and Martin. During the Yorkshire documentary, "Kinsey's Paedophiles," Jones stated:

Kinsey and the people who were close to him were very proud of the [sex] filming... [and] the risk that felon behavior entailed.... The filming that goes on involves both staff members themselves and a few invited guests.[12]

Yet Pomeroy insists:

> Speaking for myself, I cannot recall a single instance of sexual arousal on my part when I was observing sex behavior, and I am certain this was equally true of Kinsey and the other

staff members. We were so busy observing, and recording what we observed, that we had no time to think of anything else.[13]

The layman can scarcely imagine viewing a sexual scene without having feelings either of stimulation or of disgust, depending on the state of his inhibitions. We experienced neither emotion. There was, for us, no more erotic content in viewing the sexual activities of the human animal than in observing any other mammal.[14]

Indiana University publicity photo. Kinsey watches "animal" films.

[T]he situations were completely non-erotic; it was just a job, to which there was no subjective reaction.... If I appear to be overemphasizing this point, it is because I know how hard it is for the layman, or even the scientist in nonsexual fields, to believe it... Since there is something of the voyeur in nearly everyone, it is understandable that nonscientists find it hard to accept that scientists may not react the way they do; some would even consider it a kind of condescension.[15]

Despite his alleged objectivity, Pomeroy notes that Kinsey controlled all photographs of himself, and once threatened a Conde' Nast photographer with slander to prevent one from being published. He claimed: "There are a good many people who would go to any lengths to put a stop to the research we are doing, and publication of the sort of picture you have taken would materially help their cause."[16]

SEX FILMS AT IU, IN KINSEY'S ATTIC

For years, Kinsey filmed and photographed sex acts in the attic of his family home, with Paul Gebhard, then with professional cinematographers Bill Dallenback and Clarence Tripp behind the cameras. Pomeroy describes one such session:

He [Kinsey] would move quietly round the room, never intruding, occasionally whispering a direction to Bill [Dallenback]. He always complimented the subjects after a session and reassured them about the quality and value of what they had done. If they had failed to perform satisfactorily whatever act was involved, Kinsey would say, "You did very well. Just great." On one occasion... the subject went on and on with the act until the camera began to overheat and Bill knew he was about to run out of film. He made a despairing gesture to Kinsey, indicating what was happening. Prok leaned forward to the subject and said gently, politely, "If you would just come now..." "Oh, sure," the subject said, and immediately came to orgasm just as the film ran out. The man had misunderstood and thought Kinsey wanted a lengthy sequence of masturbation, which he was prepared to keep up indefinitely.[17]

It was risky business. Pomeroy explains:

> In spite of the importance Kinsey attached to what our cameras were recording, he was constantly apprehensive about this aspect of the research, and fearful of the possible consequences of discovery. Unquestionably, he had every right to be worried. If it had become publicly known, there is little reason to believe the Institute would have survived the publicity. But no one outside the inner circle knew about this phase of our work. We did not talk about it to anyone and the filming was mentioned only once in the books we compiled—a single cryptic reference in the Female volume.[18]

Indiana University publicity photograph of Kinsey and his IU staff. Second woman from left posed as an "average" 1940s housewife in interview publicity photos may be Kinsey's librarian and biographer, Cornelia Christenson - here without her glasses.

Pomeroy reprised a common Kinsey claim, noted to introduce this chapter, that many respectable people participated in the Institute's sex films because they shared his interest in such "documentaries." However, as it turns out, most of those "eminent scientists" were Kinsey's own team. The force involved in obtaining most of the wives and several of Kinsey's own team suggests that here to, Kinsey dissembled. Repeating:

> [T]he public would have been astounded and disbelieving to know the names of the eminent scientists who appeared at the Institute from time to time to examine our work and talk with Kinsey, and who volunteered before they left to be photographed in some kind of sexual activity.[19]

The "public" might indeed have been "astounded," since the "eminent scientists" who appeared in the Institute's sex films included all of the carefully selected Kinsey team, including Kinsey, his wife, the wives of all or most of Kinsey's coauthors, the timid Martin, the eager Pomeroy (who occasionally performed sexually with Kinsey *and* his wife), and a sexually-coerced Dallenback. In a brazen example of sexual workplace harassment parading as "science," Kinsey hired only those who would yield to his demands for "primary" sources.[20] His methodology included secrecy and deception, which he deemed necessary to accomplish his goals while hiding his techniques from the public.

The histories were taken in soundproof facilities constructed, according to Jones, between 1942 and 1943 (approximately when Pomeroy joined the team), with additions in 1950. Christenson writes:

> The 'lab'—as we always called it—presented a uniform, trim, antiseptic appearance… all well locked. At Wiley Hall where the Institute was housed on the ground floor, windows… were carefully fitted with strong metal grills…. All doors to private offices had to be soundproofed and special locks were installed to insure privacy in discussion and interviewing.[21]

According to Pomeroy, Kinsey was "adamant" about the soundproofing:

> [The University] had no experience in soundproofing, since such privacy did not exist anywhere else [on campus]… [A]nything above forty decibels could be heard plainly… Kinsey said that would not do; the figure had to be eighty…. They would have to tear down the whole thing and do it over…. His insistence was characteristic; he was a perfectionist… coming as close to perfection as a human being could.[22]

"Wylie Hall. Kinsey's 'laboratory' took up most of the basement from 1950 onwards." (Caption and photo taken from Gathorne-Hardy's *Sex, the Measure of All Things*.)

Samuel M. Steward

The 1996 *World Book Almanac and Book of Facts* states that 40 decibels are comparable to "light traffic," 70 decibels to "normal traffic, quiet train," and 80 decibels to "rock music or a subway."[23] Kinsey's "eighty decibels" would conceal quite a lot, including the shrieks and screams of the sadomasochistic acts performed by Samuel M. Steward, whom Kinsey labeled a "masochist." Steward would later become a well-known homosexual psychologist whose special interests included boy "hustlers" and tattooing.[24]

SEX-TORTURE EXPERIMENTS

Writing in the November 13, 1980, issue of *The Advocate*, a homosexual monthly, Steward recalled the time he was flown to Indiana to be filmed in a sex sadism film produced and directed by Kinsey. Pomeroy described Steward as a "partner" in a "homosexual couple,"[25] but Steward wrote that he had never met the "partner" (Mike Miksche) until they were introduced in Kinsey's garden. Shortly thereafter, the two prepared for the filming of an act of sexual sadism as Kinsey's "scientists" watched and took notes.

Pomeroy claims that the sadism filmed that day was merely part of the couple's "normal" sex life. He recalls that Kinsey, while in New York observing men battering one another in sadistic rituals, "was particularly intrigued by the intercourse of a homosexual couple in which one of the partners had an orgasm," so he invited Steward to his "lab" for a demonstration.[26]

Dallenbeck filmed Samuel Steward, a Kinsey "research" aide in brutal, and criminal, sadomasochistic encounters at the Kinsey Institute. One such episode was detailed in the November 13, 1980 issue of the homosexual magazine *The Advocate*.

Steward wrote that by the time he arrived on campus, Kinsey had gotten Miksche "half-drunk on gin." The subsequent sadism film sequences were not quite what Steward had anticipated:

> I was marked and marred, all muscles weakened... my jaws were so tired and unhinged... Mike slapped me hard and [unprintable]... During the sessions I was vaguely conscious of people dropping in now and then to observe, while Mrs. Kinsey, a true scientist to the end... sat by, and once in a while calmly changed the sheets upon the workbench.[27]

Years later (September, 1973), Wardell Pomeroy, who was then Dean of the Institute for the Advanced Study of Human Sexuality in San Francisco, told a gathering of sexuality specialists from *Playboy* magazine how he viewed the performance.[28] He asserted that brutality involving the use of genital organs can be both loving and sexually exciting:

> [I]n the ordinary situation it's the victim-the masochist-who is controlling the action. He's determining how much pain is inflicted upon himself. Some years back at the Kinsey Institute, we were filming for our archives, two homosexual males-a sadomasochistic couple. The sadist had manacled the masochist and tied him up... and burned his nipples with a lighted cigarette. The masochist was writhing around in pain. Then the sadist took a lighted candle and let the hot wax drop onto his partner's penis and testes, sending him into paroxysms of anguish[29] ...But all the time, the sadist was carefully watching the face of the masochist. When he saw that it was just too much to bear, he would raise the candle up and give the wax a chance to cool. It suddenly dawned on me that the masochist was almost literally controlling the sadist's hand. When they were finished, I asked who was in charge. Both answered that, of course, the masochist was. They had it straight.[30]

While Pomeroy suggests that the "partners" had a clear idea of who was in charge, operationally speaking Kinsey and Pomeroy were in charge of the entire scenario. The Kinsey team admittedly solicited victim and offender, paid for the service, and engaged in deception to bring it about.

Jones confirmed Kinsey's own sadomasochistic inclinations, which were evident in, for example, his claim (*Male* volume, p. 161) that the infants and children who fainted and convulsed during sexual experiments "derive definite pleasure from the situation." Jones writes of the man whom the nation was told would enhance male-female relationships,

> According to Gebhard, Kinsey was already having trouble with erectile impotence... [For the sex films, Dallenback said Kinsey] "had to go into the bathroom to work himself up." .... Mr. Y [a Kinsey partner] revealed.... "[H]e liked for me to beat him with a cat-o-nine tails.... put ropes around his testicles." Kinsey enjoyed oral sex (both giving and receiving), [but] he "loved anal intercourse," particularly... as the active rather than the passive partner. Kinsey would "get a kind of long-suffering look on his face when he was having sex.... some of the [other] sex partners and I used to kind of smile about it because he... looked almost grotesque."

> Kinsey's decided preference was for sadomasochists... "We had many people who came to visit who did lots of s/m." ..."Tell your sadomasochistic friends to observe great caution" ...Kinsey was speaking from experience. He "put ropes around his testicles" [and once] "climbed into a bathtub, unfolded the blade of his pocketknife, and circumcised himself

without benefit of anesthesia." ...Dallenback confirmed that it happened.... "God, it must have been damn painful. It must have bled a hell of a lot."[31]

WIVES AS SUBJECTS

All the while, like a "true scientist," Clara Kinsey would allegedly bring "pudding or milk and cookies or something" and change the sheets which, according to Steward and Pomeroy, were soiled with secretions from male reproductive organs containing spermatozoa, as well as sweat, blood, and hot wax. But Mrs. Kinsey did much more than that. James Jones confirms that she was filmed masturbating and engaging in varied forms of sex with Alfred Kinsey's young coauthors and assistants, including Wardell Pomeroy and Clyde Martin. There is no information as to whether Mrs. Kinsey was expected to act out sexually with the team's wives:

> No one felt the force of [Kinsey's] unyielding demands more strongly than Clara [who] went along with the filming... as befitted the wife of the high priest of sexual liberation. Clara was filmed masturbating, and she was also filmed having sex with Pomeroy... Martin and his wife, Alice, flatly refused to be filmed as a couple.... [O]ne of the staff wives refused to have sex with Kinsey. Perhaps it was Alice [Martin's wife].... One staff wife had an even stronger reaction. Complaining of "the sickening pressure" she was under to have sex on film with her spouse and other staff members, she told an interviewer, "I felt like my husband's career at the Institute depended on it."

> I saw some of the films.... when I took Paul Gebhard's class on human sexual behavior, when I was a graduate student... [After Reisman's] charges were made that Kinsey was a pedophile I was asked by the director of the Kinsey Institute at that time, to investigate those charges and report back to her... I did see films of Kinsey masturbating. I saw films of Mrs. Kinsey masturbating. If memory serves, I saw some films of staff having sex.[32]

Fifteen leading women's magazines—including *Redbook, Pageant, McCall's, Ladies' Home Journal, Today's Woman, Woman's Home Companion,* and *Cosmopolitan*—urged their readers to learn from Kinsey's *Female* volume how to rear their children sexually, how to please their husbands, and how to evaluate themselves as sexually healthy women. Yet we now know that one wife complained about being coerced into making sex films and participating in experiments, while Pomeroy described an instance in which the team filmed a woman who, despite her visible distress, was bullied into a sexual performance by her husband.

Pomeroy writes,

> Sometimes people from whom we had taken histories volunteered to be photographed, and one must suppose that an element of exhibitionism was involved in a few of these cases. That was true of the male partner in one couple who volunteered, although his wife was merely compliant and would never have come forward on her own initiative. *Whatever the motive we were not likely to refuse these fortuitous happenings.* We believed we were demonstrating something that would help us better to understand what human sexual behavior, particularly orgasm, was like.[33] [Emphasis added]

Kinsey found that homosexuals were often eager to perform gratis, while others expected payment for their services. "Payment," wrote Kinsey in the *Male* volume, "has been confined to prostitutes, pimps, exhibitionists or to others who have turned from their regular occupation and spent considerable time in helping make contacts."[34] Pomeroy writes that Kinsey would have "done business with the devil himself if it would have furthered the research."[35]

Kinsey and his team also collected films of children engaged in sex acts, a fact confirmed in 1981 by Kinsey's coauthor Paul Gebhard. In a letter to this author, while he was director of the Kinsey Institute, Gebhard stated:

> Since sexual experimentation with human infants and children is illegal, we have had to depend upon other sources of data. Some of these were parents, mostly college-educated, who observed their children and kept notes for us. A few were nursery school owners or teachers. Others were homosexual males interested in older, but still prepubertal, children. One was a man who had numerous sexual contacts with male and female infants and children and, being of a scientific bent, kept detailed records of each encounter. Some of these sources have added to their written or verbal reports photographs and, in a few instances, cinema.... The techniques involved [included] adult-child contacts—chiefly manual or oral.

> [While "Esther," appearing on the British documentary, stated:] My father did mail some questionnaires... I believe to the Kinsey Institute about the sexual abuse he was doing on me... since 1938, which makes me about four years old... I know he had a... camera that he used.... There was one time when I do remember a movie camera was running and he says, oh, don't pay attention to that.... You could only be a little girl to understand that it couldn't possibly be enjoyed. That was *slavery*.[36] [Emphasis in original.]

That the Kinsey team permitted, and possibly filmed and/or participated in, the sexual abuse of infants and children is confirmed by its own writings and reports. Members readily admitted that, methodologically, they viewed *all* human beings as mere animals, and often boasted that they did not recognize any moral or legal restraints on their research.

Gebhard now denies that Kinsey and his team personally conducted illegal experiments on infants and children. But for years the Kinsey Institute and the University vehemently denied that any sex films were ever made, despite the fact that Kinsey's filming had been extensively discussed and documented. When syndicated columnist Patrick J. Buchanan mentioned the films in a 1983 column about this author's earlier work, lawyers for the Kinsey Institute threatened his syndicate with legal action. They described the column as "false and incorrect in just about every respect... libelous and malicious," and demanded that the "the record be set straight at once." The missive further claimed that "The archives of the Kinsey Institute contain no films of any human sexual experiments conducted by the Institute."[37]

Buchanan responded with a second column, quoting at length from Wardell Pomeroy's 1972 memoir, *Kinsey and the Institute for Sex Research*,[38] where he pointed out that not only were sex films being made on the Indiana University campus, but Kinsey was producer and director of the films. The charges against Buchanan's syndicate were dropped.

While denying the Institute's involvement in sexual demonstrations, Pomeroy acknowledged one unusual incident:

> [The old man] said he was able to masturbate to ejaculation in ten seconds from a flaccid start... [then he] demonstrated it to us. I might add, in case this story confirms the worst fears of any surviving critics, it was the only sexual demonstration among the 18,000 subjects who gave their histories.[39]

A few pages earlier, Pomeroy had admitted that team members collected "sufficient data" about female orgasm by "direct observation:"

> [O]ne investigator asked if we could find subjects in his area who were capable of repeated ejaculation and who would come to his laboratory. On our next trip to that part of the country we located a number of men willing to cooperate.... Some [women] who had multiple orgasms... were willing to have coitus under observation....[40]

Writing in *The Pied Pipers of Sex,* Vernon Mark, a professor at Harvard Medical School, noted that the introduction of pornographic films into medical training, and the unwholesome influence of the films on individual doctors and the profession as a whole, were brought about by Kinsey. Physicians had traditionally been a highly respected class of spokesmen for sexual conservatism. Kinsey's obscenity training served to erode that standard. Dr. John Money's creation/production of child pornography and his arrangement of brutal sex change operations have just been revealed in John Colapinto's book, *As Nature Made Him* (2000). It was John Money who established obscenity as medical instruction, Dr. Mark writes:

Writing in the pseudo-academic *Journal of Paedophilia,* leading sexologist Dr. John Money of Johns Hopkins University espoused the legalization of incest and adult sex with children.

> Kinsey seems to have provided the impetus for showing sex movies to medical students and in 1967 they got to look at the materials from the archives of the Institute for Sex Research. Soon afterwards, Professor John Money compiled an illustrated presentation called Pornography in the Home, which became very popular with students at Johns Hopkins Medical School. Since Johns Hopkins enjoys a leadership role among American medical colleges it is not surprising that [roughly 90% of] medical schools followed its lead in initiating explicitly sexual films as part of the curriculum for their students. (After all, if it's good enough for Johns Hopkins!)[41]

In a letter to this author, psychiatrist Linnea Smith of Chapel Hill, North Carolina, commented on the Kinsey sex tapes:

> As unsettling as this primitive and clandestine recording of sexual performance in pursuit of "scientific knowledge" is, it has influenced many sexologists who recently identify pornography as "potent aphrodisiacs" and then go on to claim the wave of the future, cutting edge of marital and sex therapy will be to have dysfunctional couples videotape their sexual behaviors for review and critique by their therapists.[42]

Dr. Smith's observations about the medical and therapeutic use of Kinsey's sex-filming protocol are confirmed by a section in Pomeroy's book that further describes Kinsey's impact on the medical world:

In 1963, when the [Rockefeller] foundation was celebrating its fiftieth anniversary, [IU president Herman] Wells was among the six hundred guests at a dinner in the Plaza Hotel in New York. [Secretary of State Dean] Rusk was the principal speaker, the Rockefeller family was present, and the guest list included, among others, university presidents and scientists from all over the world. Robert Sproul, who had recently retired as president of the University of California, sat next to Wells, and as the two men chatted amiably together, Wells inquired, "Do you know why we're here, Bob?" Sproul said he assumed it was because their universities had been involved with research grants which the Foundation had made and considered important.

After dinner, Wells repeated this conversation to Dr. Robert S. Morison, head of the medical division of the Foundation. "Yes," Morison agreed, "I can tell you exactly why you're here." He went on to relate that each division had been asked to look over its records for the fifty years and determine what grants had been most significant.

A young assistant in Morison's division had brought him the Institute records and inquired, "Dr. Morison, just what is the significance of this?"

On his desk that morning Morison happened to have the newest and best gynecology book for medical students. He turned to a chapter and said, "Look here," and then went on to another chapter and still another. "Young man," he said, "this is pure Kinsey. It couldn't have been written before Kinsey, and it has profoundly affected this branch of medicine." After relating the anecdote, Morison said to Wells, "You're here because we consider the Institute financing one of the most significant things we ever did."

Wells agreed. He still believes that the project was one of the monumental scientific ventures of the twentieth century in America. How ironic, then, that it could have been virtually destroyed by one reactionary congressman, a tiny band of fanatic moralists and a foundation president who talked about principles that he and his board readily abrogated under pressure.[43]

Dean Rusk, was the president of the Rockefeller Foundation during Kinsey's tenure.

Herman Wells, was president of Indiana University and staunch supporter of Kinsey's studies.

The Kinsey Institute began its live obscenity productions prior to publication of the 1948 *Male* volume. Kinsey received Rockefeller monies for his "library" activities in 1946. Just as Kinsey "paid Martin out of his own pocket" until 1941, so too did he apparently pay photographer Dallenback personally until the Rockefeller funds arrived. Then both men appear to have become "permanent member[s] of the Institute staff," and expensive film equipment was purchased.[44] It is likely that some of the Rockefeller largesse was earmarked for the pornographic productions. After all, they were a passion which Kinsey eagerly shared with visiting "scholars" from the Foundation, whom James Jones asserts became "hooked" on Kinsey.[45] Moreover, in his May 7, 1951 letter to "CIB," Warren Weaver complains that Kinsey's "library of erotic literature, and a collection of pictures and other 'art' objects of erotic significance" were essentially funded by Rockefeller. Writing in 1951, Weaver recalled his 1946 objection to the funding of Kinsey's "erotica:"

> The latter phase has become sufficiently important so that they have installed and equipped a complete photographic laboratory, and have a full-time photographer *(I almost said full-*

time pornographer) who receives $4,800 per year.... This library was started with the aid of a grant, additional to his then general support, made directly from the RF to Kinsey and for the specified purpose. As a matter of record, I remind you that I opposed that grant when it was discussed in officers' conference. Now this library-art aspect of their work surely requires, out of his total general budget... more than the total annual amount the RF is contributing. I contend that *it is perfectly realistic to say that the RF is paying for this collection of erotica and for the activities directly associated with it*. And I say further that I don't think we need to, or ought to [Emphasis added.][46]

INSTITUTE FOR THE ADVANCED STUDY OF HUMAN SEXUALITY

After Kinsey died, Paul Gebhard became head of the Institute for Sex Research, while Wardell Pomeroy moved on to The Sex and Drug Forum, which later evolved into the Institute for the Advanced Study of Human Sexuality (IASHS). Now the leading institution in the sexology field (controlling conference selections, journal publications, lectures, etc.), IASHS has trained more than 100,000 sex educators, doctors, and "safe sex" instructors. IASHS is a Kinseyan filter through which almost all "accredited" persons in the sexuality field are screened at some point during their careers. The more formal course work includes such topics as "erotic sensate and massage therapy," including sexual films; how to use surrogates (prostitutes) in sex therapy; analysis of the Kinsey reports; how to create "sex-education curricula"; child sexuality (taught by Dr. Pomeroy); "forensic sexology"; and teaching students how to give expert-witness court testimony favoring obscenity, pornography, and reduced penalties for sex crimes.

As academic dean at the IASHS, Pomeroy also required staff members to participate in a variety of sex acts to break down their inhibitions and ensure that his team would be comprised of true-believing Kinseyans.

In 1977, the IASHS produced a book entitled *Meditations on the Gift of Sexual-*

Meditations on the Gift of Sexuality

text by
Rev. Ted McIlvenna, Ph.D.

photographs by
Rev. Laird Sutton, Ph.D.

Specific Press

After leaving Bloomington, Wardell Pomeroy became Academic Dean of the Institute for the Advanced Study of Human Sexuality in San Francisco alongside the Rev. Ted McIlvenna, a Methodist minister. Like the Kinsey Institute, the IASHS filmed sexual acts among staff members, including scenes of these sex professionals engaged in graphic homosexual and heterosexual orgies seen in *Meditations*, an IASHS by-product. The IASHS sold its child pornography to *Hustler* magazine for widespread publication.

BASIC SEXUAL RIGHTS

1. The freedom of any sexual thought, fantasy or desire.
2. The right to sexual entertainment, freely available in the marketplace, including sexually explicit materials dealing with the full range of sexual behavior.
3. The right not to be exposed to sexual material or behavior.
4. The right to sexual self determination.
5. The right to seek out and engage in consensual sexual activity.
6. The right to engage in sexual acts or activities of any kind whatsoever, providing they do not involve non-consensual acts, violence, constraint, coercion or fraud.
7. The right to be free of persecution or societal intervention in private sexual behavior.
8. The recognition by society that every person, partnered or unpartnered, has the right to the pursuit of a satisfying consensual socio-sexual life, free from political, legal or religious interference and that there needs to be mechanisms in society where the opportunities of social-sexual activities are available to the following: disabled persons; chronically ill persons; those incarcerated in prisons, hospitals or institutions; those disadvantaged because of age, lack of physical attractiveness, or lack of social skills; the poor and the lonely.
9. The basic right of all persons who are sexually dysfunctional to have available non-judgmental sexual health care.
10. The right to control conception.

The IASHS would legalize adult/child pornography and prostitution. Dr. John Money argues that "rough sex"–even resulting in death–be legal if the adult or child victim's prior "consent" was somehow obtained.

> **PRINCIPAL POINTS OF THE LEAGUE'S PLATFORM**
>
> The League advocates:
>
> 1. Equal privileges and obligations for men and women in regard to their sexual lives as in their political and economic lives.
> 2. Liberation of the marital relationship from Church domination. Reforms of the laws regulating marriage and divorce.
> 3. Control of conception (Birth Control, Prevenception) so that procreation may be undertaken deliberately and only with a due sense of responsibility.
> 4. Application of the knowledge of Eugenics towards improvement of the race through Birth Selection. (Encouragement of propagation of the fit and gifted, and sterilization of the unfit.)
> 5. Protection of the unmarried mother and the "illegitimate" child.
> 6. Proper, scientific understanding of variations in sexual constitutions (intersexuality) and a correspondingly rational attitude, for instance, toward homosexual men and women.
> 7. Systematic education in the biology of sex, especially regarding the problems of venereal disease, masturbation and abstinence. To promote a healthy attitude towards sex, including the knowledge of sane sex living, and not complicated by any sense of guilt.
> 8. Legal and social reforms regarding prostitution in order to eliminate its dangers (especially venereal disease).
> 9. Disturbances and abnormalities of the sexual impulse to be regarded as more or less pathological phenomena and not as crimes, vices or sins.
> 10. Reform of the penal code in regard to sexual offenses. Only those sexual acts to be considered criminal which violate the rights of another person. Protection of minors and feebleminded persons. Sexual acts between responsible adults, undertaken by mutual consent, to be regarded as their private affair (and not liable to legal actions).
>
> Differentiation between crime and vice: the former—as antisocial—being an object of the law; the control of the latter—as a personal problem—being an object of education.

The difference between the European eugenic-sexology model and that espoused by the IASHS is that the former allowed sex "between responsible [consenting] adults" but excluded minors. (10).

ity.[47] The sexual pedagogy of Institute founder Dr. Ted McIlvenna, who was trained as a Methodist minister, is evident throughout. McIlvenna appears in photos with other nude IASHS faculty members, staff, and students. A nude McIlvenna carrying a nude woman (reportedly an Institute secretary) into a hot tub is featured at the beginning of the book. Roughly half of the pages are filled with graphic didactic photographs of persons performing all variations of sexual acts alone, with others, and in groups. Many of the acts portrayed are still illegal in many states.

IASHS publications pioneered an early version of what became a formal program of "Sexual Attitude Restructuring," or SAR. It was a spin-off from Kinsey's attic and the Indiana University soundproofed facilities. Films and other images were employed to desensitize and condition students of medicine, justice, sexuality and other professionals as part of their formal 'sexology" training.

The SAR indoctrination films included not only sadism, masochism, homosexual and heterosexual coitus, sodomy, and bestiality, but child pornography (until tougher laws were passed). Examples of the latter still appear in *The Sex Atlas*, by IASHS director Erwin Haeberle.[48] Some of the child pornography photos were sold to *Hustler* magazine publisher Larry Flynt, who printed them. They present nude young children, and graphically displayed nude girls, smoking marijuana and exhibiting their genital areas. The *Atlas,* as did the *Hustler* article, advocates adult-child sex, the legalization of incest, and elimination of the age of consent.[49]

The IASHS' "Basic Sexual Rights Oath" is a virtual clone of the 1933 European oath of the World League for Sexual Reform. The key difference is that the 1933 oath restricted sex to "responsible adults, undertaken by mutual consent," while the Kinsey/Pomeroy platform would permit "every person" to have sex with whomever, and however, they wish, including "those disadvantaged because of age, lack of physical attractiveness," etc. Hence, the new sexologists would legalize adult-child sex, incest, child prostitution, and child pornography, providing that such practices are purportedly "consensual." IASHS' graduates often testify in court and elsewhere as "experts" on issues of human sexual behavior. Such testimony has boosted the billion-dollar sex/porno industry and has undermined antiobscenity laws by portraying obscenity/pornography[50] as harmless and victimless.

I have written in more detail in *"Soft Porn" Plays Hardball* (1991) on the way sexually explicit images override cognition and alter the viewer's brain, mind and memory. Since then, an increasing body of medical evidence continues to confirm the neurochemical harm inflicted by all pornography. High resonance sexual and/or violent images alter human beings neurochemically. As neuroscientist Dr. Gary Lynch has written,

What we're saying here is that an event which lasts half a second, within five or ten minutes has produced a structural change that is in some ways as profound as the structural changes one sees in [brain] damage... [51]

Pomeroy tells us that Kinsey had a "grand scheme,"[52] and that sexualized images were vital to his dream of moving American society from its traditional moral standard based on marriage, to one predicated on "free love." Images intended to promote and legitimize deviant behaviors were critical to this moral and cultural conversion – what the IASHS calls the brain's "restructuring."

The widespread availability of limitless varieties of pornographic magazines, videos, and computer graphics has institutionalized an assault on the fabric of our country that is, among other things, alienating an increasing number of men from real-life women, their wives, and their families.[53] As the institution of marriage has eroded, sexual violence toward women and children has escalated.

Today, even some Kinseyans are questioning the bizarre suggestion that compulsive masturbation is benign and arguably superior to the marital act. In 1976, Paul Robinson cautioned readers about the unforeseen consequences of Kinsey's excessive romanticization of autoerotic pleasure:

Kinsey disciple Hugh Hefner launched the "other" revolutionary book, Playboy, in 1953, the same year that Kinsey's Female volume was published. Hefner said that Kinsey was the researcher and that he was the "pamphleteer." Hefner marketed Kinsey's view of men as "Playboys," and women and children as their sexual "Playmates."

> It would seem safe to conclude that the reaction against the Victorian theory of masturbation is now complete. Indeed, the near future will probably bring a critical re-examination of the supposed benefits of autoeroticism.[54]

This Author's own earlier book on pornography noted that,

> [T]he critical re-examination predicted by Robinson is now underway, due to increasing problems of compulsive masturbation leading to impotence in normal coitus, trauma to the genitalia, and even "autoerotic fatalities" resulting from dangerous masturbatory techniques, often an attempt to enhance erotic pleasure by inducing asphyxiation. Citing figures obtained from the Federal Bureau of Investigation, the *American Journal of Orthopsychiatry* estimated the annual toll of "autoerotic fatalities" at between 500 and 1,000, mostly of younger males and always involving pornography.[55]

Such youngsters are victims of the limitless sexuality that Kinsey and his team helped to spawn. Kinsey's own death is instructive, as it appears to have been directly related to his autoerotic obsessions. Also revealing is the portrayal of obscenity in the October, 1997, issue of the Kinsey Institute publication, *Kinsey Today*. A pornographic exhibition ("The Art of Desire") was announced as part of a pending celebration of the 50th anniversary of the initial Kinsey report:

> While the anniversary exhibition is a testament to the power and pervasiveness of human sexual expression... events surrounding the exhibition also attest to the persistence of fear of knowledge of sexuality. The Art of Desire opened on the evening of a protest on the Bloomington town square by the Concerned Women of America, one in a series of demonstrations across the country calling for the closure of the Kinsey Institute. Their objective appears to be to

discredit Alfred Kinsey, and, in the process, to undermine and eventually eliminate sex education in public schools. Their overarching charge is that Kinsey is responsible for a decline in sexual morals and in the importance of the family in American society.... Surely others had the training, the research background, the ability to ask the sometimes frightening questions Alfred Kinsey asked us about ourselves.... Yet only he dared.[56]

In the same issue, the editors of *Kinsey Today* complained that their collection of 75,000 prints, 218 amateur albums, and 1,732 vintage negatives depicting aspects of human sexuality is "deteriorating."

[Hence the Institute needs public] funding from the National Endowment for the Humanities (NEH)... to catalog and process these collections... to build an automation database that will have finding AIDS with brief, item-level entries.

The Kinsey Institute calls for federal funds to protect its obscenity and pornography "collection" for future "researchers."

In the same way that America refurbished and maintains at public expense, say, President Abraham Lincoln's boyhood home, the Kinsey Institute apparently believes that Alfred Kinsey's "free love" library also qualifies as a national treasure worthy of restoration and upkeep at taxpayers' expense. It is somewhat ironic that Lincoln signed a law on March 3, 1865, which outlawed obscenity[57] within the United States.[58] And years earlier, he warned during an address at Springfield, Illinois (January 27, 1838): "If destruction be our lot we must ourselves be its author and finisher. As a nation of freemen we must live through all time, or die by suicide."[59]

CHAPTER 4 NOTES

[1]. Jonathan Gathorne-Hardy, "It's Time To Ditch The Dirt," *London Independent*, August 10, 1998.
[2]. Wardell Pomeroy, *Dr. Kinsey and the Institute for Sex Research*, Harper & Row, New York, 1972, p. 179.
[3]. The British Broadcasting Company, Biographies, "Reputations," August 14, 1996, story of Alfred C. Kinsey. This video, a copy of which is in the author's archive, includes the testimony of such Kinsey colleagues as Paul Gebhard, former Kinsey Institute director, and Kinsey coauthor, and former Kinsey senior researcher John Gagnon. Also appearing are Kinsey's daughters, *Playboy* publisher Hugh Hefner, and this author. This BBC production, though designed to maintain the Kinsey myth, did document the first public admission that Kinsey's co-workers had performed in the pornography produced in Bloomington. The documentary was repeated in the U.S.A. as "Biography", Arts & Entertainment.
[4]. James H. Jones, *Kinsey, A Private/Public Life*, W. W. Norton, New York, 1997, p. 835, f. 40. Urolaglia refers to sexual addiction/arousal from observing people urinate. See also Jack Douglas, *The Family in America*, Mount Morris, IL, The Rockford Institute, May, 1947, pp. 2-4.
[5]. Pomeroy, p. 67.
[6]. Pomeroy, pp. 68-70.
[7]. Jack Douglas, *The Family in America*, pp. 2-4.
[8]. Wardell Pomeroy, in Brecher and Brecher, *An Analysis of Human Sexual Response*, Andre Deuch, London, 1967, pp. 118-119. See also Pomeroy, *Dr. Kinsey*, p. 172.
[9]. Pomeroy, p. 174.
[10]. Pomeroy, p. 175.
[11]. Pomeroy, p. 175.
[12]. In *Alfred C. Kinsey*, James Jones documents a broad spectrum of illegal, and what are still widely viewed as immoral, behaviors within mainstream American society. Book cites are from pages 604-605. See pp. 605, 669, 689 and 775 for documentation of the Kinsey team's ability to become sexually aroused for film/pornography. Jones's Yorkshire television quotes are from the documentary, "Secret History; Kinsey's Paedophiles," broadcast August 8, 1998 throughout Great Britain.
[13]. Pomeroy, p. 176.
[14]. Pomeroy, p. 176.
[15]. Pomeroy, p. 176.
[16]. Pomeroy, p. 173.

17. Pomeroy, p. 175. See Jones, who confirms that "Gebhard was assigned to photograph erotic drawings." Gebhard told Jones: "Since we looked upon this as an extremely touchy thing, the existence of our collections, and the fact that we did photography was a deep state secret.... Consequently we set up a little amateurish darkroom in Kinsey's basement, down in his fruit cellar... for a couple of years."
18. Pomeroy, p. 186.
19. Pomeroy, p. 179.
20. Jones, pp. 605-14, 669, 684, and 775.
21. Cornelia Christenson, *Kinsey: A Biography*, Indiana University Press, Bloomington, 1971, p. 134. Also see Jones' *Alfred C. Kinsey*: "In February 1943, Pomeroy reported for work.... To meet the peculiar needs of the research, Kinsey arranged with the Office of Buildings and Grounds to have these rooms soundproofed to eighty decibels..." (p. 482). The soundproofed facility also had "steel wire on the windows and venetian blinds" (p. 673).
22. Pomeroy, p. 105
23. *World Book Almanac and Book of Facts*, World Almanac Books, Funk & Wagnalls Corp., Mahwah, New Jersey, 1996, p. 604
24. Samuel M. Steward is author of *Bad Boys and Tough Tattoos*, Harrington Park Press, New York, NY, 1990. See Steward's discussion of his filming sequences in "Remembering Dr. Kinsey," *The Advocate*, November 13, 1980, pp. 21-23.
25. Pomeroy, p. 176.
26. Pomeroy, p. 176.
27. *The Advocate*, pp. 21-23.
28. *Playboy* Magazine, "The Playboy Panel," September 1973, p. 98.
29. *Playboy*, p. 98
30. *Playboy*, p. 98
31. James Jones, *Alfred C. Kinsey*, pp. 607, 604, 605. Part 2 of endnote 30 excerpts are 612, 609, 607. Jones' admission of having seen the films during his student days, etc., is found in Yorkshire's "Kinsey's Paedophiles," with confirmation for the citation to the resisting wife seen in both Jones' book and in *The New Yorker*, "Dr. Yes," September 1, 1997, pp. 99-113. Also relevant is Dallenback's remark: "I remember masturbating to climax by myself in front of the others because Kinsey wanted it. Somebody else probably did it too, you see. And so I stood there on tiptoes or leaning against the wall or something." Looking back on that evening, Dallenback lamented, "I didn't enjoy it," adding that the entire experience was "against my sense of propriety, I think." (p. 607). After agreeing to masturbate for the camera as Kinsey required, Martin told Jones, "I really wasn't interested, the idea kind of offended me." (p. 607). Jones notes that "most" of the sex films, not all, were "done at Kinseys' home in one of the finished bedrooms in the attic" (p. 607). All of Kinsey's men, however, did as they were told.
32. Jones, p. 607. See also "Kinsey's Paedophiles" for Jones' remarks in the second paragraph of quotes.
33. Pomeroy, p. 180.
34. "Payment", wrote Kinsey in the *Male* volume, "has been confined to prostitutes, pimps, exhibitionists or to others who have turned from their regular occupation and spent *considerable time* in helping make contacts." pp. 40 - 41.
35. Pomeroy, p. 198.
36. Letter from Paul Gebhard, Kinsey Institute Director, to Judith Bat-Ada (Reisman) in Israel, dated March 11, 1981, in the author's archive. Also see "Esther," who testified in the 1998 British Yorkshire television documentary, "Kinsey's Paedophiles," part III, documented as Barbara Whitacre, in our discussion of the child sexual abuse protocol, Chapter 7, extensive endnote 42.
37. Letter from Weil, Gotshal & Manges, Fifth Avenue, New York, to Robert Reed, Tribune Company Syndicate, May 25, 1983, in the author's archive. See Patrick Buchanan, "Shocking new look at Kinsey," *New York Post*, May, 12, 1983.
38. Patrick Buchanan, "Buchanan vs. Kinsey: Round Two," *The New York Post*, June 16, 1983.
39. Pomeroy, p. 122.
40. Pomeroy, p. 179.
41. Alexandra and Vernon Mark, *The Pied Pipers of Sex*, Haven Books, Plainfield, New Jersey, 1981, pp. 124-125.
42. Linnea Smith, M.D., Personal correspondence with the author, February 10, 1997.
43. Pomeroy, pp. 380-381.
44. Pomeroy, p. 87 and Jones, *Kinsey*, p. 606-607.
45. James H. Jones, *The Origins of the Institute for Sex Research*, UMI Dissertation Services, Ann Arbor, Michigan, 1973, pp. 256, 259.
46. Warren Weaver letter to CIB, May 7, 1951, pp. 8-10, Rockefeller Center Archive.
47. Ted McIlvenna, *Meditations on the Gift of Sexuality*, The Institute for the Advanced Study of Human Sexuality, Specific Press, San Francisco, Calif., 1977. See S.H.A.R.P. brochure, 1989, p. 2 for cite to numbers of people trained via the IASHS.
48. Erwin Haerberle, *The Sex Atlas*, Seabury Press, New York, 1978.
49. *Hustler*, "Children, Sex and Society," December 1978, pp. 82-124.
50. *RSVP* Parents Training Manual, First Principles Press, Brownsboro, Kentucky, p. 19-33.
51. Dr. Gary Lynch, in "The Brain: Learning and Memory," The Annenberg CPB Collection, Santa Barbara, California, WNET, 1984.
52. Pomeroy, p. 155.
53. See Judith Reisman, *"Soft Porn" Plays HardBall*, Huntington House, LA, 1991.
54. Paul Robinson, "Dr. Kinsey and the Institute for Sex Research," *The Atlantic Monthly*, May, 1972, pp. 97-100.
55. Ann Burgess and Robert Hazelwood, "Autoerotic Asphyxial Deaths and Social Network Response," *American Journal of Orthopsychiatry*, January, 1983, pp. 166-170, and Park Dietz and Robert Hazelwood, "Atypical Autoerotic Fatalities," 1982, pp. 307-319.
56. *Kinsey Today*, Kinsey Institute for Research in Sex, Gender, and Reproduction, Fall 1997, Volume 1, Number 2.
57. *Kinsey Today*, p. 5.
58. Terrence J. Murphy, *Censorship, Government and Obscenity*, Helicon, Baltimore, Maryland, 1963, p. 75.
59. John Bartlett, *Familiar Quotations*, 14th Edition, [Ed.] Emily Morison Beck, Little, Brown and Company, 1968 [1855], p. 635.

CHAPTER 5

AMERICAN MEN: ELIMINATING FATHERS

The whole of our laws and customs in sexual matters is based on the avowed desire to protect the family, and at the base of the family is the father. His behavior is revealed by the Kinsey Report to be quite different from anything the general public had supposed possible or reasonable.[1]

Morris Ernst, 1948

By the end of 1940 he had recorded more than 450 homosexual histories[2].... His Chicago and Saint Louis contacts began to spread.... "like the branches of a tree." With 700 histories recorded at this point (1940), his tabulations, curves and correlation charts began to be impressive[3].... In autumn of 1940 he describes his prison work: "I have 110 histories from inmates there and can get as many hundreds more as I want."[4]

Wardell Pomeroy, Co-Author
***Sexual Behavior in the Human Male*, 1948**

The publication of *Sexual Behavior in the Human Male* claimed to describe the sexual behavior of the general American male population. The 200,000 copies that were sold within two months began to change the public's regard for "dear old Dad." But were the men in Kinsey's study actually the fathers and grandfathers that most Americans knew, trusted and loved? Were they the present and future fathers as Kinsey implied?

In Aldous Huxley's *Brave New World* (1932), the population rate was regulated by the government. Workers at various class levels were "decanted" from test tubes in government laboratories, all without the need or benefit of mothers and fathers. The mere mention of the words "mother" or "father" was considered a gross obscenity. Similarly, Kinsey's research taxonomy had no data categories for "fathers" or "mothers." Yet, at the time, Americans mistakenly assumed that *Sexual Behavior in the Human Male* and *Sexual Behavior in the Human Female* reported the sexual behavior of average dads and moms, grandfathers and grandmothers. Kinsey and his associates did not disabuse the public of that specious belief. The introductory quote bears repeating. Morris Ernst, his ACLU attorney, described the report's fatherhood findings as "the facts," adding,

> The whole of our laws and customs in sexual matters is based on the avowed desire to protect the family, and at the base of the family is the father. His behavior is revealed by the Kinsey Report to be quite different from anything the general public had supposed possible or reasonable.[5]

What were the "facts" about "father" that Ernst thought so compelling? Kinsey proclaimed that his data showed that 95 percent of American men had violated sex-crimes laws that could land them in jail. Ernst asserted, based on Kinsey, that 85 per cent of American men had engaged in premarital sex, 69 percent had patronized prostitutes, 45 percent had committed adultery, 10 to 37 percent had experienced orgasm in a homosexual act, and 17 percent had engaged in sex with animals.

Ernst correctly acknowledged that fathers are "at the base of the family," yet Kinsey targeted and debased fathers, as well as laws and customs intended to protect the institutions of marriage and the

Kinsey's book was released three years after young American men, dreaming of marriage, children and a little house with a picket fence, returned from World War II. (*Arbutus*, 1948).

family. Laws against divorce, adultery, sodomy, prostitution, bestiality-even incest-came under attack. Citing Kinsey, New York magistrate and attorney Morris Ploscowe stated,

> Marriage does not solve the sexual problems of the male animal, for between 30 per cent and 45 per cent of the male population has had extramarital or adulterous intercourse. About 17 per cent of the boys raised on farms [have] sexual contacts with animals. ...[W]here animals are more readily available, incidence figures for such contacts run as high as 65 per cent.... These premarital, extramarital, homosexual and animal contacts, we are told, are eventually indulged in by 95 per cent of the population in violation of statutory prohibitions. If these conclusions are correct then it is obvious that our sex crime legislation is completely out of touch with the realities of individual life.[6]

A study of the 15-page index finds the word "father" or "fatherhood" absent. "Family, basis of" merely describes "marital intercourse," due to its important in "maintenance of the family." In fact Kinsey's exclusion of normal fathers had an inordinate effect upon American law.[7]

WHOM DID KINSEY ACTUALLY INTERVIEW?

In Chapter 3 we examined the erratic figures for the male subjects selected for the first Kinsey report. The map on page five claimed that Kinsey's team collected over 21,350 "sex histories," but only "about 6,300" are listed as male while "about 5,300" of these are white males, including boys, who have "provided the data for the present publication" (p. 6). So Kinsey does not say he *has* 6,300 male subjects, but "about" that number. Using "about" may account for missing "about" 1,180 men and boys from his basic statistical tabulations. Yet, as Wallis pointed out, no more than 4,120 of the alleged 6,300 males appear in Kinsey's *Male* tables.

Nowhere did Kinsey adequately describe this "male" population. Instead, he obscured figures for the various groups sampled, forcing friends

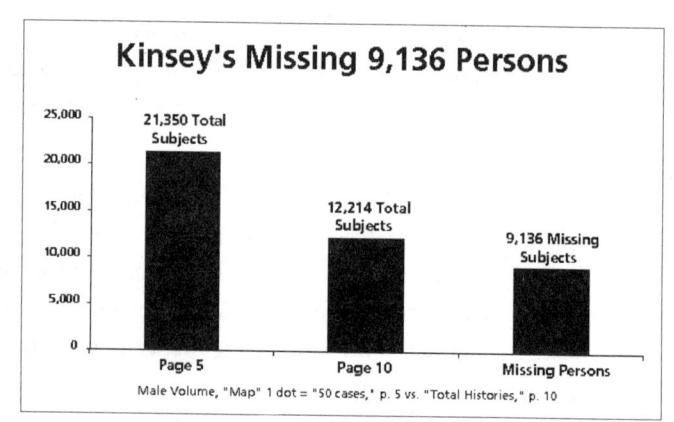

Kinsey's Missing 9,136 Persons

- Page 5: 21,350 Total Subjects
- Page 10: 12,214 Total Subjects
- Missing Persons: 9,136 Missing Subjects

Male Volume, "Map" 1 dot = "50 cases," p. 5 vs. "Total Histories," p. 10

and foes alike to guess at each. Recall that a fragment of a letter published in Pomeroy's biography of Kinsey suggested why the team sought to obscure such data. The following should be read within the context of what we now know was the Kinsey team's effort to discredit fatherhood:

> You ask about the percentage of our histories who were sex offenders and other low characters. I will tell you as a good friend exactly why we did not publish the exact figures of the constitution of our population. We anticipated that there would be a good many people like Lewis Terman who would have their own ideas as to the exact percentage of barbers and college professors of one rank and another rank who should be included. We anticipated that we would spend the rest of our lives arguing exactly who should be accepted as a normal individual, and who should be ruled out as a low character.[8]

Kinsey claimed that convicted criminals, including sex offenders, were no different than most men, they had merely been caught. Included in his "human males" sample were incarcerated pedophiles, pederasts (homosexual pedophiles), homosexual males, boy prostitutes, and other sexual riffraff. Yet the team regularly wrote and testified to the "average" nature of their male sample – just like dad. Kinsey coauthor Paul Gebhard admitted as much:

> Kinsey did mix male prison inmates in with his sample used in *Sexual Behavior in Human Male*.... *As* to generalizing to a wider population, in his first volume Kinsey did generalize to the entire U.S. population. See, for one example, the tables on page 188 and 220 where he clearly extrapolates to the U.S. Subsequently he realized this error and no such extrapolation is found in his second volume.[9]

One can enter Kinsey's statistical maze via Martin's claim that the inmates of the Indiana State Penal Farm were "misdemeanants, serving sentences of a year or less for drunk, petite [sic] theft," while slipping in the fact that these convicts also were imprisoned for "contributing to delinquency, etc." Martin knew this would include such offenses as child molestation and soliciting boys or girls for sundry types of vice. According to Gebhard, "At the Indiana State Farm we had no plan of sampling-we simply sought out sex offenders and, after a time, avoided the more common types of offense (e.g. statutory rape) and directed our efforts toward the rarer types."[10]

While Terman apparently did not notice, as Dr. Warren Weaver points out, that Kinsey misused statistics to the point of occasionally depicting a single case as a group "average," he was concerned that Kinsey's wizardry had hidden necessary age breakdowns:

> One of the most puzzling omissions in the book is the author's failure to give the complete age distribution of his subjects at the time they were interviewed. Mention is made of subjects who were in their 70s and 80s, but [the sample is so small that it is] not summarized.... The reviewer has found no statement about the lowest age limit of the younger subjects.... [Although] some types of outlet down to the age of 8 years [are given] we are not specifically informed whether any data obtained from 8-year-olds (or for that matter from 9-, 10-, 11-, or 12-year-olds) have been reported for these 5,300 males.[11]

> [Terman guessed that] this proportion would be high in the late teens and early twenties, because of the large (though unstated) number of students who were interviewed while they were attending college; *but for all we know, the proportion may be zero* [Emphasis added].[12]

Terman, an early fan who appreciated Kinsey's call for a liberal sexuality policy, wrote to Kinsey prior to publication of the *Male* volume. He was eager to see the results:

> I can hardly wait to see your first volume and shall be just as much interested in the second one. From all that I have learned about your investigation I feel sure your data will be by far the most valuable that anyone has published. Your material on homosexuality among boys is convincing evidence that rigid classifications of the traditional kind are simply not valid… that homosexuality is largely a matter of conditioning.[13]

Terman wrote to Indiana University President Wells, asserting,

> I am strongly of the opinion, however, as are also my psychological colleagues at Stanford, that Dr. Kinsey should take account of some of the criticisms in preparing his later volumes. Some of his sources of error and confusion present in the first report could easily be avoided in those which are to follow.[14]

Indiana University President Herman Wells continued to support Kinsey in his private and public life, and worked to present him and his team to the world as conventional men and honest, trustworthy academicians.

Kinsey's data in the *Male* volume do not add up to his population claims. Even Clyde Martin, his late-blooming "statistician," has estimated that only 46 percent of "college level" men were included, while Terman assumes that college men account for "more than half." Actually, however, none of the data can be validated. Only be a process of elimination can we come up with so much as an educated guess. If we begin with 4,201 men as the data base, and deduct the *admitted* prison and other outlaw populations, the remainder reasonably qualifies as his pool of "college level" (but not necessarily college-attending, as explained earlier) males.

KNOWN SUBJECTS

Such critical concepts as "outlet" sex, homosexual normality, child sexuality, and "Kinsey Scale" (sexual orientation ratings from fully heterosexual [0] to fully homosexual [6]) have emerged from the flawed data obtained during Kinsey's interviews. The "Kinsey Scale," best known for its ludicrous "10 percent" homosexuality claim. In fact, Kinsey cooked his 10 percent out of whole cloth, including the word of bisexual and homosexual interviewers who decided a subject was homosexual if they had "overt experience," or if they had some -any- thoughts about homosexuality, which the Kinsey men called "psychological reactions." So, someone thinking negatively or recalling a homosexual assault becomes part of the homosexual 10%. Such an assessment is ludicrous and misleading. Even a diligent sleuth like Terman could not identify the interviewees by reading reports and other writings produced by the Kinsey team, while statistician Paul Sheatsley and sociologist Herbert Hyman state in *An Analysis of the Kinsey Reports* (1954) that,

> one of the most telling criticisms of [Kinsey's] first report was that no one could tell how good or bad his sample actually was because nowhere was there any systematic account of the distribution of the 5,300 males in terms of such factors as age, religion, etc.[15]

The Kinsey documents are now sufficiently complete to reveal convincing evidence of meticulous deceit. We know, for instance, that Kinsey had problems convincing people in the Bloomington area to talk about their sex lives. Christenson notes that "the offers of towns people to volunteer as subjects were surprisingly slow." She quotes Kinsey as writing on one occasion: "All told then, damn few histories yet…. It is going to be hell to get older, well-established business men to jeopardize their positions by confessing even to me: businessmen are very wary about exposing themselves."[16]

We also know that, despite claims to the contrary, Kinsey was not welcome on many college campuses. According to Pomeroy,

> While it was not difficult in most cases for Kinsey to get histories from prisons, other kinds of institutions occasionally gave him trouble, especially colleges and universities, where the religious and scientific biases of administrators or faculty could operate more freely against him than they did at his Indiana base.[17]

Kinsey and his team had little alternative but to talk to sex offenders, since so many American men, including fathers, were serving their country in World War II. Prison inmates and homosexual enclaves in large cities were an ideal source for wartime interviews. Christenson writes,

> [T]here is a steady supply of readily available subjects who have plenty of free time on their hands. Thus the investigator wastes no time in making contacts or arguing to work out convenient interview schedules. There are no cancelled, late, or forgotten appointments, and few interruptions. Furthermore, the inmates are chiefly from a social economic level that is difficult to tap in the outside world. These are some of the practical reasons why Kinsey early sought prison cases for his sex histories… to do it as economically and efficiently as possible.[18]

Pomeroy recalls that by 1946, Kinsey, Gebhard, and he,

> had interviewed about 1,400 convicted sex offenders in penal institutions scattered over a dozen states…. [J]ust before the publication of the *Male* volume… [Kinsey interviewed] about two hundred sexual psychopath patients.[19]

Another 329 prisoners who were interviewed prior to 1948 were *non*-sex offenders, according to Gebhard and others.[20] Which brings the total of incarcerated interviewees for the *Male* volume to 1,929.

The Kinsey team's tome, *Sex Offenders*, has been used as a resource worldwide by legislators, penologists and law enforcement authorities. It, too, was based on the disgracefully flawed database. One of the original team members was high school teacher Glenn Ramsey of Peoria, Illinois, who is cited throughout *Sex Offenders* and in other Kinsey texts. Ramsey's reports covered at least "350 aberrant high schools boys" whom he had "interviewed." According to Pomeroy,

"Glenn Ramsey at Bloomington in September 1951, carefully posed for the new photographic collection of helpers." (Caption and photo taken from Gathorne-Hardy' *Sex, the Measure of All Things*.)

> Glenn Ramsey… interviewed seventh and eighth graders… [with techniques] similar to the adult records Kinsey was compiling and subsequently 350 of them

AMERICAN MEN: ELIMINATING FATHERS

were incorporated into the files. The parents were given a general notification of the project but were not specifically asked for permission. This was a calculated risk... Ramsey began taking personal interviews-two hours during school time and an hour after school.[21]

Ramsey began teaching in 1939, but was fired in 1942 after evidence surfaced that he had lied to parents and school administrators to gain access to youngsters for sex information. There were also rumors of additional improprieties at the high school. Nevertheless, Kinsey defended Ramsey vociferously, and obtained Rockefeller Foundation money to pay his legal fees. He warned,

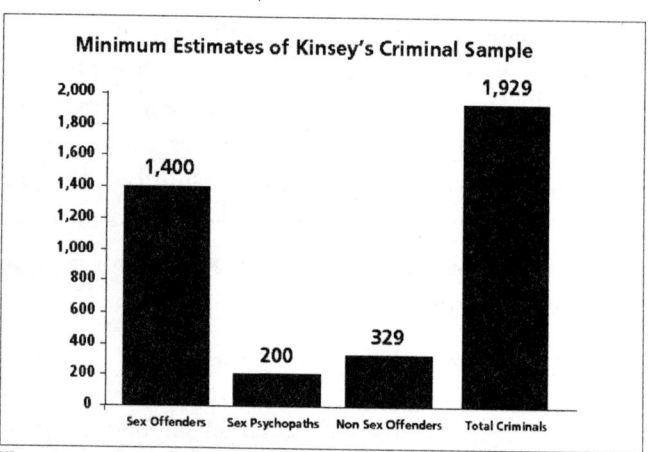

Minimum Estimates of Kinsey's Criminal Sample

Sex Offenders	1,400
Sex Psychopaths	200
Non Sex Offenders	329
Total Criminals	1,929

Kinsey's sample of "average" men, included large numbers of sex offenders, psychopaths and incarcerated criminals.

> If we let them get away with this in Peoria now... this precedent will encourage Boards elsewhere to do similar things... Catholics elsewhere [will] try the same tactics against us here and against the entire research program. [22]

Kinsey also paid for Ramsey's return to Bloomington to work at the Institute.

The inclusion of Ramsey's 350 boys in the *Male* volume data is confirmed by Christenson.[23] And Gagnon labeled the boys "aberrant," noting that Ramsey identified a 50-percent homosexual rate among them.

The 350 figure is conservative, by the way, since we know that Kinsey also interviewed children in "the ghetto" without parental consent,[24] as well as in the "Feeble Minded" Institution at Coldwater, Michigan, and in "an exclusively Negro township in a sparsely settled section of Kansas." He also queried "one hundred per cent of the boys and girls who go through the Ohio Bureau of Juvenile Research at Columbus, Ohio."[25] Kinsey refers to these and other youthful "volunteer sources" in the *Male* volume.[26] Without exact numbers, however, it is impossible to count or evaluate them. We *can* count the 317 boys cited in Kinsey's Table 31 as victims of laboratory sex experiments by adult males. It is captioned, "Pre-Adolescent Experience in Orgasm," and a note at the bottom reads: "Based on actual observation of 317 males." The "males" ranged in age from two months to 15 years, with 28 under one year of age.[27]

Were we to use "accumulative incidences" as does Kinsey, we would have to conclude that *Sexual Behavior in the Human Male* exploited 1,475 infants and boys for information about alleged infant and child orgasm. The actual child population is anyone's guess, but the minimum number of boys Kinsey cites is 667, including the 317 victims of sodomy recorded in Table 31, and the 350 cited as Glenn Ramsey's subjects.

SEX CRIMINALS NOT IN KINSEY'S "UNDERWORLD" CATEGORY

Another 300 aberrant subjects were selected from a population Kinsey called "the underworld," which he defined as persons "*[d]eriving a significant portion of their income from illicit activities: e.g., bootleggers, con men, dope peddlers, gamblers, hold-up men, pimps, prostitutes, etc."28* For Kinsey, the only sex crimes which qualified as "underworld" were those that involved economic gain, such as prostitution and pandering.

Consistent with his eugenic training and beliefs, which typically disregarded marital status and parenthood while focusing on occupational and economic status, Kinsey conjured up ten human resource categories,[29]

0. Dependent
1. Underworld
2. Day Labor
3. Semi-Skilled Labor
4. Skilled Labor
5. Lower White-Collar Group
6. Upper White-Collar Group
7. Professional Group
8. Business-Executive Group
9. Extremely Wealthy Group

Author Gore Vidal, one of Kinsey's homosexual interviewees, would be part of Kinsey's "extremely wealthy group," a "9" on his occupational chart. (1997 BBC TV Kinsey biography in, "*Reputations*")

He claimed to have interviewed at least 300 persons from each. However, only the "Underworld" population would likely have provided the degree of sexual deviance he typically sought. If we accept that he did indeed interview at least 300 members of the "Underworld," it is a safe assumption that he included them in his *Male* volume data. But since few sex predators perpetrate their crimes for economic profit, they would have been excluded from the "Underworld," and would instead have resurfaced in other categories. This statistical sleight-of-hand had the advantage of increasing the number of males in apparently normal occupations, while decreasing their numbers in deviant/sex offender populations. *For Kinsey, homosexuals, as a special (or "coded") category, did not exist.*

MISSION IN CHICAGO: COLLECT "HOMOSEXUAL HISTORIES"

The homosexuals included in Kinsey's sample were identified largely through homosexual bars, baths, and networks in New York and elsewhere. He argued that choosing a partner by "gender" is foolish and trivial. In his critical review of the *Male* volume, Terman writes,

> On p. 661 the author [Kinsey] apropos of an individual's preference for a sexual partner of the same or opposite sex, says that "This problem, is after all, part of the broader problem of choices in general: the choice of the road that one takes, of the clothes that one wears, of the food that one eats, of the place in which one sleeps, and of the endless other things that one is constantly choosing." That it is a problem of choosing is evident enough, but to many a reader the implication of the passage will be that the sex chosen as partner in a sexual activity is as unimportant as one's preferences regarding food or the cut of one's clothes.[30]

Much of Kinsey's work was designed to advance several revolutionary notions about homosexuality, including,

- clandestine homosexuality is relatively commonplace;

- most normal Americans hypocritically and secretly engage in illicit sex of various kinds, including homosexual sex;
- people are commonly bisexual, meaning they are both homosexual and heterosexual;
- prejudice against homosexuality is hypocritical and based on ignorance of normal sexual behavior; and
- children and adults should experience and experiment with both their homosexual and heterosexual sides.

Kinsey and his team expressly focused on, and solicited, "units" brought together by common deviant and perverse sexual interests, while feigning to *exclude* groups "brought together by a common sexual interest."[31] They were found in bars, bathhouses, "tearooms,"[32] and "rooming houses." Pomeroy writes,

Kinsey's anonymous tour guide into New York's homosexual milieu. After obtaining the most intimate details about his subject's sexual lives, Kinsey never published their data on homosexual incest and child sexual abuse. ("*Reputations*")

> [His] first assignment originated with a trip Kinsey made to New York for the purpose of taking the histories of a homosexual group consisting chiefly of writers, artists, architects and others occupied with creative work. This group held frequent sex sessions, to one of which Kinsey was invited as an observer.[33]

Pomeroy then describes the films Kinsey made of numerous homosexual "units" performing sodomy and sexual sadism. As discussed earlier, Kinsey even paid to have two males fly to Bloomington to be filmed performing sadistic sex acts.[34] As described by Pomeroy,

> On subsequent New York trips we spent many hours in gay bars.[35] Gebhard was once taking histories in a famous music school where we knew there were a great many homosexuals.... [O]ften... we would plunge into a subculture that was unknown to people... the world of homosexual prostitution in the Times Square area of New York.... [I]n the evening we took homosexual histories from the Near North Side.... His [Kinsey's] mission in Chicago was to collect homosexual histories.... [S]oon he had half-dozen centers in the city from which he could make contacts.[36]

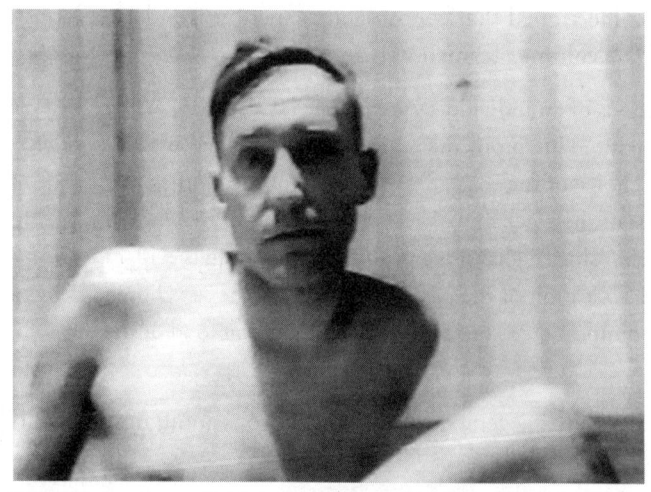

William Burroughs, another homosexual Kinsey interviewee, filmed for the BBC's biography, described his visits with Kinsey. ("*Reputations*")

We now have admissions by members of the Kinsey team that Pomeroy was dissembling. Kinsey did not merely "observe" and record homosexual sex on these trips; he was an active, obsessed, and irrational participant. In the Yorkshire television interview, Jonathan Gathorne-Hardy, Kinsey's English biographer (*Sex the Measure of All Things; A Life of Alfred C. Kinsey*, London: Chatto & Winds, 1998) who had complete access to Kinsey's files at Indiana University, reported:

We know in 1940 that he was telling his team you should experiment sexually.... He was astonished at the number of homosexuals.... [Kinsey was] sexually excited.... He [went] to urinals... had sex in... tearooms.... He could have gone to prison.... [He] was emerging with a religion he believes in, a scientific religion ....towards sexual behavior.... This is a field where you are not going to hurt people.... [P]rovided everyone consents it doesn't matter what you do.

In a letter to his friend Ralph "Mr. Man" Voris, Kinsey wrote:

Homosexual "bathhouses," where males engage in indiscriminate sexual activity, are infamous from New York to Berlin.

> Have been to [homosexual] Halloween parties, taverns, clubs, etc., which would be unbelievable if realized by the rest of the world.... Why has no one cracked this before? *There are at least 300,000 involved in Chicago alone...* I have diaries... albums of photographs of their friends, or from commercial sources-fine art to putrid. Some of the art model material is gorgeous. I want you to see it... have a total... of 120 H - histories.... The subject which you and I have been studying is one in which all possible information needs to be pooled... to affect public understanding.[37] [Emphasis added]

Addressing the issue of "units" sharing common sexual interests, "units" which would come to stand for average men, fathers, and grandfathers, Pomeroy notes:

> By the end of 1940 he [Kinsey] had recorded more than 450 homosexual histories[38] ...His Chicago and Saint Louis contacts began to spread... "like the branches of a tree." With 700 histories recorded at this point (1940), his tabulations, curves and correlation charts began to be impressive[39] ....In autumn of 1940 he describes his prison work: "I have 110 histories from inmates there and can get as many hundreds more as I want."[40]

In 1940, Kinsey was already constructing "tabulations, curves and correlation charts" when his sample clearly showed an overwhelmingly aberrant homosexual bias (as much as 80 percent), as well as at least 110 sex offender inmates from Indiana prisons.[41] Martin tells us that many of these early graphs ended up in the 1948 *Male* report for (as Pomeroy admits) the team did not generally correct graphs when new data arrived.[42]

In a letter fragment to Voris, while in Chicago collecting homosexual histories, Kinsey exulted that the "570 histories" he had completed comprised "the most exhaustive record ever had on single individuals."[43] The reference was to homosexual interviewees. Having secured at least 450 homosexual subjects by 1940 (i.e., an average of 225 homosexual subjects per year when it was difficult to obtain such interviews), Kinsey aggressively struggled to fulfill his mission and continued to gather the sex stories from among the "300,000 involved in Chicago alone."[44]

There may have been males among his prison subjects that Kinsey also counted as homosexuals. Avoiding the methodological problem of "double-counting" Kinsey's homosexual population is impossible. Volunteers already identified as incarcerated and underage must be excised. Then there is the question of what percentage of the remainder fits Kinsey's definition of "homosexual."

While the Kinsey team claimed that both prisoners and youths included large homosexual populations, the total percentage of homosexual histories remains unknown because the Kinsey team, as Martin admits, did not have a code that would pinpoint homosexuality. On the basis of available data, the two groups can only be counted as part of Kinsey's 1,400 sex offenders and 317-667 youths, not as homosexual "units."

Intense security at the Kinsey archives begins with bars on the windows and locks on the doors. Indiana University closes the Institute to critics, while opening it to trusted colleagues and "safe" individuals. How, then, can we establish the likely number of homosexuals in Kinsey's database? If we count only the 450 homosexuals interviewed by 1940, the known homosexual "unit" accounts for 10.9 percent of Kinsey's probable overall total of 4,120 males. Similarly, 570 males would account for 9.0 percent homosexuals in Kinsey's claimed 6,300-male sample. Both numbers are strikingly close to the discredited 10 percent often cited, on Kinsey's authority alone, as the percentage of males in our society who are exclusively homosexual.

According to Kinsey, the males in his group, and/or their partners, experienced arousal/orgasm physically or *psychically* during a homosexual encounter at some time in their lives. The number of permutations possible in such a definition are limitless, from a rape victim reporting that his *rapist* had an orgasm, to the Kinsey team's speculative conclusion that a subject was psychically aroused.

In the *Male* volume, Kinsey claims that people are evenly distributed along a scale from zero to six, with zero representing a small group of between 4 and 6 percent of American males who are "exclusively heterosexual" (in 1988 Georgia's state-mandated sex education program cited that claim[45]), and six representing a somewhat larger group that is "exclusively homosexual." Everyone in between those extremes, he alleged, is "bisexual" to varying degrees. Fully 18 percent of the male population is identified with "as much of the homosexual as the heterosexual in their histories ... for at least three years between the ages of 16 and 55."

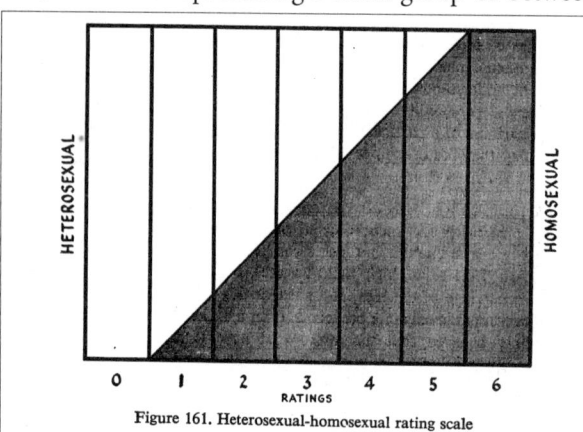

Figure 161. Heterosexual-homosexual rating scale
Based on both psychologic reactions and overt experience, individuals rate as follows:
0. Exclusively heterosexual with no homosexual
1. Predominantly heterosexual, only incidentally homosexual
2. Predominantly heterosexual, but more than incidentally homosexual
3. Equally heterosexual and homosexual
4. Predominantly homosexual, but more than incidentally heterosexual
5. Predominantly homosexual, but incidentally heterosexual
6. Exclusively homosexual

"The Kinsey scale" used worldwide, proposes human beings are naturally bisexual, fluctuating throughout their lives between homosexual and heterosexual behavior.

Kinsey claimed that he averaged about five "histories" per day after the first year. Pomeroy calculated that they had compiled 450 homosexual histories in 1940. Assuming a total of 1,692 (as Kinsey claims on page ten of the *Male* volume), 26.6 percent would have been homosexual. However, since the 1,692 people allegedly included both women and men, Kinsey's pre-selected homosexual male population would likely have been significantly higher than 26.6% in 1940.

For the sake of argument, let us accept Pomeroy's figure of 450 homosexuals in 1940, and add only 30 new cases for the years 1941-1946. That very low probability estimate yields a total of 630 homosexual histories. But the total figure for homosexuals surveyed for the *Male* volume is more than double that number.

Adding the 630 homosexuals to the other aberrant categories (see accompanying chart) brings the total to 3,526, which is absurdly unrepresentative of normal male sexuality. It accounts for 86 percent of Kinsey's known sample of 4,120, with a mere 14 percent reserved for *normal* males!

"NORMAL" REMAINDER

And what of that 14 percent? Unfortunately, few figures are available. "The *N*'s [*N*umbers] of contributing groups are almost never stated," Terman complained in his 1948 review. Kinsey claimed to have surveyed supposedly normal people who attended his lectures across the country, but Terman observes:

> We are told (p. 38) that about [6,000] histories... resulted from several hundred lectures by [Kinsey]... to perhaps 50,000 persons. We do not know how those who attended the lectures differed from those who might have attended but did not, nor how the 6,000 who heard the lectures and allowed themselves to be interviewed differed from the 44,000 who heard them but did not cooperate.... On p. 16 we learn that subjects were obtained from "homosexual communities" in Chicago, New York, Philadelphia, Indianapolis, and St. Louis; also from "underworld communities" in Chicago, Peoria, Indianapolis, New York City, and Gary (Indiana).[46]

Among the 62 groups for which Kinsey claimed to have collected 100 percent samples, Terman counted "four delinquent groups, two penal groups, and one group in a 'mental' institution... three classes of junior high school students... three rooming-house groups, two groups of conscientious objectors and a group of hitchhikers." He notes that "it is unlikely that [these men were] representative of the U.S."[47]

The Kinsey Team's Estimated 86 percent Aberrant Sample in *Male* Numbers

Aberrant Population	Estimated Sample
Prison Sex Offenders and Psychopaths (documented above)	1,600
Prison Non-Sex Offenders (documented above)	329
Experimental Child Subjects (Chapter 7, at minimum)	317
Experimental School Boys (Chapter 7, at minimum)	350
"Pimps, Thieves, Ne'er-do-wells" (Kinsey's terms), etc.	300
Homosexuals	630
Total Aberrant Population	**3,526**

– Roughly 86 percent of the 4,120 Male Population were Sexual Deviants

WHY "COLLEGE LEVEL," NOT "COLLEGE"?

Kinsey identified 42 of the 62 groups as "college level," but his definition encompassed more than college students. Indeed, there is good reason to believe that it may

AMERICAN MEN: ELIMINATING FATHERS

have included the aberrant males in his prison and homosexual samples. Demographic studies usually define a "college" population as one comprised of those who attend a college or university. At no point does Kinsey define the terms "college" or "college level." His definition of "educational level" was sufficiently vague to allow many males who had never completed high school, much less attended a college class, to be included. It reads in part:

> Educational Level... the number of years in a completed educational history, by two-year periods... made for those who have permanently stopped their schooling... but it cannot be made for those who are still in school.... The last group includes all those who have done any graduate work.
>
> The classification depends upon the educational level attained by the individual, rather than upon the number of years required to reach that level... *In cases of persons who have acquired their education through... their own independent reading and travel... the educational rating should approximate the level to which the individual's achievements would have carried him in a formal school system.*[48] [Emphasis added.]

Kinsey claimed that about 6,000 male interviews originated from university lectures.

Using this definition, Kinsey claims a total population of 2,799 males who have attained an educational level of "13+," but this would include boys "who ultimately go to college." Statistician Allen Wallis writes: "To Kinsey æ13-plusÆ means 'ultimately more than 12 years,' i.e., that at least a start has been or *ultimately will be* made to college."[49] (Emphasis in original.)

Wallis notes that page 331 of the *Male* volume states, referring to high school boys, that "there is no certainty how far they will go before they finally terminate their education." By page 682, "13+" relates to "the males who at least *start* to college," which means that merely planning to enroll, or doing so and dropping out, was sufficient to qualify for the "college level" category. Further, the "clinician may sometimes predict, on the basis of his home background, the amount of future schooling."

Kinsey's self-serving definition allowed his team to educationally upgrade whomever they wished to the "college" level, including those who merely "acquired their education through...their own independent reading and travel." [50]

Even in Kinsey's day, many prisons offered college level training programs for inmates. The Federal Bureau of Prisons had a long history of educational programs that would have qualified many of Kinsey's prisoners as "college level." In 1940, inmates at Alcatraz could take courses from the University of California in foreign languages, psychology, commercial law, philosophy, logic, and even Kinsey's own field of zoology.

Other federal prisons offered courses from Pennsylvania State College, Bucknell University, the University of North Dakota, and other institutions. Though prison travel is limited, inmates had ample time for "independent reading" during the period when Kinsey conducted his prison interviews. A 1932 report by the director of the Bureau of Prisons noted that the Bureau had purchased "14,300 new books… which brings the total of new books purchased in the past three years to about 31,000."[51]

At Minimum 86% Of Kinsey Male Interviewees Were Sexually Aberrant

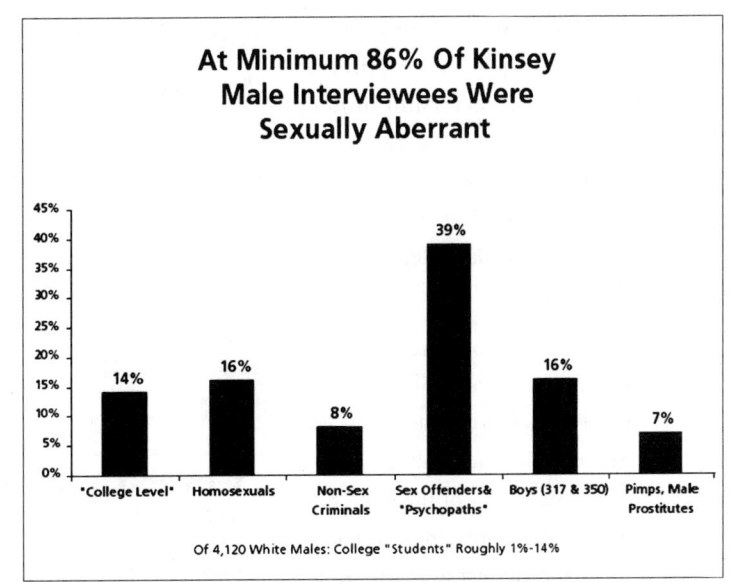

Category	Percentage
"College Level"	14%
Homosexuals	16%
Non-Sex Criminals	8%
Sex Offenders & "Psychopaths"	39%
Boys (317 & 350)	16%
Pimps, Male Prostitutes	7%

Of 4,120 White Males: College "Students" Roughly 1%-14%

Kinsey implied that about 6,000 male interviews originated from university lectures. His disciples continue to make similar unsubstantiated claims today.

Kinsey's prison subjects could also have included scholars, lawyers, doctors, businessmen, judges, and scientists who were imprisoned for sex offenses. In recent years, quite a few "college level" men have been arrested for sex crimes. Nobel-prize winner Dr. Daniel Carleton Gajdusek headed his own research laboratory at the U.S. National Institutes of Health before his 1997 conviction for child sexual abuse.[52] Dr. Richard Berendzen, who resigned in 1990 as president of American University in Washington, DC, subsequently pleaded guilty to making obscene phone calls suggesting sex with children, including incest. Elliott McGinnies, chairman of AU's psychology department, was convicted of sexually abusing a 9-year-old girl in a nudist trailer park. And in 1992 former Federal Communications Commission member Stephen Sharp was convicted of sexually assaulting a young boy.[53]

WERE ONE PERCENT NORMAL?

Moving in homosexual circles, Kinsey would have likely met many educated sexual deviants eager to tell him about their sex lives. Pomeroy reported that one of their technically trained "observers" was a man who collected detailed data on orgasm from as many as 800 children. He was "a college graduate who had a responsible government job,"[54] while the current Kinsey director, John Bancroft, euphemistically described the same man as an "elderly scientist."[55] Kinsey, Pomeroy, and Bancroft acknowledge that Kinsey directed at least two serial child rapists—one a lawyer and the other described as a "college" man.

AMERICAN MEN: ELIMINATING FATHERS

Kinsey's conjured numbers were the basis for his apocryphal attribution of high rates of sexual perversion among "college level" males, who were viewed as the nation's leadership class. Yet his own writings reveal that *real* college students, rare in his sample, were far more traditional:

> I have been going to the State Penal Farm at Putnamville two or three times every week for the last two months and shall continue so through most of the winter. I have 110 histories from inmates there and can get as many hundreds more as I want.... More important... these histories are giving me a look-in on a lower social level, *and the patterns of sexual behavior are totally different from those of college students.* After all, our college students constitute less than 1% of the population and it is the great mass of the population which is reported in the group that I am now working.[56] [Emphasis added.]

Nobel Laureate Is Sent to Jail
Tape Helped Decide Fate in Sex Abuse Case

By Justin Gillis
Washington Post Staff Writer

FREDERICK, Md., April 29— The conversation was drifting toward sensitive matters, specifically the subject of sex with minors. The Nobel Prize-winning scientist put his caller on hold to switch to a more secure line at his government office.

"I hope I'm on a private line," Daniel Carleton Gajdusek said into the phone. "I hope it's not being tapped."

It was. The tape became the strongest piece of evidence in a case that sent Gajdusek to jail today for child abuse.

The caller that day was a young man who grew up in Gajdusek's household, one of 56 youths whom the National Institutes of Health scientist had brought to live with him in the United States from distant lands. The young man, who had heard from investigators, wanted to talk about the past. That much Gajdusek knew that morning, at 11:16 a.m. March 15, 1996. What he didn't know was that the young man was sitting in the company of an FBI agent, Patricia L. Ferrante, and that her tape recorder was rolling.

"You did some stuff to me," the young man said.

"Well, forget it," Gajdusek replied.

See GAJDUSEK, A14, Col. 1

Daniel Carleton Gajdusek will spend nine months to a year in jail.

Cover-Up at American University?
Sex Expert Skeptical of Treatment of Scandalized Former President

When Richard Berendzen left his post as president of The American University (AU) in Washington, D.C., in May, 1990, there was an attempt to conceal the fact that he had been forced to resign due to his role in making obscene, child-related telephone calls to women in the area. Many speculated that the revelation of these facts would herald the end of the high-profile career that elevated him to national prominence.

Now, however, Berendzen's reputation is in the process of being rehabilitated. He still holds tenure in his teaching position at AU, and is being celebrated as a survivor of his own victimization as a child. In May, 1992, he will be speaking on his experiences from a "survivor's perspective" at the National Symposium on Child Victimization in Washington, a conference co-sponsored by several federal agencies.

While media profiles have described Berendzen as cured, Dr. Judith Reisman, who has written and lectured extensively on sexual perversion and pornography, questions the efficacy of the cure. She points out that Berendzen's conduct indicates a deep-seated psychological disorder for which there is no simple remedy. She says that the way the Berendzen case was handled by AU, Johns Hopkins University and the Washington, D.C. police appears to have been contrived more to protect Berendzen than to cure his perversion.

Susan Allen, a mother who tutors children in her home and had advertised her services, received obscene phone calls during the day from a man who told her that he kept a four-year-old girl in a cage in his basement and had her sexually abused. He also described child pornography to her, saying he had a collection of such material. Allen, who had been a victim of incest, was determined to catch the caller. She was aided by her husband, a policeman, who was able to help set up the tracing of the calls. They were found to originate from President Berendzen's private phone in his AU office.

Reisman, who interviewed both Allen and her lawyer, found them to be very critical of the response of the police

See BERENDZEN, page 5

Richard E. Berendzen

Not all sex criminals are from the disadvantaged segment of society. Here a Nobel Prize winner and a university president, both world-famous academicians, and respected members of society were found to be involved in pedophile-related crimes.

To justify his interest in prison and homosexual/city populations, Kinsey claimed on one hand that college students represent only one percent of the population. On the other, he defined the term "college level" so loosely that many of his aberrant populations easily qualified, thereby giving him an excuse to claim that the college level category was the largest sampled. He wrote:

> Again it should be emphasized that most of these calculations of validity have been based on the college segment of the population, which is the only group represented now by large enough series to warrant such examination.[57]

THE KRONHAUSENS' FINDINGS

Fortunately, Kinsey's findings were *not* duplicated in the work of Drs. Phyllis and Eberhard Kronhausen, a sexually radical couple[58] who also worked to free the world from sexual repression. They created the world's first "erotic" museum in Holland and, in an effort to further Kinsey's cause, conducted a sex survey of 200 male college students which they reported in their book *Sex Histories of American*

College Men (1960). But whereas Kinsey sought to create the impression that "college level" men were virtual clones of prison populations, the Kronhausens found that even as late as 1960 Joe College was commonly a virgin:

> NO SEX WITHOUT LOVE: Many of the students were as blushingly romantic about sex morals as any girl of their age would be. To these young men, sex without love seemed utterly unethical. Some of them did not even think it right to kiss a girl unless they were "in love."[59]
>
> PREMARITAL INTERCOURSE: In the college group as a whole one still finds considerable resistance toward premarital intercourse. What has changed in terms of sex mores between the attitudes of the older generation... [has been] as Kinsey puts it, the "rationalizations" which serve to justify this resistance against premarital intercourse.
>
> In our sample: premarital intercourse is considered highly objectionable for reasons which are primarily derived from religious tenets and beliefs and... overvaluation of virginity with particular respect to the female. This overvaluation of female virginity also prevails in the lower educational groups but there it is apparently not taken quite as seriously as in the upper educational groups.... [I]t remains a fact that this group engages in relatively little premarital sexual intercourse.... *The average modern college man is apt to say that he considers intercourse "too precious" to have with anyone except the girl he expects to marry and may actually abstain from all intercourse for that reason.*
>
> In keeping with this philosophy, the typical college man will say that he feels that marriages work out better if there has been no premarital intercourse and considers himself much "emancipated" as compared to the previous generation because, to him, his reasoning appears to be sounder than that of the older group. However, as Kinsey remarks, this change in the form of their rationalizations has not affected the overt behavior of the two generations in the least.[60] [Emphasis added.]

Even by 1960, the Kronhausens found that oral sodomy was rare among college males, while anal sodomy and bestiality (intercourse with animals) was unheard of. And while Kinsey had claimed "the homosexual incidence at college age to be about 20 percent," the Kronhausens found that only *one-half of one percent* (one in 200 college men) could be considered homosexual.

The Kronhausens caught the fact that Kinsey did not report on "college men," but on "college level" men, "including those younger males who will ultimately go to college, those in college, and those having had college background."[61] Hence, the embarrassing secret of the sexual libertarians was that as much as the Kronhausens wanted to justify Kinsey's claims of widespread sexual promiscuity among college males, they were unable even by 1960 to locate such activity on campus. Not until a decade of *Playboy* (which was launched December 1953), and indoctrination of the pertinent professions (education, psychiatry, psychology, health, law, and the mass communications and entertainment media) with Kinseyan sexuality training, did a dramatically changed societal attitude begin to take place.

Although this book does not scrutinize the *Playboy* phenomenon in depth, two earlier works by this author ("*Soft Porn" Plays Hardball*, (1991) and *Images of Children, Crime and Violence in Playboy, Penthouse and Hustler* (1989)) resulted from a U.S. Department of Justice (Office of Juvenile Justice and Delinquency Prevention) grant to study the causes of sex crimes by and against children. Both document the role of the named magazines (and pornography in general) in promoting and normalizing the Kinseyan "anything goes" view of human sexuality, including child sex abuse and incest.

As stated before, the fact that Kinsey was the cradle of the *Playboy* philosophy was confirmed by publisher Hugh Hefner, who reported during a 1996 BBC telecast that Kinsey was the researcher, but "I" was his "pamphleteer." The budding *Playboy* empire provided early and generous financial support for the Kinsey Institute.

Playboy publisher Hugh Hefner became a major Kinsey benefactor. He attributed his own sexual radicalism to having read the *Male* Kinsey reports in college.

During five decades of saturation with the Kinsey-Hefner view of human sexuality, America has witnessed a significant and disturbing change in the conduct of men and boys in general. Kinsey's misleading data have helped justify the "Me" generation and the general lowering of the status of women from helpmates to playmates. No longer divided into "virgins or whores," girls and women have increasingly become defined as "whores" in terms of their expected sexual conduct, and they and their children treated accordingly, undermining the moral order on which our nation was founded - our laws, institutions, and social attitudes. The accompanying erosion of the role of fathers has cost the nation dearly.

In June, 1999, the Washington, DC-based National Center for Public Policy Research (NCPPR) released a report which noted that "72 percent of Americans believe that fatherlessness is the most significant family or social problem facing America." Figures cited in the report paint a disturbing picture of the post-Kinsey view of fatherhood. For instance:

- Forty percent of the children of divorced parents haven't seen their dads in the past year.
- Thirty-six percent of children, approximately 24.7 million, don't live with their biological father. In 1960, just nine percent of children lived with only one parent.
- The number of live births to unmarried women increased from 224,300 in 1960 to 1,248,000 in 1995, while the number of children living with never married mothers grew from 221,000 in 1960 to 5,862,000 in 1995.
- National Fatherhood Initiative analysis found that of the 102 prime-time network TV shows in late 1998, only fifteen featured a father as a central character. Of these, the majority portrayed the father as uninvolved, incompetent or both. [62]

In his biography of Kinsey, James Jones states:

> In the consensus-minded 1950s, the mothers in television family programs such as *Ozzie and Harriet, Leave It To Beaver, Father Knows Best,* and *I Love Lucy* captured the officially sanctioned image of women. Fearful that Kinsey would reveal a contradiction between fictional women and real ones, many Americans did not want to hear what he had to say.[63]

Jones ignores the fact that the "officially sanctioned" image of women was significantly less fictional that what Kinsey "had to say."

The image of men and of fatherhood captured by pre-Kinsey television programs, scripted. Fathers largely working hard for their families, faithful to their wives, spending guiding and teaching time with their children, and playing an active role in their churches, communities, and schools. This was indeed the era of "Father knows Best," and it turns out that while this model of father did have its downside, it certainly had its upside.

The NCPPR report observed that "for the kids who have them, a good dad makes a big difference." It cited as examples:

- Children with fathers are twice as likely to stay in school.

- Boys with dad and mom at home are half as likely to be incarcerated, regardless of their parents' income or educational level…

- Girls 15-19 raised in homes with fathers are significantly less likely to engage in premarital sex, and 76 percent of teenage girls surveyed said their fathers are very or somewhat influential over their decisions regarding sex.

- Girls raised in single-mother homes are more likely to give birth while single and are more likely to divorce and remarry…

- Paternal praise is associated with better behavior and achievement in school, while father absence increases vulnerability and aggressiveness in young children, particularly boys.

- Young children living without dads married to their moms are ten times as likely to be in poverty.

- Children living in households with fathers are less likely to suffer from emotional disorders and depression…

- A white teenage girl with an advantaged background is five times more likely to be a teen mom if she grows up in a household headed by a single mom instead of with her biological dad and mom.

- Children with involved dads are less susceptible to peer pressure, are more competent, more self-protective, more self-reliant and more ambitious.[64]

Our nation is experiencing an epidemic of criminal sexual conduct, a coarsening of society, loss of manners, multiple venereal diseases, adultery, homosexuality, anal sodomy, anonymous fornication, pornography, obsessive masturbation, rape, child sex abuse, and incest. A 1989 assessment by The National Research Council stated that Kinsey had "established, to some degree, social standards of what was acceptable common practice."[65] His crimes have indeed had consequences.

CHAPTER 5 NOTES

[1]. Morris Ernst and David Loth, *American Sexual Behavior and The Kinsey Report*, Greystone Press, New York, 1948, pp. 83, 81.
[2]. Wardell Pomeroy, *Dr. Kinsey and the Institute for Sex Research*, Harper & Row, New York, 1972, p. 75.
[3]. Pomeroy, p. 72.
[4]. Pomeroy, p. 70.
[5]. Ernst, pp. 83, 81.
[6]. Morris Ploscowe, "Sexual Patterns and the Law," in *Sex Habits of American Men,* Ed. Albert Deutsch, Prentice Hall, New York, 1948, p. 126.
[7]. *Male*, p. 563.
[8]. Pomeroy, p. 293.
[9]. Letter from Paul Gebhard to Director June M. Reinisch at the Kinsey Institute, December 6, 1990. In the author's archive.
[10]. Bertram Pollens, *The Sex Criminal*, The Maculay Co., New York, 1938.
[11]. Gebhard, Gagnon, Pomeroy and Christenson, *Sex Offenders*, Harper & Row, New York, 1965, pp. 31-33.

12. Louis Terman, "Kinsey's Sexual Behavior in the Human Male: Some Comments and Criticisms," *Psychological Bulletin 45*, 1948, p. 449-450.
13. Terman, p. 450.
14. Terman quoted in Pomeroy, p. 247.
15. Terman quoted in Pomeroy, p. 293.
16. Paul Sheatsley and Herbert Hyman, "The Scientific Method," in Donald Porter Geddes, Ed., *An Analysis of the Kinsey Reports*, A Mentor Book, New York, 1954, p. 98.
17. Cornelia Christenson, *Kinsey: A Biography*, Indiana University, Bloomington, IN., 1971, p. 117.
18. Pomeroy, p. 144.
19. Christenson, p. 116.
20. Pomeroy, pp. 208, 211. In fact, in his 1949 testimony before the California legislature, Kinsey boasts that, "Our survey of sex offenders began 10 years ago, early in the research.... working rather closely with courts... [in] New York we have had constant contact over a long period of years.
21. Gebhard, *et al., Sex Offenders,* pp. 18, 27. The authors claim that between 1940 and 1945 they collected 37 percent of 888 men in a non-sex offender Indiana prison population.
22. Pomeroy, p. 83.
23. Pomeroy, p. 85.
24. Christenson, p. 135.
25. Pomeroy, p. 219.
26. Christenson, p. 135, and Pomeroy, p. 143.
27. Kinsey, Pomeroy, Martin and Gebhard, *Sexual Behavior in the Human Male*, W.B. Saunders Co., Philadelphia, 1948, pp. 13-16.
28. *Male*, p. 176.
29. *Male*, p. 78.
30. *Male*, p. 331.
31. Terman, p. 457.
32. *Male*, p. 93.
33. Laud Humphreys, *Tearoom Trade*, Aldine Publishing Company, New York, 1970, 1975. "Tearooms" are public toilets where homosexual males perform sex acts, often via "glory holes" drilled in the wall of the stalls to allow anonymous sodomy.
34. Pomeroy, p. 175.
35. Pomeroy, p. 176.
36. Pomeroy, p. 134..
37. Pomeroy, p. 78.
38. Pomeroy, p. 78. Pomeroy's explanation of Kinsey's care in not using the word "homosexuality" is in the original parenthesis.
39. Pomeroy, p. 75.
40. Pomeroy, p. 72.
41. Pomeroy, p. 70.
42. Christenson, p. 115.
43. Clyde Martin letter, responding to June Reinisch's December 12, 1990 request for aid in the author's archive.
44. Pomeroy, p. 62.
45. Pomeroy, p. 64.
46. On February 13, 1992 the author appeared as an expert witness before Georgia's Congressional Education Subcommittee. Upon viewing the child sexual abuse charts from Kinsey's *Male* volume, the Committee halted the mandated curriculum. Following an effort to inform legislators about the Kinsey frauds, the House voted 150-1 (and the Senate 48-6) to prohibit teaching youths about such illegal conduct as sodomy, adultery and fornication. However, since many Georgia teachers had been trained in AIDS prevention and sex education seminars to view any challenge to the Kinseyfied curriculum as, among other things, the work of sexually-repressed right-wing fundamentalists, the curriculum continued to surface in classrooms as Xeroxed pages utilized by such radicalized teachers.
47. Terman, p. 447.
48. Terman, p. 447.
49. *Male*, p. 77.
50. W. Allen Wallis, "Statistics of the Kinsey Report," *Journal of the American Statistical Association*, December 1949, p. 474-457.
51. *Male*, p. 77.
52. The Federal Bureau of Prisons, *1932 Report on Prison Education Programs: Activities and Purchases.*
53. *The Washington Post*, February 19, 1997, A1.
54. *The Washington Post*, May 4, 1990, C3. The Berendzen case received extensive press and television coverage, primarily due to the persistence of his victim in prosecuting the matter. He served no jail time and eventually returned to AU as a full professor. His victim

received no compensation and eventually moved from her neighborhood due to the trauma. The McGinnies case was reported only in the *Baltimore Evening Sun*, June 19, 1986, D16. For an account of the Sharp case, see the *Washington Post*, September 4, 1992, B1.

[55]. Pomeroy, p. 122.

[56]. *The Indianapolis Star*, "Kinsey Report May Be Flawed," September 19, 1995, A1, 4., Bancroft said "likely all based on sessions with lone elderly scientist."

[57]. Christenson, p. 116.

[58]. *Male*, p. 153.

[59]. Eberhard emigrated to the University of Minnesota from Berlin, Germany in 1945.

[60]. Drs. Phyllis and Eberhard Kronhausen, *Sex Histories of American College Men,* Ballantine Books, New York, 1960, p. 219.

[61]. Kronhausen, p. 255.

[62]. Kronhausen, p. 15.

[63]. Amy Ridenour, "Be Thankful for Dads," National Policy Analysis #252, National Center for Public Policy Research Analysis, June, 1999.

[64]. James Jones, *Alfred C. Kinsey; A Public/Private Life*, W.W. Norton, New York, 1997, p. 679.

[65]. Ridenour, op cit.

[66]. Turner, Miller, Modes, Ed. *AIDS, Sexual Behavior and Intravenous Drug Use*, The National Research Council, National Academy Press, Washington, D.C. 1989, p. 79.

CHAPTER 6

AMERICAN WOMEN: ELIMINATING MOTHERS

Not only is sex, in Dr. Kinsey's presentation, as meaningless as a sneeze, it is also equally unproductive.... It seems almost incredible, but is nevertheless true, that gestation, birth, and nursing of children are completely ignored. Motherhood, for Dr. Kinsey, has no sort of connection with sex.
Sociologist, Geoffrey Gorer, 1955[1]

Essentially, he [Kinsey] had characterized women as undersexed moralists who served as willing agents of social control.
James H. Jones, Kinsey biographer, 1997

Researching sexually aggressive people attracted Alfred Kinsey as he interviewed male prostitutes and other deviant men for *Sexual Behavior in the Human Male*. The *Female* volume was more of a challenge, since he was not particularly interested in women or their sexuality. He sought out similar unconventional types so that he could portray American girls, wives, and mothers as wildly sexual, though he actually believed otherwise. Jones writes,

> There can be little doubt that Kinsey would have preferred to follow the male volume with a major book on homosexuality or a study of sex offenders. For him, the personal had always been political. Yet he was enough of a realist to know that the public expected a volume on women to follow his book on men. The blows he wanted to strike on behalf of homosexuals would have to wait... Kinsey brought heavy baggage to the task.... In the male volume, Kinsey had made a number of digs that betrayed his attitude. Essentially, he had characterized women as undersexed moralists who served as willing agents of social control. Indeed, he had repeatedly discounted both their interest in sex and their capacity for high rates of sexual outlets.... He saw women as largely uninterested in sex, morally pure, and devoted to reforming men.... Kinsey believed that women were simply not as sexually responsive as men.[2]

Despite Kinsey's coming to maturity during the White Slave Trade days and knowing of the harm to a society when women were forced to support themselves by prostitution, the sex lives of normal women, whether married or single, held little interest for him. Indeed, as Jones notes, Kinsey was openly and aggressively antagonistic toward "prudish" women, as demonstrated by his boorish treatment of Indiana University Dean of Women Kate Mueller, who refused to force IU girls to answer his invasive, sexually intimate questions. In his quest to remove the

This photo of "innocent victims of the 'White Slave Trade'" appeared in *Fighting the Traffic in Young Girls* (1910).

stigma from abnormal sexual behavior in females, he claimed that his data scientifically proved the "normality" among women of numerous outlawed sexual behaviors.

Sociologist Geoffrey Gorer observed that, while the Kinsey charts detailed the demographic background of his female population (age, religion, marital status, residence, etc.), important data (especially regarding childbirth and comparisons between childless, single, married, and fertile women) were strangely absent.

> In the tables on the behavior of married women, we are told on all occasions the amount of their education, their age, and their relative religious devoutness; but not in a single table are we informed whether they be sterile or fertile, whether they have living children or no. Even from the sociological point of view, one would expect interesting and consistent differences in adultery and other post-marital carryings-on between the mothers and the childless.[3]

Yet, true to the nature of the academic enterprise at that time, even Gorer seemed to view these missing data as sloppy, disinterested or, at worst, perhaps misogynist work. Somewhat stunned, Gorer adds: "Consider the implications of this passage! The link between intercourse and procreation is either purely intellectual, or else excretory!"[4]

The Kinsey team allegedly recorded the sexual conduct of 7,789 total women in their sample, but the only births recorded were from *single* women, *unmarried* women and children borne through *adulterous* unions; as in the graph shown here.

Kinsey gave no data on normal marital birth, no data on normal mothers. By examining hundreds of charts, tables and narratives in the *Female* volume, one can patch together three rather cryptic citations describing 476 single mothers, 333 premarital pregnancies and 16 adulterous pregnancies,[5] but Kinsey provided no data on whether these babies lived or were aborted, or how these pregnancies affected the lives of the mothers—even sexually. As a "taxonomic classification," any babies or children in the Reports appear only as sexual subjects, that is, as potential sex "partners" for adults and other children.[6]

None Of Kinsey's 7,789 Interviewees Are Defined as Normal Mothers
Facilitating Arguments to End "Fornication" Laws

Total Women	7,789 Interviewees
Single White Pregnancies	476 ("Illicit")
PreNuptial Moms	333 ("Illicit")
Adulterous Moms	16 ("Illicit")
Married Moms	0 legitimate Births

10% Are Perhaps Mothers, Unwed, Adulterous, Premarital, pp. 22, 327, 434, 434.

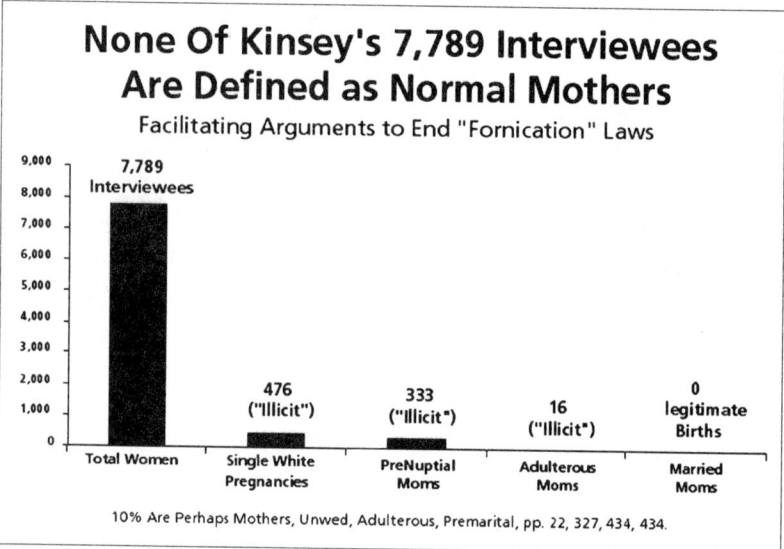

In report above, none of Kinsey's subjects are found to be normal mothers.

Females of any age—children, married, or mothers—were presented as largely sexually promiscuous. Since the Kinsey data was to present American women as sexually indiscriminate, the data had to also present no negative consequences to promiscuity. Thus Kinsey's *Sexual Behavior in the Human Female* did not report any complicating factors attendant to widespread recreational sex practiced by his female population. Rape, jealousy, venereal disease, pregnancy, out-of-wedlock birth, and abortion are largely non-existent in the Kinsey data. Thus, Kinsey created the possibility of a carefree, aggressive female sexuality. Perhaps the most damaging outcome to be based on Kinsey's fraudulent data was the myth that women could, and should, separate responsibility and commitment from sex and sex from fertility and childbirth.

THE FEMALE DATA

Rather callously Kinsey claimed to have found sexual abuse of young girls to be harmless, claiming that adult women were *never* traumatized by childhood sexual abuse and incest. Of 4,441 females interviewed about adult-child sex, he reported that 1,075 (24 percent) had been "sexually approached" in childhood. He claimed:

> [W]e have only one clear-cut case of serious injury done to the child, and a very few instances of vaginal bleeding which, however, did not appear to do any appreciable damage.[7]

The Kinsey team claimed that by January 1, 1950, it had secured data from 7,789 females (p. 22) between "two to ninety years" (p. 31), including 216 minors (calculated from the school-age and underage girls on p. 32), and seven girls who were apparently under the age of four (p. 105). Further, 1,849 (24 percent) were removed from the non-random sample because they were either nonwhite (934 (12 percent)) or prison inmates (915 (11.7 percent)) (p. 22). Some of these subjects, as we shall see, may have been returned to the sample when their data proved particularly useful in promoting Kinsey's "grand scheme."[8]

Until recently, it was assumed that the 5,940 females formally selected for the survey were young, white, middle-class, and well educated. To the contrary, 147 subjects are described as "preadolescent," ranging in age from two to 15 years, while the remainder are categorized as "adolescent and adult females," ranging in age from 11 to more than 70 years. At a minimum, 69 other minors were recorded as 16 to 18 years of age (p. 32). It appears, then, that roughly one-half of the respondents (3,051) were ages 16 to 25, with the greatest number between 16 and 35 (4,342 (73 percent)). This is hardly representative of age distribution for the American female population.

Lumping unrelated groups of young girls and elderly women into one massive group is inexcusable. Kinsey contended that his technique for collecting "human material" did not differ from that employed by public opinion pollsters to predict a group's behavior. One would be hard pressed, however, to find a polling organization that would lump infants with sexagenarians (and older) to predict an election.

What Did Kinsey Say About Child Sex Abuse?

4,441 Interviewees

"only one clear-cut case of serious injury ... a very few instances of vaginal bleeding .... Did not appear to do any appreciable damage."

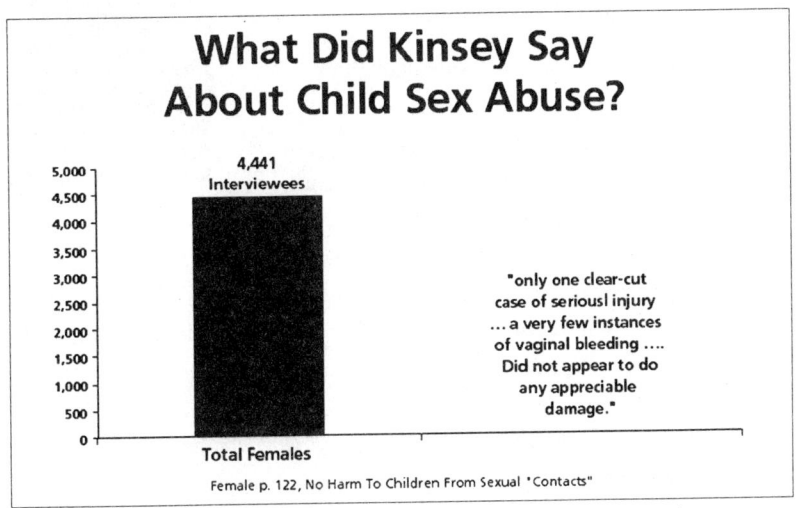

Total Females

Female p. 122, No Harm To Children From Sexual "Contacts"

It is surprising that scientists accepted these data, and even more so that its authors are today reputable sources for sex education in the nation's schools.

AMERICAN WOMEN: ELIMINATING MOTHERS

DEFINING "MARRIED"

There are no data in the entire 842 pages of *Sexual Behavior in the Human Female* that identify the percentage of women who were *legally married*. According to the report, 1,695 (30 percent) of those interviewed were (or had been) married, including 785 who were also "widowed, separated, or divorced." To make it appear that the sample included a large married population, an ambiguous definition of "married" was adopted:

> **Marital Status.** In most calculations in this volume, sexual activities have been classified as occurring among single, married, or previously married females. Individuals were identified as single up to the time they were first married. *They were identified as married if they were living with their spouses either in formally consummated legal marriages, or in common-law relationships which had lasted for at least a year.* They were classified as previously married if they were no longer living with a spouse because they were widowed, divorced, or permanently separated. These definitions are more or less in accord with those in the US Census for 1950, *except that common-law relationships have been more frequently accepted as marriages in our data*, and we have considered any permanent separation of spouses the equivalent of a divorce.[9] [Emphasis added.]

The Indiana University graduation photo of a coed reading Sexual Behavior in the Human Male *suggests the future influence of Kinsey's fraudulent data.* (*Arbutus*)

With "married" women redefined to include those who had lived with a man in a relationship "which had lasted for at least a year," Kinsey's female data would be, in the vernacular, off the charts. None of the minimum standards established by states in which common-law marriages were legal during that era were included. For instance, states that *did* tolerate common-law marriage required that the couple hold themselves out to the community as married for a number of years, and "implicit in the relationship is an understanding that a marital arrangement exists."[10] Kinsey ignored that standard, including as "married" a group of sexually radical women "cohabiting" with men at a time when that unstable lifestyle was rare and socially unacceptable. There was

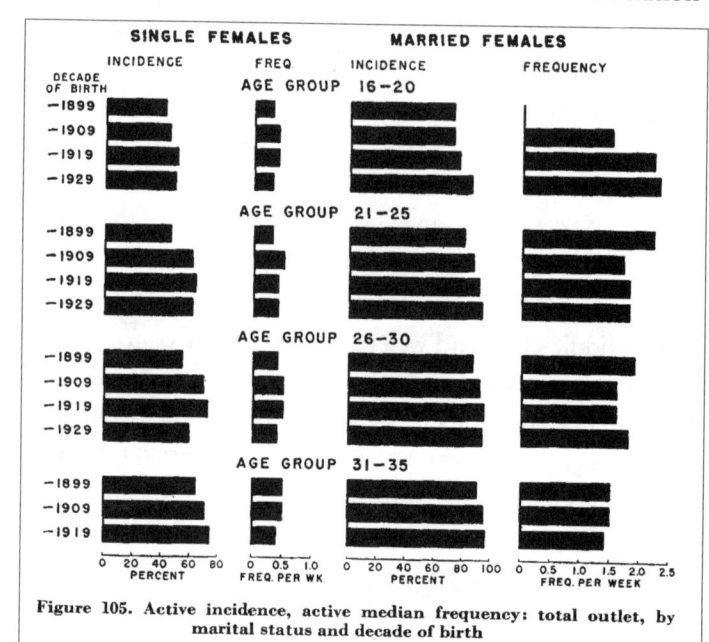

Figure 105. Active incidence, active median frequency: total outlet, by marital status and decade of birth
Data from Table 160.

The Kinsey team writes of "active incidence" for "orgasm" by "marital status" as if the women charted above were normal "married" women. Based on the Kinsey definition, these women were neither normal nor married. Kinsey's claim that their data were "more or less in accord with... the U.S. Census for 1950" also was invalid.

no requirement of a definitive "marital arrangement."[11]

Even today, the sexual behavior of couples cohabiting without benefit of matrimony differs in statistically significant ways from that of couples who marry. Also, married mothers differ significantly from women in looser arrangements. In the 1940s and 1950s, only the most radical and sexually "liberated" women cohabited with men. The strong pre-Kinsey laws protecting women and marriage labeled premarital sexual activity "fornication," or cohabitation. It was punishable by fines and/or imprisonment in 35 states, while tolerated in only 13 states.[12] Even by 1996, fornication and cohabitation remained legal offenses in 19 states.[13]

"Four authorities on female sex are (*left to right*) Wardell Pomery, Paul Gebhard, Dr. Kinsey and Clyde Martin. These four did all the questioning, hence presumably know more about women than any other men in the world." (*Life Magazine*, August 24, 1953, p. 48)

Melding three such distinct groups into one may have been *politically* expedient, but it was scientifically and taxonomically unjustified. Why would Kinsey do it? The Kinsey team well knew that classifying an unwed, yearlong sexual relationship (with or without fidelity) as "marriage" would *inflate* the married and adulterous databases while *reducing* the number of single and chaste subjects. Kinsey's definition of "married" indicates that the team had such a dearth of legally married women that it was forced to artificially inflate the married population. So few *normal* married women would talk to Kinsey and his interviewers that the team depicted untold numbers of sexually unconventional women as "married."

Since the Kinsey team did not insist that a "married" woman be limited to one man, its definition of "married" could encompass prostitutes living with their pimps. Indeed, virtually the entire "married" population could have been prostitutes, since Kinsey actively sought out, paid, and worked with subjects belonging to that category.[14] Berkeley University's Judson Landis notes the apparent influence of prostitutes on Kinsey's findings:

> A careful reading of the book, especially the chapter on premarital petting, emphasizes the fact that types of behavior that seem to approach the behavior of prostitutes were largely reported by one group of women—those who had more than 25 experiences and in most cases with many partners. It is the record of this group, when included along with the other groups, that skews the findings concerning types of behavior, just as inclusion of the atypical group discussed above skews findings in percentages of premarital and extramarital activity.[15]

By mixing in prostitutes, Kinsey was able to present sexual promiscuity as "normal," including perversions such as sex with animals. Although he excluded 934 black women as unrepresentative of that population, he *included* 31 females who copulated with animals. (In the *Male* book, he had all but recommended bestiality for lonely boys.)

AMERICAN WOMEN: ELIMINATING MOTHERS

Kinsey's attempt to normalize bestiality has surfaced in sex education and pornography, including Kinsey co-author Wardell Pomeroy's bestselling sex education text, *Boys and Sex*:[16]

> [Having sex with] the male animal, whether it is a dog, horse, bull, or some other species, may provide considerable erotic excitement for the boy or older adult.... His enjoyment of the relationship is enhanced by the fact that the male animal responds to the point of orgasm....
>
> Psychically, animal relations may become of considerable significance to the boy who is having regular experience... [and] in no point basically different from those that are involved in erotic responses to human situations.[17]

Kinsey, Pomeroy, and Martin essentially held that "sexual contacts between the human and animals of other species are at no point basically different from those that are involved in erotic responses to human situations."[18] This gives perspective to the disordered admissions of Kinsey colleague Dr. Clarence Tripp during his interview for the August 1998 Yorkshire documentary "Kinsey Paedophiles." Dr. Tripp, sexologist and psychologist-author of *The Homosexual Matrix* (1975), candidly stated,

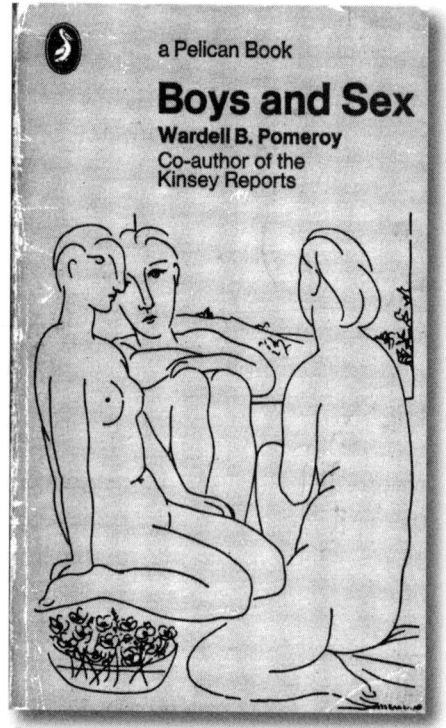

Pomeroy's books *Girls and Sex* and *Boys and Sex* are recommended by Planned Parenthood and SIECUS. Both books are used nationwide in public, private, and parochial schools as basic sex-education texts.

> *If you go out and masturbate dogs—I was very good at this when I was a boy*—the dog will love you to pieces because the dog has no efficient way to masturbate. He loves the orgasm as much as anybody else but he can't self-produce it. Now you just do this a time or two. The dogs do various... things. You try this on all the neighborhood dogs.... Some dogs will always expect or try to talk you into doing it.... Other dogs will come to any human and say, please touch me here in a certain kind of way.

That snippet from the interview was not broadcast, but the documentation is in this author's archive.

Kinsey seemed disappointed by the minuscule number of girls in his sample who had engaged in sex with "other animals:"

> [M]any of the farm-bred females had been oblivious to the coital activities which went on about them [and] had not learned that coitus was possible in any animal, let alone the human, until they were adolescent or still older. As a result, the animal contacts which the females had made were usually the consequence of their own discovery of such possibilities, whether the first experiences were had in preadolescence or in more adult years. Most of the farm boys had acquired that much information some years before adolescence.... Among the 659 females in the total sample who had reached orgasm prior to adolescence, 1.7 per cent had experienced their first orgasm in contact

with other species of animals.... Among adult females, some 3.6 per cent of the females in the sample had had sexual contacts of some sort with animals of other species after they had become adolescent.[19]

The team also identified subject units of "burlesque performers," models, artists, and "taxi dancers" (strippers).[20] The discrepancies between the real world and the Kinsey data are apparent at every turn. Sociologist Herbert Hyman points out a "striking deficiency" in Kinsey's use of the scientific method:

> Perhaps the most striking deficiency is the failure to interview enough females with no more than a grammar school education [sic]... [A] tiny three percent of the women interviewed had not attended high school.... [S]eventy-five percent of the total female sample had attended college, and a surprising nineteen percent—practically one woman in five—had gone on to postgraduate work. A rather unique group to sample so heavily and without apparent reason... [T]hree-fourths of his sample was composed of the thirteen percent of American women who have gone to college... the forty percent who never went beyond the eighth grade comprised only three percent of those he studied.... [While] Jews represent only about four percent of the U.S. population, they account for more than one quarter of Kinsey's sample.... No figures are given on the proportion of "refusals" to be interviewed.[21]

Merely correcting the population distribution, however, would not have solved Kinsey's data problems. Conventional, normal females *did not*, as Maslow had pointed out to Kinsey, voluntarily report their most intimate thoughts and acts. *Normal* American women and girls would understandably register the highest proportion of refusals.

CENSORING MASLOW

Many authors have criticized the non-random sample for the *Female* volume, noting that it does not accurately reflect American female sexuality.[22] Hyman and Sheatsley commented,

> It remains a fact that neither his sample of men nor that of women accurately represents even the whole population of this one nation, and both combined are far from a representative picture of the "human male and female." Some critics have condemned the whole sampling design, arguing that a more systematic and precise method could have been devised which would have permitted unqualified statements about the population as a whole.[23]

As noted earlier, renowned psychologist Abraham Maslow of Rutgers University published an article in 1952 criticizing the Kinsey data. That critique does not appear in Kinsey's extensive bibliography, but an earlier (1942), favorable article by Maslow *is* included. Maslow's 1952 paper has also been censored from other human sexuality literature.

Few of the typical IU coeds (pictured) answered Kinsey's questions. One California coed who did, reported she felt "raped," and that the interview negatively affected her for years thereafter.

AMERICAN WOMEN: ELIMINATING MOTHERS

Coauthored by James M. Sakoda, the paper was entitled "Volunteer-Error in the Kinsey Study." Maslow and Sakoda exposed Kinsey's entire female research population as a self-selected, dominant, sexually unconventional, and atypical group of subjects. Their tone was remorseful, since they shared Kinsey's desire for greater sexual license. They published the paper only because Kinsey declined to correct his volunteer errors. Approximately 90 percent of the sex-research volunteers tended to be what Maslow and Sakoda labeled "high self-esteem groups," while 10 percent fell into the "low self-esteem group." An extremely high proportion of the "low self-esteem subjects" were virgins, non-masturbators, and low in unconventional sexual attitude, especially oral-genital behavior.[24]

Maslow and Sakoda correlated the sexually unfettered behavior of what they termed "high dominance" women with feelings of high self-esteem. Whether this correctly portrays the anti-conventional women of the era is not at issue here. Rather, based on Maslow's decades of research on dominance-feeling and sexuality in women, he had identified such qualities as atypical and outside the norm. As noted earlier, he had volunteered to assist Kinsey in developing a valid research sample. Concerned about serious volunteer error, he had urged Kinsey to conduct sample surveys prior to analyzing and releasing the *Female* volume. Kinsey agreed to cooperate, but never did. For Maslow, correcting for volunteer error was imperative:

> These considerations were urged upon Dr. Kinsey about five or six years ago [1946 or 1947] since his now well-known research at that time rested almost entirely on data derived from volunteers. A crucial experiment was jointly designed and executed by Dr. Kinsey and Maslow to employ the self-esteem test to evaluate the extent of the volunteer-error in Dr. Kinsey's study and to check on the correlations between self-esteem and sexual behavior which had been found previously.... The second part of the experimental design which was to test the correlation between self-esteem score and sexual behavior in Dr. Kinsey's subjects has not been reported to date by Dr. Kinsey.[25]

Based on their own research, and other studies on "volunteer-error" in sex research, Maslow and Sakoda concluded that young women with histories of unconventional (radical) sexual behavior would volunteer for the sex studies, while those whose histories were conventional (the norm) would generally not participate. They also warned that while the timid and those especially vulnerable to pressure might participate, they would be inclined to give answers intended to please interviewers. Despite Kinsey's claims to the contrary, the personalities of female sex volunteers correlated with unconventional sexual behavior. According to Maslow and Sakoda, "When subjects are selected by any procedure other than random sampling, the possibility of systematic bias in selection must be considered."[26] When validating one of his own studies on female sexuality,

> [Maslow] had used volunteers for the study and stumbled across the disquieting fact that: (a) the volunteers were predominantly high in self-esteem (i.e., self-confident, sure of themselves, forward), and (b) the score of those high in self-esteem differed considerably from the score of those low in self-esteem in their sexual behavior.

> The self-esteem score correlated with unconventional sex attitude .71, with virginity .66, and with masturbation .41. To correct for the volunteer-error a special effort was made to obtain subjects who were low in self-esteem score. In addition, a simple statistical technique for correcting for volunteer-error was utilized and described in this paper.[27]

Maslow and Sakoda hoped that the so-called "100 percent sample groups" Kinsey was seeking might offset the students' unconventional ratio set. It never seemed to occur to them, however, that the 100 percent ratio also applied to groups of prostitutes, "burlesque performers," models, artists, and "taxi dancers." Indeed, the key problems with the study seemed to escape most critics. Kinsey listed in alphabetical order the categories he claimed to have interviewed. Included were missionaries, Salvation Army workers, and a large variety of groups, clubs, high school students, and the like. Though the groups were listed, Kinsey did not in fact receive cooperation from many of the individuals involved.

For instance, while he claimed to have interviewed grade school students and high school students from both public and private schools, only 147 girls from birth to age 15 are included in his final report—hardly representative of the thousands allegedly interviewed.[28]

Kinsey published a five-page list of "Occupations of Female Subjects," but were the list reliable, it means nothing statistically if, for example, he interviewed one architect, one auditor, one acrobat, one artist, etc.

Maslow warned that Kinsey's findings would inflate "the percentage reporting unconventional or disapproved sexual behavior—such as masturbation, oral sexuality, petting to climax, premarital and extramarital intercourse."[29] As we have seen, Kinsey questioned thousands of incarcerated and unfettered sex offenders and homosexual males about their behavior, then reported to the world that most men engaged in high rates of homosexual activity and other sexual crimes. The Kinsey team continued in a similar vein for the *Female* volume, allegedly questioning thousands of non-virgins and other sexually unconventional females who reported that they engaged in premarital sex, masturbation, and oral sodomy. Kinsey then told the world that most women engaged in high rates of premarital sex, adultery, masturbation, and oral sodomy and that sexually happy and orgasmic women sleep in the nude.

The Kinsey team also claimed that women with high school "backgrounds" are not "materially" different from college women.[30] The demographic evidence revealed that single, non-college females typically lived close to home and were significantly more conventional in the late 1940s than were their college sisters, who might live far from parental authority and influence. But were such non-college women barmaids and "taxi dancers," or secretaries and beauticians?[31]

Maslow predicted that sex survey volunteers would resemble the college sexual radicals. What would the sexually unconventional ratio be across Kinsey's entire female sample? The Kinsey team stated,

> The inadequacy of the educational distribution in the sample would be more serious if we had found that educational backgrounds affect the sexual patterns of females. . . . Comparisons of our high school, college, and graduate school samples of females show few differences in the behavior of these three groups; but our limited samples of the grade school group suggest that their sexual behavior may be more different.[32]

Let us momentarily disregard Simon's report that the total coded population was only about 4,500 (see footnote 8). Accepting that thousands of the 5,940 women *allegedly* interviewed would have

A Madison-Avenue style publicity campaign blanketed the nation for Kinsey's Female Report.

AMERICAN WOMEN: ELIMINATING MOTHERS

been atypical, with the remaining "conventional" females including at least 216 minors aged two to 18,[33] the Kinsey report might have contained a minute number of conventional adult women. Whether such women spoke candidly (if at all), and whether Kinsey recorded and transcribed their accounts honestly, depends on one's confidence in the veracity of his research team.

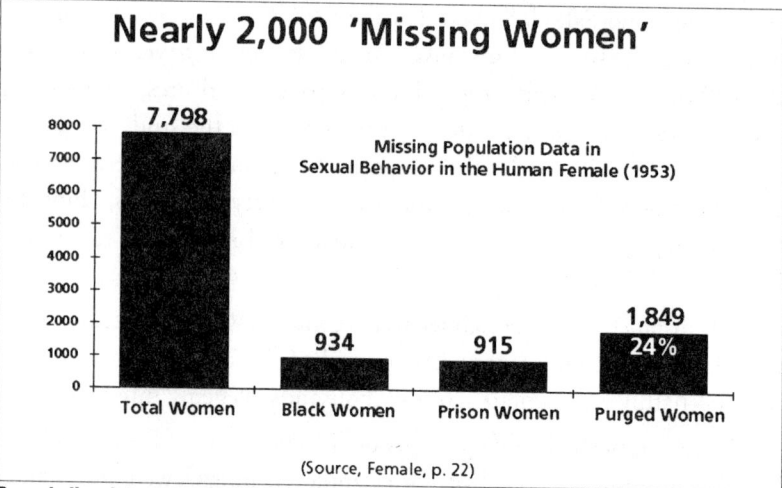

Nearly 2,000 'Missing Women'

Missing Population Data in Sexual Behavior in the Human Female (1953)

Total Women	7,798
Black Women	934
Prison Women	915
Purged Women	1,849 (24%)

(Source, Female, p. 22)

By excluding data on nearly 2,000 women comprising the two populations having the highest rate of early sexual activity, Kinsey censored the data on its injury, thereby conjuring up support for eliminating or "lightening" child protection laws, and for legalizing obscenity and other vices.

If 3,460 women were single and generally "unconventional" college volunteers, what percentage of the remaining 2,480 were normal? In addition to prostitutes and common-law volunteers, Kinsey's normal, "married" group included staff members, wives, children, friends, and colleagues of the Kinsey team. Some had already been filmed in sex scenes, and as Pomeroy has stated, "[N]o one could have come to work for Kinsey without giving his history first. It was a condition of employment which a few employees in the lower echelons resented."[34]

Such coercive personal association would raise questions about the validity of *any* findings, much less those relating to a sexually sensitive study.

WHY EXCLUDE FEMALE PRISONERS?

The removal of prison inmates from the female sample stands in stark contrast to the inclusion of male prisoners in Kinsey's initial report. The use of male prisoners had been criticized, but Pomeroy later explained that they had been included because Kinsey considered them to be no different than the general population:

> We were under attack at different times from people who insisted that we should not have included in our [male] sample the history of anyone who had ever been in a penal institution. That, as Kinsey liked to point out was based on the old fallacy that criminals are made of different stuff from the rest of the population.[35]

Gebhard later revealed in the Kinsey team's 1965 book, *Sex Offenders: An Analysis of Types*, what Kinsey and the world knew all along: the "old fallacy" was quite true. The prison population did indeed differ significantly from the non-prison population.[36] At least 1,400 sex offenders in the Kinsey sample were sex predators; many were child molesters. By *including* male prisoners (offenders) and *excluding* female prisoners (many of them victims), Kinsey could *increase* reports of favorable sexual acts between children and male adults, and *decrease* reports of harm resulting from adult sexual assaults on children. While incarcerated child rapists would usually describe their crimes as harmless, the testimony of incarcerated male or female victims of child rape would "have seriously distorted the calculations" on harm from adult-child sex.[37]

A low incidence of the former (harmful outcomes from adult sexual abuse of girls), and overemphasis of the latter (beneficial outcomes from adult sexual abuse of boys and girls), are aspects of both Kinsey reports. We now know that incest victims, and sexually abused boys and girls, are prone to respond to their abuse by resorting to drugs, prostitution, crime in general, and are subject to lifelong trauma and failure.[38]

While including unincarcerated prostitutes as married or single women in the *Female* report, the Kinsey team *excluded* the 915 felons who were imprisoned primarily for prostitution. Kinsey writes,

In 1965, Paul Gebhard gave the Kinsey team's data an additional boost with publication of *Sexual Offenders: An Analysis of Types*.

> To date, we have secured the histories of 7,789 females and of 8,603 males. Our more general information and thinking on female sexual behavior are based on this entire body of material, even though the statistical analyses have been restricted to a portion of the female sample. Because the sexual histories which we have of white females who had served prison sentences (915 cases) prove, upon analysis, to differ as a group from the histories of the females who have not become involved with the law, their inclusion in the present volume would have seriously distorted the calculations on the total sample. Neither has the nonwhite sample (934 cases) of females been included in the calculations, primarily because that sample is not large enough to warrant comparisons of the subgroups in it. The statistical analyses in the present volume have, therefore, been based on our 5,940 cases of white, non-prison females. In order to standardize the statistical calculations, histories acquired since January 1, 1950, have not been used.[39]

Nevertheless, Kinsey included information from imprisoned prostitutes here and there (e.g., their rates of adultery, early sex, and higher tolerance for oral sodomy) while excluding other pertinent information (e.g., early rape by kin and non-kin, the relationship of such abuse to their lives of crime, and other dysfunctions).[40] Gebhard stated in 1979 that "he [Kinsey] agreed to omit prison females from *almost* all of the volume...."[41] [Emphasis added.] Moreover, on page 75 Kinsey writes, "Table [5] is based on all available paired spouses, including both white and Negro, and both prison and non-prison histories." Since the database held no more than "706

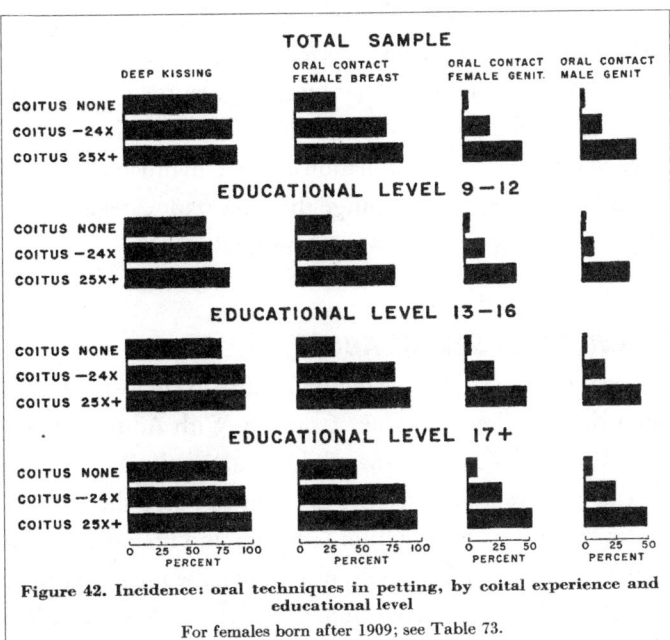

Figure 42. Incidence: oral techniques in petting, by coital experience and educational level
For females born after 1909; see Table 73.

Kinsey's data claiming that oral sodomy was common among well-educated, sexually-experienced females–with no untoward consequences–helped promote the acceptance of what had been understood as perversion as "normal."

AMERICAN WOMEN: ELIMINATING MOTHERS

Paired Spouses," it seems clear that some were married, common-law, black, prisoners, and so on.

Kinsey's warped data arguably triggered the increasing acceptance of homosexual sex acts (oral sodomy) among American women and girls. Kinsey's "Figure 42" suggested that up to 50 percent of sexually active women engaged in oral sodomy as a sexual "variation." [42] His vague narrative suggested that while rates were low (2 percent) among the chaste, "38 percent to 43 percent" of his allegedly average female coital group had engaged in oral sodomy.

Today, the promotion of oral and anal sodomy is encouraged by Kinseyan-trained school teachers and marriage counselors. *Playboy* currently markets a buxom blonde female video demonstration of both for the mail-order catalogue market. Ads subtly simulating sodomy have even appeared on the covers of some women's magazines at the grocery checkout counter. In the 1940s, even prostitutes were paid extra to perform such acts. Histories of prostitution reveal that oral sodomy paid well because such conduct was viewed as repugnant and involved humiliating postures of subjugation. A recent scholarly homosexual history, *Gay New York*, noted,

> [The] Committee of Fourteen investigators regularly reported that even prostitutes were unwilling to engage in oral sex; see for example, the reports on [a series of "tenement" house numbers were cited here, including the month, day and year for 1927 and 1928.][43]

Even major critics of Kinsey's *Female* volume, such as psychiatrists Edmund Bergler and gynecologist William Kroger (*Kinsey's Myth of Female Sexuality* (1954)[44]), failed to perceive the implications of Kinsey's definition of prostitutes as "married," and other data manipulations. They did not, for instance, address Kinsey's dubious child sex abuse, incest, or sodomy data, opting to focus instead on more Freudian psychiatric issues such as "frigidity" and vaginal versus clitoral orgasm.

WHY EXCLUDE "NONWHITE" WOMEN?

Kinsey also eliminated data collected from 934 black women. Information about black college women would have revealed many hard-working, churchgoing families with parents who had struggled to provide their daughters a college education. Elsewhere, we document Kinsey's racial bias, including his belief that the black population engaged in much more "uninhibited" sex than did the white population. Why, then, did he purge the important category of black college women from his database? Did they give "wrong" answers to his questions?

HIDING CHILD SEXUAL ABUSE

The claim that the data were purged due to small sample size is refuted by Kinsey himself. In the discussion of "Pre-Adolescent Contacts With Adult Males; Incidence and Frequency of Contacts with Adults,"[45] he claims that child sexual victimizations are harmless. A strong pro-pedophile bias appears to have influenced the decision to purge the data about poor black women and prisoners. The subjects were largely from fatherless and unconventional homes with a high incidence of early sexual experience. Conversely, black college women may have been purged due to a high percentage of biological fathers in their homes, therefore a lower incidence of early sexual activity.

The Kinsey team describes sexual "contacts" between children and adults, speculating that such incidents of abuse appear to have occurred,

In 1952 *Ebony*, the most popular black magazine of the time, mailed a sex questionnaire to Negro college students and found "much lower rates" of non-marital sex than did Kinsey. Kinsey said this was due to "more cover up" for he had "more rapport" with black women than did *Ebony*. (Pomeroy, p. 225) (*Arbutus*). (Indiana University black sorority above).

in poorer city communities where the population was densely crowded in tenement districts.... We would have found higher incidences of preadolescent contacts with adults if we had more cases from lower educational groups, or if we had included the data which we have on females who had served penal sentences, and on Negro females. These latter groups, however, were excluded from the calculations... [because they] would have *seriously distorted the calculations* on the total sample.[46] [Emphasis added.]

This statement is an amazing admission of bigotry and open disdain for both the black community and the well-being of children. If the data showed that the poorer "tenement" black community was experiencing higher levels of early child sex abuse and greater dysfunction, why did Kinsey hide this information? Was it not essential to inform the poor black community—in 1948 and again in 1953—of the need to protect their children from sex abuse, and to urge judges to disallow parole for convicted child abusers? Was it not imperative for black parents to know that sexual abuse of their children could lead to a life of crime, drugs, homosexuality, and/or prostitution?

If a large number of imprisoned women were victims of early child sex abuse, as confirmed by the literature on child abuse and prostitution,[47] then early sexual abuse is implicated as a causative factor in creating female felons. Why wasn't the nation told? Why would Jones, Pomeroy, and Christenson testify that Kinsey would "weep" for sex offenders in prison, even as he was purging the testimony of child-abuse victims from his data? From his 18,000 alleged interviews of women and men, Kinsey tallied only *one* possible child abuse victim.[48]

Post-Kinsey Trends in Child Abuse And Neglect 1950-1986

Source, 1976-1982, Trends in Child Abuse and Neglect, The American Humane Association, p. 13; 1986 Datum, Study Findings, National Incidence and Prevention of Child Abuse and Neglect, 1988, US Dpt. of HHS, p. 3-11

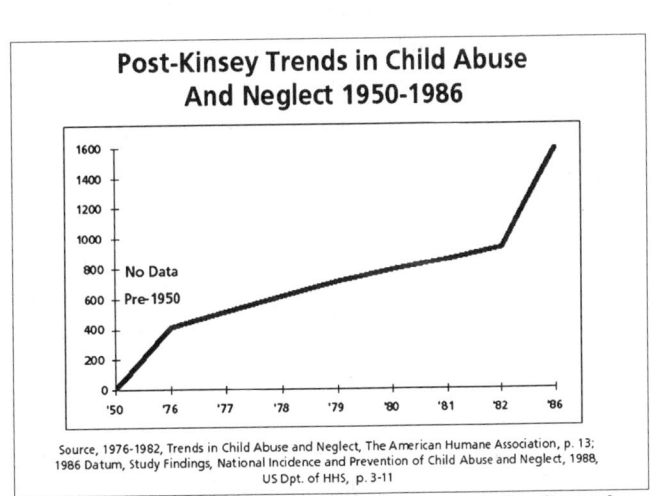

The post-Kinsey era spirals upward in virtually every area of sociosexual disorder.

AMERICAN WOMEN: ELIMINATING MOTHERS

NOTHING ABOUT ABORTION OR NARCOTICS

Kinsey said little about obscenity, venereal disease, pregnancy or abortion, and nothing about the use of drugs by prostitutes. He has nevertheless been credited by some with instigating the legalization of abortion by providing data purporting to show that nearly all pregnant single women, and 22% of those married, secured abortions despite existing statutes barring the procedure. Since the women he interviewed were so "sexually active," he and his team sought to portray abortion as so common and harmless that it should be legal.

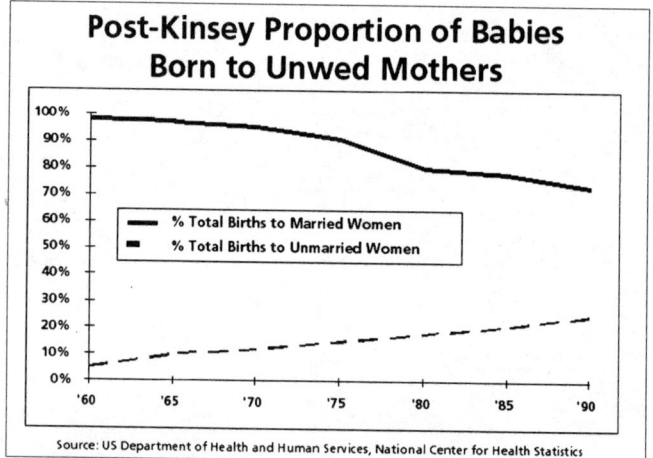

Post-Kinsey Proportion of Babies Born to Unwed Mothers

Source: US Department of Health and Human Services, National Center for Health Statistics

Post-Kinsey "sexual freedom" was accompanied by a nearly sixfold upward surge in "illegitimacy" between 1960 and 1990, despite the widespread availability of abortion (after 1973) as well as inexpensive contraception.

The most "sexually active" women were and are prostitutes, who are also major abortion and drug customers. Law enforcement was engaged in a major attack on the narcotics trade during Kinsey's survey period. Narcotics were rife among the "underworld" figures from whom Kinsey sought sex histories. Even Kinsey's good friend Harry Benjamin, who refers to the pedophile judge Rene Guyon as "the great Frenchman,"[49] admits in his book *Prostitution and Morality* (1965):

> Some young addicts become "street-walkers" at ten, twelve, fifteen. So far as we have been able to determine most young prostitute-addicts are members of impoverished families, and usually of minority groups such as Negroes, Puerto Ricans, etc. The vast majority are to be found in a few large cities…. [Researchers declare] approximately 50 per cent of all prostitutes are addicts. Other estimates have ranged as high as 75 per cent.[50]

While the Kinsey team spent a massive amount of time discussing the use of prostitutes by men, and interviewed hundreds of male and female prostitutes, they said nothing about the consequences of prostitution, such as sexually transmitted diseases (STDs), drug addiction, battery, murder and suicide. Benjamin and Masters, after describing the horrors of prostitution and extensively citing Kinsey's interviews with prostitutes, *called for legalizing prostitution as an outlet for men!*

Kinsey largely whitewashed the drug-violence-prostitution connection. Though Benjamin and Masters also trivialize drug and alcohol use by prostitutes, they describe what the Kinsey team must have learned from their in-depth interviews:

> An unknown number of the drug addicts [prostitutes] are murdered by "pushers" by means of the "hot shot," an overdose of heroin, or narcotics laced with strychnine or some other lethal poison. According to addicts, such murders are numerous, but they seem almost never to be mentioned in the newspaper. The addicts explain this by saying that the police policy is to consider "a dead junkie, good riddance."[51]

Such murders are numerous in "the trade," but they are never mentioned in *Sexual Behavior in the Human Male* or *Sexual Behavior in the Human Female*. Kinsey specialized in collecting histories from poverty-ridden areas of New York City and Chicago. Yet he makes no mention of the STD's, alcoholism, drug addiction, pregnancy, abortion, homosexuality, battery, and murder common among 200 male, and an unknown number of female prostitutes. There is no mention of the causes of prostitution or of drug use in the *Female* volume and only two citations in the index for the *Male* volume. One citation explains that some men have sexual problems when they are denied a drug to which they have become addicted.[52] The other assures the reader that,

> Persons who are under the immediate influence of drugs, particularly of some narcotic that induces sleep, are impossible as subjects. A person who is heavily intoxicated with marijuana (which is not a drug) [sic.] is similarly unreliable.[53]

MARITAL ORGASM DATA

One of the more bizarre figures cited in the *Female* volume is a high rate of *marital* orgasm satisfaction. Jones reports that Kinsey was committed to showing females to be as sexually aggressive as males. Kinsey claimed that 75 percent of the "married" subjects reached orgasm "within the first year of marriage" (during 63 percent of their marital coitus), increasing "to 90 percent" after twenty years of marriage[54] (see accompanying graph, reproduced from the *Female* report.)

Kinsey seemed to be disappointed by the figures, however, since "[a]t fifty years of age... only 93 per cent of the females reported coitus. By sixty years of age the record included 94 per cent of the males in contrast to 80 per cent of the females."[55]

Kinsey's apocryphal data on children, homosexuality, masturbation, sodomy, etc. are continually quoted and referenced in sexuality literature; in secular, parochial and religious journals; and in reports, lectures, tapes, and textbooks. Why then, are his equally questionable findings regarding high rates of pleasurable marital coitus almost never quoted or referenced by sexologists?

Texts, for example, seldom mention the "90 percent" marital orgasm rate after 20 years of marriage. Sex education books ignore it, and the data have even disappeared from the "Blue Book" on Kinsey: *The Kinsey Data: Marginal Tabulations of the 1938-1963 Interviews Conducted by the Institute for Sex Research*.[56] Tables reflecting bizarre types of orgasm by age, year, and place are prominently displayed, but there is no reference to marital orgasm in this work by Kinseyans Gebhard and Johnson. A key issue of American family life, *the satisfaction of married women* as calculated by rates of "orgasm," is conspicuously missing.[57]

Kinsey's revolutionary focus on "orgasm" to measure sexual, marital, dating, and general emotional satisfaction, has become so accepted in the Western world that it is no longer questioned. Yet, while there is a body of literature confirming that orgasm is helpful in marriage, it has never been shown to be a valid measure of sexual success or marital bliss. The data on pedophiles, rapists, and rapist-murderers[58] indicate that while the perpetrators commonly began "petting" to

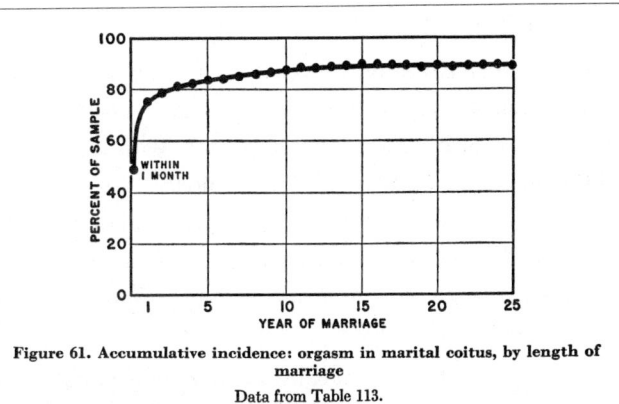

Figure 61. Accumulative incidence: orgasm in marital coitus, by length of marriage
Data from Table 113.

Marital "orgasm" data from Kinsey's *Female* volume, p. 352. It alleges virtually immediate "orgasm" among the supposedly inhibited female population, contradicting Kinsey's claim that our traditional approach to "sex education" must be radicalized in order to improve marital sex.

AMERICAN WOMEN: ELIMINATING MOTHERS

orgasm as youths, their libidos soon required more danger and perversion to attain orgasmic release. The goal may be "orgasm," but the method often becomes increasingly antisocial and violent.

The Kinsey team argued in 1948 and 1953 that sex education was needed to decrease sexual inhibition and increase orgasm, thereby enhancing marriages. Largely disregarding out-of-wedlock pregnancy, abortion, STDs, rape, and other negative factors, Kinsey claimed that women were like men, and "were it not for social restrictions, girls and women would be constantly sexually active, from birth to death."[59] He contended that "breaks" in sexual activity (i.e., periods of abstinence) were abnormal:

> Such breaks do not occur between the early and more adult sexual activities of lower mammalian females; they do not occur among most of the primitive groups upon which sexual data are available; and they do not occur among the females in lower level and less inhibited segments of our own American population.[60]

Any biologist would know, as would any animal breeder, that female mammals only copulate when they are in estrus (which is seasonal), and only reach estrus when they are physically mature. The Kinsey team, led by a zoologist, knowingly misled the nation. And why did the Kinsey team purge the "lower level" and "less inhibited segments of the American population" from its findings? Would the additional data have altered the claim that "adult-child sex play" or "play" with "adult partners" was harmless and beneficial?[61] According to psychiatrist and child specialist Dr. Iago Galdston,

> One of Kinsey's obsessive convictions is that premarital experience in orgasm favors the female's effective sexual performance in marriage. The entire work is colored by the authors' conviction that experience with premarital orgasm, preferably in coitus, is the most promising *therapy* for successful sexual performance in marriage... Kinsey contemplates the sexual function quite as on a par with any other function of the organism, such as eating or defecating. It is pleasurable—when it is good.... He seemingly applauds the Lepcha, primitive people, among whom "sexual activity is practically divorced from emotion; it is pleasant and an experience, and as much a necessity as food and drink; and like food and drink it does not matter from whom you receive it, as long as you get it...." (Page 412) This description also fits some of our most neurotically sick individuals, those who are promiscuous and loveless.[62]

If orgasm is a measure of sexual satisfaction, the 75 percent of American women (Kinsey's figure) who reached orgasm in the first year of marriage, and 90 percent who did so by the 20th year, were sexually satisfied. It would therefore be difficult to blame inhibition, or not having sex as a child or adolescent, for sexual dysfunction in marriage. *It would make no sense to carry out a sexual revolution if married people were sexually satisfied, orgasmic, and happy.*

By 1974, in the wake of Kinsey's early impact on American sexual behavior, the famous Hunt research (*Sexual Behavior in the '70s*) would report a marital orgasm rate of only 53 percent among that decade's more sexually uninhibited women—

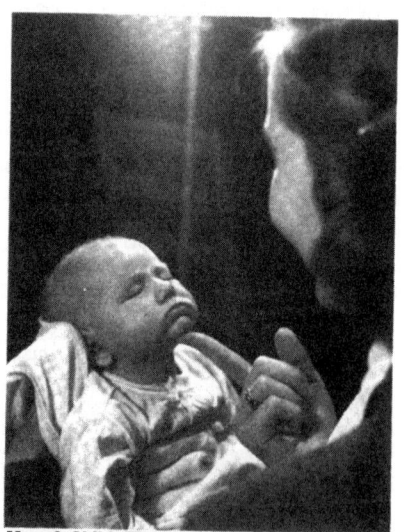

Mom & Child: Kinsey's view of normal American women is seen in his exclusion of all data documenting normal marital birth.

down 22 percent from Kinsey's earlier figure. The Hunt study was published by *Playboy*.

Amazingly, Kinsey himself claimed to have identified a high rate of marital orgasmic *failure*, despite his own contrary data. Why would he do so? The official Kinsey Institute "erotic" library bibliographer, Gershon Legman, wrote in *The Horn Book* (1964),[63]

> Kinsey's real activity has been generally misunderstood, owing to the cloud of statistical hokum

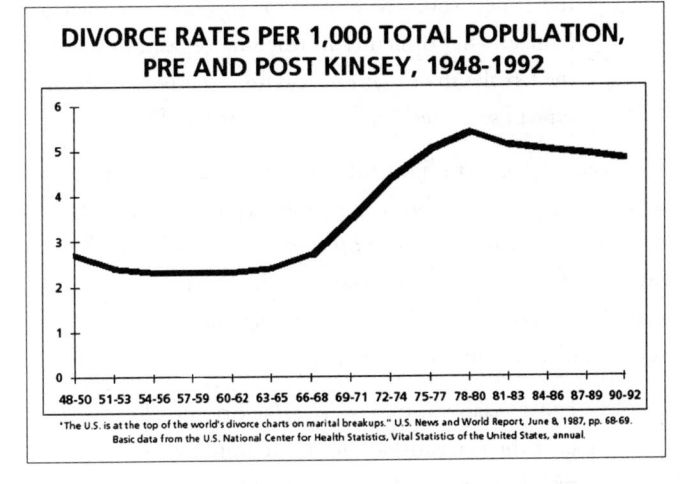

and tendentiously "weighted" population sampling in which the propagandist purpose of his [work was] disguised.... Kinsey's not very secret intention was to "respectabalize" homosexuality and certain other perversions.[64]

Which "other perversions" beyond homosexuality would Kinsey make respectable, and what was standing in his way? The latter included organized religion, organized American women, and a truly free press. Aided by small newspapers in every city, town, and hamlet, the women of the Purity Movement had brought to a screeching halt the golden profits of prostitution traffic nationwide. A still virtuous and reading public, which understood its role in self-government, brought legislators to heel. From the Comstock Act of 1873 to the Mann Act of 1910, "physicians and purity crusaders"[65] brought about public awareness and control of venereal disease, prostitution, pedophiles and other forms of vice. With Prohibition (1920-1933),[66] the American people demonstrated their capacity for action as they sought to cripple the traffic in alcohol, and thereby curb the related problems of obscenity, brothels, and drug dealing which posed threats to the institutions of marriage and family, and to the nation.

PEAK EXPERIENCES

In his "misogynist" view, conditioned by his own boyhood sexual obsessions, Kinsey concocted the notions of a male sexual "peak" in youth and of a female "peak" by mid-20's or shortly thereafter. He concluded that, "from a sexual standpoint, men and women were badly mismatched," meaning that men and women should have sex with their own gender, based on their "internal clocks."[67] This "peak" mythology, which has yet to be scientifically confirmed, has become accepted sexology dogma. It appears to have been based on Kinsey's own childhood sexual habits, increasing addictions, eventual impotence, and other personal sexual pathologies:

> Whereas men reached their sexual peak in their late teens and then gradually went downhill for the rest of their lives, women peaked in their late twenties and early thirties, maintaining this plateau into their fifties and sixties, at which point they, too, faded from the sexual picture.[68]

Having manipulated numbers to conjure up a marital problem, he pin pointed its cause: *women who had not masturbated as girls*:

> It has been pointed out repeatedly, and our own data confirm this... that the average female... has difficulty in reaching orgasm in her marital coitus.... Some 36 percent of the females in our sample had not experienced orgasm on even a single occasion, from any type of sexual activity, prior to marriage.[69]

Some 36 percent hadn't had orgasm *prior* to marriage? Until Kinsey, most of America recognized *marriage* as providing both the amorous life and its satisfaction. Kinsey suggested that his 75 percent orgasm rate *in the first marital year* was a problem that could be eliminated by women having sex outside of marriage earlier. To cure his mythical sexual disorder, Kinsey recommended such early sexual "outlets" as regular masturbation and peer sex accompanied, when deemed appropriate, by "erotic aids." Robinson writes,

> Kinsey claimed to have observed tremendous psychic damage in those who had fretted over their masturbation or attempted vainly to give it up.... This claim was largely impressionistic. He had undertaken neither a systematic survey of his subjects' health nor any controlled experiments that might have established the etiological significance of masturbation. Yet his commitment to autoeroticism was such that he spoke as though his generalizations were supported by unimpeachable statistical evidence... arguing that masturbation actually helped the individual achieve a satisfactory sexual adjustment in marriage. This was particularly true, he argued, in the case of women. The girl who did not masturbate was at a serious sexual disadvantage [developing] habits not easily unlearned after marriage.[70]

Kinsey's early-sex recommendations, then, were based on statistically invalid data compiled by an obsessive-compulsive, masturbating researcher who was himself a sexual deviant.

KINSEY ON CAMPUS

Kinsey's report had an immediate and significant impact. In 1956, writing about the *Female* volume, Dr. Millicent C. McIntosh, president of Barnard College at Columbia University, expressed some serious concerns about its influence on young men and women:

> [T]he American people approach the findings of scientists with complete faith that they must be true. Having accepted them as true, they attribute to them a validity which endues them with moral sanctions.... The Kinsey report uses all the techniques to which Americans are especially vulnerable.... I am certain that Dr. Kinsey's books contribute materially to the difficulties encountered by young people in establishing good relations between the sexes. All boys and girls are pathetically anxious to be normal.... So, if the Kinsey Report announces that ninety-one percent of females have done petting by age twenty-five, and eighty-one percent by age eighteen, the girl who is being pressed by a boy to go further than she thinks proper feels herself trapped by these statistics. If she is not erotically aroused, or does not wish to be, she begins to wonder if she is normal. A counselor in a university recently stated that many boys he knew felt that they were not actually virile if they could not keep up with the statistics Dr. Kinsey presents of sex experience for males of their age group.[71]

Dr. McIntosh continued her discussion of the effect of Kinsey's "unconventional" female subjects on the general college female population:

> [T]he evidence as he presents it makes claims for an entirely new moral code. So, he clearly believes himself that women who have had premarital experience of orgasm, either through petting or through coitus, have a markedly improved chance of success in marriage.[72]

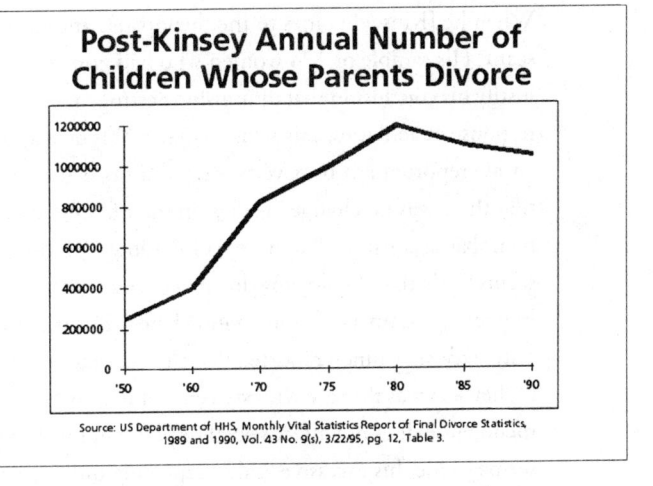

Post-Kinsey Annual Number of Children Whose Parents Divorce

Source: US Department of HHS, Monthly Vital Statistics Report of Final Divorce Statistics, 1989 and 1990, Vol. 43 No. 9(s), 3/22/95, pg. 12, Table 3.

Adding to college male and female frustration and disappointment, Kinsey suggested in his usual contradictory way that college women were freer than their more conventional non-college sisters, but that many "college-level" boys and girls were still "awkward and ineffective in their sexual response." He writes: "It is therefore, not surprising to find sexually unresponsive wives in startling high proportion of the marriages, especially in the better educated segments of the population."[73]

But most "educated wives" (those "high self-esteem" and "high dominance" volunteers Maslow wrote about) were also allegedly sleeping in the nude, engaging in oral-genital contact, having orgasms, and enjoying illicit sex.

Dr. McIntosh's concern about students reading Kinsey, then concluding that they were unsatisfactory lovers, was underscored by the Nevada case of *Sisson v. Sisson*, in which the wife in a child-custody dispute testified that her husband had become convinced that she was sexually unresponsive, based on what he had read in Kinsey:

> Q. Was the defendant ever critical of you?
>
> A. He is very critical. He believes in running his life by what he reads, by what other people do, and what they write about. And now when I say this, I mean particularly in sex life. He read the Kinsey Report and told me that I was not normal because I did not come up to the specifications on page so and so that was recorded in this book. And he runs his life as the Navy runs him, by certain rules that are set down; and to me, to continually be nagged at about your sex life, and to be continually told that you are not normal because you are not doing this or that according to what he has read, I think is very nerve-wracking and after a while it becomes, a complex with you. I know it certainly did with me.[74]

Even for older women, Kinsey caused problems by encouraging the idea that women are supposed to retain an aggressive libido well into old age. Women report anxiety and depression triggered by their belief that they should, despite hormonal changes, still be sexually aggressive. Yet, the blessings of the aging process *naturally* incline them toward the joyful role of grandmother, with the many rewards that noble calling implies. According to 1950s journalist and researcher Dorothy Dunbar Bromley,

> When he [Kinsey] comes to the menopause and its effect on a woman's libido, his data are scant. His sample of 174 women who had gone through natural menopause is too small to justify his conclusion that diminishing estrogen secreted by the ovaries does not reduce sexual response or activities. Also, his analysis of his data appears faulty. Of the 174 women, forty-six are reported not to have experienced orgasm for a year or two "before menopause"—so that there was no change, he says, in their failure to respond sexually. But at what point was menopause considered to have set in? Only with the complete cessation of menstruation? It seems likely that the slowing down of ovarian activity has both a physiological and emotional impact on numbers of women long before this point in time. Actually, in the group of 174 only sixty-six women reported that their sexual responses had continued at the same level or higher—as was the case with sixteen women. By concluding, on such thin evidence, that the menopause does not affect sexual response in most women, Dr. Kinsey shows once again, it seems to me, his excessive zeal in reporting unflagging sexual activity.[75]

The long-term negative impact of the Kinsey *Male* and *Female* reports may never be fully understood by the generation most affected by it: the Baby Boomers. The reports are still extensively cited as a litmus test for human sexual behavior, to the exclusion of both common sense and natural affection. Noted psychiatrist Dr. Karl Menninger has written,

> Kinsey implies that normality means that which is natural and most prevalent, conceives of sex as something to be let out, and also implies that orgasm is "the total goal and ultimate criterion of sexual satisfaction." But as everyone knows, "one orgasm can differ from another as widely as do kisses.... The muscles, nerves and secretions may be the same.... They may add up to the same numbers on an adding machine, but they don't add up to significant totals in human love."[76]

And, despite being unaware of Maslow's report on volunteer error, Dr. McIntosh intuits:

> Dr. Kinsey seems to find complete justification for our ignoring the higher values in the fact that the lower mammals have no knowledge of them. He is perfectly content with the behavior of his fantastic collection of females because this behavior (1) occurs very often among the 5000-odd specimens he has collected; and (2) because it is similar to that found in animals.... Dr. Kinsey comes along, *setting woman in his animalistic world, lining up statistics which seem to show that she is not really different from the bitch or the cow or the female goat.*[77] [Emphasis added.]

THE LOVELESS, CHILDLESS PAJAMA GAME

The average married woman in the 1950s had children. What was sex like for the married mothers Kinsey allegedly interviewed about their sexual lives? If he asked no questions, does this mean the women volunteered no answers themselves about the impact of children on their sex lives? Were there queries about orgasm or sexual feelings following the birth of a child? And what of sex when the children slept in the same room or nearby? Suddenly, squeezed in among the data on 2,451 women engaged in "marital" coitus, Kinsey announced,

> Half of the married females in the sample had regularly slept nude.... Some 37 per cent of the females born before 1906 recorded such experience; but there had been a considerable

development of this practice within more recent years, and 59 per cent of the females... born after 1920 recorded nudity in sleep.[78]

Half of these "repressed" and "inhibited" women had "regularly slept nude"? Apparently Kinsey did not inquire, and none of his female subjects offered their own comments, about how nude slumber fits in with small children wandering into the bedroom at 2 a.m., or the necessity of quickly running to assist a child involved in an emergency. Most of Kinsey's interviews were conducted during the 1930s and 1940s in the East and Midwest, where winters were long and cold and heating systems were less efficient than today's. Central heating was a luxury unavailable to many. While it was illogical nonsense to claim that prior to 1953 one-half of women in the northern United States slept regularly in the nude, Kinsey contended that women who have sex in nightgowns are guilty of "a perversion,"—the only "perversion" he recognizes. He asserted,

> Considering these advantages in nude coitus—and not forgetting the evolutionary emergence of the human species out of unclothed mammalian stock—it seems reasonable to conclude that the avoidance of nudity during coitus is a perversion of what is, in a biologic sense, normal sexuality.[79]

Kinsey does not define rape, incest, pederasty, bestiality, sodomy, peeping, exhibitionism, sadism, or masochism as perversions "of what is, in a biologic sense, normal sexuality." But this "scientist" and his colleagues (and by implication his funders) agreed that women who wear nightgowns during sex are guilty of "a perversion" of "normal sexuality." (You will recall his claim on other occasions that, sexually speaking, there is no such thing as "normal" or "abnormal.")

In the *Male* volume, Kinsey claimed that roughly 30 percent of married males slept in the nude "frequently."[80] Are we to believe that more than 20 percent of married women were sleeping nude "regularly" while their inhibited husbands wore pajamas? Were 20 percent of American women less inhibited than their men? Men masturbate more, earlier and have more illicit and homosexual sex with adults, children, and animals, but are less "perverted" than women who wear pajamas?

Applying Kinsey's method of analysis, it could be assumed that the Kinseys slept naked. Jones notes that he and Clara had separate bedrooms.[81] He recalls an anonymous visitor to the Kinsey household (now identified as Earle Marsh):

> During his visits to Bloomington, Mr. Y always stayed at the Kinsey's.... Kinsey's relationship with Clara was no longer passionate.... "They slept in different bedrooms," he continued. "I don't think he had sex with Mac to have sex, but if I was there we'd all have sex." Elaborating, Mr. Y. revealed, "Kinsey and I'd be having sex upstairs and I'd go down[stairs] and have sex with Mac in the same house. She accepted what went on, you know." Indeed, Mr. Y was surprised by how liberated Clara was sexually.... "She looked like she was a little pip-squeak, you know. Her hair was straight and she didn't look like she was all loose or open and she was open as hell." ...Not that Clara had much choice, [says Jones] not if she wished to remain with her husband.[82]

As is common among women married to "bisexual" or homosexual males, Clara would accept sodomy—the only form of sexual union possible in a homosexual union. In Kinsey's case, Jones reports that Clara would be subject to all forms of sodomy, as well as any other perversions Kinsey chose for film, live performance, or as an "outlet." And it is indeed possible that she, like many of those catalogued in her husband's "nature library," slept nude as well.

VENEREAL DISEASE

The Rockefeller Foundation allegedly had a great interest in venereal disease and its prevention. Thus, the venereal disease infection rate at Indiana University before 1948 is instructive. In his dissertation, Jones describes efforts to offer the Wassermann test for venereal disease on the campus during the 1930s:

> [T]he office of the Daily Student received numerous complaints about the anti-syphilis campaign. Irate critics denied that Wassermann tests were needed and asserted that few, if any, students had venereal disease. They accused the editors of sensationalistic journalism and warned that people of the state would get the impression that syphilis was rampant at Indiana University. The editors replied that, *while there were three known cases of syphilis on campus* [they did not specify whether the three cases were students or faculty] stamping out the disease was not their motive. Rather... they wanted the university to exercise leadership in developing a franker attitude toward the dread disease that numbers countless thousands of American's among its victims.[83] [Emphasis added.]

Like her husband, Clara Kinsey was misrepresented in all publicity photographs (as above) as a conservative, average homebody. Instead, we know now that Clara Kinsey, as well as other wives and staff, were coerced into filming and performing sex for Kinsey.

With only "three known cases of syphilis on campus," there is some justification for Kinsey's failure to report it. However, very few of his female "volunteers" were normal American coeds, and many had wide-ranging sexual experience as prostitutes. Kinsey claimed that his team had asked 1,753 "cases" about venereal disease, and that "only 44 females [2.4%] had ever had any type of venereal infection."[84] It is difficult to accept that widespread secret sexual license resulted in virtually no venereal disease, as is the notion that in this intimate, in-depth sex study Kinsey asked only 23 percent of the women if they had contracted a venereal disease.

The Kinsey Institute team assured its audience that "the medical techniques which are now available can prevent overall disease from becoming a matter of much social importance."[85] That reassurance helped hide the fact that herpes simplex can mutate into genital herpes during orogenital activ-

SEXUALLY TRANSMITTED DISEASES GONORRHEA: CASES PER 100,000 TOTAL AGE GROUP 10-14, PRE AND POST KINSEY

Basic data from the Census for Disease Control and Department of Health and Human Resources

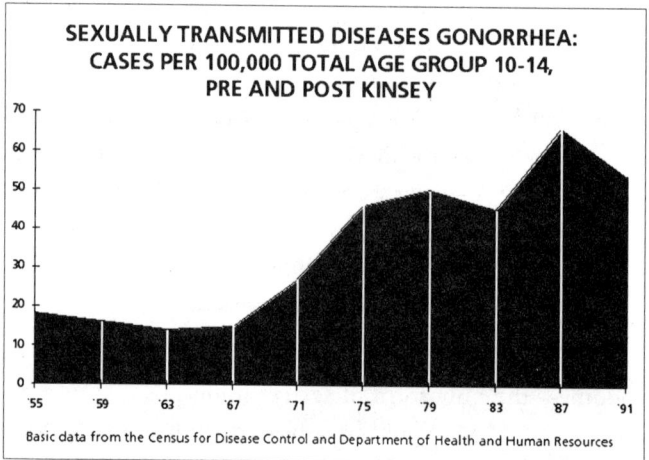

Kinsey's data indicated widespread sexual activity, but sparse venereal disease. The real truth of "sexual freedom" is evident in the post Kinsey increases of crippling and fatal sexually-transmitted diseases (STDs)

ity,[86] with the result that oral sodomy has spawned an epidemic of painful genital herpes. The treatment of both new and old strains of venereal disease costs taxpayers billions annually, while causing untold suffering and human tragedy, adding yet another dimension to the harm wrought by the Kinsey reports. Barnard College sociologist Bernard Barber has noted,

Post-Kinsey Trends in Child Abuse And Neglect 1950-1986

Source, 1976-1982, Trends in Child Abuse and Neglect, The American Humane Association, p. 13; 1986 Datum, Study Findings, National Incidence and Prevention of Child Abuse and Neglect, 1988, US Dpt. of HHS, p. 3-11

> Many people... fear the bad consequences of the Kinsey report for the behavior of American youth. Of course it is not enough for the scientist simply to disclaim a responsibility.... Scientists who know that the results of their work will affect people for both ill and good usually want to tell the public about these diverse consequences.... This new knowledge will change the very situation that the scientists are themselves studying. There can be no question that the Kinsey Reports will change the patterns of sexual behavior in American society.... In the former case, that of "self-fulfilling prophecies," the scientist gets the results he predicted partly because he predicts them. As it has been wittily, though inaccurately, said, the Kinsey volume on Men produced the results of the Kinsey volume on Women.[87]

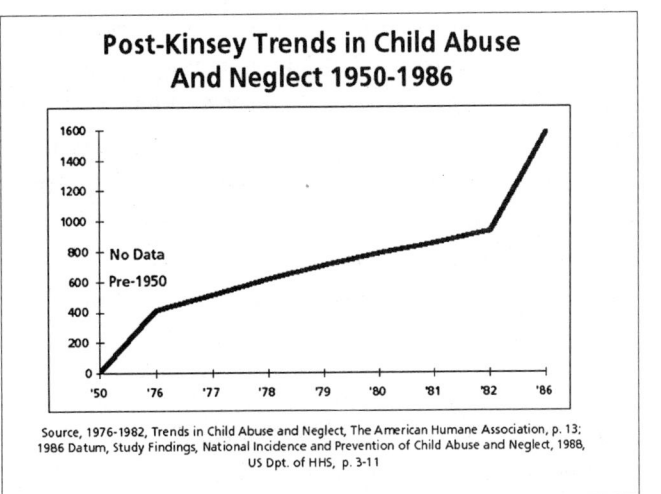

In recent decades, as oral and anal sodomy—the bridge activities between heterosexuality and homosexuality—have become increasing acceptable, Kinsey's self-fulfilling prophecies of increasing bisexuality and homosexuality have come to pass. More than two decades ago, Hunt reported in *The People's Almanac*,

> [F]or the past generation, a major—and permanent reevaluation of sexual attitudes has been occurring throughout our society... things unseen and unheard of a generation ago or even a decade ago are now to be seen and heard on every side... 75 percent of the single women had intercourse before they were 25.... More than 50 percent of the divorced males and females who had extramarital relations say that such activities caused their separations or divorces... young wives are much more likely (24 percent) to engage in extramarital sexual activities than they were in Kinsey's day.
>
> Heterosexual anal intercourse [sodomy] is much more widely used today than formerly.... Nearly 25 percent of all females and more than 25 percent of all males... experienced anal intercourse and nearly 25 percent of married couples under 35 had used it at least once in the last year.... Oral sex is far more widely used—an average of half again as much as it was in Kinsey's sample; 90 percent of married persons under 25 had practiced cunnilingus or fellatio, or both, in the past year. Premarital sex has become acceptable and widespread.[88]

Current sex education programs focus even on elementary school children, in part to help them prepare to avoid venereal diseases. During the Kinsey era, the only STDs commonly experienced were syphilis and gonorrhea. Today, after 50 years of Kinseyite conditioning, we can add to the list genital herpes, chlamydia, pelvic inflammatory disease (PID), bacterial vaginosis, trichomoniasis, hepatitis (A, B and C), cervical cancer, and many other maladies.

There was a 30 percent increase in reports of syphilis from 1985-1987, and about two million new cases of gonorrhea are reported annually. At least a quarter of the homosexual population is reportedly afflicted with gonorrhea of the tonsils. Chlamydia-related health costs are running around $1.3 billion annually; genital herpes reportedly afflicts about 25 million Americans; cervical cancer and genital warts are estimated at 12 million or so cases nationally; there are around 200,000 new cases of hepatitis B annually; and on and on.[89]

"EROTICA" IN THE FEMALE VOLUME

Kinsey carefully sidestepped the evils of pornography and obscenity in his section on "erotic" art, which includes discussions of drawings based on such criteria as observations of the opposite sex (and one's own sex,) graffiti, sex discussions, arousal from sadomasochistic stories, being bitten, fetishism, etc. He makes light of obscenity, euphemistically terming it "erotica," and claims that men are very interested—and women uninterested—in such materials. He admits that there were people in his "histories" who became sadistic after exposure to "erotic" stories, but there is no indication of disapproval, or recognition of social problems arising from the training of people to be sexually sadistic.

Jones briefly mentions Kinsey's own lifelong addiction to pornography, his use of it as a tool for recruiting his young students into sex, and its utilization later in life as a stimulus for his increasing impotence. And just as Kinsey employed sexually explicit and obscene materials to desensitize others and usher them into the world of "anything goes," Hugh Hefner, founder of *Playboy* magazine, can be credited with popularizing the Kinseyan concept of the "ideal woman"—not as wife and mother, but as a *Playmate*, with a new one every month.

Kinsey worked to undermine marriage as a sacrament in which a man and woman commit to each other to generate and nurture new life. This was in keeping with the eugenic thinkers of his day, who sought to remove the "archaic" impediment of the traditional family from the road to their sexual utopia. Kinsey was uniquely qualified for the job of devaluing "pure" women, thereby hamstringing the family. The extensive propagation of his devious data has contributed significantly to the breakdown of heterosexual love, tenderness and parenting. Kinsey's legacy is truly appalling. For the model of the 60s recreational man and woman led directly to the current disorder and despair among American children.

CHAPTER 6 NOTES

[1]. Geoffrey Gorer "Nature, Science and Dr. Kinsey," in Himelhoch and Fava, *Sexual Behavior in American Society*, W.W. Norton & Co., New York, 1955, p. 52.

[2]. James H. Jones, *Kinsey: A Public/Private Life*, W.W. Norton, New York, 1997, pp. 330.

[3]. Gorer, p 52.

[4]. Gorer, p. 53.

[5]. Kinsey, Pomeroy, Martin and Gebhard, *Sexual Behavior in the Human Female*, W.B. Saunders Co., Philadelphia, 1953, pp. 434, 327, 345. In *Kinsey: A Public/Private Life* (1997), James Jones correctly notes that the personal was political for Kinsey. He also confirms that the Kinseys commonly engaged in multiple acts of adultery in the family home, depending on Dr. Kinsey's sexual desires.

[6]. See this Chapter seven, "The Child Experiments."

[7]. *Female*, p. 122.

[8]. As noted by Simon, Gebhard and Johnson in *Marginal Tables*, W.B. Saunders, Philadelphia, 1979, p. 29.

9. *Female*, p. 53.
10. Robert Rothernberg, *The Plain Language Law Dictionary*, Penguin Books, New York, 1981, p. 61.
11. *Female*, p. 53.
12. Morris Ernst & David Loth, *American Sexual Behavior and the Kinsey Report,* Greystone Press, New York, 1948, pp. 128-131.
13. Richard A. Posner, *A Guide to America's Sex*, The University of Chicago, Chicago, Illinois, 1996, p. 99.
14. *Female*, pp. 62, 79, 300, 323, 503, 614.
15. Judson Landis, "The Women Kinsey Studied," in *Social Problems,* in Himelhoch and Fava, Ibid. p. 112.
16. Wardell Pomeroy: coauthor of the Kinsey Reports; *Boys and Sex*, A Pelican Book, New York, 1981, reprinted recently and printed seven times prior, recommending sundry forms of sexual deviation for children, including bestiality, pp. 134-135.
17. Pomeroy, p. 134-135.
18. Kinsey, Pomeroy and Martin, *Sexual Behavior in the Human Male*, W.B. Saunders, Philadelphia, 1948, p. 667.
19. *Female*, p. 505.
20. *Female*, p. 39.
21. Hyman and Sheatsley, "The Scientific Method," in Donald Porter Geddes, Ed., *An Analysis of the Kinsey Reports*, A Mentor Book, New York, 1954, pp. 100.
22. E.G. Montagu, "A Most Important Book, But…" and Hyman and Sheatsley, "The Scientific Method," both in Himelhoch and Fava, 1954; Andrea Dworkin, in Laura Lederer, *Take Back the Night,* Bantam, New York, 1981; Judith Herman, *et al.,* in *Father Daughter Incest*, Harvard University Press, Cambridge Massachusetts, 1981. See especially Oliver Jensen, *The Revolt of American Women,* Harcourt, Brace and Jovanovich, Inc., 1952, from which selected visuals of women were taken for this publication, and *Arbutus,* 1948, the Indiana University yearbook.
23. Hyman and Sheatsley, in Geddes, p.98.
24. Maslow and Sakoda, "Volunteer Error in the Kinsey Study,*"Journal of Abnormal and Social Psychology,* 47, pp. 259-262, 1952, a general critique of methods, and especially see Warren Weaver letter to CIB, May 7, 1951, The Rockefeller Archive Center.
25. Maslow "Volunteer-Error in the Kinsey Study," in Himelhoch and Fava, pp. 120, 123.
26. Maslow in Himelhoch and Fava, p 119.
27. Maslow, p. 220
28. *Female*, p. 32.
29. Maslow, in *Journal of Abnormal and Social Psychology,* p. 259-262.
30. *Female*, pp. 31-32.
31. *Female*, p. 39.
32. *Female*, pp. 31-34.
33. *Female*, p. 32.
34. Wardell Pomeroy, *Dr. Kinsey and the Institute for Sex Research*, Harper & Row, New York (1972), p. 461.
35. Pomeroy, Ibid. p. 202.
36. Gebhard, Gagnon, Pomeroy and Christenson, *Sex Offenders*, Harper & Row, New York, 1965 p. 865-867. The copyright is cited to the Kinsey Institute and the front cover of the book jacket quotes Morris Ernst describing this book as "more significant than all prior publications."
37. *Female*, p. 22.
38. See Judith Reisman, *Images of Children, Crime and Violence in Playboy, Penthouse and Hustler,* IME, Arlington, VA, 1948, and *National Legislation of and International Trafficking in Child Pornography*, Center on Speech, Equality and Harm, University of Minnesota Law School, 1996, and references therein.
39. *Female*, p. 22.
40. See Judith Reisman, *Images*, and *"Soft Porn" Plays Hardball*, Lafayette, LA, 1991. See also Lederer and Delgado, Eds., *The Price We Pay*, Hill and Wang, New York, 1995.
41. Gebhard and Johnson, *The Kinsey Data: Marginal Tabulations of the 1938-1963 Interviews Conducted by the Institute for Sex Research*, W.B. Saunders, Co., Philadelphia, 1979, p. 29.
42. *Female*, p. 255.
43. George Chauncey, *Gay New York*, Basic Books, HarperCollins, 1994, f. 45, p. 396.
44. Edmund Bergler and William Kroger, *Kinsey's Myth of Female Sexuality*. Grune & Stratton, New York, 1954.
45. *Female*, p. 117.
46. *Female* pp. 117-118 and 22.
47. *Female*, as footnote 38. See also massive body of documentation used in the Canadian Supreme Court Decision, *Butler v. The Queen*, February 27, 1992, declaring all pornography illegal in Canada.
48. *Female*, p. 122.
49. Harry Benjamin and R.E.L. Masters*, Prostitution and Morality*, Souvenier Press, London, 1965, p. 5.
50. Benjamin, pp. 15, 18.

51. Benjamin, p. 114.
52. *Female*, p. 521.
53. *Male*, p. 49.
54. *Female*, p. 352.
55. *Female*, p. 348.
56. Gebhard and Johnson, 1979.
57. Gorer, p. 52.
58. See data from The Missing and Exploited Children's Center in Arlington, Virginia and also, Reisman, *Images of Children, Crime and Violence in Playboy, Penthouse and Hustler*, 1989 and *"Soft Porn" Plays Hardball*, 1991. For much of the data on increased violence included in this chapter see William J. Bennett, *The Index of Leading Cultural Indicators*, Empower America, the Heritage Foundation, Free Congress Foundation, Washington, D.C., Vol. 1, March 1993, pp. 2-22 and Patrick Fagan, *The Root Causes of Violent Crime: The Breakdown of Marriage, Family and Community*, The Heritage Foundation, Washington, DC, B-10265, March 17, 1995.
59. *Female*, pp. 115-116.
60. *Female*, p. 116.
61. *Female*, p. 118.
62. Iago Galdston, "So Noble an Effort Corrupted," in Donald P. Geddes, *An Analysis of the Kinsey Report*, A Mentor Book, New York, p. 42-6.
63. Gershon Legman, *The Horn Book*, University Books Inc., New Hyde Park, New York, 1964.
64. Legman, p. 125.
65. Jones, *Kinsey: A Private/Public Life*, p. 330.
66. Prohibition, 1917-1933.
67. Jones, p. 693.
68. Jones, p. 693.
69. *Female*, p. 172.
70. Paul Robinson, *The Modernization of Sex*, Harper & Row, New York, 1976, p. 65.
71. Millicent C. McIntosh, "I Am Concerned," in Geddes, pp. 138-142.
72. McIntosh, p. 140.
73. *Male*, p. 543.
74. *Sisson V. Sisson* 77 Nev. 478, 367 P.2d 98 (1962). Cited in his concurring opinion in *Roth v. Goldman* [172 f.2d 1788 (2d. Cir., 1949)] by Judge Frank, who described the Kinsey report as excellent science.
75. Dorothy Bromley, "Dr. Kinsey's *Summem Bonnum*" in Geddes, 1954, p. 150.
76. Karl Menninger, writing in the *Saturday Review of Literature*, September 26, 1953, in Geddes, 1954, p. 302.
77. McIntosh, in Geddes, p. 141.
78. *Female*, p. 365.
79. *Female*, p. 365.
80. *Male*, p. 372.
81. Jones, p. 604.
82. Jones, p. 604.
83. Jones, *Dissertation*, p. 64.
84. *Female*, p. 327.
85. *Female*, p. 327.
86. Beyond the common medical knowledge of herpes simplex and genital herpes, see the special health report in the December 23, 1997 *The Advocate*, on "What's New in Lesbian Sex?"
87. Bernard Barber, "The Three Human Females," in Geddes, p. 61.
88. David Wallechinsky and Irving Wallace, *The People's Almanac*, Doubleday & Co., Garden City, New York, 1975, pp. 989-991.
89. See Reisman, *et al, Kinsey, Sex and Fraud: The Indoctrination Of A People*, Huntington House, Lafayette, LA, 1990, pp. 92-100 for a brief summary of current data on these venereal diseases.

CHAPTER 7

THE CHILD EXPERIMENTS

Dr. Balluseck... [made measurements] of his crimes committed against children... while in correspondence with the American sexual researcher Kinsey... [doing this] research... over three decades.

[*Frankfurter Allgemeine Zeitung*, **May 22, 1957**]

The nazis knew...[he] practiced his abnormal tendencies in occupied Poland on Polish children, who had to chose between Balluseck and the gas ovens. After the war, the children were dead, but Balluseck lived. Today the court has got four diaries ... [where] he recorded his crimes against 100 children.... He sent the detail of his experiences regularly to the US sex researcher, Kinsey. The latter... with Balluseck kept up a regular and lively correspondence.

[*National-Zeitung*, **May 15, 1957**].

Balluseck... corresponded with the American Kinsey Institute for some time, and had also got books from them which dealt with child sexuality.

[*Tagespiegel*, **October 1, 1957**]

Sexual Behavior in the Human Male[1] included 23 chapters of supposedly scientific data and analysis. Perhaps the most baleful was Chapter 5, "Early Sexual Growth and Activity," where Kinsey claimed to show that the tiniest of infants have the "capacity"[2] for orgasm. He contended that his data confirmed that sexual activity is natural to the human "animal" from birth, and that human children are therefore unharmed by sexual activity even from birth. Prior to Kinsey, sexual information ("sex education") focused on marriage, sexual hygiene (venereal disease) and family living, and was widely recognized as the responsibility of parents or legal guardians. After Kinsey, this crucial responsibility was gradually transferred to school teachers.

Kinsey's philosophy of early childhood sexual development became the standard for today's graphic sex instruction materials in many, of not most, American public, private, and parochial schools, usually camouflaged by such euphemistic captions

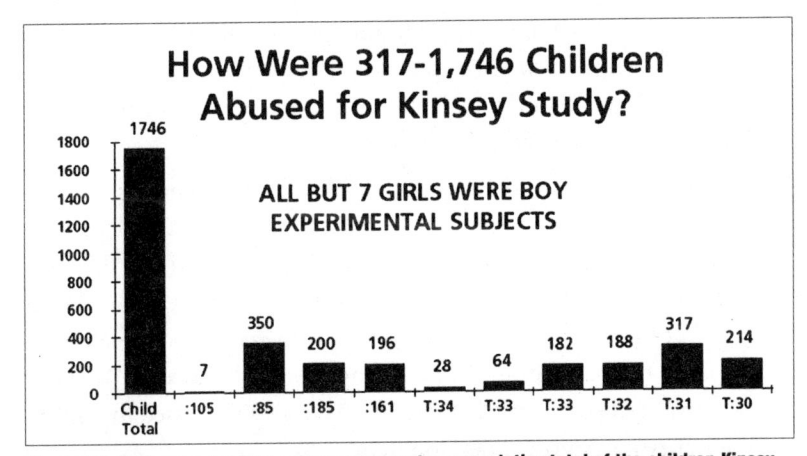

How Were 317-1,746 Children Abused for Kinsey Study?

ALL BUT 7 GIRLS WERE BOY EXPERIMENTAL SUBJECTS

Child Total	:105	:85	:185	:161	T:34	T:33	T:33	T:32	T:31	T:30
1746	7	350	200	196	28	64	182	188	317	214

The 1,746 children in the Table above represents a cumulative total of the children Kinsey cites as sex subjects for the team's Male and Female volumes. The second column cites to the page number in the Female volume for 7 small girl test subjects. The next column represents 350 children mentioned in Pomeroy, and the remaining columns are data from Kinsey's Male volume with the page (:) or Table (T) numbers cited below the bar.

Indiana University's numerous publicity pictures of Kinsey and his staff were posed to promote the impression that the researchers were honest, stable, and normal.

as sex education, AIDS prevention or awareness, family life, health, hygiene, home economics, physical education, even "abstinence" education.[3] Public health data confirm that as Kinseyan-based sex education has metastasized, levels of sexual disease and dysfunction have rocketed upward.

Kinsey asserted that "Erotic arousal could... be subjected to precise instrumental measurement if objectivity among scientists and public respect for scientific research allowed such laboratory investigation."[4] It is reasonable to assume that he meant what he wrote. He and his team did, in fact, conduct what he called "scientific research" on children involving the "precise instrumental measurement" of what he interpreted as "erotic arousal" in infants, toddlers and children. Whether "public respect" is due his "laboratory investigation" is for you, the reader, to judge.

His research was indeed groundbreaking. Prior to Kinsey, no child developmental specialists suggested that children were either sexual from birth or that they benefited from early sexual activity. One education professional, Mary Shivanandan, summarized the "developmental theories of the 20th century" as they relate to children, recalling that while Sigmund Freud (1856-1939) had argued that children were "polymorphus perverse" at birth, psychosocial identity was the childhood goal, with children going through various "stages" in their development, including the wholly asexual "latency" stage, on their way to maturity. Similarly, psychoanalyst Eric Erikson (1902-1994) stressed the child's goals of trust, autonomy, industry, identity and spiritual development.

Cognitive theorists Jean Piaget (1896-1980), Lawrence Kohlberg (1927-1987), and Albert Bandura (1925-) focused on mutual cooperation, moral thinking, and social learning as the child's major

Indiana University's favorable publicity on behalf of Kinsey helped soidify his position as the head of the emerging field of human sexuality.

objectives. Humanists Carl Rogers (1902-1987) and Abraham Maslow (1908-1970) stressed the child's drive toward "self-actualization" as the motivating purpose. Learning theorist B.F. Skinner viewed the child's chief end as learning reason and obedience. And maturational theorists Arnold Gesell (1880-1961) and Robert Havighurst (1900-1991) cited "normal" development and task achievement as childhood goals.

Alfred Kinsey alone argued that sexual satisfaction was a childhood goal.[5]

PART I: THE LITTLE BOY EXPERIMENTS

The number of male infants and young boys observed undergoing sexual stimulation, as reported in the *Male* volume, is between 317 and 1,739 (seven girls were similarly tested). The child-subject totals may be calculated several ways, depending on the manner in which chart figures are tallied. In *Ethical Issues in Sex Therapy*, Volume II (1980), influential sexologists Masters, Johnson, Kolodny, and Weems present a series of papers reprising the history of the research on the "Ethics of Sex Research Involving Children and the Mentally Retarded." One important essay, by Albert Jonsen and J. Mann, states that Kinsey "included observational reports on the speed of reaching orgasm in 1,888 boys, ages 5 months to adolescence, who were timed with a stop watch," and "147 pre-adolescent" girls, for a total of 2,035 children.[6] The authors cite their "personal communication" with Kinsey and co-author Wardell Pomeroy, who validated the 1,888 boys in the Kinsey reports.[7]

Where could the Kinsey team have found from 1,746 to 2,035 boys and girls for "instrumental measurement" of "erotic arousal" data, "timed with a stop watch," from infancy to teen years, without parental objection? And what about Kinsey's "trained observers"? The *Male* volume tells us virtually nothing, except,

> Better data on pre-adolescent climax come from the histories of *adult males who have had sexual contacts with younger boys* and who, with their adult backgrounds, are able to recognize and interpret the boys' experiences. Unfortunately, not all of the subjects with such contacts in their histories were questioned on this point of pre-adolescent reactions; but 9 of our adult male subjects have observed such orgasm. Some of these adults are technically trained persons who have kept diaries or other records, which have been put at our disposal; and from them we have secured information on 317 pre-adolescents who were either observed in self-masturbation, or who were observed in contacts with other boys or older *adults*.[8] [Emphasis added.]

Kinsey's record of what he perceived to be infant and child orgasmic potential is presented in Table 30 of the *Male* volume.[9] Explanatory notes for Table 30 state,

All data based on memory of older subjects, except in the column entitled "data from other subjects." In the later case, original data gathered by certain of our subjects were made available for use in the present volume. Of the 214 cases so reported, all but 14 were subsequently observed in orgasm.[10]

Before reviewing the alleged child sexuality "data" about "preadolescent climax," let us take a brief look at some new information about "Kinsey's Paedophiles" that was uncovered in 1998 by the Yorkshire Television investigators. We will meet a few of the "adult males" whom Kinsey enlisted for his research team when compiling data for the chapters on "Early Sexual Growth and Activity" and "Pre-Adolescent Sexual Development" in his *Male* and *Female* volumes, respectively.

The Yorkshire documentary, entitled *Secret History: Kinsey's Pedophiles*, was broadcast in Great Britain on August 10, 1998. In a review, England's *BBC Radio Times* wrote that "this deeply unsettling documentary... makes a strong case that Kinsey cultivated [pedophiles whose crimes] he presented as scientific data." London's *Daily Mail* for August 11, 1998, agreed: "An academic study admitted the... repugnant... evidence of a child abuser as though this were a respectable scientific contribution." In the Yorkshire interview, Gebhard confirmed that "certain of our subjects," who joined Kinsey's child sexuality research team, were child molesters:

Yorkshire Television British documentary, Secret History: "Kinsey's Paedophiles," August 10, 1998.

> *Interviewer:* How did Kinsey come in contact with, say, the paedophiles?
>
> *Gebhard:* That was rather easy. We got them in prisons, a lot of them.... We'd go after them.... Then there was also a paedophile organization in this country... not incarcerated... they cooperated... You had one in Britain... a British paedophile organization.

So, the Kinsey team found pedophile organizations and asked them to help with its child sex experiments. James Jones, in his Yorkshire interview, admitted the pathology of the man he called "Mr. X," or "Mr. Green" but who was in fact the U.S. federal government land surveyor named Rex King:

> Kinsey relied upon [King] for the chapter on childhood sexuality in the male volume... I think that he was in the presence of pathology at large and... Kinsey... elevated to, you know, the realm of scientific information... what should have been dismissed as unreliable, self serving data provided by a predatory pedophile... I don't have any doubt in my own mind that man wreaked havoc in a lot of lives. Many of his victims were infants and Kinsey in that chapter himself gives pretty graphic descriptions of their response to what he calls sexual stimulation. If you read those words, what he's talking about is kids who are screaming. Kids who are protesting in every way they can the fact that their bodies or their persons are being violated.

The interviewer asked, "Do you think it is right that the Kinsey Institute continues to protect him? Which is more important, confidentiality or those children?" Jones replied, "In my mind those children," and continued,

I don't think the Christian right is wrong on that. I think they have their right to be outraged... political ideology really doesn't have much to do with people's reactions to child abuse.

Countering the Kinsey Institute's defense that the children did not "complain" about their abuse, Jones asked,

How did they know they didn't complain? The person who was rendering that information is the same person who abused them. It seems to me that they have as much credibility as a rapist would have, saying that the victim enjoyed the rape.

James Jones. Outcut from interview for "Kinsey's Paedophiles."

Jonathan Gathorne-Hardy, a recent Kinsey biographer (*Sex the Measure of All Things; A Life of Alfred C. Kinsey*, London: Chatto & Winds, 1998), reveals that Kinsey Institute Director John Bancroft secretly allowed him to read and copy Kinsey's pedophile team reports:

[Kinsey] was deeply affected by five paedophile headmasters who... had... loving relationships with young adolescent boys of twelve or thirteen.... The reason the Kinsey Institute is so careful....is that... they have... evidence of sexual behaviors that even now are illegal. They are nervous that sons or grandsons will sue them if they let this information out. So they had to be very, very careful that names are not revealed in that way.

Jonathan Gathorne-Hardy. Outcut from interview for "Kinsey's Paedophiles."

Gathorne-Hardy perused Rex King's records. He confirmed that King was indeed the individual whom Wardell Pomeroy said raped at least 800 infants, children, kin, and strangers:

Eight or nine typewritten volumes [were] typed up by Kinsey's wife... prior to 1945, which was, you know, before Kinsey admitted [he had employed King. King] went on having sex with everybody until the end... long after Kinsey got the journals. The material in that chapter almost entirely came from [King's] journals which Kinsey got in 1944/45.

I daren't put this on film. I did read [King's records] but Bancroft doesn't want me to say I read them. Bancroft says that if the people know I read them they will go to him and say, you've let one scholar have them, and I'm not going to do that. So what I had to say in my book is that I closely questioned Bancroft and Gebhard about the contents of the journals, but I didn't read them. In fact, I did read them. *But I can't say I read them.*

Kinsey photographer, psychologist, and implicit sex partner Clarence Tripp said that such pedophile researchers were cooperative and happy to demonstrate and share their activities:

You don't find out about what pedophiles think and do [unless] you talk to a man who has done pedophile... there is nothing like going to first sources and photographing you see.... I photographed everything in the human animal when we could arrange it.... If the FBI were to come, demand to see our histories, I would destroy them first.

After graphically describing his own hands-on sexual activity with dogs, Tripp said,

I got hold of a young German boy prostitute... who I photographed with one of the younger ones.... This is the picture. This would probably be the epitome of child corruption in Reisman's mind.... Kinsey had a huge store of films done by myself, Bill Dallenbeck and other people.... Kinsey... would say "Show me," or "Do you mind if I watch?" Or "Let me come over."...Whenever possible Kinsey did validate it."

Interviewer: what you're saying then is that it is possible that Kinsey personally validated [King's] material [the sex with children]?

Tripp: Almost always... there is no mention of his observing people. But he did. He wanted to see everything. This is a hands-on scientist... he had to see it to really believe it.... He poked into, he looked at everything. He often had to have these things photographed because he simply didn't have time.... [Kinsey] was in the market for everything... people who are into special things, love to document it. And it seems to rev them up if they mark it down on a calendar.

Clarance Tripp. Outcut from interview for "Kinsey's Paedophiles."

Dr. Fritz von Balluseck, Nazi pedophile who contributed his on-going child sexual abuse "data" to Kinsey.

Until the Yorkshire investigators located the reports in Berlin, only a few knew about Dr. Fritz Von Balluseck, the Nazi pedophile who contributed his child abuse data (from roughly 1936-1956) to Kinsey's research database. Their exchange of information is discussed later in this chapter. Meanwhile, Tripp confirmed Pomeroy's claim that Kinsey was collecting "early adolescent sperm" to study motility, and "had at least ten motility studies going."

As noted earlier, "motility" studies entail the microscopic evaluation of sperm to pin point the earliest age at which boys are fertile. This required that Kinsey and/or his aides masturbate young boys and/or monitor the self-masturbation of older boys for ejaculate to be examined for sperm count and motility. Paul Gebhard testified that their group recruited pedophiles and pederasts to collect child "orgasm" data wherever they could:

[King] had sex with men, women, children and animals.... Nursery school people... parents... couldn't give us the extraordinary detail that [King] did. It was illegal and we knew it was illegal and that's why a lot of people are furious... they say we should have turned him in instantly... *If we had turned him in it would have been the end of our research project.*

During his Yorkshire interview Tripp said that "we" ought to "rev up" children sexually "at an early age." He and his colleagues hoped that it would "fix" people like this author by "proving" that children have orgasms, thereby reducing disapproval of, and eliminating laws against, "molestation," "abuse," and the like:

If we could only get those children with some kind of masturbation or something that would rev up their sexual substrate at an early time it would fix people like Judith Reisman immediately because then they'd respond and then they'd know what the rest of the world was like....

Neither Kinsey nor members of this team used the terms "molestation" or "abuse" in a negative manner; they believed that their experiments were entirely acceptable, added Tripp:

> Paedophilia is an almost non-existent kind of crime.... For instance they use words like child molestation. What is that? Nobody knows. Abuse of children? Are they talking about boxing them against the ear or hitting them with a stove pipe? Are they talking about tickling them a little? Are you talking about fondling? I hesitate to even call [Rex King] a paedophile.

Based on the evidence, child sex abuse was a prominent research protocol for the child "data" from Kinsey's two volumes authoritatively cited as fact, worldwide.

TABLE 30: "PRE-ADOLESCENT EROTICISM AND ORGASM"

Table 30 deals with "first" orgasm data. Pomeroy asserts that "age of first orgasm" was "one of the most important parts of the sex history."[11] Child developmental professionals prior to Kinsey pinpointed puberty-related physiological factors as signs of budding sexual maturation. For Kinsey, sexual maturation was evident on the occasion of first "orgasm" experienced by the 214 little boys listed in Table 30. For his entire male sample, Kinsey reported a (for him) disappointing 93 percent who did not answer the interview question about when they had their first orgasm. Only 7 percent, he lamented, recalled orgasms prior to age 14.

Kinsey's conclusion from these skimpy and unsupported data was that *most* pre-adolescents *can* experience orgasm. He writes of the "normality" of orgasm for little boys (despite the absence of memories or ejaculate), claiming that it is "not at all rare among pre-adolescent boys, and it also occurs among pre-adolescent girls." He defines this as a "significant fact" which is not "well established in scientific publication," therefore "profitable to record here…in some detail."[12]

First Pre-Adolescent Erotic Arousal and Orgasm
Number of Cases

AGE	EROTIC AROUSAL — In Any Sex Play	In Heterosexual Play	In Homosexual Play	ORGASM — Data from Present Study	Data from Other Subjects	Total Cases	% of Total
1					12	12	2.5
2					8	8	1.6
3				2	7	9	1.8
4	10	9	2		12	12	2.5
5	30	23	8	5	9	14	2.9
6	26	21	8	15	19	34	7.0
7	32	29	6	21	17	38	7.8
8	38	29	12	27	21	48	9.9
9	38	37	3	24	26	50	10.3
10	83	71	17	56	26	82	16.8
11	72	67	13	54	22	76	15.6
12	92	84	13	51	23	74	15.2
13	37	37	3	15	9	24	4.9
14	10	10		3	3	6	1.2
15	3	2	1				
Total	471	419	86	273	214	487	100.0
Mean Age	10.28	10.41	9.62	10.40	8.51	9.57	
Median Age	9.75	9.87	9.26	9.77	8.10	9.23	

Table 30. Pre-adolescent eroticism and orgasm

Kinsey quickly rebounded from this numerical setback by reporting that children who cannot experience orgasm are have probably been rendered psychologically incapable due to environmental (read, parental) inhibitions:

> The observers emphasize that there are some of these pre-adolescent boys (estimated by one observer as less than one quarter of the cases), who fail to reach climax even under prolonged and varied and repeated stimulation; but even in these young boys, this probably represents psychological incapacity more often than physiologic incapacity.[13]

THE CHILD EXPERIMENTS

Neither sexology's ethical guardians nor most of Kinsey's critics have sought further details about the "prolonged and varied and repeated stimulation" to which the children were exposed. And when the children did not respond with "orgasm," *how did they respond?* When this author's 1981 paper, "Child Sexuality or Child Sexual Abuse: A Critical Evaluation of the Kinsey Reports," was retrieved from the Kinsey Institute files during the 1993 deposition of their then director, one of the many handwritten "corrections" found on that trip was that child orgasm tests were for the orgasmic "capacity" and not the "potential" of infants and children.

The Kinsey team embellished the data even further, stating that the toddlers required a *fresh* social climate, and concluding that, in an "uninhibited" society, the majority of boys could be having orgasms by three or four years of age:

> In the population as a whole, a much smaller percentage of the boys experience orgasm at an early age, because few of them find themselves in circumstances that test their capacities; but the positive record on these boys who did have the opportunity makes it certain that many infant males and younger boys are capable of orgasm, and it is probable that half or more of the boys *in an uninhibited society could reach climax by the time they were three or four years of age,* and that nearly all of them could experience such a climax three to five years before the onset of adolescence.[14] [Emphasis added.]

Evolutionarily speaking, what use would infants or young children ages three to four years have for an orgasmic capacity without a physiological basis for early sexual maturity? Even current Kinsey Institute Director John Bancroft acknowledges that there is a "biological basis" for the genitals, and that it is generative. Testosterone is inhibited in the male until roughly 12 years of age and, Bancroft says, a young boy's "first ejaculation occurs" at about 13 years of age.[15] To sexualize toddlers and young children without any "biological basis" for doing so renders them freaks of nature.

TABLE 31: "PRE-ADOLESCENT EXPERIENCE IN ORGASM"

Kinsey believed that human beings and their responses could be categorized like the gall wasps he had collected earlier. This taxonomic technique is evident in Table 31 of the *Male* volume, "Pre-adolescent experience in orgasm," which is a carbon copy in theory, structure, and groupings of his 1936 insect table on "Cynips." In Table 31, Kinsey reported the little boys' ages and "orgasm" responses to stimuli.[16] Bancroft claims that Kinsey's "meticulous" boy tables report the "data" Kinsey received from King, who he called an old "technically trained" forester[17] and who, Pomeroy and others claim, had sexual relations with 800 children of both sexes).

Kinsey stated that "some of the younger boys who have contributed to the present study" also described their "orgasm." However, the charts show that 28 of Kinsey's "younger boy" contributors/participants were infants, so unable to speak. Kinsey claimed in Table 31 that "orgasm" was "observed" in a male infant of five months, although the table further notes failure to produce orgasms in male babies of two, three, four and nine months. Each age category included children tested for orgasm; that is, Kinsey confirmed 22 toddlers up to two years old, were test subjects. He claimed that 11 of these tykes "reached climax," while 11 others did not. These could have been some of Rex King's little victims, described by Gathorne-Hardy in his Yorkshire interview.

Two three-month-old babies were tested and coded as not having reached "climax." Of twelve four-year-olds, Kinsey claims five were anorgasmic while seven were successfully orgasmic.

Such is the view of those collecting sex "data" on 317 boys in Table 31, men engaged in "actual observation" of the children. Some of the little boys were tracked for years. Kinsey writes, "In 5 cases of young pre-adolescents, observations were continued over periods of months or years, until the individuals [child subjects] were old enough to make it certain that true orgasm was involved."[18] In other words, at least five little boys continued to be subjected to experimentation "over periods of months or years" so that scientists and/or technically trained observers could know if what these men called "true orgasm was involved."

SPRING 1997
Director's Column
by Dr. John Bancroft

This is an exciting time for the Kinsey Institute. We are in the midst of the first of two consecutive fiftieth anniversary years—this year, the founding of the institute; next year, the publication of *Sexual Behavior in the Human Male*, Alfred Kinsey's first groundbreaking volume. We intend to celebrate these occasions in a variety of ways, starting with a public exhibition and lecture series, which you can read about on page 2 of this newsletter.

After a period in which the Kinsey Institute has spent too much time defending itself against outside attack, we are ready to show the world our pride in the institute and its mission, which is to promote interdisciplinary research and scholarship in the fields of human sexuality, gender, and reproduction. Our mission, and the work we do in support of it, is more important today than at any time in the past, and with the developments and projects now underway, our leadership in this area will be even stronger as we enter the next century.

But we do need help. Indiana University is supporting us wholeheartedly, but at the present time, financing academic enterprises such as ours is becoming increasingly difficult. We must find additional sources of funding, and we are working hard on that right now.

We also need the support of people who recognize the Kinsey Institute's importance in this sexually troubled time, and who care about advancing knowledge of human sexuality. There are some people in the United States who object to research into sexuality and who attack our efforts and those of other serious sex researchers.

AGE WHEN OBSERVED	TOTAL POPULATION	CASES NOT REACHING CLIMAX	CASES REACHING CLIMAX	CUMULATED POPULATION	CUMULATED CASES TO CLIMAX	PERCENT OF EACH AGE REACHING CLIMAX
2 mon.	1	1	0			
3 mon.	2	2	0			
4 mon.	1	1	0			
5 mon.	2	1	1			
8 mon.	2	1	1			
9 mon.	1	1	0			
10 mon.	4	1	3			
11 mon.	3	1	2			
12 mon.	12	10	2			
Up to 1 yr.	28	19	9	28	9	32.1
Up to 2 yr.	22	11	11	50	20	
Up to 3 yr.	9	2	7	59	27	57.1
Up to 4 yr.	12	5	7	71	34	
Up to 5 yr.	6	3	3	77	37	
Up to 6 yr.	12	5	7	89	44	
Up to 7 yr.	17	8	9	106	53	
Up to 8 yr.	26	12	14	132	67	63.4
Up to 9 yr.	29	10	19	161	86	
Up to 10 yr.	28	6	22	189	108	
Up to 11 yr.	34	9	25	223	133	
Up to 12 yr.	46	7	39	269	172	80.0
Up to 13 yr.	35	7	28	304	200	
Up to 14 yr.	11	5	6	315	206	
Up to 15 yr.	2	2	0	317	206	
Total	317	111	206	317	206	65.0

Table 31. Ages of pre-adolescent orgasm
Based on actual observation of 317 males.

In Spring 1997, Bancroft, still refusing to name either victims or perpetrators of the Kinsey crimes, complains that the Institute has spent "too much time defending itself against outside attack."

THE CHILD EXPERIMENTS

TABLE 32: "SPEED OF PRE-ADOLESCENT ORGASM"

Table 32 details the "speed of pre-adolescent orgasm."[19] The table's legend states: "Duration of stimulation before climax: observations timed with second hand or stopwatch. Ages range from five months of age to adolescence." We read in *Ethical Issues in Sex Therapy*, Volume II, that Wardell Pomeroy confirmed the "observation" data on these boys and that the 1,888 boys from age five months to fifteen years were observed being "erotically stimulated" in order to record "speed of reaching orgasm" while "timed with a stop watch."[20] In an audio-taped interview, Kinsey associate Paul Gebhard was asked who collected such illegal data?

Gebhard: ...Most of it was done by one individual, a man with scientific training, and not a known scientist. The other cases were done by parents, at our suggestion, and, let's see, then there were some that were done by nursery school personnel.

Interviewer: Was that at your suggestion too?

Gebhard: Yes... we would ask them to watch, and take notes, and if possible, time it and report back to us.... Once we asked people about giving us their observations, we would ask them later too. if [the pedophiles] got in contact with us later we would ask them more about it. We follow up by re-interviewing people occasionally...

Interviewer: So, do pedophiles normally go around with stop watches?

Kinsey's Table of wasps, he states, was based on the actual observation of 124,512 gall wasps he collected in the wild.

Complexes	Number of Species	Insects Examined Before 1930	Insects Examined 1930-1936	Total Insects	Total Galls
Cynips					
Folii	4	646	51	697	1,200
Longiventris	2	129	6	135	370
Divisa	2	1,090		1,090	1,090
Agama	1	57		57	180
Disticha	1	13		13	5
Cornifex	1	4		4	12
Antron					
Echinus	6	589	786	1,375	7,400
Guadaloupensis	3	18		18	140
Teres	3	55		55	190
Besbicus					
Multipunctata	4	175		175	1,200
Maculosa	2	29		29	70
Mirabilis	2	26	32	58	420
Atrusca					
Dugèsi	29	164	3,306	3,470	18,000
Bulboides	5		840	840	1,500
Aggregata	5		318	318	1,500
Bella	5	56	2,410	2,466	15,000
Centricola	4	118	61	179	405
Philonix					
Plumbea	13	30	1,122	1,152	3,300
Fulvicollis	9	5,170	1,987	7,157	22,550
Acraspis					
Arida	11	27	1,071	1,098	3,800
Melles	11	431	147	578	1,640
Nubila	9	64	2,088	2,152	6,100
Villosa	9	367	191	558	2,280
Gemmula	5	746	10	756	660
Pezomachoides	9	5,890	1,554	7,444	23,500
Hirta	10	1,457	2,030	3,487	12,000
Totals 26	165	17,351	18,010	35,361	124,512

Kinsey claimed that his wasp Table was based on actual observation of 124,512 gall wasps.

TIME	CASES TIMED	PERCENT OF POPULATION	CUMULATED PERCENT
Up to 10 sec.	12	6.4	6.4
10 sec. to 1 min.	46	24.5	30.9
1 to 2 min.	40	21.3	52.2
2 to 3 min.	23	12.2	64.4
3 to 5 min.	33	17.5	81.9
5 to 10 min.	23	12.2	94.1
Over 10 min.	11	5.9	100.0
Total	188	100.0	

Mean time to climax: 3.02 minutes
Median time to climax: 1.91 minutes

Table 32. Speed of pre-adolescent orgasm

Gebhard: *Ah, they do if we tell them we're interested in it.... When we interview pedophiles, we would ask them, How many children have you had it with? What were their ages? Do you think they came to climax or not?... Are you sure it really was climax or not?* (see [44].)

Gebhard was unusually candid for a member of the Kinsey team. A former director of the Kinsey Institute, he admitted collaborating in the child abuse. The Institute has understandably been extremely protective of the data, and refuses to reveal who collected them. Additionally, Gebhard admits that the team collaborated and interacted with their "observers" before and after the commission of criminal acts against children.

As recorded in *Ethical Issues in Sex Therapy and Research,* Volume 2, Gebhard was asked about the ethics of coercing people of all ages to participate in the Kinsey research. He replied that the Kinsey team did indeed coerce people, and that he would have no qualms about doing it again. He asserted:

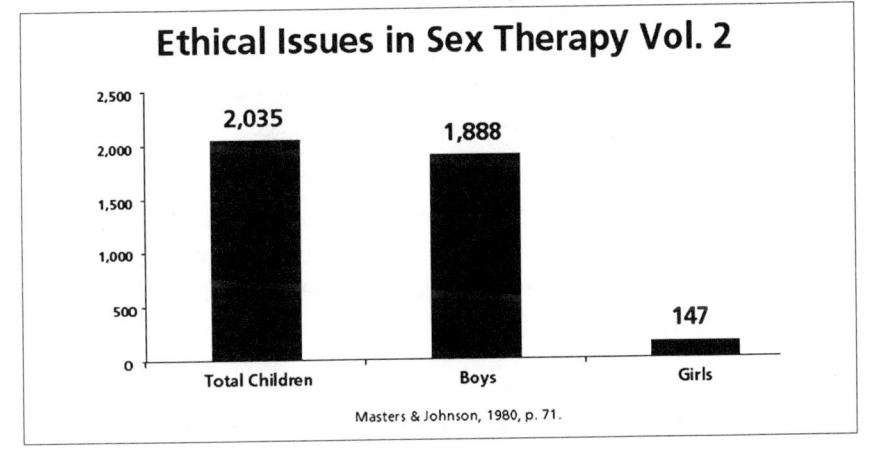

> Well, it is definitely coercion.... I think a certain amount of coercion is acceptable in the interest of encouraging research participation. I wouldn't hesitate to use that tactic again– though I might not spell it out in my proposal to the committee on human subjects.[21]

Whether or not coercion is part of a sex-research protocol, child responses remain subject to interpretation by the adult, for as Kinsey himself admitted, "Pre-adolescent boys, since they are incapable of ejaculation, may be as uncertain as some inexperienced females in their recognition of orgasm."[22] He claimed that he and his team could precisely interpret a child's response, and could unerringly recognize orgasm without ejaculation.

Kinsey testified that it had "been necessary to test the reliability of every... technique, at every point of the program."[23] How, then, did he and his team "test the reliability" of child "orgasms" and the competence of their "technically trained observers"?

THE CHILD EXPERIMENTS

TABLE 33: "MULTIPLE ORGASM IN PRE-ADOLESCENT MALES"

Kinsey's Table 33 presented data about the number of orgasms among 182 pre-adolescent boys, as well as the time between orgasms for another 64. The legend for the table reads: "Based on a small and select group of boys. Not typical of the experience, but suggestive of the capacities of pre-adolescent boys in general."[24] Kinsey wrote,

NO. OF ORGASMS	CASES OB-SERVED	PERCENT OF POPULA-TION	CUMU-LATED PERCENT	TIME BETWEEN ORGASMS	CASES TIMED	PERCENT OF POPULA-TION	CUMU-LATED PERCENT
1	81	44.5	100.0	Up to 10 sec.	3	4.7	4.7
2	17	9.3	55.5	11 to 60 sec.	15	23.5	28.2
3	18	9.9	46.2	Up to 2 min.	8	12.5	40.7
4	10	5.5	36.3	Up to 3 min.	10	15.6	56.3
5	14	7.7	30.8	Up to 5 min.	7	10.9	67.2
6–10	30	16.5	23.1	Up to 10 min.	11	17.2	84.4
11–15	9	4.9	6.6	Up to 20 min.	7	10.9	95.3
16–20	2	1.1	1.7	Up to 30 min.	1	1.6	96.9
21+	1	0.6	0.6	Over 30 min.	2	3.1	100.0
Total	182	100.0	100.0	Total	64	100.0	100.0

Mean No. of Orgasms: 3.72
Median No. of Orgasms: 2.62

Mean Time Lapse: 6.28 minutes
Median Time Lapse: 2.25 minutes

Table 33. Multiple orgasm in pre-adolescent males

> The most remarkable aspect of the pre-adolescent population is its capacity to achieve repeated orgasm in limited periods of time. This capacity definitely exceeds the ability of teen-age boys who, in turn, are much more capable than any older males.…It is certain that a higher proportion of the boys could have had multiple orgasm if the situation had offered.… Even the youngest males, as young as 5 months in age, are capable of such repeated reactions.[25]

Kinsey's "interviewers" allowed a "time lapse" of from 2.25 minutes to 6.28 minutes between orgasm trials, which suggests that they were stimulating the boys to bring about "orgasms" as swiftly as possible. Just as Kinsey described adult sexual abuse of children as "sex play," Tripp saw such tests on young boys as play: "If you have paedophilia between an older male and a young boy is that homosexual?…It's that they are playing in a way."

TABLE 34: "EXAMPLES OF MULTIPLE ORGASM IN PRE-ADOLESCENT MALES"

Gebhard acknowledged during his Yorkshire interview that "science" was not part of Kinsey's agenda for the child chapters. He cited Table 34, admitting that they used the records of "Kinsey's though the deviates involved were ordinary parents and physicians. "Judith Reisman… [saw] this famous table 34 that had the data on children… [She] hit the ceiling… [A] good piece of it came from [King].

Table 34 was truly grotesque. It reported around-the-clock experimental "data" on infants and young boys.[26] The Kinsey team seemed completely at ease when describing the extraordinary data:

> Even the youngest males, as young as 5 months of age, are capable of such repeated reactions. Typical cases are shown in Table 34. The maximum observed was 26 climaxes in 24 hours [in a 4-year-old and a 13-year-old], and the report indicates that still more might have been possible in the same period of time.[27]

Gathorne-Hardy recalls that the "five month old boy in table 34 [King] did with a woman… Kinsey, however, did not use all of his figures." What figures did Kinsey disregard? Table 34 is said to show typical instances of the orgasmic "capacity" of male infants and children. As with the adults, however, the precise number of children subjected to testing is impossible to determine. Kinsey states

AGE	NO. OF ORGASMS	TIME INVOLVED	AGE	NO. OF ORGASMS	TIME INVOLVED
5 mon.	3	?	11 yr.	11	1 hr.
11 mon.	10	1 hr.	11 yr.	19	1 hr.
11 mon.	14	38 min.	12 yr.	7	3 hr.
2 yr.	{ 7	9 min.	12 yr.	{ 3	3 min.
	11	65 min.		9	2 hr.
2½ yr.	4	2 min.	12 yr.	12	2 hr.
4 yr.	6	5 min.	12 yr.	15	1 hr.
4 yr.	17	10 hr.	13 yr.	7	24 min.
4 yr.	26	24 hr.	13 yr.	8	2½ hr.
7 yr.	7	3 hr.	13 yr.	9	8 hr.
8 yr.	8	2 hr.	13 yr.	{ 3	70 sec.
9 yr.	7	68 min.		11	8 hr.
10 yr.	9	52 min.		26	24 hr.
10 yr.	14	24 hr.	14 yr.	11	4 hr.

Table 34. Examples of multiple orgasm in pre-adolescent males

there were "some instances of higher frequencies" than those shown. Why were they not given? A two-, 12-, or 13-year-old may have been tested more than once. Also lacking is an explanation of why orgasms claimed for the five-month infant are recorded, but not the time required to attain them. Moreover, Kinsey reports in detail, as an observer, about a "fretful babe" "distracted [from] other activities" by the experimenter. The "weeping" and "convulsive action" of the baby is labeled "orgasm" by the Kinsey team.

Kinsey admits that some of the children were tracked for months or years:

> A fretful babe quiets down under the initial sexual stimulation, is distracted from other activities, begins rhythmic pelvic thrusts, becomes tense as climax approaches, is thrown into convulsive action, often with violent arm and leg movements, sometimes with weeping at the moment of climax. After climax the child loses erection quickly and subsides into the calm and peace that typically follows adult orgasm. *It may be some time before erection can be induced again after such an experience.* There are observations of 16 males up to 11 months of age, with such typical orgasm reached in 7 cases. In 5 cases of young pre-adolescents, observations were continued over periods of months or years, until the individuals were old enough to make certain that true orgasm was involved; and in all of these cases the later reactions were so similar to the earlier behavior that there could be no doubt of the orgiastic nature of the first experience.[28] [Emphasis added]

First of a series of child photos from Darwin's Expressions of Emotion that illustrate fear, anger, and rage.

In *Kinsey's Pedophiles*, the camera moved in for a close up of Rex King's records of "the orgiastic nature" of infant, child, and juvenile responses to manipulation. "Willy Price" is cited as one of King's 15-year-old victims. Gebhard stated in a phone interview that the Kinsey Institute has "names" of some child victims. Willy Price would be in his late 60s by now and may still be alive. Gathorne-Hardy reads, on camera, from hard copies of King's reports. The interview appears in the transcript of the Yorkshire documentary. Some of the brutally graphic language spelt out in Hardy's reading from the original has been excised for this book.

> Out of 317 cases [King] records having to force cooperation on five occasions: aged 2, 4, 7, 10 15 (Willy Price).... He likes to arouse boys... King records in the history the color, taste and smell of the semen. Also, when he can, examines adolescent semen for sperm.... Does it with mother and son... Some of his women masturbate their children for him...."
> [Gathorne-Hardy reads from record] "Experimented with baby.... Could take head of

THE CHILD EXPERIMENTS

[male sex organ] in mouth easily.... His success in getting his huge range was, like Kinsey that he not only did not disapprove, he was happy to join in... seducing boys and men.... In a few minutes [the boy] was laughing and did not hold it against me. Fact is he seemed proud he had done it. I praised him and told him he was some kid to take a 7" **** down his throat and up his *** *the same night*.... [Got boys] round to discussing sex... excited them... [show graphic sex]. Listened.... They felt safe and warm and happy."

Such activity easily qualifies as the delusional frenzy of a dangerous sexual psychopath. For Kinsey, his team and his disciples, including Dr. Bancroft, current Kinsey Institute president, Kinsey's was quality "scientific research" that deserves "public respect."

For Darwin, an expression interpreted as "horror." For Kinsey, a fretful babe's "convulsive" orgasm.

DARWIN VERSUS KINSEY: INTERPRETING PHYSIOLOGICAL RESPONSES

The Kinsey Institute insists that Kinsey's pedophiles were "technically trained" adult "observers" who could reliably "interpret the boys' experiences." From King's descriptive entries, Kinsey teased out the numbers that appear in the descriptions which follow. Kinsey described the "erotic stimulation" of 196 children to create "erections." which he reported as orgasms. The standard definition of for normal male "orgasm" includes ejaculation:

> The highest point of sexual excitement, characterized by strong feelings of pleasure and *marked normally by ejaculation of semen by the male* and by vaginal contractions in the female. Also called climax.[29] [Emphasis added.]

While adults supplied the following "data" about the boys' experiments, the six types of "orgasm" described *refer only to boys, not men.* Kinsey's repeated references to "adult males" is *deliberately* confusing. There are *no* "adult males" in the group of pre-adolescents he studied, so each mention of "older males" refers to boys *under 13-years of age*. Since Kinsey claimed that Charles Darwin was his methodological, scientific, and "biologic" mentor, a study of Darwin's *Expressions of the Emotions in Man and Animals* (1904), in regard to Kinsey's descriptions of "orgasm" is very illuminating. Darwin's *negative* descriptions of children's rage, terror, anger, and fear, etc., mirror and conflict with Kinsey's *positive* descriptions of "orgasm" in children.[30] The *Male* volume states,

> Our several thousand histories have included considerable detail on the nature of orgasm; and these data, together with the records supplied by...older subjects who have had sex...with younger boys, provide material for describing the different sorts of reactions which may occur. In the pre-adolescent, orgasm is, of course, without ejaculation of semen.[31] *In the descriptions which follow, the data supplied by adult observers for 196 pre-adolescent boys are the sources for the percentage figures indicating the frequency of each type of orgasm among such young males....six types are listed....* [Note, no "adult males" are studied.]
>
> 1. *Reactions primarily genital:* Little or no evidence of body tension... penis becomes more rigid and may be involved in mild throbs, or throbs may be limited to urethra alone; semen (in the adult) seeps

from urethra without forcible ejaculation; climax passes with minor after-effects. A fifth (22%) of the pre-adolescent cases on which there are sufficient data belong here, and probably an even higher proportion of older males. [Recall, no "adult males" are studied.]

2. *Some body tension...twitching* of one or both legs, of the mouth, of the arms, or of other particular parts of the body... rigidity of the whole body and some throbbing of the penis; orgasm with a few spasms but little after-effect... involving nearly half (45%) of the pre-adolescent males, and perhaps a corresponding number of adult males. [Recall, no "adult males" were studied.]

For Darwin, an expression interpreted as "fear." For Kinsey, an expression interpreted as orgasm.

3. *Extreme tension with violent convulsion:* Often involving the sudden heaving and jerking of the whole body... that the legs often become rigid, with muscles knotted and toes pointed, muscles of abdomen contracted and hard, shoulders and neck stiff and often bent forward, breath held or gasping, eyes staring or tightly closed, hands grasping, mouth distorted, sometimes with tongue protruding; whole body or parts of it spasmodically twitching, sometimes synchronously with throbs or violent jerking of the penis... still more violent convulsions of the whole body; heavy breathing, groaning, sobbing, or more violent cries, sometimes with an abundance of tears (especially among younger children), the orgasm or ejaculation involving several minutes (in one case up to five minutes) of recurrent spasm... the individual is often capable of participating in a second or further experience. About one sixth (17%) of the pre-adolescent boys, a smaller percentage of adult males. [Recall, no "adult males" were studied.]

For Darwin, an expression interpreted as "hysterical." For Kinsey, an expression interpreted as orgasm.

4. As in either type 1 or 2; but with *hysterical laughing, talking, sadistic or masochistic reactions*, rapid motions (whether in masturbation or in intercourse), culminating in more or less frenzied movements which are continued through the orgasm. A small percentage (5%) of either preadolescent or adult males. [Recall, no "adult males" were studied.]

For Darwin, an expression interpreted as "pain." For Kinsey, an expression interpreted as orgasm.

5. As in any of the above; but culminating in extreme trembling, collapse, loss of color, and sometimes fainting of subject. Sometimes happens only in the boy's first experience, occasionally occurs throughout the life of an individual. Regular in only a few (3%) of the pre-adolescent or adult males. [Recall, no "adult males" were studied.] Such complete collapse is more common and better known among females.

6. Pained or frightened.... The genitalia... become hypersensitive...*some males suffer excruciating pain and may scream if movement is continued or the penis even touched.* The males in the present group become similarly hypersensitive before the arrival of actual orgasm will fight away from

the partner and may make violent attempts to avoid climax, although they derive definite pleasure from the situation. Such individuals quickly return to complete the experience, or to have a second experience if the first was complete. About 8 per cent of the younger boys are involved here, but it is a smaller percentage of older boys and adults [Recall, no "adult males" were studied] which continue these reactions throughout life.[32]

Rex King, hidden away as "Mr. X." Outcut from interview with Gathorne-Hardy in "Kinsey's Paedophiles."

Gathorne-Hardy states that Rex King constructed the "six kinds of orgasm" stated above by Kinsey as fact. Hardy also claims that Kinsey (himself a clinically defined sado-masochistic sexual psychopath) then "verified" King's descriptions of orgasm, apparently including the fainting, convulsing, and striking of the "partner:"

> Kinsey... has a thing in there defining six kinds of orgasm... alerted to by [King]. Then he [Kinsey] looked for himself... and it turned out that[King's] observations were terribly feasible.... So, before the book was published, they packed off the galleys to [King]... [and] he patched it all up again.... *Kinsey was himself a super-expert at child sexuality, a super observer....* [King] was the only man I ever knew who could, who was *more sensitive than Kinsey at looking at that [child sex] material...* King had sex with all these relatives and brothers and sisters and aunts... but nobody is objecting. He makes it pleasant... He rented himself out as a baby sitter part of the time... [and abused the children] Most of this material eventually got transferred to the Institute for Sex Research.

In the *Male* volume, Kinsey refers to another aspect of the sexual maturation of young boys, gleaned "from certain of our subjects who have *observed* first ejaculation in a list of several hundred boys."[33] Pomeroy has noted that the Kinsey team tested for sperm motility, with microscopic examination of seminal fluid for "mature" sperm, and Kinsey claimed to locate "11 out of 4,102 adult males in our histories" who allegedly had "orgasm" without ejaculate.[34]

If Kinsey's "trained observers" are to be believed, such orgasmic but non-ejaculating men are either freaks of nature or men who have severe psychological and/or physical maladies. We are left to wonder what Pomeroy meant when he wrote that Kinsey believed students in the sexology field had all been "too prudish" to make an actual investigation of sperm count in early adolescent males.[35] Even Kinsey's harshest critics failed to realize, or did not understand, that the young ejaculate-less subjects were fainting and/or convulsing in pained response to sexual molestation.

SOME CHILDREN STRAPPED OR "HELD DOWN"

A review of the child data by prominent pediatricians and other health professionals confirms what most mothers and fathers know instinctively: children, especially the very young, would not willingly submit to such abuse. Dr. Lester Caplan, a Baltimore physician and member of the American Board of Pediatrics, confirmed in a letter to this author that the children could not have been voluntary participants in the Kinsey research protocol:

> Regarding the data in Chapter 5, I have come to the following conclusions:

1. That the data was not the norm—rather was data taken form abnormal sexual activities, by sex criminals and the like.
2. Unnatural stimulation was used by the researchers to get results.
3. The frequencies and the number of orgasms in 24 hours was not normal nor the mean.
4. One person could not do this to so many children—these children had to be held down or subject to strapping down, otherwise they would not respond willingly.[36]

Dr. Caplan was merely confirming common sense, empirical observation, and pediatric training. During their Yorkshire interviews, both Gathorne-Hardy and Gebhard stated that Kinsey's books were meant to convince the public that we are all sexual, womb to tomb, so Kinsey had to "prove" infants were lustful, even if it meant tying them down and labeling their "hysterical weeping" an "orgasm":

> *Gathorne-Hardy:* [King] would masturbate little boys, tiny little boys, babies at 15 or 16 months. People don't normally do that.... Very small children can have orgasms, tiny children. There are even scans of a boy sort of playing with his cock in the womb. Kinsey knew the material would be less scientifically considered if he did reveal his source.
>
> *Gebhard:* Children are sexual beings... [L]ittle males get erections even in the uterus. They are sexual from the word go.... [King] contributed a fair amount to our knowledge... and medicine's knowledge of sexuality in children. We made our point that children are sexual from birth.

Crooks and Baur's 1983 college human sexuality text, *Our Sexuality* (Benjamin/Cummings Publishing Co.), a typical example of such works-cites the Kinsey team's findings on child sexuality as applicable to today's children:

> In many Western societies, including the United States, it has been traditional to view childhood as a time when sexuality remains unexpressed and adolescence as a time when sexuality needs to be restrained.... However, with the widespread circulation of the research findings of Alfred Kinsey and other distinguished investigators, the false assumption that childhood is a period of sexual dormancy is gradually eroding. In fact, it is now widely recognized that infants of both sexes are born with the capacity for sexual pleasure and response.
>
> *Signs of sexual arousal in infants and children, such as penile erection, vaginal lubrication, and pelvic thrusting, are often misinterpreted or unacknowledged.* However, careful observers may note these indications of sexuality in the very young. In some cases, both male and female infants have been observed experiencing what appears to be an orgasm. The infant, of course, cannot offer spoken confirmation of the sexual nature of such reactions.... *The following two quotations [from Kinsey's Male and Female Reports] are offered as evidence for this conclusion.*

Actually, the "misinterpretation" of certain physiological reactions in infants and children is entirely the authors'. The placing of a sexual connotation on these reflexive nervous and vascular reactions reflect hurtful, unethical, illegal and, consequently, invalid research.

But the acceptance of infant and childhood sexuality is powerfully entrenched in sexology circles. The "given" factor can be clearly seen in statements from Mary Calderone (past president and co-founder, with Lester Kirkendall, of SIECUS). Speaking before the 1980 annual meeting of the Association of Planned Parenthood Physicians, Dr. Calderone reportedly explained that providing today's society "very broadly and deeply with awareness of the vital importance of infant and childhood sexuality" is now the primary goal of SIECUS.[38] In 1983, Calderone wrote of the child's sexual capacities that,

> [these should] be developed-in the same way as the child's inborn human capacity to talk or to walk, and that [*the parents*] *role should relate only to teaching the child the appropriateness of privacy, place, and person-in a word socialization*[39]

With knowledge to the contrary, Indiana University consistently presented Kinsey as working under their safe and respectable auspices.

Or, in a typical Christian set education resource, "Children are Sexual Beings, Too." It may be surprising to realize that our children are *sexual beings from birth*. For instance, a parent changing a male infant's diaper may accidentally stimulate the child and be shocked to realize the *child is having an erection*. Similarly, *researchers tell us* that *baby girls have vaginal lubrication regularly*. In fact, a little girl being bounced on her parent's knee may feel pleasant sensations and bgin to make natural pelvic thrust movements.[40]

Which "researchers tell us" these things about children? Who is Buth's source? Only those trained by "sexologists" "tell us" about "child sexuality." The author first read the above dogma, eroticizing a baby girl's "vaginal lubrication" and a baby boy's erection in a 1977 pro-pedophile essay. But, all mucosal exit/entry organs; ears, mouth, vagina, anus, (even eyes) "have lubrication regularly," while the reflexive nervous and vascular reactions of the penis, "erectile tissue," respond to *many* biological stimuli; urinary build-up, friction, infections, (or fear), all wholly unconnected to libido. Clearly, Buth relies upon Freud's discredited child sexuality theories but, like Kinsey, Buth guts Freud's latency period.

Yes, children can be sexually abused and *prematurely* disturbed and aroused, by fear-sex stimuli like pornography as well as genital trauma due to antibiotics, medication or yeast infections and (more likely) pinworms. Even *Webster* states that ejaculation is required for the male "orgasm" and that eliminates babies, prepubertal children, from this category. Would God so mock His people so as to, or nature, the animal world, make little children "sexual" when an early libido could cripple the child's development?

"SCIENTIFICALLY TRAINED OBSERVERS"

So, Kinsey was not merely an "interviewer" as his supporters would have us believe. He and his team had long conducted laboratory experiments on human sexual response. Kinsey acknowledged that they had "unpublished gynecologic data that have been made available for the present project... some special data on the... detailed anatomy... involved in sexual response... physiologic experiments on the sexual activities of... the human animal."[41] The experiments occurred both in the field and at Indiana University, where perverts of all sorts kept detailed records of their child molestations and sent them to Kinsey for inclusion in his studies. As Kinsey explains in the *Female* volume,

It is difficult... to acquire any adequate understanding of the physiology of sexual response from clinical records or case history data, for they constitute secondhand reports which depend for their validity upon the capacity of the individual to observe his or her own activity, and upon his or her ability to analyze the physical and physiologic bases of those activities. In no other area have the physiologist and the student of behavior had to rely upon such secondhand sources, while having so little access to direct observation. This difficulty is particularly acute in the study of sexual behavior because the participant in a sexual relationship becomes physiologically incapacitated as an observer. Sexual arousal reduces one's capacities to see, to hear, to smell, to taste, or to feel with anything like normal acuity, and at the moment of orgasm one's sensory capacities may completely fail.[42]

It is for this reason that most persons are unaware that orgasm is anything more than a genital response and that all parts of their bodies as well as their genitalia are involved when they respond sexually.... The usefulness of the observed data to which we have had access depends in no small degree upon the fact that the observations were made in every instance by scientifically trained observers. Moreover, in the interpretation of these data we have had the cooperation of a considerable group of anatomists, physiologists, neurologists, endocrinologists, gynecologists, psychiatrists, and other specialists. The materials are still scant and additional physiologic studies will need to be made.[43]

We've shown that Kinsey and his pedophiles reported on the sexual "responses" of between 317 and 1,739 or 1,888 male infants and children.

Let us now turn to Kinsey's treatment of little girls.

PART II: THE LITTLE GIRL EXPERIMENTS

Adult Offenders: The accompanying table presents figures regarding adult offenders whom Kinsey euphemistically labeled "Partners." Chapter 4 of the *Female* volume, entitled "Pre-Adolescent Sexual Development," contains the Kinsey data on female *child* sexuality. They vary considerably from that having to do with male children. For instance, there are no data about tests of "speed to orgasm." Most of his female child "data" are obtained from adult recall. Pomeroy and Gebhard confirmed Jonsen and Mann's report[44] that the boys were timed to orgasm with a stop watch by adults and that "147 pre-adolescent females ranging in age from 2 to 15 years" were similarly "observed." So, Kinsey's data on the "Adult Partners" of 609 girls (unnumbered table) claims that, as pre-adolescents, 24 percent of his subjects were approached by adults in a sexual manner. He reports that 84 percent of those "approaches" were by non-kin and 23 percent by kin, and that *all were harmless*.

Of the 609 girls, 52 percent were victimized by strangers; 32 percent by friends (family friends, brothers of a friend, and others); and 140 (23 percent) by relatives. That latter figure translates to an incest rate of roughly 2.4 percent of the 5,940 females sampled (percentages for the various Kinsey categories add-up to 107 percent).

While Kinsey included all sorts of arcane data in his tables on male and female sexuality, there are *no* similar tables for child molestation or incest.

As noted earlier, Kinsey termed adults who had sexual intercourse with their children the children's "partners." Sexual activity was called "play." In his listing of relatives, Kinsey does not differentiate the non-biological family (live-in, step, adopted relations) from biological relations. This is critical information for a nation told by sexologists that divorce and live-in partners are harmless and preferable for children over that of a strained marriage.

The Kinsey team presents a small sample of seven girls under four years of age on whom direct sexual experiments had allegedly been performed: "We have similar records of observations made by some of our other subjects on a total of 7 pre-adolescent girls and 27 pre-adolescent boys under four years of age (see our 1948 study: 175-181)."[45]

The public deserves to know more about those seven (or 147) little girls. In a letter dated March 11, 1981, Gebhard claimed that no follow-up information on any of the children was available. Regarding the 27 boy "subjects" who were also under "'four years of age," Kinsey had stated that "observations made by some of our other subjects" strongly suggesting these small children were sexually tested by older "persons."[46] Subsequent investigation by Yorkshire Television confirmed that speculation.[47]

"ESTHER," INCEST SURVIVOR INTERVIEW FOR "KINSEY'S PAEDOPHILES"

Esther: My grandfather was a student here... when Alfred Kinsey was here... in a biology class in 1922... My father actually did mail some questionnaires... I believe, to the Kinsey Institute about the sexual abuse that he was doing on me... since 1938, which makes me about four years old... I had to meet with him and with Alfred Kinsey... Alfred Kinsey asked me some questions, was I happy... did I love my daddy? Of course, I was instructed... to be very nice to this man, that he was a very famous man... the conflict of emotions [in the sex abuse] actually ended up in convulsions... it was crying and uncontrollable shaking...

At the very peak of when all the abuse was going on, there was a time when there was a paper in a brown envelope and it... had little questions on it, with little blocks in front of it... but I didn't understand one of the words... orgasm... my father explained to me what an orgasm was. And he asked me to let him know when there was an orgasm. He always looked at his watch... he said, he had a deadline to meet and you had to send [the paper] away. So he put it in this envelope and I have never seen it since...

...I know he had a... camera that he used, but I don't know how much he took... one incident he could have taken... in the act... There was one time that may have been photographed... there was one time when I do remember it [a movie camera] was running and he says, oh, don't pay attention to that.

...I think what he did, at least in my case was use the figures for incest in the 1953 book... Now I understand, they have

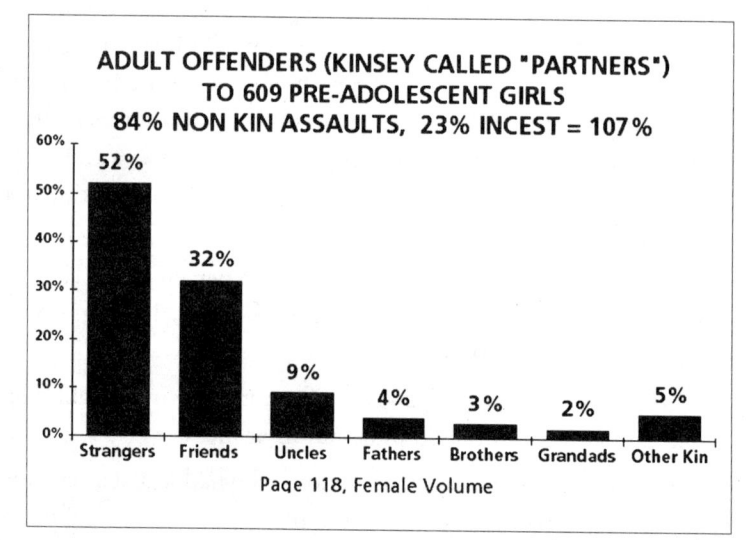

ADULT OFFENDERS (KINSEY CALLED "PARTNERS") TO 609 PRE-ADOLESCENT GIRLS
84% NON KIN ASSAULTS, 23% INCEST = 107%

Category	Percentage
Strangers	52%
Friends	32%
Uncles	9%
Fathers	4%
Brothers	3%
Grandads	2%
Other Kin	5%

Page 118, Female Volume

Alleged Kinsey incest survivor, "Esther," at about age 9. (Yorkshire Television outtake.)

"Esther" at Indiana University, recently, which still houses and supports the Kinsey Institute. (Yorkshire Television outtake.)

passed on that incest information onto someone else who is publishing a book and that makes me angry... They didn't ask my permission to publish...

...I went into a psychologist myself and I found Kinsey's lies coming right back at me. And then I realized that the Kinsey Institute is teaching the psychologist, I just got through paying money to see.. most people seek [help] from a psychologist or psychiatrist that was trained by [Kinseyans].

[The Kinsey books] are republished... reams of that information is going to be used in our public schools and perpetuate the lie again. Who is financing it...?

Those archives need to be opened up so people can understand that if they feel they were connected with the Kinsey Institute that they can go back and know for sure... **they used me** and they used those children and that is a terrible way to feel, to feel that you've been used for a lie, and they perpetuated it *so that it would happen again...*

My grandfather's perpetuation to my father was generational, and I think that's what Alfred Kinsey was after...

They didn't think that molesting children was wrong, so they didn't want to interrupt it, the abuse that was going on. They wanted that to continue, that is what they are doing this book for... [re-release of the Kinsey Reports, 1998]

The names of some or all of the children are in the Kinsey records. In fact, during his November 2, 1992, phone interview, Gebhard stated that the Institute has the names of "some" of the children who were so used: "Most of the cases we don't have the names of the children, but there are a small number of cases where we do have some names."[48]

RECORDS OF 23 YOUNG GIRLS IN "ORGASM"

There are justified concerns about what happened to these little boys and girls. First, if it is indeed true that seven girls less than three years old were directly observed by the Kinsey team reaching "orgasm," why are they not recorded as a separate group? No precise information (age, family data, race, religion, and other basic demographics) is provided for this unique, and apparently unprecedented, "population sample."

Hyman and Sheatsley have noted that "[o]ne's credulity is occasionally strained by a reported datum which Kinsey presents without qualification."[49] And the "actual observation" of three-year-old girls "masturbating" entailed a highly unethical indeed criminal procedure in the 1930s, even today. Hyman was a Rockefeller grantee and a highly respected interview specialist, while Sheatsley was well-known in the world of military analysis. Their article appeared in *An Analysis of the Kinsey Reports*,[50] where they remarked that it was scientifically irresponsible for the Kinsey team to combine direct experimentation with memories gleaned from adult interviews.

THE CHILD EXPERIMENTS

The Kinsey team claimed to have witnessed four infant girls reach "orgasm" at less than one year of age. Developmentally, such infants would be nursed or bottle-fed at one year, [perhaps could walk, but perhaps could walk,] but could not speak, could not yet control their bowels, jump, or eat with a fork or spoon, etc. But the Kinseyites were certain that they had attained orgasm!

Kinsey's Table 10[51] produces the following numbers on "pre-adolescent orgasm from any source."

KINSEY'S ALLEGED GIRL "ORGASM" DATA (FEMALE, P. 127)

"Table 10. Accumulative Incidence: Pre- Adolescent Orgasm From Any Source"

AGE	% OF TOTAL SAMPLE	CASES
3	-	5,908
5	2	5,862
7	4	5,835
9	6	5,772
10	8	5,762

Having claimed that it had "just recorded" "orgasm" data on one-year-old and three-year-old infants, the Kinsey team later indicated that no orgasm was recorded by age three "from any source."[52] Combining information from Kinsey Table 21[53] and 25 (see below) yields the following information about girls who *allegedly* masturbated to orgasm. Whether the girls had the adult "help" that Kinsey admits in the *Male* volume is concealed:

GIRL "MASTURBATION" DATA (FEMALE, PP. 177 & 180)

AGE	PERCENTAGE	ORGASM
	(Table 21, P. 177)	(Table 25, P. 180)
3	1% (of 5,913)	0% (of 5,913)
5	4% (of 5,866)	2% (of 5,866)
7	7% (of 5,841)	4% (of 5,838)
10	13% (of 5,808)	8% (of 5,802)
12	19% (of 5,784)	12% (of 5,778)

While fluctuating totals are not explained, another contradiction emerges: the sample size for orgasm from one source—masturbation (Kinsey's Table 25; Figure 5 above)—is larger than the sample size for orgasm from all sources (Tables 10 and 147) for ages three, five, seven, 10, and 12. If lack of orgasm by age three is *explained as a problem of recall*, as Kinsey claimed (Table 25; Figure 5 above), then the 23 girls under three years of age to whom Kinsey referred on page 105[54] (not merely the seven noted earlier) would also have been "direct observation" subjects.

Typically, according to Kinsey, the statement about "just" recording the baby "orgasms" was made alongside *recollections* by adult women of orgasms they allegedly experienced as children.[55] Such information is essentially worthless unless we know the truth about the interviewers and those interviewed. Following is an oft-quoted graphic description from the *Female* volume about an "intelligent mother" who allegedly frequently observed her three-year-old masturbating:

Lying face down on the bed, with her knees drawn up, she started rhythmic pelvic thrusts, about one second or less apart. The thrusts were primarily pelvic, with the legs tensed in a fixed position. The forward components of the thrusts were in a smooth and perfect rhythm which was unbroken except for momentary pauses during which the genitalia were readjusted against the doll on which they were pressed; the return from each thrust was convulsive, jerky. There were 44 thrusts in unbroken rhythm, a slight momentary pause, then 10 thrusts, and then a slight momentary pause, 87 thrusts followed by a slight momentary pause, then 10 thrusts, and then a cessation of all movement. There was marked concentration and intense breathing with abrupt jerks as orgasm approached. She was completely oblivious to everything during these later stages of the activity. Her eyes were glassy and fixed in a vacant stare. There was noticeable relief and relaxation after orgasm. A second series of reactions began two minutes later with series of 48, 18, and 57 thrusts, with slight momentary pauses between each series. With the mounting tensions, there were audible gasps, but immediately following the cessation of pelvic thrusts there was complete relaxation and only desultory movements thereafter.[56]

Another picture from Indiana University's "Uncle Kinsey" publicity series (with Martin's daughter).

And on the Yorkshire Television interview, said Gathorne-Hardy:

[Kinsey] was an established professor who could go anywhere and do anything.... [M]oralists go around, horrified at the fact that quote unquote, Kinsey used pedophiles to get information.... Well, it's true that [King]... had intercourse with hundreds of males and females of every conceivable age... His girlfriend did the whole thing with her own daughter.

Apparently, King's "girlfriend" did not merely *record* her daughter's bizarre conduct. This is an admission that she and/or King *caused* the child's behavior.

This alleged "scientific" record has been cited by professionals in law and medicine worldwide. Typically, college sexuality texts by such authors such as Crooks and Bauer cite this page in Kinsey as evidence that children under age three are capable of orgasm. Future teachers, doctors, and other professionals, as well as parents, are told that "intelligent" parents should not be disturbed by such activities.

Though graphic, anecdotal stories are hardly science, when they were couched in scientific verbiage by Kinsey they helped pave the way for intimate

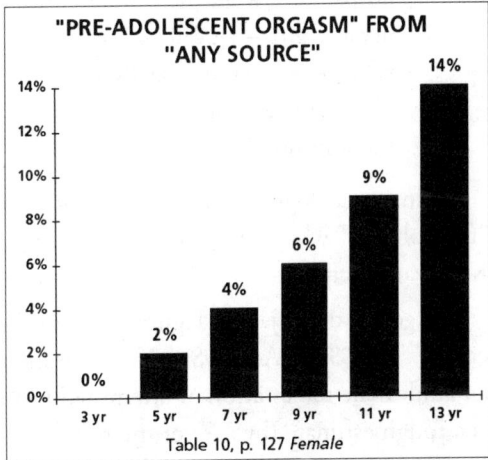

"PRE-ADOLESCENT ORGASM" FROM "ANY SOURCE"

Age	Percentage
3 yr	0%
5 yr	2%
7 yr	4%
9 yr	6%
11 yr	9%
13 yr	14%

Table 10, p. 127 *Female*

THE CHILD EXPERIMENTS

physical examinations of children in their schools. For instance, the "Tanner Maturation Guide"[57] claims the areola size of the breast and the presence of pubic hair determine whether a child is physically mature enough to play school sports. Using that guide, children in New York were required to strip so they could be examined to see if they were qualified for team sports. One New York mother was impelled to file suit against her daughter's school, rather than allow her youngster to undergo the humiliation and embarrassment of a nude examination by her female coach.[58]

GIRL'S SEXUALLY VICTIMIZED BY MEN AND OLDER BOYS (FEMALE, P. 118]

"Ages of Females Having Adult Contacts"

AGE	% OF ACTIVE SAMPLE	Author's Analysis	%TOTAL SAMPLE
4	5	52	1
5	8	83	2
6	9	94	2
7	13	135	3
8	17	177	4
9	16	166	4
10	26	270	6
11	24	249	6
12	25	260	7 [sic, should be 6]
13	19	197	6 [sic, should be 4]
	1,039	**1,682 Girls Molested**	4,407 Females

Another Kinsey table of girls under age 13 "Pre-Adolescents" is captioned "Age of Females Having Adult Contacts" (p. 118). It includes figures for pre-adolescent females who were sexually molested by males over *15-years-old*. (My daughter would not count as a molestation victim since her rapist was 13-years-old.) Similar to other Kinsey team data, it entails a confusing and incoherent set of numbers. Clarence Tripp offers a few thoughts beyond quantification; beyond Kinsey's numbers. It would have been helpful to the public in 1948 to read his descriptive narrative about King's "fit problem,"

> The children thought he was wonderful.... There was no force, no damage, no harm, no pain.... Well, there were two instances in which a young boy or girl – I think it was a girl— agreed to the sexual contact but then they found it very painful and yelled out when it actually took place. This was because they were very young and had small genitalia and [King] was a grown man with enormous genitalia and there was a fit problem.

Kinsey catalogued some adult-child "contacts" of his girl victims, but such details as Tripp's "fit problem," when "they were very young" were not revealed to the millions of Kinsey readers and Kinseyan disciples.

"Age" in the adjacent Figure refers to that at which a sexual approach by an adult male was recalled. The "% of Active Sample" appears to refer to 1,039 women who, Kinsey claimed, recalled an adult male molestation or attempted molestation. The shadowed column, added by this author, is a rough estimate (by age) of the number of girls who allegedly recalled molestations. And "% of

Total Sample" refers to the 4,407 women who are not viewed as "active" molestation victims. The figures leave much to be interpreted by the reader.

This crucial and revealing table, as does virtually all of Kinsey's data, falls short of the "meticulous" taxonomic "perfection" attributed to Kinsey by Indiana University, the Rockefeller Foundation, and almost all of Kinsey's supporters. Kinsey's child data were never challenged by anyone—other than this author.

It should be noted that 32 girls were actually raped, even according to Kinsey's data (3% of 1,075), while the rest were subjected to exhibitionists or fondling. Kinsey states on page 120 that the men and boys exposed themselves specifically to upset the little girls, and that the offenders gained pleasure from seeing the "fright or surprise or embarrassment" on the children's faces. He discounted the "harm" factor, claiming that the procedure provided "a source of pleasure to some children." According to Kinsey:

- 5% of the molested girls appeared to be "aroused";
- 1% were brought to "orgasm" by the offender(s);
- 80% reported some fear, terror, and/or guilt.

It is unclear why the total number of molested female child victims was reduced from 1,075 (as noted elsewhere) to 1,039, or why the total sample dropped from 4,441 (also noted elsewhere) to 4,407. Moreover, it is a mystery why so much of the scientific world has accepted Kinsey's claim that only one child out of 4,441 *perhaps* suffered some "serious injury" by adult sexual abuse. Or, why the word abuse or molestation never occurs in Kinsey's two books.

INCEST OFFENDERS DEFINED AS CHILDREN'S SEXUAL "PARTNERS"

One technique for hiding information is failure to list relevant words in a book's index. The *Female* volume claimed to be an objective report on female sexual behavior. Yet the term "incest" does not appear in its 31-page index of some 4,300 entries. (It was, however, listed once in the *Male* volume.)

The Kinsey team allegedly recorded when children were molested by Kinsey's "adult partners," as recalled by female interviewees from childhood. You will recall Pomeroy's claim that Kinsey chose terms meticulously, avoiding "euphemisms" that would distort meanings. Kinsey used the euphemism "partner" to mask adult molesters, pedophiles, and others who sexually assault children. The use of the term "partner" suggests the activity was mutually agreed upon. It serves to discount the harm resulting from adult sexual abuse of children. As reported by Donna Friess and Esther White (see extensive endnotes), Kinsey's incest data had, and continues to have, a dramatic impact on children. In fact, those who have suffered from the abuse perpetrated by Kinsey's pedophiles may yet

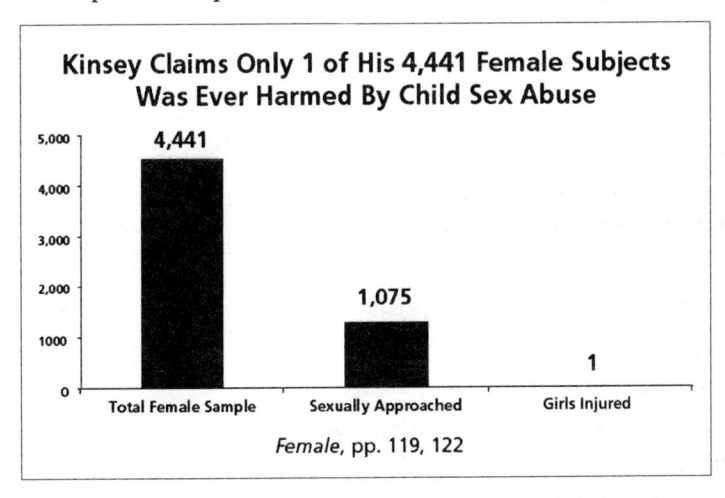

Kinsey Claims Only 1 of His 4,441 Female Subjects Was Ever Harmed By Child Sex Abuse

Total Female Sample	Sexually Approached	Girls Injured
4,441	1,075	1

Female, pp. 119, 122

THE CHILD EXPERIMENTS

obtain access to the files sequestered at the Kinsey Institute. According to Gathorne-Hardy, who believes that "As a scientist I thought Kinsey was marvelous, exemplary," the Institute fears that some of Kinsey's victims may yet come forward:

> [The Kinsey Institute] is nervous, people will read the journals and identify someone in them. [King] described having sex with this... little girl, this little boy or this man or this pig.... I think the Kinsey Institute felt... right wing figures... would pluck out things.... I think they are right to keep them undercover because they are not dealing with scrupulous scholars, they are dealing with people out to wreck them... there are descriptions of [King] buggering boys nigh on 13 ...[who] doesn't enjoy it. I mean it's quite sort of harsh stuff some of it.

The pedophile claim that adult sex with children is harmless has obtained a large following during the last half-century. Current estimates of "one in four females (and one in seven boys) having been molested by age 18"[59] suggest that American children are today experiencing unprecedented rates of sexual abuse.

Figure 9 presents figures from Kinsey's table on prepubescent girls and their adult "partners." This author has added a "victim" data column for clarification. As noted earlier, an incest rate of 2.4 percent (147 cases among the 5,940 female subjects) was indicative of a serious problem for society in general and law enforcement in particular. From the Kinsey team's child-sex normalcy perspective, however, there was a motive to obscure the data. And again, Kinsey's "% of Active Sample" category totaled 107 percent, which reflects Kinsey's pattern of well-funded bad statistics. Are there 645 child abuse victims (based on his percentages) or are the added 36 cases multiple abuses? For a study alleged to be the most "meticulous" work on sexuality ever conducted, Kinsey actually hides the number of child victims in both his *Male* and *Female* volumes.

RELATIONSHIP OF ADULT TO GIRL INCEST "VICTIMS" ADDED TO KINSEY'S ORIGINAL UNNAMED TABLE [FEMALE, P. 118]

ADULT "PARTNERS"	% OF ACTIVE SAMPLE	[AUTHOR'S ANALYSIS] [Number of Girl "Cases"]
Strangers	52	317
Friends/Acquaintances	32	195
Uncles	9	55
Fathers	4	24
Brothers	3	18
Grandfathers	2	12
Other Relatives	5	30
Cases Reporting	609	651

"Author's Analysis:" This column was added to show the actual number of children represented by Kinsey's percentages.

Among the many aspects of incest that the Kinsey team opted to ignore were,
- number of resulting pregnancies;
- number of resulting abortions;
- relationship of victim to perpetrator (father, brother, uncle, stranger, etc.);
- instances of venereal disease;

- number of girls victimized by more than one relative;
- duration of the incestuous relationship;
- number of offenses per child;
- number of girls who reported their ordeal to parents and/or authorities;
- ages at which the offenses occurred;
- number of victims battered, blackmailed, or photographed for pornography;
- number of girls given pornography as model behavior to copy;
- number of victims attempting suicide;
- number of victims subsequently entering prostitution or becoming substance abusers.

The list could to on and on. Failure to raise such points suggests a strong—indeed pathological—bias aimed at blinding readers and other researchers to the critical, often life-threatening situations facing boy and girl victims of incestuous abuse. Kinsey purged all homosexual incest from his report.

Many persons responded to Kinsey's call for diaries and sexual calendars. They were "solicited" and "urged" to keep records of any future or on-going "outlets." One woman's recollection of her grandfather[60] includes the "forms" he mailed to the Kinsey Institute, on which he apparently recorded his sexual abuse of his granddaughter, and her alleged "responses." Kinsey states,

> Many of the calendars have come from scientifically trained persons who have comprehended the importance of keeping systematic records. Many of the calendars are a product of our call for such material in the Male volume…. Persons who… are willing to begin keeping day-by-day calendars showing the sources and frequencies of their outlet, are urged to write us for instructions.[61]

Follow-up data on the child molestation and incest cases have, according to the Kinsey Institute, been maintained from time to time, but are yet to be made public. It is understandable, since the team sought-out actual and potential offenders and urged them to keep records of their future planned sex acts with children to "help science." The recent admissions by Gathorne-Hardy, Paul Gebhard, and Kinsey Institute Director Bancroft that the Institute has some of the abused children's names, and some of the original child abuse data, confirms that the information has been, and is being, deliberately suppressed.

If, as the Kinsey team claimed, a parent was always present during interviews, and if the name of each subject was coded in the Institute data base, why cannot the children be traced? And why was there apparently no follow up to determine their subsequent physical and emotional status? Such data could have helped to confirm or refute Kinsey's allegation that adult sex with children is harmless.

Childhood incest and the sexual abuse of women has been shown to result in; divorce, battery of wives and children, jealousy and rivalry between mothers and siblings, obesity, anorexia, venereal disease, pregnancy, abortion, attempts to run away, suicidal ideation, and suicide, promiscuity, "voluntary" and forced prostitution and/or pornography, addiction to alcohol and drugs, early marriage, incest on younger siblings and later child victimization.[62] All are current, commonly recognized variables of the incest victim profile.[63]

As academic dean of the Institute for the Advanced Study of Human Sexuality, Kinsey co-author Wardell Pomeroy sanctioned incest as beneficial when advising readers of *Penthouse*, *Chic*, and other pornographic magazines. He based his position on Kinsey Institute data supposedly supporting the notion of "positive incest." Pomeroy stated in his sexuality text, *Girls and Sex* (1969), that the "medical" reasons for "the incest taboo" are that "the children of an incestuous union will be likely to inherit the outstanding good characteristics of both [parents]."[64]

Hardly. The *British Medical Journal*, reporting on studies of first generation father-daughter and brother-sister incest births, ignoring the emotional costs, found 42 percent to be apparently normal, 58 percent diseased, retarded, or still-born.[65]

During a December 1977 *Penthouse* interview, past Kinsey Institute Director Paul Gebhard also claimed that incest was harmless. With their reputations enhanced as Kinsey co-authors, the opinions of Pomeroy and Gebhard have been widely quoted by others, and cited authoritatively in state and federal court decisions (see Chapter 9, "Kinsey and the Law").

Kinsey publicly claimed that his "scientific" findings showed children "derived definite pleasure" from their experiences.

Kinsey's incest data were requested from the Institute by this author in 1981. In his reply, Director Gebhard stated that it had been passed along to Warren Farrell, who was said to be working on a book entitled, *The Last Taboo: The Three Faces of Incest*:[66]

> We omitted incest (in the *Female* Report), except for one brief mention, because we felt we had too few cases: 47 white females and 96 white males, and most of the incest was with siblings. We have turned our incest data over to Warren Farrell to supplement his larger study which I think is still unpublished.[67]

Gebhard's letter underscored the contradictions of the Kinsey incest data. The *Female* volume listed 147 instances of female incest victims, (23 percent of the 609-subject "Active Sample"), not 47.[68] Moreover, most of the incest alleged by the team was committed by uncles and fathers not by "siblings." Again, Kinsey says nothing about whether these incest offenders were biological or non-biological (step family/adoption) kin.

As of this writing, Farrell's "positive incest" book remains unpublished.

SEXUALIZED IMAGES OF CHILDREN

According to *Newsweek*, Kinsey Institute Director June Reinisch once stated that she found the Institute's "collection of child pornography so distasteful... that she cannot bear to look at it."[69] Yet Pomeroy and Gebhard both reassure their audiences that adult sex with children, including incest, is not only harmless, but in some instances beneficial. Dr. Pomeroy is on the Board of Consultants for *Penthouse Forum Variations*, a periodical which refers to incest as "Home Sex."

Along with articles and images recommending and demonstrating bestiality, sadism, homosexuality, and bisexuality, *Penthouse Forum Variations* published Pomeroy's article, "A New Look at

While incest was largely committed by adults in the past, as "soft" pornography entered the home, sexual abuse by older children has become an increasing problem.

Incest."[70] It appeared alongside a letter from a supposedly happy incest daughter who wrote, "My early memories of a typical morning when I was five or six are of getting in bed with dad when my mother left for work." The *Penthouse* editor graphically described sex with "father" as "marvelous."[71] In his book, *Boys and Sex* (1981) Pomeroy recommended sex with animals as "potentially joyous," unless one is discovered by the inhibited and sexually repressive "Mrs. Grundys" of the world.[72]

Pomeroy wrote about the "benefits" of incest for *Penthouse Forum* consumers.

Also accompanying Pomeroy's *Penthouse Forum Variations* article was a letter-to-the-editor from an anonymous woman. Entitled, "Another Look at Incest," it graphically described a five-year-old girl, deserted by her mother, who lived sexually with her father for years. The youngster was described as healthy and loved. Indeed, the writer claimed that after dating and sleeping around with a number of boys, she planned to marry someone wonderful—like her dad.

Pomeroy "scientifically" reinforced what the reader had just learned about the benefits of incest and adult sex with children. He wrote:

Pomeroy sits on the *Penthouse Forum* board, alongside a veritable "Who's Who" in the human sexuality traffic.

> When we look at a cross-section of the normal population (rather than look at a selection of those in prison for incest), we find many beautiful and mutually satisfying and healthy relationships between fathers and daughters. These may be transient or ongoing, but they have no harmful effects.[73]

Needless to say, Pomeroy never had a "cross-section of the normal population." So, the Kinsey team did not provide any reliable data confirming that "we find many beautiful and mutually satisfying relationships between fathers and daughters... [that] have no harmful effects." Writing about "positive incest" in the December 1977 issue of *Penthouse*, Philip Nobile, erstwhile *Penthouse Forum* editorial director, advocated an end to the incest taboo by calling on the expertise of then-Kinsey Institute Director Gebhard:

> Actually, Kinsey was the first sex researcher to uncover evidence that violation of the [incest] taboo does not necessarily shake heaven and earth. Unpublished data taken from his original sex histories (some 18,000 in number) imply that lying with a near relative [incest] rarely ends in tragedy. "In *our basic sample, that is, our random sample, only a tiny percentage of our incest cases had been reported to police or psychologists*," states Kinsey collaborator Dr. Paul Gebhard, currently director of the Institute for Sex Research in Bloomington, Indiana. "In fact, in the ones that were not reported, I'm having a hard time recalling any traumatic effects at all. I certainly can't recall any from among the brother-sister participants and I can't put my finger on any among the parent-child participants." The nation was hardly prepared for such talk in the '50s, but Gebhard is releasing Kinsey's startling incest material for incorporation in Warren Farrell's work-in-progress, *The Last Taboo: The Three Faces of Incest [Emphasis added]*.[74]

Interestingly, that was presumably the same "incest material" that Gebhard, in his later letter to this author, claimed entailed "too few cases [so that] we omitted incest, except for one brief mention" in the *Female* volume.

WHO CONDUCTED, TIMED, AND FILMED THE EXPERIMENTS?

Kinsey's experiments were understandably conducted in secrecy. His zoologist's taxonomic categorization methods are evident everywhere. Many subsequent schools of "sex science" have adopted his zoological methods of collecting, organizing, and classifying. In Kinsey's words:

> The techniques of this research have been... born out of the senior author's long-time experience with a problem in insect taxonomy. The transfer from insect to human material is not illogical, for it has been a transfer of a method that may be applied to the study of any variable populations.[75]

Such human sex measurements and categorizing were virtually unknown in the 1940s. According to Kinsey,

> None of the older authors, with the possible exception of Hirschfeld, attempted any systematic coverage of particular items in each history, and consequently there was nothing to be added or averaged, even for the populations with which they dealt.... The present study is designed as a first step in the accumulation of a body of scientific fact that may provide the basis for sounder generalizations about the sexual behavior of certain groups and, some day, even of our American population as a whole.[76]

Kinsey effected the sexual reform of "our American population as a whole" via zoological quantification, accumulating copious statistics, tables, charts, measurements and percentages. Kinsey senior researcher John Gagnon, speaking of himself and his colleagues, noted that as a teenager:

> [A local homosexual] plied us with beer and evidence from the Kinsey Report showing that although homosexuality might be a crime and a sin, it was statistically common, phylogenetically normal, and might indeed be pleasurable and profitable. This was my first experience in the use of sexual science for practical goals.... Kinsey wished to justify disapproved patterns of sexual conduct by an appeal to biological origins.... Putting a percentage in front of the topic made it speakable.[77]

A young John Gagnon, sex researcher for the Kinsey Institute and current human sexuality science authority.

If Kinsey was not responsible for any experimentation on children, as maintained by Kinsey Institute Director John Bancroft and former Director June Reinisch,[78] who was? In their attempt to minimize the public outcry over Kinsey's scientific solicitation and collaboration with pedophiles, Bancroft, Reinisch, the Kinsey Institute, and Indiana University pointed to a single, anonymous individual. But they never produced a name. Why?

Pomeroy first introduced the mysterious "gentleman," or "elderly scientist," in 1972. The man we now know, (thanks to the Yorkshire television investigative team) to be Rex King, the traveling government surveyor, is called "Mr. X." by James H. Jones in his Kinsey biography. Pomeroy described him as a "quiet, soft-spoken, self-effacing... unobtrusive fellow... a college graduate." In his 1972 book on Kinsey, Pomeroy firmly stated that this "unobtrusive fellow" had sex with 800 children, had been initiated into sex by his grandmother and his father, and had sex with various animals. John Bancroft called their mystery man an "elderly scientist,"[78] "educated in some technical field, perhaps holding a college degree,"[80] and most interesting, as "an omniphile, an extraordinarily active man" whose "training was in forestry."[81] Jones writes:

> Kinsey began his courtship of Mr. X in the fall of 1943... [He] correctly divined that Mr. X longed for recognition and approval. From the beginning, therefore, Kinsey treated him like a colleague, a fellow seeker of truth who had compiled valuable scientific data. In a letter that combined flattery and praise, Kinsey wrote, "I congratulate you on the research spirit which has led you to collect data over these many years."...[H]e was "very much interested in your account [of certain illegal behaviors Mr. X had practiced in hotels, such as drilling holes in walls to film people engaged in sex in adjacent rooms].... There are difficulties enough in this undertaking to make it highly desirable for all of us who are at work to keep in touch. I hope we keep in touch with you." Much to Kinsey's delight, the materials arrived by return mail, the first of many shipments over the next several years. "Your instant willingness to cooperate and your comprehension of the problems involved in these studies make me all the more anxious to meet you," replied Kinsey.... "Mrs. Kinsey and I should be glad to entertain you in our home.... Everything that you accumulated must find its way into scientific channels."[82]

Kinsey offered to cover the expense of bringing the serial child molester to his family home in Bloomington, and expressly hoped "to work out further plans for cooperating with you." Jones continues:

> Kinsey's benign view of pedophilia does not fully explain why he was so taken with Mr. X. To fathom their relationship, one must understand that Kinsey considered Mr. X not merely a sexual phenomenon but a scientific treasure. Privately, Kinsey had long believed that human beings in a state of nature were basically pansexual. Absent social constraints, he conjectured, "natural man" would commence sexual activity early in life, enjoy intercourse with both sexes [any and all ages] eschew fidelity, indulge in a variety of behaviors, and be much more sexually active in general for life. To Kinsey, Mr. X was living proof of this theory. Describing Kinsey's joy in discovery, Nowlis [a junior Kinsey staffer] declared, "This was like finding the gall wasp which would establish not a new species but a new genus" ....As Nowlis put it, *Kinsey looked upon Mr. X as a "hero" because "the guy had the courage and the ingenuity and the sexual energy and the curiosity to have this fantastic multi-year odyssey...and never get caught."*[83] [Emphasis added.]

Kinsey claimed that children's screams of pain, and struggles to escape from their "partners," were evidence of the children's pleasure.

Jones admits that Kinsey's "hero," Rex King, copulated with "countless adults of both sexes."[84] Hence, he would be at the very least a statistical vector for sexually transmitted diseases. Jones records Pomeroy's testimony that Mr. X could "masturbate to ejaculation in ten seconds from a flaccid start... [which] our subject calmly demonstrated,"[85] meaning that he was, as we now know, still an active serial, not merely nostalgic, child molester. Jones does not, however, directly relate

THE CHILD EXPERIMENTS

King's sexual feats to the abuse of even a single child. He does not tell us, for instance, the age of the youngest girl and boy molested by Kinsey's "hero," whom the Kinsey Institute considered to be an expert on the "truth" about child sexuality.

Jones writes:

> Kinsey [was determined] to exhaust Mr. X's collections and personal expertise. In March, 1945, *Kinsey offered to pay Mr. X's salary if he would take a leave from government and pull together his materials....* Confessing that his own data on preadolescent orgasms were "definitely scant," Kinsey wrote to Mr. X in March, 1945, "Certainly you have very much more material than we have in our records." Specifically, Kinsey asked for information about the average age at which orgasm occurred in preadolescent boys, their capacity for multiple orgasms, and the earliest age at which orgasms have been observed in boys... it took months for him to... pull this material together. "This is one of the most valuable things we have ever gotten and I want to thank you most abundantly for the time you put into it and for your willingness to cooperate.... Anyone who is scientifically trained must comprehend how valuable the data are."[86] [Emphasis added]

James H. Jones, another Rockefeller grantee, worked closely with the Kinsey Institute while writing his Kinsey biography.

That Kinsey admired this criminal serial child molester whose "courage and ingenuity" in his child sexual "odyssey" were outstanding because he was not "caught," is further documented in Kinsey's personal correspondence, where child sexual abuse is transmogrified into acts of virtual heroism. Only Vincent Nowlis, then a junior Kinsey staffer, appeared to have voiced any objection to the Kinsey team's support of Mr. X and his "research." Jones recalls,

> Nowlis saw things differently. He regarded Mr. X as a monster pure and simple and thought it was wrong to use data that came from immoral research. Decades later, he recalled telling Kinsey, "Look, that material on timing infants and youngsters to orgasm—I don't think that belongs in this book." But Kinsey was adamant.... Kinsey meant to change the public's thinking on sexual matters... Kinsey was determined to provide those data.... The end justified the means.[87]

Indiana University records confirm that Kinsey did not report Mr. X to authorities. Indeed, for over fifty years the entire Indiana University Kinsey Institute team collaborated in covering-up sex crimes perpetrated against children involved in its research.

During an appearance on the *Donahue* television talk show in December 1990, Kinsey colleague Clarence Tripp stated that several pedophiles gave testimony about their sex crimes to Kinsey, but they were not criminals because they had not been prosecuted or served prison time. This author asked Tripp, as we waited in the Green Room prior to our joint appearance on the program, "Are you saying that if one kills an unarmed person, a child or two, unless one is caught, tried and convicted one is not a murderer, a criminal?" Tripp repeated the Kinsey position: that one is not an offender, not a criminal, unless one is caught and convicted. And while Kinsey, Pomeroy, and Gebhard emphatically admitted the involvement of the Kinsey team with *several* pedophiles,[88] and Gebhard affirmed that their team was "amoral" and "criminal," and Pomeroy documented Kinsey's own personal collection of "early adolescent...sperm,"[89] Jones neglects to report such critical information. We are told only of the dead Kinsey, while information that could trigger prosecution of the living remains in limbo.

During a 1995 Canadian television program, Kinsey Institute Director John Bancroft stated that the reason he had determined that there was "only" one man who had experimented on hundreds of children was that "some otherwise" reasonable people were asking how Kinsey could have gotten specific information about "speed" of climax, time between "climaxes," and so on. Yet, Gebhard and Bancroft both spoke of "Mr. X" as "pedophiles" (plural). And in the *Male* Volume, Kinsey asserts that there were "nine" men involved in the laboratory experiments:

Paul Gabheard, Director of the Kinsey Institute.

> Better data on pre-adolescent climax come from the histories of adult males who have had sexual contacts with younger boys… 9 of our adult male subjects have observed such orgasm… in contacts with… adults.[90]

But, we now know that it was Kinsey's mentor and colleague Robert Dickinson who "trained" Kinsey and King in the "proper" techniques of child sexual abuse. Yorkshire Television investigators discovered that Dr. Robert Dickinson, Kinsey's famous "mentor in sex research," had "collaborated with the pedophile [King] for several years, and taught him how to record his child abuse in scientific detail." Tripp reported:

> Dickinson taught him [Rex King] how to measure things, and time things, and *encouraged* him to—he knew he was going to do his ordinary behavior anyway, Dickinson couldn't have stopped him from being a pedophile—but he said, at least you ought to do something scientific about it so it won't be just your jollies, it'll be something worthwhile, so he gave him some training by letter and correspondence. [Emphasis added.]

Obviously, by reporting this serial child rapist to law enforcement authorities, Dickinson and Kinsey could have "stopped him from being a pedophile" who harmed children.

Dickinson confirmed in his Foreword to Ernst and Loth's *American Sexual Behavior* (1948) that "nine" men were involved in the study:

> The total of the case histories carrying rather full details of sex experience, gathered by nine different investigators during twenty-five years, [Kinsey, Pomeroy, Martin, Gebhard and five other men] is something like two-thirds of the present Kinsey collection of 12,000.[91]

We were left to wonder exactly who those "nine" men were, and why the identity of the notorious "Mr. X" was kept a secret. Thanks to the Yorkshire documentary, we now know that "Mr. X" was Rex King, and we also know the name of at least one other key Kinsey pedophile. In a classic case of truth being stranger than fiction, one of Kinsey's child sex experimenters was a World War II Nazi Storm Trooper. Yorkshire Television researchers uncovered his name, photograph, history, and court records. After the war, Dr. Fritz von Balluseck became a respected lawyer.

THE CHILD EXPERIMENTS

PART III: KINSEY'S NAZI PEDOPHILE

Yorkshire investigators had followed up this author's original questions regarding Kinsey's association with Nazis and the possibility that some of the abused children were obtained from WWII Germany and/or Russia. At least one of Kinsey's sex collaborators was a documented Nazi, the infamous George Sylvester Viereck, a convicted German spy who had worked among Washington D.C. power brokers. David Brinkley in his history of the period, *Washington Goes to War* (1988: 26) wrote that Viereck was "one of the...masterminds of the propaganda cabinet that Germany set up here early in the war." Yorkshire researchers flew to Berlin (as did this author), interviewing and digging through old files and press reports. There they discovered Dr. Friedrich Karl Hugo Viktor von Balluseck, who was tried in Berlin in 1957 for a child sex murder. According to Paul Gebhard who took over serving as the prestigious Director of Indiana University's Kinsey Institute, just after Kinsey's death:

> [Kinsey] wrote him questions in the letter and they carried on quite a correspondence.... Police [seeking a child sex murderer] went through his possessions... found his correspondence with Kinsey.... They got Interpol.... The FBI put pressure on Kinsey to reveal the guy's sexual diary. Kinsey said, absolutely not. [T]he poor paedophile... had his reputation destroyed... finally quit corresponding with us.

Like Kinsey, fascist scientists in Germany[92] believed that they had a right to experiment on anyone. Dr. von Balluseck[93] was an incest offender who raped and sodomized not only his own offspring, but Jewish, Polish, and German children as well, from roughly 1927 to 1957. The German press reported Kinsey's visit to Frankfort during his world tour in 1956. Little else is available regarding the German stopover, or if Kinsey met with Balluseck, and there was no mention of Kinsey's visit to Frankfort in the approved writings about Kinsey's European travels.

"THE MOST IMPORTANT PEDOPHILE IN THE CRIMINAL HISTORY OF BERLIN"

Dr. von Balluseck's trial for the murder of 10-year-old Loiselotte Has, who was "found... naked and throttled... on a piece of wasteland," was widely covered in Germany. It was "completely unprecedented in the moral history of the post war era," and von Balluseck was described as "the most important pedophile in the criminal history of Berlin." Kinsey collaborator Balluseck was tried for the abuse of 50, or "more than 100," or "several hundred" children. As noted, he had sexually violated children for "over the last three decades" (*Frankfurter Allgemeine Zeitung*, May 22, 1957).

Dr. Fritz von Balluseck. Outcut from Yorkshire Television's "Kinsey's Paedophiles."

News of Kinsey's role in the case was splashed across the headlines of Germany's largest newspapers. Judge Heinrich Berger "emphasized again and again the important function played by the press in warning the public against paedophiles like Balluseck, who approach children as understanding friends and helpers in their sexual need" (*Frankfurter Allgemeine Zeitung*, May 22, 1957). Despite Alfred Kinsey's shocking role in the explosive case, the U.S. press was uniformly silent about it.

According to Yorkshire Television's research department, from 1942 to 1944 Dr. von Balluseck was the Department of Justice District Kreishauptmina, the commandant of the small Polish town of Jedrzejow. It was there that he targeted the children he sexually assaulted, warning them, according to German news accounts, that "It is either the gas chamber or me." *The Encyclopedia Judaica*[94] reports that all Jedrejow Jews ended up in the gas chambers. All, including the children, were under the control of Dr. von Balluseck.

The German press described early attempts to "cover up" who Balluseck really was, including efforts to keep his photograph under wraps and the court description of the influential attorney as a "shop-worker." And commenting on the experiments recorded in volumes found in von Balluseck's desk, Judge Berger exclaimed: "This is no longer human! What was this all for? To tell Kinsey about?" (*Morgenpost*, May 16, 1957). Here are additional excerpts from German press accounts:

> The Nazis knew and gave him the opportunity to practice his abnormal tendencies in occupied Poland on Polish children, who had to chose between Balluseck and the gas ovens. After the war, the children were dead, but Balluseck lived. [*National-Zeitung*, May 15, 1957]

> Balluseck's career catapulted because he was a fanatical member of the Nazi party... he was a Nazi Occupational officer in Poland and he abused 10-12 year old girls. [*Neues Deustschland*, May 17, 1957]

> Balluseck... corresponded with the American Kinsey Institute for some time, and had also got books from them which dealt with child sexuality [*Tagespiegel*, October 1, 1957]

> [N]ot only did he commit his crimes in Germany, but also during the war as an occupation officer, he committed numerous sexual crimes against Polish girls of between 10 & 14 years old. [*Der Morgen*, May 15, 1957]

> Dr. Balluseck... [recorded measurements] of his crimes committed against children between 9 and 14 years old... in four thick diaries... of a pseudo-scientific character... while in correspondence with the American sexual researcher Kinsey... about his research results which as he said himself, took place over three decades. [*Frankfurter Allgemeine Zeitung*, May 22, 1957]

> **Judge Berger:** "I had the impression that you got to the children in order to impress Kinsey and to deliver him material."
>
> **Balluseck**: "Kinsey himself asked me for that [asked me to do so]"
>
> As a role model for his perverse actions Balluseck named the so-called sexual psychologist Kinsey.... [*Neuess Deutschland*, May, 17, 1957]

> Today the court has got four diaries, and in these diaries, with cynicism and passion, he recorded his crimes against 100 children in the smallest detail. He sent the detail of his experiences regularly to the US sex researcher, Kinsey. The latter was very interested and kept up a regular and lively correspondence with Balluseck [*National-Zeitung*, May 15, 1957]

> Sharp criticism of American sex researcher by presiding Judge... Heinrich Berger... because of the correspondence between Regierungsrat Dr. Fritz von Balluseck, accused of many counts

of sexual crimes, and Kinsey. The presiding judge exclaimed, *"Instead of answering his sordid letters, the strange American scholar should rather have made sure that Mister von Balluseck was put behind bars."* [*Morgenpost*, May 16, 1957]

"KINSEY...ASKED THE PAEDOPHILE SPECIFICALLY FOR MATERIAL OF HIS PERVERSE ACTIONS"

The connection with Kinsey, towards whom he'd showed off his crimes, had a disastrous effect on [von Balluseck]... [I]n his diaries he'd stuck in the letters from the sex researcher, Kinsey in which he'd been *encouraged to continue* his research.... He had also started relationships... *to expand his researches*. One shivers to think of the lengths he went to. [*TSP*, May 17, 1957, emphasis added]

Indeed, the German press reported that Post WW II von Balluseck sexually assaulted his own daughter, and the 11-year-old son of a vicar, and forced the boy to write down the acts for Kinsey.

Kinsey had asked the paedophile specifically for material of his perverse actions. The presiding judge, Dr. Berger noted that it was Kinsey's duty to get Balluseck locked up, instead of corresponding with him. [*Berliner Zeitung*, May 16, 1957]

He made statistics of all these experiences and he sent them with comprehensive reports to the American sex researcher, Kinsey. In one reply, which apart from a "thank you," contained the warning "be careful" (or "watch out") Balluseck cut out the signature from this letter, and stuck it in his diary. [*TGSP*, May 16, 19957]

In the diaries, described as volume 1 & 4, he described with pedantic exactness, how he committed his crimes....Balluseck had close contact with the so called American sex researcher, Kinsey, to whom he'd repeatedly and explicitly reported his perverse crimes. Balluseck had also described those in pedantic detail in his diaries. [*National-Zeitung*, May 15, 1957]

So Balluseck was not only sending Kinsey his old child abuse data, recorded during his days as a Commandant in Jedrzejow; he was also seeking to "continue" and "expand" his sexual seduction of children for Kinsey's use.

The University of Indiana press office regularly forwards international articles about the school (especially those containing damaging information) to the administration. According to Paul Gebhard, the University and its president, Herman Wells, were aware of Kinsey's collaboration with Balluseck. Kinsey refused to provide evidence that the FBI knew he had regarding Balluseck's crimes.

After serving his sentence for child sex abuse (he was not convicted on the murder charge), Balluseck continued his correspondence with Gebhard, while the latter indignantly protested that this "poor pedophile" had trouble obtaining a job after his release from prison.

During a seminar on *The Ethics of Sex Research* (Masters, Johnson & Kolodny, 1972), Gebhard told the assembled sexology "experts" that it was ethical to use Balluseck's child data. None registered disagreement, nor did any protest when Gebhard revealed how the Kinsey team had covered up for the erstwhile Nazi.

> We [were] amoral at best and criminal at worst.... An example of our criminality is our refusal to cooperate with authorities in apprehending a pedophile we had interviewed who was being sought for a [child] sex murder.[95]

The sort of conjecture that enabled the Yorkshire researchers to uncover Balluseck's connection to Kinsey seems once again in order. Were some of Kinsey's 317 to 2,035 boys and girls mentioned in the *Male* and *Female* volumes exterminated in Treblinka? Were sexually abused and murdered children included in the records that Balluseck "repeatedly and explicitly" mailed to Kinsey? If so, these war-crime "data" have been used by psychopathic sexual revolutionaries to uproot American laws and culture.

Current Kinsey Institute Director Bancroft, a medical doctor with a behavioral modification background, has described Alfred Kinsey as his own youthful "model." At first, he refused to be interviewed by Yorkshire Television, but subsequently agreed, provided that all questions were submitted for his advance approval. His carefully crafted answers to the 14 questions were still revealing.

Yorkshire producer Tim Tate, a long-time Socialist, asked Bancroft: "If its scientific value is uncertain, why have you republished [Kinsey's] material?" Bancroft replied, "We haven't republished, we have reprinted" Kinsey's books. Yet in the next figurative breath he stated that he was "very keen that these books are being republished," since he wanted critics to read "what Kinsey actually says." He then defended adult sex abuse of children as a method of avoiding "ignorance":

Dr. John Bancroft. Outcut from interview in "Kinsey's Paedophiles."

> [I]f you want to remain in ignorance then so be it... But for many of us, there is the belief that there is a need for better knowledge and... you can't do that if you then turn round and report [child molesters] to the police.[96].

Tate then asked: "But what has the material in Table 31 to Table 34 actually contributed to science's understanding of sexuality in children?" Bancroft replied that it showed that boys "before puberty were capable of experiencing more than one orgasm, whereas, after puberty that is not the case." Otherwise, he said, Kinsey's child sex data have been scientifically "irrelevant."[97]

Bancroft's justification for immoral and unethical conduct is that facts are needed to dispel "ignorance," yet he falsely claims that Kinsey made no "moral judgments"; that Rex King died before Kinsey's books were completed; that the 40-year-old King was an adult molester "for about 30 years before Kinsey met him,"[98] and so on. Bancroft became increasingly hostile, finally blurting:

> All this crap about Table 31 and 34!.... [Kinsey] opened up the subject... made it possible to talk about in a sensible way... He has de-mystified the subject of sexuality.... He stands... above the rest of researchers in the field.... He is a superb scholar... a fine mind... a pioneer. I have great respect for the man and for his integrity.[99]

In fact, however, Kinsey's devious and deviant data has "opened up" children to precocious early sex activity (encouraged by pornography in our homes, schools and libraries), based on Kinsey's widely repeated and wholly unproven mantra that children are sexual from birth. These data from child rapists now influence our courts, education, medicine, theology, and politics, generating laws which violate parental rights to protect their children while undermining our culture in ways too numerous to count.

THE CHILD EXPERIMENTS

PART IV: THE "NEW BIOLOGY" AND "THE KINSEY'S MODEL"

The Kinsey team contended that if Americans would follow their analysis of human sexual conduct, they would eventually arrive at a socio-sexual paradise. Here is a summary, prepared by this author, of the key findings that were to pave the way to Kinsey's nirvana:

- All orgasms are "outlets" and equal— whether between husband and wife; boy and dog; man and boy, girl, or baby—since there is no such thing as abnormality or normality.
- As the aim of coitus is orgasm, the more orgasms from any "outlet," at the earliest age, the healthier the person.
- Early masturbation is critical for sexual, physical, and emotional health. It can never be excessive or pathological.
- Sexual taboos and sex statutes are routinely broken, so they should be eliminated. That includes laws against rape and child rape, unless serious "force" is used and serious harm is proven.
- Since sex is, can be, and should be commonly shared with anyone and anything, jealousy is passé.
- All sexual experimentation before marriage will increase the likelihood of successful long-term marriage, while venereal diseases and other socio-sexual maladies will be reduced dramatically.
- Human beings are naturally bisexual. Religious bigotry and prejudice force people into chastity, heterosexuality, and monogamy.
- Children are sexual and potentially orgasmic from birth and are not harmed by "consensual" incest or sex with adults. Indeed, they often benefit from such practices.
- There is no medical or other reason for adult-child sex or incest to be forbidden.
- All forms of sodomy are natural and healthy.
- Homosexuals represent ten to thirty-seven percent of the population or more. (Kinsey's findings were fluid on this point.) Some educators have interpreted his findings to mean that only four to six percent of the population is exclusively *heterosexual,* so it is "heterosexual" bias that should be eliminated.

Each of these "findings," gleaned from Kinsey's reports, has been disproven by credible research and actual human experience over the past fifty years. Yet "accredited" AIDS and sex education in elementary, secondary, college, graduate, and post-graduate schools is almost entirely predicated on the Kinseyan "variant" sex model.

"[Alan] Bell [on floor] meeting with group facilitators before the [sexual] attitude reassessment workshop. Dallenback." These are the "laid back" teachers who teach our teachers who teach our children about sex. Photographs of "nude body workshops" in which "reassesment" learners commonly participate were not published in this book. (Martin Weinberg, Ed, Sex Research Studies from the Kinsey Institute, Oxford University Press, New York, 1976, p. 245.)

In 1948, the Kinsey model began to permeate the educational establishment. It would indoctrinate doctors, teachers, ministers, social workers, attorneys, the military, and United States Supreme Court Justices. The accompanying chart tracks the development of America's sex establishment, beginning with the research base, the funders, and Indiana University. Notice how often the same names show up on the boards of societies and accrediting agencies.

THE RESEARCHERS

It began at Indiana University and included the men who formed the official Kinsey Institute research base: Kinsey, Pomeroy, Martin, Gebhard, and later Gagnon, Simon, Weinberg, Bell, and Money, among others. All were Ph.D.s and sexual pedagogical (teaching) authorities. They stood, and stand, four-square on the false data base compiled by Kinsey.

THE FUNDERS

The original patron of the Kinsey research in 1938 was publicly-funded Indiana University. Thereafter, the tax-exempt Rockefeller Foundation backed Kinsey's work through the National Research Council. By the 1960s, the pornography industry, primarily *Playboy,* supported the Kinsey team's "New Biology."

Martin Weinberg trains attendees. Ibid.

THREE PIONEERING CENTERS

Of the three pioneering sex-study centers,[100] the National Sex & Drug Forum in San Francisco, established in 1968 and later renamed The Institute for the Advanced Study of Human Sexuality (hereafter Sex Institute), offers the most extensive training and advanced degrees. It was directed by Kinsey co-author and *Penthouse Forum* board member Wardell Pomeroy (now retired) and *Hustler* magazine contributors Ted McIlvenna and Erwin Haeberle.

Colin Williams lectures on nudism. Ibid.

In 1964, an accredited sexology degree became available from the New York University Health Department's School of Education, under youthful homosexual activist Deryck Calderwood, who died of AIDS. In 1978, the University of Pennsylvania Department of Health's School of Education began offering similar Kinseyan New Biology training and degrees, directed by homosexual advocate Kenneth George.

As of this writing, the Sex Institute offers a doctorate of education, four graduate programs, and seven basic credentials (including a "Safe Sex Certificate") which can be obtained swiftly with little or no prior training. Pomeroy, the Institute's then-academic dean, acknowledged that advanced sex degree applicants are accepted "off the street," provided that they do not have traditional preconceptions about sexual mores. The demand for Kinseyan-only standards is evident in the Institute's codified "Basic Sexual Rights" ethical oath, which legitimizes the Kinsey New Biology model of "consensual" adult-child sex, incest, child prostitution, and child pornography.

THE CHILD EXPERIMENTS

The Sex Institute's degree program includes "advanced graduate" studies such "erotic sensate and massage therapy," and focuses most of its scholarly training on student viewing (and making) of "erotic" films. Other key credit courses include how to use sex surrogates (prostitutes) in sex therapy and an analysis of the Kinsey reports including Chapter 5 on the children. The Institute provides training in the design and implementation of "sex education curricula" for all ages largely directing America's classroom sex education. Dr. Pomeroy, an original SIECUS official, teaches child sexuality. "Forensic sexology" is a popular course. And "accredited" Sex Institute "experts" are trained to testify on behalf of sex offenders and businesses which specialize in the production of obscenity and pornography.[101]

In 1980, Pomeroy himself testified on behalf of a pornographer in *Happy Day v. Kentucky*, a court case in which Pomeroy admitted under oath that he had sought funds from the sex industry to produce his own child pornography.[102]

The March 1991 "Department of Defense Report on Homosexuality and Personnel Security" cited Kinsey, Pomeroy, Gebhard, Martin, Gagnon, Ford, Beach, and Bell as DoD consultants, along with *Journal of Pedophilia* editor Vern Bullough and pedophile advocate John Money.[103] Such men helped give a cover of "science" to the subsequent DoD decision to recommend the acceptance of homosexuals in the military. A 1993 Rand study of

Scientific Authority for Human Sexuality Education in the Second Half of the 20th Century

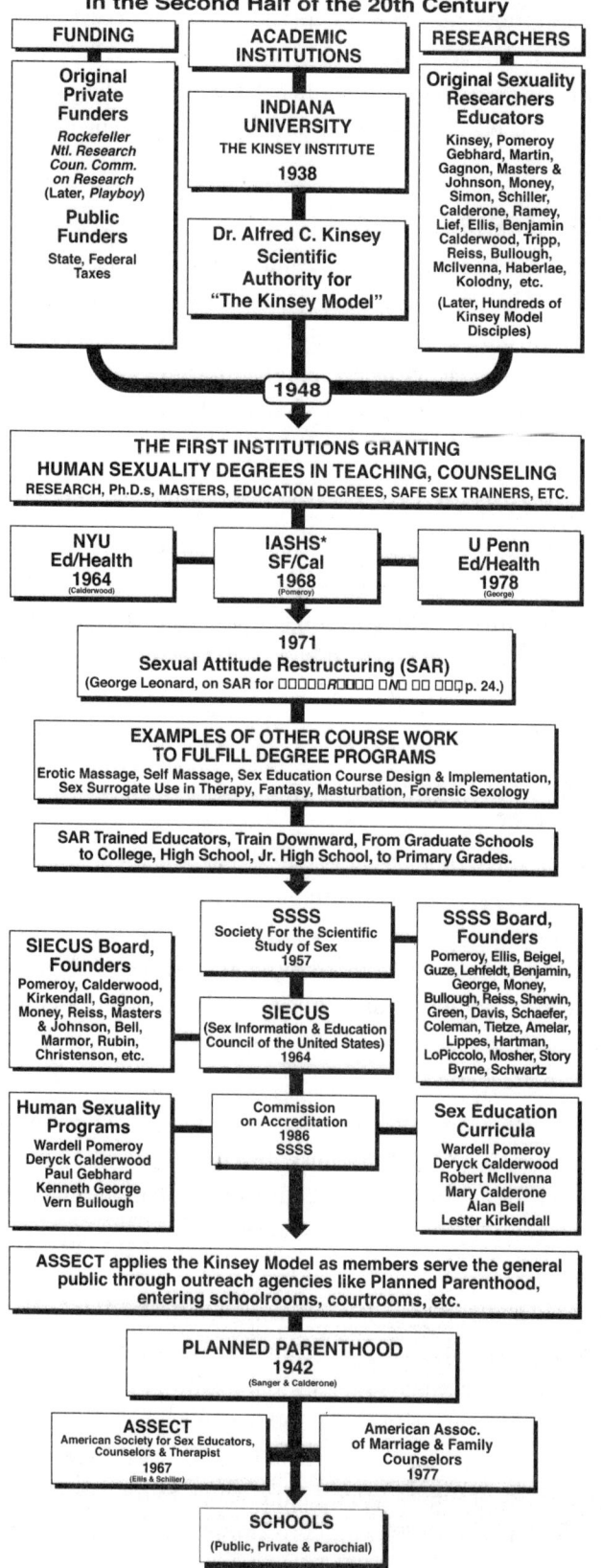

FUNDING	ACADEMIC INSTITUTIONS	RESEARCHERS
Original Private Funders Rockefeller, Ntl. Research Coun. Comm. on Research (Later, Playboy) **Public Funders** State, Federal Taxes	**INDIANA UNIVERSITY** THE KINSEY INSTITUTE 1938 — Dr. Alfred C. Kinsey Scientific Authority for "The Kinsey Model"	**Original Sexuality Researchers Educators** Kinsey, Pomeroy, Gebhard, Martin, Gagnon, Masters & Johnson, Money, Simon, Schiller, Calderone, Ramey, Lief, Ellis, Benjamin, Calderone, Tripp, Reiss, Bullough, McIlvenna, Haberlae, Kolodny, etc. (Later, Hundreds of Kinsey Model Disciples)

1948

THE FIRST INSTITUTIONS GRANTING HUMAN SEXUALITY DEGREES IN TEACHING, COUNSELING
RESEARCH, Ph.D.s, MASTERS, EDUCATION DEGREES, SAFE SEX TRAINERS, ETC.

| NYU Ed/Health 1964 (Calderwood) | IASHS* SF/Cal 1968 (Pomeroy) | U Penn Ed/Health 1978 (George) |

1971 Sexual Attitude Restructuring (SAR)
(George Leonard, on SAR for □□□□□R□□□□ □M□ □□ □□□ p. 24.)

EXAMPLES OF OTHER COURSE WORK TO FULFILL DEGREE PROGRAMS
Erotic Massage, Self Massage, Sex Education Course Design & Implementation, Sex Surrogate Use in Therapy, Fantasy, Masturbation, Forensic Sexology

SAR Trained Educators, Train Downward, From Graduate Schools to College, High School, Jr. High School, to Primary Grades.

| SIECUS Board, Founders Pomeroy, Calderwood, Kirkendall, Gagnon, Money, Reiss, Masters & Johnson, Bell, Marmor, Rubin, Christenson, etc. | SSSS Society For the Scientific Study of Sex 1957 — SIECUS (Sex Information & Education Council of the United States) 1964 | SSSS Board, Founders Pomeroy, Ellis, Beigel, Guze, Lehfeldt, Benjamin, George, Money, Bullough, Reiss, Sherwin, Green, Davis, Schaefer, Coleman, Tietze, Amelar, Lippes, Hartman, LoPiccolo, Mosher, Story Byrne, Schwartz |
| Human Sexuality Programs Wardell Pomeroy Deryck Calderwood Paul Gebhard Kenneth George Vern Bullough | Commission on Accreditation 1986 SSSS | Sex Education Curricula Wardell Pomeroy Deryck Calderwood Robert McIlvenna Mary Calderone Alan Bell Lester Kirkendall |

ASSECT applies the Kinsey Model as members serve the general public through outreach agencies like Planned Parenthood, entering schoolrooms, courtrooms, etc.

PLANNED PARENTHOOD 1942 (Sanger & Calderone)

| ASSECT American Society for Sex Educators, Counselors & Therapist 1967 (Ellis & Schiller) | American Assoc. of Marriage & Family Counselors 1977 |

SCHOOLS (Public, Private & Parochial)

172   KINSEY: CRIMES & CONSEQUENCES • CHAPTER 7

Kinsey Institute & The Human Sexuality Researchers

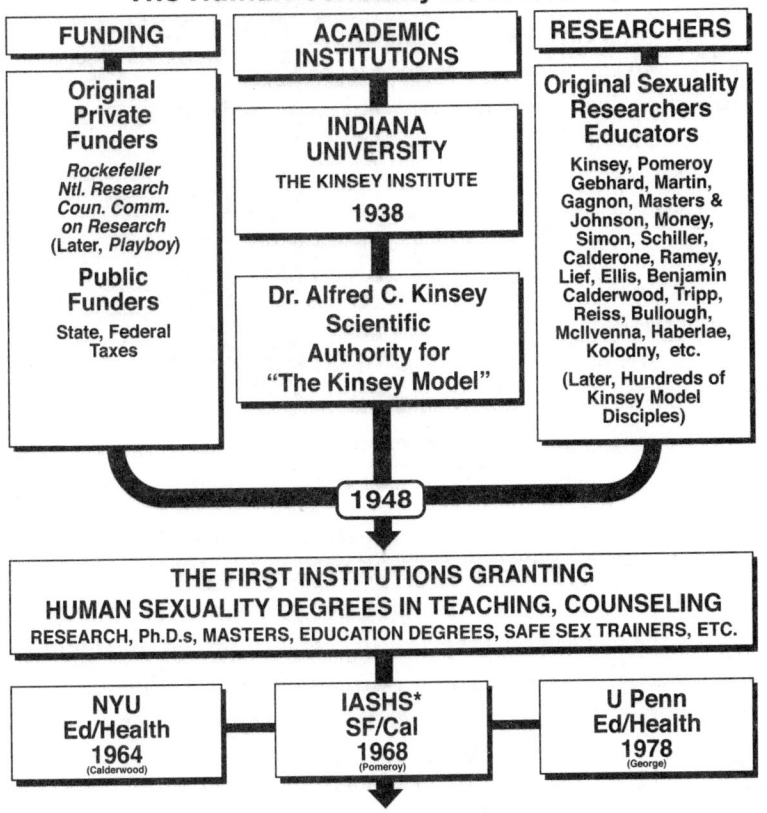

FUNDING
- **Original Private Funders**: Rockefeller, Ntl. Research Coun. Comm. on Research (Later, *Playboy*)
- **Public Funders**: State, Federal Taxes

ACADEMIC INSTITUTIONS
- **INDIANA UNIVERSITY** — THE KINSEY INSTITUTE 1938
- **Dr. Alfred C. Kinsey** — Scientific Authority for "The Kinsey Model"

RESEARCHERS
- **Original Sexuality Researchers Educators**: Kinsey, Pomeroy, Gebhard, Martin, Gagnon, Masters & Johnson, Money, Simon, Schiller, Calderone, Ramey, Lief, Ellis, Benjamin, Calderwood, Tripp, Reiss, Bullough, McIlvenna, Haberlae, Kolodny, etc. (Later, Hundreds of Kinsey Model Disciples)

↓ **1948** ↓

THE FIRST INSTITUTIONS GRANTING HUMAN SEXUALITY DEGREES IN TEACHING, COUNSELING
RESEARCH, Ph.D.s, MASTERS, EDUCATION DEGREES, SAFE SEX TRAINERS, ETC.

- **NYU** Ed/Health 1964 (Calderwood)
- **IASHS*** SF/Cal 1968 (Pomeroy)
- **U Penn** Ed/Health 1978 (George)

---

homosexuality in the armed forces was similarly based in large part on Kinsey's data and conclusions.

Many of the Sex Institute's sex films and videos have been distributed by Focus International (FI) to universities and colleges nationwide. Among its other "erotic" media, FI offers "The Kinsey Three (Hetero, Homo & Bisexuality)" and "About Your Sexuality" (for junior high children). The latter features scenes of condomless heterosexual and homosexual oral and anal sodomy. All three centers (Sex Institute, NYU, and the University of Pennsylvania) have long taught sex using the Sexual Attitude Restructuring (SAR) technique. Dr. Pomeroy has noted, "The SAR is designed to desensitize," that is to disinhibit, all viewers.

The editorial board of PAIDIKA: The Journal of Paedophilia boasts major leaders in American sexology. All of its editors are self-admitted pedophiles. The magazine is published in Amsterdam.

SEXUAL ATTITUDE RESTRUCTURING (SAR)

In December 1982, George Leonard reported his Sexual Attitude Restructuring (SAR) experience at The Institute for the Advanced Study of Human Sexuality (IASHS) in *Esquire* magazine. Noting that at least 60,000 people had been trained in colleges and universities by the SAR since the early 1980s, Leonard viewed his experience as typical:

The sensory overload culminated on Saturday night in a multimedia event called the F—korama... in the darkness... images of human beings—and sometimes even animals—engaging in every conceivable sexual act, accompanied by wails, squeals, moans, shouts, and the first movement of the Tchaikovsky Violin Concerto. Some seventeen simultaneous moving pictures.... Over a period of several hours, there came a moment when the four images on the wall were of a gay male couple, a straight couple, a

THE CHILD EXPERIMENTS

lesbian couple, and a bestial group. The subjects were nude.... I felt myself becoming disoriented... was she kissing a man or a woman? I struggled to force the acts I was watching into their proper boxes... and now I couldn't remember which was which. Wasn't I supposed to make these discriminations? I searched for clues. There were none. I began to feel uncomfortable. Soon I realized that to avoid vertigo and nausea I would have to give up the attempt to discriminate and simply surrender to the experience.... The differences for which lives have been ruined, were not only trivial, but invisible. By the end... [n]othing was shocking... [b]ut nothing was sacred either. But as I drove home, I began to get a slightly uneasy feeling. It was almost as if I had been conned... by my own conditioned response of taking the most liberated position... whatever my deeper feelings... love had not been mentioned a single time during the entire weekend.

The SAR has served as a critical tool to reshape views of human sexuality. The New Biology media, an orgy of pornographic couplings on film and video, is regularly utilized in academia to restructure students' modest sexual attitudes into the bizarre Kinseyan alternative. To understand how this works, it is useful to study the mechanics of the SAR in desensitizing and disinhibiting the human brain to allow a shift in pedagogical attitude and performance. The SAR literally scars the viewer's brain as it circumvents, short-circuits, his or her cognition and conscience. Neuroscientist Dr. Gary Lynch says of all high resonance stimuli: "What we're saying here is that an event which lasts half a second, within five or ten minutes has produced a structural change that is in some ways as profound as the structural changes one sees in (brain) damage."[104]

SAR AS SEX EDUCATION IN "THE DECADE OF THE BRAIN"

The 1990s were declared "The Decade of the Brain" by the U.S. Congress. More has been learned about this vital organ during the last three decades than in all prior history. Of special import to the discussion of classroom sexuality curricula is that the brain knows no present. Relevant experience "conjures up images of scenes witnessed...in the past." What does it mean for sex education courses, then, if "*inhibition*" rather than "*excitation*" is the hallmark of the healthy brain.[105]

Functionally speaking, the SAR, (and to a lesser degree, yet with more consistency, today's mass media) breaks down the "inhibitions" of "the healthy brain." The SAR is effective because all human brains obey what neurologists call "a law of strength." Simply put, this means that novel, scary, exciting stimuli from the outside world are processed faster and with more force than non-threatening, pleasant stimuli. Neurochemical pathways in the brain are chemically imprinted by hetero-and homo-erotic media stimuli; hence, they fuse sex, violence, fear, and anxiety into one felt emotion. The SAR reprograms students in education, medicine, psychology, criminals sexology and so on, by reconfiguring their neurochemistry—their human "nature"—producing a cadre of educated leaders who are part of Kinseyan deviance.

The effect of television experiences, and other modern media stimuli on the developing brains of children, is addressed convincingly by educational psychologist Dr. Jane Healy in her book, *Endangered Minds* (1984).[106] The neurochemical impact of sexualized media, whether commercial or educative, upon children's nascent brains, minds, and memories, is producing a new breed of children, hence a new breed of adults and a new type of society.

In *The Brain* (1984),[107] Richard Restak reported that a visual image passes from the eye through the brain in three-tenths of a second. The brain is structurally changed and memories are created. We literally "grow new brain"[108] with each experience, and we have no choice in the matter; we are designed to believe what we see. What sexologists and pornographers call sexual "fantasy" is sexual reality to the human brain. Visual data are processed as memories and emotions, and as such they are *really* neurochemically etched into the pathways of the brain as real.

Our brain controls our body, as well as our emotional and physical health, so "false" visual stimuli recorded as "real" can change our vital signs (heart rate, perspiration, intensified breathing, etc.) the same as "real" images. Neuropsychologist Margaret Kemeny states:

> [A]nytime we feel anything...think anything...imagine anything, there is activity in the brain that is taking place...that can then lead to a cascade of changes that have an impact on health.[109]

One wonders how have days and nights of SAR films portraying anal and oral sodomy, bestiality, and sadistic sex (as well as homosexual, heterosexual, group, child, and child-adult coitus) affected and changed the brains of the medical professionals, psychologists, criminologists, educators, sociologists, ministers, and sex "experts" exposed?

THE PROFESSIONAL SEX FIELD ACCREDITING AGENCIES AND SOCIETIES

Human Sexuality Programs at the three major academic centers mentioned above are designed to produce SAR-conditioned sexperts and sexologists from all pertinent disciplines. Sexuality "experts" have generated dozens, then hundreds, then thousands of three-unit AIDS prevention and other sex accreditation seminars, schools, and conferences. The Society for the Scientific Study of Sex (SSSS) established a Commission of Accreditation for the field, originally controlled by key Kinseyans Pomeroy, Gebhard, George, Calderwood, and Bullough.

> Founded in 1957, the Society for the Scientific Study of Sex (SSSS) is an international organization of professionals dedicated to the advancement of sexual knowledge...it publishes the Journal of Sex Research, sponsors programs to award research excellence, holds annual and regional conferences to promote interdisciplinary cooperation among researchers, educators and clinicians.[110]

Growing out of the Kinsey model, this sexology monopoly set standards in the field of sexology. It annually grants the Alfred C. Kinsey Award for Excellence in Scientific Study. Operationally, the SSSS largely directs and controls who is, or is not, recognized as a sexology professional. It influences who is hired, fired, or promoted within academia. In 1989, homosexual advocate Kenneth George headed both the SSSS board of directors and the University of Pennsylvania's Human Sexuality Program.

Today, students hoping to advance in fields dealing with issues related to human sexuality are expected to acknowledge agreement with Kinsey's scientific-variant view of sexuality, as taught in their schools. This, for all practical purposes, has long eliminated from the sexuality field those who might insist on maintaining a virtuous, moral standard of sexuality.

Let us close our brief look at the SSSS by noting that during its 1987 AIDS conference in Atlanta, Georgia, it successfully jumped onto the AIDS gravy train, giving SSSS access to copious AIDS prevention research funds. Sexology fundamentally promotes all of the sexual activity said to result in AIDS, including anal sodomy. For years their sexology films produced at San Francisco's Sex Institute modeled and promoted unprotected multiple heterosexual and homosexual sex acts, inclusive of both sodomies. Under the guise of AIDS education, this profession has become even more aggressive in modeling its variant-sexuality standard for our nation's schoolchildren. For example, the late Deryck Calderwood, a onetime SSSS president who headed New York University's School of Education Sexuality Department, created a curriculum for middle-school children (subsequently a film-strip and video) entitled, *About Your Sexuality,* which graphically glamorized unprotected homosexual and heterosexual anal sodomy. As noted in the *New York Tribune,* Calderwood, who died young of AIDS, was "a disciple of sex pioneer Alfred Kinsey (who) believed, with Kinsey, no type of sexual behavior is abnormal or pathological."

Another accrediting organization, the American Society of Sex Educators, Counselors and Therapists (ASSECT), was formed in 1967 by Drs. Phyllis Schiller and Albert Ellis. ASSECT has also long utilized the SAR technique as a desensitizing educational tool. Dr. Ellis served on the board of *Penthouse Forum.* Both the SSSS and ASSECT joined together to sponsor the 1998 "World Pornography Conference" held at California State University at Northridge, which was branded, by the Democrat-controlled California legislative committee that investigated its origins, a "pornography trade show." Hardly surprising, the CSUN's "Center for Sex Research" had been dubbed "The Kinsey Institute of the West." Its director, James Elias, is a Kinsey Institute

Kinseyan Professional Sexological Societies & Accrediting Agents

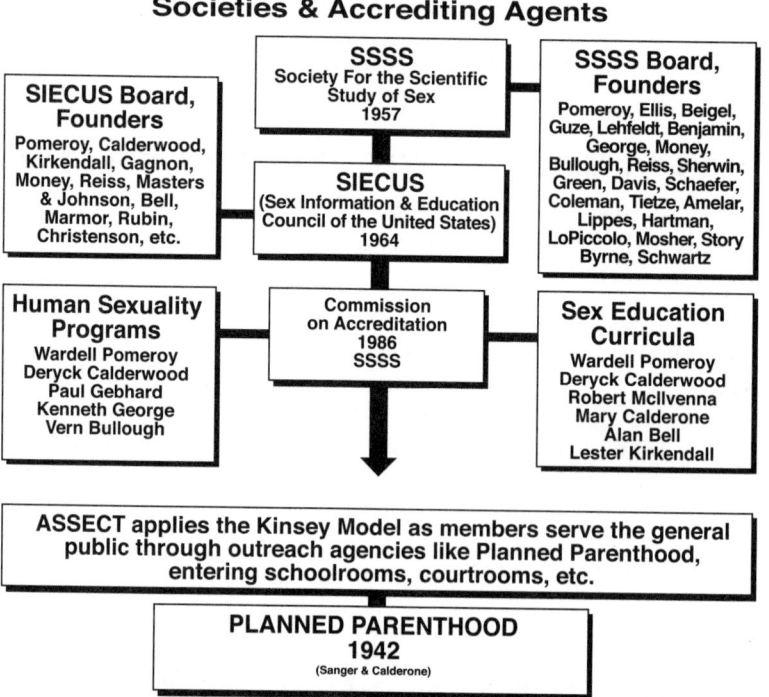

SSSS — Society For the Scientific Study of Sex, 1957

SIECUS Board, Founders: Pomeroy, Calderwood, Kirkendall, Gagnon, Money, Reiss, Masters & Johnson, Bell, Marmor, Rubin, Christenson, etc.

SSSS Board, Founders: Pomeroy, Ellis, Beigel, Guze, Lehfeldt, Benjamin, George, Money, Bullough, Reiss, Sherwin, Green, Davis, Schaefer, Coleman, Tietze, Amelar, Lippes, Hartman, LoPiccolo, Mosher, Story, Byrne, Schwartz

SIECUS (Sex Information & Education Council of the United States) 1964

Human Sexuality Programs: Wardell Pomeroy, Deryck Calderwood, Paul Gebhard, Kenneth George, Vern Bullough

Commission on Accreditation 1986 SSSS

Sex Education Curricula: Wardell Pomeroy, Deryck Calderwood, Robert McIlvenna, Mary Calderone, Alan Bell, Lester Kirkendall

ASSECT applies the Kinsey Model as members serve the general public through outreach agencies like Planned Parenthood, entering schoolrooms, courtrooms, etc.

PLANNED PARENTHOOD 1942 (Sanger & Calderone)

ASSECT American Society for Sex Educators, Counselors & Therapist 1967 (Ellis & Schiller)

American Assoc. of Marriage & Family Counselors 1977

and Institute for the Advanced Study of Human Sexuality alumnus. Its founder, Vern Bullough sent threatening letters to this author for identifying him as a pedophile editor of *Paidika: The Journal of Paedophilia*.

Kinsey's data laid the groundwork for the academic pornography produced by gynecologist William Masters who left his wife to marry Virginia Johnson. By 1957, utilitarian research on orgasms was being publicly advocated by the Kinseyite first couple of sex therapy (now divorced) at Washington University's Medical School. The Masters & Johnson studies fell into disfavor following a spousal lawsuit which publicly exposed their use of therapeutic prostitutes (called "sex surrogates" by sexologists).

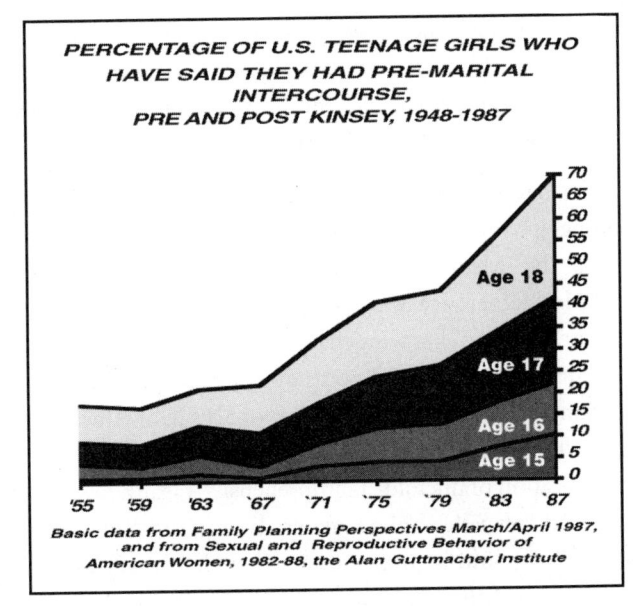

PERCENTAGE OF U.S. TEENAGE GIRLS WHO HAVE SAID THEY HAD PRE-MARITAL INTERCOURSE, PRE AND POST KINSEY, 1948-1987

Basic data from Family Planning Perspectives March/April 1987, and from Sexual and Reproductive Behavior of American Women, 1982-88, the Alan Guttmacher Institute

In the 1980s, the Masters and Johnson, *Playboy* Foundation grant recipients, appeared in *Playboy* to reveal their finding that "some" women (seven anonymous female subjects identified elsewhere as probably prostitutes) enjoy anal sodomy (the key known source for AIDS). Many *Playboy* consumers who undoubtedly read this as an oral and anal sodomy endorsement, would have been angry and resentful at wives or girlfriends who did not respond "properly" to the dangerous, painful and historically unnatural act as "love."

SIECUS

In 1964, the Sex Information and Education Council of the United States (SIECUS) was launched at the Kinsey Institute. Its objective was to teach Kinseyan ideology as sex education in our schools. SIECUS (which now calls itself the *Sexuality* Information and Education Council of the United States) imprinted the new Kinsey variant standard on almost all sex education curricula. Its early leader, Dr. Mary Calderone (past medical director of Planned Parenthood) was the direct link between Kinsey's university-based research, Planned Parenthood's grassroots outreach, and SIECUS. SIECUS was a "Resource Center [operating] Specialized Programs to Distribute Information about Human sexuality [through] learned journals, research studies, training materials for health professionals and sample classroom curricula."[111]

IS THE SIECUS/Playboy PARTNERSHIP A RICO CASE IN THE MAKING?

As SIECUS is regularly funded by the State, questions need to be asked about the January 1979 *Annual Playboy* which announced that *"Playboy* Foundation provide[d] the first of several major grants to The Sex Information and Education Council of the United States to support its nationwide educational programs."

As Christie Hefner added, *Playboy* also provided the original seed money for SIECUS:

Through the *Playboy* Foundation, Hefner put his money where his mouth was. It made the initial grant to establish an Office of Research Services of the Sex Information and Education Council of the U.S. (SIECUS) in the late 60s.

So, has such funding been a covert form of taxpayer-subsidy for the pornography industry (remember, *Playboy* was the corporate spokesperson for the "Media Coalition," with its seedier pornography members). Did Mr. Hefner give SIECUS its "initial grant to establish an Office of Research Services" knowing that SIECUS would serve his corporate product interests in the schoolrooms of America? Did Mr. Hefner know the "nationwide educational programs" of SIECUS "education" would push "sexually explicit materials" to school children? For, under SIECUS's sex education brainchild "Comprehensive Health Education," Planned Parenthood and colleagues have delivered "sexually explicit materials" to Tom Sawyer and Becky Thatcher for decades. Remember, SIECUS sex information is directed at elementary and secondary school children, not college youths. Listen to the SIECUS February/March 1996 "Position Statement" on "Sexually Explicit Materials":

Christy Hefner of Playboy Magazine, and SIECUS patron.

> When sensitively used in a manner appropriate to the viewer's age and developmental level, sexually explicit visual, printed, or on-line materials can be valuable educational or personal aids helping to reduce ignorance and confusion and contributing to a wholesome concept of sexuality [p. 21].

It is still illegal to sell "sexually explicit materials" (pornography) to children under the age of 18 years. Posturing as an independent scholastic group training school teachers, has SIECUS been covertly desensitizing and recruiting millions of vulnerable, child consumers for the pornography trade? Is this pornography insider-trading with stock options, funded with taxpayer dollars? In an undated 1980s SIECUS press release, SIECUS claimed it sought donations to *combat* children's exposure to sexually explicit materials:

> The overwhelming majority of parents had never discussed sexual issues with their children at all.... That's why SIECUS exists.... [I]t must not be left to X-rated movies, TV ads, and sleazy magazines, as the Moral Majority would have us do.

SIECUS director Mary Calderone and other SIECUS associates have been advantaged by the pornography commerce—appearing as interviewees in *Playboy* and other sex trade materials, and receiving other promotional benefits from their alliance. Rather like the current government investigation of the unfair marketing of beer, cigarettes and "R-rated" movies to children, marketing "sexually explicit material" to schoolchildren subverts parent approval and is very possibly criminal. For example:

This Planned Parenthood booklet, "You've Changed the Combination," typifies the organization's use of the Kinsey Model in sex education circa 1974 (The author has blacked-out some explicit imagery.)

- Does SIECUS use the Kinsey Model, providing inaccurate, false advertising and fraudulent information about sex to teachers and children, facilitating confusion and trauma?
- Does SIECUS use the Kinsey Model to "contribute to the delinquency of minors" by exposing children to material illegal for them to purchase until age 18?
- Has SIECUS disclosed its corporate pornography connections in its grant applications?
- Would SIECUS and *Playboy* share corporate responsibility for sex crimes committed by schoolchildren whose sexual inhibitions and "confusion" were compromised after exposure to the Kinsey Model via SIECUS' "sexually explicit materials?"

One of several illustrations in Playboy magazine indicating distress regarding the discrediting and debunking of Alfred Kinsey (circa 1998).

As noted, in the early 1980's *Time* dared twice to expose SIECUS matriarch Mary Calderone and other key sex educators who claimed "anything goes," for and with children. The April 14, 1980 issue of *Time* cited the SIECUS paper on incest, "Attacking The Last Taboo," which claimed, "We are roughly in the same position today regarding incest as we were a hundred years ago with respect to our fears of masturbation." Concluded *Time*, SIECUS was part of an academic "pro-incest lobby... conducting a campaign to undermine" the "taboo against incest" and all other sexual inhibitions--the Kinsey Model.

In 1991, SIECUS launched its series of "Guidelines for Comprehensive Sexuality Education." The guidelines were aimed at institutionalizing Kinseyan sexuality nationwide and influencing legislation dealing with sexuality issues. SIECUS claimed they would "provide accurate information about human sexuality." Building on a virtual sex education monopoly, only Kinseyan-trained teachers would be permitted in American schoolrooms (K-12) to develop "sexuality literacy:"

> Sexuality education should only be taught by specially trained teachers. Professionals responsible for sexuality education must receive specialized training in human sexuality, including the philosophy and methodology of sexuality education. Ideally, teachers should graduate from academic courses or programs in schools of higher education that provide the professional with the most time-intensive and rich training. At a minimum, teachers should participate in extensive in-service courses, continuing education classes, or intensive seminars.[112]

What "human sexuality information" has SIECUS provided to children, parents, school boards, teachers, doctors, nurses, clergy, psychologists, social workers and the general culture?[113] In full agreement with the Kinsey Model, the organization suggested,

> A partial list of safe sex practices for teens could include... massaging caressing, undressing each other, masturbation alone, masturbation in front of a partner, mutual masturbation.... By helping teens explore the full range of safe sexual behaviors, we may help to raise a generation of adults that do not equate sex with intercourse, or intercourse with vaginal orgasm, as the goal of sex.[114]

Like Kinsey, nowhere in this "expert advice" does SIECUS mention marriage, or indicate that it should play a part—much less a central part—in the sexual scheme of things. Nowhere does it caution that the suggested activities might undermine love and trust, not to mention mental and physical health. Like Kinsey, SIECUS discourages "intercourse as the goal of sex," instead offering youngsters masturbatory activity with erotic entertainment (endorsed in their 1991 Guidelines as "erotic literature" and art"). In 1992, SIECUS produced a pamphlet, "Talk about Sex," which urged children not to reject the sexually exploitive media that surrounds them, but to "use" it as a sexual aid:

> When talking to a friend or a possible sex partner, speak clearly.... Movies, music and TV... often have a message about sexuality and can help possible sexual partners express their affection and sexual interest.... Use entertainment to help talk about sexuality, TV, music videos... magazines are a good way to begin to talk about sexuality....[115]

Like Kinsey, the *SIECUS Report* (1996) urged the use of "sexually explicit visual, printed or on-line materials" for schoolchildren in order to "reduce ignorance and confusion" and to help the children develop "a wholesome concept of sexuality." The official SIECUS position equates sodomy with marital sex as "any type of unprotected sexual intercourse (oral, anal or vaginal)."

> Few people realize that the great library collection of... the Kinsey Institute... was formed very specifically with one major field omitted: sex education. This was because it seemed appropriate, not only to the Institute but to its major funding source, the National Institute of Mental Health, to leave this area for SIECUS to fill. Thus we applied and were approved for a highly important grant from the National Institute for Mental Health that was designed to implement a planned role for SIECUS to become the primary data base for the area of education [indoctrination] for sexuality."[116]

The SIECUS Sex Education Curriculum Board was also led by Pomeroy, Bell, Calderwood, Calderone, and McIlvenna—all Kinseyans and all committed to Kinsey's research findings, deviant standards and pedophile promotions. What has been the damage of the ideas unleashed by the documented SIECUS/*Playboy* partnership? Has SIECUS violated the 1992 *Federal False Claims Act*, which provides damages and civil penalties for individuals or persons who knowingly submit a false or fraudulent claim to the United States government for payment or approval?

Beyond fraud and child endangerment, do such violations rise to the standard of a criminal conspiracy, as in the *Racketeer Influence Corrupt Organizations* (RICO) statute? Or, at minimum does the evidence unite the recently estimated $11.5 billion sex syndicate with SIECUS? That *Playboy* and other "sexually explicit materials" do encourage illegal juvenile sexual activity and copy-cat crimes, including incest and child sex abuse, is documented in my peer-approved US Department of Juvenile Justice report, obtainable via the US Department of Justice website.

Did Playboy partner with SIECUS in its "initial grant to establish an Office of Research Services" so that SIECUS would be a stealth invader, serving the sex trade at the expense of America's children? The question deserves to be on the Congressional floor.

PLANNED PARENTHOOD, BRIEFLY

Planned Parenthood (PP) has a history as fraught with special interests as has SIECUS and scores of books have been written about its movement into the schools, carrying the SIECUS banner of pseudo-science. PP was given a boost by Kinsey's claims that children are sexual and that "normal" women commonly have sex prior to marriage. Kinsey also urged that abortion be legalized, based on his wholly spurious data on the commonality of abortion in the USA, and in April 1955 he delivered a preliminary report on his abortion data at a PP abortion conference at

Columbia University's Arden House which became a foundation for the pro-abortion movement.[117]

A Planned Parenthood booklet given by teachers to secondary level schoolchildren, entitled "You've Changed the Combination!!!" was decorated with illustrations of nude, *Playboy*-like, large-bosomed women towering over small, wimpy nude males. It recommended that children have sex—but only with their "friends." It also equated virginity with prostitution since some girls remained virgins until they married:

> Do you want a warm body? Buy one. That's right. There are women who have freely chosen that business, buy one.... Do you want a virgin to marry? Buy one. There are girls in that business too. Marriage is the price you'll pay, and you'll get the virgin. Very temporarily.[118]

One of several other "special interest" associations whose economic and social base now includes "sexuality instruction" is the American Association of Marriage and Family Counselors. The current decisions by the American Psychiatric Association (1994) in its *Diagnostic and Statistical Manual IV* to remove pedophilia, masochism and sadism as mental or psychological disorders and a 1999 article in the *American Psychological Association Bulletin* which would normalize adult sex with "willing" children, means these two powerful mental health agencies have joined forces with Kinsey's other pedophile advocates.[119]

Virtually without exception, the basis of professional training is Kinsey's duplicitous data, and that of his disciples who have built upon the false foundation he established.

From the "informal" sex education reaching nearly all children via pornography, to the "formal" sex education from doctorate to kindergarten, the Kinsey Model <u>is</u> the monopoly. The foundation of the modern sex industry then, from sex commerce to the sex "expert" who serve as expert witnesses for pornographers, all stand on the legitimacy of wholly illegitimate pseudoscience. Next we will examine how this "education" process has been used to reshape our laws on sex offenses, to fit the Kinsey Model, impacting the lives of every American.

CHAPTER 7 NOTES

1. Kinsey, Pomeroy, and Martin, *Sexual Behavior in the Human Male*, W.B. Saunders, Philadelphia, 1948, is *Male* volume in each chapter citation section; Kinsey, Pomeroy, Martin and Gebhard, *Sexual Behavior in the Human Female*, W.B. Saunders, Philadelphia, 1948, is *Female* volume in each citation section.
2. The handwritten notations by the Kinsey Institute representative were made on a copy of a proposed book chapter, from the paper given by Reisman (Bat-Ada) at the 5th World Congress of Sexology in Jerusalem, 1981. There were several titles, but the one at issue was "'The Empirical Study and Statistical Procedures' on 'Child Sexuality' Undertaken by the Institute for Sex Research and Dr. Alfred Kinsey: A Critical Analysis of Child Sexual Experimentation." The document was obtained during a deposition of Kinsey Institute Director June Reinisch on December 7, 1993.
3. SIECUS, *Sexuality in Man*, Scribners, New York, 1970, pp. 6-7.
4. *Male*, p. 157.
5. Mary Shivanandan, "Childhood and Educational Development" in *Foundations for Family-Life Education*, Educational Guidance Institute, Inc. Arlington, VA., 1991.
6. Masters, Johnson, Kolodny, and Weems, *Ethical Issues in Sex Therapy*, Volume II, Little Brown and Company, Boston, 1980, p. 71. Albert Jonsen is Professor of Ethics in Medicine, School of Medicine, University of California, San Francisco. Jay Mann is Associate Clinical Professor of Medical Psychology, School of Medicine, University of California, San Francisco and Stanford University.
7. Ibid., p. 106.
8. *Male*, p. 177.
9. *Male*, p. 175.
10. *Male*, p. 175.
11. Wardell Pomeroy, Carol Flax, and Connie Wheeler, *Taking a Sex History*, The Free Press, New York, 1982, p. 5.
12. *Male*, p. 175.
13. *Male*, p. 178.
14. *Male*, p. 178.
15. John Bancroft, M.D., *Human Sexuality and its Problems*, Churchill Livingstone, Edinburgh, Scotland, 1989.
16. *Male*, p. 176.
17. *The Washington Post*, December 8, 1995, p. F1-4.

18. *Male*, p. 177.
19. *Male*, p. 178.
20. Masters, et. al, p. 71.
21. Masters, et al, p. 256.
22. *Male*, p. 176.
23. *Male*, p. 11. Note that the author has removed the word "other" and inserted ellipsis to aid the reader in avoiding the language maze constructed by Kinsey in his two reports. Kinsey told readers that he verified *all* of his data, not just "some" or "other" parts it.
24. *Male*, p.179.
25. *Male*, p. 179.
26. *Male*, p. 180.
27. *Male*, p. 180.
28. *Male*, p. 177.
29. *The American Heritage Dictionary of the English Language*, Houghton Mifflin Company, 1992.
30. Charles Darwin, *The Expression of the Emotions in Man and Animals*, John Murray, London, 1904, pp. 65-67.
31. *Male*, p. 160. Orgasm in the normal male is specifically defined as including ejaculation. "The highest point of sexual excitement, characterized by strong feelings of pleasure and marked normally by ejaculation of semen by the Male and by vaginal contractions in the Female. Also called climax." This is not possible for boys prior to physical/sexual maturity. *The American Heritage Dictionary of the English Language*, 1992.
32. *Male*, pp. 160-161. [Emphasis added.]
33. *Male*, p. 185.
34. *Male*, p. 158.
35. Wardell Pomeroy, *Dr. Kinsey and the Institute for Sex Research*, Harper & Row, New York, p. 315.
36. Letter to Dr. Judith Reisman from pediatrician Lester Caplan, M.D., November 29, 1983.
37. *Female*, pp. 410 and 570. [Emphasis added.]
38. *Obstretical Gynecological News*, December 1, 1980, p. 10.
39. [SIECUS Report, May-July 1983, p. 9. [Emphasis added.]
40. (Lenore Buth, *How to Talk Confidently with Your Child about Sex*, Concordia, 1998, page 23. [Emphasis added.])
41. *Female*, p. 570.
42. *Female*, p. 570.
43. Albert Jonsen and Jay Mann, "Ethics of Sex Research Involving Children and the Mentally Retarded," in Masters, Johnson, Kolodny, and Weems, *Ethical Issues in Sex Therapy*, Little Brown & Co., Boston, Massachusetts, p. 1980.
44. *Female*, p. 105.
45. The Case of "*Esther*," Esther White: The Kinsey team had the name of at least one of their victims. According to an affidavit by Esther White, they were in regular contact with her abusers and even arranged to meet with them on one occasion. Mrs. White is a lovely, quiet lady with a tragic past who prefers to avoid publicity. She has kindly agreed to the inclusion of her story here. It details incestuous violations by her father and grandfather, whom she believes were two of Kinsey's "observers." Mrs. White appears as "Esther White" in the Yorkshire television documentary, *Kinsey's Paedophiles*.

Esther White's sworn statement identifies her as "a victim of acts of sexual abuse perpetrated upon me by both my paternal grandfather and my father between the years of 1938 and 1946," the years of Kinsey's sex research project, when he was soliciting sex "histories" nationwide. Her abuse "began when I was four years of age and continued until I was age 12," when her mother found out (1946) stopped it. Mrs. White's grandfather was a graduate of Indiana University, 1922, and "learned of the Institute's existence and its subject area of studies from alumni bulletins or some similar communications."

Mrs. White had reason to believe her grandfather was "personally acquainted with Alfred Kinsey." She adds, "My father did not tell me that he was sharing information about the acts of abuse with the Kinsey Institute *until it had stopped*. My first knowledge that he was providing information about his abuse to the Institute occurred in 1947, when I was age 13." Her father asked her if she had had "orgasm as a result of specific acts of abuse." She believes "this questioning was done at the behest of the Kinsey Institute. He was documenting on papers (kept in an envelope) that he sent away. *There was a deadline by which he had to return them*. I had no idea at the time what they were for, or what he wrote."

Mrs. White states that in or about 1943 she was taken by her father to meet a man she recalls as "Mr. Stockman," and another man named "Pomeroy." In an interview with this author on October 3, 1997 in Washington, D.C., she stated that a third man, whom she did not know, was also in the room. He asked her several questions relating to her emotional state:

"He wanted to know if I was happy, if my life was good with my father. I had been told what to say, of course and I answered in the affirmative. This seemed to satisfy the man. I had never seen a picture of Dr. Kinsey and recently received a brochure with his photograph on it and I definitely recognize that man as being Dr. Kinsey."

Following the interview, Mrs. White states that her "father and grandfather then left with these men to attend a meeting at Ohio State University." A few years later, her father gave her a "signed copy" of the Kinsey report and "suggested that I read it to *see the contributions he had made to the scientific findings it contained* that would revolutionize the way the world would view sexuality in the future." When her father died, Mrs. White threw the book away. She would now like to know what part Indiana University, through its Kinsey Institute, may have played in encouraging the abuse to which she was subjected. Mrs. White recalls films her father made of her abuse.

We also have the testimony of Donna Friess, Ph.D., detailing her father's use of the Kinsey report as justification for the sexual abuse of her and her sisters. Friess wrote of her traumatic experiences in her book, *Cry the Darkness: One Woman's Triumph Over the Tragedy of Incest* (Health Communications, Inc., Deerfield Beach, Florida, 1993). It is not known if her father supplied Kinsey with information. In a letter to this author, Dr. Friess wrote that her father admitted that he "decided a long time ago to allow myself anything that dogs do." Kinsey "advocated the animal model of human sexual behavior. My father subscribed to it. Everyone of his children own their own copies of the Kinsey reports. He forced me to make a gift of the *Male* report to my boyfriend (now my husband) when I was in college." Writing in the July, 1992 issue of *The California Psychologist* Dr. Friess stated her belief that Kinsey was fully aware of the abuse of children, yet insisted on calling it "play." She noted: "Kinsey does not distinguish between child-to-child sexual contact and child-to-adult sexual contact" (p. 27).

46. See Gebhard's telephone interview, his testimony in the Masters and Johnson seminar on *Ethics in Sex Research and Therapy*, his articles in the press cited throughout this book, John Gagnon's admission of the Kinsey Institute team's crimes in his book Human Sexualities, Wardell Pomeroy's statements in his biography of Kinsey, etc.

47. Gebhard, November 2, 1992, telephone interview with J. Gordon Muir, M.D., editor of Reisman et al., *Kinsey, Sex and Fraud,* 1990.

48. *Female*, p.105.

49. Herbert Hyman and Paul Sheatsley "The Scientific Method," in, Donald Geddes, Ed., *An Analysis of the Kinsey Reports*, A Mentor Book, New York, 1954, p. 106.

50. Hyman, Ibid., pp. 91-117.

51. *Female*, p. 127.

52. *Female*, p. 544.

53. These girls are typical of the youngsters about whom the Kinsey Institute claims it has no records. The location of these children remains an issue.

54. *Female*, p. 180.

55. *Female*, p. 104-5.

56. *Female*, p. 104-5.

57. The "Tanner Maturation Rating" questionnaire authorized by the New York Board of Education follows the Kinseyan pattern of sexuality "measurement": "Starting this year, schools require applicants for everything from football to cheerleader to fill out the new form.... The definitions of the five stages include descriptions of the amount of pubic hair, and the size and shape of the penis, breasts and areolas.... Deputy Health Commissioner Mark Rapaport, whose office requires the form, defended it as perfectly sensible... it applies to kids who may be immature, a small kid who may be 14 and wants to compete" (*NY Post* June 28, 1988). The size of the areola has as little relationship to physical maturity as does hair color. One wonders why coaches and health teachers would want to read and rate the sizes and shapes of their student's genitals and the pigment surrounding their nipple area? In this modern extension of the Kinsey "measurement sexuality" mentality, as children develop in growth spurts, would boys classified as "too immature" for sports have an option to make the team should they "prove" sudden penis maturation? It seems preposterous to point out that a boy's penis size and a girl's breast size are irrelevant to their ability to swim, jump, kick a ball, or play a sonata.

58. *New York Post*, June 28, 1988.

59. Judith Reisman, *SoftPorn Plays Hardball*, Huntington House, Lafayette, LA, 1991.

60. *Female*, p. 84.

61. Ibid.

62. See the growing body of literature on incest research and data.

63. Reisman, *SoftPorn.*, Ibid.

64. Wardell Pomeroy, *Girls and Sex*, Pelican Books, New York, 1969, pp. 133-4.

65. *The British Medical Journal*, 282:250, 1981. Scrutinizing combined data from two 1967 studies, the Journal reported that "of 31 children born to father-daughter (12) and brother-sister matings (19) only 13 were normal," and, "[T]wo died from recessive disorders (optic fibrosis and glycogen-storage disease) and one from an almost certainly recessive disorder causing progressive cerebral degeneration and loss of vision. Two of those alive probably had disorders, both with severe mental retardation with cerebral palsy, and one a possibly recessive disorder, severe non-specific mental retardation. Two others died in the neonatal period...Two had congenital malformations.... Eight others...were mentally retarded, with IQs in seven ranging from 59 to 76."

And this excerpt from *Female*, pp. 121-122: "There are, of course, instances of adults who have done physical damage to children with whom they have attempted sexual contacts, and *we have the histories of a few males who had been responsible for such damage*. But these cases are in the minority and the public should learn to distinguish such serious contacts from other adult contacts which are *not likely to do the child any appreciable* harm if the child's parents do not become disturbed." [Emphasis added.]

66. Gebhard's letter to Reisman, March 11, 1981, in the author's archive.

67. Ibid.

68. *Female*, p. 118.

69. *Newsweek*, "Keepers of the Flame," June 18, 1984, p. 15.

70. Wardell Pomeroy, Penthouse Forum Variations, "A New Look at Incest," 1977, pp. 85-90.

71. Penthouse Forum "Letters," Ibid.

72. Wardell Pomeroy, *Boys and Sex*, Penguin Books, New York, 1981, pp. 134-135.

73. Pomeroy in *Penthouse Forum* , ibid.

74. *Penthouse*, "Incest, the Last Taboo," December 1977, p. 181. Kinsey did not call it incest, or sex with kin, but (according to Nobile) "lying with a near relative." Pomeroy, in his 1977 Penthouse Forum Variations article, "A New Look at Incest," claimed that adult-child incest could not only be harmless, but could benefit the child emotionally. He wrote: "Incest between adults and younger children can also prove to be a satisfying and enriching experience....When there is a mutual and unselfish concern for the other person, rather than a feeling of possessiveness and a selfish concern with one's own sexual gratification, then incestuous relationships can--and do--work out well....[Incest] can be a satisfying, non-threatening, and even an enriching emotional experience, as I said earlier." (*Penthouse Forum Variations*, 1977, pp. 86-90).

75. *Male*, p. 9.

76. *Male*, p. 9.

77. John Gagnon, "Reconsiderations," Human Nature, October 1978, Volume 1, No. 10, pp. 93.

78. See May 7, 1993 deposition materials re: *Reisman vs. The Kinsey Institute*, in the author's archive.

79. *Indianapolis Star*, September 19, 1995, A1-4.

80. *The Humanist*, "Sex, Science and Kinsey," September/October, 1996, pp. 23-26.

81. *The Washington Post*, December 8, 1995, F1-4.

[82]. James Jones, *Alfred C. Kinsey: A Public/Private Life*, WW Norton, New York, 1997, pp. 507-513.

[83]. Jones, pp. 512-513.

[84]. Jones, Ibid. Pomeroy reported this information in his 1972 biography of Kinsey (ghost-written, reports Gathorne-Hardy, by John Toffel, as were all Pomeroy's books). See: Alfred C. Kinsey: *Sex, the Measure of All Things*, Chatts & Wendres, London, 1998, pp. 231, 444.

[85]. Jones, Ibid.

[86]. Jones, pp. 510-511.

[87]. Jones, p. 513.

[88]. Gebhard admitted his (and the team's) collaboration with the several pedophiles in a telephone interview, and in several press articles, all in this author's archive.

[89]. Pomeroy, p. 315.

[90]. *Male* p. 177.

[91]. Robert Dickinson, Forward in Ernst and Loth, *American Sexual Behavior*, The Greystone Press, New York, 1948, p. vii-viii.

[92]. Max Weinreich, *Hitler's Professors: The Part of Scholarship in Germany's Crimes Against the Jewish People*, Yiddish Scientific Institute, Yivo, New York, 1946

[93]. A photocopy of Dr. von Balluseck's Nazi membership card, dated August 1, 1930, obtained from the German document center, is on file in the author's archive. Max Weinreich, *Hitler's Professors: The Part of Scholarship in Germany's Crimes Against the Jewish People*, Yiddish Scientific Institute--Yivo, New York, 1946

[94]. *The Encyclopedia Judaica*, Keter Publishing, Vol. 9, 1972, p. 1310-1311.

[95]. Masters, Johnson, and Kolodny, Ed., *Ethical Issues in Sex Therapy and Research*, Little Brown and Company, Boston, 1977, p. 13.

[96]. Tim Tate video interview with John Bancroft at Indiana University, excerpted from the complete interview transcript, July 21, 1998, p. 18.

[97]. Ibid., p. 4.

[98]. Ibid., p. 9.

[99]. Ibid. p. 20.

[100]. The discussion of the sexology profession is extracted from *RSVP America*, 1996, First Principles, Inc., and The Institute for Media Education, Crestwood, Ky. Complete citations available in RSVP document.

[101]. Word of one California college-level sex course taught by Barry Singer, board member of the Society for the Scientific Study of Sex's *Journal of Sex Research*, reached the press. It provides insight into the procedure for receiving extra credit for some sexology courses. Dr. Singer taught his students as he had been taught. Hence, his field work included extra credit for married students who would engage in adultery, and "straight" students who would engage in homosexual sex. The "field" research, including trips to gay bars, swingers' clubs, etc., is typical of the courses offered through other credentialed sexuality institutes. Time, June 7, 1982, p. 49.

[102]. To illustrate the shift in standards from absolute obscenity to the variant "pornography," an historical context is helpful. "Pornography" was not included in the 1828 edition of *Webster's Dictionary*. Only "obscenity" was defined in the words, images, and concepts that we term pornography today. Pornography, from the Greek pornea, means "fornication"; "writing about or drawing on prostitutes." Somewhere between 1828 and 1857, pornography was transported to America from England and Europe.

[103]. *Paidika: Journal of Paedophilia*, "Statement of Purpose," Amsterdam, The Netherlands, September 1987, Vol. 1, pp. 2-3.

[104]. *The Brain: Learning and Memory*, The Annenberg CPB Collection, Santa Barbara, CA., WNET, 1984.

[105]. Richard Restak, *The Mind*, Bantam Books: New York, 1988, p. 283.

[106]. Jane Healy, *Endangered Minds*, New York City, Bantam Books, 1984.

[107]. Bill Moyers interviewing Gary Lynch in Richard Restak's Public Broadcasting System program, The Annenberg/CBP Collection, *The Brain*, eight documentaries on brain behavior, 1984.

[108]. Ibid.

[109]. Bill Moyers, *Mind & Body*. Public Broadcasting System Television, February 1993.

[110]. Quote taken from the SSSS program brochure *Expanding the Boundaries*, Toronto, Ontario, Canada, 1989.

[111]. SIECUS brochure, "Are you going to stand by; will you?" undated, circa late 1980s.

[112]. SIECUS "Guidelines for Comprehensive Sexuality Education, the National Guidelines Task Force, 1991, p. 9.

[113]. See *Time* magazine article citing this issue of SIECUS ("Attacking the Last Taboo," April 14, 1980) for a discussion of "sex researchers" promoting incest.

[114]. "Safe Sex and Teens," by Debra W. Haffner, *SIECUS Report*, September/October 1988, p. 9.

[115]. SIECUS, "Talk About Sex," 1992.

[116]. Mary Calderone, writing about SIECUS' role in promoting Kinsey's message, *SIECUS* Report, May-July 1982, p. 6.

[117]. Wardell Pomeroy, *Dr. Kinsey and the Institute for Sex Research*, Harper & Row, New York, 1972, p. 394.

[118]. Distributed by Planned Parenthood and published by Rocky Mountain Planned Parenthood, Colorado, 1974.

[119]. *Los Angeles Times* for July 19, 1999 published an article by libertarian Carol Travis entitled "Uproar Over Sexual Abuse Study Muddies the Waters." Travis writes: "I guess I should be reassured to know that Congress disapproves of pedophilia and the sexual abuse of children. On July 12, the House voted unanimously to denounce a study that the resolution's sponsor, Matt Salmon (R-Ariz.), called 'the emancipation proclamation of pedophiles.' .... What got Congress riled was an article last year in the journal Psychological Bulletin, which is to behavioral science what the *Journal of the American Medical Assn.* is to medicine." The authors of that article--Bruce Rind, Philip Tromovitch and Robert Bauserman--concluded, from their meta-analysis of a non-random selection of 59 "studies" of child sexual abuse, that if the child is "willing," sex with an adult may be rewarding and harmless and that "non-judgmental" language should be used when referring to child molesters (i.e., terming sex with children "adult-child sex" rather than "child sexual abuse). Following the Congressional resolution and massive pressure from "Dr. Laura," the APA apologized and backed down from its publication of this pedophile promotional piece. Recent revelations that two of the three supposedly objective APA authors have ties with Paidika: The Journal of Paedophila raise serious questions about their objectivity. An article by Robert Buserman, entitled "Man-Boy Sexual Relationships in a Cross-Cultural Perspective," appeared in the Summer 1989 issue of *Paidika*. The Winter 1995 issue includes a book review by Bruce Rind, and recommends an article by Bauserman and Rind.

STOLEN HONOR
STOLEN INNOCENCE

PART III:
Consequences

CHAPTER 8

KINSEY'S IMPACT ON AMERICAN LAW

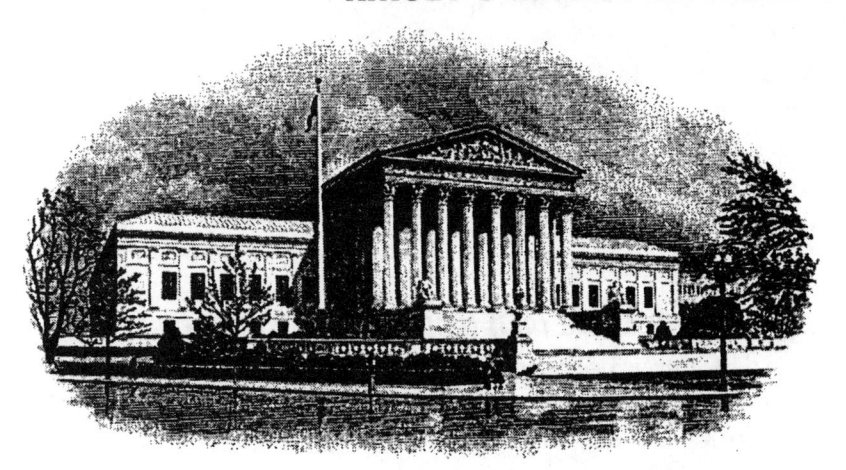

The U.S. Supreme Court

A law is that which is laid, set or fixed, like a statute, constitution.... Laws are imperative or mandatory, commanding what shall be done; prohibitory, restraining from what is to be forborne; or permissive, declaring what may be done without incurring a penalty.
Webster's 1828 Dictionary[1]

[T]he propitious smiles of Heaven can never be expected on a nation that disregards the eternal rules of order and right which Heaven itself has ordained.
George Washington, First Inaugural Address, 1789.[2]

The legal system has started to judge by ideology, not law.
Judge Robert Bork[3]

Kinsey's Sexual Revolution was not designed just as a trend meant to liberate America's libido by influencing culture, as many may mistakenly think. Rather, Kinsey meant to undermine the legal protections for the institution of marriage, the smallest building block of American society. It is difficult in a single volume to untangle each tentacle of Kinsey's effect on American law and public policy. This chapter, however, describes something of the far-reaching legal legacy of Kinsey's specious data.

PART I: "THE AMERICAN LAW INSTITUTE'S MODEL PENAL CODE OF 1955 IS VIRTUALLY A KINSEY DOCUMENT"

It begins with the influence of these data upon Kinsey's collaborators in the American Law Institute (ALI), founded in 1923. By 1947 the American Bar Association (ABA) joined with the ALI to begin a "national program of continuing education of the bar."[4] The Model Penal Code produced by the

ALI and adopted by the ABA in 1955 was vital to altering our nation's sex-crime statutes, state by state. How influential were Kinsey's data in the preparation of the new penal code?

According to Kinsey's authorized biographer, Jonathan Gathorne-Hardy, "The American Law Institute's *Model Penal Code* of 1955 is virtually a Kinsey document.... At one point Kinsey is cited six times in twelve pages."[5] In 1954, Hardy reports, after reviewing "a list of the council of the American Law Institute," Kinsey marked in red the name of Judge Hand, suggesting Hand "would probably support Kinsey's attempts to change the sex laws."[6] In the end, the new code's sex law reform was largely based on Kinsey's data and would undermine the protections for marriage, then the only lawful place for coitus.

THE AMERICAN LAW INSTITUTE (ALI) MODEL PENAL CODE (MPC)

After a "grant from the Carnegie Corporation in 1948" aided the ALI in establishing joint educational efforts with the ABA, the Rockefeller Foundation stepped in to aid Carnegie. Stanford University Law School professors Kaplan and Weisberg wrote in *Criminal Law* (1991):

> In 1950, the infusion of a large grant from the Rockefeller Foundation stirred the model penal code project to life again. An advisory committee, made up of distinguished scholars in the field of criminal law was assembled by the American Law Institute. Wechsler was appointed chief reporter [author] of the enterprise, and Louis Schwartz, another eminent authority in the field, was named co-reporter [author].[7]

The ALI's claimed goal is found in its mission statement crafted in 1923 "to promote the clarification and simplification of the law," to better adapt law to contemporary social needs, to achieve agreement among lawyers on "the fundamental principles of the common law," and to correct the legal "uncertainty and... complexity." Kaplan and Weisberg support the ALI claim that there was a "general dissatisfaction with the administration of justice,"[8] although nowhere do these writers note that this dissatisfaction centered on the public desire for tougher enforcement of extant criminal laws. Stanford law professor, Gerald Gunther, said the ALI, "is the elite incarnation of the American legal establishment, a select group of leading practitioners, scholars, and judges committed to "the improvement of the law." Gunther notes that Judge Hand was an ALI founder, and held "major positions in it for the rest of his life."[9] The 1996 Annual Report proclaimed:

> The Institute's reputation for objectivity is one of its most valuable assets. The respect accorded the Institute's texts depends in major part on that reputation. The Institute's reputation will suffer if an accusation is made with any colorable basis that Institute texts were crafted to aid the personal interests of the Institute's Reporters. If the accusation were justified, the Institute's reputation would suffer justifiably.[10]

The American Bar Association's American Law Institute Model Penal Code, Draft 4, "Sex Offenses."

At the very time the ALI's Model Penal code was being developed, there was a growing public outcry for tightening, *not loosening*, what were called "sexual psychopath" laws. But respected magistrate Morris Ploscowe, one of the Model Penal Code's principal authors, argued—based on Kinsey's findings—that "When a total clean-up of sex offenders is demanded, it is in effect a proposal to put 95 percent of the male population in jail.... Of the total male population 85 per cent has had pre-marital intercourse...."[11] Ploscowe introduced to the legal profession what Kinsey had certainly envisioned:

> One of the conclusions of the Kinsey report is that the sex offender is not a monster... but an individual who is not very different from others in his social group, and that his behavior is similar to theirs. The only difference is that others in the offender's social group have not been apprehended. This recognition that there is nothing very shocking or abnormal in the sex offender's behavior should lead to other changes in sex legislation.... In the first place, it should lead to a downward revision of the penalties presently imposed on sex offenders.[12]

Judge Learned Hand, ALI founder.

Recall that both Kinsey books, as "scientific," were allegedly embargoed from all press coverage in order to provide fair access to this allegedly scientific document. The premiere and trusted *Life Magazine* was one of many American news sources to maintain that mythology. Wrote *Life Magazine*:

> [W]e have rarely reviewed a book—and never before under such strange circumstances as our article about the Kinsey report on pages 41 through 56. Until last June, the new Kinsey report had been clothed in almost as much secrecy as the blueprints for the atomic submarine. Part of it was still in a locked desk... the secret Dr. Kinsey had kept from the world until today.[13]

FOUR KINSEY BOOKS CALL FOR "SCIENCE-BASED" SEX-LAW REFORM IN 1948

Yet, the "blueprints for the atomic submarine" were covertly given to friends long before critics might read Kinsey's books. For example, Kinsey had quietly aided legal and scientific scholars in their publication of four books, which were published in tandem with Kinsey's *Male* volume. Each of the four books called for "reforms" which were in reality massive changes in long-settled law based on Kinsey's findings which, as the books demonstrate, were widely received as truthful accounts of the sexual behavior of American men.

(1) *Sex Habits of American Men: A Symposium on the Kinsey Report,* early 1948

The first book, *Sex Habits of American Men: A Symposium on the Kinsey Report*, was dedicated to Kinsey and edited by journalist and author Albert Deutsch. Deutsch thanked "Dr. Kinsey" for "the many hours" he spent to discuss the book during its preparation.[14] This multi-disciplinary mix of essays included opinions by a number of leading scholars and citizens who advocated a shift in standards relating to marriage, sex, and family. They cited Kinsey as scientific authority for the necessity of the proposed changes. One essay in Deutsch's symposium was by the aforementioned New York Magistrate Morris Ploscowe, who published his own tome in 1951—based on Kinsey's science—entitled "*Sexual Patterns and the Law.*" This latter work was used for decades in criminal and civil cases relating to human sexual behavior.

Despite the four books and the many voices trumpeting Kinsey's research, there were a few voices of concern over Kinsey's acceptance in academia and the promotion of Kinsey's science, more accurately termed "scientism," including sociologist Albert Hobbs. Hobbs wrote in *Social Problems and Scientism* (1953) that, "conclusions of the Kinsey report are already contained in college textbooks with the interpreter in one text being none other than Albert Deutsch." Hobbs reported on Kinsey's early influence with university pedagogues and their receptivity to his work,

> More recently Mr. Deutsch has written several articles for *Look Magazine* [on Kinsey].[14] As another indication of gullibility, Mr. Deutsch reports that the faculty of Yale University included Kinsey's first volume among the 191 world classics of all time, and designated it as one of the fifteen most important books written by an American![15]

Ironically, after 50 years of saturating America with Kinsey's science and the Sexual Revolution it incited, the *Intercollegiate Review* in 1999 ranked Kinsey's *Sexual Behavior in the Human Male* as the 3rd "worst book of the century." It stated: "So mesmerized were Americans by the authority of Science, with a capital S, that it took 40 years for anyone to wonder how data is gathered on the sexual responses of children as young as five." Added the *Review*, "A pervert's attempt to demonstrate that perversion is "statistically" normal."[16]

(2) *The Ethics of Sexual Acts,* March 1948

The second of the four Kinsey-assisted books was republished in 1948 and again in 1958 from an earlier 1934 edition. It was *The Ethics of Sexual Acts* by French jurist, Rene Guyon. Kinsey supplied early manuscripts of his *Male* volume to Guyon, who utilized some of Kinsey's allegedly embargoed figures and charts to supplement his own comprehensive legal and legislative analysis of marriage and family law. An acknowledged pedophile, Guyon viewed children as viable sexual objects—and women as "parasites." Until Kinsey, Guyon had no "scientific" authority for his sexual utopia. Kinsey's statistics purported to show a discrepancy between "prescribed and actual behavior," and no sexual abnormality. They strengthened Guyon's arguments for abolishing laws restricting sexual conduct in concert with sympathetic acceptance of sex offenders, including rapists and pedophiles.

Rene Guyon: French jurist, pedophile, and Justice of the Supreme Court of Thailand.

Guyon's writings on the unfair incarceration of sex offenders, especially the elderly child molester, are repeated nearly intact in Kinsey's own writings. Dr. Harry Benjamin, an endocrinologist and internationally acclaimed sexologist, was a close friend and correspondent of both Kinsey and Guyon. He wrote in his introduction to Guyon's book: "Guyon speaking as a philosopher, and Kinsey, judging merely by empirical data" are upsetting our most cherished conventions. Benjamin went on to say:

> Many... sex activities, illegal and "immoral," but widely practiced, are recorded by both investigators.... Unless we want to close our eyes to the truth or imprison ninety-five percent

of our male population, we must completely revise our legal and moral codes.... It comes probably as a jolt to many, even open-minded people, when they realize that chastity cannot be a virtue because it is not a natural state.[17]

(3) *About the Kinsey Report,* May 1948

Donald Porter Geddes and Enid Curie edited *About the Kinsey Report,* the third swift arrival citing Kinsey in its call to lighten sex laws. Geddes' book was released in May, a few months after Guyon's book and only four months after the arrival of *Sexual Behavior in the Human Male*. *About the Kinsey Report* was published as a "Signet Special Book."[18] There was a second printing in July 1948 and several thereafter. Contributing to Geddes' essays, like Deutsch's "Symposium," were 11 renowned intellectuals[19] representing major Ivy League universities. They instilled confidence in the Kinsey Report as a collection of factual, objective data. It was presented, they said, by a conservative and impartial American academic, whose only interest was to set the sexual record straight.

Popularizing the Kinsey Male Report in 1948.

Sexual Behavior in the Human Male was said to be embargoed until its release in January 1948. Thus, Kinsey's book had allegedly been available for only four months when the Geddes' essays were published. Few of the authors could have read or thought seriously about their written assessments of Kinsey's work. Yet, Erich Fromm rebuked Kinsey's academic critics, asserting that Kinsey showed us our "social character."[20] With such distinguished scholarly support mounting, Kinsey's impact on the law would be immense. Professor Montagu rightly noted that, "during the period of a whole generation" Kinsey's sexual findings "will be more or less continually discussed…. There has never been anything like this before in the history of any country."[21] In the naïve ambience of his era, before the plagues now attending the Sexual Revolution, Montagu eagerly predicted "the outcome of all this discussion" will surely be "beneficial" for law and society.[22]

In "The Limits of Sexual Law," Columbia University law professor Karl F. Llewellyn echoed Fromm and Montagu, saying this "carefully and shrewdly gathered and analyzed body of fact" forces "severe rethinking of deep-cutting problems of our law."[23] "*Sane*" people must organize and pressure lawmakers to carry out the Kinsey-Pomeroy-Martin (K-P-M) recommendations, ignoring past views of normal, moral, right or wrong, giving authority, said Llewellyn, to the K-P-M statistics:

> Not the least value of this Kinsey-Pomeroy-Martin study is to suggest the degree to which an individual scholar, or physician, or psychiatrist, or educator, or legal official tends unwisely to… [rely on] his private experience coupled with his own peculiar type of background. No, this K-P-M material, though still far from giving the whole picture, is solid, broad, novel in range, accuracy, and discrimination, and is to be taken very seriously indeed.[24]

With under four months to read, write and analyze 804 pages of K-P-M statistics, charts, graphs and narrative, Professor Llewellyn dubbed the study as "solid," adding:

> To reach [K-P-M's] bearing on our law, one must first back off from the material itself and look at law. The first ideal and task of law is the general organization of man's conscious

> struggle to direct and control those portions of man which threaten to interfere with man's right development. That job, of necessity, sets some of us against others of us....
>
> The second task of law is less fine or ideal than practical and tough. If greed or hate or envy, or mere self-will and impatience or meanness or ambition or depravity? or mental queerness? or indeed anything else, including fine idealism that heads into conflict with law? if any of these, in any person or group, get in law's way, that fact has to be dealt with, somehow...
>
> Law is a Must. Without it (until man becomes different) either a group or a nation or a civilization just ceases to be.... So long as this machinery works, its every part plays together with its every other part to keep people in line. But let it fail to work in any case, and its whole force turns to keeping the offender [in] line.[25]

One can only wonder whether Llewellyn, or others in the legal profession at that time, suspected that Kinsey's "shrewdly gathered and analyzed data" reflected men of "ambition... depravity [and] mental queerness,"[26] whose "self-will and impatience or meanness" were set "against us" in order to get "in law's way" to see to it that the pre-1948 American "civilization just ceases to be." James Jones' 1997 Kinsey biography reveals that Kinsey himself trolled homosexual bars and bath houses.[27] Kinsey gathered 86 percent of his male subjects from those engaged in sexual crimes. Kinsey's mission, Jones writes, was to free America from Victorian "repression." To accomplish this mission required a thorough revision of American sex laws—a legal revolution.

(4) *American Sexual Behavior and the Kinsey Report,* July 1948

The fourth book published in tandem with Kinsey's Report was *American Sexual Behavior and the Kinsey Report.* This very important contribution to the growing "free love" legal debate was co-authored by ACLU attorney, Morris L. Ernst, and historian David Loth. The book's dedication was to the accommodating Kinsey team who "enriched the market-place of thought."[28] Ernst advocated legalization of adultery, obscenity, and abortion throughout his career, as well as Kinsey's full panoply of sex law changes:

> Let me mention a few items on which law must say thank you [to Kinsey]. Our laws have attempted to abolish all sexual outlets, except marital intercourse,... [including] sodomy [and] seduction... Forty-four states have laws against adultery. ...Yet the Kinsey report may well... show that one third of all husbands [commit adultery] ...Those who are concerned with juvenile delinquency, treatment of homosexuals, and the frightening attitudes of our penal institutions will have a glimmer of what the Kinsey report will do to the stream of law.[29]

Morris Ernst, ACLU attorney for Kinsey and Planned Parenthood.

Ernst was influential. He served as a "personal representative for President Roosevelt during World War II."[30] Moreover, he was well credentialed as a legal radical for serving as a founding member of the American Civil Liberties Union (ACLU).[31] Ernst was also the attorney for Kinsey, Margaret Sanger, the Kinsey Institute, the Sex Information and Education Council of the United States (SIECUS), and Planned Parenthood of America. Ernst had close ties to influential and progressive Supreme Court

Justices Louis Brandeis, Brennan, Frankfurter and Judge Learned Hand,[32] among others. Through the considerable efforts of Ernst, the Kinsey study would have special salience in the courtroom as its findings were plied there. In 1945, Ernst declared, "[w]e had fun educating juries and judges" with their new "scientific" sex information:

> Soon it will be proved that homosexuality, masturbation, and petting are more prevalent among the sophisticated, or what is called the upper stratum of society, than among other people, who show a higher percentage of premarital sexual relationship. The figures on sexual relations with girls under eighteen years of age—which acts, no doubt, run into millions of incidents a year—may cause a reappraisal of headlines concerned with juvenile delinquency. But the law in the main... is administered by judges stemming from one stratum of life, unconsciously applying their codes vis-à-vis, the other stratum. All of which not yet reduced to scientific terms is nevertheless the ever-changing basis of the law of changing obscenity.[33] [Emphasis added.]

While Marxists pander to class warfare, in 1948 Marxism was not yet part of the accepted American academic curriculum. No scientist or social critic before Kinsey had implied that sex offenders were treated too harshly because judges were unconsciously applying their "upper" religious and moral codes to the "lower stratum." Kinsey wrote in the *Male* volume:

> Judges often come from better educated groups, and their severe condemnation of sex offenders is largely a defense of the code of their own social level... [T]he judge, the civic leader, and most of the others who make such suggestions, come from that segment of the population which is most restrained on nearly all types of sexual behavior, and they simply do not understand how the rest of the population actually lives.[34]

In true ACLU fashion, as early as 1945, Ernst alluded to an anonymous study finding the "upper level judge" was a key impediment to national serenity. In 1948, as Ernst predicted, Kinsey "reduced to scientific terms" his sex data, then Ernst parlayed the data and intimidated conventional judges and juries with the latest "science." *Three years* after Ernst's "better educated" judges, essay, Kinsey declared that "judges stemming from one stratum" could not rule accurately in cases involving those in other social strata.[35] Kinsey wrote:

> The penalties visited upon persons who are convicted of sex offense may be peculiarly severe, *just because the judge does not comprehend the lower level background of the offender*. The judge may give a long sentence because he believes that such a stay in prison will reform the [person] being punished, but... Data *which we have on more than 1,200 persons who have been convicted of sex offenses indicate that there are very few who modify their sexual patterns as a result of their contacts with the law*, or indeed, as a result of anything that happens to them after they have passed their middle teens.[36] [Emphasis added.]

"A BOOK CAN END AN ERA"

By 1989, a Rockefeller-funded National Research Council AIDS report said America could be divided into "pre-Kinsey" and "post-Kinsey" eras.[37] The nation's Founders had woven fixed laws and principles into the fabric of the new nation. Kinsey and his associates considered the legal prohibitions and societal restrictions in Judaism and Christianity as "repressive," archaic and harmful. He and his legal colleagues embarked on a voyage to reopen as "new," the old pagan world. In his Foreword to Ernst and Loth's *American Sexual Behavior and the Kinsey Report*, Kinsey mentor, Robert Dickinson predicted:

> A book can end an era. An era of Hush-and-Pretend in the life of our nation may end through the Kinsey Report.... For the voluminous first section of the Kinsey study of human sexual behavior, the two authors of this book [Ernst and Loth] present many implications and applications which further serve to make the Kinsey statistics come alive, giving them a heart-beat and close touch with live people. A lawyer of note, champion of forthright speech, arbiter of controversies at many levels and writer of searching texts on social trends, has joined in a happy collaboration....

Dr. Robert Dickinson

> Surely new programs are indicated. We need to start with parents, educating them to educate their children. Then we can educate the educators—teachers, doctors, ministers, social workers and all concerned in the sexual patterns which Professor Kinsey finds are set so early in life.... Later we will teach techniques. Thus we may learn to build character and health and happiness, honoring equally all bodily activities which conform to the life of the spirit.[38]

DID ERNST AND/OR GUYON WRITE KINSEY'S "LAW" ARGUMENTS?

It will be shown that while the ALI-MPC authors quote Kinsey to the American judiciary, Kinsey gained his legal counsel from seriously tainted sources. As noted, in his 1945 book, *The Best is Yet...,* Morris Ernst provides a preview of the forthcoming sex information that will, he says, change the nature of society. Ernst and Guyon had each prepared legal constructs to replace America's sex offender laws *before* these arguments and Kinsey's science appeared in the 1948 *Male* volume. Sections of Kinsey's language regarding law reform appear to be copied from Guyon's 1934 *The Ethics of Sexual Acts*, discussed later in this chapter. Ernst's 1945 biography sheds further light on the source of Kinsey's legal construct in the *Male* volume. Kinsey's second authorized biographer, Christenson, reports that Ernst and Loth were taken to task in a Kinsey Institute press release for revealing their privileged access to the Kinsey data prior to the publication of the allegedly embargoed *Male* report. Kinsey biographer Cornelia Christenson, states:

> "The authors of this vitally significant article have long worked closely with Dr. Kinsey and his associates... Here they present for the first time the facts to be revealed in the new report." [Christensen protests] In view of this [claim] the Institute issed a press release stating that the authors had not been given any special access to the material for the forthcoming book.[39]

That Ernst was Kinsey's lawyer[40] was hushed up. On the evidence, Ernst was a trusted Kinsey aide years before he admitted to knowing the zoologist. Upon analysis, Kinsey's law language dips deeply into that of the ACLU lawyer and the French pedophile judge, discussed further on.

> **1948 Ernst & Loth Crimes List (52 Sex Sex Crimes for Civil Order) Targeted for Abolition or Lightening by the Kinsey Legal Cadre**
>
> Crimes against Nature
>   a. Sodomy
>   b. Bestiality
>   c. Buggery
>   d. Cunnilingus
>   e. Fellatio
> Adultery
> Indecent Exposure
> Disorderly Houses
> Nuisance
> Disorderly Conduct
> Pornographic Literature
> Immoral Shows and Exhibitions
> Contraception – Indecent Articles
> Bastardy
> Bigamy
> Chastity*
> Lewd Cohabitation
> Incest
> Lewd Acts with Infants [oft defined as under 18-years-of-age]
> Crimes Against Infants [Minors]
>   a. Impairing morals of a minor
>   b. Prostitution
>   c. Abduction
>   d. Seduction
>   e. Statutory Rape
> Abortion
> Fornication
> Contacts (Sexual Immorality)
> Compulsory Prostitution of Wife
>
> Transportation for Immoral Purpose
> Nudist Camps
> Abduction
> Seduction
> Prostitution
> Rape
>   a. By force
>   b. Statutory
> Lewd Behavior
> Obscene Books, Letters, Communications
> Assault with Intent to Commit Sodomy
> Assault with Intent to Commit Rape
> Solicitation with Intent to Commit Sodomy
> Solicitation with Intent to Commit Prostitution
> Illicit Intercourse
> Publication of Sex Crimes Magazines
> Advertisements Relating to Certain Diseases
> Exposure of Person
> Males Living on Proceeds of Prostitution
> Sending Messages to Places of Prostitution
> Allowing Children to Remain in Houses of Prostitution or Any Place Where Opium or Other Such Preparations is Smoked
> Smoking Opium and Other Preparations
> Concealing Birth of a Child
> Libel of Sexual Behavior
> Slander of Sexual Behavior
> Compulsory Prostitution by Parents of Children (female and in some States, male)
> Miscegenation
> Obscene Language
>
> * Here the authors include "chastity" as a sex crime. One assumes this "joke" was a reflection of the authors specific views.

IN 1948 ERNST & LOTH TARGET 52 SEX CRIME LAWS

Kinsey's false data first entered, as Ernst said, in "the stream of the law" through the ALI-MPC, "Tentative Draft No. 4," dealing with "Sex Offenses," on April 25, 1955. Other drafts covering other areas of law followed. All found their way into legislation and judicial decisions. With the ALI-MPC drafts and the four books previously mentioned by such notable professionals and academics, the legal profession and state legislatures thereafter began to gradually ignore, lighten, or repeal the 50 sex-related crimes that Ernst and Loth had included in their book, *American Sexual Behavior and the Kinsey Reports*.[41] A "separate volume could be written about each statute in relation to the Kinsey data." [See following chart.] Standing on the notion of the alleged right of privacy, the Kinsey legal cadre judged the 52 protective laws as largely illegitimate. By accepting Kinsey's data, almost all sex acts would be "restated" as private and not subject to social control.

In summary, the four 1948 Kinsey books, (1) *Sex Habits of American Men: A Symposium on the Kinsey Report*; (2) *The Ethics of Sexual Acts*; (3) *About the Kinsey Report*; and (4) *American Sexual Behavior and the Kinsey Report;* all say "thank you" to Kinsey for his legal aid in "educating juries and judges." The statement often repeated by Indiana University, Kinsey's employer, that Kinsey's "findings" were embargoed to media and scholars-at-large is refuted by these four complex books, released within a very few months of Kinsey's 1948 volume. Although he did not want to do so, Kinsey was expected to write the *Female* volume instead of his tome calling for a repeal of sex laws. However, these four books by legal and social science elitists launched the *legal* revolution better than Kinsey could have done himself as a mere zoologist. They, as academics, legal experts and scholars, spoke for Kinsey.

Then, by 1950, under cover of the American Bar Association and funded by Carnegie and Rockefeller grants, the tiny cadre of American Law Institute-Model Penal Code authors did not "clarify" America's common law, but rather radically changed its sex laws based on Kinsey's data. Kinsey would indeed impact the American justice system at-large by being cited as the "scientific" expert by both the authors of the four books and the MPC authors as supposedly proving that "sex offenders" were 95 percent of America's fathers and beloved male family members. The ALI authors demanded and facilitated "a downward revision" of sex offender penalties because Kinsey said reality was out-of-step with the law. This was all based on Kinsey's aberrant groups of criminals, homosexuals, pedophiles and the like which fortified the ALI's Model Penal Code. The revision led to the weakening and deconstruction of the 52 sex offender laws targeted for change, undermining marriage as the single legitimate source of all coitus.

These distinguished ALI-MPC authors hailed from august institutions and were leaders in their professions. They are culpable. They knew or should have known that Kinsey was a fraud. (The Rockefeller Foundation knew his data were totally unreliable.) The ALI authors' actions and writings reveal a "colorable bias," thereby seriously compromising the work and reputations of the Model Penal Code's "Institute's Reporters."

After Kinsey's bogus data entered "the stream of the law" through the ALI-MPC draft on "Sex Offenses" in 1955, the Kinsey sexuality model became codified as "normal" in mainstream America. It was taught by many unsuspecting law professors in America's most prestigious law schools. If Kinsey's science is any indication of the reliability of the ALI-MPC, one can only wonder at the efficacy of the entire effort. One might summarize the process by quoting Judge Robert Bork, "The legal system has started to judge by [a libertarian] ideology, not law."[42]

PART II: THE HISTORY OF AMERICA'S "FIXED" LAW ORDER: THE PURITY CRUSADE & COMSTOCK ERA

Anthony Comstock

Let us briefly reprise the early 1900s, the era from which Kinsey sprang as a young man. The ladies of the Purity Movement of the 19th century, both secular and sectarian, understood (as did America's Founders) that all law is moral. The period from 1871 to 1920 was dubbed the "Comstock Era" named for Anthony Comstock, the crusading New York social reformer. Based upon the evidence that "vice shortens human life," and undermines the civil society, Comstock joined with the ladies of the Purity Movement to support the enforcement of laws which preserved marriage and encouraged virtuous conduct. This "Purity" alliance between the ladies and Comstock was established to protect society's most defenseless segments.[43] women, children, the elderly and the unborn. While the nation's laws protected society's most defenseless, their advocates had the law to stand on. Kinsey and his legal colleagues began the effort to remove the supports of American law from the Purity movement and from subsequent generations.

The nation and the laws that Comstock and the Purity ladies sought to uphold and enforce were drawn from a law order created with fixed boundaries and a separation of powers. However, the success of the American law order required an informed, self-disciplined and virtuous people. Said John Quincy Adams, 6th President of the United States and son of John Adams, the 2nd President,

> [T]he highest glory of the American Revolution was this; it connected in one indissoluble bond the principles of civil government with the principles of Christianity. From the day of the Declaration… they (the American people) were bound by the laws of God, which they all, and by the laws of the Gospel, which they nearly all, acknowledge as the rules of their conduct.[44]

When the Founders presented the Declaration of Independence to the British aristocracy in the 18th century, war was required to enforce its terms. In 1948, Kinsey and his collaborators delivered a radical declaration of *sexual* independence from moral constraints. This elitist group then instigated a culture war to change society's concept of "sexual rights." The Kinsey group's strategy included the incremental gutting of American law. Generally unknown to law school graduates today, the father of our "American" language, Noah Webster, explained that our peace and prosperity are based on "a love of virtue, patriotism and religion." In the Preface to his History of the United States he wrote,

> Republican government loses half its value, where the moral and social duties are imperfectly understood, or negligently practiced. To exterminate our popular vices is a work of far more importance to the character and happiness of our citizens than any other improvement in our system of education.[45]

This chapter addresses the way in which "popular vices" have been encouraged in the law and "virtue, patriotism and religion," "moral and social duties" have been neglected or undermined. America's founders crafted a civil society and its treatment of sex in United States law upon a faith base. What does it mean for law, justice and public safety to document American governance as *built* upon the Ten Commandments of the Old Testament, as well as other key New Testament laws which formed the Christian faith? This was confirmed in *Church of the Holy Trinity v. United States,* 143 U.S. 457 (1892).[46] The U.S. Supreme Court unanimously agreed, "These and many other matters which might be noticed, add a volume of unofficial declarations to the mass of organic utterances that this is a Christian nation."[47]

The language was clear and unambiguous. This 1892 Supreme Court decision has never been overturned. It implies an adherence to laws largely based on fixed moral standards—designed to encourage marital fidelity and to strengthen the family. Why then, throughout most of the 20th Century, has its historic messag been largely ignored in the law?

Justice David Josiah Brewer

THE HISTORY OF AMERICA'S "FIXED" LAW ORDER: ORIGINS OF THE EVOLUTIONARY "STREAM OF THE LAW" AT HARVARD

For Sir William Blackstone, whose books and teachings on the common law were foundational to American law, and for America's founders, the law was "revealed" and thus "eternal." Recognizing the limitations of human observation and reason, their view of the law was not determined on the basis of the scientific method of the time.[48] However, as science embraced Darwin's evolutionary theory of a changing or unfolding universe, the evolutionary view of law was seen as "progressive." Thus, it began following the evolutionary stream of relativism. Relativism became "positive" law, which in the 20th century became confused with "the rule of law."

Charles William Eliot

Christopher Columbus Langdell

The principle of "fixed" law gave way to a process of constant change. This departure from fixed legal principle was championed by such learned men as scientist Charles William Eliot. From 1869-1909, as president of Harvard,[49] Eliot sought to apply the Darwinian scientific method to education and legal study. It appears that only professors who accepted the evolutionary law view were welcome at Harvard Law School. In 1870, Eliot selected Christopher Columbus Langdell to guide the prestigious law school into the evolutionary "stream of the law":

> This philosophy ("positivism") was introduced in the 1870s when Harvard Law School Dean Christopher Columbus Langdell (1826-1906) applied Darwin's premise of evolution to jurisprudence. Langdell reasoned that since man evolved, then his laws must also evolve; and judges should guide both the evolutions of law and the Constitution. Consequently, Langdell introduced the case-law study method under which students would study judges' decisions rather than the Constitution. Under the case-law approach, history, precedent, and the views and beliefs of the Founders not only became irrelevant, they were even considered hindrances to the successful evolution of a society…. Other law schools gradually embraced Langdell's case-law approach, and the result was a diminishing belief in absolutes. In fact, within a few short years (by the 1930s), *Blackstone's Commentaries on the Law* had been widely discarded. *Blackstone's* was deemed to present an outdated approach to law since it taught that certain rights and wrongs—particularly those related to human behavior—did not change.

Roscoe Pound (1870-1964) strongly endorsed the positivistic philosophy introduced by Langdell. As a

Jacque Loeb

prominent twentieth-century legal educator, Pound helped institutionalize positivism.... According to Pound, no longer should it be the mission of jurisprudence to focus on the narrow field of legal interpretation; the goal should be to become a sociological force to influence the development of society. The effects of these teachings by Langdell and Pound—and others like them—had a direct effect on the Supreme Court as individuals who embraced this philosophy were gradually appointed to the Court. For example, Oliver Wendell Holmes, Jr. (1841-1932), appointed to the Supreme Court in 1902, explained that original intent and precedent held little value: "[T]he justification of a law for us cannot be found in the fact that our fathers always have followed it. It must be found in some help which the law brings toward reaching a social end."[50]

As a student at Harvard (1916-1920), Kinsey entered the stream of the elite academic world where the new religion of relativism and scientific evolution was firmly rooted. Kinsey learned about Jacque Loeb's "New Biology" and the possible transformation of the world that was said to be the scientist's right and responsibility. In time, Kinsey would, like Eliot before him, join law with science to transform America's "fixed" laws regarding sexual offenses. Kinsey provided the evolutionary "scientific" justification for the arguments of legal revolutionaries, pioneering the legalization of all sexual "outlets."

THE HARVARD LAW REVIEW HERALDS THE CALL FOR THE MODEL PENAL CODE

The ALI-MPC's chief author, Professor Herbert Wechsler, was a distinguished legal academic at Columbia University. Like Ernst, Wechsler was well credentialed having served as a confidential assistant to President Franklin D. Roosevelt and as Assistant Attorney General under Attorney General Francis Biddle. Wechsler also served as an aide to Biddle and American judges during the Nuremberg trials of Nazi war criminals.

In 1952, Wechsler wrote an important article for the *Harvard Law Review* entitled, "The Challenge of a Model Penal Code." In it he lamented that for nearly two decades the concept of a new model code had languished on "the American Law Institute's agenda of unfinished business."[51] After the 1948 storm of publishing whipped up its support for Kinsey's "social science" research, Wechsler weighed in. He was

Professor Wechsler, second from left, Francis Biddle and unidentified colleagues.

KINSEY'S IMPACT ON AMERICAN LAW

gratified, he said, that the ALI "project was renewed in 1951, with the support of an Advisory Committee drawn from the law and other disciplines concerned with social aspects of behavior." But, Wechsler knew, two years before his Harvard call for the production of the Model Penal Code, that after the requisite planning, proposals and indispensably numerous meetings, in 1950[52] the Rockefellar Foundation "granted funds which will permit the undertaking to proceed."[53]

Another distinguished ALI-MPC author, Manfred Guttmacher, was drawn from the Group for the Advancement of Psychiatry ("GAP"). As chair of that group, Guttmacher explained that after meeting with Kinsey the GAP decided most sex offenders were "neither socially dangerous nor psychopathic." Why? Kinsey's "data" showed that these criminals did not differ from every man. Said the ALI-MPC's psychiatrist, Guttmacher: "Kinsey's findings were the points by which we steered. The debt that society will owe to Kinsey and his co-workers for their researches on sexual behavior will be immeasurable."[54]

Dr. Manfred Guttmacher

It is well to remember here that during the early 1950s, Kinsey became a focal point for the Reece Committee, convened during the 83rd Congress in 1953 and 1954. As a part of its report, Congressman Reece issued a warning regarding the enlarging role of Foundation-supported social scientists, like Kinsey, in changing American society to a place where,

> There are no absolutes, that everything is indeterminate, that no standards of conduct, morals, ethics, and government are to be deemed inviolate, that everything, including basic moral law, is subject to change, and that it is the part of the social scientists to take no principle for granted as a premise in social or juridical reasoning, however fundamental it may hereto have been deemed to be under our Judeo-Christian moral system.[55]

The Rockefeller Foundation's 1950 funding of the MPC worked for the legal applications of Kinsey's false "data." A congressional finding of Kinsey's research as criminal and fraudulent would destroy decades of labor for a legal revolution. While Kinsey was livid when Rockefeller pulled his bountiful fortune, the possibility of exposure by Congress more than justified the Kinsey defection. Those in the "inner circle" all knew that Kinsey's contribution to the legal revolution would literally prove to be immeasurable. For as Reece wisely discerned, the Kinsey Reports gave "scientific" cover for the ALI authors to jettison America's sexual "absolutes." Future "social or juridical reasoning" would find rulings largely based on Kinsey's fantasies, delusions and distortions of the sexual life.

THE CODE MUST BE CHANGED—IT RELIES UPON THE "COMMON LAW"

Wechsler claimed that state criminal laws had been experiencing "neglect" for decades because they were fixed and rooted in the common law. Since the Magna Carta, in 1215, the common law had served England and America. For, while societies, technologies, or "times" may change, human nature, human interaction and their resulting legal disputes were fixed and predicable through the ages. Wechsler says:

> [R]elying on the common law to pour content into the main concepts used... even in states such as New York and California, which have attempted a full legislative restate-

ment of penal law [Kinsey had aided these states in these changes] the statutes draw a large part of their meaning from the older concepts of the common law, and the gloss provided by decisions is extremely large. These are the formal indications of neglect and inattention.[56]

Eventually the 52 laws Ernst advocated for change in his 1948 book would be addressed in the new code, but Wechsler begins safely in the more virtuous 1950s pointing to the divison between major crime and minor criminality. Wechsler explained that new "scientific" information justified the removal of the many differences in criminal punishments among the states because the "penal law is ineffective, inhumane and thoroughly unscientific."[57] He continued:

> The further impeachment based on science rests in part on these contentions but in larger part on the submission that the law—or at least some of its important aspects—employs unsound psychological premises such as "freedom of will" or the belief that punishment deters; that it is drawn in terms of a psychology that is both superficial and outmoded, using concepts like "deliberation," "passion," "will," "insanity," "intent"; that even when it takes the evidence of psychiatric experts, as on the issue of responsibility, it poses questions that a scientist can neither regard as meaningful or relevant nor answer on his scientific terms; and, finally, that though the law purports to be concerned with the control of specified behavior, it rejects or does not fully use the aid that modern science can afford.[58]

Even to a layman Wechsler's above statement (published in the legally prestigious *Harvard Law Review*) signals a powerful shift in criminal and moral standards. His reasons for replacing the Common Law seemed to be because of "harsh or anarchical penalty provisions."[59] Wechsler says these constituted nothing more than "vengeance in disguise."[60] Wechsler also cites the "fundamental criticism emanating from without the legal group—especially the psychological and social sciences."[61] Kinsey was counted among the "fundamental" critics influencing Wechsler, especially concerning the need to liberalize the penalties for sex offenders.

The American Common Law was based on fixed legal principles, a jury of one's peers where everyone knew "right from wrong" and the jury could judge cases by the unmoving standards of the Common Law. But Wechsler here begins to diminish this very American institution by elevating the right of peer-reviewed "scientists" and experts over the jury system. Wechsler seemed to believe that the laws restrictive of sexual activity were misplaced and even a serious threat to America's social institutions. Citing Kinsey's *Male* volume, Wechsler asked rhetorically, "Does Dr. Kinsey's data [sic] and other modern insight with respect to sexual activity have a bearing on what may significantly be regarded as an injury which should be classified as criminal?"[62]

COMMON LAW SEX OFFENSES YEILD TO KINSEY'S "SOCIAL SCIENCE" DATA

In 1948, ALI-MPC author Morris Ploscowe claimed—based upon Kinsey's findings—"It is obvious that our sex crime legislation is completely out of touch with the realities of individual living."[63] That same year, Ernst and Loth wrote about the infamous 95 percent of American men in Kinsey's *Male* Report:

These are the facts.... The whole of our laws and customs in sexual matters is based on the avowed desire to protect the family, *and at the base of the family is the father*. His behavior is revealed by the Kinsey Report to be quite different from anything the general public had supposed possible or reasonable.[64] [Emphasis added.]

It has been rather complacently assumed by a great many Americans that sexual activity for men outside the marriage bond is as rare as it is offensive to the publicly proclaimed standards of the people... strengthened by the bulk of popular literature and entertainment... [and] the almost savage penalties which many State laws attach to such activities [as adultery].[65]

Kinsey's Report dealt with "males" and implicitly, with fathers. Yet, advocates for criminal law reform like Wechsler, Ploscowe, Guttmacher, Schwartz, Tappan, Ernst and Loth, etc., libeled American husbands and fathers, who fought in World War II, as sexual offenders and deviants. They based this on Kinsey's "95 percent sex offenders" statistic. Kinsey assisted his colleagues greatly in undermining the role of "fathers" in their moral and legal responsibilities as providers for and protectors of their families. In 1955, state legislatures received the fourth draft of the Model Penal Code. Based on the recent "objective, scientific" research, it was portrayed merely as a restatement and "clarification" of the Common law. The codes sponsored by the American Law Institute, writes Lawrence M. Friedman—celebrated author of *A History of American Law*—were "meant for persuasion of judges, rather than enactment into law."[66] Eventually, the United States Supreme Court justices and every law school accepted the new Code as authoritative.

PART III: THE ROCKEFELLER FOUNDATION: "WITHIN THE STATE A STATE SO POWERFUL"

Like Congressman Reece, Supreme Court Justice Louis Brandeis—while supportive of the concept of evolutionary law—was concerned about philanthropies such as the Rockefeller Foundation. He issued this warning about their powerful special-interest influence under the guise of benevolence: "*There develops within the State a state so powerful that the ordinary social and industrial forces existing are insufficient to cope with it.... [Their power is] inconsistent with our democratic aspirations.*"[67] [Emphasis added.]

Supreme Court Justice Louis Brandeis

The Foundation enthusiastically supported the concept of "eugenics," which encourages the reproductive efforts of those deemed to have "good" ("eu" from the Greek for good) genes, while discouraging or stopping procreation by undesirables. This view had motivated the Foundation's earlier support of Planned Parenthood founder Margaret Sanger, and her eugenic and birth control movement. But Rockefeller and others were anxious to go even further to mold America's breeding patterns along evolutionary lines.

The Foundation considered Kinsey's "quantitative content" sex research of critical importance to the "grand scheme." As Professor Christopher Simpson wrote in *Science of Coercion:* The Foundation sought "quantitative" data to provide "a tool for social management" that is postwar "psychological warfare" with which to impose the will of the elite "on the masses."[68]

The *Greenwood Encyclopedia of American Institutions* (1984), volume #8, describes the origin and a brief history of tax-exempt foundations in America, and the seminal role of the Rockefellers:

The idea of establishing a foundation independent of the donor and his family, professionally managed, and with the mandate "to attempt to cure evils at their source" without regard to national boundaries probably came from Fredrick T. Gates, a former Baptist minister and long time associate of John D. Rockefeller, Sr., who exerted considerable personal influence on all the Rockefeller philanthropies.

Originally it was hoped that such a Rockefeller trust would be chartered by the Congress of the United States, with its organization and program subject to continuing congressional review. Legislation was introduced to this end in 1910, 1911, and 1912, but the Congress, strongly influenced by hostility toward large corporations and their founders, was not receptive to such a proposal.

The result was that Rockefeller Foundation was finally incorporated by the New York State legislature in 1913 with an initial endowment of $35 million "to promote the well-being of mankind throughout the world."[69]

THE ROCKEFELLER FOUNDATION'S SUPPORT OF THE SEXUAL REVOLUTION IN THE NAME OF CODIFICATION

According to Manfred Guttmacher, in the mid-1920s the ALI sought Rockefeller funds to carry out a legal "codification project" but held off until "the behavioral sciences" could aid in legal recommendations:

> In 1950 the American Law Institute began the monumental task of writing a Model Penal Code. I am told that a quarter of a century earlier the Institute had approached the Rockefeller Foundation for the funds needed to carry out this project, but at that time, Dr. Alan Gregg, a man of great wisdom counseled the Foundation to wait, that the behavioral sciences were on the threshold of development to the point at which they could be of great assistance. Apparently, the Institute concluded that the time had arrived.[70]

Thus, the Rockefeller Foundation had great hope for developing a social scientist who would provide quantified data that could overturn the old moral order. In 1942, Kinsey and his behavioral "sex science" were receiving funds from The Rockefeller Foundation.

KINSEY'S THIRD VOLUME WAS TO BE A LEGAL REPORT

In a letter dated July 7, 1950, Warren Weaver, head of Rockefeller Foundation's Natural Sciences Division, revealed that Kinsey was considering the retention of several favored attorneys to assist him in completing a third report. One of those suggested was Harriet Pilpel, assistant to Kinsey's ACLU lawyer Morris Ernst. Another was Paul Tappan of New York University. Pilpel became a Kinsey lawyer and Tappan an ALI-MPC author. The evidence shows *all* 1955 MPC authors, Wechsler, Ploscowe, Schwartz and Tappan, to be Kinsey partisans. Following a 1950 visit to the Indiana University campus and Kinsey's home, Dr. Alan Gregg, who had been the principal Rockefeller mover and shaker behind Kinsey's *Male* and *Female* volumes, wrote in his diary about Kinsey's "personnel" needs, and the lawyers that the Rockefeller Foundation might suggest for the Kinsey Institute's planned law volume:

Past and present needs remain unsatisfied in point of anatomy, physiology, psychology and statistics... M. might be available for staff. K. [Kinsey] believes he should add to staff now so as to prepare for Volume 3, the legal volume. He has in mind <u>Alice Field</u> of New York, a woman with legal training who is now in Magistrates Court.... <u>Harriet Pilpel</u> now in Morris Ernst's office... Paul Tappan at New York University has degrees in law and sociology; would be excellent in the field of European laws and interstate laws relating to sex.[71] (Underlined in original.)

Ms. Field contributed to *Sexual Habits of American Men, A Symposium on the Kinsey Report* (1948), which also included Morris Ploscowe's essay on Kinsey and sex-offender laws. Paul Tappan joined Kinsey disciples Guttmacher and Ploscowe, as well as other Kinsey admirers, to form the Rockefeller-funded ALI-MPC team which created the MPC. While biographer James Jones reports that Kinsey's treatise on law is available at the Kinsey Institute, the Institute refuses to release any such documents to researchers it perceives as critics.

Attorney Harriet Pilpel, assistant to Kinsey's ACLU lawyer Morris Ernst.

Kinsey's findings on human sexuality permeated the final (1980) version of the MPC. He was cited as the primary authority on sex research, and his co-author, Wardell Pomeroy, was added as an authority in various areas of suggested law revision.[72]

"VIRTUALLY EVERY PAGE OF THE KINSEY REPORT TOUCHES ON THE LEGAL CODE"

Other legal citations in the ALI-MPC included Britain's Wolfenden Report on sex law reform and Ploscowe's *Sex and the Law* (1951).[73] Scores of other books and journals also relied heavily on Kinsey. Princeton's David Allyn, author of "Private Acts/Public Policy: Alfred Kinsey, the American Law Institute and the Privatization of American Sexual Morality," said, "*Sex and the Law* translated the sociological contents of the Kinsey Report into legal principles for the reform of America's moral economy."[74] Allyn also discussed Ploscowe's ALI-MPC activities in some detail. In 1948, Morris Ernst wrote that "Virtually every page of the Kinsey Report touches on some section of the legal code... a reminder that the law, like our social pattern, falls lamentably short of being based on a knowledge of facts."[75] In 1955, he added that the "Kinsey investigators discovered that a good many of the sex offenders who had been convicted were the victims of a certain amount of personal spite."[76]

The shift from "fixed" laws based primarily on the case-law method, to laws reflecting "slowly formed habits" or reactions to "spite," was underway.[77] Without the stability of fixed common law authority, cases began relying heavily upon non-legal mental-health authority and special interest experts to implement a new legal process. Roughly one-third of the 1955 MPC's social science citations were to Kinsey. And 100 percent of its references to empirical U.S. social science data about "sex offenses" cite Kinsey's apocryphal findings.

PART IV: APPROXIMATELY 650 CITATIONS TO KINSEY IN LAW REVIEW ARTICLES 1982-2000; 90 MORE BY 2011

How could a man who has been dead for over 40 years have an impact in America today? *Westlaw* is the most widely used database for legal cases and law review journals. A preliminary search for the years 1982-2000 yielded roughly 650 citations to "Alfred Kinsey." And another 90 citations by 2011. For comparison, citations for the famed Masters and Johnson sex research team during the same period turned up only 92 citations. The Kinsey list does *not* include the many additional cites to the ALI-MPC. Combining Kinsey's *Westlaw* citations with those located via the *Social Science Citation Index* and *the Science Citation Index*[78] yields a total of approximately 5,796—compared to about 3,716 for Masters and Johnson. Kinsey is roughly double the citations for such luminaries as Sigmund Freud, Abraham Maslow and Margaret Mead.

To further understand Kinsey's importance to "law-making in our lifetime," compare his citations to those for Herbert Wechsler, chief author of the MPC and author of the second most cited law review article in history. In *Overcoming Law* (1995), Judge Richard Posner, Chief Justice of the U.S. 7th Circuit Court of Appeals (which includes Indiana), recalled that an article by Wechsler "published in 1959," had been cited by the end of 1992 "a remarkable 1,102 times in law reviews."[79]

In his chapter, "Economics and Homosexuality," Judge Posner cited to Kinsey as his credible legal authority. Referring to the Kinsey Scale, Posner asserted:

> Kinsey devised a scale of zero to six to represent the range of homosexual preferences. A zero has only heterosexual preference, a six only homosexual preference. A three is a perfect bisexual, indifferent to the sex of his partner. Kinsey proxied preference by "fantasy": what kind of sexual relations do we (day) dream of having? Our fantasies reveal preferences that have a certain (though not the only or even primary) authenticity because they are not affected by costs and benefits stemming from our interactions with other people. They are in a rough sense pre-social, biological preferences.[80]

Judge Posner, a zealous obscenity-as-harmless advocate, continued at some length venerating Kinsey's discredited homosexuality, bisexuality and heterosexuality "scale" as though the drawing were a real scientific instrument. So, it's no surprise that such a view is held by roughly 6,000 general social science and science citations and approximately 650 law review references to Kinsey. Moreover, articles citing to the MPC are exponentially greater than the 650 direct citations to Kinsey. Lawyers and judges will cite the original "case" for authority, spinning off into copy-cat citations impossible to ascertain. Since the publication of the first edition of *Kinsey: Crimes & Consequences*, a follow-up search of *Westlaw* yielded a dozen new Kinsey citations from September 1997 to March 2000. Descriptions of some of the law review articles citing Kinsey as a legitimate authority follow:

NONCOMPREHENSIVE "KINSEY" WESTLAW CITES, 1982-2011

2000		*Stanford Law Review*: Bisexuality as a Norm, "Erased" from Cultural Discussion
1999	May	*Cornell Law Review*: Children's Suggestibility
1999	Spring	*William & Mary Journal of Women and the Law*: Pan-sexuality
1999	Winter	*Hastings Women's Law Journal*: Political Feminist Jurisprudence
1999		*University of Illinois Law Review*: Homosexuality
1998	Fall	*Urban Lawyer Fall*: Government Operations and Liability Law
1998	Summer	*Northwestern University Law Review*: Symposium: Legal Responses to Child Molesters
1998	Spring-Summer	*UCLA Women's Law Journal*: Women, Morality, and Sexual Orientation

1998	June	*New York University Law Review*: Gay Rights Litigation Strategies
1998	June	*Psychology, Public Policy, and Law*: Sex Offender Law, "Homophobia" and Sexual Psychopath Legislation Postwar Society
1998	Spring	*Case Western Reserve Law Review*: Reverse Incest Suits
1998	Spring	*Law and Psychology Review*: Evolutionary Biology And Rape Liability
1998	April	*New York University Law Review*: (Homosexual) Male Rape Victims and the Rape Shield Law
1998	Winter	*Case Western Reserve Law Review*: First Amendment Protection for Homosexuals
1998	Winter	*Hastings Women's Law Journal*: Female Juvenile Delinquency… Gender Bias
1998		*Cardozo Arts and Entertainment Law Journal*: Artists Intellectual Property
1998		*Denver University Law Review*: InterSEXionality, Homosexuality
1998		*Denver University Law Review*: Marriage, Bisexuality
1998		*Santa Clara Law Review:* The Defense Of Marriage Act: "According to the Kinsey Report, 37% of the male population has had some homosexual experience, 13.7% has had more homosexual than heterosexual experience, and 4% were exclusively homosexual. The numbers were similar but lower for women." [p.939, f. 1]. For purposes of this comment, and for ease of calculation, the author uses the common belief that 10% of the population is homosexual.
1998		*University of Illinois Law Review*: Homosexuality, "Social Science and Gay and Lesbian Parents"
1997	September	*Practicing Law Institute*: Gender Discrimination
1997	August	*UCLA Law Review*: Gender Discrimination
1997	Summer	*Common Law Conspectus*: First Amendment
1997	Summer	*New England Journal on Crime & Civ. Confinement*: Human Rights
1997	Summer	*Yale Journal of Law and the Humanities*: Gender Issues Law Journal
1997	Summer	*Family Law Quarterly*: Child Custody
1997	June	*Minnesota Law Review*: Gender Issues
1997	June	*Yale Journal of Law & the Humanities*: Gender Issues
1997	June	*Practicing Law Institute*: Sex Harassment
1997	May	*Stanford Law Review*: Culture
1997	Spring	*Columbia Journal of Law and Social Problems*: Rape
1997	Spring	*Duke Journal of Gender Law & Policy*: Gender Issues
1997	April	*Fordham Law Review*: Criminal Rights
1997	Spring	*Harvard Women's Law Journal*: Gender Issues
1997	Spring	*Hofstra Law Review*: Homosexuality
1997	Spring	*Indiana Journal of Global Legal Studies*: Gender Issues
1997	Spring	*Journal of Contemporary Legal Issues*: Culture
1997	Spring	*Mercer Law Review*: Law
1997	Spring	*Michigan Journal of Race and Law*: Discrimination
1997	April	*North Carolina Law Review*: Child Abuse
1997	Spring	*Oregon Law Review*: Courtroom Science
1997	Spring	*Saint Louis University Law Journal*: Courtroom Science
1997	Spring	*Saint Louis University Law Journal*: Incest Cases
1997	Spring	*South Carolina Law Review*: Child Custody
1997	Spring	*Southern California Interdisciplinary Law Journal*: Child Custody
1997	Spring	*Southern Illinois University Law Journal*: Child Custody
1997	Spring	*Women's Rights Law Reporter*: Marriage Law
1997	March	*Federal Probation*: Offender's Rights
1997	March	*Fordham Law Review*: Homosexual/Legal History
1997	March	*Harvard Law Review*: Laws
1997	February	*Michigan Law Review*: Race/Gender
1997	Winter	*Boston College Third World Law Journal*: Child Rights/Custody
1997	January	*California Law Review*: Hearsay/Speech
1997	January	*Cardozo Law Review*: Gay/Lesbian
1997	January	*Cardozo Law Review*: Family Law
1997	Winter	*Case Western Reserve Law Review*: Female Circumcision
1997	Winter	*Case Western Reserve Law Review*: Genital Mutilation
1997	Winter	*Georgetown Journal of Legal Ethics*: Attorney/Client Sex
1997	Winter	*Marquette Law Review*: Naturalism/Humanism
1997	Winter	*University of Colorado Law Review*: Child Custody/Protection
1997	Winter	*Virginia Journal of Social Policy and the Law*: Child Sexual Abuse
1997	Winter	*Women's Rights Law Reporter*: Class/Gender
1997	Winter	*Yale Journal of Law and the Humanities*: Female Juvenile Delinquency
1997		*Albany Law Review*: Individual Responsibility
1997		*Animal Law*: Animal Rights
1997		*Catholic Lawyer*: Euthanasia

1997		*Houston Law Review*: International Health
1997		*Idaho Law Review*: Children/Conflict Divorce
1997		*Loyola of Los Angeles Entertainment Law Journal*: Identity Question
1997		*Maine Law Review*: Child Sexual Abuse/Repressed Memory
1997		*Medicine and Law*: Compulsory Hospitalization/Criminal Acts
1997		*New York University Review of Law and Social Change*: Education and Race
1997		*North Dakota Law Review*: Indian Child Welfare Act
1997		*Notre Dame Law Review*: Race
1997		*Ohio State Law Journal*: Child Custody
1997		*Seton Hall Law Review*: Genetic Testing
1996	Winter	*Arizona Law Review*: Sentencing Policy
1996	December	*California Law Review*: Pornography
1996	November	*Cardozo Law Review*: Moral Slavery
1996	November	*New York University Law Review*: Custody/Termination of Parental Rights
1996	Fall	*American University Journal of Gender and the Law*: Repressed Memory/Child Sex Abuse
1996	September/October	*Boston Bar Journal*: Grandparent's Rights
1996	Fall	*California Western International Law Journal*: Abortion/Islamic Response
1996	Fall	*California Western International Law Journal*: Capital Punishment, Pornography, Drugs
1996	Fall	*Connecticut Law Review*: Time/Culture
1996	Fall	*Cornell Journal of Law and Public Policy*: Child Custody
1996	Fall	*DePaul Law Review*: Race
1996	Fall	*Dickinson Law Review*: Anti-Semitism
1996	Fall	*Duquesne Law Review*: Suicide
1996	Fall	*Hastings Constitutional Law Quarterly*: Discrimination
1996	Fall	*Law and Social Inquiry*: Social Control
1996	Fall	*Mississippi Law Journal*: Free Society
1996	Fall	*Oregon Law Review*: Identity Politics and Law
1996	Fall	*Oregon Law Review*: Socialization
1996	Fall	*Pacific Law Journal*: Child Abuse
1996	Fall	*Texas Journal of Women and the Law*: Sexual Orientation
1996	Fall	*University of Colorado Law Review*: Reform
1996	Fall	*University of Dayton Law Review*: Cultural Feminism
1996	Fall	*Virginia Journal of Social Policy and the Law*: Trust, Lies, and Interrogation
1996	Fall	*Washington University Journal of Urban and Contemporary Law*: Parental Rights
1996	Fall	*Willamette Law Review*: Ideology
1996	Fall	*Women's Rights Law Reporter*: Women's Roles
1996	September	*Cornell Law Review*: Abuse
1996	July	*Current Developments in Employment Law*: Workplace Claims
1996	Summer	*Arizona State Law Journal*: Custody
1996	Summer	*Connecticut Law Review*: Parental Rights
1996	Summer	*Dickinson Law Review*: Rape
1996	Summer	*Family Law Quarterly*: Adoption/Parental Rights
1996	Summer	*Harvard Civil Rights—Civil Liberties Law Review*: Civil Rights
1996	July	*Iowa Law Review*: Property Rights
1996	Summer	*University of Chicago Law Review*: Parent Rights
1996	Summer	*University of San Francisco Law Review*: Law's Inversion
1996	Summer	*University of San Francisco Law Review*: Lawyer Lovers
1996	Summer	*Yale Journal of Law and the Humanities*: Culture
1996	Summer	*Yale Journal of Law and the Humanities*: Representation
1996	Summer	*Yale Journal of Law and the Humanities*: Legal Realism
1996	Summer	*Yale Journal of Law and the Humanities*: Empathy
1996	July	*Practicing Law Institute*: Child Physical and Sexual Abuse
1996	June	*Practicing Law Institute*: Libel
1996	June	*Columbia Law Review*: Race
1996	June	*Law and Inequality: A Journal of Theory & Practice*: Feminism
1996	June	*Loyola of Los Angeles Law Review*: Religion
1996	June	*New York University Law Review*: Juvenile Status
1996	June	*Psychology, Public Policy and Law*: Workforce
1996	June	*Psychology, Public Policy and Law*: Informal/Formal procedures
1996	May	*Boston College Law Review*: Repressed Memory/Child Sexual Abuse
1996	May	*Columbia Law Review*: Legal Rights

1996	May	*Georgetown Law Journal*: Jurisprudence
1996	May	*Minnesota Law Review*: Religious Liberty
1996	Spring	*American Business Law Journal*: Law
1996	Spring	*American Journal of Comparative Law*: Obscenity
1996	April	*American University Journal of Gender and the Law*: Consensual Relationships
1996	Spring	*Boston College Environmental Affairs Law Review*: Animal Rights
1996	April	*Defense Counsel Journal*: Client-Patient Privilege
1996	April	*Hastings Law Journal*: Reproduction
1996	Spring	*Houston Law Review*: Paranoia
1996	Spring	*Journal of Contemporary Health Law and Policy*: Memory
1996	Spring	*Journal of Criminal Law and Criminology*: Polygraph
1996	April	*North Carolina Law Review*: Separation of Church and State
1996	Spring	*Nova Law Review*: Sterilization of the Mentally Disabled
1996	Spring	*Southern California Review of Law and Women's Studies*: Cultural Rape
1996	Spring	*Tennessee Law Review*: Political Correctness
1996	Spring	*Transnational Law & Contemporary Problems*: Transplants
1996	Spring	*U. C. Davis Law Review*: Religion/Politics
1996	Spring	*University of Chicago Law Review*: Victim Impact
1996	Spring	*University of Pittsburgh Law Review*: Tyranny
1996	Spring	*Wayne Law Review*: Ethics/Morality in Medicine
1996	Spring	*Widener Law Symposium*: Childhood Sexual Abuse
1996	Spring	*William and Mary Law Review*: Third-Party Custody
1996	March	*Cardozo Law Review*: Law/Democracy
1996	March	*Cardozo Law Review*: Law/Democracy
1996	March	*Columbia Law Review*: Criminal Law
1996	March	*Columbia Law Review*: Child Separation
1996	March	*Duke Law Journal*: Society System
1996	March	*Fordham Law Review*: Child Protection
1996	March	*Fordham Law Review*: Children/Civil Litigation
1996	March	*Fordham Law Review*: Parents in Child Welfare Cases
1996	March	*Fordham Law Review*: Children's Legal Representation
1996	March	*Fordham Law Review*: Child & Adolescent Ethical Issues
1996	March	*Virginia Law Review*: Law & the Individual
1996	February	*Duke Law Journal*: Women in the Military
1996	February	*Stanford Law Review*: Love
1996	February	*University of Kansas Law Review*: Privacy/Intimacy
1996	January	*Harvard Law Review*: Sexual Abuse
1995	October	*Washington Law Review*: Same-Sex Marriage/Separation
1995	Fall	*American Journal Trial Advocate*: Expert Witness
1995	Fall	*University of Chicago Law Review*: Judicial Opinion
1995	October	*Columbia Law Review*: Adoption/Law
1995	April	*Stanford Law Review*: Pornography
1995	Spring	*Duke Journal of Gender Law & Policy*: Homosexuality/Adoption
1995	January	*Stanford Law Review*: Homosexuality ("Outing")
1995		*Berkeley Women's Law Journal*: Bisexuality
1995	Fall	*Journal of Contemporary Health Law and Policy*: Homosexuals/Military
1995	October	*Yale Law Journal*: Homosexuality In Law
1995	July	*Iowa Law Review*: Homosexuals/Military
1995	May	*Harvard Law Review*: Homosexuals/Military
1995	May	*Southern California Law Review*: Same-Sex Marriage
1995	April	*Stanford Law Review*: Pornography
1995	April	*New York University Law Review*: Homosexuals/Military
1995	February	*Stanford Law Review*: Adultery
1995	January	*Stanford Law Review*: Homosexuality ("Outing")
1995	Winter	*Journal of Criminal Law and Criminology*: Hate Crime (Homophobia)
1995	January	*California Law Review*: Homosexuals (Law and Society)
1995	Winter	*Yale Journal of Law and Human*: Bisexuality
1995		*Berkeley Women's Law Journal*: Bisexuality
1995		*Columbia Journal of Gender and Law*: Homosexuality
1995		*Washington University Law Quarterly*: Homosexuality ("Outing")
1995		*Yale Journal of Law and Feminism*: Same-Sex Sexual Harassment
1995	Fall	*Emory Law Journal*: Same-Sex Marriage
1994	Fall	*J. Marshall Law Review*: Homosexuality/Military

Year	Season/Month	Citation
1994	Summer	*Fordham Urban Law Journal*: Sodomy
1994	June	*Colorado Law*: Legal Workplace
1994	Spring	*SMU Law Review*: Criminal Law
1994	Spring	*William & Mary Law Review*: National Origin Discrimination
1994		*North Dakota Law Review*: Punitive Damages
1994		*Stanford Law & Policy Review*: Homosexuality/Military
1994	Summer	*Harvard C.R.-C.L. Law Review*: Homosexuality (First Amendment Rights)
1994	Summer	*Harvard C.R -C..L. Law Review*: Homosexual Immigrants
1994	Summer	*Fordham Urban Law Journal*: Sodomy
1994	May	*Columbia Law Review*: Disabilities/Moral Code
1994	Spring	*Golden Gate University Law Review*: Homosexuality & Law
1994	Spring	*Oregon Law Review*: Homosexuality ("Outing")
1994	April	*Texas Law Review*: Pornography
1994	Spring	*Catholic University Law Review*: Same-Sex Marriage
1994	Spring	*S.U. Law Review*: State v. Baxley
1994	Winter	*Suffolk Transnational Law Review*: AIDS, Law Reform
1994	Symposium	*Utah Law Review*: Homosexuality Legislation
1994		*Berkeley Women's Law Journal*: Homosexuality/Feminist Legal Theory
1994	Symposium	*Ohio State Law Journal*: Anti-Gay Legislation
1994	Symposium	*Utah Law Review*: No-Fault Divorce
1994		*University of Toledo Law Review*: Therapeutic Divorce
1993	July	*Georgetown Law Journal*: Sexuality
1993	June	*Georgetown Law Journal*: Sexuality
1993	May	*Stanford Law Review*: Sexuality
1993		*Yale Law & Policy Review*: Homosexuality/Affirmative Action
1993	December	*Florida Law Review*: Sexual Conduct/Model Penal Code
1993	November	*Vanderbilt Law Review*: Homosexuality [Employment Discrimination]
1993	October	*Virginia Law Review*: Gay Rights
1993	July	*Georgetown Law Review*: Sexuality
1993	Summer	*Dickinson. Law Review*: Homosexuality/Law
1993	June	*Georgetown Law Journal*: Gay Rights
1993	May	*Stanford Law Review*: Sexuality
1993	May	*Michigan Law Review*: Sexuality
1993	Spring	*New York Law School Journal of Human Rights*: Same-Sex Marriage
1993	Winter	*U.C. Davis Law Review*: Homosexuality/Employment Law
1993	Winter	*Texas Journal of Women and Law*: Women/Violence
1993		*St. Louis University Publication Law Review*: Abortion
1992/1993		*University of Louisville Journal of Family Law*: Homosexuals/Domestic Violence
1992/1993		*New York University Review of Law & Social Change*: Indecency
1993		*Seton Hall Law Review*: Same-Sex Marriage
1993		*Yale Law & Policy Review*: Homosexuality/Affirmative Action
1992	October	*Yale Law Journal*: Sexuality
1992	October	*Yale Law Journal*: Gay Legal Agenda
1992	Spring-Fall	*Women's Rights Law Report*: Lesbianism
1992	Spring-Fall	*Women's Rights Law Report*: Sexual Orientation
1992	Fall	*Stetson Law Review*: Parental Custody
1992	Summer	*SMU Law Review*: Homosexuality—Military
1992	Summer	*Virginia Tax Review*: Generation Shifting
1992	May	*California Law Review*: Statutory Rape
1992	April	*University of Pennsylvania Law Review*: Criminal Liability
1992	Winter	*Buffalo Law Review*: Ethics
1992		*Santa Clara Law Review*: Privacy
1992	Fall	*University of Michigan Journal of Law*: Homosexuality/Employment Discrimination
1992	Spring-Fall	*Women's Rights Law Report*: Homosexuals/Minority Status
1992	Spring	*Journal of Contemporary Health Law & Policy*: Homosexuals—Military
1992	January	*California Law Review*: Homophobia—Manslaughter
1992	Winter	*California Review of Law & Women's Studies*: Teen Pregnancy
1992	January	*University of Miami Law Review*: Homosexuality ("Outing")
1992	Winter	*University of Toledo Law Review*: Homosexuality/Military
1991/1992		*Journal of Family Law*: Adultery
1991	January	*Los Angeles Law Review*: Benshalom v. Marsh
1991	Winter	*Vermont Law Review*: Homosexuality/Employment Discrimination

1991	Winter	*Military Law Review*: Homosexuality/Military
1991	Fall	*University of Richmond Law Review*: Incest
1991		*Indiana Law Review*: Sexuality/Law
1990	December	*Cardozo Law Review*: Same-Sex Marriage
1990	Fall	*Journal of Law & Politics*: Homosexuality/National Security
1990	July	*Pacific Law Journal*: Drugs/Employee Rights
1990	April	*Columbia Law Review*: Statutory Interpretation
1990	April	*Los Angeles Law Review*: Same-Sex Marriage
1990	March	*Boston College Law Review*: Homosexuality/Equal Protection
1990	Fall	*Buffalo Law Review*: Morality & Values
1990	January	*NY University Review of Law & Social Change*: Homosexuals/Military
1989	Fall	*University of Pittsburgh Law Review*: AIDS
1989	June	*UCLA Law Review*: Homosexuality/Equal Protection
1989	May	*Harvard Law Review*: Sexual Orientation/Law
1989	May	*Harvard Law Review*: Criminal Justice/Homosexuality
1989	April	*UCLA Law Review*: Public Disclosure (Privacy)
1989	Winter	*Dickinson Law Review*: Homosexual Fathers/Child Custody
1989	January	*Harvard Law Review*: Homosexuality/Child Custody
1989		*Ohio State University Law Journal*: AIDS
1989		*Nebraska Law Review*: Expert Testimony/Child Sexual Abuse
1988	May	*Yale Law Journal*: Homosexual Agenda (Historical/Political)
1988	April	*NYU Law Review*: Bowers v. Hardwick
1988	January	*North Carolina Law Review*: Criminal Law
1988		*St. Louis University Public Law Review*: AIDS
1987	May	*Yale Law Journal*: Prostitution
1987	April	*Columbia Law Review*: Ethics
1987	March	*Yale Law Journal*: Punishment
1987	March	*University of Miami Law Review*: Obscenity
1986	November	*NYU Law Review*: Privacy
1985	January	*Yale Law Journal*: Moral Character
1985	April	*UCLA Law Review*: Homosexuality/Child Custody Battles
1984	July	*California Law Review*: Homosexuality/Equal Protection
1984	May	*NYU Law Review*: Religion & Morality Legislation
1984	Spring	*Columbia Human Rights Law Review*: Homosexual Aliens
1984	Spring	*Family Law Quarterly*: Cohabitation
1984	Spring	*NYU Journal of International Law & Policy*: Homosexual Aliens
1983	November	*Columbia Law Review*: Child Sex Abuse/Child Witness
1982		*Ohio State Law Journal*: Intimate Association

Kinsey's more than 6,000 citations in law, social science, and science journals attest to his considerable influence. But they do not indicate the extent to which his views have been further magnified by such key change agents as Ernst, Ploscowe, Wechsler, Tappan, Guttmacher, and the Rockefeller Foundation. Note, for instance, how Ploscowe uses a snippet of Kinsey's misleading data to call for a change in U.S. law regarding sex:

> These pre-marital, extra-marital, homosexual and animal contacts, we are told, are eventually indulged in by 95 per cent of the population in violation of statutory prohibitions. If these conclusions are correct, then it is obvious that our sex crime legislation is completely out of touch with the realities of individual living and is just as inherently unenforceable as legislation which prohibits the manufacture and sale of alcoholic beverages or legislation which attempts to prohibit gambling. For in each case the law attempts to forbid an activity which responds to a wide human need. [81]

Reviewing, Kinsey was born in an era remembered for the great purity campaigns to preserve marriage and protect women and children. These largely volunteer groups battled to preserve America's founding virtues and first principles. Running concurrently with the great temperance movements, which began in the second half of the 19th century, culminating with the end of prohibition in 1933, was the titanic struggle for supremacy between Christianity and Science. The overcoming of fixed religious foundations and the ascendancy of evolutionary science in America was exemplified by President Eliot's Harvard legacy when he retired in 1909. In 1916, the Harvard Kinsey entered had abandoned its original religious moorings and embraced a Darwinian worldview. Thus, Kinsey was a perfect fit. He had left a religious home to embrace science as the answer to life's eternal questions.

Kinsey's data were used by legal elites to abolish America's common law protections for women and children in the area of sex offenses. The well-respected attorney, Herbert Wechsler, ushered Kinsey onto the legal stage in 1952 by writing in the *Harvard Law Review*, "Dr. Kinsey's data" bring "modern insight with respect to sexual activity." Wechsler called for revising sex offender laws to fit the "reality" Kinsey's data described. That reality was grounded in the fact that Kinsey said 95 percent of American males are sex offenders—breaking one or more laws according to the Common Law standard. Therefore, the ALI wanted to eliminate the "almost savage penalties" which had discouraged crimes like adultery.

While many legislators and judges were concerned about the influence of tax-exempt foundations on American life, The Rockefeller Foundation funded Kinsey and then funded the American Law Institute's production of the Model Penal Code (MPC). The Rockefeller Foundation knew that Kinsey's data, compiled by rapists, incest offenders, pedophiles, homosexuals, prostitutes, etc., were unreliable. Yet the American Law Institute MPC authors—Wechsler, Ploscowe, Guttmacher, Tappan, and Schwartz—used Kinsey's aberrant population to frame the 1955 model code on sex offenses. The MPC was designed to be sent to state legislatures and especially to influence judges.

The evidence of the supremacy of science in sex offender laws over the Biblically rooted American Common Law can be measured by Kinsey's *Westlaw, Social Science Citation Index*. Law is important because it points the way. Kinsey understood the need to deconstruct the Common Law. And the Model Penal Code did, in fact, largely abolish it.

PART V: "PENALTIES SHOULD BE LIGHTENED" FOR SEX OFFENDERS AND VIOLENT FELONS

> When a total clean up of sex offenders is demanded, it is in effect a proposal to put 95 per cent of the male population in jail.... Of the total male population 85 per cent has had premarital intercourse.... Some of the males studied by the authors may have obtained sexual intercourse with a girl of previous chaste character by means of various deceptions, artifices or promises. This might make them guilty of seduction.[82]
>
> One of the conclusions of the Kinsey report is that the sex offender is not a monster... but an individual who is not very different from others in his social group, and that his behavior is similar to theirs. The only difference is that others in the offender's social group have not been apprehended. This recognition that there is nothing very shocking or abnormal in the sex offender's behavior should lead to other changes in sex legislation. ...In the first place, it should lead to a downward revision of the penalties presently imposed on sex offenders.[83]
>
> **Morris Ploscowe,** *Sexual Patterns and the Law*

In 1949, Kinsey told a special session of the California legislature that his Indiana University team had determined that most child sex offenses result from *sexual repression*. He and his team were, by definition, secret "sexual psychopaths" fearful of prosecution and prison, public condemnation, and ruin of their scientific careers. Therefore, Kinsey energetically advocated against the legislative and judicial move toward tougher sex offender penalties. The data, he said, proved the "sexual psychopath" laws invalid since *all* sexual conduct was normal, "mammalian," and thus largely non-criminal.

As public outrage often sways laws and public policies, legislatures had responded to the people in the volatile area of sex-crime legislation. In early America, records confirm that a "rape" charge commonly resulted in conviction and swift public whipping or death. By the 1870s, as the strictures of American Puritanism gave way and widespread migration to cities and urban areas occurred, rape increased and punishment decreased. This triggered the Purity Movement during the late 1800s. And the battle began against "The White Slave Trade" prostitution, drinking, gambling and other "vice." Sociologist Peggy Sanday writes that following the sexual libertarianism of the "Roaring '20s" a "wave of brutal, seemingly sexually motivated child murders" swept the land:

> [T]he public panicked. A 1937 article in The Nation conveyed the hysteria attached to the subject of sex… [T]he author claimed that the pendulum in America was swinging "from sex repression to sex obsession." *** Institutionalization of the male sexual psychopath became the reform movement of the thirties. Politicians, law enforcement official, and psychiatrists all got into the act… in 1937 Hoover called for a "war on the sex criminal" and charged that "the sex fiend, most loathsome of all the vast army of crime, has become a sinister threat to American childhood and womanhood."

> Historian Estelle Freedman notes that between 1935 and 1939 five states passed sexual psychopath laws. After World War II, twenty-one additional states and the District of Columbia enacted such laws between 1947 and 1955.[84]

KINSEY TESTIFIES TO THE CALIFORNIA LEGISLATURE

The passage of tough "sexual psychopath" laws "*between 1935 and… 1947 and 1955*, resulted from public outrage at media reports of particularly heinous sex crimes—including a famous rape-murder of two little California girls. Kinsey's Herculean behind-the-scene efforts to *reduce sex crime* penalties would seem to have faced an uphill battle. However, by 1981, former President Ronald Reagan wondered about our justice system, our violent society and the contempt of the judiciary for the *victims* of crime:

> For most of the past thirty years [since 1951] "justice has been unreasonably tilted in favor of criminals and against their innocent victims. This tragic era can fairly be described as a period when victims were forgotten and crimes were ignored."[85]

A look at Kinsey's role as sex expert can help clarify that revolution in judicial attitudes toward the sex offender. Pre-Kinsey, "seduction" had been a sexual crime but by 1948 Kinsey emboldened by his data urged *reduced* penalties, even parole, for violent sex offenders. Concealing his own sexual activities was paramount for Kinsey. How sympathetic would legislators have been to Kinsey's pleas had they known that he concealed the fact that roughly one year earlier his team denied assistance to police regarding a Kinsey aide who was a child sex-murder suspect. Said Gebhard *"An example of criminality is our refusal to cooperate with authorities in apprehending a pedophile we had interviewed [who was] being sought for a sex murder."*[86] [Emphasis added.]

WHAT RIGHTS SHOULD THE PAROLEE HAVE?

After claiming that their massive database found most children harmed more by hysterical parents, police and social workers than by sexual molestation, Kinsey used his false data to argue for paroling rapists and even child sex offenders:

> DR. KINSEY: For the last 11 years we have had a research project, as you know, under way at the university on human sexual behavior… [providing] a picture typical in the population as a whole as well as a special study of the persons who have been involved with the law as sex offenders. The research is supported by Indiana University, by the medical division of the Rockefeller Foundation, and by the medical division of the National Research Council at Washington… [W]e find that 95 percent of the [male] population has in actuality engaged in sexual activities which are contrary to the law.
>
> MR. BECK: [W]hat are your recommendations… at the present time?
>
> DR. KINSEY: by lessening the penalty—still arresting, still convicting, but lessening the penalty….
>
> MR. BECK: You mean by granting parole?
>
> DR. KINSEY: They grant parole immediately in 80 percent of… sex cases….[87]

U.S. Supreme Court Justice Earl Warren, governor of California during Kinsey's perjured testimony to the California legislature.

Kinsey's argument for elder parolees was false and disingenuous. He elsewhere enthused over his "sixty-three-year old" pedophile who molested 800 children and could come to climax faster than anyone else Kinsey and Pomeroy had ever witnessed.[88] Kinsey did *not* reveal these facts to the Assembly Interim Committee on Judicial System and Judicial Process of the California Legislature. The future U.S. Supreme Court Justice, Earl Warren, was then governor of California.

Finally, in a 1981 conference on "Victim's Rights," the family survivors of victims of murder and the survivors of rape and rape torture met to take action against the Justice system's documented leniency for sex *offenders* versus its disdain for their innocent victims. Kinsey's impact on attitudes, behavior and law regarding paroling violent sex criminals is seen in the following report:

> In 1990, Tacoma, Washington, a paroled child sex offender raped and sexually mutilated a 7 year-old-boy, causing the state to form a "task force on sexual predators." This called for life imprisonment without parole for any violent sexual act against a child. Prior to his latest atrocity, Shriner had murdered a 15-year-old girl and savagely molested seven other children. Apparently, there are yet other cases in which he beat the rap. Shriner was free on the streets after his earlier crimes despite the authorities' knowledge of his plans to build a "death van" equipped with shackles and a cage for the capture and torture of young children and tools with which to mutilate them. He was well known to the police, who are accustomed to questioning him frequently in connection with attacks on young people. Nevertheless, Shriner lived next door to an elementary school. Shriner was free to attack again because

miscarriage of justice has been institutionalized. His series of serious crimes drew minuscule punishments and legal rulings, which gave him the benefit of the doubt, ensured his presence on our streets.[89]

The disinterest by the justice profession in the *victims* of these heinous crimes reflects a Kinseyan view of the natural "mammalian" rights of all offenders. Kinsey would be in complete agreement with two heated "evolutionary psychologists" whose data are designed to show, scientifically, the normalcy of rape. Craig Palmer, of the University of Colorado, and Randy Thornhill, a sexuality maven at the University of New Mexico, write:

> We fervently believe that, just as the leopard's spots and the giraffe's elongated neck are the results of aeons of past Darwinian selection, so also is rape. [R]ape is... a natural, biological phenomenon that is a product of the human evolutionary heritage.[90]

Post-Kinsey, brutal sex predators saw a growing judicial concern for their "rights" and were treated "therapeutically," receiving shorter sentences and parole. Upon release, parolees so commonly repeat and accelerate their sex/hate crimes, that ineffectual statutes like "Megan's law" have been introduced nationwide to try to keep track of where violent child abusers live in one's neighborhood. This provides political cover for politicians feeling real public pressure against a failed Kinsey-driven justice system.

WHAT RIGHTS SHOULD VICTIMS HAVE?

On June 25, 1996, then President Bill Clinton, joined by Senator Howell Heflin (D-Al), announced a proposed amendment to the U.S. Constitution. Instead of properly incarcerating violent criminals for life or imposing the death penalty, the amendment said:

> Each year about 43 million Americans are victims of serious crimes. Our criminal justice system will never be truly just as long as criminals have more rights than victims. We need a new definition of justice, one that includes the victim.... Victims ought to have rights.[91]

While governmental agencies define sex crimes differently, the "time served" for even rape-murder remains uniformly low. On January 21, 1997, a "Victims Rights Amendment" to the Constitution of the United States was proposed which would:

> [Provide rights] to protect the victims of violent crime that they currently do not enjoy, including: the right to be notified of a parole hearing, the right to speak or present written testimony, the right to be notified of the release of the criminal and the right to restitution from the defendant.[92]

Meanwhile, just as the Kinsey legal and "social science" team had desired, the "privacy" rights of rapists and murderers continue to take precedence in most states over the rights of their innocent victims. AIDS has brought Kinsey's unjust offender bias to the forefront. As of this writing, about five states inform rape victims if the rapist had AIDS. Georgia allows its district attorneys to inform victims. An Orlando, Florida rape victim recently sued Florida for her attacker's medical records but was told "she can't access them due to privacy considerations." "Why does he have any privacy rights?" the victim said. "He certainly disregarded mine." A major concern among victims centers upon the rapist's parole and his attempt to further harm the victim or her family.

The view of "privacy" as protecting the rights of a rapist to keep his diseases secret—and the parole of such diseased offenders—may be seen as a direct result of the ALI-MPC shift in focusing its protection on the offender rather than his victim. The violence of many rapes further endangers women due to the additional blood contact. "It's something that crosses every victim's mind," says Debbie Andrews, executive director for the Rape Abuse & Incest National Network.[93]

Writing in 1952, before the consequences of Kinsey-influenced sex-crime legislation would be known, Professor Herbert Wechsler picked up on Kinsey's leniency theme:

> What rights ought the parolee to have? How can law best contribute to effecting readjustment after release from an institution?... To the extent—and the extent is large—that legislative choice ought to be guided or can be assisted by knowledge or insight gained in the medical, psychological and social sciences, that knowledge will be marshalled for the purpose by those competent to set it forth.[94]

Which social scientists were "competent to set it forth." Kinsey's view was that in the vast majority of instances adult-child sex is harmless. Recall Pomeroy's comment:

> Kinsey pointed out that what the nation and the FBI were calling heinous crimes against children were things that appeared in a fair number of our total histories, and in only a small number of cases was public attention ever aroused or the police involved. Kinsey numbered himself among those who contended that, as far as so-called molestation of children was concerned, a great deal more damage was done to the child by adult hysteria.[95]

But "adult hysteria" was not responsible for the increase of murderers and mutilators of children. As a Darwinian, Kinsey's adherence to the notion of the inherent good of humankind urged penologists to help all such felons readjust "back into society." Kinsey urged society to adjust its values and morals to those of the sex criminal, not vice versa. "Common sense," he insisted, was all that sex criminals needed to keep from offending society. In a letter to an official at San Quentin Prison, quoted by Pomeroy, he asserted:

> Apart from the question of institutional discipline, there is this issue of sexual readjustment of men after they get back into society... We hope that our research will help point the way on that score.[96]

Women and children have paid a dear price for penologists' reliance on Kinsey's data to "point the way" toward elimination of pre-Kinsey penalties—including life imprisonment and the death penalty—for rape and other heinous crimes, while allowing parole for murderers and other violent criminals.

THE ALI-MPC NORMALIZING FORNICATION AND ADULTERY

Louis Schwartz was allegedly "the man responsible for drafting the model penal code's sections relating to sex offenses." At the ALI committee's annual meeting in 1955, Schwartz stated that the new MPC would treat most sex crimes as "private." There would be no societal consequences—were they consenting adults—even if this included carnality in a "public place."

> Schwartz defended his position by appealing to the authority of the social sciences. "If we have changed a lot here," he told his audience, "we have not done so just on our authority

as lawyers." He called attention to the distinguished [ALI-MPC] Advisory Committee. "Included are experienced trial judges, a number of leading psychiatrists and sociologists of the country," he pointed out.[97]

Those psychiatrists and sociologists included Sanford Bates, Manfred Guttmacher, Morris Ploscowe, all with a thorough knowledge of the Kinsey Reports. While half the states in the Union prohibited even a single act of intercourse outside of marriage, Schwartz would legalize all aspects of fornication—"based on the authority of the 'social sciences'." While most of the ALI attendees accepted Schwartz's authorities, the proposed legalization of adultery drew some objection from the floor:

> [A] lawyer from Nebraska remained indignant about the proposed decision to decriminalize adultery in the model penal code. "I come from a section of the country," he told his fellow committee members, "where we still try to preserve the home and sanctity of the marriage"… The committee voted with Ploscowe to eliminate adultery from the model penal code. In fact, by the time the code was published in 1960, it closely matched Schwartz and Ploscowe's original intentions, *which were based on the logic of the Kinsey reports…* Regarding homosexuality, Schwartz cited the Kinsey Reports as evidence of the frequency of homosexual activity and the senselessness of trying to control it…. *When the American Law Institute's model penal code was published, it proposed a major reconstruction of the law of sexual behavior. The suggested reconstruction was made possible by the first and second Kinsey Reports….* Justice William Brennan developed the Court's [Roth] definition of obscenity by referring to the ALI's model penal code.[98] [Emphasis added.]

FORNICATION AND ADULTERY LAWS

Under "Sexual Offenses" in the MPC,[99] fornication and adultery are blended together as the same crime. In fact, adultery specifically refers to infidelity in marriage. To lump adultery and fornication together devalued marriage. In any event, the MPC redefined these acts as "Illicit Cohabitation and Intercourse." Authors of the ALI-MPC eliminated any penalty for "single" acts of adultery. Instead, the authors would require that the injured spouse prove "cohabitation" and "habitual" betrayal. Liberalizing the standards for adultery—marital betrayal—has predictably contributed to the erosion of marriage and the protections afforded previously to wives, children and family. Shortly, the prior stringent compensatory legal awards of home, alimony and other resources commonly granted to the abandoned wife and children would be similarly terminated.

In fact, the first "scientific" citation on the third page of the ALI-MPC on Sex Offenses is to the Kinsey data. Here the authors cite Kinsey's adultery statistics to claim:

> The reluctance to prosecute finds some justification in evidence that a large proportion of the population is guilty at one time or another of this breach of sexual mores. Kinsey reports that one-half of the married males and one-fourth of the married females commit at least one adulterous act during married life, and one of every six of the females who had never had such relations wanted or would consider having them.[100]

Kinsey's statistical defamation of wives and husbands—and implicitly mothers and fathers—in the 1940s was stunning. For, needing to fully establish the immorality of women in order to legitimize no-fault adultery, Kinsey claims most women "wanted" to commit adultery but were just fearful. This begins the affectation that adultery is a vague issue of "mores." Rather, adultery is the betrayal of the nation's most important legal contract maintaining the good order of society.

On the fourth page of the code (page 207), the authors—Wechsler, Ploscowe, Schwartz, Tappan, Guttmacher, *et al*, sounding rather like Kinsey's law students, provide two "scientific" citations. First, citing Kinsey, they declare, "Pre-marital intercourse is also very common and widely tolerated, so that prosecution for this offense is rare."[101] And, on the same page, the authors cite Kinsey to support their argument:

Even in the early 1960's most college men still wanted to "wait" for love and marriage.

> [I]n a heterogeneous community such as ours, different individuals and groups have widely divergent views of the seriousness of various moral derelictions....[102] The immorality of the extra-marital fondle or kiss may have to receive legislative concern once we embark on the task of enforcing morals.[103]

Finally, on the next page of the MPC, the legal community reads Kinsey's finding that *"in an appreciable number of cases an experiment in adultery tends to confirm rather than disrupt the marriage...."*[104] [Emphasis added]

Kinsey's claim in the *Female* volume that a sizable percentage of women were sexually promiscuous bolstered the argument that laws against fornication and adultery should be abolished, since fornication was supposedly widespread. Most deceptively, it also implied that related factors such as illegitimacy, venereal disease, and divorce were either insignificant or irrelevant because the data on disease and dysfunction were so low. And by implication it raised questions about the relevancy of laws against bigamy, polygamy, sex with minors, breach of promise, and many others statutes such as "fault" divorce, that had served primarily to protect women, children and society. The ALI-MPC authors claimed that the single most significant reason for criminalizing "illicit intercourse" has been our nation's adherence to anachronistic religious prohibitions. By citing *only* biblical sources for the laws prohibiting fornication and adultery, while ignoring and purging the myriad and significant historical, medical and sociological data which underpin such laws, the ALI-MPC authors revealed that they were bent on undermining rather than clarifying and codifying American statutes.

ADULTERY'S "RIPPLE EFFECT"

The harmful "ripple effect" of fornication and adultery is costly to society in ways too numerous to cite. The secretive conduct of adultery, in particular, confirms that this is not a "private" or "victimless" crime. Besides injuring the betrayed spouse, adultery demoralizes friends and family and commonly scars the children of the union who often remain leery of marriage and commitment. Many victims enter into troubled and harmful conduct. After 50 years of Kinsey-era disordered and broken families, some states are re-assessing their position on adultery. A few, for instance, have initiated legislation to repeal "no-fault" divorce statutes, and to reestablish adultery as grounds for "fault" divorce.[105]

What types of men were habitual adulterers prior to 1948? Not even renowned playboy Hugh Hefner was "sexually active" at the time. Indeed, his biographers tell us that he remained a virgin until he read Kinsey just prior to his marriage.[106] And the statistics on venereal disease and out-of-wedlock births were a fraction of what they are today.

As noted earlier, sexual libertarian researchers Drs. Phyllis and Eberhard Kronhausen reported in 1960 very different data and findings than did Kinsey, in their Kinsey-inspired book *Sex Histories of American College Men* (1960).[107] Contrary to the Kinsey Report, most college males were found to be quite traditional toward any sexual contacts prior to, and outside of, marriage. Joe College preferred to wait.[108] And, regarding Kinsey's data on "working class" males, the Pre-Kinsey national "hard data" statistics on abortion, venereal disease, illegitimacy and such, fully disprove the Kinsey-ALI-MPC claims for a nation of promiscuous women and men—especially among those mothers and fathers purged from his data base.[109]

KINSEY: ONE-HALF MARRIED MALES, ONE-FOURTH FEMALES, COMMIT ADULTERY

Few Americans could avoid hearing of the data on adultery created by the four Kinsey authors. In its August 24, 1953, edition, *Life Magazine* placed the announcement of "Kinsey Report on Women" just above a photo of two little girls collecting seashells on the beach. Unaware of the four Kinseyans' closet life as adulterous, bi-homosexual misogynists, *Life Magazine* gave them full credibility. Said *Life*, they know more "about women than any men in the world." *Life* published Kinsey's "facts" about common rates of "fornication" and "adultery."

Based on such a widespread publicity, by 1955 the authors of the ALI-MPC cited Kinsey's "new science" to justify their call for eliminating long-standing American laws. At the top of the list was legalizing fornication, cohabitation and adultery in most states. For, according to the ALI-MPC, Ploscowe, *et al.*, women were deeply involved in adulterous activity. These claims had serious repercussions for the treatment and view of marriage and commitment. Kinsey seemed to know all:

Kinsey sought to mislead the nation into believing that the average Joe College was a sex offender.

> The pattern of adulterous relations is extremely sporadic. There are typically many acts within a short time period and then none for long periods. One-third of the females reported less than a total of ten acts; two-fifths had only one partner. The male seldom had extra-marital intercourse with the same partner for more than a brief period (a summer, a vacation). Adulterous relationships are often idealized in literary representations, and are revealed in the

intimate biographies of prominent and respected figures.[110]

Citing Kinsey's findings of widespread fornication among his "typical" female population, the MPC authors argued that laws against "fornication" and "adultery" are unjust, unfair, unconstitutional—and must be changed.

PROFOUND SOCIETAL CONSEQUENCES FROM DECRIMINALIZING ADULTERY, COHABITATION AND FORNICATION

The argument was that legalizing fornication and adultery would have little negative effect on society since, according to the four Kinsey men, fornication and adultery were already common among all socioeconomic groups. However, the maxim that women give sex to get love (a.k.a., marriage) and men give love in order to get sex, was unmistakable in the profound, unanticipated fallout from de-stigmatizing adultery and legalizing fornication, and cohabitation.

Once believed, Kinsey's fornication and adultery data created widespread distrust between women and men. "Love" became the reason for engaging in sex without a marriage license—a mere contract, a "piece of paper." In fact, the covert suspicion that "good" women were secretly sexually promiscuous dramatically weakened women's historic negotiating power to withhold sex until men contracted to love, honor and cherish via marriage, children, protection and provision. Once women lost their virginity as a marital bargaining chip, their sexual ability and availability became their backup bargaining tool.

And, once women's sexual favors were easily available—as the Kinsey team claimed they were all along—"shot gun" weddings were outmoded. Instead, women of all races and religions were suddenly suspect, increasingly abandoned in single mother poverty. Or, having survived venereal diseases and traumatic abortions, they were too often left sterile, their health and welfare sorely compromised. The subsequent fallout from millions of fatherless children subjected to abuse and neglect has become a modern tragedy of epic proportions.

Following release of the ALI-MPC, the marital and financial obligations of many husbands and wives to their spouses and children diminished. "No-fault divorce" de-stigmatized adultery, and the payment of alimony, which had hampered the potentially errant husband and father, was ridiculed as an old-fashioned anachronism of sexual repression and Puritanism.

Gebhard, Martin, Kinsey, Pomeroy (Life August 24, 1953)

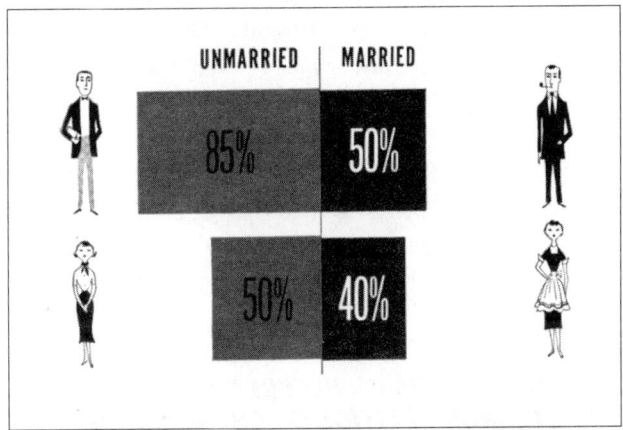

Citing to Kinsey, Life states: "The measure of indiscretion is shown in Dr. Kinsey's findings: 85% of men and 50% of women have had premarital sex experience; 50% of men and 40% of women have been or will be unfaithful after marriage." (Life, August 24, 1953, pg. 45.)

KINSEY'S IMPACT ON AMERICAN LAW

Writing in *The Family in America* (January 2000), Bryce Christensen addressed some of the appalling societal consequences from "no fault divorce." One of these has been the often draconian laws to collect child support from alleged "deadbeat dads." The U.S. Census Bureau reported that in 1950, 43 percent of children were at home with Mom while Dad worked full-time. By 1990, only 18 percent of American children had such a stable home.[111] Christensen observed the concern, regarding the recent "public consensus" about children reared without a father, the "poverty and deprivation of children in female-headed households." Turning to that massive increase in single moms and inevitable child poverty, Christensen writes:

> America's policymakers have given little or no regard to the social ideal of wedlock. Though zealous to reduce the child poverty which parental divorce has caused, they have shrunk from the task of preventing divorce in the first place. Indeed, the policy-makers pushing for tougher measures to collect child support have generally acquiesced in the liberal no-fault divorce statutes, which helped to drive up the divorce rate in the first place....
>
> Few Americans would dispute a father's obligation to provide for his children. Throughout American history, any man who bore the title father bore also the title of provider....
>
> It was because of this perceived linkage between wedlock and a man's obligation to act as a provider that in the case of an out-of-wedlock pregnancy, the extended family and local community often pressured the responsible young man into a shotgun wedding. Marriage made the young man publicly take upon himself the duty to provide for the unborn child and its mother.[112]

"DEADBEAT DADS OR FLEECED FATHERS?"
THE STRANGE POLITICS OF CHILD SUPPORT

The above title by Christenson centers on "fault-based divorce," noting that pre-Kinsey, the adulterous male or female spouse forfeited child custody, while dad supported his children in any case. Once "fault" was eliminated from custody proceedings, adulterous, promiscuous moms have retained custody of children while the wronged father continued to pay child support. On the other hand, based on their higher incomes, under "no-fault" divorce, felons—even convicted incestuous fathers—have gotten custody of their children. This has placed children in dire situations. Christensen is incredulous:

> For unlike traditional divorce statutes, no-fault divorce undermines rather than reinforces marriage as a social ideal... no-fault divorce trivializes marriage, making it weaker than the weakest of contracts-at-will. It is now easier to dispose of an unwanted spouse of twenty years than to fire an unwanted employee of one year... Thomas B. Marvell calculated in 1989 that the adoption of no-fault statutes had driven up state divorce rates "by some 20 to 25 percent." And in a 1999 analysis, a team of statisticians determined that in the 32 states which had enacted no-fault laws by 1974, these laws "resulted in a substantial number of divorces that would not have occurred otherwise... Undermining marriage as a social ideal was not one of the objectives identified by the activists who pushed no-fault statues through in the 1960's and 1970's. Indeed, many of these activists claimed that their legal innovation would actually strengthen wedlock by helping men and women trapped in bad marriages to

move into good marriages… [But] casual divorce has actually made men and women less likely to "commit fully" to a marital union, thus reducing the likelihood of marital success…

*   *   *   *

It is largely because no-fault has weakened the economic status of victimized former wives that feminist Betty Friedan, formerly a supporter, now admits, "I think we made a mistake with no-fault divorce"…

Most of all, recognizing wedlock as a social ideal will compel the surrender of the dangerous illusion that the bureaucratic machinery, of child-support-collection can somehow obviate the need for the personal virtues that sustain marriage and family life. Once we have all surrendered this illusion, then we can—with T.S. Eliot—finally break out of the spells woven by politicians "dreaming of systems so perfect no one will need to be good."[113]

"No-fault" divorce encouraged crime. The ALI-MPC role in encouraging fornication and adultery demoralized marriage and families and harmed millions of women and children financially, morally and physically. With "no-fault" divorce, women who had given their virginity, youth, dreams, labor and fidelity—their most significant "property" under common law—could be shabbily dismissed, their betrayal legally and socially trivialized. "No-fault" divorce swelled the ranks of "displaced homemakers," and their troubled and increasingly dangerous children.

If, as Kinsey claimed, almost *everyone* engaged in pre-marital sex, then virginity was not a practiced virtue. Hence, condemnation of the crimes of seduction, fornication, cohabitation and adultery became antiquated and the ability to maintain a stable marriage and family for the individual and society significantly weakened.

NORMALIZING RAPE

Feminist lawyer and former Democratic presidential Campaign Manager for Michael Dukakis (1988), Susan Estrich was perplexed by the influence of the Carnegie/Rockefeller Foundation-funded ALI's new MPC on rape.[114] Before the MPC promoted Kinsey's research, rape had been punishable by death in almost half of American states. The rape "innovations" of the ALI-MPC confounded Estrich. Unmindful of Kinsey's fraud, she was incensed by the liberal changes to rape laws.

Reprising our earlier discussion, when as the "weaker vessel," women's charges of sexual molestation were commonly believed, men often faced severe—possibly fatal—punishment from their peers. When the "White Slave Trade" was eradicated by moralists, young college men—as recorded by the Kronhausens—frequently brought *themselves* virginally to their brides. This helped men to hold to an ideal of "first love." The new rape laws dismissed such egalitarian chastity, offering a new vision of who and what was natural to man. Under the new ALI-MPC, "cases of rape and sexual assault only,"[115] protested Estrich, "require corroboration of the victim's testimony."

THE FRESH COMPLAINT AND FORCIBLE RAPE

Rene Guyon, Harry Benjamin, John Money (who fraudulently pioneered surgical sex change operations for newborns) and others of the sexology elite edited the influential *Sexology* magazine. Writing an article in it, Columbia law professor, Beryl H. Levy, LL.B., Ph.D., asked "What is Rape?" He argued that by 1961 the courts recognized "what we may call the "absence-of-consent" theory or the "utmost resistance" theory." Levy, clearly advocating for leniency in rape notes that in the latter theory:

> [I]t must be shown that the woman fought back like a tiger (so to speak). She must be shown to have resisted with all her might and main and with every means at her disposal: punching, scratching, biting, kicking, screaming, etc.... *Some experts have expressed the opinion that it is well-nigh impossible for a man to rape a woman of ordinary good health and strength....* Women may have rape fantasies: they think they have been raped even though the man may have been nowhere near them.... *The law of statutory rape might well bear some re-examination to determine if it is still carrying out the old common-law idea, which was protection of innocent young maidens....* In this field of law, as in many others, we must constantly re-study the law on the statute books to see the extent to which it accords with present day practices and social behavior widely followed and approved.... [R]espect for the law requires an effort to bring it into correspondence with contemporary values and contemporary ways of acting.116 [Emphasis added.]

Kinsey's data defining "contemporary values" were clearly being codified by Levy and *Sexology* as the means by which "experts" might judge rape and statutory rape. Kinsey saw sexual assaults as easily forgotten by victims. Therefore, rapists were inappropriate for imprisonment. Feminist Susan Brownmiller in *Against Our Will, Men, Women, and Rape*, recalls Kinsey's statement that "the difference between a rape and a good time depends on whether the girl's parents were awake when she finally came home."117

These self-serving falsehoods confirm Kinsey's claim that out of 4,441 female interviewees, "one" *may* have been injured by a child sexual assault. The Kinsey-ALI-MPC plan was to eliminate "unrealistic" rape and statutory rape laws. According to Morris Ploscowe, in the 1948 "Pre-Kinsey era" (see chart below), three states gave mandatory death sentences for simple rape—that is, one man convicted of raping one woman. Nineteen states provided the death penalty, life, or very long terms. Twenty-eight states gave the rapist 20 years or more, and one state gave 15 years or more. Post-Kinsey's "data" stated that 95 percent of men were already sex offenders and most women were promiscuous—or wanted to be. Therefore, the justification for tough rape, child abuse and obscenity laws was largely moot.

Estrich wondered at the "fresh complaint" clause that said, "a complaint must be filed within three months," if the crime were sexual. This clause had not been part of America's common law.118 There was more. Even if it was a "fresh complaint," the ALI-MPC ordered that the jury receive "cautionary instructions" regarding the victim's possible tainted testimony.119 In addition, said Estrich, "[f]orcible rapes are graded." "If serious bodily injury is inflicted, forcible rape is a first degree felony."120 Who was the ALI-MPC protecting? In fact, homosexual rapes "were at best classified as a lesser felony," observed Estrich.121

Moreover, noted Estrich, the ABA/ALI's lawyerly libidos established new regulations for deciding if a girl could be raped. Were the victim shown to have had a "racy" past (not exactly defined by the ALI-MPC), for purposes of adjudication she might be labeled a "prostitute." Therefore, even when she was the victim of a "gang" or fraternity "group" rape, the guilty predator might be cleared of any crime. These followed on Kinsey's claims that men were animals and rape a natural and normal reaction to a seductive female.

ALI-MPC lawyers redefined "prostitute" with the accuracy that Kinsey exhibited in redefining "married" woman.[122] With the ALI acceptance of Kinsey's supposedly scientific findings, and with wide ALI-MPC acceptance by state legislatures and law schools, Kinsey's image of sexually active women and girls became reality. Legal authorities increasingly distrusted charges of rape and rapists got neither harsh punishment nor corrective therapy. With the stringent requirements for rape conviction, it became clear that once on the stand the child or woman victim often had fewer rights than the accused. For example, college coeds raped while unconscious after their drinks were "spiked," regularly lost their cases and left college. The rapists, however, remained on the same campus, free and untainted.

CONSEQUENCES: A "RAPE EPIDEMIC"

The current epidemic of sexually violent crime—rape, gang-rape, date-rape, rape-mutilation, serial rape-murder, kidnapping-rape, "rough-sex" rape-murde—is victimizing the elderly as well as younger boys and girls. Moreover, younger and younger offenders are committing the crimes.[123] Based on his intimate association with 1,400 sex offenders—a large percentage of them rapists—Kinsey advocated loudly and repeatedly for rapist leniency. Kinsey's silence was reserved for the notion of punishment.

In 1,146 pages on male and female sexual conduct, the Kinsey team stated no opposition to rape. Remember, Kinsey believed that convulsions and screams of pain even by infants and children were not signs of "force or undue intimidation." As the Kinsey group argued that all sexual violence was part of the normal mammalian heritage, it was in the area of rape that we began to see a growing interest in protecting the predator rather than the victim.

Ploscowe reports that of 324 New York murders of females in 1930, 1935 and 1940, (average 108 per year) 17, or six per year, involved rape or suspicion of rape of women or children. FBI data for 1995 show that New Yorkers experienced 4,654 murders in 1995 and 3,333 rape/murders. The latter data do not appear to include rape and murder of children under 12 years of age. At the time of this writing, these children are not located in the sex crime database.[124]

NEW YORK RAPE DATA PRE- AND POST-KINSEY ERA

The authors of *Transforming a Rape Culture* ask if "rape and sexual assault truly permeate this society, or are we hearing about the sensationalized, isolated cases? Has the rate of sexual violence really increased?" Sociologist Peggy Sanday in *A Woman Scorned* reports, "Between 1935 and 1956, arrest rates for rape nearly doubled, as did the rates for other sexual offenses."[125] Sanday further notes the current rape dilemma:

> For Puritans there were many restraints on male sexual license, not the least of which

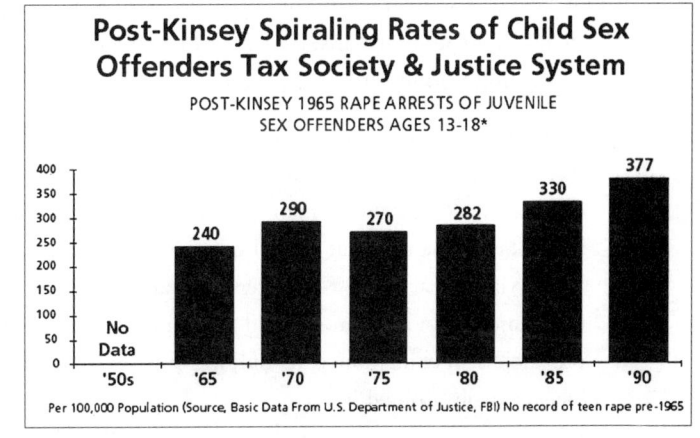

Post-Kinsey Spiraling Rates of Child Sex Offenders Tax Society & Justice System

POST-KINSEY 1965 RAPE ARRESTS OF JUVENILE SEX OFFENDERS AGES 13-18*

'50s	'65	'70	'75	'80	'85	'90
No Data	240	290	270	282	330	377

Per 100,000 Population (Source: Basic Data From U.S. Department of Justice, FBI) No record of teen rape pre-1965

KINSEY'S IMPACT ON AMERICAN LAW

were the fornication laws of Colonial Times. For feminists the only restraint on sexuality is mutual consent and the expectation of sexual self-determination. Sex outside of marriage was forbidden by the law and by the church in all the early colonies, not just in Puritan New England. However, despite the legal constraints against "fornication," the evidence suggests that Puritan women were not prudes. It was assumed that women had a sexual appetite, which gave them sexual agency in ways that would be denied nineteenth and early twentieth-century women. The sexual agency of Puritan women meant that a man believed a woman who said no. *When women charged men with rape, the authorities tended to believe them because of the assumption that women had no reason to lie.*[126] [Emphasis added.]

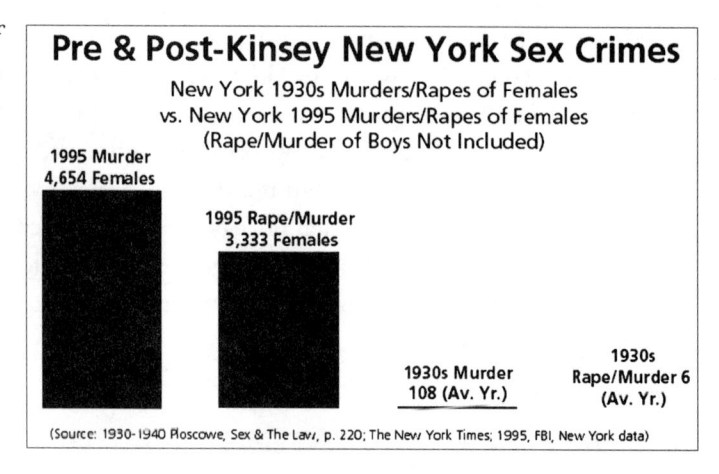

Pre & Post-Kinsey New York Sex Crimes
New York 1930s Murders/Rapes of Females vs. New York 1995 Murders/Rapes of Females
(Rape/Murder of Boys Not Included)

- 1995 Murder: 4,654 Females
- 1995 Rape/Murder: 3,333 Females
- 1930s Murder: 108 (Av. Yr.)
- 1930s Rape/Murder: 6 (Av. Yr.)

(Source: 1930-1940 Ploscowe, Sex & The Law, p. 220; The New York Times; 1995, FBI, New York data)

NORMALIZING STATUTORY RAPE AND INCEST

Kinsey's claims about the harmlessness of even child rape have had ongoing repercussions. In 1948, Morris Ernst called upon "every bar association in the country" to "establish a Committee on the Laws of Sexual Behavior and consider its own State's legal system in this field… to adjust our laws[127] to the growth of scientific knowledge and the changing needs of the people. The *Male* volume, Ernst declared, "has enabled us to graduate into the butterfly stage of science," and "has already started history on a new course."

Meanwhile, just as the ALI-MPC would normalize rape, Albert Deutsch *urged* future ALI-MPC attorney Morris Ploscowe—and other participants in a seminar entitled, *Sex Habits of American Men*—to accept children's sexual desires. When speaking to the ALI about the MPC, Ploscowe, unable to distinguish between a husband promising to love, honor and cherish, etc., and a Don Juan soliciting a good time, "ridiculed the statutory rape laws. He pointed out that in Tennessee the legal age of marriage was sixteen while the legal age of consent for [non-marital] intercourse was twenty-one.[128] Deutsch wrote that Kinsey had confirmed that children were sexual from birth. Therefore, sex laws protecting youngsters were predicated on fantasy, not reality:

> The Kinsey group… [supports] the Freudian thesis of infantile sexuality—affirmed on a mass-basis study for the first time. The significance of the Kinsey findings in this regard is enormous.… [It] explodes many popular notions as to when sex activity begins and reaches its peak in humans… that sex attitudes and habits start in infancy and that sex life, in fact, begins virtually at birth. Kinsey reports that a complete orgasm (except for ejaculation) has been observed in a five-month-old male, and in a girl infant of only four months.… One pre-adolescent child [four-years-old] was observed to experience 26 orgasms within 24 hours when sexually aroused.[129]

Kinseyans Gebhard, Gagnon and Pomeroy, writing in *Sex Offenders*, reveal their collective view of child sex abuse, although they know full well that female mammals copulate only during estrus, which is when they are mature:

> The horror with which our society views the adult who has sexual contact with young children is lessened when one examines the behavior of other mammals. Sexual activity between adult and immature animals is common and appears to be biologically normal.[130]

"YOUNG PERSONS ARE PLACED IN PENITENTIARIES MERELY BECAUSE THEY INDULGED THEIR SEXUAL FEELINGS"

Kinsey lectured to lawyers, district attorneys, judges and legislators.

A major inroad into legitimizing all forms of sexual license would be the claim that women and children wanted to be sexually free. But they were repressed by their social mores. Moreover, they were unharmed by explicit or raw sex. In 1932, French jurist and philosopher Rene Guyon, credited with coining the phrase "sex by age eight or else it's too late," developed a comprehensive theoretical and legislative strategy to abolish sex-offender laws. Many of his recommendations and data were later integrated and adopted by the ALI-MPC. Guyon, who shared Kinsey's misogynist views of women and children, considered human sexual conduct as devoid of any spiritual or moral trappings. He declared:

> Our social life is seething with uneasiness; young persons are placed in penitentiaries merely because they indulged their sexual feelings; good folk, useful citizens, are tracked down, threatened with dismissal or prevented from getting a better job, denounced by sex prohibitionists, because these honest workers believe they have the right to gratify their sexual impulse to the full; sentences are pronounced in court so cruel that they are capable of ruining a man's whole career because he has performed a natural act which the law itself upholds if certain formalities have preceded it; …thousands of abortions are procured to avoid the slur our moralists would impose upon an illegitimate offspring; a natural physiological act, much on a line with feeding, but so distorted from its original purpose that some people find it impossible to perform and have preferred death to its accomplishment; so many being sacrificed—sent to prison, into exile, into a convent, to death—because they have exercised their sexual functions outside the bounds of conventional forms; in a word, almost universal delirium brought about by an illogical, an unscientific system which has overreached the limits of the possible.[131]

The following excerpts allegedly written by Kinsey in his 1953 *Female* report, mirror Guyon's treatise,

> In many instances the law, in the course of punishing the offender, does more damage to more persons than was ever done by the individual in his illicit sexual activity.… The intoxicated male who accidentally exposes his genitalia before a child, may receive a prison sentence which leaves his family destitute for some period of years, breaks up his marriage, and leaves three or four children wards of the state and without the sort of guidance which the parents might well have supplied. The older, unmarried women who prosecute the male whom

they find swimming nude, may ruin his business or professional career, bring his marriage to divorce, and do such damage to his children as the observation of his nudity could never have done to the woman who prosecuted him. The child who has been raised in fear of all strangers and all physical manifestations of affection, may ruin the lives of the married couple who had lived as useful and honorable citizens through half or more of a century, by giving her parents and the police a distorted version of the old man's attempt to bestow grandfatherly affection upon her.[132]

As Morris Ernst predicted, the ALI-MPC was generally sympathetic to sex offenders. After all, if Kinsey was right in claiming that 95 percent of American males *were* sex offenders, then it is not only natural to be a sex offender, but necessary to protect such adventurers from recrimination. The flyleaf of Rene Guyon's *Sex Life and Sex Ethics* (1933), which was restricted for sale to members of the medical profession, psychoanalysts, scholars and interested adults, stated that the book:

> begins with a careful study of sexuality in infancy and childhood, continues the study among primitive races, and then among more civilized peoples.... M. Guyon comes to some startling conclusions concerning sexual responsibility, modesty and justifiability of the general taboos affecting the sexual organs and sexual acts. He makes a penetrating study of the phenomenon of modesty, traces the origin of sexual taboos, discusses chastity and condemns its exaltation as a virtue, and proceeds to attribute to our present sexual ethic, the prevalence of unhappiness and neuroses....[133]

Pedophile Guyon brazenly portrayed adult-child sex as an act as natural and necessary as eating or breathing.[134]

NORMALIZING SEXUAL ASSAULTS AS "VICTIMLESS CRIME"

The view of even child rape as a "victimless crime" coincides with Kinsey's analysis of the harmlessness of all sexual acts. Recall in his *Female* report he says:

> If a child were not culturally conditioned, it is doubtful if it would be disturbed by sexual approaches... It is difficult to understand why a child, except for its cultural conditioning, should be disturbed at having its genitalia touched, or disturbed at seeing the genitalia of other persons, or *disturbed at even more specific sexual contacts.*[135]

Such "approaches" and "more specific sexual contacts" began to be viewed as "victimless crimes" of "sex education" with children only victimized by hysterical adults:

> When children are constantly warned by parents and teachers against contacts with adults, and when they receive no explanation of the exact nature of the forbidden contacts, they are ready to become hysterical as soon as any older person approaches, or stops and speaks to them in the street, or fondles them, or proposes to do something for them, even though the adult may have had no sexual objective in mind. Some of the more experienced students of juvenile problems have come to believe that the emotional reactions of the parents, police officers, and other adults who discover that the child has had such a contact, may disturb the child more seriously than the sexual *contacts* themselves. The current hysteria over sex offenders may very well have serious effects on the ability of many of these children to work out sexual adjustments some years later in their marriages.[136]

Kinsey's citations to researchers like himself (whose personal sexual biases we now may infer) lent additional acceptance to the view of child sexual abuse as harmless "pleasure" for the victims:

Violent Offenders in 1992 Served 48% of Their Sentence
All Violent Crimes Involved Threat or Imposition of Harm.

Category	Years Served
Average	3.6 yrs.
Homicide	5.9 yrs.
Forced Rape	5.4 yrs.
Kidnapping	4.3 yrs.
Robbery	3.7 yrs.
Sexual Assault	3 yrs.
Assault	2.4 yrs.
Other	2.3 yrs.

(Source: Bureau of Justice Statistics, DoJ, April 1995, No.4)

The effects on children of sexual contacts with adults are also discussed in:

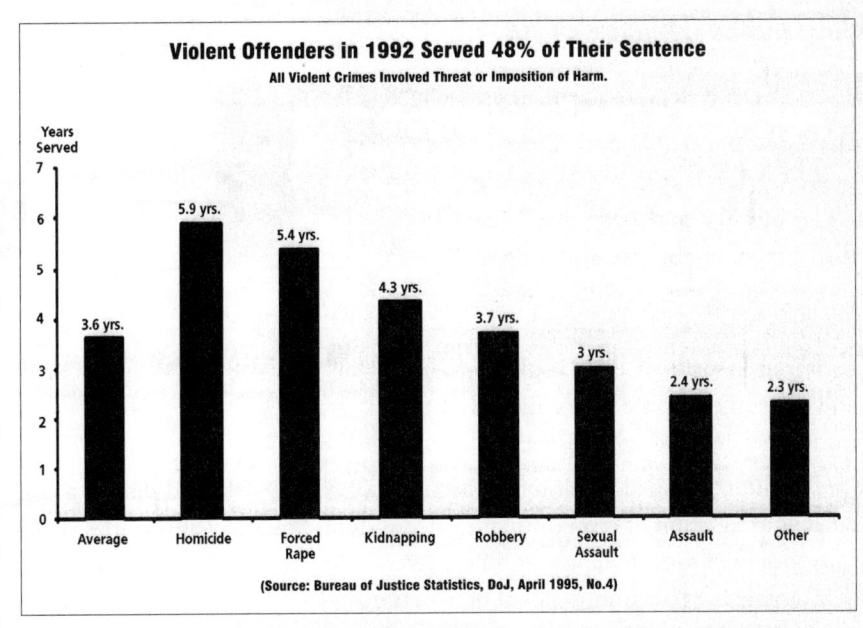

Abraham (1907) 1927:52-57 (such events often not reported to parents because of child's guilt feelings at pleasure in the experience). Bender and Blau ...(11 girls, ages 5 to 12, free of guilt and fear). Rasmussen 1934 (follow-up of 54 cases in Denmark showed little evidence of ill effects). Landis, et al, 1940:279 (no unpleasant reactions in 44 per cent of 107 cases; worry, shock, or fright in 56 per cent)... David M. Levy 1953... (concludes from experience with numerous cases that psychological effects are primarily the result of the adult emotional disturbance, and are likely to be negligible if there is no physical harm to child).[137]

And, said Kinsey sex researcher, John Gagnon, later of the National Research Council:

The Kinsey research "normalized" many kinds of sexual conduct.... [As people] practiced a wide variety of forbidden sex techniques, it was difficult to continue believing that they represented a moral or psychological minority. It was apparent that such conduct was common.... [T]he Kinsey research opened up discussion of homosexuality, prostitution, and pornography, which were found to be sufficiently widespread that it became more difficult to argue their abnormality.[138]

THE NATIONAL SURVEY OF CRIME SEVERITY

Rape crisis centers join in such protests by pointing out that the sentencing data available from the Department of Justice reveal a small portion of American criminals as actually apprehended and brought to trial with only half of the convicted criminals receiving prison sentences. Those who do receive "time," serve about half their sentence prior to parole. And of those paroled, half are *recorded* as recidivists (breaking parole, or committing new crimes when free). Here again, the Kinseyan concept of "consent" by the victim creates an atmosphere, which makes rape harder to prosecute.

It is especially noteworthy that both government and private studies confirm the frustration of feminists and non-feminists, liberals and conservatives in identifying sex crimes as significantly under-prosecuted in the justice system—and once prosecuted—as meagerly penalized. Wolfgang and Figlio's, *The Department of Justice's National Survey of Crime Severity Sentencing Guide* of 1977 and 1985, has been distributed to the nation's judges, prosecuting attorneys and criminologists. It is as a typical translation of Kinseyan theories of child sexuality and "victimless crime" maneuvered into the "rule-making" process.

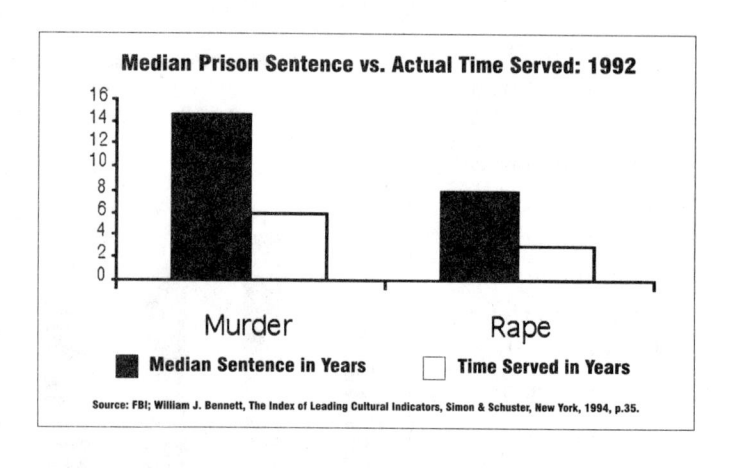

Median Prison Sentence vs. Actual Time Served: 1992

Murder: Median Sentence ~15 years; Time Served ~5 years
Rape: Median Sentence ~8 years; Time Served ~3 years

Source: FBI; William J. Bennett, The Index of Leading Cultural Indicators, Simon & Schuster, New York, 1994, p.35.

Again, continued belief in the accuracy of Kinsey's skewed data is a contributing factor to the current exhaustion of our criminal justice system. Some say authorities that permit the release back into society of sadistic rapists and murderers—free to repeat their crimes—represent a system adrift in a moral abyss bent on national destruction.

In 1977, following on the heels of the ALI Model Penal Code, the developing concept of "a victimless crime" arrived full-blown into America's courtrooms via Thorsten Sellin, an ALI Model Penal Code author. Working under a grant from the U.S. Department of Justice, Sellin and his student, Marvin Wolfgang, crafted the first "National Crime Severity" scale for judges and juries. Sociologist Sellin had been Morris Ploscowe's law student. Wolfgang took his sexuality training at the Kinsey Institute.

While on the Attorney General's Commission on Obscenity and Pornography in 1970, Dr. Wolfgang advocated child access to pornography. In 1977, he and Sellin created the Justice Department's criminal sentencing guides, ranking 204 "serious" crimes which *excluded* child rape, gang rape, homosexual rape, and the like. The Justice Department's Sellin/Wolfgang "National Survey of Crime Severity"[139] even excluded criminal use of children in prostitution or pornography. Excluding these common law child protection provisions moved child protection backward, toward the so-called voluntary "White Slave Trade" child abuse status of the pre-1910 Mann Act era.[140]

The judicial acceptance of sex crime as "victimless crime" was a revolutionary change in legal theory. Kinsey was explicitly relied upon to support the invalid conclusion that "sexual intercourse between unmarried persons" is "widespread,"(see *Pettit v. State Board of Education*, 1973;[141] *Carter v. U.S*, 1968;[142] and *State v. Silva*, 1971[143]) suggesting that illegal forms of heterosexual activity are inevitable, normal and therefore should be tolerated. This notion grew into the current acceptance of widespread sexual activity among children as being common, inevitable, normal and, therefore, beyond parental or governmental control.

A "MODEST SEX OFFENDER" IMAGE

Soon, Gagnon reported, educated people were echoing Kinsey's theories. Therefore, Kinseyan sex crime opinions became accepted cultural givens:

> A more modest and less violent image of the sex offender began to appear in the public press.
> Rather than focusing on rare violent events, attention began to be paid to the majority of

people whose offenses were occasional, who had no criminal pasts, and who were responsive to treatment... With an increase in public sexual knowledge about people who have and have not fallen afoul of sex law, new ways of thinking about the relationship between sex and law began to emerge... Pivotal to these conceptions was the distinction between victim and victimless crimes. This distinction has been latent in criminology for some time, but application to sexual offenses began in the 1950s.[144]

Yet, hundreds of thousands of rape victims can testify to the fact that paroled sex predators commonly repeat their crimes. They are largely unresponsive to "treatment." And, we've learned, through the increasing brutality of rape, that such predators increase their levels of barbarity to behave with the levels of sexual violence depicted in the sexual media.[145] The allegedly knowledgeable sex therapist often responds "to treatment" by predators convinced that once paroled, this kindly, modest, sex offender will never rape again. Writing in *Human Sexualities*, co-author and Kinseyan disciple John Gagnon said:

> Such research into sex offenders characterized the 1950s, and was followed in the 1960s by research into homosexuality, prostitution, and pornography, which undermined the stereotypes of these offenses as well...Fewer influential people thought that all sexual problems could be solved by the law and law enforcement. Both legal change and redefinition of sex offenses began to emerge.[146]

If one percent of the male population was arrested for acts common to all men, as Kinsey claimed, then government would need to arrest the entire nation or pardon the persecuted one percent. Justice should move from punishment to a self-help mode, said Kinseyans. Gagnon recalled Kinsey's impact in building our current views of "victimless crime":

> The Kinsey studies stimulated further research into unconventional sex... Criminological studies undermined the belief that there was some single type called the "sex offender." The major publication of the Institute for Sex Research during the 1960s was titled *Sex Offenders*... Most sex offenders were not "sex fiends" and only a few of them were violent or dangerous, or likely to repeat their crimes.[147]

THE "PEER SEX PLAY" DEFENSE

Penologists, legislators, and lawyers were on record as visiting Kinsey regularly, with the ideas and language of Ernst and Guyon reflected in Kinsey's final discussion of law. Writing in his diary following a visit with Kinsey on July 7, 1950, the Rockefeller foundation's Alan Gregg shed additional light on Kinsey's furtive collaboration with law and justice professionals:

> [Kinsey] averages about one well-qualified visitor a day; penologists, sociologists, legislative experts, psychologists, doctors of medicine, lawyers and directors of welfare and social work, ministers and teachers.... These actual visitors to Bloomington mark a new phase, I think, in the whole affair.[148]

The fingerprints of Kinseyan influenced "penologists... legislative experts... lawyers" and judges are visible throughout the ABA-ALI Model Penal Code. Not only would Kinsey's falsified data on women's sexuality undermine the marital life of women, his child sexuality data would eroticize children. His data would undermine some children's right to life, liberty and the pursuit of happiness. In 1948, Magistrate Morris Ploscowe, writing on Kinsey's claims of widespread premarital sex, ridiculed the battle against rape and child sexual abuse:

> J. Edgar Hoover's estimate that a criminal assault by a sex delinquent occurs *every forty-three minutes* is based on the number of rapes reported to the Federal Bureau of Investigation by local police forces. In 1948, on the basis of these reports, the F.B.I. estimated that there were 16,180 rapes throughout the country. But most of such offenses are statutory rapes, involving an act of sexual intercourse with the consent of a girl who is under age… In New York City… 82 per cent were for statutory rape involving acts of sexual intercourse with girls under eighteen. If most rapes simply involve consensual acts of sexual intercourse with under-age girls, they are not the products of degenerates and psychopaths who force their attentions upon unwilling victims.[149]

Efrem Zimbalist, Jr., meeting with J. Edgar Hoover, long-serving Director of the FBI. Zimbalist appeared in the video, The Children of Table 34, produced by Family Research Council.

New York Magistrate Ploscowe does not mention why, out of "16,180 rapes throughout the country" roughly *13,300* girls "under eighteen" *reported* they were raped. Were these "consensual acts of sexual intercourse?" Some false charges might be expected *but not 13,300*. On the other hand, recall that no one doubted Kinsey's claim that of 4,441 women interviewees, *none really* experienced rape or sexual harm. Magistrate Ploscowe then outlines the pioneering "peer sex play" defense favored by the Kinsey team. This theory of "peer sex play"— grounded on Kinsey's child "orgasms"—now dominates most sex-offender laws, effectively *legalizing rape of children and youths* by those within three to five years of their own age. Says Ploscowe,

> Only where the age disparity between the man and the girl are very great is it possible to say that the rape may be the work of a mentally abnormal individual, a psychopath, or a potentially dangerous sex offender.[150]

In most states now a ten-year-old raped by a 13-year-old can be said to have been engaged in "peer sex play." Ploscowe warns of "the problem of credibility in the complainant's testimony in statutory rape." In the ALI-MPC Karpman insists "a majority of authorities find that the sex offender in general is not a recidivist," with "statistics indicating that recidivism is lower for lewd and lascivious conduct with children than for many other types of sex offenses." The latter citation is provided by the *California Sex Crimes Report 1950-1953*, for which Kinsey testified in 1949 on the harmlessness of child sexual abuse. (Such claims have been discredited. Recidivism is *highest* among sex offenders.)[151]

Ignoring the decades of struggle to enact and/or enforce laws protecting children from predators and cite prostitution in the "White Slavery" of women and children, the ABA/ALI-MPC authors criticize the Mann Act, which finally crippled the sex traffic in girls across state lines. In an amazing bit of eccentricity the ALI-MPC warn that The Mann Act was used to nab "alleged racketeers" who merely took "girl friends on trips to Florida," a technique that could "easily be turned against other vulnerable individuals or groups."[152]

GUYON, A PHILOSOPHER, AND KINSEY, AN EMPIRICIST

Guyon's 1933 book was reprinted in 1948 with a new title, *The Ethics of Sexual Acts*. It included Kinsey's allegedly embargoed data and a new introduction by Kinsey colleague, Dr. Harry Benjamin, that effused:

> Writing an introduction to a new edition of a book by Rene Guyon is a signal honor... There is hardly an author anywhere with qualifications comparable to those of Guyon... personal experience... philosopher... world traveler, and a student of human behavior... familiar with... [p]assion.... [D]ecades later American scientists would supply statistical confirmation of many of his revolutionary theses... Guyon's "message of sexual freedom" is a clarion call to all the "victims of anti-sexualism and puritanical terror."[153]

> Guyon, speaking as a philosopher, and Kinsey, judging merely by empirical data, do not subscribe to the theory that the sex urge can be "sublimated."…. There are other analogies between some of Guyon's contentions and Kinsey's figures. For instance, the astounding universality of self-gratification (masturbation) in adolescents and its prevalence in adults even after marriage; the widespread indulgence in homosexual acts after adolescence; the fact that adultery is conceded by about half of all married men; and, finally, the sex activity of children and "teen-agers." Guyon... wrote several chapters emphasizing the sex life of the young and regretting its prolonged neglect....

> Kinsey's data reveal the surprising frequency of pre-adolescent sex-play, both hetero- and homo-sexual, and also of coitus itself. He also reveals that, contrary to popular belief, men are most sexually active in their teens... Unless we want to close our eyes to the truth or imprison ninety-five per cent of our male population, we must completely revise our legal and moral codes. Faced by Guyon's disconcerting candor (and also by Kinsey's unimpeachable figures) even the liberal-minded scientist, believing himself quite free of prejudices, may suddenly discover that he too has retained childhood inhibitions and... repressions.

> Thanks to the Herculean labors of Kinsey and his co-workers [Guyon's contribution] will take its place among the books rightly called classic.... The present volume contains many building stones upon which to rear a happier world, the world of tomorrow, although it may be generations before the edifice is completed.

Similarly, in the original introduction to Guyon's book, sexologist Norman Haire wrote:

> The author rejects the usually accepted conception of normality and abnormality, and asserts that the many-sided sexuality of the child (what Freud has called its "polymorph-perversity") is really normal, not only for the child but also for the adult... He accuses [psychoanalysts

of erroneously trying] to "cure" the patient by teaching him to adapt himself to a sexual ethic that is really faulty, instead of assuring the patient that it is not he, but the faulty sexual ethic which has produced his neurosis, that is in need of cure.

He proceeds to the discussion of onanism, incest, homosexuality, fetishism, and even such "extraordinary" variations as necrophilia and coprophilia, all of which he considers to fall within the limits of the normal....[154]

Guyon's sex-offender-law abolition program was now quantified with Kinsey's "proofs" about human sexuality, which ALI-MPC authors—such as chief reporter Wechsler, and legal advocates, such as ACLU attorney Ernst—helped launch into the "stream of law." The emerging legal process, including doctrines of the new sexual ethic would be, in the words of Langdell, government by science and an evolutionary principle of "growth."[155]

LEGISLATIVE AND JUDICIAL CLOUT

Sex offenders committing "crimes against nature" gained ground with introduction of the emerging legal doctrine of "consent." As expounded by Guyon and Kinsey, if a victim were enticed or tricked by a sexual predator, he or she would become a collaborator. Therefore, there would be no grounds for legal charges. Or, were the perpetrator charged and convicted, there would be grounds for reduced punishment. This philosophy has wormed its way into statutes and legal decisions, producing such legal anomalies as "date rape." Kinsey, after all, had "proven" that women, girls, children, and infants were both seductive and unharmed by rape and other sexual offenses. No harm, no crime.

Kinsey's reports have been cited as authoritative in at least 50 major court cases. In countless instances, the Kinsey-laden ALI-MPC has led to significant readjustments of existing law. Kinsey's influence at the state legislative level is evident in this account by Pomeroy:

> Kinsey not only studied the histories of people who had been convicted as sex offenders. He carried on an elaborate study of the procedures involved in the handling of sex offenders....
>
> As a result of this work... Kinsey could point to some concrete results in state legislatures. In California, for example, the lawmakers appropriated $75,000 per year for a study of sex offenders, supplementing his own work and placed it under the direction of Kinsey's friend Dr. Karl Bowman... [whose] research program made abundant use of our material... Kinsey himself met with the California legislature's committee on sex laws, and he prepared special documentary material for the consideration of several other committees. Governor Pat Brown, whom he came to know well, worked with him closely in developing the state's program.
>
> In 1952 Kinsey collaborated with an Illinois state legislative committee which was working on a revision of sex laws in that state. He spent much time in gathering factual data for the committee's use. This action followed a pattern he had already established with legislative committees and special research groups set by the governments of New Jersey, New York, Delaware, Wyoming and Oregon.
>
> All this, said Kinsey, ought to be a lesson to the governor and legislature of Indiana, who could profit from what he was doing instead of being alarmed by the publication of his book.[156]

THE ALI-MPC URGED AGE OF CONSENT AT TEN-YEARS-OLD

In 1948, Morris Ernst parroted Kinsey and claimed,

> For most children, the phase of earliest sexual activity occurs between the ages of eight and thirteen. But some *boys* begin it in babyhood, and 10 per cent by the time they are five years old.... In childhood, as in youth and manhood, the Kinsey Report shows there is such a wide range of behavior at any age that the word "normal" cannot be applied.... It is plain that the first problem is to educate the educators and the parents so that we can have someone to teach the children. The Kinsey Report offers a factual basis on which to begin revision and improvement.
>
> For instance... boys are capable of orgasm at ages much earlier than most people had supposed. *The book reports authentic examples of orgasm (of course without ejaculation, but all the other factors were plainly present) in boys of only a few months of age....* [T]he investigators found that more than half of these boys were able to reach a second climax within a few minutes after the first, and 30 per cent achieved as many as five in quite rapid succession... [and] teen-age youths have a higher frequency of sexual activity than adults...
>
> [Kinsey reports] some 40 per cent of the boys who had some sort of sex experience.... Sixty percent of the boys who were not yet adolescent when their histories were taken had had some homosexual activity.... For about 12 per cent... it began at five years old or earlier, and the average age for this was nine years, two and a half months.... *These statistical data may shock many parents.... The Kinsey report undoubtedly will result in a good deal of soul-searching in regard to sex education for the very young.... The Report has set forth the facts....* [We must] consider seriously the very great amount of children's sexual activity that the Kinsey Report reveals.[157] [Emphasis added.]

Dr. Wardell Pomeroy often testified across the country saying obscenity is harmless and children are unharmed by sex acts or exposure.

The homosexual movement has long been campaigning for a lowered or eliminated age of consent, arguing that boys (and girls) are fully capable of "orgasm." Thus, they should be allowed full sexual "rights," including the "right" to sex with adults. New York University Press's publication, *Lavender Culture*, by Jay and Young, was first published in 1978 and republished in 1994. It argues for this "right" in the chapter, "Gay Youth and the Question of Consent."[158] These activists base their arguments on Kinsey's "children are sexual from birth" dogma, as well as the claim that men and women who have sex with children are largely harmless and in control of their abuse—if they are merely counseled. The ABA-ALI-MPC Code cites the California Sex Crime Reports, 1950-1953, which accepted Dr. Kinsey's claims of low "recidivism" rates for child sex predators, pedophiles, and pederasts. The ALI-MPC also utilized Kinsey as its premier sex-science authority on the early sexual capacity and proclivities of children. The ALI-MPC author claims that 10-year-old girls may "wisely" be adjudicated as mature. He explains that, at that age, their sexuality may taint the girl's conduct in adult-child sexual crimes:

Despite the indication that 12 is the commonest age for the onset of puberty, it seems wise to go well outside the average or model age, and it is known that significant numbers of girls enter the period of sexual awakening as early as the tenth year.[159]

The ALI-MPC author justified the conclusion that it is "wise" to assume that 10-year-old girls are sexually "awakened." A footnote states: "Kinsey's statistics based upon the recall of adults indicate the following median for development: 12.3 years for pubic hair; 12.4 years for breast development; 13.0 years for first menstruation."[160] The ALI-MPC authors lowered the age of consent from Kinsey's apparent 12-13-year-old, citing to Kinsey's view of benign incest. The ALI-MPC itself is cited in legislative and court decisions involving rape, child sex abuse, and incest. The scientific authority of record is Kinsey and his team. The ALI-MPC author puts into the legal record Kinsey's minimization of incest *offenses* despite what he says may be the commonality of male incestuous desires:

> ***Heterosexual incest occurs more frequently in the thinking of clinicians and social workers than it does in actual performance***. There may be a good many males who have thought of the possibilities of sexual relations with sisters or mothers or with other close female relatives, but even this is by no means universal, and is usually confined to limited periods in the boys' younger years.... Because the cases are so few, it would be misleading to suggest where the high incidences might be. The most frequent incestuous contacts are between pre-adolescent children, ***but the number of such cases among adolescents or older males is very small***.[161] [Emphasis added.]

Despite his 1,400 sex-offender subjects and his known tendency to exaggerate the sexually unconventional, Kinsey testified that the incidence of adult-child sex abuse and incest is "very small"—so small that his team just incidentally noted its occurrence. And although from 317 to 1,888 boys and almost 200 girls in his sample experienced sexual contact with adults, they (he claimed) experienced no trauma.[162] Kinsey observed, he said, that "sexual contact," even with "relatives," was often repeated because the children (not the adults) "had more or less actively sought repetitions of their experience."[163]

This view is seen in what the ALI-MPC included—as well as what it excluded and where it placed its information. The ALI-MPC Report's concluding two-page report on the "Swiss Penal Code, Offenses Against Morals." Switzerland, largely considered a peaceful, civilized country, is cited by their ALI-MPC colleagues as viewing a month or so of prison or "reclusion," ("the state of being in solitary confinement")[164] as an adequate penalty for child rapists, incestuous batterers and the like.

Using the Swiss as a model, the ALI-MPC says Swiss offenders who fornicated with a "feeble-minded" or mentally ill woman can receive "up to" five years of reclusion "or" prison "*for at least a month*" (apparently in one's home). Intercourse "or analogous act" with any age *child under 16 years*, can result in "reclusion *or* imprisonment *of at least 6 months*." Intercourse with an adopted child or stepchild "over 16… below the age of 18" may result in reclusion "for *up to* five years or" prison "*for at least 3 months*." Intercourse "with a person committed to a hospital or asylum, or held in an institution under official authority" can result in "reclusion up to three years *or* prison… for at least *one month*." "*If the victim died*" from the sexual assault, the killer *may* be reclused "for 5 years… if the actor might have foreseen that."[165] Compared to the Swiss, the ALI-MPC would seem to be actually Draconian.

KINSEY'S HOMOSEXUAL INCEST DATA CONCEALED FROM THE LAW

The Model Penal Code excludes homosexual (man-boy) incest and sex abuse. Kinsey concealed his data comparing heterosexual to homosexual child sexual abuse.[166]

However, based on the then-Kinsey Institute Director Paul Gebhard's March 11, 1981, letter to this author, homosexual boy abuse/incest was double that of heterosexual incest. Says Gebhard, Kinsey's research "sample" had "47 white females and 96 white males" who were incest victims.[167] Pomeroy said they interviewed about 1,400[168] sex offenders including prisoners who were child rapists:

> If the list was short for some offenses—as in incest, for example—we took the history of everybody on it. If it was a long list, as for statutory rape, we might take the history of every fifth or tenth man... [then we would go] to a particular prison workshop and get the history of every man in the group, whether he was a sex offender or not.[169]

Kinsey had meaningful information on incest victims and offenders to aid in the understanding of this criminal conduct. Yet, in 1950, when then FBI director, J. Edgar Hoover warned of a "terrifying" increase in sex crimes:

> Kinsey scoffed at the idea... Kinsey pointed out that what the nation and the FBI were calling heinous crimes against *children were things that appeared in a fair number of our total histories, and in only a small number of cases was public attention ever aroused or the police involved.* Kinsey... contended that, as far as so-called molestation of children was concerned, a great deal more damage was done to the child by adult hysteria [than by the sex crime against the child].[170]

While "a fair number" of Kinsey's 5,300 or 4,120 men committed what "the nation and the FBI" thought were "heinous crimes against children," Kinsey hid this child sexual abuse data from "the nation and the FBI."

NORMALIZING ALL ADULT-CHILD SEX

The ALI-MPC had properly prepared their readers for the concluding and conclusive Swiss sex offenders penalties. The ALI-MPC cites a California study on sex predators, one of many relying on Kinsey's data, that claims "the degree of recidivism was lowest for those convicted of incest, of lewd and lascivious conduct with children, and of rape."[171] The report stated:

> The majority [of rapists] were given [light] penalties.... This reflects the fact that the bulk of rape convictions result from statutory offenses and not forcible rape of the type committed by so-called sex fiends...."[172] The rule of "slightest penetration" has been criticized by Ploscowe as punishing attempt rather than the completed rape.[173]

The California study was actually repudiated by sex predator statistics existing during Kinsey's era, and even more discredited by contemporary data.[174] Sex offenders in general, and child molesters in particular, are more likely to re-offend than are other criminals. A 1982 U.S. Justice Department report found:

> Recidivism appears to be high among youthful sex offenders. Noting a recidivism rate of 50 percent for juvenile rapists, Wenet and Clark (1977) point out that youth tend to repeat the same sexual offense for which they were originally caught.[175]

Additionally, it appears that not only are sex crimes repeated by youths, but the offenses (consistent with the disturbing trend in all youth crimes) are increasingly "more lethal and threatening a wider sector of people since the mid-1970s."[176] Moreover, although the Kinsey team and their disciples claim incest is largely harmless or beneficial, the medical facts find between 30 and 50 percent of children of incestuous unions to be born abnormal.[177]

The Kinsey Institute team tried to paint a statistical portrait similar to that in *Brave New World* of happy young boys and girls interacting sexually in the open. Yet, the hard data confirm that children are increasingly placed in harm's way by—and are more vulnerable to violent abuse from—older juveniles and adults.

PART VI: NORMALIZING PEDOPHELIA AND PORNOGRAPHY

Kinsey's *Female* volume excluded data and discussion about female pedophiles. While this law chapter has focused primarily on adult *male* sexual abuse of children, it should not be misread to suggest that there is not a growing problem of women who victimize children as well.[178] When you eroticize an environment, you erotically charge those within it. When erotically charged stimuli are permitted in schools—unless there is conscious resistance toward the material—teacher-student relationships are affected; the presence of erotically charged stimuli alters the nature of relationships in the home, in the workplace, in church, courtrooms institutions, and clubs. While female pedophiles are not as common as their male counterparts, women have more ready access to children than do men. There must be concern about *both* types of child predators.

In 1973, the American Psychiatric Association (APA) removed homosexuality from its list of "disorders." In another bold move, the APA in 1995 removed both sadism and pedophilia from its disordered list. It stated that the desire to do violence or to have sex with children becomes a disorder only if the pedophile feels "guilty" or has anxiety about his sexual desire or actions toward children. The APA published "study," in line with the Kinseyan model, has reportedly already been used in the courtroom to erode legal protections that currently penalize child sex offenses—or, as some sexologists euphemistically term it, "age-discrepant sexual intimacy."

As we pay the bills and endure the consequences of the post-Kinsey sexual revolution,[179] many Americans are asking: "How could it have come to this?" If "the rule-making part of the law in my lifetime" was, as Kinsey's ACLU Lawyer Morris Ernst claimed, dramatically altered by the Kinsey cadre's efforts, then the nation's sex and marital laws were radically restructured on a body of lies. In 1983, Notre Dame University legal historian and constitutional law Professor Charles Rice commented on the groundbreaking changes in laws relating to homosexuality:

> Homosexuality is no longer treated as an automatic and conclusive bar to public employment, including the armed forces and public schools… no longer excluded solely on that account from the legal, medical and other professions, or from immigration and citizenship. Liquor licenses may no longer be denied to establishments merely because they cater to homosexuals. Mere solicitation of homosexual activity is no longer punishable…. Student homosexual clubs now have the same rights as other groups… [and homosexual activity is] no inherent bar to the custody and adoption of children.[180]

Revolutionary changes in the '90s have supported the continued liberalization of laws on sodomy, sex and reproduction. Based on the disproven assumption that sexual arousal can never be toxic, even laws against public nudity are often not enforced. In fact, the use of any age child in pornography, in sodomy, sadism and bestiality, was made legal in *New York v. Ferber* (1980) and unanimously reversed by the United States Supreme Court in 1982. The legitimizing of pedophilia lends support to the unrelenting efforts to legalize child pornography at the same time that children are widely exposed to pornographic stimuli in the mass media, schools and public libraries.

Few of the early pioneers working for uncensored media envisioned the current consequences, when children access obscenity by phone, Internet or in the school or public library. And few child advocates understand the role mainstream erotica/pornography has played in legitimizing, marketing and supplying child pornography. This author's study for the United States Department of Justice, Juvenile Justice and Delinquency Prevention, *Images of Children, Crime and Violence in Playboy, Penthouse and Hustler,* (1989) established that link. Even now child pornography can be ordered from *Playboy's* earlier editions and from other mainstream pornographic magazines as well as via the *Playboy Press* productions.[181]

The most notable mainstreaming of child pornography may still be the infamous 1976 *Playboy Press* pictures of the then 6-or-7-year-old child, Brooke Shields, in *Sugar and Spice, Surprising and Sensuous Images of Women. Playboy Press* posed a naked, oiled Brooke Shields in the context of other sadistic, pseudo-lesbian and racist pornography. All would "stir the sex impulses or… lead to sexually impure and lustful thoughts" (thought being the neurochemical "action" changing the brain structure).[182]

OBSCENITY: BOOKLEGGERS AND SMUTHOUNDS

The repudiation of obscenity has been the hallmark of every civil society. In *Violence as Obscenity* (1996), Kevin Saunders observes "the Greek view that violence was obscene and that 'obscene' meant 'off-stage.'"[183]

Professor Jay Gertzman, writes about the period between the two world wars when New York was the center of American obscenity production—much of which was still "literature," as in the written word. Morris Ernst, the key lawyer seeking to legalize these materials, argued for their banality. The public view, that sexually "impure" materials led to sexually impure "copy cat" conduct, resulted in tough penalties for this new, growing business. With the press still largely independent, cartoons and stories treated "unclean literature" as contributing to public disorder, coarsening men and society. Toxic smut contributed to sexual disease, early death and violent crime.

In *Bookleggers and Smuthounds: The Trade in Erotica 1920-1940,* Gertzman fills in some of the blanks between the era ending the "White Slave Trade" and the "Mann Act" in 1912 and the mainstreaming of "unclean literature." For the first time in modern history large numbers of ordinary people, not only the idle rich, could afford to purchase obscene materials. Meanwhile, the press focused on the questionable censorship of actual "literature" such as *Elmer Gantry*, and the works of Faulkner, Hemingway and H.G. Wells.

Mr. Summer (in hat) is shown here "burning pornographic magazines, pamphlets, postcards, and lending-library sex-pulp novels in the furnace of police headquarters." March 28, 1936, press photo from the Mirror's Extra 3- Star Edition.

KINSEY'S IMPACT ON AMERICAN LAW

But some critics woefully note that, based on today's runaway traffic in pictorial obscenity at the schoolroom level, "blue noses" such as John Saxton Sumner, the secretary of the New York Society for the Suppression of Vice (NYSSV), may have been on to something.

Titillating—and just crude materials—were hauled off by police officials, their producers tried, convicted and imprisoned. Mr. Sumner (in hat) is shown here "burning pornographic magazines, pamphlets, postcards, and lending-library sex-pulp novels in the furnace of police headquarters."[184] Police raids like this March 28, 1936, photo from the *Mirror's Extra 3-Star Edition*, more clearly identify the combatants. The battle is raging between the "anything goes" sexual revolutionaries (man is just an animal) and the crowd protecting "home and hearth" (man is made in the image of God). The police are confiscating sexual materials destined "for hundreds of peddlers from coast to coast."[185]

The Common law criminalized and strictly punished those producing and purveying obscene materials. *Black's Law Dictionary* (1968) included the historical pre-Kinsey definition of obscenity, which remained largely intact until 1957:

> OBSCENITY: Offensive to chastity of mind or to modesty, expressing or presenting to the mind or view something that delicacy, purity and decency forbids to be exposed; calculated to corrupt, deprave, and debauch the morals of the people, and promote violation of the law; licentious and libidinous and tending to excite feelings of an impure or unchaste character; tending to stir the sex impulses or to lead to sexually impure and lustful thoughts; tending to corrupt the morals of youth or lower the standards of right and wrong especially as to the sexual relation.[186]
>
> OBSCENE BOOK or PAPER: An obscene book or paper within the act relating to non-mailable matter means one which contains immodest and indecent matter, the reading whereof would have a tendency to deprave and corrupt the minds of those whose minds are open to such immoral influences.[187]
>
> OBSCENITY: The character or quality of being obscene; conduct tending to corrupt the public morals by its indecency or lewdness.[188]

Terrence J. Murphy in *Censorship, Government and Obscenity* recounts President Abraham Lincoln's contribution to our understanding of virtue and purity:

> During the Civil War the volume of such mail [obscenity] increased greatly. Pornographers were attempting to exploit the loneliness of the Union soldiers away from home. Consequently… President Lincoln signed into law… legislation controlling obscenity on March 3, 1865.… [T]he Lincoln Law… outlawed obscenity within the United States.[189]

The public and the 1933 and 1934 court in Ulysses understood "obscene" as "tending to stir the sex impulses or to lead to sexually impure and lustful thoughts.…"[190] This is, as Lincoln's postal laws said, material "of a vulgar and indecent character," signifying "lustful" as well as "sexually impure."

In "CHAP. LXXXI—Act relating to the postal Laws Sec. 16," the Lincoln Law read:

> And be it further enacted, that no obscene book, pamphlet, picture, print, other publication of a vulgar and indecent character, shall be admitted into the mails of the United States any person or persons who shall deposit or cause to be deposited, in any post-office

or branch post-office of the United States, for mailing or for delivery, an obscene book, pamphlet, picture, print, or other publication, knowing the same to be of a vulgar and indecent character, shall be deemed guilty of a misdemeanor, and, being duly convicted thereof, shall for every such offense be fined not more than five hundred dollars, or imprisoned not more than one year, or both, according to the circumstances and aggravations of the offense.[191]

LAW DICTIONARY DEFINES OBSCENITY PRIOR TO 1957

This definition of obscenity held until *U.S. v. Roth* (1957),[192] when the United States Supreme Court accepted the revolutionary ALI-MPC.

The Kinsey team was first to break the legal principle of government confiscation of obscenity. It was allowed to legally receive obscene materials through the mail in 1957 on the grounds that its status as a "scientific" body gave it scientific immunity from the "prurient interest" standard, thereby placing the Kinsey team beyond the bounds of prosecution.[193] The legal notion that "educative" sex stimuli are non-prurient eventually justified the introduction of sexually obscene materials into classrooms for viewing by school children under the guise of "sex education." In the words of a 1995 SIECUS position statement, "When sensitively used...sexually explicit visual, printed, or on-line materials" are "valuable educational or personal aids"… "reduc[ing] ignorance and confusion and contributing to a wholesome concept of sexuality."[194]

The Kinsey Institute and Indiana University played a major role in ignoring, undermining, and eventually overturning America's obscenity laws. The Institute pornography was shown and explained in 1970 to the President's Commission on Pornography, bolstering the Commission's Kinseyan conclusions about the harmlessness and usefulness of pornography for children and society.[195] As for harm to women, in his 1968 autobiography, *A Love Affair With The Law*, the anti-censorship ACLU lawyer Ernst conceals his role as Kinsey's attorney-at-law saying instead that Kinsey:

> Clinched some of the theories that I, as a lawyer, had been proceeding on by way of hunch. He produced the proof that women are not really interested in reading or viewing the pornographic. All too long, courts dominated by males had argued: This is all right for us men—but we have to protect our women. Now it became clear that we need not thus save the women. They are not taken one step nearer to bed by any book.[196]

Although repeatedly noting that males "are conditioned by the social groups in which they live,"[197] Kinsey argued that the use of pornography by homosexual and sadistic males was normal, and thus advantageous. Many such researchers have concealed their autoerotic desires under the guise of art and research.[198] On that note, commemorating its 50th anniversary, the Institute opened an obscene exhibition called "The Art of Desire." The Institute, the first "seemingly serious academic voice" to view obscenity/pornography as "sex science," magically transformed obscenity, by redefinition, into legitimate sexual information.

PORNOGRAPHY AND THE REPEAL OF RETICENCE

In *The Repeal of Reticence, A History of America's Cultural and Legal Struggles over Free Speech, Obscenity, Sexual Liberation, and Modern Art*, Rochelle Gurstein, of New York's Bard Graduate School, states,

"The greatest authority on sexual behavior at the time, the Kinsey Reports," showed "the minor degree to which literature serves as a potent stimulant."[199] Gurstein deserves to be quoted extensively:

> In fact, he [Justice Harlan] pointed out… "there is a large school of thought, particularly in the scientific community, which denies any causal connection between the reading of pornography and immorality, crime, or delinquency." Justice Douglas reached the same conclusion: "The absence of dependable information on the effect of obscene *literature* on human conduct should make us wary."[200] [Emphasis added]

Of course, glossy color picture books and videos decipherable to children and illiterates alike— have long since replaced the use of cognitive brain activity required in the past by obscene "literature." In "The Kinsey Report: The Sociological Approach to Intimate Life," Gurstein identified Kinsey as the "scientific community" to whom these esteemed justices referred as they opened the floodgates to legalize and popularize pornography:

> That the linchpin of modern obscenity law turned out to be scientific study of sexual behavior is ironic, given that this had once been understood as a species of obscenity in its own right; sex-reform and birth-control materials were the prime suspects in obscenity prosecutions through the 1920s… For sex reformers, the demystification of sex through scientific method had been both the animating vision and the missing link of their project, and with the publication of *Sexual Behavior in the Human Male* by Alfred C. Kinsey, Wardell B. Pomeroy, and Clyde E. Martin in 1948, their aspirations were finally realized.[201]

Here Gurstein quotes the now famous words of Ernst and Loth, "The Kinsey Report has done for sex what Columbus did for geography." And, she adds, "The Kinsey Report's candor, unexpected findings, and enormous popularity ensured that 'it will be impossible to go back to the old folkway of reticence about sex':

> While Ernst and Loth raised many of the same issues that would make their way into Lockhart and McClure's [famous obscenity] article six years later—the constitutional status of obscenity, the clear and present danger test, and the need for scientific proof of actual harm—the timing of the publication introduced a new and distinctive dialect into the legal discourse that has persisted into the present day…. Due to the highly charged atmosphere of the cold war, the authors politicized two of the most cherished mechanisms of liberal society—free speech and the marketplace: "This book is dedicated to a people who, not under a dictator, can still work out their own salvation by the free spread of knowledge, and to Alfred C. Kinsey, Wardell B. Pomeroy, and Clyde E. Martin, who have enriched the marketplace of thought."[202]

Gurstein identifies the use of the Cold War to legalize the Kinsey model by equating his books with pornography access and the "free spread of knowledge."[203]

> So perhaps the greatest achievement of the Kinsey Report is a reaffirmation of our freedom to talk; freedom for the individual to talk in confidence and have it respected, freedom for the scientist and the commentator to propound facts and interpretations which are deeply shocking to certain sections of the community.[204]

Following Kinsey's male book, a "positive rash" of media appeared calling for freedom from parental controls. Ernst said, "In some respects, the publication of this sober, scientific work marks the…

beginning of the era of emancipation from the Victorian taboos in regard to sex." And, Gurstein adds:

> The line of rebellion… [of] youthful cultural radicals at the turn of the century, now apparently culminated with the "sober" and bloodless jargon of sociologists working out of Indiana University in the 1940s: "Professor Kinsey and his associates are representatives of this kindlier age. With a wealth of data which would have given narrower minds a handle to strip the hide from human complacency, they have chosen the less sensational role."[205]

Sociologist Lionel Trilling, one of a small group of intellectual dissenters, is cited by Gurstein as suspecting Kinsey's legal, change-agent design, when Trilling notes:

> [Kinsey] holds that judgments express nothing but private whims and subjective preferences, and, as they belong to the individual, are always self-interested and manipulative… sheer power struggles, and judgment, distinction, and discrimination are modes of domination.[206]

Gurstein, by no means a "conservative," concludes:

> Without this respect for the limits as to what can be spoken, private and public had collapsed into one another, leaving in their wake a strange new realm, at once as noisy and promiscuous as a circus and as sterile and solemn as a laboratory. In this new world, the protection afforded by cultural conventions such as privacy and modesty no longer held sway. An amorous couple could be wrenched from each other's arms and dragged naked before the court of public opinion, where they would be asked by experts in white coats, laboriously taking down their every word, to describe every detail of their erotic life. And "the human male" does not protest that his privacy is violated or that it is a breach of fidelity to speak of those moments that belong exclusively and completely to his loved one and himself; instead, he enthusiastically tells all.[207]

In fact, in *Private Acts/Public Policy: Alfred Kinsey, the American Law Institute and the Privatization of American Sexual Morality*, Princeton historian and Kinsey admirer, David Allyn, writes that Kinsey challenged "the very legitimacy of public morality itself," by eradicating public awareness of the societal consequences of "private" sexual acts:

> *Kinsey's 1948 study… played a critical role in the mid-century privatization of morality. In the post-WWII era, experts abandoned the concept of "public morals," a concept which had underpinned the social control of American sexuality from the 1870's onward. In the 1950's and 60's, however, sexual morality was privatized, and the state-controlled, highly regulated moral economy of the past gave way to a new, "deregulated" moral market.* [Emphasis added.]

*   *   *   *

> Kinsey's text aided the privatization of morality in a more subtle manner by downplaying the problem of public sexual expression. The text gave the impression that sexual behavior only occurred in the private space of the home. [Kinsey] was virtually silent when it came to questions of public sexuality; this silence served Kinsey's deregulatory ends.
>
> *In the 1950's the American Law Institute attempted to shape its model penal code in accordance with Kinsey's scientific discoveries*—by privatizing most moral questions [seen when]

the Supreme Court ruled on *Roth v. the United States* (1957) and *Griswold v. Connecticut* (1965)... Both cases drew on the American Law Institute's model penal code's distinction between public and private sexual expression, *which, in turn, drew on the work of Alfred Kinsey.*[208] [Emphasis added.]

Despite the massive problems associated with child sexual abuse, "S & M," prostitution, pornography, public sexual solicitations, abortion, etc., Kinsey offered no "data" on these crimes—thus creating the illusion that sexual conduct was harmless and a purely private matter.

"LOCAL DRIVES AGAINST SO-CALLED OBSCENE MATERIALS"

By ridiculing those who challenged him as sexually fearful and hypocritical, Kinsey and his cadre could testify authoritatively as sex experts to sway public opinion and change sex laws. Kinsey eagerly defamed the vice squads and crusaders who were forcing "smut peddlers" out of business:

> Local drives against so-called obscene materials, and state, federal, and international moves against the distribution of such materials, are not infrequently instituted by females who not only find the material morally and socially objectionable, but probably fail to comprehend the significance that it may have for most males and for some females.[209]

As supposedly *bona fide* sexologists, the Kinsey Institute team and its minions testified before courts and legislators, guiding the ALI-MPC adoption process to liberalize laws against obscenity. In *Censorship, Government and Obscenity*, author Terrence J. Murphy writes:

> The Model Penal Code proposal states it rejects the common legal definition of obscenity.[210] ...Until such time as the American Law Institute satisfactorily clarifies its proposal the courts would do well to hold fast to the definition which they clarified over many years and through a long series of cases....[211] The first legislative body to act upon the recommendation of the American Law Institute, North Carolina, accepted the provisions.... This occurred just fourteen days before the Roth decision was handed down.[212]

According to Murphy, the United States Supreme Court wrongly believed the ALI-MPC to be consistent with the Common Law definition of obscenity.

U.S. SUPREME COURT HEEDS ALI-MPC'S "PRURIENT INTEREST" STANDARD

In explaining its June 24, 1957 decisions in *Roth v. United States* and *Alberts v. California*, the High Court adopted the new and confusing term "prurient interest" and attempted to explain that prurient was the *same* as lewd or lascivious desire or thought:

> We perceive no significant difference between the meaning of obscenity developed in the case law and the definition of the A.L.I. Model Penal Code.... A thing is obscene if, considered as a whole, its predominant appeal is to prurient interest, i.e., a shameful or morbid interest in nudity, sex, or excretion, and if it goes substantially beyond customary limits of candor in description or representation of such matters.[213]

The Court thereby established a standard for *accepting*, rather than *denying*, the value of material that might arouse "prurient interest." To say that a judge or juror does not have an "itch or longing to see or desire that which is lewd or lascivious" (the definition of "prurient" is "itch") to the point of "excitement of feeling, accompanying special attention to some object" (the definition of "interest") means that he or she deems that object to be "of no prurient interest," and therefore acceptable rather than objectionable! So violent scenes of torture or rape, for example, become acceptable if the juror does not experience (or, just as likely, is ashamed to admit he or she *does* experience) an "itch or longing to continue to experience the excitement of feeling" accompanying the viewing of what may very well be the lewdest of lewd and obscene material that should be "off-stage."

Here again we see the perverse influence of Kinsey—whose personal hatred of traditional morality has enticed our nation to tolerate increasing extremes of degradation. The subjective line between "soft-core" (legal) and "hard-core" (arguably illegal) pornography was to be drawn by the "itch" and "the eye" of each judge and juror.

"HARD CORE" INJURY FELT BY THE JURIST

Although "hard-core" pornography is sometimes ruled obscene or illegal, many Americans do not understand what the term meant to the Supreme Court. In essence, it meant the erect male genitalia presented in penetration. Such a definition is amazingly literal. The Court banned such images, with no more logic, it appears, because they "titillated" or embarrassed the Justices and made them feel uncomfortable. Before the 1957 *Roth* decision, the law censored "lewd" materials that stirred any "impure or prurient thoughts." Since *Roth*, it has become increasingly acceptable and incrementally legal to show nude and semi-nude women and girls sadomasochistically tied up and abused, stabbed, and raped, with their sexual organs subjected to sundry types of abuse, including burning, searing, and other forms of torture. Such depictions have frequently been deemed by a majority of Justices to be "soft core" legal, pornography. And with the spread of the homosexual movement and its imagery, the erect male genitalia in penetration has emerged as a more prevalent occurrence as well.[214]

As "erotica" plays an increasing role in the lives of Americans, including institutional and professional leaders, their ability honestly and objectively to evaluate pornography as harmful to vulnerable children and others has become seriously compromised. In *The Brethren* (1979), journalist and author Bob Woodward reports that Justice William O. Douglas believed that *nothing* should be banned, in public or in private, to protect *anyone*, including children. He writes of other Justices:

> White did not loathe pornography, as Blackmun and Burger did. It was simply that these were things for his son's eyes, perhaps, but never for his wife's or daughter's…. Brennan, like White, had his own private definition of obscenity: no erections. He was willing to accept penetration as long as the pictures passed what his clerks referred to as the "limp dick" standard. Oral sex was tolerable if there was not erection… Stewart… had seen it during World War II, when he served… in Casablanca… locally produced pornography. He knew the difference between that hardest of hard core and much of what came to the Court. He called it his "Casablanca Test." ["I know it when I see it."] Marshall, as usual, [was] more amused than shocked by the exhibits.[215]

LAW CLERKS DISAPPOINTED

Credit is due the somewhat capricious Woodward as one of the few to even mention such intimate or private particulars.[216] He also notes that most of the young law clerks that do legal research and draft opinions for the Justices have long been voluntarily or involuntarily exposed to obscene material "which stirs lust and impure thoughts." Woodward claims that after viewing a pornographic Danish film, Justice Marshall quipped:

> "Well, Harry, I didn't learn anything, how about you?" Blushing, Blackmun joined the rest of the room in a hearty laugh. The second reel had the first hard-breathing segment as two women made love [sic]. Then the film returned to its clinical, documentary style. Blackmun found it distasteful. The film's tone, if not its content, degraded women. That alone was enough to predispose him against all pornography.[217] *...The clerks were disappointed that the movie was such soft core....* Back in chambers, *Powell's clerks remarked to him that Vixen had been disappointing.* Two clerks confessed that *they had seen all the movies of the director, Russ Meyer—the master of sex-exploitation films. Yale Law School had even presented a Russ Meyer festival.*[218] [Emphasis added.]

Woodward inadvertently revealed the successful pornography conditioning process by which the Yale, Harvard, etc., U.S. Supreme Court clerks—future judges and prosecutors—had succumbed. He added:

> [Justice] Powell's gaunt face was expressionless. He had never before seen such a film, he explained slowly. He had had no idea such movies were even made. He was shocked and disgusted. He did not wish to discuss it further. Powell's clerks were amazed. There could not have been a milder movie for him to see. There had been nothing more than nudity, and facial and bodily expressions that suggested orgasm. *How would he have reacted to the hard-core peep-show reels with nothing but explicit sex from beginning to end? His clerks decided not to let any other clerks know of Powell's reactions. His vote was crucial. He was a reasonable man. Perhaps when the shock had faded a bit, his initial distaste could be overcome.*[219] [Emphasis added].

NORMALIZING OBSCENITY IN THE CASE LAW
JUSTICE DOUGLAS: THINGS "STIMULATE SEXUAL DESIRE" MORE THAN READING

In his *Roth* dissent, joined by Justice Hugo Black, Justice William O. Douglas quoted favorably from a 1954 *Minnesota Law Review* article entitled, "Literature, the Law of Obscenity, and the Constitution," which relied on Kinsey. Co-authored by legal scholar William Lockhart, it asserted:

> The many other influences in society that stimulate sexual desire are so much more frequent in their influence, and so much more potent in their effect, that the influence of reading is likely, at most, to be relatively insignificant in the composite of forces that lead an individual into conduct deviating from the community sex standards. The Kinsey studies show the minor degree to which literature serves as a potent sexual stimulant. And the studies demonstrating that sex knowledge seldom results from reading indicates the relative unimportance of literature in sex thoughts as compared with other factors in society.[220]

Reprising here, "reading" has long been an anachronism in pornography that focuses on glossy color pictures, film and videos with few words. Lockhart subsequently served as director of the

1970 President's Commission on Pornography, sending the Commission to the Kinsey Institute for information.

In 1985, a dissenting opinion in a Texas court case involving a statute forbidding the sale of obscene devices cited Kinsey in defense of such devices:

> We have come too far in the study of human sexual behavior of the human male and female since the day Kinsey, Pomeroy, and Martin wrote their work... [a]nd their sequel.... And have learned too much.... To turn the clock back to more unenlightened times.[221]

NORMALIZING BESTIALITY

Kinsey's "enlightened" data have also served to diminish abhorrence of sexual contact between humans and animals. From his interview for the Yorkshire documentary, "Kinsey's Paedophiles," we now know that at least one of Kinsey's team, Clarence Tripp, admitted to being sexually active with dogs.[222]

> In general, Kinsey notes, the upper level condemns lower level morality as lacking in the proper ideals and righteousness... [citing bestiality] figures in the Kinsey report those have received wide publicity.... One out of every six American farm boys has sexual contacts with animals.
>
> [Deutsch reiterates] Only a very small proportion of males imprisoned as sex offenders are involved in behavior materially different from that of most males in the general population, the Kinsey group states.... [F]ully 95 out of 100 Americans are involved in one or more illicit sexual activities.... Judge Ploscowe, in his chapter on this subject, points out the existing contradictions in our sex laws and the pressing need for revision.[223]

Kinsey biographer James Jones recalls that Kinsey wrote extensively about sex laws, calling for their overhaul:

> A month later, the attorney wrote to say that he had succeeded in getting the original charge of sodomy, which would have carried a fifteen-to-twenty-year sentence upon conviction, reduced to a minor offense. Noting that his client had received a one-year sentence, the attorney declared, "Your book was of considerable assistance to me in the preparation and disposition of this case." Clearly pleased by the outcome, Kinsey replied, "I am very glad if our studies were of use to you in this particular trial. I hope they can be of increasing use to many people in regard to our sex laws."[224]
>
> Kinsey got his wish. For the remainder of his life, virtually every week's mail brought similar letters from attorneys and judges and in each instance he did his best to show how his research could be used to push the law toward an ethic of tolerance. Pleased by the rush of legal reformers to his doorstep, Kinsey boasted to a friend, "I think a very great many people have done a good deal of thinking about our American sex laws since our data was [sic] published."[225]

Had Kinsey been given his way, he would have overhauled America's sex offender codes completely. To his mind, they were archaic, unscientific, inhibited, mean-spirited, and punitive. "There is no scientific justification for the definitions of sex perversion which are customarily made under the law," he wrote a court official:

> Almost without exception the several examples of behavior, which are known as perversions, are basic mammalian patterns. [He continued,] In non-inhibited societies and in non-inhibited portions of our own society, the so-called sex perversions are a regular part of the behavior pattern, and they probably would be so throughout the population if there were no traditions to the contrary. This statement applies to such things as mouth-genital contacts, anal coital acts, homosexuality, group activities, relations between individuals of diverse age, and animal intercourse."

Current sex offender laws, he explained, were based on English-American common law traditions, which in turn were "a direct continuation of the Talmudic proscriptions on such activities and not the product of scientific judgments." Still, Kinsey estimated that if these archaic laws were to be enforced, most of the male population would be in jail. As things stood, however, ubiquitous behavior all but precluded effective enforcement:

> Our sex laws are so far from the normal biologic picture, and so remote from the actual behavior of the population. [Warned Kinsey] that it is physically impossible to enforce them in any but the most capricious fashion.[226]

PART VII: HOW DID WE COME TO PARTIAL-BIRTH ABORTION?

With "seduction" and "breach of promise" seldom held to be crimes, men were being freed from any legal duty to women, which in turn paved the way for the legalization and increasing acceptance of contraception and abortion on demand. Women became consenting "partners" responsible for both creating and terminating a baby's life. Previously when American society understood these matters from scriptural authority, men were held legally and socially responsible for creating the life of a child.

In *Sexual Behavior & the Law* (1965), Samuel Kling lauds the ALI-MPC and the jurists who followed Kinsey's lead. He provided "expert" support for ALI-MPC's liberalization of sex-offender laws and its call for changes in abortion laws. His book, written in an easy-to-read, question-and-answer style for laymen and professional "lawyers, physicians, psychiatrists, and social workers," cites Kinsey throughout. To the question, "Are most criminal abortions successful?" he answered in the affirmative, noting:

> The Kinsey Institute reported that between one-fifth and one-fourth of the white married American women interviewed in their sample had had at least one induced abortion. Three-fourths of them reported no unfavorable consequences. Most did not regret the experience.[227]

Kinsey's ACLU attorney, Morris Ernst, was a key Planned Parenthood lawyer, while Kinseyan Dr. Mary Calderone had served as medical director of Planned Parenthood. Dr. Calderone was a founder and first executive director of the Sex (now Sexuality) Information and Education Council of the United States (SIECUS). Mary Calderone and Kinsey co-author, Paul Gebhard, would be very influential authorities in the *Roe v. Wade* decision. It includes a footnote citation to Draft No. 9 (May 8, 1959) of the ALI-MPC, which in turn states: "Major sources of Information on abortion include two sources: Calderone, *Abortion in the United States* (1958); Gebhard and others, *Pregnancy, Birth and Abortion*, chap. 8 (1958)."

WHERE DID KINSEY'S 90 PERCENT (UNMARRIED) AND 22 PERCENT (MARRIED) ABORTIONS COME FROM?

Abortion Wars, (1998) a collection of writings from libertarian essayists, journalists, lawyers, scholars, activists, physicians and philosophers, celebrates 50 years of legal and social victories leading to widespread acceptance of abortion in America. These sexual revolutionaries thank Kinsey as the first entry (page xi) for serving as the first agent of change in the *Abortion Wars'* chronology of events—leading to the view of the unborn as quasi or non-human. States *Abortion Wars*:

> **1953**: Alfred Kinsey's *Sexual Behavior in the Human Female* reports that 9 out of 10 premarital pregnancies end in abortion and 22 percent of married women have had an abortion while married.[228]

In over 20 years of research into the Kinsey data, this author found no such abortion data in the 1953 Report, indeed no index reference to "abortion" in *either* Kinsey Report (*Sexual Behavior in the Human Male*, 1948 or *Sexual Behavior in the Human Female*, 1953). Where did these critical "data" come from? The ALI-MPC carried the first major "scientific" support for legalizing abortion in America. The ALI-MPC was cited as a national authority on abortion three times in Justice Blackmun's written opinion in *Roe v Wade*. Blackmun, writing for the majority, explains that most states are patterning their rulings on abortion after the ALI-MPC:

> A short discussion of the modern law on this issue is contained in the Comment to the ALI's Model Penal Code s 207.11, at 158 and at. 35-37 (Tent. Draft No. 9).
>
> In the past several years, however, a trend toward liberalization of abortion statutes has resulted in adoption, by about one-third of the States, of less stringent laws, *most of them patterned after the ALI Model Penal Codes.*
>
> *Fourteen States have adopted some form of the ALI statute.*[229] (Emphasis added).

Justice Blackmun cites to page 147 of Draft 9 of the ALI-MPC, to Planned Parenthood Medical Director Mary Calderone and her misinformed claims, which were considered by "about one-third of the States," and by the Supreme Court in *Roe v. Wade*. Calderone stated that the Kinsey scientific data, showed:

> *"(4) 90 to 95% of pre-marital pregnancies are aborted."* [230]

Kinsey's fraudulent claims at that conference, "that 90 per cent of all illegal abortions are done by physicians," implied that family physicians commonly aborted the unwanted babies of massive numbers of single women as well as respectable wives.

Gebhard and Calderone are supported by abortion data that are *not in the over 18,000 pages of Sexual Behavior in the Human Male and Female* books. In their book, *Blessed are the Barren*, authors Marshall and Donovan reference the famous Kinsey's Planned Parenthood speech,

> At the 1955 abortion conference sponsored by the Planned Parenthood Federation of America… the question of physician-induced abortion came up. The discussion leader on this point was the famed sex researcher, Alfred Kinsey.[231]

That "90 to 95% of pre-marital pregnancies are aborted," in the 1920s through 40s is a stunning claim for a time when not only abortion, but birth control was largely illegal. In fact, the claim was fraudulent. Kinsey's database had so few normal women that he had to redefine "married" to include females who had lived over a year with a man. This definition would allow for Kinsey's large prostitute population, more desirous of talking to an agreeable "scholar" about their illegal and socially condemned acts of fornication and cohabitation, than were normal, conventional, emotionally healthy American women.[232]

The key citation for Kinsey's suddenly discovered abortion "data" was published in *Pregnancy, Birth and Abortion*, by co-author Paul Gebhard, *et al*. The "Introduction," to *Pregnancy, Birth and Abortion* states,

> The Institute for Sex Research… has produced two major publications, *Sexual Behavior in the Human Male* (1948) and *Sexual Behavior in the Human Female* (1953). Both volumes dealt with sexual behavior per se; the reproductive consequences of a part of such behavior were scarcely touched upon… This omission may seem strange to those of purposivistic thought to whom sex and reproduction are essentially synonymous.…

> * * * *

> However, despite much writing, estimating, and guessing, there have been very few factual data on conceptions among unmarried females and the prevalence of induced illegal abortion among both married and unmarried females in this country. It is precisely on these subjects that we can provide much needed, factual information.

> *As the Institute for Sex Research continues to produce work of value, the debt science and society in general owe to Dr. Kinsey will continue to increase.*[233] [Emphasis added.]

KINSEY'S SUDDEN ABORTION DATA

Having claimed that "roughly half of the women from the middle and upper socio-economic levels, who married had had coitus prior to marriage"[234] during the 1920s-1940s, the Kinsey team later claimed that their "data" also found more that 25 percent of married women had abortions as did 89 percent of single, pregnant women.

Who was "married"? The Kinsey team, sans Kinsey himself, producing *Pregnancy, Birth and Abortion* claimed their "Terms Relating to Social Phenomena" were the same as the Kinsey team's definition of "married" women in *Sexual Behavior in the Human Female*.[235] Under the chapter entitled, "The Sample and Its Statistical Analysis," the original Kinsey team provides their definition of "Marital Status":

> They were identified as married if they were living with their spouses ***either*** in formally consummated legal marriages, ***or*** *in common-law relationships that had lasted for at least a year*… These definitions are *more or less in accord with those used in the U. S. Census for 1950, except that* common-law relationships have been more frequently accepted as *marriages* in our data.…

This definition conflicts with the U.S. Census where women were not considered "married" if they were just in common-law relationships. Since Kinsey's idiosyncratic definition did not qualify as a common-law relationship, the abortion writers, post-facto, changed the team's bad definition adding the U.S. Census standards for a marriage ignored in *Sexual Behavior in the Human Female*:

Married: persons were considered married if they were living with their spouses *either* in a legal marriage *or* in a common-law relationship that had existed continuously for at least one year. *In the latter instance, both spouses had to consider themselves married, and live together openly as man and wife.* [236]

So, the Kinsey team producing *Pregnancy, Birth and Abortion* says the couple "had to consider themselves married and live together openly as man and wife." However, neither of these two variables, a) considering themselves married or b) living together openly as man and wife, were part of the "married" definition in *Sexual Behavior in the Human Female*—the book from which these abortion data were said to be obtained.

PREGNANCY, BIRTH AND ABORTION

One cannot scientifically create a new definition years after data have been collected (if such information were collected). Since the bogus definition of "common law" relationships differs dramatically from the conduct of normal married women, Gebhard's, *et al*, abortion data would create legal, "husband and wife" data base. Gebhard, makes the following claims:

WIVES

Our white non-prison married women, taken as a unit, approximate the socio-economic upper 20 per cent of the urban population, but include an overrepresentation of women who have been separated, divorced, or widowed. ...*In the course of a lifetime... between one quarter and one fifth had an induced abortion.*[237]

SINGLES

Our white non-prison females when taken as a unit correspond to the socio-economically upper 20 per cent of the U.S. population... Of the pre-marital pregnancies that ended before marriage, 6 per cent were live births, 5 per cent spontaneous abortions, *and 89 per cent induced abortions.*[238] {Emphasis added.]

Moreover, the Kinsey team "showed" abortions may make happier marriages:

The data showed that orgasm in the first year of marriage for those who had a pre-marital induced abortion was about the same *or a little higher than for those without that experience. It was also found that females with a pre-marital induced abortion became separated, divorced, or widowed slightly less often than those without such an abortion.*[239]

"PLANNED PARENTHOOD: A PRACTICAL HANDBOOK OF BIRTH-CONTROL METHODS"

In 1965, the late Dr. Abraham Stone[240] and the late Dr. Norman Himes wrote *Planned Parenthood: A Practical Handbook of Birth-Control Methods*. The authors cite:

The problem of induced abortion in the United States was covered in depth at the 1955 Arden House Conference on Abortion sponsored by the Planned Parenthood Federation of America. *An attempt was made to determine the extent and size of the problem.* The late

Dr. Alfred C. Kinsey reported to this conference the results obtained by *his group sampling methods*. Abortion data was gathered by the Kinsey group as part of the total record of female sexual activity; the sample reported consisted of 4,248 pregnancies occurring in 5,299 white females. The proportion of *premarital conceptions in this group terminated by induced abortion was in the range of 88 to 95 per cent! Of the married women in the sample, 22 per cent had at least one abortion of an unwanted pregnancy by age forty-five.* Among all the single women who had had coitus, the abortion incidence was 20 per cent.[241]

The attempt to show massive abortions—and the harmlessness of abortion—required that the Kinsey team find, as they did, that abortions were largely beneficial. They actually improved marriages, and were found safe and morally acceptable to the medical profession. But, to do so meant that almost all abortions had to be carried out by "physicians" with largely favorable results.[242] To accomplish this flight of fancy, the Kinsey team returned to their successful ploy of redefining the common English language—like that of "married" women—which inevitably misled and confused legislators, the public and other scholars, as well as judges and juries. The Gebhard abortion team reported:

> *"Physicians" accounted for about 85 per cent of the abortions in our white non-prison sample, although in some of these cases the "physician" did not have a medical license.* Although operative techniques were reported to have been used in over 90 per cent of our white non-prison sample, they were reported in only 72 per cent of the white prison sample...[243] [Emphasis added.]

THE NATIONAL COMMITTEE ON MATERNAL HEALTH (NCMH)

So, the Gebhard team claims a "physician" (their quotes) is a physician even without a medical license (ignored in the pro-abortion debate). And, how many were "some physicians"? Were 50 percent, 75 percent, 90 percent, 99 percent, "some" without a license? The claim that most abortions were so uncomplicated and morally neutral that they were customarily performed illegally by medical doctors, got wide distribution via Planned Parenthood and SIECUS:

> [A]t the 1942 abortion conference sponsored by the National Committee on Maternal Health (NCMH) at the New York Academy of Medicine, NCMH chairman Dr. Robert L. *Dickinson stated that 75% percent of all illegal abortions were performed by physicians*. His remark went unchallenged.[244]

As a relevant aside, recall that Pomeroy—speaking at the New York Academy of Medicine—explained this same chairman of the NCMH, Dr. Robert L. Dickinson, originally found and "trained" Rex King. King was the child rapist who provided Kinsey with hundreds of child "orgasms." Pomeroy's admission was confirmed by Kinsey colleague Paul Tripp on Yorkshire television's *"Kinsey's Paedophiles."* Dickinson directed King in his child abuse research protocol because, said Tripp, science might as well "get something out of" King's rape activities so that he did not merely satisfy "his jollies." Is this NCMH the derivation of today's Child and Maternal Health Bureau, CMHB, which oversees America's health care workers on issues of child sexuality, abstinence, abortion and the like?

At the 1955 abortion conference sponsored by the Planned Parenthood Federation of America and attended by a host of birth control proponents and others who would play major roles in the legalization of abortion, the question of physician-induced abortion came up. *The discussion leader on this point was the famed sex researcher, Alfred Kinsey, who was introduced by conference chairman Guttmacher as someone who could "give us the naked facts." Providing a breakdown of illegal abortions, Kinsey stated that 87% of induced abortions were performed by doctors* and about 8% were self-induced, and these could be ignored and it would not change the overall illegal abortion picture [Emphasis added.][245]

Dr. Mary S. Calderone, an editor of the Planned Parenthood conference proceedings, parlayed Kinsey's conclusions. She wrote in 1960:

The conference estimated that 90 percent of all illegal abortions are done by physicians. Call them what you will, abortionists or anything else, they are still physicians, trained as such; and many of them are in good standing in their communities.... Whatever trouble arises usually comes after self-induced abortions, which comprise approximately 8 %, or with the very small percentage that go to some kind of non-medical abortionist. Another corollary fact: physicians of impeccable standing are referring their patients for these illegal abortions to the colleagues they know are willing to perform them...

Planned Parenthood president Dr. Alan E Guttmacher acknowledged that in… 1970, after abortion laws had passed several states [he had a] query from an Ohio physician [seeking an abortionist]. Guttmacher responded within a fortnight [with] two proficient abortionists in New York City.

* * * *

In light of Kinsey's figure that 90% of all abortions were done by bona fide doctors, Guttmacher's reference to only two physician abortionists in all of New York City [versus hundreds in the Ohio area] leads to an interesting situation: either illegal abortion was not as big a problem as Planned Parenthood claimed it was, or even doctors could not do them safely. But as Guttmacher believed in the safety of physician-induced abortion, that leaves a smaller illegal abortion problem. Cross checking these various "stories" at the time could have put the illegal abortion thesis to rout.[246]

PREGNANCY, BIRTH AND ABORTION

The Kinsey team producing *Pregnancy, Birth and Abortion* discusses abortion data on black women and women who were in prison. Kinsey purged all data on black women in *Sexual Behavior in the Human Female* and avoided the glaring data on early sexual abuse among incarcerated women, especially among prostitutes. However, the Kinsey team that produced *Pregnancy, Birth and Abortion* also claims that teenagers were using (illegal) contraception regularly and responsibly. Indeed, these "experts" resolved that in 1958, adolescents appeared to be sterile until they reached about age 17, no doubt in order to explain America's low rates of out-of-wedlock births.

> While frequency of coitus is an obvious factor in whether or not a female becomes pregnant, there are numerous other factors, some of which are of prime importance ... *There is evidence that adolescent females under seventeen are relatively sterile.* Anthropologists have noted this so-called "adolescent sterility" in other cultures and it has received some attention in our own....
>
> [And] of the 156 girls on whom we have detailed contraceptive information and who experienced pre-marital coitus within three years following their menarche, only *11 per cent failed to use contraceptives* while 11 per cent used them occasionally *and 78 per cent used them regularly*.[247] [Emphasis added.]

These "observations" are absurd. The age of menses was slightly higher in the 1920s-1940s than the current 13 years. Yet the notion that 78 percent of these girls walked to the corner drug store to ask Mr. Jones, the family pharmacist, for condoms and then efficiently used this contraband, flies in the face of history, logic and hard data. So the question is—whose interests would be served by data showing massive numbers of harmless abortions?

If sex education was to become a reality, the team producing *Pregnancy, Birth and Abortion* had to convince the public and the judiciary that child sexual activity was harmless. The team's data showing almost no childhood pregnancy, abortion or venereal disease accompanied that end. Like Kinsey, Gebhard's Kinsey team producing *Pregnancy, Birth and Abortion* defied logic, human experience and medical science. There was no evidence for the "adolescent sterility" concocted by Gebhard and his "anthropologists." The rate of births to unmarried teenagers, 15-19 years old, jumped from 12.6 percent in 1950 to 44.6 percent in 1992.[248] And the increase in teenage sexually transmitted diseases is significantly higher.

Since the sale of contraception was restricted until 1960, one wonders whether the entire scientific, literate world was intellectually paralyzed following the release of the Kinsey reports. Scientists claimed widespread teen sexual activity, without venereal disease, childbirth or abortion. "Seventy-eight percent" of young girls use contraception *regularly*, they said, and in this unique era, girls are temporarily, "sterile."[249]

NORMALIZING PROSTITUTION AND NARCOTICS

Kinsey's books on women and men said nothing about drug abuse. And little was said about obscenity except that it is harmless and some women object because of sexual repression. As noted, venereal disease, pregnancy and abortion were barely mentioned. Even drug and alcohol use by prostitutes rated no data. Yet, the Kinsey-Gebhard group claimed that *normal* women were commonly premaritally active sexually, resulting in massive harmless abortions. And these abortions required legalization.

Of course, prostitutes—the most sexually active women and girls—were also major abortion and drug customers. Law enforcement was in the midst of a vigorous attack on the narcotics trade during the Kinsey survey period. Yet narcotics were rife among the "underworld" figures from whom Kinsey collected sex histories. Even Kinsey's good friend, Harry Benjamin, who refers to the pedophile judge, Rene Guyon, as "the great Frenchman," admits in his book *Prostitution and Morality* (1965):

> Some young addicts become "street-walkers" at ten, twelve, fifteen. So far as we have been able to determine most young prostitute-addicts are members of impoverished families, and

usually of minority groups such as Negroes, Puerto Ricans, etc. The vast majorities are to be found in a few large cities...[250] [Researchers declare] approximately 50 per cent of all prostitutes are addicts. Other estimates have ranged as high as 75 per cent.[251]

The Kinsey team interviewed hundreds of male and female prostitutes and spent a massive amount of time discussing men's use of prostitutes.[252] But they said nothing about the origins of—or consequences of—prostitution, STDs, alcohol, drug addiction and suicide. Benjamin and Masters, after describing the horrors of prostitution and extensively citing Kinsey's interviews with prostitutes, *called for legalizing prostitution as an outlet for men.* They suppress all data about homosexual abuse of boys.

Kinsey covered up the drug-abuse-prostitution connection. Benjamin and Masters largely trivialize drug and alcohol use by prostitutes. Yet, they describe what the Kinsey team must have learned from in-depth interviews with prostitutes:

> An unknown number of the drug addicts [prostitutes] are murdered by "pushers" by means of the "hot shot," an overdose of heroin, or narcotics laced with strychnine or some other lethal poison. According to addicts, such murders are numerous, but they seem almost never to be mentioned in the newspaper. The addicts explain this by saying that the police policy is to consider "a dead junkie, good riddance," and never to bother with investigating such homicides or listing them as such.[253]

Such murders, numerous or rare in "the trade," are unmentioned in *Sexual Behavior in the Human Male* or *Sexual Behavior in the Human Female*. Kinsey specialized in collecting histories from prostitutes in poverty-ridden areas of New York City and Chicago. Yet he ignored the early sex abuse, STDs, alcoholism, drug addiction, pregnancy, abortion, homosexuality, battery, and murder common among 200 male and unknown numbers of female prostitutes. There is no mention of the causes of prostitution or of drug use in *Sexual Behavior in the Human Female*, and only two citations in the *Sexual Behavior in the Human Male* index. One cite explains that some men have sexual problems when they are denied a drug to which they have become addicted.[254] The other assures the reader that marijuana is not a drug. Yet it admits that those who are intoxicated with it are "unreliable."[255] All these claims were continually reinforced by a litany of world-renowned scholars and sundry other experts.[256]

PART VIII: NORMALIZING SODOMY AND MASTURBATION

Alfred Kinsey fathered not only the sexual revolution in general, but the "bisexuality/gay rights" movement in particular. Movement leaders have cited the "pioneering" work of Kinsey and his team as the scientific basis for normalizing sodomy, the only "intimate" form of homosexual "intercourse."

Webster's 1828 dictionary defined "sodomy" as simply "a crime against nature." *Black's Law Dictionary* (1963) more precisely defined it as "carnal copulation, against the order of nature, by man with man, or, in the same unnatural manner, with woman or with a beast," including "penetration of the mouth," which as "fellatio" was considered sodomy by a majority of states, though excluded by others.

Kinsey claimed that nearly everyone practiced masturbation. Moreover, no harm could ever result from it. This has led to widespread excuses to teach children about masturbation—even "how to" in school classrooms, while facilitating its use in graphic pornographic productions. Solicitations for masturbation either as voyeurs or participants became largely decriminalized, leading to increased solicitation and seduction of boys into part-time and homosexual prostitution. Moreover, Kinsey's own death, arguably from brutal masturbatory obsessions, coincides with the roughly 1,000 deaths said to occur annually due to autoerotic asphyxia. Most of the dead are young boys and men, raising questions about the inherent "harmlessness" of normalizing masturbation for individuals and society.

KINSEY SCALE #1

Another book could be written about Kinsey's influence on second-generation legal and social articles which are driving changes in laws. These laws involve sex education, "gay" marriage, "gay" adoption, the codification of "hate crimes," "hate speech," and the proliferation of special non-discrimination laws requiring unrestricted "gay" access to housing and employment.

Such legal support of sodomy and homosexuality is largely based on perhaps the most oft-cited graph in social science history: the "Kinsey Scale." The "scale" supplanted the prevailing biological and legal understanding of the creation of two separate sexes with a radical different notion. It claimed to show "scientifically" that there are many "sexualities," and that normal human sexuality is a changing, androgynous bisexuality.

Figure 161. Heterosexual-homosexual rating scale
Based on both psychologic reactions and overt experience, individuals rate as follows:
0. Exclusively heterosexual with no homosexual
1. Predominantly heterosexual, only incidentally homosexual
2. Predominantly heterosexual, but more than incidentally homosexual
3. Equally heterosexual and homosexual
4. Predominantly homosexual, but more than incidentally heterosexual
5. Predominantly homosexual, but incidentally heterosexual
6. Exclusively homosexual

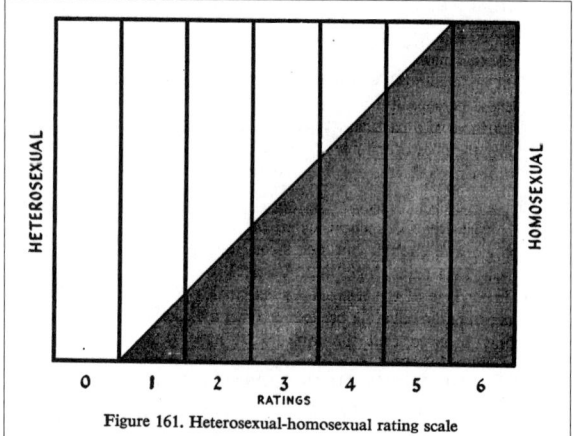

The scale slides from exclusively homosexual ("6") to exclusively heterosexual ("0"). It is the basis for the apocryphal claim that 10 percent to 37 percent of men are "sort of" homosexual.[257] The law has reacted to this concept of bisexuality in a number of ways. Protections for women and children, and penalties for sexual offenses based upon the pre-Kinsey notion of the inherent differences between the sexes have largely diminished or eliminated in these "gender neutral" times. Moreover, schools teach children that they may be homosexual—*and* they are just as likely bisexual. As a result, teachers and students nationwide are organizing "Gay, Lesbian, Bisexual and Transgendered" youth groups in schools nationwide.

THE APA YIELDS TO KINSEY AND THE LAW TO THE APA

A watershed in the drive to normalize sodomy was reached when the American Psychiatric Association, largely on the basis of Kinsey's research, opted to change its diagnostic manual. The medical profession uses this manual to uniformly define pathologies in both the clinic and the courtroom. In 1973, homosexual advocates instigated a violent and extortionate political confrontation at a meeting of the APA. This disruption served to push Kinsey's data into the forefront as justification for a transformation in APA professional standards and sexual attitude.

As mentioned earlier, homosexuality was removed as a "disorder" from the *Diagnostic and Statistical Manual of Psychiatric Disorders*.[258] Soon thereafter, the American Psychological Association adopted the Kinseyan view of sodomy as harmless. Furthermore, social work and most other professional mental health organizations eventually fell in line. Today, in many elite circles sodomy is viewed as a sexual expression equivalent to normal marital relations—and quite possibly superior.

Sodomy was a crime in every state until 1961. However, Illinois became the first to decriminalize sodomy between consenting adults, assuming incorrectly, that sodomy only took place in the privacy of one's bedroom.[259] In 1988, new ground was broken in the sexual revolution.[260] A Maryland court upheld a conviction for sodomy committed between unmarried heterosexuals. But a dissenting opinion cited both Kinsey reports to argue for a more lenient approach to sex offenses:

> [P]ublic morality… condones rather than condemns this activity, and the degree… has not only dramatically increased over the past 40 years but is approaching universality, at least among married couples. *The conduct, in other words, is no longer regarded by the people as unnatural, or perverted, or unorthodox.*

Several key cases had earlier relied on Kinsey's data to support the conclusion that sodomy and other forms of illegal sex are common. In 1969,[261] an Alaska court had held:

> The epochal work of Sigmund Freud, the taxonomic studies of Alfred Kinsey, and the work of countless others, despite the controversy over their theories and conclusions, have nevertheless created a social and intellectual climate in which some of the revolutionary ideas of a generation ago have become the commonplaces of today.
>
> A re-examination of our entire regulation of sexual behavior by the criminal law may well be in order. The courts cannot, of course, perform such a comprehensive task, as it is beyond the capabilities of only the judiciary. But the widening gap between our formal statutory law and the actual attitudes and behavior of vast segments of our society can only sow the seeds of increasing disrespect for our legal institutions.

A footnote accompanying that last sentence reprised and summarized Kinsey's claim that "if all infractions of sexual laws were punished, 95 percent of the male population would have to be convicted of a crime at one time or another, and a majority of the males would be in the category of repeated offenders."[262]

Continuing the "harmless sexual revolution" scenario—in 1951, a Minnesota court held that it was an error to permit a witness to testify that the husband had engaged in a homosexual act prior to his marriage. In a footnote, the court stated:

> The rule, which excludes evidence of one wrongful act for the purpose of showing that the accused has a propensity to commit similar acts, is one of long standing. As applied to the field of homosexual offenses, the continued application of the rule is justified by the results of recent scientific studies. See, Kinsey Pomeroy Martin, *Sexual Behavior in the Human Male* (1948) c. 21. [See *Luley v. Luley*, 48 N.W.2d at 330, n.4].[263]

In a 1977 New York Family Court case, a law forbidding "deviate" prostitution was held to be unconstitutional. The court relied on Kinsey in concluding that sodomy is neither harmful nor contrary to nature.[264] A few years earlier, in a 1973 Tennessee case, the court had upheld a sodomy statute, but a dissenting judge relied on Kinsey to argue that the proscribed activity is "approved by almost 90 percent of adults between 18 and 34." To hold it is a crime," he said, "would seem to me to be judicial legislation of the plainest kind."[265]

In increasing numbers of court cases and legislative challenges to sodomy statutes, Kinsey, the ALI's MPC, and/or the American Psychiatric Association manual have been cited to bolster the conclusion that fornication, adultery, abortion, sodomy, homosexual activity, and prostitution are all common and innocuous. (See *Wasson v. Commonwealth*, 843 S.W. 2d 487 (Ky. 1992)).

KINSEY SCALE #2

The "Kinsey Scale" also surfaced in the District of Columbia case, *Gay Rights Coalition v. Georgetown University* (1987).[266] The court cited Kinsey in holding that Georgetown University could be compelled to provide recognition to a homosexual student group:

> From Kinsey's study of twelve thousand white males, still the largest of its kind, Kinsey reported that only 50% had neither overt nor psychic homosexual experiences after the onset of adolescence.[267] Another 37% had at least some overt homosexual experience to the point of orgasm between adolescence and old age, while the remaining 13% reacted erotically to other males without having physical contacts. Almost half of his sample had both heterosexual and homosexual experiences at some point during their lives.[268] Kinsey's findings challenged the popular assumption that the vast majority of people are either exclusively heterosexual or exclusively homosexual and suggested that instead individual sexual responses and behavior fall somewhere between extremes for some 46% of the population.[269] While stressing the existence of a continuum, for convenience Kinsey adopted a seven-point scale, with zero denoting the exclusively homosexual and six the exclusively heterosexual.[270] The Kinsey scale continues to be relied upon today. Shortly afterwards, Kinsey found a similar diversity of sexual responses and behavior among women.[271] At a minimum, Kinsey's research claimed a diversity of human sexual orientations and prompted considerable further inquiry.

Here, from the thousands of cases involving obscenity, homosexuality, sodomy, and related issues, is a sample of cases that further reveal the ALI-MPC-Kinsey in the APA legal revolution.

In *Acanfora v. Board of Education of Montgomery County* (1973),[272] a Maryland court upheld the discharge of a teacher[273] for speech and other non-sexual activities. But it asserted he could not be discharged merely because he is a homosexual. The court argued, "Assuming further no significant decline in homosexuality since the famous Kinsey report, the law raises additional concern over the impossibility of compliance, contributing to contempt for the legal system."[274]

In *Rowland v. Mad River Local School District*,[275] the U.S. Court of Appeals for the Sixth Circuit upheld the discharge of a homosexual employee. But a dissenting opinion (dissents often portend future case law and may be cited as authoritative in other cases) relied on Kinsey, claiming that Kinsey had proven that homosexual activity by both sexes is common—thus normal, thus legal.[276]

In *Boutilier v. Immigration and Naturalization Service* (1966), which was subsequently affirmed by the Supreme Court,[277] the U.S. Court of Appeals for the Second Circuit held that a homosexual was properly found to be a person of "psychopathic personality" and could be refused entry to the United States. The majority, however, cited Kinsey's data on homosexual behavior,[278] and a dissenting judge stated:

> [T]hat the legislative history [of the 1952 amendments to the Immigration and Nationality Act] should not be read as imputing to Congress a purpose to classify under the heading

> "psychopathic personality" every person who had ever had a homosexual experience. *Professor Kinsey estimated that "at least 37 per cent" of the American male population has at least one homosexual experience, defined in terms of physical contact to the point of orgasm, between the beginning of adolescence and old age.*[279]

Kinsey's *Male* volume, given as the reference at that point and lengthy quotation from the report, was included in a footnote.

When the U.S. Supreme Court affirmed the lower court's ruling, the majority specifically held that Congress did indeed intend to include homosexuals among those deemed to be afflicted with a "psychopathic personality," and therefore excludable under our immigration laws. But in a dissent, Justice William O. Douglas quoted from Kinsey to support his argument that,

> It is not possible to insist that any departure from the sexual mores, or any participation in socially taboo activities, always or even usually, involves a neuroses or psychosis, for the case histories abundantly demonstrate that most individuals who engage in taboo activities make satisfactory social adjustments. There are, in actuality, few adult males who are particularly disturbed over their sexual histories. Psychiatrists, clinical psychologists, and others who deal with cases of maladjustment, sometimes come to feel that most people find difficulty in adjusting their sexual lives; but a clinic is no place to secure incidence figures. The incidence of tuberculosis in a tuberculosis sanitarium is no measure of the incidence of tuberculosis in the population as a whole; and the incidence of disturbance over sexual activities among the persons who come to a clinic, is no measure of the frequency of similar disturbances outside of clinics. The impression that such "sexual irregularities" as "excessive masturbation," pre-marital intercourse… mouth-genital contacts, homosexual activity, or animal intercourse, always produce psychoses and abnormal personalities is based upon the fact that the persons who do go to professional sources for advice are upset by these things.

> It is unwarranted to believe that particular types of sexual behavior are always expressions of psychoses or neuroses. In actuality, they are more often expressions of what is biologically basic in mammalian and anthropoid behavior and of a deliberate disregard for social convention. Many of the socially and intellectually most significant persons in our histories, successful scientists, educators, physicians, clergymen, business men, and persons of high position in governmental affairs, have socially taboo items in their histories, and among them they have accepted nearly the whole range of so-called sexual abnormalities. Among the socially most successful and personally best adjusted persons who have contributed to the present study, there are some whose rates of outlet are as high as those in any case labeled nymphomania or satyriasis in the literature, or recognized as such in the clinic.[280]

In *One Eleven Wines & Liquors, Inc. v. Division of Alcoholic Beverage Control* (1967),[281] a New Jersey court reversed the denial of a liquor license which had been refused on the grounds that homosexuals were allowed to congregate at the bar. It relied on the "expert" testimony of Wardell Pomeroy, Kinsey's co-author and a current leader in the sex therapy and AIDS education industry. Appearing in court, Pomeroy said he:

> was associated with the Kinsey Institute for twenty years and was the co-author of several books dealing with sexual behavior and offenses. He referred to the Kinsey studies, which

contained startling indications that 13%t of the males in the country were more homosexual than heterosexual and that 37% had at least one homosexual experience to the point of orgasm in the course of their life. He also referred to indications that 55 percent of the population was neutral on the subject of homosexuality and there is now a more acceptance attitude than there was twenty years ago.... In response to an inquiry by the division's hearing, Dr. Pomeroy voiced the opinion that no adverse social effects would result from permitting homosexuals to congregate in licensed establishments.[282]

NORMALIZING SODOMY/HOMOSEXUALITY IN THE MILITARY

Political decisions approving homosexuality in our Armed Forces under the guise of a "don't ask, don't tell" policy may be viewed as the result of Kinsey-based studies. Prior to July 19, 1993, Rand's National Defense Research Institute submitted a report to then-Secretary of Defense Les Aspin, purporting to provide current information, research, and analysis that would "end discrimination on the basis of sexual orientation in the Armed Forces." The 518-page study was entitled *Sexual Orientation and U.S. Military Personnel Policy: Options and Assessment*. It claimed to be an independent, multi-disciplinary, million-dollar, taxpayer-funded study of the most volatile political issue of President Clinton's first year in office. Citing Kinsey, it claimed that sexual orientation is "not germane" to military service:

> Kinsey and associates (1948) did not use "homosexual" or "heterosexual" as nouns characterizing people, but rather as adjectives characterizing an act. In their landmark study, they created a seven-point scale—which came to be known as the "Kinsey scale"—to place individuals along a continuum ranging from exclusively heterosexual (0) to exclusively homosexual (6), according to his or her current or cumulative lifetime sexual experiences and sexual feelings. All intermediate points indicated personal histories with a mixture of homosexual and heterosexual acts and/or feelings. Kinsey, et al[283] found that most of those who ever engaged in homosexual acts had engaged in a greater proportion of heterosexual acts. In contemporary society, it appears that bisexuality is still more prevalent than exclusive homosexuality; the probability studies presented in the previous section support the generalization that a majority of men who report male-male sexual contacts in adulthood also report female sexual partners in adulthood.[284] ...Rand researchers re-analyzed a 1982 reader survey that appeared in *Playboy*.[285]

> Dr. Kinsey says: "You have correctly interpreted the data, which you are using from our book. Certainly, there is no question that the reality of the total situation needs to be drawn to the attention of the country. Hysteria thrives best when only a small segment of the picture is understood." The Senate subcommittee investigating employment of "homosexuals and other moral perverts" by the Federal government had better read the Kinsey report before it goes very far. Dr. Alfred C. Kinsey and his associates found, for instance, that 4% of the white males of this country are "exclusively homosexual throughout their lives after the onset of adolescence." ...If this figure can be applied to the 1,419,674 male Civil Service employees, it means that 56,787 federal employees are "exclusively homosexual." If it were legitimate to apply the figure to the white male

members of Congress, it would mean that 21 Senators and Representatives are "exclusively homosexual."[286] ...Selective Service boards and Armed Forces sources give a total figure of about 1% of our wartime military strength officially identified as "homosexual." The Kinsey figures show nearly 30% of men of the age group included in the Armed Forces as having some homosexual experience at that period in their lives. "The most obvious explanation of the very low figures of the Armed Forces sources," Dr. Kinsey went on, "lies in the fact that both the Army and Navy had precluded the possibility of getting accurate data on these matters by announcing at the beginning of the war that they intended to exclude all persons with homosexual histories... Consequently, few men with any common sense would admit their homosexual experience to draft boards or to psychiatrists at induction centers or in the services."[287]

The historic origin of U.S. sodomy statutes, including those applicable to the military, was included in *Military Necessity & Homosexuality* (1993), a book provided to the Joint Chiefs of Staff and most active duty flag and general officers prior to implementation of the "don't ask, don't tell" policy.[288]

How the Joint Chiefs accepted such a revolutionary change in military law is documented by former Defense Department official, Colonel Ronald D. Ray in "Lifting the Ban on Homosexuals in the Military: The Subversion of a Moral Principle."[289]

> The President, the Congress, and the Joint Chiefs, relying on the Kinsey-driven Rand Study, ignored and overturned the historic first principles of the U.S. military written by General George Washington for the Continental Army, and John Adams for the U.S. Navy, and adopted by the Continental Congress on November 28, 1775. Those principles were in effect by U.S. statute and military regulation when Bill Clinton was sworn in as president in January 1993.
>
> They consisted of "virtue, honor and patriotism," and specifically charged all U.S. commanding officers, "to guard against and suppress all dissolute, immoral and disorderly practices" and "to take all necessary and proper measures... to promote and safeguard the morale, the physical well-being, and the general welfare... [of those] under their command."[290] Acceptance of "don't ask, don't tell," by the Joint Chiefs relying on Kinsey's skewed research amounted to a surrender of that standard that had served the nation long and well.[291]

SUMMING UP

It is left to others to fully document the scores of additional cases citing Kinsey and his disciples that have emerged since this author gathered the information for this chapter. In sum, the American Law Institute should revisit all uses of Kinsey's skewed data and the data from his disciples, and their disciples, etc., in the ALI-MPC. Moreover, a neutral task force should initiate a full and open public investigation of the impact of Kinsey's false data on our nation's laws, the military, our schools, churches, the news and entertainment media, academia, our families—all of our cultural, political, and religious institutions.

Once the facts are gathered, the task force should draft the needed corrections to our current legal system. Scientific fraud has been acknowledged and investigated in several areas. The Office of Scientific Inquiry at the National Institutes of Health recently reported that it was reviewing nearly 100 cases of alleged fraud or misconduct. In 1988, the renowned scholar Dr. Stephen Breuning was convicted of a crime and punished for scientific fraud because, the prosecutor argued:

> His well-established reputation was considered instrumental in forming public health policy nationally. The NIMA panel said last spring that several states amended treatment practices as a result.... There was no evidence presented in the indictment that the therapy advocated by Breuning actually helped or hurt the children... just that the research wasn't done...[292]

Dr. Stephen Breuning was convicted and punished for scientific fraud because "his well-established reputation was considered instrumental in forming public health policy nationally," despite the fact that there was no evidence that "Breuning actually helped or hurt the children." Therefore, the Kinsey Institute team and Indiana University should be held accountable for their actions and omissions, including a pattern of scientific fraud, the protection of pedophiles and their employment as molesters as "trained observes."

Paralleling the Breuning case, the Kinsey team and the Kinsey Institute also have a "well established reputation" in the field of human sexuality/sexology, and are "considered instrumental in forming public health policy nationally."

Writing in the journal *Science*,[293] Daniel E. Koshland, Jr., observed that fraud is "unacceptable," especially since all of science is "based on trust," but seemed certain that "an important finding [of fraud] will become exposed." Koshland claimed that "there is no modern equivalent of Piltdown man, a fraud that took years to uncover." Yet, as we have seen, Kinsey likely is. Scores of letters, phone calls, and faxes to *Science* and Koshland resulted in silence about Kinsey's findings. Official public scrutiny of the Kinsey record could expose perhaps the greatest scientific scandal of all time.

With that in mind, the time has come for a full investigation of the Kinsey Institute and everyone involved who knew or should have known about the false authorities that they relied upon to make judgments affecting the American public. The American Law Institute, the APA and our most prestigious and influential law schools have a huge moral and legal obligation to recall the laws and policies made that were based on fraudulent scientific authority. All Kinsey-influenced laws and judicial decisions should be revisited with the goal of crafting new statutes and rulings based on accurate information. This would necessitate opening all Kinsey Institute records to an independent investigation of Professor Alfred Kinsey and his team who operated on the taxpayer payroll for Kinsey's entire career at Indiana University. An honest, public investigation could pave the way for correcting the consequences of a half-century of lies, deception and unconscionable crime.

UPDATE 2011

Since January 2000 over 90 commonly laudatory citations to Kinsey's data have appeared in USA Law Review Journals. Their 90 authors use Kinsey's "data" to continue shaping our laws on marriage, adultery, abortion, sexual "orientation," sodomy, housing, adoption, child custody, sex offense reductions, registration, education, "compulsory monogamy," counseling, obscenity, pornography, child hearsay, homosexual immutability, natural law, cyber-predators, the sex industry, anti-discrimination statutes, family in prisons, behavioral addictions, due process, informational privacy, civil justice, opportunistic bias crimes, hemophilic mandates for health care providers, Lawrence v TX, "Gays" in the Military, Transgender immigration, cohabitation, sex trafficking, econometric abortion analyses, sex torts, homosexual parenting, securities class actions, sexual psychopath law, indecency censorship, school safety for "gays", race and "gay" identity, cinematic psychological conceptions, personal v community, gay pornography, the first amendment, polygamy, global human rights protection, transgendered prisoners, a breach of vows, homophobia and sexism, states' rights, transgender health care, religious liberty, Title VII, pedophiles and cyber-predators, unborn victims of violence act, federalism, Wechsler and the Model Penal Code, prostitution, teen oral sex felons, pro-life suppression, science identity, sexual harassment, etc..

E.g., in 2004, the Alabama district court "replete with cites to the Kinsey studies" found "a constitutionally inherent right to sexual privacy... premarital intercourse, marriage," citing Kinsey's impact on the "imagery and implements of adult sexual relationships" via "the availability of "pornography," etc., while in 2007, Australia's High Court Justice Kirby thanked Kinsey for shaping his views and rulings on human sexuality and for laying "the fault lines of civilizations." Indeed. Yes. Indeed.

To get more updates on this matter, please visit:

DrJudithReisman.com/laws

CHAPTER 8 NOTES

[1] Noah Webster, "Law, 1," *American Dictionary Of The English Language* 1928 www.lexrex.com/catalog/webster 1828.htm.

[2] George Washington, "First Inaugural Address In the City of New York, April 30, 1789," *Inaugural Address Of The Presidents Of The United States* 1989 (www.bartleby.com).

[3] Quote from speech by Judge Bork, cited in Barbara Olson, *Hell To Pay*, Regnery Publishing, Washington, D.C., 1999, p. 52.

[4] *This is ALI-ABA*. Brochure, unpaginated, The American Law Institute, Philadelphia, Penn., October 18, 1995, p. 1.

[5] Jonathan Gathorne-Hardy, *Sex, Alfred C. Kinsey, The Measure of All Things*, Chatto & Windus, London, 1998, p. 449.

[6] Id., p. 158.

[7] John Kaplan and Robert Weisberg, *Criminal Law, Cases and Materials, Second Edition*, Little, Brown and Company, Law Book Division, Boston, Mass., Appendix B, "A Note on the Model Penal Code", 1991, pp. 1165-1168.

[8] *This is the American Law Institute*, Rev. Brochure, unpaginated, The American Law Institute, Philadelphia, July 1995, p. 1.

[9] Gerald Gunther, *Learned Hand: The Man and the Judge*, Alfred A. Knopf, New York, 1994, p. 410.

[10] The American Law Institute Annual Reports, May 14-17, Washington, D.C., 1996, p. 19.

[11] Morris Ploscowe, "Sexual Patterns and the Law," in *Sex Habits of American Men, A Symposium on the Kinsey Report* (Albert Deutsch, editor), Prentice Hall, New York, 1948, pp. 125-126.

[12] Id., pp. 133-134.

[13] *Life Magazine*, August 24,1953, p. 11.

[14] See Albert Deutsch, "Foreword," in *Sex Habits of American Men: A Symposium on the Kinsey Report* (Albert Deutsch, editor), Prentice Hall, New York, 1948, p. viii..

[15] Albert Hobbs, *Social Problems and Scientism*, The Telegraph Press, Harrisburg, PA, 1953, pp. 101-102.

[16] "The Fifty Worst Books of the Century," *The Intercollegiate Review*, Intercollegiate Studies Institute, Delaware, Fall, 1999.

[17] Dr. Harry Benjamin, "Introduction" to Rene Guyon, *The Ethics Of Sexual Acts*, Alfred A. Knopf, New York, 1948, pp. h-i.

[18] *About the Kinsey Report*, Donald Porter Geddes and Enid Curie, editors, The New American Library of World Literature, 1nc., New York, 1948.

[19] The titles and names of the authors should be of interest to some readers: *New Light on Sexual Knowledge*, By Donald Porter Geddes; *Sexual Behavior Among Primitive Peoples* By Clellan Ford, Ph.D., Associate Professor of Anthropology, Yale University; *Sex is God-Given*, By Frederick C. Kuether, B.D., Director, Council for Clinical Training; *Sex and Character: the Kinsey Report Viewed from the Standpoint of Psychoanalysis*, By Erich Fromm, Ph.D., Lecturer at Yale University, Bennington College, and the New School for Social Research; *Understanding Our Sexual Desires*, By M. F. Ashley Montagu, Ph.D., Professor of Anatomy, Hahnemann Medical College and Hospital, Philadelphia; *Sex on the Campus*, By G.M. Gilbert, Ph.D., Associate Professor of Psychology, Princeton University; *Sex: and Social Attitudes*, By Robert M. MacIver, Ph.D., Lieber Professor of Sociology, Columbia University; *Sex and Human Love*, By O. Spurgeon English, M.D., Professor of Psychiatry, Temple University; *The Limits of Sexual Law*, By Karl N. Llewellyn, J.D., Professor o! Law, Columbia University, *Sex and Class Behavior*, By Eli Ginzberg, Ph.D., Professor of Economics, Columbia University, *Who Educates Our Children?* By Benjamin C. Gruenberg, Ph.D., Biologist and Educator; *'The End of "Hush and Pretend"* By Robert L. Dickinson, M.D., Honorary Chairman, National Committee on Maternal Health.

[20] Fromm, supra, n. 19, in Geddes, supra, n. 18, pp. 48, 56. For example, Erich Fromm says Kinsey showed us our "social character," reprimanding those who had warned, "Kinsey could not possibly have unearthed such wealth of data in so short a time" when mental health professionals have much less success after much longer interviews.

[21] Montagu, supra, n. 19, in Geddes, supra, n. 18, p. 69.

[22] Id.

[23] Llewellyn, supra, n. 19, in Geddes, supra, n. 18, p. 113.

[24] Id., p. 116.

[25] Id., pp. 116-117.

[26] The Kinsey team can be clinically certified as "sexual sociopaths:" "Sociopath: One who is affected with a personality disorder marked by aggressive, antisocial behavior, " The American Heritage Dictionary of the English Language.

[27] See James Jones, *Alfred C. Kinsey: A Public/Private Life*, W.W. Norton & Company, New York, 1997, pp. 385, 502-503.

[28] Morris Ernst and David Loth, *American Sexual Behavior and The Kinsey Report*, Graystone Press, New York, 1948.

[29] Morris Ernst, "The Kinsey Report and the Law," in *Sexual Behavior in American Society*, Jerome Himehach and Sylvia Fava, editors, W.W. Norton, New York, 1948, pp. 247-248.

[30] Morris Ernst, *A Love Affair With The Law*, The MacMillan Company, New York, 1968, back cover.

[31] Claire Chambers, *The SIECUS Circle*, Western Islands, Belmont, Massachusetts, 1977, p. 29.

[32] Ronald D. Ray, "Kinsey's Legal Legacy," *The New American,* January 19, 1998, pp. 31-32.

[33] Ernst, *The Best is Yet......*, Harper & Brothers, New York, 1945, pp. 113-114.

[34] Alfred Kinsey, Wardell Pomeroy, Clyde Martin, *Sexual Behavior in the Human Male*, W.B. Saunders Company, Philadelphia, PA, 1948, pp. 390-392 (hereinafter "*Male*"). See full discussion of "upper level" judges, pp. 389-393.

[35] Ernst, supra, n. 30, pp. 103-104. Ernst always avoided juries in obscenity cases (p. 104) because, as Kinsey "proved," "the sexual activities of the poor and uneducated differ drastically from those of the wealthy and educated."

[36] *Male*, supra, n. 34, p. 392. The judge who is considering the case of the male who has been arrested for homosexual activity, should keep in mind that nearly 40 per cent of all the other males in the town could be arrested at some time in their lives for similar activity, and that 20 to 30 per cent of the unmarried males in that town could have been arrested for homosexual activity that had taken place within that same year. Id, p. 664.

[37] C.F. Turner, H.G. Miller and L.E. Moses, Eds. *AIDS, Sexual Behavior and Intravenous Drug Use,* National Research Council, National Academy Press, Washington, D.C., 1989, p. 79.

[38] Robert Dickinson, "Foreword" in Ernst and Loth, supra, n. 28, pp. vii-viii.

[39] Cornelia V. Christenson, *Kinsey: A Biography*, Indiana University Press, Bloomington, Indiana, 1971, p. 156.

[40] Wardell Pomeroy, *Dr. Kinsey and the Institute for Sex Research*, Harper & Row, New York, 1972, p. 344.

[41] Ernst and Loth, supra, n. 28, p. 127.

[42] Quote from speech by Judge Bork, cited in Barbara Olson, *Hell To Pay*, Regnery Publishing, Washington, D.C., 1999, p. 52.

[43] Timothy J. Gilfoyle, *City of Eros, New York City, Prostitution, and the Commercialization of Sex*, W. W. Norton, New York, 1992, p. 181.

[44] Speech by John Quincy Adams, July 4, 1821, found in William J. Federer, *America's God and Country*, Fame Publishing, Coppell, TX, 1994, p. 18.

[45] Intoduction, *Webster's 1828 Dictionary*, republished by Rosalie J. Slater, Foundation for American Christian Education, San Francisco, California, 1987, p. 10. (Quoting "*Preface to the History of the United States.*")

[46] *Church of the Holy Trinity v. United States,* 143 U.S. 457 (1892).

[47] Id., p. 471.

[48] Herbert W. Titus, *God, Man and Law: The Biblical Principles,* Institute in Basic Life Principles, Oak Brook, Illinois, 1994, p. 5.

[49] Id., p. 2.

[50] David Barton, *Original Intent: The Courts, The Constitution, & Religion*, WallBuilder Press, Aledo, Texas, 1996, p. 228-229.

[51] Daniel Lawrence O'Keefe, *Stolen Lightening: The Social Theory of Magic*, Continuum: New York, 1982. In 1982, Philosopher O'Keefe sheds some interesting light on the way in which Wechsler's call for "new" codes of sexual conduct is worked out in a republic such as ours. Said O'Keefe, "New legislation is produced by a new experiment; it is endlessly repeated and if it not only works but fits existing scientific paradigms it is gradually agreed upon, the various stages of "hypothesis," "theory," "law," etc., being like the stages of the bill going through Congress. Once the "bill" finally passes, the rule is of law and the experiment that legislated it is packaged to become part of the curriculum for all science students, who endlessly repeat it. The teacher-guided student group performing the experiment reproduces the social structure of the magical séance. Outside of the laboratory, deductive proofs are used which cite the experiment as a picture. And common speech arguments, carried on within the frame if paramount reality, cite these proofs and these experiments as ultimate authorities, more ultimate today than scripture. Why then are we surprised as the thing unfolds? Because as part of the game, we agree to psyche ourselves," pp. 106-107.

[52] Id.

[53] Herbert Wechsler, "The Challenge of a Model Penal Code", 65, *Harvard Law Review,* May 1952, 1097.

[54] David Allyn. "Private Acts/Public Policy: Alfred Kinsey, the American Law Institute and the Privatization of American Sexual Morality, " *Journal of American Studies*, 30, 1996, pp. 3, 405-428. [Emphasis added.]

[55] Ray, "Kinsey's Legal Legacy," supra, n. 32, p. 31.

[56] Wechsler, supra, n. 53, p. 1100.

[57] Id., p. 1103.

[58] Id.
[59] Id., p. 1102
[60] Id., p. 1103
[61] Id., p. 1102
[62] Id., p. 1106.
[63] Ploscowe, supra, n. 11, in Deutsch, *Sex Habits of American Men*, supra, n. 11, p. 126.
[64] Ernst and Roth, supra, n. 28, p. 83.
[65] Id., p. 81.
[66] Lawrence M. Friedman, *A History of American Law*, New York, New York, Simon & Schuster, 1985, p. 406.
[67] Brandeis' concern about the subversive nature of "philanthropies" is found in Rene Wormser, *Foundations: Their Power and Influence*, Covenant House, Sevierville, Tennessee, 1993, p. 6.
[68] Christopher Simpson, *Science of Coercion: Communication Research & Psychological Warfare* 1945-1960, Oxford University Press, New York, 1994, pp. 29-31. Eugenicists would close the book on the "fixed" view of human life, that is, the view of man and woman as in the image of God, as His agents, producing–within a protective and prescribed marital act–their own offspring and conferring to them "life, liberty and the pursuit of happiness," fundamental to the American way of life. Eugenicists bring the ancient theology to America. So while science was the method, religion was the aim.

Man in control and moving irreversibly closer to the *Brave New World is* detailed in Aldous Huxley's "fiction" where the words "mother and father" are obscenities; family's non-existent; adults totally promiscuous never marrying; and private property non-existent. Controlled offspring are produced in efficient state-run hatchery laboratories, "decanted" from test tubes, and raised in state sponsored institutions where they are encouraged to engage in "erotic play" on the playground. When depression and the meaninglessness of this life overwhelm them, the inhabitants self medicate at will using "soma," a drug to enhance and relax or to relieve anxiety or any cowardly reaction to their existence in the "brave new world." The Rockefeller agencies appear to be working toward a similar eugenic world for American law, medicine, social sciences, mass communications, and government, while neutralizing the Church and the ministry as effective representatives of the Creator's fixed order.

[69] Harold Keele and Joseph Kiger, editors., *The Greenwood Encyclopedia of American Institutions,* Vol. 8, *Foundations*, Greenwood Press, Westport Conn., 1984, pp. 364 .
[70] Manfred S. Guttmacher, M.D., *The Role of Psychiatry in Law*, Charles C. Thomas, Springfield, Illinois, 1968, Introduction, pp. v, vi.
[71] Alan Gregg Diary, July 7, 1950, pp. 1- 2, Rockefeller Archive Center.
[72] For the record, in the following year, in 1981, this author presented a paper entitled "The Scientist as Contributing Agent to Child Sexual Abuse: A Preliminary Consideration of Possible Ethics Violations" to sexuality specialists at the Fifth World Congress of Sexology in Jerusalem. This was the first public presentation of the child sex experiment data from the Kinsey report. There was standing room only in the conference session, and after the audience viewed the slides taken from Kinsey's own book of all of his child "orgasm" tables, a stunned silence followed the presentation. Finally, the exclamation from a Swedish reporter cut into the anxious room. He declared to those present, all leaders of the human sexuality "field" from many countries including England, Norway, Sweden, Denmark, Ireland, France, Canada, Germany and the United States, that this revelation on Kinsey's involvement with children is an "atomic bomb" and he demanded to know how they could just sit there. At that point, a Kinsey Institute representative stood (identified as "Joan Brewer") and challenged my presentation, saying these child data were from interviews and from one woman who watched her daughter. Then, conference keynoter, John Money of Johns Hopkins University, pushed open the main conference room double doors, strode into the room straight to the podium and was immediately handed the microphone from Richard Green the panel moderator. Money took this opportunity given to him at the podium by the moderator to advise all present whose livelihood depends on the study of sex that if "this woman [referring to this author] is allowed to continue sexology and sex education will be set back 200 years." Dr. Money, (recently exposed for his brutal, lying and botched role in coercing the parents of a baby boy to allow a sex change operation on the child, thereafter claiming the boy was a "happy" little girl) while in Israel for the Conference, would go on record in the *Jerusalem Post* as an advocate of "age-discrepant sex" or "man-boy love." The child data in Kinsey's own report had the ability, if widely known and understood, to undermine Kinsey's authority, largely halting the "free love" movement from intrusion into American institutions. The effort to stop this information in this book from reaching the American public and the legal profession has been monumental.
[73] Morris Ploscowe, *Sex and the Law,* Prentice Hall, New York, 1951.
[74] Allyn, supra, n. 54, p. 422.
[75] Ernst and Loth, supra, n. 28, p. 132.
[76] Id., p. 125.
[77] Titus, supra, n. 49, p. 2.
[78] The *Social Science Citation Index* and *the Science Citation Index* provide the most prestigious database in social science for references to specific scientists and scholars. Thus, when Kinsey or Freud are named in key books or articles in the science publications (not popular journals or press), one may be fully certain that the cited persons are impacting upon attitudes and behavior among reviewers and their readers ("behavior" means action). Simply citing Kinsey versus "God," for authority in addressing moral issues, for example, like adultery or pre-marital sex, may be seen as a definite action reflecting a body of belief. A complete breakdown of these citations and the history of the database are on file in the author's archive.
[79] Richard Posner, *Overcoming Law*, Harvard University Press, Cambridge, MA, 1995, pp. 54, 70.
[80] Id., p. 555.
[81] Ploscowe, "Sexual Patterns and the Law," in *Sex Habits of American Men*, supra, n. 11, p. 126.
[82] Id., pp. 125-126, 130.
[83] Id., pp. 133-134.
[84] Peggy Sanday, *A Woman Scorned, Acquaintance Rape on Trial*, Doubleday, New York, 1996, pp. 144-145. (Emphasis added).

85 Ronald Reagan, Preface to the *California Department of Justice, Crime Victims Handbook*, U.S. Department of Justice, 1981.
86 Paul Gebhard, "Designated Discussion" in *Ethical Issues in Sex Therapy and Research*, edited by William Masters, Virginia Johnson and Robert Kolndny, Little Brown & Co., Boston, 1977, p. 13.
87 Preliminary Report of *The Subcommittee on Sex Crimes of the Assembly Interim Committee on Judicial System and Judicial Process*, California Legislative Assembly, 1949, (Created by HR 232 and HR 43), pp. 103, 105, 117.
88 Pomeroy, supra, n. 40, p.122.
89 June 14, 1989, *The Washington Times*, F4.
90 *The Sciences*, "Why Men Rape," by Thornhill and Palmer, January/February 2000, pp. 31, 30. See also widespread coverage in press and on television typified by Roger Highfield, Science Editor, "Outrage as professors claim rape is natural," *London Telegraph*, Issue 1747, March 7, 2000.
91 Press release, Senator Heflin, Washington, D.C., June 27, 1996.
92 James Wootton, *Safe Streets*, Washington, DC. April 14, 1997.
93 *The Courier Journal*, February 27, 2000, A11.
94 Wechsler, supra, n. 53, pp. 1129-1130.
95 Pomeroy, supra, n. 40, pp. 207-208.
96 Id., p. 206.
97 Allyn, supra, n. 54, pp. 424-425, citing transcript of 1955 ALI draft committee meetings, pp. 86-133.
98 Id., pp. 425-427.
99 The American Law Institute, *Model Penal Code, Tentative Draft No. 4*, "207.1" Sex Offenses, April 25, 1955 (hereinafter "MPC").
100 Id., pp. 206-207.
101 Id., p. 207.
102 Id., p. 207.
103 Id., p. 208.
104 Id., p. 208.
105 *The Washington Post, Parade*, June 22, 1994.
106 Judith Reisman, *"SoftPorn" Plays Hard Ball*, Huntington House, Lafayette, LA, 1990, p. 36-37, citing Thomas Weyr, *Reaching for Paradise*, Times Books, New York, 1978, pp. 195-196.
107 Phyllis and Eberhard Kronhausen, *Sex Histories of American College Men*, Ballantine Books, New York, 1960.
108 Id., pp. 291-300.
109 Kinsey has no listing for "adultery" in the *Male* volume. Rather, Kinsey substitutes the non-legal definition of "extra marital coitus" as the first sex "science" setting legal precedent. Lying throughout the *Male* volume about his "correcting" for error based on "the U.S. census for 1940" gave all of Kinsey's fraudulent data weight in the minds and laws of this nation. It is assumed that since Kinsey made no distinction between homosexuals, rapists, pedophiles and all other men, his analyses of "adultery" would include all of these perverse people as "married" should they be in legal or illegal relations for any period of time. The *Female* volume includes an Index reference to "adultery: legal penalties" and with the reference, "See coitus, extra marital."
110 MPC, supra, n. 99, p. 207.
111 *USA Snapshots*, December 27, 1999.
112 Bryce Christensen, "Deadbeat Dads," in *The Family in America*, January 2000, pp. 1-7.
113 Id
114 Susan Estrich, "Rape," 95 The *Yale Law Journal* 1087, pp. 1134-1147, May 1986.
115 Id., p. 1137.
116 Beryl Levy, "What is Rape?" in *Sexology*, June 1961, pp. 744-748 (Emphasis in original).
117 Susan Brownmiller, *Against Our Will, Men, Women, and Rape*, Simon & Schuster, New York, 1975, p. 195.
118 Id., p. 1138.
119 Id., p. 1140.
120 Id
121 Id., p. 114.
122 Alfred Kinsey, Wardell Pomwery, Clyde Martin, Paul Gebhard, *Sexual Behavior in the Human Female*, W.B. Saunders, Philadelphia, PA, 1953, p. 53 (hereinafter "*Female*").
123 Although Kinsey's most recent biographer, James Jones, attempted to deflect his readers from a view of his subject as cold and inhuman by claiming Kinsey advocated laws against rape, Jones could provide no proof of Kinsey's support of *any* rape laws.
124 Ploscowe, "Sexual Patterns and the Law," in *Sex Habits of American Men*, supra, n. 11, p. 200; 1995, FBI New York data.
125 Sanday, supra, n. 84, p. 159.
126 Id., p. 67.
127 Ernst and Loth, supra, n. 28, pp. 19, 139.
128 Allyn, supra, n. 54, p. 421.
129 Albert Deutsch, "Kinsey, the Man and his Project," in *Sex Habits of American Men*, supra, n. 28, pp. 29-30.
130 Paul Gebhard, John Gagnon, Wardell Pomeroy, and Cornelia Christenson, *Sex Offenders*, Harper & Row and Paul B. Hoeber, Inc., Medical Books, New York, NY, 1965, p. 54.
131 Rene Guyon, *Sexual Freedom*, Greenwood Press, Westport, CT, 1963, pp. 25-26.
132 *Female*, supra, n. 122, pp. 20-21.

[133] Rene Guyon, *Sex Life and Sex Ethics*, John Lane the Bodley Head, Ltd., London, 1933, Introduction, pp. v, vi.
[134] At this time, many of the sexual "rights" of children promoted by Guyon and Kinsey are now encoded into the United Nations proclamation of the "Rights of the Child."
[135] *Female*, supra, n. 122, p. 107, (emphasis added).
[136] Id.
[137] Id., p. 121, n. 20.
[138] John Gagnon, *Human Sexualities*, Scott Foreman, & Co., Glenview IL, 1977, p. 303.
[139] Sellin/Wolfgang U.S. Department of Justice "National Survey of Crime Severity," U.S. Department of Justice, 1977.
[140] Current views of prostitution: "Until the 1960s, attitudes toward prostitution were based on the Judeo-Christian view of immorality. Researchers have recently attempted to separate moral issues from the reality of prostitution. The rationale for its continued illegal status in the U.S. rests on three assumptions: prostitution is linked to organized crime; prostitution is responsible for much ancillary crime; and prostitution is the cause of an increase in sexually transmitted disease. These assumptions are now in question. Whether it is rational to make one activity criminal in order to reduce or control another merits serious inquiry. Finally, public-health officials indicate that prostitutes account for only a small percentage of the sexually transmitted disease cases in the U.S. Greater sexual freedom has made young people the major source of such cases. Furthermore, strong arguments have been made in support of legalizing prostitution. Decriminalization would free the courts and police from handling victimless crime, allowing these forces more time to deal with serious and violent crimes. The constitutional question of violation of equal protection also has been raised, since the law penalizes prostitutes but not their customers. In the U.S. today, prostitution is legal only in the state of Nevada (at the option of each county government). Polls have shown that approximately half of the U.S. population would favor decriminalization of prostitution throughout the country." (*Encarta*, 1997).
[141] 513 P. 2d 889-897, n. 3 (CA) (1973) (Tobriner, dissenting).
[142] 407 F.2d 1238, 1248 (D.C. Cir. 1968) (Danaher, dissenting).
[143] 491 P.2d 1216, 1222, n. 8 (Hawaii, 1971) (Levinson, dissenting).
[144] Gagnon, supra, n. 137, p. 304.
[145] Judith Reisman, *Images of Children, Crime and Violence in Playboy, Penthouse and Hustler*, The U.S. Department of Justice, the Department of Juvenile Justice and Delinquency Prevention, Grant No. 84-JN-AX-K007, The Institute for Media Education, Arlington, VA, 1989, pp. 114-115. See also, Id, pp. 7-33, 177-180.
[146] Gagnon, supra, n. 137, pp. 303-304.
[147] Id.
[148] Alan Gregg, Diary, July 7, 1950, following his "Visit to Dr. Alfred C. Kinsey," Indiana University, p. 4, the Rockefeller Archive Center.
[149] Ploscowe, *Sex and The Law*, supra, n. 73, p. 217.
[150] Id., p. 217.
[151] See the body of research and statistics on rape and sex offender recidivism available from the US Department of Justice Statistics, Washington, DC. See especially *U.S. Department of Justice*, Juvenile Justice and Delinquency Prevention, *Violent Juvenile Offender I*, "Sexual Exploitation of Children," Human Resources Division, April 20, 1982, p. 12.
[152] MPC, supra, n. 99, pp. 205-206.
[153] Benjamin, supra, n. 17, in Guyon, supra, n. 17, pp. a, b, h, i.
[154] Norman Haire, "Introduction," in Guyon, supra, n. 132, p. vi.
[155] Titus, supra, n. 49, p. 4.
[156] Pomeroy, supra, n. 40, pp. 210-211.
[157] Ernst and Loth, supra, n. 28, pp. 41-46.
[158] Karla Jay and Allen Young, *Lavender Culture*, New York University Press, New York, pp. 342-364.
[159] MPC, supra, n. 99, p. 252.
[160] Id.,, n. 134, p. 252.
[161] *Male*, supra, n. 34, p. 558.
[162] *Male*, supra, n. 34, pp. 160-161.
[163] *Female*, supra, n. 122, p. 118. What did the team mean, sought? How much is, "more" or "less"? On what evidence was the "more" assumption based? Did prosecutors *really* believe such blatant self-interest as fact?
Kinsey held that there is no such thing as abnormal sexual activity, since all mammalian sexual conduct is also the norm for humans. He thus considered pedophilia (adult-child sex) and incest to be entirely normal, and sought to defuse the strong American legal and societal resistance to, and criminal aura associated with, all forms of adult-child sex. In this, Kinsey and the authors of the ALI-MPC appeared in agreement.
[164] *The American Heritage Dictionary of the English Language*, 1992.
[165] MPC, supra, n. 99, pp. 301-302.
[166] Despite his disproportionately large homosexual population, Kinsey purged all homosexual incest in the *Male* volume, except *one* citation to "incest" in the *Male* index (as above, claiming it is non-existent). This would support his thesis that although Americans were promiscuous, no one was injured, and hence our sex laws were, if anything, too harsh. If children and women were not harmed by sexual interaction, public morality did not need to be protected by the force of law. Kinsey never defined "harm." With this goal of ending serious penalties for sex crimes, Kinsey has no category in the *Female* volume for reporting incest, saying children had sex with "relations," "Adult Partners, Uncles, Fathers, Brothers, Grandfathers, Other relatives." The *Male* volume mentions incest and child abuse as a footnote. Thus Kinsey eliminated incest as a result of the use of obscene materials, or as a result of any other environmental causes, legitimizing his call for *full sexual liberty from law*.
[167] March 11, 1981 personal correspondence. In the author's archive.

[168] Pomeroy, supra, n. 40, p. 208.
[169] Id., p. 203.
[170] Id., pp. 207-208. [Emphasis added.]
[171] *California Sex Crimes Report*, 1950-53, California Sexual Deviation Research, 21, 1953.
[172] Id., p. 243. Kinsey's claim of a low recidivism rate for child sex abusers is not now nor has it ever been, to this author's knowledge, the view of most child protection workers. In a typical academic study, Hanson, Steffy and Gauther looked at recidivism in a child sex abuser population of 197, from 1958 to 1974, and found 42 percent of the offenders reconvicted for sex crimes, suggesting a much more significant number had been offending, but were not caught. "Long-term Recidivism of Child Molesters," *Journal of Counseling and Clinical Psychology*, 1993, pp. 646-652
[173] Id., p. 244. The ABA/ALI author seems to share Ploscowe's empathy for convicted rapists whom Ploscowe sees as unfairly penalized.
[174] The California Sex Crimes Reports 1950-1953, Report of the Department of Mental Hygiene, California Sexual Deviation Research, 21 (1953) study had received Kinsey's expert testimony and therefore reflected Kinsey's unsubstantiated claim that child molesters did not repeat their crimes. This was *repudiated* by the sex predator data extant during Kinsey's era, and more fully repudiated by *current* sex predator data in the ABA/ALI Model Penal Code, May 1, 1953, p. 241.
[175] The U.S. Department of Justice Office of Juvenile Justice and Delinquency Prevention report, "Violent Juvenile Offenders" in "Sexual Exploitation of Children A Problem of Unknown Magnitude," p. 12, April 20, 1982.
[176] Id.
[177] See *British Medical Journal*, 282: 250, *1981,* cited in Reisman, et al, *Kinsey, Sex and Fraud*, Huntington House, Lafayette, LA, 1990, p. 71.
[178] See Karen S. Peterson, "Woman's Obsession for Boy," *USA Today,* February 5, 1998, p. 4D; 35-year-old mother of four has a baby with a 13 year-old boy.
[179] See the thousands of court cases resulting in the normalization of vice.
[180] Charles E. Rice, *Legalizing Homosexual Conduct: The Role of the Supreme Court in the Gay Rights Movement:* Constitutional Commentary No. 1, Center for Judicial Studies, 1984, p. 1.
[181] Back issues of *Playboy* and other pornographic magazines can be purchased using the toll free numbers for these materials. This author has obtained what was illegal "child pornography" from said agents.
[182] Reisman, "Soft Porn," supra, n. 106, p. 105.
[183] Kevin Saunders, *Violence as Obscenity*, Duke University Press, Durham, NC, 1996, p. vii.
[184] Jay A. Gertzman, *Bookleggers And Smuthounds: The Trade In Erotica 1920-1940,* University of Pennsylvania Press, Philadelphia, 1999, p. 136.
[185] Id., p. 89.
[186] Henry Campbell Black, *Black's Law Dictionary*, West Publishing, St. Paul. Minn., 1968, p. 1227.
[187] Id.
[188] Id.
[189] Terrence J. Murphy, *Censorship, Government and Obscenity*, Helicon, Baltimore, MD, 1963, p. 75.
[190] Id., p. 5.
[191] Thirty-Eighth Congress, See II, Ch. 89, 1865, p. 507.
[192] 354 U.S. 476 (1957). However, following the international acclaim greeting the Kinsey data (claiming sex crime both common and harmless among average Americans) on March 29, 1948, after a two-year hiatus, the U.S. Supreme Court ruled in *Winters* v. *New York* that "bloodshed, lust or crime" stories might be legally distributed. This 1948 ruling was the first of many to be based on the notion that the American citizenry could be exposed to communications of "bloodshed and lust" without causing individual or social harm, without contributing to "Offenses Against Public Order."
[193] What the U.S. Customs office did was to claim a certain class of people can receive sex stimuli, but such people are beyond the ability of pornography or obscenity to "stir the sex impulses or to lead to sexually impure and lustful thoughts." The idea that sex materials of all kinds can be non-prurient has been used to justify the legalization and distribution of documentably "lewd" materials nationwide, especially to schoolchildren under the umbrella of AIDS prevention and sex education. Indeed, one case in Massachusetts involved a young girl who was forced to remain in a classroom during a graphic sexual entertainment described as sex education. The U.S. Customs office first allowed illegal sexual materials to be imported in 1960 for the Kinsey Institute, for "scientific" research purposes. Prior to that, U.S. Customs outlawed importation and delivery of such sexual materials through the U.S. mail. Wardell Pomeroy, supra, n. 40, pp. 141, 388, 449.
[194] SIECUS 1995, Position Statement on "Sexually Explicit" materials.
[195] See the Indiana University Kinsey Institute brochures describing the visits by the Pornography Commission to their facilities. The Kinsey Institute brochure distributed during the 1980s under "Services," states "Members of the Institute have been in great demand to deliver lectures, serve on panels, and act as consultants. In many instances individuals and groups visit the Institute to confer and obtain information, such as the congressionally appointed Committee on Obscenity and Pornography (page numbers unreadable).
[196] Ernst, supra, n. 30, pp. 103-104.
[197] Kinsey had no citation to "pornography" in his books, only to "erotica," and there is no indication in his data to say that sexually stimulating media played any role in triggering unwanted sexual conduct by those so stimulated (*Female,* supra, n. 122, pp. 86, 653, 671-675 and *Male,* supra, n. 34, pp. 23, 65).
[198] See James Jones, *Alfred C. Kinsey: A Public/Private Life*, W.W. Norton & Company, New York, 1997, pp. 605-614, 669, 684, 755, documenting the Kinsey team's obsessive creation and use of pornography, as well as citations to Kinsey's "nature library" and his use of pornography to interest and seduce his young male students.
[199] Rochelle Gurstein, *The Repeal of Reticence, A History of America's Cultural and Legal Struggles over Free Speech, Obscenity, Sexual Liberation, and Modern Art,* Hill and Wang, New York, 1996, p. 249.

200 Id., p. 252.
201 Id.
202 Id., p. 253.
203 Id.
204 Id., p. 253
205 Id., p 254.
206 Id., p. 259.
207 Id.
208 Allyn, supra, n. 54, 206-207.
209 *Female*, supra, n. 122, p. 663.
210 Murphy, supra, n. 187, p. 28.
211 Id.
212 Id.
213 Id., 354 U.S. at 487, n. 20.
214 The impact of Kinsey is further seen as the evidence finds Chief Justice Earl Warren, in close touch with disciple Appeals Court Judge Justice Learned Hand (deceased, 1961), who served as an adviser to the Council for the Model Penal Code and a close associate of Morris Ploscowe, New York Magistrate, associate ABA/ALI Model Penal Code reporter, as well as legal advisor and other Kinsey disciples including Morris Ernst. Kinsey's influence on the ALI treatment of obscenity in the Model Penal Code, and, via Judge Hand and Justice Warren upon the U.S. Supreme Court in its obscenity deliberations is readily apparent.
215 Bob Woodward, *The Brethren*, Harper and Row, New York, 1979, p. 228-9.
216 While in his later years, Woodward's investigative reporting took what could be called a neglectful turn, my thirty years of research and study in the area of obscenity and related matters confirms Woodward's observations regarding the old world of educated men versus the new. Moreover, it is well documented that such film festivals are regular events on Ivy League campuses and others. Indeed, this author was an invited speaker on the Princeton campus following a celebratory pornography festival sponsored by the Women's Studies department.
217 Woodward, supra, n. 215, p. 235.
218 Id.
219 Id, pp. 117, 121.
220 354 U.S. at 511, citing *Lockhart and McClure*, "Literature, the Law of Obscenity, and the Constitution," 38 Minn. L. Rev. 295 1954.
221 *Yorko v. State*, 690 S.W.2d 260-272 (Tex. Cr. App,) 1985.
222 "Secret Histories: Kinsey's Paedophiles," Yorkshire Television, August 10, 1998.
223 Deutsch, supra, n. 14, in *Sex Habits of American Men*, supra, n. 14, pp. 32-34.
224 Jones, supra, n. 198, p. 619.
225 Id.
226 Id.
227 Samuel Kling, *Sexual Behavior & the Law*, Random House, New York, 1965, p. 9.
228 Rickie Solinger, Ed., *Abortion Wars*, University of California Press, Berkeley, CA, 1998, page ix. (Emphasis added)
229 410 U.S. 113, 140 and n. 37, 1973.
230 The American Law Institute Model Penal Code, Tentative Draft 9, May 9, 1959, § 207.11, n. 1.
231 Robert Marshall and Charles Donovan, *Blessed are the Barren: The Social Policy of Planned Parenthood*, Ignatius Press, San Francisco, CA, 1991, p. 260.
232 Id.
233 Gebhard, Pomeroy, Martin, Christenson, *Pregnancy, Birth and Abortion*, the "Science Editions", John Wiley & Sons, Inc., New York, 1958, pp. xi-xiii. [Emphasis added]. See also p.212 re: medical licenses.
234 Paul Gebhard, Wardell Pomeroy, Clyde Martin and Cornelia Christenson, "*Pregnancy, Birth and Abortion*," in *Sex Research Studies from the Kinsey Institute*, Martin S. Weinberg, editor, Oxford University Press, New York, 1976, p. 100.
235 *Female*, supra, n. 122, p. 53.
236 Gebhard, et al, supra, n. 233, p. 3. (emphasis added).
237 Id.
238 Id., p. 119.
239 Id., p. 213 (emphasis added).
240 Stone was also Director of the Margaret Sanger Research Bureau and Vice-President of the Planned Parenthood Federation of America, the International Planned Parenthood Federation, and the American Society for the Study of Sterility. Hines was an editor and contributor to the *Encyclopedia of the Social Sciences* and the *Encyclopedia Sexualis*.
241 Stone and Himes, *Planned Parenthood: A Practical Handbook of Birth-Control Methods*, Collier Books, New York, 1965, p. 235.
242 Gebhard, et al, supra, n. 236, pp. 205-206.
243 Id., p. 212.
244 Marshall and Donovan, supra, n. 238, p. 260. [Emphasis added.]
245 Id., p. 261
246 Id.
247 Gebhard, et al, supra, n. 236, p. 32.

[248] In, *Sex Education in American Schools*, Source, "Youth Indicators 1996; Indicator 7," Concerned Women For America, Washington, D.C., 1996, p. 11.

[249] Gebhard, et al, supra, n. 236, p. 32.

[250] Harry Benjamin and R.E.L. Masters, *Prostitution and Morality*, The Julian Press, New York, 1964, p. 159.

[251] Id., p. 18, n. 3.

[252] Id., p. 18.

[253] Id., pp. 14-15, 18.

[254] *Male*, supra, n. 34, p. 521.

[255] Id., p. 49.

[256] See Geddes and Curie, supra, n. 18.

[257] *Male*, supra, n. 34, pp. 638-641.

[258] Jones, supra, n. 198, p. 677. See especially content analysis data in Judith Reisman and Charles Johnson, *The Reisman-Johnson Report*, "Partner Solicitation Language as a Reflection of Male Sexual Orientation," First Principles Press, Crestwood, Ky., 1995.

[259] Ronald D. Ray, *Military Necessity & Homosexuality*, First Principles Press, Crestwood, KY, 1993, p. 108.

[260] *Schochet v. State*, 541 A.2d 183, 206 and n. 3 (Md. App.) 1988.

[261] *Harris v. State*, 457 P.2d 638, 645 (Alaska) 1969.

[262] Id., at n. 21, citing *Male*, supra, pp. 390-393. See also Kinsey, et al, *Female*, supra, n. 122, pp. 259-263, 366-370.

[263] *Luley v. Luley*, 48 N.W.2d 328, 330, n. 4 (Minn.) 1951.

[264] *In re P.*, 400 N.Y.S.2d at 455, 463, n. 15, 1977.

[265] *Locke v. State*, 501 S.W.2d 826, 828-829 and n. 2 (Tenn. Crim. App., 1973) (Galbraith, dissenting).

[266] 536 A.2d 1 (D.C. App.) 1987.

[267] Id., at p. 34, citing *Male*, supra, n. 34, p. 650-51.

[268] Id.

[269] Id.

[270] Id., pp. 636-650.

[271] Id., at p. 34, citing *Female*, supra, n. 122, pp. 173-74, 1953.

[272] 359 F. Supp. 843 (D. Md., 1973).

[273] In 1979, homosexual teachers flew to New York and publicly supported the "right" of a teacher to have sex with a boy outside of school (*New York Post*, 5, July 11, 1979). More recently, "gay and lesbian" counselors have been retained to advise students about AIDS.

[274] 359 F. Supp., supra, n. 274, at 852.

[275] 730 F.2d 444 (6th Cir., 1984).

[276] Id., at 455-56 (Edwards, dissenting).

[277] 363 F.2d 488 (2nd Cir., 1966), affirmed 387 U.S. 118, 1967.

[278] Id., at 490, n. 2.

[279] Id., at 497, citing *Male*, supra, n. 34, p. 623, 1948 (Moore, dissenting) [Emphasis added].

[280] Id., citing *Male*, supra, n. 34, pp. 201-202, 1948 (Douglas, J., dissenting) 387 U.S. at 127-28.

[281] 235 A.2d 12 (1967).

[282] Id., at 15-16.

[283] Rand, *Sexual Orientation and U.S. Military Personnel Policy: Options and Assessment*, National Research Institute, Office of the Secretary of Defense, MR/323/0OSD, 1993, citing *Male*, supra, n. 34, p. 650

[284] Id., citing Susan Rodgers and Charles Turner, "Male-Male Sexual Contact in the U.S.A.: Findings from Five Sample Surveys, 1970-1990," *The Journal of Sex Research*, Vol. 28, No. 4, 1991, pp. 505, 509.

[285] Id., pp. 51-52.

[286] Id., citing *Male*, supra, n. 34, p. 621.

[287] General Science, "Sexual 'Pervert' Probe" Science Newsletter for July 1, 1950, p. 5.

[288] Ray, supra, n. 261, p. 100.

[289] Ronald D. Ray, "Lifting the Ban on Homosexuals in the Military: The Subversion of a Moral Principle," in *Gays and Lesbians in the Military: Issues, Concerns and Contrasts*, William J. Scott and Sandra Carson Stanley, editors, Aldine DeGruyter, New York, 1994.

[290] Colonel Ronald D. Ray, "Virtue, The First Principle of American Military Service Since 1775," *Wings of Gold*, Summer 1995, p. 71.

[291] Personal interview, with Colonel Ronald D. Ray, January 1997, Crestwood, Kentucky.

[292] *The Washington Post*, April 16, 1988.

[293] Daniel Koshland, Editorial, Science, January 6, 1987, p. 141.

CHAPTER 9

ELITE AMERICAN EUGENICISTS

Kinsey concentrated on negative eugenics, calling for a program of sterilization that was at once sweeping and terrifying. "The reduction of the birth rate of the lowest classes must depend upon the sterilization of perhaps a tenth of our population."[1]

James H. Jones, *Alfred C. Kinsey: A Private/Public Life,* **1997**

In 1954, the 83rd U.S. Congress became concerned about the influence of the large tax-exempt foundations on the nation's social, economic, and political well-being. Following the infamous 1914 scandal known as "The Ludlow Massacre" of women and children in Rockefeller's Colorado coal mines, the Democrat-chaired Walsh Committee held hearings on the industrial practices of Big Business. In 1952 the Cox Committee continued the line of inquiry, but further examined certain "non-profit" foundations created by Big Business. The 1954 investigation was chaired by Republican B. Carroll Reece of Tennessee, a decorated veteran and World War I hero. The Reece Committee inquiry confirmed what Supreme Court Justice Louis Brandeis had once said about the extent to which foundation funds were being used to achieve political objectives, while the foundations themselves had become "a state within a state." The Reece Committee reported that a mix of the Old World aristocracy and heirs to the American "Robber Barons" had emerged to control extensive resources while "operating outside of our democratic processes."[2]

U.S. Congressman and World War I hero B. Carroll Reece (R-Tennessee) chaired the Reece Committee during the 83rd Congress (1953-1954).

Dr. Carroll Quigley, professor of history at Georgetown University's Foreign Service School, wrote his important and revealing book *Tragedy and Hope* in 1966. Quigley had been one of Bill Clinton's college mentors, and the President-to-be paid tribute to him by name during his acceptance speech at the 1992 Democratic National Convention. In *Tragedy and Hope,* Quigley candidly stated,

> I know of the operations of this network [of foundations] because I have studied it for twenty years and was permitted... to examine its papers and secret records. I have no aversion to it or to most of its aims and have, for much of my life, been close to it and many of its instruments.[3]

Regarding the foundations, Quigley recalled:

> It soon became clear that people of immense wealth would be unhappy if the [Reece] investigation went too far and

Cartoons in the first half of the 20th Century often depicted big business as a threat to American interests.

ELITE AMERICAN EUGENICISTS 269

that the "most respected" newspapers in the country, closely allied with these men of wealth, would not get excited enough about any revelations to make the publicity worthwhile, in terms of votes or campaign contributions. An interesting report showing the Left-wing associations of the interlocking nexus of tax-exempt foundations was issued in 1954 rather quietly. Four years later, the Reece committee's general counsel, Rene A. Wormser, wrote a shocked, but not shocking, book on the subject called *Foundations: Their Power and Influence*.[4]

Professor Carroll Quigley

In the introduction to *Foundations,* Wormser summarized the Reece Committee's findings:

It is not easy to investigate foundations, not even for Congress to attempt it: the giant foundations are powerful and have powerful friends. A special committee was created by the House of Representatives of the 83rd Congress to investigate tax-exempt organizations. It is generally referred to as the "Reece Committee" after its chairman, Congressman B. Carroll Reece of Tennessee. It was successor, in a way, to the "Cox Committee," created by the previous Congress. The Reece Committee had perhaps the most hazardous career of any committee in the history of Congress. It survived its many perils, however, to bring to the attention of Congress and the people grave dangers to our society.

These dangers relate chiefly to the use of foundation funds for political ends; they arise out of the accumulation of substantial economic power and of cultural influence in the hands of a class of administrators of tax-exempt funds established in perpetuity. An "elite" has thus emerged, in control of gigantic financial resources operating outside of our democratic processes.[5]

As described by the Congressional Committee, the network of philanthropic foundations was quite "willing and able to shape the future of this nation and of mankind in the image of its own value concepts," creating injustice due to undemocratic, "interlocking and self-perpetuating" groups. The Reece Committee concluded that, unlike corporate structures, foundations are "unchecked by stockholders"; unlike government they are "unchecked by the people"; and unlike churches they are "unchecked by any firmly established canons of value."[6] Indeed, these "Old World" American elite interests operate like the European aristocracies America's founders sought to escape. They chafed under the American democratic process, believing it left the world without a unified hand and mind to guide it safely though the global shoals of food production to feed the teeming masses (workers for their business interests in peace and war) and population control (too many of the "wrong" types of people).[7]

Rockefellers, father and son. The Reece Committee investigation of the Rockefeller Foundation was triggered by the Foundation's inclination to fund causes promoting population control and alteration of the American way of life.

The Rockefeller Foundation had primarily targeted its efforts and largess at controlling populations and manipulating mass communication. And one focus of the Congressional Committee investigation which differed from the earlier Walsh and Cox inquiries was Rockefeller Foundation support for Alfred Kinsey's Institute for Sex Research at Indiana University. Reece Committee legal counsel Wormser writes,

> The Rockefeller Foundation's statement filed with the Committee explained its connection with the Kinsey studies in this way. In 1931 it "became interested in systematic support for studies in sexual physiology and behavior" ...Its work in these areas was chiefly in connection with the "committee for research in problems of sex of The National Research Council," to which, by 1954, the Foundation had granted $1,755,000 in annual grants running from $75,000 to $240,000. Beginning about 1941, a considerable portion of these funds was supplied to Dr. Kinsey's studies, and one grant was made direct to Dr. Kinsey.... The work of the NRC produced some results of truly noteworthy importance.... [However] the much-publicized "best-seller" Kinsey studies base an advocacy of criminal and social reform on the very *un*scientific material which Dr. Kinsey had collected and permitted to be widely disseminated.[8]

During the Reece Committee hearings, Dr. Albert Hobbs, a widely published University of Pennsylvania sociologist, critiqued the "skewed" Kinsey data in scathing terms. Kinsey biographer James Jones attacked Professor Hobbs as a "right-wing sociologist"[9] for his testimony that,

> [S]ocial scientists should exercise the greatest care in informing the public when their work is not truly "scientific." The very term "social science" implies that their conclusions are unassailable because they are "scientifically" arrived at. There is the constant danger, then, that laymen will take these conclusions as axiomatic bases for social action. [Note for example]...the remarkable number of writings which appeared after the Rockefeller Foundation-supported Kinsey studies. With the assumedly "scientific" character of Dr. Kinsey's work behind us, we had such things offered to the public as this by one Anne G. Freegood, in the September 1953 issue of *Harper's*:

University of Pennsylvania sociologist Dr. Albert Hobbs warned the Reece Committee about Kinsey's "scientism" (pseudo-science).

> The desert in this case is our current code of laws governing sexual activities and the background of Puritan tradition regarding sex under which this country still to some extent operates.[10]

Later, Ann Freegood wrote that the first Kinsey report "has already been cited in court decisions and quoted in textbooks as well as blazoned from one end of the country to the other." Wormser quotes from Professor Hobbs' book, *Social Problems and Scientism*, regarding the widespread use by the professions of Dr. Kinsey's first report:

> Despite the patent limitations of the study and its persistent bias, its conclusions regarding sexual behavior were widely believed. They were presented to college classes; medical doc-

tors cited them in lectures; psychiatrists applauded them; a radio program indicated that the findings were serving as a basis for revision of moral codes relating to sex; and an editorial in a college student newspaper admonished the college administration to make provision for sexual outlets for the students in accordance with the "scientific realities" as established by the book.

Some of these Kinseyites have said that our laws are wrong because they do not follow the biological "facts." Published reports such as those of Kinsey can do immeasurable harm when they falsely pretend to disclose biological "facts." A great part of the Kinsey product is without basis in true "fact" and is mere propaganda for some personally intriguing concepts.

Wormser continues,

> Professor Hobbs pointed out that Dr. Kinsey ridiculed "socially approved patterns of sexual behavior," calling them "rationalizations," while conversely referring to socially condemned forms of sexual behavior as "normal" or "normal in the human animal." This presentation, said Professor Hobbs, "could give the impression, and it gave the impression to a number of reviewers, that things which conform to the socially approved codes of sexual conduct are rationalizations, not quite right, while things which deviate from it, such as homosexuality, are normal, in a sense right." ...Professor Hobbs stressed the fact that such pseudoscientific presentations could seriously affect public morality. Here is more of his testimony:[11]

For an illustration, in connection with the question of heterosexuality compared with homosexuality, Kinsey, in the first volume, has this statement: "It is only because society demands that there be a particular choice in the matter (of heterosexuality or homosexuality) and does not so often dictate one's choice of food or clothing."

In the second volume it is stressed, for example, that we object to adult molesters of children primarily because we have become conditioned against such adult molesters of children, and that the children who are molested become emotionally upset, primarily because of the old-fashioned attitudes of their parents about such practices, and the parents (the implication is) are the ones who do the real damage by making a fuss about it if a child is molested. Because the molester and here I quote from Kinsey, "may have contributed favorably to their later sociosexual development." That is, a molester of children may have actually, Kinsey contends, not only not harmed them, but may have [helped]. Especially emphasized in the second volume, the volume on females, is the supposed beneficial effects of premarital sexual experiences. Such experiences, Kinsey states: "provide an opportunity for the females to learn to adjust emotionally to various types of males."[12]

*　*　*　*

In addition on page 327, he contends that premarital sexual experience may well contribute to the effectiveness of one's other nonsexual social relationships, and that many females—this is on page 115—will thus learn how to respond to sociosexual contacts.... On page 328, that it should contribute to the development of emotional capacities in a more effective way than if sexual experiences are acquired after marriage.[13]

The avoidance of premarital sexual experience by females, according to Professor Kinsey, may lead to inhibitions which damage the capacity to respond, so much that these inhibitions may persist after years of marriage, "if, indeed, they are ever dissipated." That is from page 330. So you get a continued emphasis on the desirability of females engaging in premarital sexual behavior. In both these volumes there is a persistent emphasis, a persistent questioning of the traditional codes, and the laws relating to sexual behavior. Professor Kinsey may be correct or he may be incorrect, but when he gives the impression that the findings are scientific in the same sense as the findings in physical science, then the issue becomes not a matter of whether he as a person is correct or incorrect, but of the impression which is given to the public, which can be quite unfortunate. (*Hearings*, pp. 129, 130.)[14]

As discussed in Chapter 8, Hobbs was correct in fearing that the Kinsey data were being used in law and public policy and taught to college students nationwide. The results were indeed "unfortunate."

POWERFUL POLITICAL INTERVENTION AND THE KINSEY FILE "NEVER SAW THE LIGHT OF DAY"

During a conversation just prior to his death, Dr. Hobbs told this author that he could not understand how he had missed the clear evidence of child sexual abuse in Kinsey's data. Dr. Hobbs' daughter, Pamela Hobbs Hoffecker, stated during a 1996 interview: "My father told me that if the Reece Committee had had the benefit of Judith's Reisman's discovery that children were abused for Kinsey's data, that would have changed the course of American, even world, history."[15]

Certain Rockefeller business activities had supplied war-making materials to Hitler's war effort, causing then-Senator Harry Truman (D-Missouri) to use the word "treason" when describing Rockefeller (Standard Oil), during a Senate speech on March 27, 1942. Now the Rockefeller Foundation (and other foundations as well) were found to be funding questionable programs and research during the post-war era that were having a harmful impact in critical areas of America's social, educational, and political life. The Reece Committee investigation of Kinsey's sex research as it served the conspirator's special revolutionary interests, had to be stopped—and it was. Wormser writes,

> Most mysterious and disturbing was how the investigation of the Kinsey data was thwarted by a combined effort of the Republicans and the Democrats in that administration.... [Congressman Wayne] Hays [D.-Ohio] particularly [would not allow] a proposed study of the Kinsey reports... Dr. Ettinger had dug up some significant material about foundation support of the Kinsey projects. This brought Mr. Hays

The Rockefellers' international business dealings with Nazi Germany were labeled "treason" by U.S. Senator (later President) Harry Truman (D-Missouri) on March 27, 1942.

to a steaming rage, and he asked to see our entire Kinsey file. It was produced for him, and he angrily declared to Mr. [Norman] Dodd [the committee's research director] that we were to go no further with this particular investigation, contending that every member of Congress would be against our doing so. Neither Mr. Dodd nor I could see any reason why Dr. Kinsey's foundation supported projects should not bear as much scrutiny as any other foundation operation. But Mr. Hays then introduced another element into the situation. Our appropriation for 1954 had, at the time, not yet been approved, and Mr. Hays stated emphatically to Mr. Dodd that he would oppose any further appropriation to our Committee unless the Kinsey investigation was dropped. His unreasoning opposition to any study of these projects was so great that he threatened to fight against the appropriation on the floor of the House. [Fearful,] Mr. Dodd concluded that Mr. Hays must be appeased. He suggested, therefore, that Mr. Hays take the entire Kinsey file and lock it in his personal safe so that he would know the material could not be used without the express consent of the Committee. This Mr. Hays did. The file remained in his safe throughout the hearings... he may still have it.

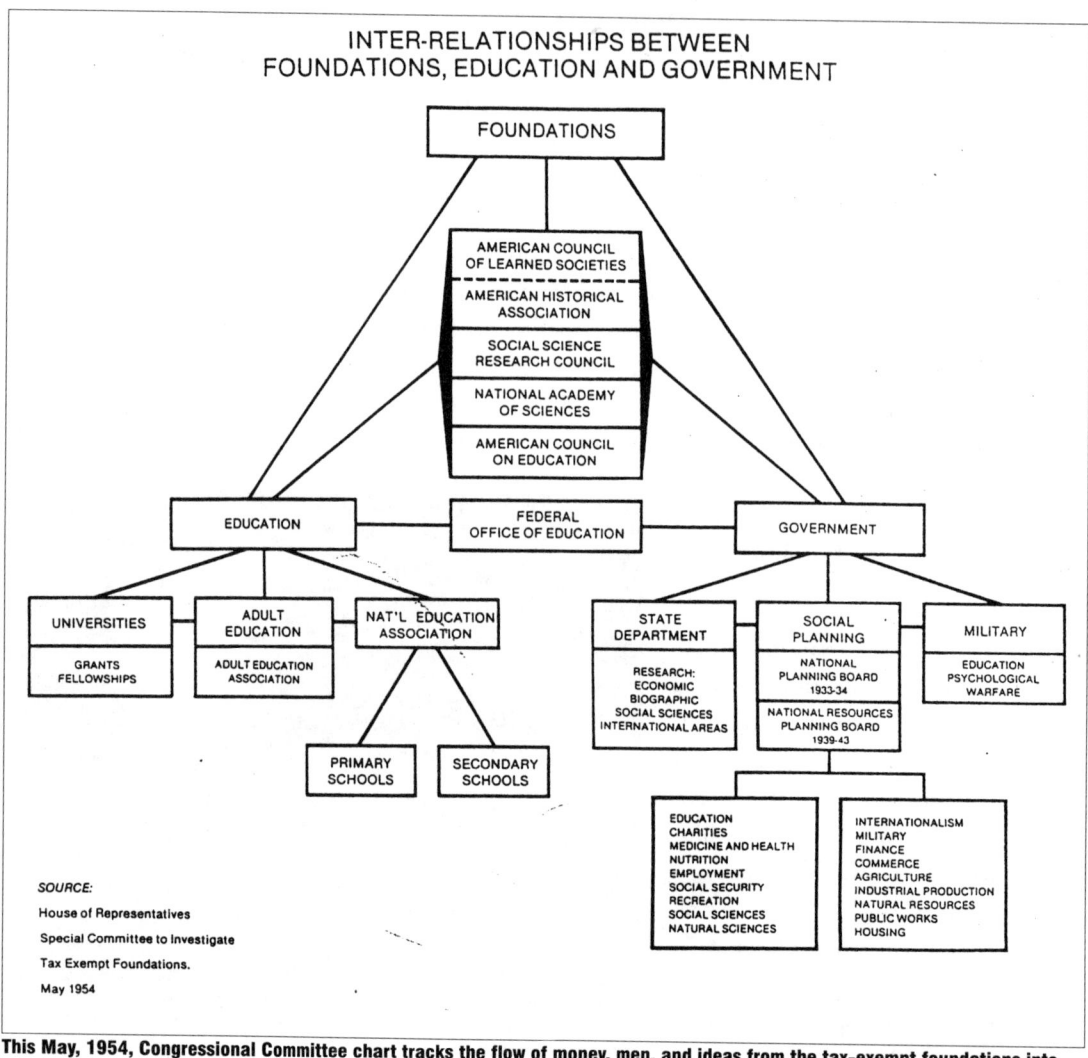

INTER-RELATIONSHIPS BETWEEN FOUNDATIONS, EDUCATION AND GOVERNMENT

```
                        FOUNDATIONS
                             │
          ┌──────────────────┼──────────────────┐
          │   AMERICAN COUNCIL OF LEARNED SOCIETIES   │
          │   AMERICAN HISTORICAL ASSOCIATION          │
          │   SOCIAL SCIENCE RESEARCH COUNCIL          │
          │   NATIONAL ACADEMY OF SCIENCES             │
          │   AMERICAN COUNCIL ON EDUCATION            │
          │                                            │
     EDUCATION ── FEDERAL OFFICE OF EDUCATION ── GOVERNMENT
```

EDUCATION branches: UNIVERSITIES (GRANTS, FELLOWSHIPS); ADULT EDUCATION (ADULT EDUCATION ASSOCIATION); NAT'L EDUCATION ASSOCIATION (PRIMARY SCHOOLS, SECONDARY SCHOOLS)

GOVERNMENT branches: STATE DEPARTMENT (RESEARCH: ECONOMIC, BIOGRAPHIC, SOCIAL SCIENCES, INTERNATIONAL AREAS); SOCIAL PLANNING (NATIONAL PLANNING BOARD 1933-34, NATIONAL RESOURCES PLANNING BOARD 1939-43); MILITARY (EDUCATION, PSYCHOLOGICAL WARFARE)

SOCIAL PLANNING leads to:
- EDUCATION, CHARITIES, MEDICINE AND HEALTH, NUTRITION, EMPLOYMENT, SOCIAL SECURITY, RECREATION, SOCIAL SCIENCES, NATURAL SCIENCES
- INTERNATIONALISM, MILITARY, FINANCE, COMMERCE, AGRICULTURE, INDUSTRIAL PRODUCTION, NATURAL RESOURCES, PUBLIC WORKS, HOUSING

SOURCE:
House of Representatives
Special Committee to Investigate
Tax Exempt Foundations.
May 1954

This May, 1954, Congressional Committee chart tracks the flow of money, men, and ideas from the tax-exempt foundations into critical sectors of American life.

The Kinsey reports were included as a small part of the committee's evidence in open hearings, thanks to the testimony of Professor Hobbs. But Wormser laments that the valuable material in the Kinsey file never saw the light of day.[16] Committee chief counsel Wormser and research director Dodd were first-hand witnesses to the intense and powerful opposition to any investigation of the tax-exempt foundations,[17] including the successful effort to prevent further public hearings. The censorship was reinforced by the major media's refusal to provide meaningful news coverage of the committee's hearings and findings or to expose the behind-the-scenes war to keep the public in the dark.

Due to massive pressure coming from the highest levels, the Reece Committee was shut down by the end of 1954.[18] Its final report was delivered on December 16, 1954. Kinsey's powerful friends in high places had again protected him and his cadre from public scrutiny.

STATISTICAL STUFF, NONSENSE, AND CONTROL

Norman Dodd, director of research for the Congressional Committee.

Kinsey's preposterous statistical data served the Rockefeller Foundation's larger purposes. You will recall that six years prior to the Reece Committee hearings the Foundation had been informed of the bad data by Warren Weaver, the head of its Natural Sciences Division. In 1948, Weaver had discussed Kinsey's lack of scientific methodology with Allen Wallis of the University of Chicago,[19] and later wrote that although monies for "the National Research Council Committee for Research in Problems of Sex were, from 1934 through 1941, recommended to the Trustees by me,"[20] the Kinsey research was a scientific farce. He had bluntly asserted, "I know of no evidence that Dr. Kinsey understands the underlying statistical character of his work," and had charged that neither Kinsey nor his assistant, Clyde Martin, had "the competence... [or] interest" in correcting this shocking fault. Weaver was, for example, appalled to discover that "Kinsey quotes an 'average,' which on examination, turns out to be an average of just one case!"[21]

Despite the exposure of Kinsey's worthless research by Weaver, Wallis, Hobbs, and other credible critics, Rockefeller Foundation trustees continued to fund the Kinsey sex studies until 1954, when the Reece Committee planned to publicly examine both Kinsey and his data.

Cultural trends author and Kinsey analyst Dr. E. Michael Jones comments on some of the ways in which Kinsey exercised control over his benefactors. He refers to Yerkes, Corner and Gregg as "the Three Wise Men." Reviewing the James Jones biography of Kinsey, Jones asserts,

> What is clearer in the book is how Kinsey used sex to control the people around him. In this regard the controllers at the Rockefeller Foundation—Yerkes, Corner and Gregg—got more than they bargained for. The method was fairly simple. To begin with all of the above mentioned men had jettisoned religion in favor of science as a better guide to how to live life. That naturally led them to see sex as just one more field of study, which led them to ignore its power over them. Hence when Kinsey jerked their chains they were unaware of what was going on until it was too late. In this Kinsey played Dionysos to their Pentheus. All the while they thought he was in their power, when all he had to do was ask if they wanted to see the women dancing naked on the mountainside to turn the tables on them.

Which is precisely what Kinsey refined into the standard treatment of those who came to visit at the Institute in Bloomington. "I want you to see our library and our collections of erotic materials in sufficient detail to understand what bearing they have on the research project as a whole," Kinsey wrote to Alan Gregg, director of the Medical Science Division of the Rockefeller Foundation and the man who held the purse strings, and on February 6, 1947, Gregg arrived in Bloomington, like Pentheus arriving on the mountain to watch the women dancing naked. Kinsey, [Jones tells us] took obvious delight in showing his visitor various books, photographs and drawings," which is not hard to understand because he understood that this was the simplest way to draw Gregg under his control as a supporter of his research.

The culmination of every trip to Bloomington was, of course, the moment when Kinsey took his victim's sexual history. (Actually, some of Kinsey's willing victims then went on to allow themselves to be photographed while engaged in sexual activity, but this was the exception and not the rule.) Yerkes had done this before Gregg arrived in Bloomington and afterward no matter how shabbily Kinsey treated him, Yerkes felt obliged to support him. The word blackmail springs most immediately to mind. Kinsey took sexual histories as a way of gaining power over people, and scientists, those who felt that sexual morality was an outdated remnant of a bygone era were his easiest picking in many ways. The threat of blackmail was never far from the practice of taking sexual histories, which is probably why, in addition to his prurient interest in the subject matter, Kinsey was so avid to take them.

His use of sex as a way of controlling people was not limited to foundation executives. He did the same thing to the press in preparation for the release of the Male volume. Reporters were invited to Bloomington, softened up by being shown pornography, then asked to sign a "contract" which would allow Kinsey to read any article they wrote before it was published, in the interest, of course, of scientific accuracy. To insure final control over this willing group of Enlightened thinkers, Kinsey persuaded them to give their sexual histories. Then in the event that one of the journalists would somehow come to his senses and write something unfavorable, Kinsey had a wealth of information on the most intimate details of his life that could be used against him.[22]

THE VICTORY TOUR: KINSEY TO THE LAND OF GUYON, HIRSCHFELD AND CROWLEY

By 1955, Kinsey was at the height of his renown. Homosexual author Gore Vidal described him as the "most famous man in America, the world, for about a decade."[23]

In the wake of the Reece Investigation, Dean Rusk, then president of the Rockefeller Foundation (and later Secretary of State) terminated the Foundation's financial support of Kinsey's sex research.[24] Kinsey had served his purpose. The Foundation had shifted its funds to the American Law Institute. There, Kinsey's research would be put to use to erode existing laws protecting marriage and the family and to craft more lenient sex-offender laws via the American Law Institute's (ALI) Model Penal Code. On April 25, 1955, the ALI released its first Model Penal Code draft (#4), modeled in large part on Kinsey's recommendations, which helped to alter and liberally revise American sex offender laws and penalties.

Kinsey had lectured nationwide to standing ovations in America's finest universities and colleges, traveling an "anything-goes" campaign trail to weaken sex-offender laws. He had escaped close scrutiny by a congressional committee that could have resulted in ruin, even prison. He and wife Clara now embarked on a trip to Europe.

In his 1972 biography, Pomeroy claims that beyond Mexico and Peru, Kinsey "had never been any farther from the continental United States than Cuba before 1955."[25] Kinsey did not speak a foreign language, yet Pomeroy suggests that during his three-week worldwide tour he was able to comprehend and authoritatively evaluate the socio-sexual intricacies of scores of exotic foreign cultures. "Somewhat to his own amazement, Kinsey found that he was a celebrity abroad."[26] A conquering hero in Scandinavia, the eugenicist began training professional groups, from law enforcement to psychiatry, about "scientific" sex by portraying his defective methodology and sham findings as authoritative and scientific.

In Denmark, Kinsey "tracked down a scholar"[27] who insisted that the entire corpus of Hans Christian Andersen's famous fairy tales were "straight-out homosexual stories." Kinsey agreed, but said the sexually permissive Danes "would have been outraged" to know what this anonymous "scholar" had discovered. Kinsey called Anderson's *The Little Mermaid* a "mute nymph" who "cannot tell the world how she feels about anything," just as "Andersen could not tell the world of his homosexual love for the people of the world."[28] His literary argument says little about Andersen, but it reveals a great deal about Kinsey, who would not tell the world of his secret life. Kinsey's notions about Andersen follow:

> Andersen is an excellent illustration of the fact that the world simply must learn that persons with homosexual histories and exclusively homosexual histories have been among the persons who were the most important.... [Homosexuals] certainly have done some of the outstanding things in the world.[29]

Kinsey was popularized in the theater and was the subject of numerous mainstream cartoons.

Kinsey, who knew he also had done some of the "outstanding things in the world," was pleased by the "socialized approach to sex" in Denmark and by their tolerant police force. As a sexologist, filmmaker, and promiscuous collector himself, Kinsey was elated that the Danish sex industry had "recently been greatly [liberated] by the repeal of the laws against pornography." A reduction of the age of consent made sex for unmarried girls over 16 and boys over 18 legal, permitting vulnerable youngsters to enter and enrich the legalized sex "industry." Expanding opportunity for exploiting ever younger "sex workers," with government approval, is something for which Denmark has earned a worldwide reputation.

Kinsey, undisturbed by prostitution, was pleased to have the chance to "talk to the boys and girls who were actually prostituting." They accepted money in an "indirect fashion." Kinsey was touched that the police did not interfere when an older man sexually solicited "a twenty-year-old boy."[30] He was gratified that "transvestitism was permitted," although disappointed that a police permit was required. Kinsey "shocked" Danish students with lectures describing restrictive American sex laws. Kinsey's great disappointment in the Danes was that, while legalizing homosexual conduct, they still largely disapproved of it. He wrote in his notebook,

> I found there was very considerable public opinion against such behavior, and it was the judgment of most of the persons with whom I talked—and I had the opportunity to talk to scores in the short time I was there—that it would do considerable damage to the social or political position of an individual if it was discovered that he had a homosexual history, even though no legal action was taken.[31]

Next on the tour was Sweden, a country where Kinsey also found himself quite at home. Shortly before he arrived, according to Pomeroy, a cabinet minister was "found to have had sexual relations with a teen-age boy. Kinsey was assured that people would be shocked at any suggestion that he be removed from his office."[32] As other Scandinavian countries, Sweden (a monarchy-based plutocracy) had no jury system, so it was easier to implement lenient sex-offender laws there than in jury-based America.

Neither Kinsey nor Pomeroy comment on the impact of politically powerful pedophiles on Swedish laws that opened the nation to adult and child pornography, thereby largely abandoning both women and children to sexual predators. (It was apparently a result also of the influence of such Swedish sex revolutionaries as Gunnar and Alva Myrdal.)[33] Premarital sex for children was condoned by the Swedes, and Kinsey reassured critics that children had sex only with those they held in "esteem." A Cabinet minister, for example, would presumably qualify.

For Kinsey, Sweden was more progressive than was Denmark, though he admired all of Scandinavia due to its open sexual license. In Norway, he enjoyed the sculptor Adolph Gustav Vigeland, whose "vital nude figures… [are] spread through a beautiful park." While heroic and

Publicity photo of Dr. and Mrs. Kinsey during their trip to Europe.

cherubic nude statuary has been common in Europe for centuries, Kinsey was especially pleased with Vigeland's nudes. Why? "Kinsey observed a high percentage of the figures were male... often depicted... wrestling against females, or animals devouring females with apparent male approval." Although Vigeland had been married, Kinsey noted a score of his letters "to a single male in a one-year period... the [homosexual] inference was clear."

From the Scandinavian countries, Kinsey traveled to England, where he helped craft the controversial 1957 Wolfenden Report. The report recommended the legalization and licensing of obscenity, homosexuality, and other activities previously understood to be perversions. After Kinsey's visit, the Wolfenden Report became a cited authority in the United States; Wolfenden cited the Model Penal Code of the United States, while revolutionary American attorneys and judges cited Wolfenden. In England,

Kinsey commands attention as he lectures to an academic audience in Denmark.

> [Kinsey attended]conferences with professional groups. The latter included prison and hospital staff as well as the British commission that was then working on the revision of the English sex law. This was the group that crafted the Wolfenden Report for Parliament in 1957. Lectures in London at the Institute of Psychiatry and at the Maudsley Hospital were high points.[34]

ROMAN HOLIDAY

France disappointed Kinsey. He had expected the French to be far more sexually liberated. In England, writes Pomeroy, Kinsey had hoped to acquire Aleister Crowley's diaries for the Institute.[35] Crowley, an "occultist" drug addict and sadist also known as "The Beast," was accomplished in homosexual magic. He conducted ritual Satanic sacrifices of such heartless cruelty that he was driven out of Italy following the revelation of fatal bloody orgies with children and their mothers in his squalid Sicilian "abbey."[36] He had died in December 1947.[37]

Kinsey was reportedly unsuccessful in obtaining the diaries, after which he made a pilgrimage to Thelema Abbey, the temple where Crowley had ministered. Crowley's first book, the pornographic *White Stains*, advocated sexual magic and was much favored by Kinsey. In fact, Kinsey was photographed in Crowley's "Chamber of Horrors," while he and Clara appear together in a photo following Kinsey's return from the Abbey. The latter appears (without identification) in Pomeroy's biography, and also in *Anger* (1995), by William Landis, a biography of Crowley disciple Kenneth Anger. The caption reads, "Dr. Kinsey with his wife in Italy, 1955. He had just visited Crowley's Thelema Abbey in Sicily and would soon die."[39]

ELITE AMERICAN EUGENICISTS

At Thelema, Kenneth Anger restored the occult and pornographic murals that adorned Crowley's temple for tantric sex (they had been whitewashed by order of the Italian government). Landis focuses on Anger's homosexual filmmaking and his relationship with Crowley, and also describes in some detail Anger's relationship with Kinsey. He confirms Kinsey's attempt to obtain Crowley's diaries in England.

"Dr. Kinsey with his wife in Italy, 1955. He had just visited Crowley's Thelema Abbey in Sicily and would soon die." (Cutline from Anger by William Landis)

Were Kinsey and Crowley correspondents? Indeed, was Crowley one of Kinsey's "technically trained observers"? We know from Pomeroy that Kinsey had carried out extensive, secretive, "confidential" correspondence with diarists in Europe and Middle Eastern countries. Kinsey and Crowley could have corresponded in English. They shared similar sexual obsessions, friends, and acquaintances, such as Kenneth Anger, the American Nazi George Sylvester Viereck, and the French pedophile Rene Guyon, to name a few. According to Anger,

> Kinsey was obsessed with obtaining the Great Beast's day-to-day sex diaries.[40] ...To obtain grant monies and maintain the support of the university, Kinsey needed the excuse of research to validate his twenty-four-hours-a-day obsession with sex. However, Prok's battle cry of "Do your best and let other people react as they will" seemed a variation on Crowley's "Do what thou wilt" maxim.[41]

The shorthand code in which Kinsey recorded his subjects' histories also is "highly reminiscent," said Anger, of Crowley's own "sex ritual" records. American Nazi traitor George Sylvester Viereck may have been Kinsey's initial contact man for Crowley during the war.[42] Pomeroy remarks only that Viereck's "admiration for Hitler had him in frequent political trouble," and that Kinsey had a "high opinion of Viereck's erotic writings," as well as those of Crowley's *White Stains*. Kinsey's judgment of Crowley as "a brilliant writer,"[43] is downplayed by the Kinsey Institute's erotic bibliographer, Greshon Legman, but one wonders about Kinsey's obsessive desire to secure Crowley's diaries. During his visit to the Sicilian temple, Kinsey registered no ethical, moral, or humane objection to the practices and paintings of satanic sex magic evident at Crowley's "Unnatural Abbey."[44] The images covering the walls garishly depict children and adults in real-life, ritual sado-sexual ceremonies.[45]

Kinsey constantly condemned those who espoused sexual self-discipline and restraint, or American founding moral principles, but he found Crowley's savage child pornography, his homosexual magic, and his human sacrifice records to be "most open."[46]

Kinsey with Kenneth Anger, a friend of Kinsey and Aleister Crowley. The photo, taken at Crowley's Sicilian temple, does not appear to be a candid photograph. Rather it seems to make a shadowy statement about Kinsey, Anger, and Crowley.

ITALY

Pomeroy devotes six pages to Kinsey's visits to France, Denmark, Norway, and Sweden, but ten pages to his trip to Italy alone. He quotes Kinsey as saying that Italian males took great pride in the size of their genitalia, and giving assurance that "on the average they were large." Pomeroy writes,

Aleister Crowley kept extensive sex diaries of great interest to Kinsey.

A Cyclops figure adorns that wall of Aleister Crowley's Sicilian temple Thelema. It is representative of the satanic and pornographic murals restored by Kenneth Anger after these murals were whitewashed by the Italian government.

Italian tailors, Kinsey discovered, made a practice of making extra room for [genitalia] in the pants they cut, so that it came near to being a pocket. Italian men told Kinsey they did not like American-style jockey shorts because they brought the genitalia up into the crotch.[47] ...This difference in male attitudes toward the genitals Kinsey had first observed in Cuba, where he saw boys openly touching their sexual parts, in contrast to America where male children are taught from an early age not to do such a thing.[48]

ELITE AMERICAN EUGENICISTS

As a sexologist in the field, Kinsey wrote that groin touching was even more common in Southern Italy, where he said men unzip their pants in public, reach in and adjust their genitals, then zip up again. Even well-dressed businessmen did this in the middle of the day, Kinsey said, and he was sure that no one paid attention. Pomeroy states that Kinsey wrote that he saw businessmen stroking their penises through their clothing when they had a sudden erection.[49] Both Kinsey and Pomeroy were quite certain that such zipping, unzipping, and related activities were excellent telltale signs of Italian health and sexual freedom.

A highly promiscuous heterosexual and homosexual environment inevitably produces a corresponding rate of venereal disease. With Kinsey himself apparently suffering from one or more sexually transmitted diseases related to his orchitis, he and Pomeroy neglected to note that venereal disease commonly locates on the groin. Regular manipulation, shifting, scratching, and rubbing is common among those infected by disease in the groin. As poverty limits good hygiene and interest in cures, disease could easily account for obsessive genital touching which tourist Kinsey attributed to "sexual freedom." In 1955, a decade after the war, Italy remained largely destitute. The poor Italian male, whom Kinsey grumbled had to pay 25 cents for sex, could not easily pay for venereal-disease medication as well. He would just scratch and pass it on to others, including any children he fathered.

Kinsey uses the word "girl" interchangeably with "woman." Italian "men" had sex with "girls," not women. Apparently many of these "girls" were indeed juveniles. Kinsey, like jurist Rene Guyon, viewed women as "parasites." Only once does Pomeroy mention a girl's age. Kinsey's European translator and colleague, cryptically known as "R.J.," took Kinsey through many houses of prostitution. In one such facility, described as bare, dirty, and crowded with "girls" exhibiting themselves for inspection by potential customers, R.J. requested that he and Kinsey have sex with a thirteen-year-old child.[50]

Their order was processed by the madam, whom Kinsey viewed approvingly as bringing no moral values into her business affairs. He claims, however, that he did not use the girl. "The madam did not even seem surprised; she let it be known that girls of almost any age were available."[51] Kinsey, it appeared, was charmed.

THE TURIN GIRL

Kinsey saw the child-sex traffic in Italy as simply sex for pleasure. He thought male prostitutes were "handsome young Italian boys," while female prostitutes were "rather sloppy, fattish Southern Italians." At the regulated brothels, girls were paid,

> twenty-five cents, on a scale going up to seventy-five cents—about as cheap as [Kinsey] had ever recorded. The men who went upstairs, came down, stopped at the desk and paid the madam as they went out.... In Naples one night Kinsey talked to a girl from Turin [who] complained that she had had only nine men that night and could not live on this kind of trade.[52]

In an observation that rivals Guyon's "parasite" comment about women, Kinsey wrote of the Turin girl: "I have never seen any sex machine who had less emotion for the Southern Italian male, than she did.[53]

Was this the "sensitive" interviewer who found out everything about 10,000 to 18,000 males and females for his reports? Or was he a Grand Inquisitor who took delight in extracting the most intimate experiences from intimidated subjects? What could Kinsey learn from questioning a "sex machine" who had little "emotion for the Southern Italian male?"

The Turin girl had serviced *only* nine men in one evening. Kinsey said she was unhappy with the slow traffic and "complained she... could not live on this kind of trade." He viewed her "kind of trade" and her life—past, present, and future—in terms of her failure as a "sex machine." There are other pertinent questions. Did the girl support others financially—her parents, siblings, or perhaps one or more of her own children? What does her apparent lack of emotion say about her life, her feelings, and any hope for the future? Were Kinsey and Pomeroy so lacking in feeling that neither questioned how she could find *pleasure* in being copulated and sodomized by parades of dirty, scratching, strange, lonely, and commonly diseased men? Such matters apparently did not trouble Kinsey or friendly biographers, all of whom had access to his travel files and letters.[54]

Kinsey and Pomeroy clearly believed that prostitution, including child prostitution, was neither wrong nor exploitive. Indeed, Pomeroy's Institute for the Advanced Study of Human Sexuality has advocated the legalization of prostitution—with no age restrictions—as an "ethic" in their formal graduate training brochures. Pomeroy quotes Kinsey's summary of the quality of Italian sexuality:

> It is a man's country... and interestingly enough, I talked to a good many women who said they do not resent it.... I have never seen males who were less interested where females were concerned... even those who went off with the girls....[55]

According to Kinsey, the reason Italian boys and men demand pay for sodomy is that while they *want* to engage in sodomy gratis, they "could not offer free sex; it would have lowered their status." "Kinsey surmised this might be a cultural holdover from their Greek and Phoenician backgrounds."[56] Pomeroy continues,

> It was perfectly apparent to him, Kinsey noted later, that most of the males he saw looking for sex would have accepted it from either males or females; the only difference was that they would be paid for it if they were brought to climax by the males, and would pay for it themselves if females accomplished it. Consequently, a man might look for males first, then go out and have sex with a girl, since the girl would cost less than he had been paid by the male, and he would make a slight profit.[57]

Reading this, some might fairly conclude that Kinsey was so blinded by his own sexual appetites that he had no ability to see reality. Italian men paid for sex with women because, despite the larger female supply, women were more naturally desired and in demand. Kinsey's opinions about the sexual status of children, and sex throughout Italy generally, were revealing. The following excerpt from one of his letters reveals his perverse delusions as the father of the sexual revolution and sex education in the United States[58]:

> I don't suppose that we spoke to any person of any age, male or female, in the city who didn't promptly offer to find sexual relations for us. Several girls came out of a house in a back alley and hung on to our hands, begging for money, and when we, came to a cross-alley, a woman came out and got rid of the girls, then we had her for two or three blocks. It was the same way with boys, who offered to find anything for us. Any child could tell you where the nearest house of prostitution was, and it was never very far away.[59]

Pomeroy further notes:

> Another prime area of sexual activity in Naples was its famous Galleria, where Kinsey found it was possible to observe any number of people out hunting for sex at any hour of the day or night. Young boys masturbated and no one paid any attention, which proved once more, Kinsey wrote, "what a hysterical fear we have acquired of male genitals." There were both male and female prostitutes in the Galleria. One girl was completely nude to the waist; she had on a gauzy, thin shawl which kept slipping off. Kinsey saw a young, slender boy of twenty or so who was doing a big business with GIs, sailors and older Italian men. There were roving smaller children who would begin by offering to take the visitor to girls, and if that did not work, they would offer boys, their younger or older brothers, and finally themselves. Gangs of young adolescent boys swarmed on American sailors.[60]

The implied meaning here, as in all of Kinsey's work, is that the United States should imitate Italian homosexuals and let sexual freedom ring here as there. On the other hand, many of those living in Italy at the same time insist that Kinsey's accounts are untrue.[61] Yet the need to portray post-World War II Italian sexual disorders as a reflection of sexual health and vigor was crucial to the Kinsey thesis. Pomeroy writes,

> Kinsey saw men from thirteen to fifty [a thirteen-year-old man?] exhibiting and indicating they were ready for sexual contact [and] a boy with an erection who followed them for several blocks until they made it clear that they were not interested.... [One man insisting] "But I have to come to orgasm, and if you are too tired now, I can see you at 2 a.m."[62]

Kinsey's foreign travels read like *The Ugly American* as a "free-sex" missionary.[63] Pomeroy continues,

> It was noteworthy, he [Kinsey] said, that boys in Rome who brought letters up to the hotel rooms were satisfied with a tip, but in Naples they might sit down and make it clear they would be glad to stay longer for other purposes.... One handsome thirteen-year-old looked at their guide, smiled and instantly came to erection.... He followed Kinsey's little party around for several hours.... The town of Taormina was filled with older men who had been photographed as boys [in sexual activities] by the baron [a local pederast].[64]

Kinsey and Pomeroy were fully comfortable with young boys allegedly following them around with erections, and suggested that the elderly baron's young victims were unharmed by his criminal obsessions. Kinsey claimed, however, that there "were no purveyors of erotica in Sicily," since when "sex is so free, you don't have this sort of thing."[65] The comment gives one pause. Elsewhere, Kinsey had claimed that the absence of "erotica" was a sign of sexual repression. But as Pomeroy once noted, Kinsey could change his position or beliefs swiftly, and then change them back again at whim.

We are not told if Kinsey toured Europe's numerous historical and cultural sites during the trip. Based on the available accounts, apparently not. He preferred lower anatomy to lofty monuments testifying to centuries of human achievement.

SPAIN AND PORTUGAL

Kinsey's enthusiasm about sexual license in Scandinavia and Italy was balanced by his aversion for Spain, where he witnessed little public sex. He wrote of the Spaniards, "Their buttocks are a totally different shape and, obviously, genitalia were being held up by inner clothing to prevent anyone noticing them."[66] He was also most disturbed by the absence of male street prostitutes: "If I had been there longer and had people to guide me, I could have found all the hypocrisy that goes with the suppression." He bought a "tremendous lot of sex books in Barcelona," apparently for his Rockefeller-funded "nature library."[67] Pomeroy observes that Kinsey would have been pleased with post-Franco Spain: "He was a few years too early. Today many of the big hotels, even the most luxurious, have prostitutes openly inhabiting their lobbies and cocktail lounges."[68]

Kinsey also found Portugal to be rather dull. When he asked a cab driver about homosexual activities, the driver replied there were none. "Men are men in Portugal," said the cabbie. Kinsey described the response in his notebook as "A grand piece of nonsense," and dubbed Portugal "a priest-ridden country." Portuguese men, he snidely added, had "low buttocks."[69]

LAST DAYS

Kinsey died in August 1956, shortly after his return from Europe. The official cause was given as pneumonia brought on by overwork and an enlarged heart. Jones writes:

> He was suffering from pneumonia, which aggravated a long-standing heart condition.... The immediate cause of death was not pneumonia or a failing heart but an embolism caused by a bruise on one of his legs, which he had sustained in a fall while working in his garden.[70]

Despite the official medical diagnosis, there is reason to believe that Kinsey's bizarre array of sexual activities may have done him in. Despite the reality of common STDs, he had often denied the dangers of the sexual perversions he advocated. Jones, acknowledging what those at the Kinsey Institute knew but kept hidden, asserts that for Kinsey:

> Sexual activities in themselves rarely do physical damage, but disagreements over the significance of sexual behavior may result in personality conflicts, a loss of social standing, imprisonment, disgrace, and the loss of life itself.[71]

Throughout his life, his sexual behavior became more and more disordered. Jones, as noted in an earlier chapter, recalled:

> William Dallenback, the institute's photographer [said] Kinsey was becoming overtly exhibitionistic... having himself filmed, always from the chest down... in masochistic masturbation. The world's foremost expert on sexual behavior would insert an object such as a pipe cleaner or swizzle stick into his urethra, tie a rope around his scrotum, and then tug hard on the rope....[72]

Kinsey with Institute photographer Bill Dellenback in a barnyard.

On one occasion... Kinsey climbed into a bathtub, unfolded the blade of his pocketknife, and circumcised himself without benefit of anesthesia.... Recalled Dellenback, "God it must have been damn painful. It must have bled a hell of lot."[73]

Kinsey was not only an obsessive masturbator, but impotent as well. According to Jones in *The New Yorker* book summary (September, 1997), Kinsey required extensive and labored private sexual activity to attain a degree of sexual arousal. By 1954, as his fame peaked, he sank into depression:

Wylie Hall at Indiana University, was the site of Kinsey's sado-sexual hanging.

> Sales of the *Female* volume were not as great as he had hoped, his research was investigated by a congressional committee amid charges that it aided subversion.... One evening in August 1954, dejected and bitter, stood in his offices in the basement of Wylie Hall... threw a rope over the pipe, tied a knot around his scrotum, and wrapped the other end around his hand. Then he climbed onto a chair and jumped off.

Medical professionals explained to this author that this sado-masochistic act likely represented a long-standing pattern of behavior for Kinsey (confirmed by Gathorne-Hardy in his 1998 biography). This act of self-mutilation occurred as the Reece Committee prepared to call him to testify. He fled committee, citing health problems as an excuse. Jones continues,

> Shortly after this episode, Kinsey... Gebhard and Dellenback traveled to Peru.... There, Kinsey took to his bed, suffering from an infection in his pelvic region. He attributed his illness to a throat infection he had contracted earlier in Los Angeles, explaining that the infection had spread to his pelvis. A physician friend, however, labeled Kinsey's illness *orchitis*, pinpointing the testicles as the site of the infection.

According to *Dorland's Medical Dictionary,* orchitis is,

> ...marked by pain, swelling... usually due to gonorrhea, syphilis, filarial disease, or tuberculosis.... Traumatic orchitis [is] orchitis following trauma, vas ligation, or surgical manipulation, without evidence of previous disease, believed to be due to an infectious process resulting from lowered resistance of the injured tissues to bacteria.[74]

Kinsey's orchitis followed the "trauma" of Kinsey's compulsive genital self-mutilation, causing "injured tissues," lowering Kinsey's resistance to "bacteria," a compromised immune system and his death from orchitis. In the same way, Kinsey's reported pneumonia and heart condition could have logically resulted from advanced syphilis or other venereal diseases.

Indiana University's biographical publicity about Kinsey says nothing about his "orchitis," or any other medical condition that could have resulted from sexual disorder or venereal disease.

The *Indianapolis Star*, whose editorial page masthead carries Abraham Lincoln's dictum, "Let the people know the facts and the country will be saved," commented on James Jones lengthy article about Kinsey in *The New Yorker* magazine for September 1, 1997:

> Kinsey gave the world a distorted—some would say sick—view of human sexuality. And what ought to enrage Hoosier taxpayers is that their money helped him do it. For years, the institute received about $500,000.00 annually from Indiana University. The funding was cut in half in 1993, largely at the behest of some university trustees. Political commentator Patrick Buchanan, never one to mince words, once called Kinsey "America's original dirty old man." The *New Yorker* article suggests Buchanan may be uncomfortably close to the truth.[75]

The press was devastated with news of his illness. The "sexual revolution" faced a potentially serious setback were it widely known that the theoretical father of the movement had died from an advanced stage of sadosexual autoerotic (masturbatory) activity. *The National Review* commented on Kinsey's untimely demise:

> As for Kinsey's own quest for personal liberation, it ended in pain and squalor: he developed a massive pelvic infection as the result of his masochistic practices, almost certainly hastening his death at the age of 62. Growing up at the turn of the century, he had been exposed to countless tracts warning that masturbation led to insanity and death. In his case, they may have been onto something.[76]

What has taken place at the Kinsey Institute in recent years? One reproductive "expert" announced plans to create a human clone under the guise of "Gender and Reproductive Technology,"[77] an especially worrisome development since the Kinsey Institute is now named "The Kinsey Institute for the Study of Sex, Gender and Reproduction." Its past director, June Reinisch, has been implicated in research that entails giving pregnant women male hormones, without their knowledge, so that gender-specific behavioral effects on the babies can be observed.[78] And, the Kinsey Institute, without apology, reprinted Kinsey's two volumes for libraries, universities, students, teachers and the public.

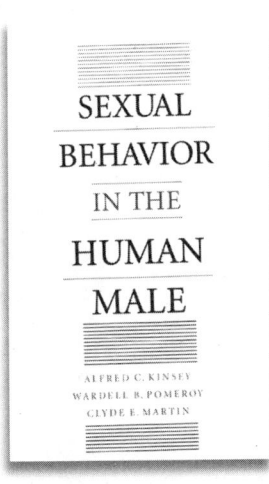

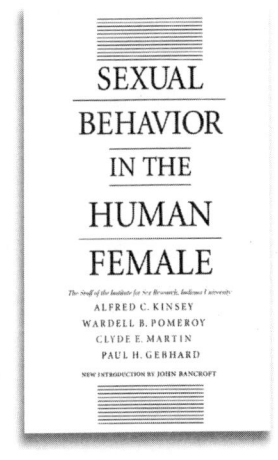

Kinsey's two books were republished by Indiana University in celebration of Kinsey's 50th jubilee in 1998.

"Mr. Tilby is in the Kinsey Report."
This cartoon suggested that Kinsey and his data were appropriate for discussion in polite, mixed company.

THE COLD, DEADLY HANDS OF KINSEY

No other report of a scientific investigation has ever been launched with such carefully planned publicity as was this volume. Newspapers and magazines were given release dates for articles about the study to be printed in advance of the book's publication, and Dr. Kinsey and his associates stipulated that manuscripts of the articles must be submitted to them for checking.[79]

The New Yorker magazine
January 3, 1948

AFTER WORLD WAR II

Kinsey's two reports ushered in the era of sexual license that he espoused. The available evidence indicates that mainstream America did not initially believe Kinsey's "findings."

It was in the face of a relentless, one-sided media assault that attitudes began to change, as Americans were pushed and prodded into the sexual revolution. The country gradually became Kinseyfied. "Science" supposedly confirmed that sex was no more than a pleasurable pastime; that masturbation was harmless; that "wife-swapping" and "swinging" could solve silly jealousies; that "no-fault" divorce could end friction and blaming—better for the children—that early premarital sex could strengthen marriages without increasing rates of out-of-wedlock births and venereal disease; that exposure to obscenity was sexually healthy; that religious strictures were either outmoded or overstated; that reducing or abolishing penalties for sex crimes, and providing parole for sex offenders, would reduce rape and other types of sex abuse; and that 10 percent of American men were homosexual, and virtually all others bisexual, so anti-sodomy laws should repealed.

No longer restrained by "Victorian" and "Puritanical" strictures, America could at last be the "Land of the Free" in every sense of that word—free from traditional morality and free from self-restraint.

Cartoon depicting the marital suspicion engendered by Kinsey's data–perhaps especially that 50 percent of American men were secret adulterers.

Were Kinsey, Hirschfeld, Crowley, and Guyon alive today, (or for that matter, those of the Marxist "Frankfort school" including the USA college guru, Herbert Marcuse) they would no doubt be delighted to find their model of sex education dominating the media, the arts, and permeating most of our schools.

They would find their sexual model, "The Kinsey Model," imbedded in laws and government policies. These sexual liberators and libertines would be pleased to see obscenity in corner drugstores, on the Internet, in public libraries, private and public schoolrooms and on roadside billboards.

Kinsey would be thrilled by the extent to which "The Kinsey Model" was entrenched everywhere, the way non-marital sex, adultery, sodomy, and bi/homosexuality are glamorized in film and on TV. He would delight in watching teachers instruct grade-school children on how to place condoms on bananas, cucumbers, and wooden penises, and how to make models of their sex organs in Play-Doh. And he would thrill at the sight of schoolrooms plastered with sexual and patently pornographic AIDS posters, while the Ten Commandments are prohibited by judge-made "law."

This 1990 Kinsey Institute book launched the current "sexual literacy" campaign in American classrooms. The Institute urged that teachers become "trained" to supplant parents who are alleged to be "sexually illiterate."

It is doubtful that any other 20th century figure can equal Alfred C. Kinsey for achieving widespread public acceptance of the disordered and destructive elements of his own troubled imagination, or in wreaking havoc on our culture in the name of "science."

However, as it turns out, Kinsey was only one of many so called "geniuses," eugencists, who sought to remake humankind in their own images. Our final chapter, good reader, introduces others of Kinsey's elitist 1930s-1950s international network. We will go back in time to Cabaret Berlin, Hitler, Germany, and Stalinist Russia, raising further questions and some answers, about Kinsey's crimes and consequences.

CHAPTER 9 NOTES

[1]. James H. Jones, *Alfred C. Kinsey: A Public/Private Life*, W.W. Norton, New York, 1997, p. 809 footnote 78.
[2]. Rene Wormser, *Foundations*, The Devin-Adair Company, New York, 1958, pp. vii-viii.
[3]. Carroll Quigley, *Tragedy and Hope*, Macmillan, New York, 1966, pp. 954-955.
[4]. Quigley, p. 950.
[5]. Wormser, pp. vii-viii.
[6]. Wormser, pp. vii-viii.
[7]. Gregory Ahlgren and Stephen Monier, *Crime of the Century, The Lindbergh Kidnapping Hoax*, Boston, Massachusetts: Braden Books, 1993. Dr. Carrell was the scientist with whom Lindbergh had maintained a relationship since their work at the Rockefeller Institute in New York. Carrell argued for the preservation of the strong. "Only the elite makes the progress of the masses possible," he wrote. There should be no interest in "encouraging the survival of the unfit and the defective...." These, he concluded, should be gassed.
[8]. Wormser, pp. 100-101, footnote.
[9]. Jones, p. 734.
[10]. Wormser, p. 100-101.
[11]. Wormser, p. 102.
[12]. Wormser, p. 103.
[13]. Wormser, pp. 102-103.
[14]. Wormer, pp. 102-103.

15. Author's interview with Pamela Hobbs Hoffecker, January 12, 1996.
16. Wormser, p. 351. See also William H. McIlhany, II, *The Tax-Exempt Foundations*, Arlington House Publishers, Westport, Connecticut, 1980.
17. Wormser, pp. 345-346.
18. While Jones suggests that the Reece Committee continued its investigation well into 1955 (p. 737), this does not appear to be what finally happened. (Personal interview with Robert Goldsbough, The American Research Foundation, Inc., Baltimore Maryland, January 5, 1998. Goldsbough's Foundation houses the Norman Dodd papers).
19. Author's interview, May 6, 1997, Washington, DC.
20. Warren Weaver memo to CIB, May 7, 1951, Rockefeller Archive Center, p. 1.
21. Weaver, footnote, p.3.
22. E. Michael Jones, *Culture Wars*, "The Gay Science" February, 1997.
23. Kinsey, on "Reputations," *Biography*, BBC-TV, rebroadcast on Arts & Entertainment, 1996.
24. Plutocracy is defined as government by a wealthy class, Encarta, 1997.
25. Wardell Pomeroy, *Dr. Kinsey and the Institute for Sex Research*, Harper & Row, New York, 1972, p. 401.
26. Pomeroy, p. 405.
27. Pomeroy, p. 409.
28. Ibid.
29. Ibid.
30. Pomeroy, p. 406.
31. Pomeroy, p .410.
32. Ibid.
33. See discussion on Mr. and Mrs. Myrdal in Claire Chambers, *The SIECUS Circle*, Western Islands, Belmont, Mass., 1977.
34. Cornelia V. Christenson, *Kinsey, A Biography*, Indiana University Press, Bloomington, Indiana, 1971, p. 195.
35. Sandy Robertson, *The Aleister Crowley Scrapbook*, Samuel Weiser, York Beach, Maine, 1994, p. 83.
36. See Robertson, Landis, Cavendish, et al.
37. John Symonds, *The Confessions of Aleister Crowley*, Arcana, England, 1979.
38. Bill Landis, *Anger, The Unauthorized Biography of Kenneth Anger*, Harper Collins, New York, 1995.
39. Landis, pp. 87-89, p. 148.
40. Landis, p. 87.
41. Landis, p. 88.
42. David Brinkley in *Washington Goes to War*, Ballantine Books, New York, 1988, reported that Viereck was convicted of treason in World War II, as a paid Nazi agent. This author verified the conviction with the extant public records.
43. Pomeroy, pp. 197, 414.
44. Robertson, Ibid, p. 83.
45. Landis, Ibid. See also, Richard Cavendish, Editor, *Man, Myth and Magic: An Illustrated Encyclopedia of the Supernatural*, Marshal Cavendish, New York, 1970. Crowley's *The Book of The Law*, which he claimed came from a spirit of one of the Secret Chiefs of Madame Blavatsky, was to spawn a new world with Crowley as prophet.
46. Landis, Ibid.
47. Pomeroy, p. 425.
48. Pomeroy, p. 425.
49. Pomeroy, p. 425.
50. Pomeroy, p. 424.
51. Pomeroy, p. 424.
52. Pomeroy, p. 422.
53. Pomeroy, p. 422.
54. Within the total pages devoted to children, neither Kinsey nor Pomeroy express any concern for the critical issues of child venereal disease, pregnancy, from kin or non-kin, emotional vulnerability and blackmail, resulting patterns of prostitution, drug and alcohol abuse, self-inflicted harm (cutting, burning of the body) or suicide, and the like, all of which is well and completely documented as the common result of children's early sexual abuse. All the more so in Kinsey's day, the "data" on the harm to children from sexual relations with adults was understood in the medical and psychological literature. Indeed, that was one of the key reasons for the unified efforts of "Puritans" and feminists at the turn of the century. It would have been impossible, however, for men on the Kinsey team, men who viewed "convulsions" in an infant being raped by a man as "definite pleasure," to hear, much less accept, much less print, the facts, about the trauma of child rape. Moreover, having interviewed the rapists and the incestuous rapists, Kinsey and his team had nothing to say about the interviews with their victims.
55. Pomeroy, p. 421.

56. Pomeroy, p. 426.
57. Pomeroy, pp. 425-6.
58. Pomeroy, p. 423.
59. Pomeroy, p. 425.
60. Pomeroy, p. 426.
61. Pomeroy, p. 425.
62. Pomeroy, p. 26.
63. While Pomeroy offers a disclaimer, there is no real evidence that Kinsey knew or cared about the true plight and economic conditions of Italian men, women, or children. "I should make it clear, I think, that Kinsey was not insensitive to the other aspects of life in Italian cities. His journal speaks often of the poverty in Naples and in other parts of Italy. He was well aware that part of the abundant sexuality directed toward him and any other obvious American was motivated by the desperate need for money" (p. 426).
64. Pomeroy, p. 427.
65. Pomeroy, p. 428.
66. Pomeroy, pp. 428-429.
67. Pomeroy, p. 428.
68. Pomeroy, p. 428.
69. Pomeroy, p. 429.
70. James Jones, "Dr. Yes," *New Yorker*, September 1, 1997, p. 113.
71. Jones, Ibid, p. 108.
72. Jones, Ibid, p. 113.
73. James H. Jones, *Alfred C. Kinsey: A Public/Private Life*, W.W. Norton, New York, 1997.
74. *Dorland's Medical Dictionary*, W.B. Saunders, Philadelphia, 1981, page 933.
75. Editorial Board, "The Kinsey Legacy," *The Indianapolis Star*, August 26, 1997.
76. Terry Teachout, "What the Doctor Saw," *National Review*, October 13, 1997, p. 69.
77. *The Washington Post*, January 1, 1997
78. Elizabeth Hall, *Psychology Today*, "Profile: June Reinisch, New Directions for the Kinsey Institute," June 1986, pp. 33-39.
79. "The Kinsey Report," *The New Yorker*, January 3, 1948, p. 60.
80. Edward Everett Hale, "Lend a Hand," in James Dalton Morrison, Ed., *Masterpieces of Religious Verse* (1948); also, John Bartlett, *Familiar Quotations*, Emily Morison Beck, Ed., 14th Edition, Little, Brown and Company, Boston, 1968 [1855], p. 717.

CHAPTER 10

FROM BERLIN TO BLOOMINGTON
KINSEY'S "SCIENTIFICALLY TRAINED OBSERVERS"

Write the laws carefully so as not to interfere with human cloning research that stops short of producing a baby but that might advance medical science. The laws also should not interfere with research in the cloning of humans.... [The commission on cloning humans] would allow any cloning research to continue that stops short of actual implantation... of a cloned egg into a woman's uterus... [Said one critic] "This means it is OK to clone as long as you kill."[3]

The Washington Times, June 8, 1997

[The] famous Krupp munitions works at Essen employed a larger staff of trained scientists than any university in the world.[1]

Edward McNall Burns, *Western Civilizations*, 1958

Better data on preadolescent climax come from the histories of adult males who have had sexual contacts with younger boys and who, with their adult backgrounds, are able to recognize and interpret the boys' experiences. Unfortunately, not all of the subjects with such contacts in their histories were questioned on this point of preadolescent reactions; but 9 of our adult male subjects have observed such orgasm. Some of these adults are technically trained persons who have kept diaries or other records, which have been put at our disposal; and from them we have secured information on 317 preadolescents who were either observed in self-masturbation, or who were observed in contacts with other boys or older adults.[2]

Kinsey, et al, *Sexual Behavior of the Human Male*, 1948

Since 1981, when this author exposed at the Fifth World Congress of Sexology the Kinsey team's collaboration with and/or involvement in child sexual experiments, the most frequently asked questions have been: Where did the children in Kinsey's *Male* and *Female* volumes come from, and where are the children of Table 34 today? And how did Kinsey's "technically trained observers" gain access to 1,888 (or even 317) boys and nearly 200 girls for illegal genital experiments in the 1930-40s?[4] To this date, the Kinsey Institute and Indiana University have refused to reveal the names of any

We now know that Kinsey and his staff engaged in sex crimes hidden from the world.

subjects or experimenters. Therefore, this final chapter presents circumstantial evidence about similar publicly-funded human experimentation in Europe during the 1930s and 1940s, when at least one elite perpetrator was permitted to avoid accountability due to intervention of a Rockefeller Foundation board member. This author will also provide a glimpse of the intent and direction of the scientific community and its pre- and postwar public and private funders. Far beyond Bloomington, a network of scientists worked and collaborated, some of whom were Kinsey's friends and colleagues and part of his "grand scheme."[5]

The who, where, how, and why of the child "orgasm" data have haunted this author since discovering Table 34 in 1977. The Kinsey team claimed to have "interviewed" children in the "ghetto," and at the Chicago Randall School for Negro Boys, the Delaware Kruse School for Negro Girls, the Mishawaka Indiana Children's Home, and several other orphanages or reformatories.[6] But filming and concealing child orgasm experiments en masse, "using manual and oral techniques" as reported by Dr. Gebhard, would have been extraordinarily difficult at the time. Many reputations would have been placed at risk.

The Table 34 video, produced by Family Research Council in 1995, echoed the question, "Where are the children in Kinsey's reports?"

Dr. John Bancroft, current director of the Kinsey Institute, insists that Kinsey was a pioneer and, above all, an honest scientist. But where could a team of honest scientists obtain access to more than 2,000 children for sex experiments apparently filmed under laboratory conditions?[7]

Following introduction of "The Child Protection and Ethics in Education Act" in Congress (1995), which called for an investigation of the Kinsey data, Dr. Bancroft became the first Kinsey Institute director to publicly repudiate a portion of Kinsey's data. Bancroft acknowledged that Kinsey was "misleading" when he reported that he had collaborated with "at least nine" trained observers on the child experiments. Dr. Bancroft claimed to have found in the Kinsey files that only "one" lone pedophile provided the data for Tables 30-34. He opined that none of the children involved would likely ever step forward, since they were more than 50 years old, and most "must be dead by now."[8]

BANCROFT'S "LONE PEDOPHILE THEORY"

Until Dr. Bancroft arrived at Indiana University in May 1995, it had been claimed that the Institute's files were entirely consistent with the Kinsey reports. The two prior Kinsey Institute directors, successive Indiana University presidents, and Kinsey's coauthors had all defended the reports as virtually flawless. Following the 1981 Jerusalem conference, then-Institute director Dr. June Reinisch temporarily closed the Institute, she said, in order to conduct her own in-house investigation of Kinsey's child sexuality data. She subsequently reaffirmed the Kinsey reports to be accurate.[9] She and the University then launched an aggressive press campaign worldwide to discredit this author for focusing attention on Kinsey's child experiments and child sexuality data.

Except for Dr. Bancroft, Institute and University academicians have claimed that at least nine "technically trained observers" collaborated with the Kinsey team in the design and conduct of the child experiments. Kinsey coauthor and one-time Institute director Dr. Paul Gebhard confirmed during a recorded telephone interview that he and other members of the team gave instructions for the "trained observers" (note the plural) to use stop watches to time the child "orgasms." And Kinsey wrote in the *Male* volume that the data on child "orgasm" came from "9 of our adult male subjects," whom Kinsey said "observed such orgasm."[10]

Gebhard admitted that some of the experimenters were "participant observers," since they themselves used "manual and oral techniques" while testing the children. Kinsey wrote that some of his "technically trained" men "kept diaries or other records" at the team's suggestion. Gebhard reported such "records" included films and photographs that were "put at our disposal." The Kinsey reports claim that at least "317 preadolescents" were subjected to sexual experiments by "older adults,"[11] while Gebhard and Pomeroy subsequently confirmed that at least 2,035 child subjects were involved.[12]

Dr. June Reinisch, former director of the Kinsey Institute. Under her Johns Hopkins mentor, Dr. John Money, Reinisch says she administered male hormones to pregnant women, without their knowledge or consent.

DIARIES OF "OLDER ADULTS"

How did Kinsey acquire sex diaries from "older adults" about children observed in various stages of adult-child sexual contact? As noted, Kinsey himself had said that his team gave "instructions" to anyone willing to keep daily records of their sexual activity with adults, children, etc. The 1,400 or more "sex offenders" whom Kinsey and his team recruited from within and without prison would likely have been included in his call for diary-keepers. Gebhard writes,

> We [were]... amoral at best and criminal at worst. Examples of amorality are our refusal to inform a wife that her husband has... an active venereal disease, and our refusal to tell parents that their child is involved in seriously deviant behavior. *An example of criminality is our refusal to cooperate with authorities in apprehending a pedophile we had interviewed who was being sought for a [child] sex murder*[13] [Emphasis added.]

So the Kinsey team was aware of its own "criminality." And with whom did it collaborate to obtain its data, even to the point of protecting a pedophile being sought for murder?[14] "We have a network of connections that could put us into almost any group with which we wished to work, anywhere"[15] wrote Kinsey. The experiments were also prospective; that is, the protocol involved a future collection of clinical research, including diaries or daily calendars solicited by the Kinsey team. The team made suggestions and asked that the research be designed and carried out to meet Kinsey Institute specifications:

> Many of the [sex activity] calendars are a product of our call for such material....
>
> Persons... who are willing to begin keeping day-by-day calendars showing the sources and frequencies of their outlet [sexual activity], are urged to write us for instructions. Many of the calendars have come from scientifically trained persons.[16]

Meeting with three American Statistical Association representatives, Kinsey defends Martin's statistical analyses with "Edmondson" pretending to be Kinsey's statistician.

Kinsey's claim that incest is essentially harmlessness served to justify his call for men across the country to sexually interact over time with their own and other children. The child who resisted sexual interaction with a parent would have little recourse to stop an incestuous guardian who faced little threat of exposure and apprehension. Incestuous adults "willing to begin keeping day-by-day calendars showing the sources" and "frequencies of their outlet" were urged to write the Kinsey team for "instructions." If the parent, guardian, or foster parent was a science teacher, doctor, or other technically-trained professional, he or she would have qualified in Kinsey's broad sense as "scientifically trained."

The team apparently had no qualms about interviewing hundreds of violent sex criminals about their sexual interaction with children. It interviewed at least one child sex murder suspect, whom it protected, despite the documented inclination of pedophile rapist-murderers to continue raping and murdering until they are caught and incarcerated.[17] Yet, Kinsey assured the world his data were sound and trustworthy because

Dallenbeck's secret job at Indiana University was to film Kinsey and his group in sex acts and to process similar sex material mailed to Kinsey by his correspondents.

> the greatly disturbed type of person who goes to psychiatric clinics has been relatively rare in our sample. We have refused to take histories from recognizable psychotics who were handicapped with poor memories, hallucinations, or fantasies that distorted the fact.[18]

COLLABORATION WITH "SCIENTIFICALLY TRAINED OBSERVERS"

Aside from the amazing implication that the 1,400 sex offenders deemed acceptable were neither "disturbed" nor "handicapped with poor memories, hallucinations, or fantasies that distorted the fact,"[19] let us turn now from the personal diary-keepers mentioned in the *Female* volume to Pomeroy, who refers to a number of "technically trained" professionals who collaborated with Kinsey on taxonomic studies.[20] Many were reputable colleagues and co-researchers. Pomeroy writes:

> We need more hands.... [In] 1943 [Kinsey] began, to push the project into high gear.... [In 1942 he] employed a half-dozen good gynecologists to make experimental tests of a long series of patients—the English doctor was one of them—to determine the extent to which women were aware of tactile and heavier stimulation in every part of the genitalia.
>
> If we could get the right collaborators to help... major objectives can be reached in a reasonable period of years... Kinsey... [worked with] scientists [who] were studying heart rate and respiration during intercourse. He wanted to hire a physiologist to study these phenomena at the Institute.... A medical school researcher... wanted to find out whether the number of sperm cells per ejaculation... was lowered in cases where a man ejaculated two or more times in rapid succession....

Kinsey worked with many doctors, including primatologist Dr. Frank Beach; gynecologists Dr. Earle Marsh (with whom, Gathorne-Hardy, Kinsey and Mrs. Kinsey had a sexual liaison) and Dr. Francis Shields; Dr. Harry Benjamin, the New York clinical endocrinologist (another pro-pedophile colleague); Rene Guyon, who worked also with Dr. Robert Dickinson, and who "had conducted a massive study" of the "physiologic effects of masturbation on the sexual organs of women"; physiologist Dr. Clifford Adams from Pennsylvania State University; Dr. Abraham Stone, New York physician and marriage counselor who helped pioneer birth-control methods; Dr. Karl Bowman of the controversial Langley Porter Clinic in San Francisco; consulting psychologist A.E. Hamilton, who headed "the Hamilton School"; Dr. John Hamon, a fertility expert in San Francisco; Dr. Philip Polatin of Columbia University; Dr. Carl Moore of the University of Chicago; and so on.

These "upper-level" scientists seem to have been in a different category than the "diary keepers."

"COORDINATING" THE WORK

Kinsey wrote in the *Male* volume: "It has been necessary to develop techniques for coordinating the work of those associated in the research, so that the data secured by the several interviewers might fairly be added together."[22] He had learned how to "observe and record by proxy"[23] the diary keepers' calendars, and the detailed systematic accounts and "physiologic" data from foreign correspondents in Europe, Russia, Italy, and Japan.[24] You will recall that his "network of connections" would reach almost "any group… anywhere."[25] Kinsey was indebted to the Rockefeller Foundation for providing such connections, and he dropped the Rockefeller name liberally (though requested not to do so) to gain entry into the networks and the halls of power.[26] Rockefeller connections were important in the scientific community. Pomeroy states that "outside the boundaries of Bloomington, his [Kinsey's] best friends were scientists like himself who, in one way or another, were a part of his grand scheme."[27]

Kinsey, known for his taxonomical precision, was said to have collected four million different specimens of gall wasps.[28] He taught his young assistants to measure wingspread and other features, and to categorize each wasp. He would guide and analyze their work himself. His reputation was built on his obsession to control every aspect of the research in which he was involved. As a "New Biology" scientist, he would seek the same control over his sex research, noting that control

Unbeknownst to the journalists (above) who popularized Kinsey's research, they aided in his outreach to adults who sexually abused children in order to be included in Kinsey's "data."

of and access to primary sources for experiments with human subjects were more limited (if more challenging) than for wasps.

The question arises whether Kinsey, in his search for primary sources, worked with English—and possibly French, German, or Soviet doctors—both before and during the war. Allen Dulles, while director of the Central Intelligence Agency, once stated that some projects were "too risky to perform within the borders of the United States." Dulles cited an institute run by a Dr. Cameron as a "good source for human guinea pigs."[29] He was referring to American-born E. Ewen Cameron, who would later serve as president of the American Psychiatric Association. Dr. Cameron was a Kinsey correspondent and part of the Rockefeller network beyond the boundaries of Bloomington.

Dr. Cameron, like Kinsey, was a Rockefeller grantee.[30] Robert Morison, the Rockefeller Foundation Medical Director who praised Kinsey as perhaps their most important grantee, was Cameron's Rockefeller patron.[31] Dr. Cameron was also a CIA mind-control researcher who conducted brutal human experiments, detailed by investigative author Gordon Thomas in *Journey into Madness: The True Story of Secret CIA Mind Control and Medical Abuse* (1989). Dulles preferred doing sensitive human experiments outside "the borders of the United States." Thomas writes,

Robert Morison

> While political terrorism has been capturing widespread attention.... Almost nothing has been made public of how doctors today use their knowledge and skills in its support. Yet they regularly medically examine political prisoners... to assess the degree of torture to be used. They attend interrogations to treat the direct physical effect of the torture they have approved so that investigation can continue. They recommend how much further torture can then be applied. Physicians... falsify autopsy reports... for persons those doctors know were tortured to death [claiming] "cardiac failure" or "pneumonia" on those certificates.... Psychiatry, in particular, is highly vulnerable to being used by the state to maintain power and control the thoughts and actions of its citizens.[32]

Let us follow the work of one scientist within the Kinsey/Rockefeller Foundation international network, where chilling clinical human experiments by "trained observers" and scientists in laboratory conditions actually took place before and during World War II, when Kinsey's research also was being conducted.[33]

SCIENTIFIC CONNECTIONS:

Kinsey came from the Bussey School at Harvard, a hotbed of the "New Biology" of which German American Jacque Loeb (1859-1924) was the foremost architect and proponent. Loeb believed that "man himself can act as a creator, even in living Nature, forming it eventually according to his will."[34] His principal idea was that "it is possible to get the life-phenomena under our control, and that such a control and nothing else is the aim of biology."[35] He would end his career at the Rockefeller Institute for Medical Research. Many men in Kinsey's scientific network beyond Bloomington shared this heady and self-important view of themselves and the "new biology." One such was Hermann J. Muller (1890-1967).

ROCKEFELLER, MULLER, GERMANY, AND RUSSIA
WHO WAS HERMANN MULLER?

The Rockefeller Foundation was part of the network that had adopted a eugenic view of human life. Writing in the November 1933 issue of *Fidelity*, Suzanne Rini described how Rockefeller's Frederick Osborn:

Hermann J. Muller

> ...devised a cleanup campaign for eugenics after the War. Complaining that people generally reject seeing themselves as inferior, he suggested... rely[ing] on other motivation... to build a system of voluntary unconscious selection ... Let's stop telling anyone that they have a generally inferior genetic quality, for they will never agree. Let's base our proposals on the desirability of having children born in homes where they will get affectionate and responsible care, and perhaps our proposals will be accepted.... The iron fist in the velvet glove was born, as well as cheery slogans to accompany the crypto-coercion, such as "Every child a wanted child."[36]

Both Hermann Muller and Kinsey appeared in the pages of *Sexology*, a pseudo-medical sex journal on whose board sat Kinsey colleagues Harry Benjamin and Rene Guyon. Muller and Kinsey agreed on the need to replace religion with scientific belief and sexual restraint with sexual license. They also shared an enthusiasm for "positive eugenics," the elimination of defective genetic stock by mass sterilization. In *The Human Agenda* (1972), medical ethicist Roderick Gorney connects eugenicist Muller with Aldous Huxley's predictions in *Brave New World*:

> The more radical method of genetic intervention is called "positive eugenics." This is a more ambitious and controversial proposal, championed, among others, by the late Hermann Muller, who [advocates] selective breeding... to eliminate the defects... [and] to increase the number of people with "superior" qualities. One way to accomplish this would be to establish sperm (and eventually egg) banks in which the reproductive cells of individuals with the exceptional health, intelligence, or special talent could be preserved. These could then be used by people who want to produce children with better endowment than would result from their own genes. Some have objected that people would not willingly agree to substitute the sex cells and characteristics of others for their own. Muller rejects "the stultifying assumption that people would have to be forced, rather than inspired, to engage in any effective kind of genetic betterment." He points out that...
>
>> seemingly "normal couples" ...would elect to use this means of having at least a part of their family.... [T]he obvious successes achieved by this method would within a generation win it still more adherents. It would constitute a major extension of human freedom in a quite new direction.
>
> [Gorney continues] But naturally, such a program poses a potential threat to our values.... It opens the door to the frightening abuses of compulsion outlined in Aldous Huxley's *Brave New World*, such as the creation of special classes best fitted to be servants to others who are rulers. With good reason, we might fear the consequences of such a system conducted according to the mad assumptions of racists.[37]

What Gorney feared had already come to pass. Muller privately advocated forced sterilization. In 1945, the eugenicist/geneticist[38] joined the small Indiana University zoology department. Like Kinsey, he was a long-term recipient of Rockefeller Foundation largess through the National Research Council.[39] In 1946 he garnered a Nobel Prize for medicine for his discovery of the use of X-rays to induce and accelerate genetic mutation. Although his major work was said to be with fruit flies (*Drosophila*), Muller declared that "the method can be applied to reproductive cells of any kind,"[40] including humans.

In his book *Out of the Night* (1935), Dr. Muller expressed his hope that he would see the day when selective breeding would allow the cloning of masses of human resources. He advocated the establishment of sperm banks to collect the sperm of geniuses for the genetic improvement of future generations.

In 1980, 13 years after his death, the Hermann Muller Sperm Bank, containing the sperm of Nobel prize winners, was established. It currently operates in California as the Repository for Germinal Choice, which stores and distributes the sperm of Nobel laureates and others of "exceptional ability."[41] It has been lauded in *Sexology* magazine by Kinsey colleagues Rene Guyon and Harry Benjamin.[42]

Nobel Prize winner Hermann J. Muller advocated forced sterilization and an elitist "Sperm Bank" in *Sexology*.

Muller was born in New York City on December 1, 1890. His paternal grandparents had emigrated from the Rhineland to America. His father had continued the grandfather's art metal works. Muller's Jewish-American mother was descended from Spanish-Portuguese forebears who settled in Britain prior to their migration to the United States. As noted in his Guggenheim grant application, Muller both read and wrote German.[43]

Kinsey with Dr. Carl Hartman at the University of Texas at Austin in 1951 where Muller was then a faculty member. Hartman later became a director of the Ortho Research Foundation in Raritan, New Jersey.

In 1920, he joined the zoology department at the University of Texas, Austin (UT-A). Kinsey and Muller had a mutual friend in the department, Professor Carl Hartman, whom Kinsey visited the same year that Muller joined the faculty. This was just prior to Kinsey's own affiliation with Indiana University's zoology department.[44] While at UT-A, Muller "helped to recruit students for the communist-supported National Student League," where he aided in publishing *The Spark*, named for Lenin's newspaper, *Iskra* ("The Spark").[45]

Muller received his first Rockefeller Foundation grant in 1925 for work on mutation and genetics. The Foundation also funded a contract that resulted in his 1935 paper on twins, heredity, and eugenics. The Archive at the Rockefeller Foundation confirmed that Muller's initial grant was $65,000, and suggested that funding continued until 1936. Some of his writings appeared *Sexology*. In 1932 he received a Guggenheim fellowship to conduct research in Berlin.

BERLIN WELCOMES MULLER

When he returned to Berlin in 1932, after an earlier visit in 1922, Muller was well aware that the German capital was the epicenter of research and experimentation on brain function and its relationship to genetics and psychiatry. He knew that for more than a decade racist genetics had been welcomed by many in American, English, and German medical and psychiatric circles. The German medical profession was wholly sympathetic with his sperm bank proposals for breeding supermen. Muller played a role in the move to eliminate the traditional family (mother and father with children), a major impediment on the road to achieving the "brave new world." Under the umbrella of the "new biology," Kinsey's grand scheme of uncontrolled human sexuality, and Muller's controlled procreation under selective breeding conditions, would become important elements of the super-race program.

Berlin's first "scientific" sex "Institute" had been established in 1919 by the famous homosexual, Dr. Magnus Hirschfeld. The first survey of homosexuality was conducted in Berlin by Hirschfeld, who treated sexual deviants referred to him by the courts. Among these were many sex perverts, rapists, pedophiles, pederasts, etc., including many patients from the Nazi Party.⁴⁶ It was in Berlin that Freud's more contentious disciple, Wilhelm Reich, had begun his "sex positive" campaign to recruit youth into sex education programs and early peer sex.⁴⁷ Since 1920, the German eugenics, birth control, and sterilization movements building on the American model, had been crusading for the sterilization of those with "bad" genes, and the breeding of "good" genes. Pornography had been mainstreamed via German "sex hygiene" films and magazines, and a booming homosexual world—rife with novels, texts, films, and the international "gay culture" of bars and baths—focused on the joys of pederasty ("man-boy love").⁴⁸ Before 1932, as the Nazis began to gain power, sex revolutionaries were strutting about Berlin in the striking uniform of the macho-male Prussian/Nazi storm trooper.

1926 Berlin, The Eldorado, a transvestite night spot, and "Monokel," a lesbian bar.

In Weimar, Germany, "Cabaret Berlin" featured nude "straight" and "gay" dance hall entertainment, while drugs dominated the urban German cultural landscape. Weimar's wide-open pan-sexual revolution preceded, indeed laid the groundwork for, the National Socialist (Nazi) takeover. As in the French and Russian revolutions, Germany's political upheaval would be preceded by a sexual revolution, with thousands of destitute boy and girl prostitutes roaming violent streets in search of customers and recruits.⁴⁹ Alex de Jonge writes in *The Weimar Chronicle: Prelude to Hitler* (1978) that after World War I, widespread inflation destroyed the stable, conservative German middle class, and predisposed its youth to cynical rootlessness and disorder. The resultant trauma,

> destroyed savings, self-assurance, a belief in the value of hard work, morality and sheer human decency.... Traditional middle-class morality disappeared overnight. People of good family cohabited and had illegitimate children.... Pearl Buck wrote that "Love was old-fashioned, sex was modern. It was the Nazis who restored the 'right to love' in their propaganda," [creating] that new decadent and dissolute generation that put Berlin on the cosmopolitan pleasure seeker's map.⁵⁰

> Some of those who looked most handsome and elegant were actually boys in disguise. It seemed incredible considering the sovereign grace with which they displayed their saucy coats and hats. I wondered if they might be wearing little silks under their exquisite gowns; must look funny I thought... a boy's body with pink lace-trimmed skirt.⁵¹

Exploiting this revolutionary upheaval, Hitler had recruited and trained his Hitler Youth since about 1922. Adult males seeking youthful boy consorts traveled to Berlin from all corners of the globe to join in the excitement of the wide-open German free-sex movement:

> Hitler conducted a whirlwind campaign. On July 15, 1932, he began an airplane tour of Germany. During the ensuing fortnight, he addressed fifty mass meetings—more than three daily.... But there was far greater coordination of effort as the nationwide network of party cells swung into high gear. Hitler's propagandists operated with the smooth efficiency of a well-oiled machine. They carried the battle to every man, woman and child. They organized mammoth meetings that were masterpieces of stagecraft. Perfect timing and skillfully contrived light and sound *effects*.... Roehm made himself invaluable as Hitler's Chief of

A Nazi mass meeting in Berlin shortly after Muller's arrival at the Brain Institute.

Staff. His handling of the Storm Troops was not always beyond criticism, and his sexual irregularities continued to be a source of embarrassment to certain of his associates. The Führer, however, seemed to love him dearly and extolled the manner in which he discharged his duties as generalissimo of the SA... the outcome of the elections of July 31, 1932, was spectacular.... [O]f 608 Reichstag seats... their 230 seats made them far and away the single biggest group in the Reichstag, ... Judged in terms of vote-getting, National Socialism... the Nazis were... at their zenith.[52]

It was in this atmosphere that Muller began his work, in September 1932, at the Kaiser Wilhelm Brain Research Institute in Berlin. The Institute was comprised of many separate research centers. The Brain Institute had been deeply involved in "new biology" research on heredity and the human brain for years prior to Hitler. It continued its work with approval of the Nazi government after Hitler ascended to power on January 30, 1933[53] (four-months after Muller's arrival). Since the early 1920s, the Rockefeller Foundation had helped to fund and maintain the Institute.

As the author of *Studies in Genetics*, Muller was a geneticist of the communist/materialist school. He believed in the existence of strict genetic class divisions, similar to the alpha, beta, gamma, delta, and epsilon classes presaged in Huxley's *Brave New World*.[54] There were those who should breed and those who should be discouraged from breeding.[55] In this scientific context, jurist Karl Binding and psychiatrist Alfred Hoche published *The Release of the Destruction of Life Devoid of Value* (1920), which "advocated that the killing of 'worthless people' be legally permitted."[56] In line with Kinsey's recommendation (as reported by biographer James Jones) that one-tenth of the "lower level" population be sterilized,[57] Binding and Hoche gave a nod to pity, and then swiftly

Studies in GENETICS

The Selected Papers of H. J. Muller

INDIANA UNIVERSITY PRESS
BLOOMINGTON   1962

Germany's long history of youth "nature" groups helped pave the way for overruling parents and the sexual seduction of an unknown number of boys.

FROM BERLIN TO BLOOMINGTON: WHO WERE KINSEY'S "SCIENTIFICALLY TRAINED OBSERVERS"?

moved to the goal of eliminating imperfect Germans (the elderly, the infirm, and the mentally defective) from the gene pool.[58] Their book influenced, "or at any rate crystallized," the thinking of a whole generation in Germany and elsewhere.[59] It laid the foundation, legally and medically, for euthanasia.

Muller lived and worked in the reigning sexual freedom of Berlin and amid thousands of Hitler Youth marching and parading daily down the main streets. In 1933, the brilliant physical chemist Michael Polanyi resigned from the Kaiser Wilhelm Institute "in protest of its dismissal of Jewish scientists."[60] It was in this explosive medical and political atmosphere that Muller, himself half-Jewish, was allowed to continue his research at the Brain Research Institute, with the Russian communist geneticist Timofeev-Ressovsky and his team, "engaging in tests for mutation… exploring the structure of the gene."[61]

On February 4, 1933, when Hitler formally assumed power, Muller wrote to Henry Allen Moe, Secretary of The John Simon Guggenheim Memorial Foundation in New York, seeking a "fellowship renewal." Muller explained that he had been working on "the artificial production of mutations… visiting other [Nazi] investigators, planning new experiments."[62] He continued,

> [I]t has now become evident to me… that a second year of the fellowship would be invaluable.… [Earlier] I stayed in Munich, where I acquainted myself with the genetic work of the Zoological Institut, and of the Institut fur Psychiatrie, under Dr. Rudin, whose very comprehensive material offers a rich field for the study of mutations in man, and of their inheritance.[63]

Dr. Ernst Rudin and several other Nazi doctors founded "the Society for Racial Hygiene… to further the cause of human racial improvement."[64] In 1933, Rudin was not researching fruit flies because, shortly thereafter, he put into place the extermination procedures for hereditarily undesirable Germans. This policy later enabled the harvesting of live "fresh" brains of adults and children for careful laboratory study.

Muller also mentions meeting and working with the well-known German scientists Erwin Baur, Eugen Fischer, and Fritz Lenz, all three authors of a major 1921 volume on racial hygiene widely used by the Nazis.[65] Lenz's special work on harm from radiation preceded Muller by roughly a decade. Muller planned to contribute an essay to the next edition of Baur's *Handbook on Heredity*, but it was not to be.[66]

Muller told the Guggenheim Foundation that he was working with his German colleagues on "various physical problems concerning the mode of effect of X and ultraviolet radiation on the genes" (a process subsequently developed and utilized for nonsurgical castration in the concentration camps). Muller said he was working on "the nature of the mutation process" and "crossing over." In his February 4, 1933 letter, he also states that he was partly aided by his assistant who was funded by the Rockefeller-supported "Committee on Radiation of the National Research Council of the U.S."[67] Rockefeller Foundation monies, he continued, were paid via the National Research Council "directly to the assistant, in checks issued by the treasurer of the University of Texas.... This assistant, Mr. Carlos Offermann... is now on his way here."[68]

Rockefeller and Carnegie had been funding genetics/eugenics research at least since 1905, when both foundations helped to establish the Eugenics Record Office at Cold Spring Harbor in Nassau County, New York, where they developed the "psychometric" studies of inherited characteristics. Eugenic researcher Suzanne Rini describes these studies as "eugenic telephone books and road maps" which, crafted in democratic America, were imitated later in Nazi Germany when such "trait" books were developed by German anthropologists who delivered them "to the SS to round up Jews and gypsies."[69]

In the midst of a growing Nazi police state, Muller gushed to the Guggenheim, "This Institute has placed its facilities at my disposal.... There is every prospect that the National Research Council [Rockefeller] will be willing to continue this arrangement for the academic year 1933-34." He looked forward to a long and exciting collaboration, based on what he called the excellent "opportunity" available in Nazi Germany. He effused,

> The further my contacts have developed the more I have realized the richness of the fields here and the desirability of staying a longer time in order adequately to assimilate and to work over the material and to make proper use of the opportunities presented by it.

The notion that Muller was speaking of his "opportunities" to work on the "material" of fruit flies seems highly unlikely, especially in light of his comment that,

> at the institute at which I am making my headquarters for the present months, there is a wealth of material for the study of mutations affecting the structure and functioning of the brain, and showing their mode of inheritance and interaction.[70]

Strangely, although Muller was "officially" a Jew under Nazi law (his mother was Jewish), and although other famous part-Jewish scientists were losing their jobs and being purged, there is no record of his background retarding his labors. Quite the contrary. Muller claims to have had a close relationship with Freiherr von Verschuer, who was infamous for his role in giving scientific credibility to the New Nordic Race Superiority concept. Indeed, Muller was pleased with the offers of help by "Drs. Verschuer and Fischer in connection with their genetic work at the Kaiser Wilhelm Institut fur Anthropologie in Berlin."[71] Stefan Kuhl writes in *The Nazi Connection: Eugenics, American Racism and National Socialism* (1994),

> In the Nüremberg Doctors Trial in 1946 only a small group of German racial hygienists was accused of participating in government-sponsored massacres[72].... Von Verschuer was accused by German physicist Robert Havemann of receiving "human material" from his assistant Josef Mengele. Before his enlistment in the SS in 1940, Mengele had worked under Verschuer in Frankfurt.[73] In 1942,

Freiherr von Verschuer

Mengele assumed responsibility for medical experiments in concentration camps.[74]

Mengele examined twins and dissected them after they were killed. He sent the results of dissections (including pairs of eyes) to Verschuer at the Kaiser Wilhelm Institute. Miklos Nyiszli, doctor and prisoner at Auschwitz who worked with Mengele in preparing the specimens, confirmed this in his autobiography and claimed that Verschuer thanked Mengele for "these rare and valuable specimens."[75]

Mengele visited his professor in Berlin and was received by Verschuer's family. Shortly after the war, Verschuer destroyed all his correspondence with Mengele and denied that Mengele had ever been his assistant in Berlin or that he had ever received biological specimens from him.[76] Furthermore, Verschuer claimed that he was "openly opposed to the National Socialist fanaticism."[77]

Figure 15. Ziel und Weg (Goal and path), official journal of the National Socialist Physicians' League. The headline in the spring 1933 issue reads: "We Take Command!"

The official poster of the Nazi "Physicians' League" (1933). It reads, "We take command."

After the war, Verschuer wrote to Mueller, his "Jewish friend at Indiana University," seeking help. He told Muller that he was committed to restoring the reputation of "our science,"[78] and argued that the first necessary step was to remove all those "who were not real scientists" from their positions. Referring to his own troubles, he asked for Muller's support with a letter of recommendation lamenting his "life of deprivation."[79] However, almost immediately Verschuer became a professor of human genetics at Muenster, while Fritz Lenz took professorships at German universities in human genetics, anthropology, and psychiatry. These scientists/architects of mass extermination, who operated with assistance from elite American tax-exempt foundations, survived Nazi oppression virtually unscathed.

DACHAU, 1933: 8,000 SLAVE LABORERS

By 1933, the German euthanasia program was under way and the groundwork was laid for unconscionable human experiments on adults and children. Dachau had been established with over 8,000 slaves, who were routinely rented out by the Nazi government to private farms, factories, and institutions. Some would likely have gone to research laboratories at the Kaiser Wilhelm Institute:

> From 1933 to 1945 the expenses for the SS for one inmate averaged about ten cents a day. That included board, clothing, "supervision," housing. Inmates were rented out to private industry at the price of $1 a day or, for skilled workers, $1.50 a day. That made a huge profit for the SS, which, as is often overlooked, became a very big commercial undertaking itself and also piled up enormous profits for the private industrial corporations from the cheap labor.... Inmates had to work long hours—usually eleven hours—including Sundays and holidays.[80]

Nazi Germany was a "police state," and Pomeroy tells us that Kinsey "would have done business with the devil himself if it would have furthered the research."[81] George Sylvester Viereck, the convicted World War II traitor and Kinsey correspondent, was the "devil" to whom Pomeroy was referring. Viereck worked for the German embassy in Washington, D.C. David Brinkley, in *Washington Goes to War* (1988), recalls that he was on Hitler's payroll as a conduit of information to and from "Hitler

using money from Germany to set up… Nazi front groups."[82] In this political environment, Hermann Muller had access to richer "fields" where "the material" and the "opportunities" were plentiful for human experimentation on children as well as adults.

By 1938, slave labor and mass murder were the order of the day in Germany. From 1934 to about 1937, Muller maintained correspondence with his German scientific colleagues as they continued their joint brain "work." Meanwhile, the euthanasia policy was taking its grisly toll:

> Thousands of children were disposed of. A special agency existed for them, consisting of a commission of three experts: one a psychiatrist and director of a state hospital, the other two prominent pediatricians. The children came from psychiatric hospitals, institutions for mental defectives, children's homes, university pediatric clinics, children's hospitals, pediatricians, et al. They were killed in both psychiatric institutions and pediatric clinics. Especially in the latter a number of woman physicians were actively involved in the murders. Among these children were those with mental diseases, mental defectives—even those with only slightly retarded intelligence—handicapped children, children with neurological conditions, and mongoloid children (even with minimal mental defects). Also in this number were children in training schools or reformatories. Admission to such child-care institutions occurs often on a social indication and not for any intrinsic personality difficulties of the child. One physician who killed such training-school boys and girls with intravenous injections of morphine stated in court to explain his actions: "I see today that it was not right.… I was always told that the responsibility lies with *the professors from Berlin*." [Emphasis added.][83]

The educated-physicians, pediatricians, psychiatrists, university professors, and local teachers-were the leaders of Germany's "Brave New World."

Pictured is Muller's well-staffed laboratory in Moscow. Muller's Rockefeller-funded assistant, Offermann (front left, next to Muller) went with him to Moscow. They were joined by Daniel and Roselee Raffel, (front right) who were Johns Hopkins University post-doctoral students.

MULLER IN STALINIST RUSSIA

In 1934, the Soviet government offered Muller his own laboratory, assistants, and all of the "material" he could hope for. In 1934, when the Guggenheim Foundation declined to renew his fellowship funds for work in Germany, Muller left the doctors and "professors in Berlin" to upgrade his academic status to that of "Senior Geneticist" at the Academy of Sciences in the Soviet Union, where he headed a "program of positive eugenics"[84] for the Moscow Institute for Genetics.

Still on leave from the University of Texas at Austin, Muller worked in Russia as a senior scientist until 1937,[85] aided by his assistant, Carlos Offermann, who had been funded by Rockefeller. Muller and Offermann were later joined by sundry Johns Hopkins students. It appears that Muller continued to receive Rockefeller Foundation during his tenure in the USSR.

Publicity photo of a well-fed group of "twins" who were being studied in Russia by a Muller colleague.

Leningrad presented Muller with other opportunities. When he arrived there, the city was being purged by Stalin. Author Alexandr Solzhenitsyn describes the Russian scene at the time, when "one quarter of Leningrad was purged-cleaned out-in 1934-1935:"

> [U]nder the notorious law of August 7, 1932, [by] May 17, 1933... many tens of thousands of peasants... even boys, girls, and small children [who took bits of wheat received]... ten years in prison.... The Kirov wave from Leningrad has begun... [in every] city and an "accelerated" judicial procedure was introduced... no right of appeal... one quarter of Leningrad was purged—cleaned out—in 1934-1935... firing from the civil service of all those whose fathers had been priests, all former noblewomen, and all persons having relatives abroad. [86]

Just as Muller never did reveal to the world the Nazi brutalities he witnessed, no word of the Soviet atrocities crossed his lips or emerged from his very active pen. Writing in *Utopia In Power: Socialism Achieved And Won, 1935-1938* (1982), world-renowned Russian historians Mikhail Heller and Aleksandr Nekrich revealed the sort of science that the Soviets expected from its scientists:

> In the late 1920s the Soviet government began to insist that there was a truth about... the universe [Marxism]... and only the party and its Leader knew it for certain.... An effort to intimidate scientists began. They were arrested one by one at first, then in groups. In 1929 a group of historians, including Sergei Platonov and Evgeny Tarle, were arrested; in 1930 it was a group of microbiologists; then it was agronomists, physiologists, aircraft designers, and so forth. Some were killed, others broken in spirit. In 1934 Professor S. Pisarev was forced to sign a denunciation of his friend, academician Vavilov.... By 1936 the devil and his numerous assistants... accomplished their task: science was under control. The Academy of Sciences passed a resolution stating, "We will resolve all problems that arise before us with the only scientific method, the method of Marx, Engels, Lenin, and Stalin."[87]

While "all persons having relatives abroad" were being arrested, Muller, a foreigner, remained one of the elite, and he and his experimental laboratory remained untouched. Pictures of happy, well-fed, clean little "twins" studied in Russia, appear in his biography. There are, however, no photographs of his Berlin laboratory or his staff of German scientists.

Despite what was taking place in Soviet science when he arrived in the Soviet Union, Muller's treatise *Out of the Night* celebrated the coming of global communism. The title page of the book proudly lists him as a member of the "Academy of Sciences of the USSR." In the midst of the "Great Terror," mass arrests, cruel tortures, and murders (to which many of his fellow scientists fell victim), Mueller remained secure and his laboratory protected.

In *Out of the Night*, Muller passingly deplored the "vested interests of church and state, Fascists, Hitlerites, and reactionaries generally," whom he viewed, in contrast to Marxist forces, as unscientific. The Marxists were clearly his heroes, and he sought to create a world of men with "the innate quality" of "Lenin, Newton, Leonardo, Pasteur, Sun Yat Sen and Marx."[88] Famed sociologist Tilman Spangler,[89] author of *Lenin's Brain*, a docu-drama about the Kaiser Wilhelm Brain Institute during Muller's tenure in Berlin, said rumor had it that Muller left Russia in 1937 due to a scandal, and that he was widely suspected of having been a longtime employee of the Comintern (Communist International) which Lenin had founded.[90]

FURTHER KINSEY/MULLER NETWORK CONNECTIONS

Muller never repudiated the racist eugenic premise of *Out of the Night*. Yet in 1946, largely abandoned by his prewar American academic colleagues due to his work in Stalinist Russia (few knew of his Nazi Germany era), he received the prestigious Nobel Prize. The Russian biologist Sergei Rotianovich Tsarapkin, who worked with Muller in Berlin, was not so lucky. He reappears, perhaps for the last time, in conversation with Alexandr Solzhenitsyn. Solzhenitsyn is first to speak in this scene from *The Gulag Archipelago* (1973):

> "Tsarapkin, Sergei Rotianovich." But, look here, I know you very well indeed. You're a biologist? A non returnee? From Berlin?"
>
> "How do you know?"
>
> "But after all, it's a small world! In 1946 with Nikolai Vladimirovich Timofeyev-Ressovsky."
>
> [Solzhenitsyn continues] In 1922, the German scientist Vogt, who had founded the Brain Institute in Moscow, had asked to have two talented graduate students sent abroad to work with him permanently [in Berlin]. And that was how Timofeyev-Ressovsky and his friend Tsarapkin had been sent off on a foreign assignment with no time limit.... In 1945 the Soviet armies entered... Berlin... Timofeyev-Ressovsky and his entire institute joyously welcomed them.... Soviet representatives came to inspect [the Institute] and said: "Hmm! Hmm! Put everything in packing cases, and we'll take it to Moscow." "That's impossible," Timofeyev objected. *"Everything will die on the way."* They were naïve. They had thought that the institute would not be able to operate without them.[91]

Solzhenitsyn in the Russian Gulag.

Muller left Russia in 1937. Aided by the Rockefeller Foundation, he landed in another hotbed of genetic research at Edinburgh, Scotland, coincidentally the site of the 1997 breakthrough in cloning the sheep "Dolly."[92] Eventually returning to the United States, he joined the faculty of Amherst College. In 1945, he moved to Indiana University, where he joined Kinsey in the zoology department. While challenging the indiscriminate use of x-rays and campaigning against nuclear armaments, Muller continued to advocate elitist "sperm banks to… improve the human gene pool"[93] and to assure that "the genetic endowment of gifted men be widely spread through space and time."[94]

The U.S. officially entered the war in December 1941, but prior to that time John D. Rockefeller's Standard Oil was helping to fuel Hitler's armies, even as the Rockefeller Foundation was promoting America's involvement in the war through an extensive mass communications propaganda campaign. So outrageous were the Rockefeller's internationalist business dealings that then-Senator (later President) Harry Truman used the term "treason" to describe them:

> [A] Senatorial investigating committee headed by Harry Truman… declared… "Standard Oil could be scarcely regarded as an 'American' business… it was a hostile and dangerous agency of the enemy."[95]
>
> Committee Chairman Truman had left the hearings snorting, "I think this approaches treason."[96]
>
> [Truman, Senate speech, March 27, 1942:] Even after we were in the war, Standard Oil of New Jersey [a Rockefeller company] was putting forth every effort of which it was capable to protect the control of the German government over vital war material. As Patrick Henry said: "If that is treason then make the most of it!" Yes, it is treason. You can not translate it any other way.[97]

Meanwhile, in Bloomington, Kinsey was still receiving letters and packages of "material" from his European network, even as he continued his correspondence with Viereck[98] and others about sexual issues. One such contact was a secret, highly trained person he labeled "R.J."[99]

Kinsey was "impatient" with "secondhand" sources. As Pomeroy notes, "[L]ike any scholar, he yearned for original sources."[100] So he conducted firsthand sex experiments, including planning, soliciting, and engaging in adult sexual activities, and collecting "ejaculate" from immature young boys.[101]

As we have noted, Kinsey and Muller were "new biologists" in the Loeb tradition, believing that man is creator and thus capable of controlling life and death. Kinsey's announcement that "Scientists must have the right to decide"[102] all things for society "in the laboratory," coupled with his published views favoring the sterilization of "lower level" people[103] and the breeding of only the select, is totally in keeping with the "new biology." But it does make

Indiana University's zoology staff. Muller (second from left) sits across from Kinsey

one wonder, in light of the extensive historical evidence of the deadly consequences in Germany, how eugenicist scientists today could continue to have their work funded by the large foundations and other "respectable" sources, and enjoy the trust and honor of society and their colleagues.[104]

BUSCHMANNSHOF: KRUPP'S CHILD CONCENTRATION CAMP

The House of Krupp, the 400-year-old German arms making dynasty, had a patriarch who lived a secret double life. Amateur zoologist Fritz Krupp collected primitive forms of life and collected homo sapiens (young boys) for sexual purposes. While Fritz, at the turn of the century, was making $25 million a year, he committed suicide when photographic evidence of his pederasty became public. Fritz's grandson, young Alfried Krupp, also committed crimes that became widely known.

Krupp biographer William Manchester said of arms merchant Krupp and his family:

> The dynasty was a continuum; one must see it in that light. Because of the family's legacy, its men had been ready to follow Hitler before he appeared to lead them. Indeed, he had been the perfect instrument for ideas carefully nursed in Essen [Krupp headquarters in Germany] three generations ago, and his [Hitler's] National Socialism had been the ultimate realization of Kruppdom.
>
> The tradition of the Krupp Firm, and the 'social-political' attitude for which it stood, was exactly suited to the moral climate of the Third Reich. There was no crime such a state could commit whether it was war, plunder, or slavery in which these men would not participate."[105]

Krupp was convicted for horrific "crimes against peace," "plunder," and crimes against humanity that included "slave labor," and "conspiracy." A 36,000-word declaration by Krupp's Harvard Law School-educated prosecutor, General Telford Taylor, contained a catalogue of crime committed by Krupp before and during the war.

To [General] Taylor, Krupp was a challenge. Both men were of the same generation, and the General felt they should be capable of understanding one another. He never reached Alfried, though. The barrier between them was impenetrable.

Alfried Krupp, seen here in the witness box during the Nuremberg trials, essentially dictated the terms of his freedom. (Manchester)

[When] Alfried joined the SS, Krupp had, in the words of an SS membership certificate, made himself responsible with [his] signature. Unlike most Nuremberg defendants including the mass murders, Krupp never expressed contrition. The most shocking testimony made no discernible impression upon him, though he never missed a word of it; in his conferences with Klanzbuher, the counsel was astonished by Alfried's memory.[106]

Alfried Krupp was arrested at Villa Hügel in Essen on April 11, 1945. At his trial, he stood in the dock flanked by his Nazi aides, his board of directors, and his legal staff. I.G. Farben, the international European conglomerate with close business ties and licensing arrangements for petroleum with Standard Oil and the Rockefeller family, stood trial upstairs on similar charges.

Some called Alfried Krupp the German equivalent of Henry Ford II. William Manchester reports that he "dominated them all in the courtroom. This was his trial. He was the most famous man in Nuremberg, and everyone in the courtroom felt his silent power." One reporter wrote, "It is hard to equate that elegant patrician face with such ruthlessness and cruelty as he, in fact, displayed during this Hitlerian period."[107]

Krupp in the dock (first from left) at Nuremberg trials. (Manchester)

Although the postwar world was vitally interested in the explosive Krupp trial, William Manchester states that it was virtually ignored by the U.S. mass media. Some newspaper stories were based on General Taylor's war crimes charges, but the actual testimony was all but unreported. A *New York Times* correspondent covered the entire nine-month Krupp trial, and wrote "objective concise and accurate reports," but little appeared in print. Manchester writes,

> somehow the *Times* rarely found room for them. Alfried's trial, like Adolph Eichmann's thirteen years later, lasted nearly nine months, longer than any ever held in the United States. The court proceedings ran over four million words. Yet, between the late winter of 1947 and the summer of 1948, when the last evidence was heard, America's news paper of record published exactly 4 of Miss McLaughlin's accounts of trial testimony - a total of 47 paragraphs less than 2 columns, all of it buried on inside pages.[108]

But, how could such a major story of historical dimensions have been ignored, while Kinsey's face and "data" graced the front pages of American newspapers coast to coast in 1948?

In *Science of Coercion*, Christopher Simpson sheds additional light on the Rockefeller Foundation's media influence. The Foundation underwrote most major academic communication research projects during the latter half of the 1930s. Its "administrators believed, however, that media constituted a uniquely powerful force in modern society." To that end, Rockefeller would,

...finance a new project on content analysis for Harold Lasswell at the Library of Congress, Hadley Cantril's Public Opin-

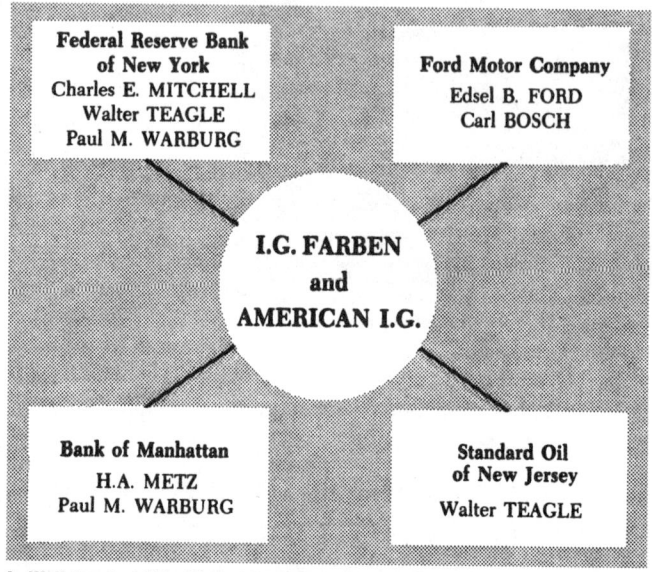

Federal Reserve Bank of New York
Charles E. MITCHELL
Walter TEAGLE
Paul M. WARBURG

Ford Motor Company
Edsel B. FORD
Carl BOSCH

I.G. FARBEN and AMERICAN I.G.

Bank of Manhattan
H.A. METZ
Paul M. WARBURG

Standard Oil of New Jersey
Walter TEAGLE

In Wallstreet and the Rise of Hitler, (1976) Anthony Sutton identifies the documented connections between Rockefeller (Standard Oil & Bank of Manhattan), Ford and other major internationalists, and the Nazi Arms business.

ion Research Project at Princeton University, the establishment *of Public Opinion Quarterly* at Princeton, Douglas Waples'… studies at the University of Chicago, Paul Lazersfeld's Office of Radio Research at Columbia University, and other important programs.[109]

This was a whole new science. Rockefeller funded communications experts such as Harold Lasswell and Walter Lippmann in the hope that they could "magically," impose the will of the elite on the masses. "For widespread literacy," said Simpson "compelled the development of a whole new technique of control, largely through propaganda… to promote… overt acts."[110]

Many Americans in the early 1900s viewed big-business "trusts" as heartless internationalist entities that worked against the best interests of the common people.

Many Americans in the 1930s and 1940s had a great distrust of the "trusts" and were of the opinion that big business, largely devoid of patriotism, would sell its goods to the highest bidders, playing all sides against each other. While the Rockefeller Foundation was funding German eugenics research in Berlin, and Rockefeller interests were fueling the Nazi war machine, the Rockefeller machine also worked to induce U.S. entry into the war. It would then profit from the sale of gas, oil, rubber, and other materials for the war effort.

> As war approached, the Rockefeller Foundation… organized a series of secret seminars with men it regarded as leading communication scholars to enlist them in an effort to consolidate public opinion in the United States in favor of war against Nazi Germany—a controversial proposition opposed by many conservatives, religious leaders, and liberals at the time.… Engineering mass consent for the elites' authority."[111]

Kinsey's 1948 and 1953 reports were headline news.

At the secret Rockefeller communications seminars, one participant voiced the concerns of several others, charging the Foundation with attempting to craft new means of totalitarian control over the American people. The critic said, "We have thought in terms of fighting dictatorships by force through the establishment of dictatorships by manipulation."[112]

FROM BERLIN TO BLOOMINGTON: WHO WERE KINSEY'S "SCIENTIFICALLY TRAINED OBSERVERS"?   313

With the Allied postwar occupation of Germany underway, Manchester describes yet another powerful Rockefeller representative. John J. McCloy, a well-connected Wall Street attorney, was a useful instrument for the elite U.S. tax exempt foundations. He came to be known as the "Chairman of the American Establishment." He had served as Assistant Secretary of War from 1944-46, and established a small, highly secret Psychologic Branch within the War Department. Christopher Simpson writes,

> [McCloy] helped define U.S. social science and mass communication studies long after the war had drawn to a close. Virtually all of the scientific community that was to emerge during the 1950s as leaders in the field of mass communication research spent the war years performing applied studies on U.S. and foreign propaganda... public opinion [research] (both domestically and internationally), clandestine OSS operations.[113]

John D. Rockefeller supplied oil to the Nazi war machine while calling for America's sons to enter the European war.

McCloy's mass communication psychological warfare agents switched from World War II propagandists to civilian mainstream media moguls, positioned in key public opinion organizations and publications. Many assisted with the brilliant public relations campaign that accompanied publication of Alfred Kinsey's *Male* and *Female* volumes. The establishment media dutifully promoted and cheered the supposed quality of Kinsey findings. The Rockefeller Foundation and the federal government jointly backed sundry propaganda activities through the Office of War Information (OWI), which in turn funded the National Opinion Research Center and such key survey organizations as Gallup. The survey organizations regularly issued favorable reports about Rockefeller Foundation activities and grantees.

Simpson continues,

> [The OWI alumni became] the publishers of *Time, Look, Fortune, and* several dailies; editors of such magazines as *Holiday, Coronet, Parade,* and the *Saturday Review,* editors of the *Denver Post,* New Orleans; *Times-Picayune,* and others; the heads of the Viking Press, Harper & Brothers, and Farrar, Straus and Young; two Hollywood Oscar winners; a two-time Pulitzer prizewinner; the board chairman of CBS and a dozen key network executives; President Eisenhower's chief speech writer; the editor of *Reader's Digest* international editions; at least six partners of large advertising agencies; and a dozen noted social scientists [as well as the] dean of the Columbia Graduate School of Journalism and founder of the *Columbia Journalism Review*.[114]

Simpson points out that those who had engaged in "wartime psychological warfare work" became a network of social science leaders who, like their new biology colleagues, sought to "promote their particular interpretations of society."[115]

In 1946, following his War Department service, McCloy was appointed to the board of the Rockefeller Foundation. Three years later he became U.S. High Commissioner of Germany, succeeding General Clay.[116] He later became chairman of the Rockefeller's Chase Bank, which he helped turn into the country's second largest bank through merger with the Bank of Manhattan to form the Chase Manhattan bank. He also served stints as president of the World Bank and of the Ford Foundation, and prior to his death in 1989 was a consultant to presidents Kennedy (he was appointed to the Warren Commission), Johnson, Nixon, and Ford.

On February 3, 1951, while High Commissioner of Germany, McCloy freed Krupp. The patriarch of the Krupp Dynasty was granted full clemency, and his entire immense private fortune was restored, after serving less than two years of his war-crimes sentence. A shocked Eleanor Roosevelt asked, *"But why are we freeing so many Nazis?"* The clemency negotiations for Krupp involved high-level discussions[117] at the Jewish Claims Conference, where it was agreed that Krupp would not be subject to further claims by Holocaust survivors.

McCloy arranged for *surviving* Krupp slaves to receive roughly $1,200 each for their years of servitude,[118] but they actually received a mere $500, while Krupp was allowed to retain his mansions, buildings, and billions in coal and steel holdings. McCloy biographer Kai Bird notes that Krupp rejected all legal liability for his slave laborers, and only paid the pittance to help "heal the wounds suffered in World War II."[119] London's *Sunday Dispatch* took note of how little the surviving slave workers were to be compensated, describing the settlement as "mean spirited and tawdry."[120]

No single act during the occupation generated greater emotional shock than McCloy's rejection of the Krupp verdict and restoration of Krupp's slave-enhanced fortune.[121] U.S. Supreme Court Justice Robert H. Jackson, who led the American prosecution team at Nuremberg, asserted that there were no grounds for the clemency: "If you were to say that Krupp was not guilty, it would be as true to say that there had been no Auschwitz fuse factory, no basement torture cage, no infant corpses, no slain, no crime, no war."[122] The records of the Krupp trial had been boxed in six crates resembling coffins and McCloy never opened them.

For those who wonder how masses of children could have been obtained for "scientific" experiments, a clue may lie with the "ruthless" and "cruel" Alfried Krupp. Despite General Taylor's comprehensive 36,000-word indictment of Krupp at Nuremberg, nary a word was said about *Buschmannshof,* Krupp's children's concentration camp. Infants and children under six years of age were torn from their Krupp-enslaved mothers and interned in *Buschmannshof,* where they died at a rate of some 50 per day for years. Krupp's older children were called "slave youth," and little is known about their lives. There are no records of the dead children, but estimates peg their number in the thousands.

Left to right: David Rockefeller, John J. McCloy, George Champion, and an unknown individual, forming the Chase Manhattan Bank in 1955. (Byrd)

So outrageous was the *Buschmannshof* camp that, according to Manchester, had its existence become widely known, the world would have been appalled and the news would have incited ghastly retribution."[123] *However, the degree of media control is best revealed, not by how a story is told, but the extent to which it is suppressed.* Only with the close cooperation of powerful European and American political and media elite was the story of the *Buschmannshof* children's concentration camp successfully buried. Manchester writes:

> The suppression of the *Buschmannshof's* story was an almost unqualified success.[124]… [The] silence went unchallenged, partly because the facts are so incredible, partly because the infants… [were far away] and chiefly because there are no known survivors. Indeed, Krupp was so confident that Buschmannshof would be forgotten that its buildings weren't even torn down. Today they still stand, seven long low dingy barracks with small windows, indistinguishable at first glance from the sheds of Auschwitz.[125]

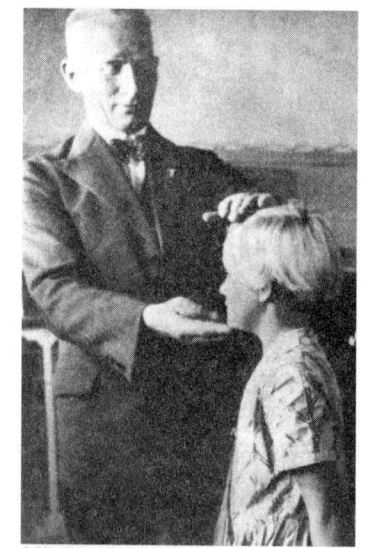

A Nazi teacher (a member of the German Socialist Teachers Association), measures the value of a child as Nordic stock. (Kuhl)

Like Krupp, the Kinsey Institute and Indiana University have avoided accountability for collaborating with and/or covering up for crimes against children. The names of the children of *Buschmannshof* are, like Kinsey's smallest subjects, known but to a select few and to God. Their gravestones rest largely unnoticed at the back of a German cemetery. Slabs marking their final resting places are engraved with numbers, not names.[126] They are like the children in Kinsey's tables, known only by their number, the number of their "orgasms." A small cadre of elite "social managers" controlled the outcomes for these children in both places.

This prominent photograph symbolizes events occurring during Muller's European tenure.

Manchester states that the vast majority of the mothers had seen their *Buschmannshof* children for but a few moments at birth, after which the infants were taken to the sheds.[127] What the social planners of the scientifically run "brave new world" did not consider was the power of human bonds and a mother's love, for as Manchester says, "the maternal yearning… produced indescribable mental agony."[128]

America was built on a challenge to the plans of entrenched nobility, plans to control and manipulate populations. Just as the elite of the international "nobility" have and do support one another in interlocking networks, American mothers and fathers today must take the lead in demanding the names of Kinsey's child subjects. These little ones, whose "indescribable mental agony" has been suppressed for more than half a century by the academic elite, should not suffer the same dishonor and ignominy as the children of *Buschmannshof*. Where are the children of Table 34? Who were Kinsey's "trained observers"? Indiana University and the Kinsey Institute must be made to answer.

Mothers, fathers, and future parents must become aware of the extent to which Alfred Kinsey, his team, his "trained observers," his funders, and his advocates in the media and elsewhere, have eroded our moral and cultural underpinnings. The time has come to dismantle the elitist "Grand Scheme" that derives to a significant extent from Kinsey's warped model of human sexuality.

Bushmanshoff-Krupp's concentration camp for children. (Munchester)

CONCLUSION

It was astonishing to read of a United States Government effort to investigate Kinsey's Rockefeller-funded studies. The nation is indebted to Dr. Stanley Monteith for republishing Rene Wormser's book on the Reece Committee, *The Foundations: Their Power and Influence*. Wormser documents Congressman Wayne Hays' "unreasoning opposition… [so] that he threatened to fight against the appropriation on the floor of the House *unless the Kinsey investigation were dropped*." Congressman Hays' vigorous opposition to any inquiry into the Kinsey Reports, coupled with other evidence in this last chapter, finds Kinsey not necessarily the darkest corner in the utopian "Brave New World" being built by the New Biologists.

We now know that Kinsey was not a "lone" research pursuing a perverse personal agenda. Rather, he operated within a vortex of such privileged and often interlocked power brokers, that their covert special interest agents stopped a Congressional investigation cold. Within this vortex, Hermann Muller seamlessly maintained his *on-going Rockefeller-funded* genetic "mutation" research--from Austin, Texas to Nazi Germany to Stalinist Russia to Bloomington, Indiana--without interruption or interference. This, at the same time that Rockefeller's attorney John J. McCloy as High Commissioner of Germany confidently sprung Nazi arms merchant Alfried Krupp from prison, his slave labor-enhanced fortune fully restored to him intact.

The far-ranging impact of Kinsey's admittedly atrocious deeds give pause. Could Kinsey have conducted screaming, sadomasochistic experiments in Wylie Hall, on the bucolic Indiana University campus while collaborating with international and domestic pedophiles in the 1930-40s, without being detected by University officials and exposed by law enforcement and the media? Kinsey certainly had the complicity of university chieftains. But, Congressman Hays confirms that Kinsey's funders and guardians extended to the nation's capitol. Individually, the members of this elitist scientific network operated as a law unto themselves. They still do. They believe themselves above others. In this they share a unified world view, a belief in their imperial right to all of the earth's human and natural resources, including children, and a hatred of any counterforce that would attempt to restrict their ambitions, power or control.

In 1954, having barely survived exposure by Reece's Congressional investigation, Kinsey's Rockefeller money was redirected to the American Law Institute for the production of the Model Penal Code, designed to abolish and supplant America's Common Law legal system. Confirming Kinsey as their "most important" grant, Rockefeller's enduring tribute to the zoologist was Kinsey's role as the sole sex science authority for the new code. The strict "Sex Offense" laws that had outlawed all sexual expression outside of the marital act would be "restated" to fit Kinseyan sexual liberation and preferences.

But, not *only* Kinsey's sexual liberation. The eugenic power vortex is more fully documented in the book, *Psychiatrists: The Men Behind Hitler*. Authors Roder, Kubillus and Burwell report on a 1962 London symposium on genetics attended by Muller, his fellow Communist comrade and Kinsey's London host, J.B.S. Holdane, Sir Julian Huxley, and others. These "superior" men, like Kinsey, saw themselves as eugenic royalty, or the new genetic hegemony. Their network of interlocking scholarly elitists is one of a mutually supportive cadre for whom the world is their laboratory, thus all "science" is "good" by definition. Under the banner of Darwinian progress, their plans are chilling indeed and they are underway at this moment, good reader, with official sanction, encouragement, and public funds. Rodger, et al, reprint several of the London seminar remarks:

NOBEL LAUREATE, CO-DISCOVERER OF DNA, FRANCIS CRICK:...

> I'd like to concentrate on a certain issue. Do people even have the right to have children? As we have heard, *it would not be difficult for governments to add something to the food supply which would prevent procreation. In addition, and this is hypothetical, the government could keep another substance at hand which would counteract the effect of the first one, and only people whose procreation is desired* could receive it. This is definitely not out of the question.
>
> At this point in time, mankind will certainly not submit to compulsory sterilization measures. But if you begin with a few, of course, voluntary experiments and show that they work, you could within one generation achieve results on the whole population. *Because moral values grow and mature just as everything else.*
>
> If you could convince people that their children are not a private matter, that would be a tremendous step forward. *I suspect that through the results of science, we will in time become less and less Christian.*

NOBEL LAUREATE HERMANN MULLER:

> Probably close to 20 percent of the population, if not more, have inherited a genetic defect. If that is right, in order for us to avoid genetic degeneration, then that *20 percent of*

the population should not be allowed to reach sexual maturity or, if they live, they would not be allowed to procreate. Finally, there are certainly great opportuitys available for improvement in our transformation of the genetic makeup itself. [Perhaps anticipating the opportunities for, again?, experiementing with - preborn-baby parts, Muller goes on.] To investigate these problems, *we have to free ourselves from our prejudices and open our minds to the new possibilities that sicnece and technology are offering* us.

Muller then explains that some people would be "proud" to forfeit children of "their loins," a mere "stimulus-response" by-product. This would aid "the welfare of their children and mankind."

NOBEL LAUREATE JOSHUA LEDERBERG:

> I can foresee, for example, having the fundamentals very soon to develop a technique to enlarge the human brain *through prenatal or early postnatal interventions.*

THE ULTIMATE ELITIST PLAN GOES TO KINSEY'S AND MULLER'S FRIEND, HOLDANE:

> It might be possible to synthesize new geners and to insert them into human chromosomes... our descendants could acquire many valuable properties of other species *without losing their specific human qualities...* Under such circumstances *it might be good to have four legs,* or, at least, very short legs... [From this] I might conclude that *many parents would be ready to risk the life of their small child* if there was a chance it would develop extraordinary strength. I have designed my own utopia, or as others might suppose, my own private hell. *I justify myself with the fact that utopian designs have influenced the course of history.*[130]

Roder, Kubillus and Burwell note that this symposium was sponsored by a major pharmaceutical corporation (a producer of the psychiatric drug, Ritalin).[131]

> Moreover, the assembled scientists shared reflections that are strikingly similar to the thoughts expressed by highly influential men known now as Nazis, geneticists and racial hygienists[132] ....There is a fear, therefore, that is amply justified--that we could be heading for a new and molecular Auschwitz... a new brand of space-age eugenics.[133]

Until now, it has been unthinkable to consider the doctrinaire ties between western scholars and researchers in Hitler Germany or Stalinist Russia, much less the clandestine international eugenicist network documented by Roder, et al. It was equally unthinkable that *any* American academician would willingly engage in biomedical experiments on human beings.

However, Kinsey's totalitarian links are a missing piece to a larger, sinister puzzle. The Department of Health and Human Services[134] revealed a systematic abuse of the defenseless as the raw material for a billion dollar "biomedical and behavioral research" industry. Discussing the growing call for "informed consent," the HHS reported the forty-year syphilis experiments on trusting black men, initiated in 1932 and continued during WWII, and "long after penicillin was demonstrated to be an effective treatment of the disease."[135] HHS admitted the abuse of women for "miscarriage" research in the "early 1950s"[136] resulting in cancer-ridden daughters. We know of the experiments with psychotropic drugs sponsored by the CIA,[137] and the injection of "cultured cancer cells into debilitated, elderly patients" by two physicians at "Jewish Chronic Disease Hospital in Brooklyn, NY." Just as important, these killer-doctors received all of "one year's probation," their medical licenses maintained intact.[138] The report continues, saying Pappworth, in *Human Guinea Pigs* described "risky procedures not intended to benefit" patients:

In chapter after chapter, [Pappworth] described the insertion of catheters and biopsy needles into important organs of the body (bladder, kidney, heart, liver) and resulting meningitis, shock, liver damage and cardiac arrest. The subjects of these procedures were newborns, infants and children (both healthy and diseased), pregnant women, prisoners, patients undergoing surgery, the mentally disabled, the aged, the critically ill, and the dying. The published articles revealed little concern on the part of the investigators for their subjects.... The authors somewhat surprisingly noted that "There were no serious complications. Several findings were encountered!" They mention, however, that in three patients the needle accidentally pierced the bowel; in two instances, it punctured a main artery; another patient had his gall bladder punctured; one patient had syncope (shock); and three had large haemorrahages"[139] [and] experiments... involved injecting hepatitis virus into mentally retarded children at teh Willowbrook State School in New York.[140]

Using captive children for personal "experimentation" is, on the evidence, not necessarily abhorrent to eugenic-minded scholars. Dr. John Money, world-renowned sexology professor emeritus at Johns Hopkins University was finally exposed in a year 2000 book for his demonic "Frankenstein" experiments. *The New York Times Book Review* had prophetically hailed Money's work, *Man & Woman, Boy & Girl* as "the most important volume in the social sciences since the Kinsey Reports." The *NYT* said of Money's claim that nature could be conquered by nurture, that, "[I]f you tell a boy he is a girl, and raise him as woman, he will want to do feminine things."[141]

Money's Mengele-abuses were belatedly revealed due to the bravery of one of his "patients," a young baby twin whose parents were manipulated into permitting Money's disciple to surgically alter their little boy into a "girl." The "brilliant" Money, a Kinsey disciple and mentor of former Kinsey Institute director June Reinish, pretended for decades that he "proved" one's biological sex can be altered harmlessly and agreeably physical and emotional mutilation by the illustrious Money.[142] Tragically, "David" (he renamed himself after the Biblical David who slew Goliath), the courageous young man is one of thousands of infants annually victimized by Money's global disciples in the medical and mental health fields.[143] That this steady surgical ravage of innocent babies is still a largely well-kep global secret-like the real story of the Kinsey cabal--can be credited to the world media monopoly originally designed by Rockefeller and now controlled by a few elite families and global corporations.[144]

Illegally barred from access to the Kinsey archive, "unfriendly" scholars can find no answers about Kinsey's support of Rex King who systematically assaulted over 800 children for Kinsey's *Male* volume. It is absurd to ignore evidence implicating the Rockefeller-German-Russian eugenic network in providing Kinsey's "aides" access to children destined for death in places like *Bushmanshoff*.

For, one would think cannibalism--the use or consumption of human flesh--would be beyond the pale for American industry. Yet, a mere fifty-two years after Kinsey launched the Sexual Revolution, "scientists" and businessmen openly traffic in the use of pre-born baby parts for "good" research, as did the Nazis.[145] This booming scientific service industry requires commercial orders to ship fresh or frozen pre-born babies *whole or* in parts, via UPS, Federal Express, Airborne and other carriers. Paul Likoudis describes this "economically important by-product of the sexual revolution" in "Dead Baby Parts Business Booming" for AIDS and other research:

> Human embryonic and fetal tissues are available from the Central Laboratory for Human Embryology at the University of Washington. The laboratory, which is supported by the

National Institutes of Health, can supply tissue [as in Muller's letters, "material"] from normal or abnormal embryos and fetuses of desired gestational ages between 40 *days and term.*

Partial-Birth abortions seemed to be so horrible that most of us wondered how such procedures could be defended.... But now we have evidence of a very clear additional reason why they want these late-term abortions to continue. *The reason is that this is the one method that gives them intact fetal bodies from which they can obtain organs for research.*[146] ...A full-color, glossy brochure invites abortionists to "find out how you can turn your patient's decision into something wonderful." It's printed by... a wholesale trafficker in aborted baby parts... his current "Fee for Services Schedule" offers eyes and ears for $75 to $999 for a brain.... An "intact trunk (with/without limbs)" costs $500, for example, a liver, $150, ("30% discount if significantly fragmented").

Here, courtesy of the Internet's National Institutes of Health, in taxpaper-funded black and white, is the reality of America's culture of death. The commerical cannibalism of the human young has quietly gone mainstream as a coalition of major medical and health organizations, businesses, and associations press for federal funding of lethal embryo research.[147]

Muller and Kinsey would be gratified to know that American scientists can now acquire human "material" right at home--from one's office computer--on the Internet. Muller had to go to Nazi Germany and Stalinist Russia to get fresh "material," and Kinsey had to locate pedophiles around the world to get the data he wanted on child "orgasms."

A myriad of examples are available, but the airing this spring of ABC's 20/20 broadcast on the trafficking in baby parts is a prime illustration of the cognitive dissonance existing in our nation of "In God We Trust." It was satisfying to think that the truth would be revealed on prime time and in time for Congressional hearings on embryo research. While the program reflected an abhorrence of this new enterprise, it was less for the primitive violations of these babies than due to a residual revulsion against profits being earned from selling cannibalized eyes, hearts, brains, livers, thymuses, etc. That "scientists" purchase pre-born baby parts for their "good" experiments appears to be growing in acceptance.

In World War II, scientists justified the depraved experiments on Christians, Jews and others by the fact that these prisoners were going to die anyway and their deaths could be of medical benefit for others. That same "good" logic could justify killing someone to harvest their organs, particularly if they are a tissue match. There is evidence that this is done in China, with prisoners' executions timed to supply organs to waiting recipients. Is there a right to "donate" someone else's "tissue"? Seen from a purely naturalistic, materialistic or evolutionary world-view, with "survival of the fittest" as doctrine, this appears a "logical" decision. When each person is a law unto themselves, each person is the law--until of course we cannot speak for ourselves or when other more powerful folks speak for us.

Too many of the roads from Kinsey's victimized children lead to the self-anointed scientific elite. Just as important is the evidence that this cabal, largely directing higher education, medicine and media, have a similar plan for us common folk deemed "genetically defective" by self-styled "geniuses" like the Nobel prize winners we just heard from. The results of eugenic, genetic, psychiatric leadership and power surround us, from commonly Ritalin'd school boys to our epidemic infertility among young women, and impotent males needing little blue pills to do what Grandpa did naturally after working twelve-hours at the mill. The "human resources" designers are in place, aggressively crafting a "New World" with out tax dollars.

American is no longer under limited government with the consent of the governed, but directed by internaitonal leaders, with their myriad human failings, and also by great "scientists" of superior seed who, like Holdane, will genetically patch together beings with "four legs" to do specialized work, or to simply amuse their perverse sense of creative potential. These new creatures will be permitted life--so long as they obey and make no unreasonable demands of their creators.

In *Frankenstein, The Modern Prometheus,* Mary Shelley warned of those who plotted to obstruct God's created order so as to unhinge life from the divine. In her 1827 foreword, Shelley reports "the event on which this fiction is founded has been supped by Dr. Darwin, and some of the physiological writers of Germany, as not of impossible occurrence."[148] In 1851, Dostoyevsky declared in *The Brothers Karamazov*, "if there is no God, then everything is permitted." Dostoyevsky's description of London's Great Exhibition, displaying the triumphs of science and technology at the Crystal Palace, embodied the axiom for which he is so well known.

> For what is being celebrated as the culmination and very last word of European civilization is, in his view, nothing but the triumph of the old flesh-god of materialism over the spiritual principle (Christianity) which had once inspired European mankind.[149]

Kinsey's personal motive for his research was no mystery. He hated the way America's Christian-based law constrained America's sexual and moral life. All nations are inherently religious, even under the mask of atheism. The "Grand Scheme" shared by Kinsey and like-minded eugenic and legal elites, would do no less than gut the Old and New Testaments as America's founding common law order. Kinsey's closeted cadre were at war. They would deconstruct the common law, anointing science as the nation's religion and scientists as the new priest class. But, the renowned Jewish authority Rabbi Daniel Lapin, author of *America's Real War* has summarized what is at risk when the Christian roots of this nation are destroyed:

> I desperately want my children, and one day (God willing) my grandchildren and their descendants, to have the option of living peacefully and productively in the United States of America. I am certain this depends upon America regaining its Christian-oriented moral compass.... American Jews in particular, owe a debt of gratitude to Christians for the safe haven America has been since its founding.

Kinsey was, no doubt, proud of his key position in the science clergy. In the end, it is not surprising that an official finding of Reece's Congressional Committee was that the Foundation-sponsored Kinsey Reports were "deliberately designed as an attack on Judaic-Christian morality." Kinsey's human experiments on children give us the glimpse into the widespread, far-reaching network of New Bioloty scientists while their current traffic in fetal parts hints at where the new/old religion is going. American can no longer deny the reality of what the sexual revolution has wrought on our own shores.

Crick rightly noted at the 1962 London symposium on genetics, "I suspect that through the results of science, we will in time become less and less Christian." As what is known as science has increased in influence in America, Biblical Christianity has decreased. This chapter further documents our movement back to the dark, "where everything is permitted" or "anything goes." In 1828, Noah Webster, like Mary Shelley, issued a warning to the nation when he coined *only one original word* for his new, uniquely American Dictionary of the English Language. The word was "demoralize" ("to undermine the confidence or morale of; dishearten; to corrupt"). Our national morality and self-government, hence our confidence and morale, have been our only historical defense against powerful external and internal invaders. Given the "scientific" and materialistic influence upon our nation's moral compass, we are no longer "One Nation, Under God." As man does what he will, with no honor to the sacred and no limit to the profane, all Americans are in peril in our now unwalled cities.

Please do what you can to help!

> *I am only one,*
> *But still I am one.*
> *I cannot do everything,*
> *But still I can do something;*
> *And because I cannot do everything,*
> *I will not refuse to do the something that I can do.*
>
> —Edward Everett Hale[129]

CHAPTER 10 NOTES

1. Edward McNall Burns, *Western Civilizations: Their History and Their Culture*, Fifth Edition, W.W. Norton & Co., Inc., New York, 1958, p. 653.
2. Kinsey, Pomeroy and Martin, *Sexual Behavior in the Human Male*, W.B. Saunders, Philadelphia, 1948, p. 177.
3. *The Washington Times*, June 8, 1997, "The Commission on cloning recommends," p. A6.
4. Masters, Johnson et. al, *Ethical Issues in Sex Therapy and Research, Volume 2*, Little Brown and Company, Boston, 1980, p. 71.
5. Pomeroy, p. 155.
6. Frederic Lilge, *The Abuse of Learning: The Failure of the German University*, Macmillian Company, New York, 1948.
7. See Gebhard letter to Reisman, March 11, 1981 (in this author's archive), in which Gebhard, then-director of the Kinsey Institute, writes: ""Some of these sources have added… photographs and, in few instances, cinema."
8. Kinsey Institute Internet site, October 10, 1997. An open letter from Dr. Beverly LaHaye, Director of Concerned Women for America, October 2, 1997, in which LaHaye called for an investigation of the child sex abuse. Bancroft responded.
9. Extensive documentation exists, following the May 7, 1993 deposition of Dr. Reinisch, to confirm that no such investigation actually took place.
10. Kinsey, Pomeroy and Martin *Sexual Behavior in the Human Male*, W. B. Saunders, Philadelphia, 1948, p. 177.
11. *Male*, p. 177.
12. Masters, Johnson and Kolodny, Ed., *Ethical Issues in Sex Therapy and Research, Reproductive Biology Research Foundation Conference*, Little, Brown and Company, Boston, 1977, p. 13.
13. Masters, Johnson and Kolodny, Ed. Ibid. p.13.
14. Masters et al, pp. 18-19. Not only does Gebhard say that it is all right to lie and coerce persons into research, and that if his team knew of a child sex murderer they would protect the miscreant, but he further confirms that were mass murders being planned within his earshot he would not warn the potential victims or authorities. He would merely "count the heads as they came in," p. 19.
15. *Male*, p. 39.
16. *Female*, p. 84. While the ellipses point out that this illegal "call" was given "in the male volume," the ellipses are inserted here to restrict further confusion by the Kinsey Institute. The Kinsey team admitted soliciting day-to-day "diaries" of sex acts with all subjects about all sex "outlets" (including children). It therefore provided "day-to-day… instructions" to their solicited sex collaborators about conducting sexual experiments, under their guidance, for "science."
17. See investigative reporter Anne E, Schwartz *in The Man Who Could Not Kill Enough*, Girch Lane, Carol Publishing, New York, 1992, a book on Jeffrey Dahmer. Schwartz includes a list of serial murders and cites Albert Fish who, in about 1940, killed 15 to 200 children in the New York area. She also recalls Mack Edwards, who killed 6 children in California during the Kinsey research era. Their deaths followed sexual abuse (p. 220.), Schwartz cites Dr. Ron Holmses of the Southern Police Institute as her document source for the data.
18. *Male*, p. 37.
19. *Male*, p. 37.
20. Wardell Pomeroy, *Dr. Kinsey and the Institute for Sex Research*, Harper & Row, New York, 1972, p. 70 and pp. 172-187.
21. Kinsey worked with other such "elites" in human experiments. See prior chapters.
22. *Male*, p. 11.
23. Pomeroy, p. 402.
24. Pomeroy, pp. 403-05.

25. *Male*, p. 39.

26. James Jones, *Origins of the Institute for Sex Research*, UMI Dissertation Services, Ann Arbor, Michigan, 1973, pp. 238-242.

27. Pomeroy, p. 155.

28. Pomeroy, p. 16. Pomeroy notes that Kinsey "presented his collection to the American Museum of Natural History, in New York; it was the largest collection of any kind ever given to that institution, numbering more than four million different specimens."

29. Gordon Thomas, *Journey into Madness: The True Story of Secret CIA Mind Control and Medical Abuse*, Bantam Books, New York, 1989, p. 35.

30. Thomas, Ibid.

31. Thomas, Ibid.

32. Thomas, Ibid, p. 1

33. Recall the Reece Committee's conclusion that a group of the largest charitable, tax-exempt foundations had established an American plutocracy, a shadow government symbolized by Ford, Carnegie, Rockefeller, Russell Sage, and several other "philanthropies." The Reece Committee found this plutocratic control was largely accomplished by funding the "right" university research by the "right" researchers, then funding mass media dissemination of the "right" science data while ignoring or censoring the "wrong" data. A breakthrough in our understanding of this plutocratic strategy is credited to Christopher Simpson, an obscure, liberal American University professor. In *Science of Coercion: Communication Research & Psychological Warfare 1945-1960*, he revealed records obtained via the Freedom of Information Act. He reported that after World War II Rockefeller financed experts in "wartime psychological warfare work" to "promote their particular interpretations of society" to Americans. This "remarkably tight circle of men and women," wrote Simpson, understood "mass communication as a tool for social management." What role did flawed Kinsey sex data serve in the Rockefeller-funded strategy for "social management"? The Rockefeller media elite retailed Kinseyan sexual morality in the service of "social control" by focusing on "the usefulness of quantitative research-particularly experimental and quasi-experimental effects research—opinion surveys, and quantitative content analysis as a means of …social management."

34. Philip J. Pauly, *Controlling Life, Jacques Loeb & The Engineering Ideal in Biology*, Oxford University Press, New York, 1987, p. 4.

35. Pauly, p. 4.

36. Suzanne Rini, *Fidelity*, "The Rockefellers and the Eugenics Movement," November, 1933, p. 23. Rini writes: "In the 1920s, [Henry Fairfield] Osborn was chief of the Rockefeller-funded Museum of Natural History in New York City…. In the Nixon years, Osborn became Assistant Secretary of the Interior and later was ensconced as head of the Environmental Protection Agency. His relative, Frederick Osborn, was the pick to head up John D. Rockefeller's Population Council in 1952, the same year that Rockefeller money beefed up Planned Parenthood to global stature when it hooked 'International' to its name. People would do well to understand that a kind of 'land ethic,' which conflates Darwinian evolution doctrines, population and quite frankly, death, has been articulated by population control ideologues for years. In fact, environmental eugenics is possibly the most lethal, for through its triage system, 'There will be less concern for rights for… parents when human rights themselves begin to move down the scale in relation to the rights of other species, or the "biotic community."'"

37. Roderick Gorney, *The Human Agenda*, Simon & Schuster, New York, 1972, p. 215.

38. Pauly, p. 5.

39. *Male*, p. vii. Acknowledgments, letter from Muller to Guggenheim, February 4, 1933, p. 2. and National Academy of Sciences, Research Council. This author's confirmation in a phone conversation with NRC reference archivist, Janice Goldblum, June 23, 1997.

40. Muller Feb. 4 1933 letter to Henry Allen Moe, Guggenhiem Foundation, Guggenhiem Foundation Archives.

41. Robert K. Graham, the entrepreneur who began "a sperm bank utilizing Nobel Prize winners as donors… became the focus of attention Feb. 29 when he revealed that three Nobel Prize winners had contributed sperm to the Hermann J. Muller Repository for Germinal Choice. One prizewinner, Dr. William Shockley, confirmed the claim." *The Boston Globe*, March 18, 1980.

42. *Sexology*, Sexology Corp., New York, H. Gernsback, President, Harry Benjamin, Rene Guyon, Lester Kirkendall, John Money, and others were on the board of the magazine when Muller's article appeared, June 1962, pp. 725-728. Part two appeared in the July 1962 issue.

43. Muller attended public school in the Bronx and entered Columbia College on a scholarship, receiving his B.A. and MA from Columbia, and his Ph.D. from the University of Chicago.

44. Elof Axel Carlson, *Genes, Radiation, and Society: The Life and Work of H.J. Muller*, Cornell University Press, Ithaca, New York, 1981, p. 120.

45. Carlson, p. 177.

46. See Judith Reisman "Somewhere Ernst Roehm must be laughing," book review in *Culture Wars*, April 1996, pp. 16-17.

47. See the vast body of sexological work by Wilhelm Reich, especially *The Mass Psychology of Fascism*, Farrar, Straus & Giroux, New York, 1980.

48. See Scott Lively and Kevin Abrams, *The Pink Triangle*, Founders Publishing Co., Keiger, Oregon, 1996, and Scott Lively, *Poisoned Stream, The "Gay" Influences in Human History 1890-1945*, Founders Publishing Co., Keiger, Oregon, 1997.

49. Robert Elson, *Prelude to War, World War II*, Time Life Books, New York, 1976, pp. 78-82.

50. Alex de Jonge, *The Weimar Chronicle: Prelude to Hitler*, New American Library, Times Mirror, New York, 1978, pp. 100-101: "1923 was the year that the Hotel Adlon first hired gigolos, professional male dancers, to entertain the lady clients at so much per dance. It was also a period when prostitution boomed. A Frenchman accustomed enough to the spectacle of Montmartre was unable to believe his eyes when he beheld the open corruption of Berlin's Friedrichstrasse. Klaus Mann remembers: *Some of them looked like fierce Amazons strutting in high boots made of green glossy leather. One of them brandished a supple cane and leered at me as I passed by.* 'Good evening, Madame,' I said. She whispered in my ear: 'Want to be my slave? Costs only six billion and a cigarette. A bargain, Come along, honey.'"

51. De Jonge, Ibid.
52. S. William Halpern, *Germany Tried Democracy*, W.W. Norton, New York, 1946, p. 491-498.
53. William Shirer, *Rise and Fall of the Third Reich*, Simon & Schuster, New York, 1960, p. 5.
54. Aldous Huxley, *Brave New World*, Harper & Row, New York, 1932.
55. Caroll Quigley, *Tragedy and Hope*, Macmillan Company, New York, 1966, p. 1240. "The application of Darwinism to human society toward the end of the nineteenth century... provided the ideological justification for the wars of extermination of Nazism and Fascism. Only after the middle of the twentieth century did a gradual reappearance of the old Christian ideas of love and charity modify this view, replacing it with the older idea that diverse human interests are basically irreconcilable." (p. 1240)
56. Fredric Wertham, "The German Euthanasia Program," excerpted from *A Sign for Cain*, Hayes Publishing, Cincinnati, Ohio 1973, p. 33.
57. James Jones, *Kinsey: A Public/Private Life*, W.W. Norton, New York, 1997, p. 809 f. 78.
58. Wertham, p. 33.
59. Ibid.
60. Peter Coleman, *The Liberal Conspiracy, The Congress for Cultural Freedom and the Struggle for the Mind of Postwar Europe*, Free Press, New York, 1989, p. 105.
61. *The Dictionary of Scientific Biographies* (American Council of Learned Societies, 1919), Hermann Muller, Vol. ix, 1974, p. 565.
62. Muller-Guggenheim letter, in the author's archive.
63. Muller-Guggenheim letter, Ibid.
64. Robert N. Proctor, *Racial Hygiene, Medicine Under the Nazis*, Harvard University Press, Cambridge, Massachusetts, 1988, pp. 17-18, 26, 40.
65. Muller-Guggenheim letter, Ibid.
66. Muller-Guggenheim letter, Ibid.
67. Regarding collaboration between—and conduits for— science, industry, and business, readers are referred to a revealing *Frontline* telecast entitled "Nazi gold" (June 18-19, 1997). Switzerland is cited as a pass-through for Nazi sympathizers who purchased gold extracted from the bank accounts (and teeth) of Nazi victims. The gold served as a medium of exchange for funding Hitler's war machine, since no governments were accepting German marks.
68. Muller-Guggenheim letter, Ibid.
69. Suzanne Rini, "The Rockefellers and the Eugenics Movement," *Fidelity*, November, 1993, p. 22.
70. Muller-Guggenheim letter, Ibid.
71. Muller-Guggenheim letter, Ibid.
72. Stefan Kuhl, *The Nazi Connection: Eugenics American Racism and German National Socialism*, Oxford Press, New York, 1994, p. 101.
73. Kuhl, Ibid, p. 102.
74. Kuhl, Ibid, p. 102.
75. Kuhl, Ibid, p. 102.
76. Kuhl, Ibid, p. 103.
77. Kuhl, Ibid, p. 103.
78. Kuhl, Ibid, p. 103.
79. Kuhl, Ibid, p. 103.
80. Wertham, pp. 14, 15.
81. Pomeroy, p. 198.
82. David Brinkley, *Washington Goes to War*, Ballantine Books, New York, 1988, p. 26.
83. Wertham, p. 32.
84. *The Dictionary of Scientific Biography*, vol. ix 1974 p. 565.
85. *Who Was Who in America*, 1968, Volume 4, p. 687.
86. Aleksandr Solzhenitsyn, *The Gulag Archipelago*, Harper & Row, New York, 1973, pp. 58-59.
87. Mikhail Heller and Aleksandr Nekrich, *Utopia In Power: Socialism "Achieved and Won, 1935-1938*, Simon and Schuster/Summit Books, New York, 1982, pp. 290-291.
88. Hermann J. Muller, *Out of the Night*, The Vanguard Press, New York, 1935, Ibid, p. 113.
89. On December 12, 1997, while in Germany, this author interviewed Dr. Tilman Spengler in Berlin. Spengler authored *Lenin's Brain* (Farrar, Strauss & Giroux, New York, 1993), in which he described Hermann Muller's stay at the Kaiser Wilhelm Brain Institute. Having worked for several years at the Institute, Spengler crafted a nonfiction book based on the historical facts of the case. While agreeing that it was possible that children may have been victimized in the facility during Muller's tenure, Spengler suggested that it was also likely that the abuse took place in Moscow, where Muller had access to extensive laboratory facilities. Muller, Spengler said, was suspected of being a Communist agent in Berlin and a spy for the Comintern, while the Rockefeller-funded Brain Institute was viewed as a communist operation. Spengler was astonished to find no reference to Muller's Storm Trooper arrest, or to the horrible events taking place in Germany during his stay, in Muller's *Out of the Night*. He noted that there were rumors circulating about a "less honorable" reason for Muller's departure from Russia in 1937 than Muller claimed in his book.

90. "Comintern: acronym for Communist International, founded (1919), by V.I. LENIN to claim Communist leadership of the world socialist movement. Its conditions for membership excluded non-Communist socialists. Its efforts to foment revolution failed, and in 1935 it began to form coalitions, or popular fronts, with bourgeois parties. The Comintern dissolved (1943) as a gesture of support for the Allied war effort. The Cominform (Communist Information Bureau) was organized in (1947) by the USSR to coordinate the exchange of information between E[astern] European and some W[estern] European Communist parties, formerly a function of the Comintern. It was disbanded in 1956." *The Concise Columbia Encyclopedia,* 1991, Columbia University Press.

91. Solzhenitsyn, p. 600.

92. *Newsweek,* March 10, 1997.

93. *Cambridge Dictionary of Scientists,* 1996, p. 237.

94. *Asimov's Biographical Encyclopedia of Science and Technology,* 1972, pp. 634-5.

95. Anthony Sutton, *How the Order Creates War and Revolution,* Research Publishing, Phoenix, Arizona, 1984, p. 86. See also William Stevenson, *A Man Called Intrepid: The Secret War,* Ballantine Books, New York, pp. 65, 91, 307, 308, 311.

96. Stevenson, Ibid.

97. Harry Truman, March 27, 1942, Congressional Record.

98. Stevenson, Truman, et al.

99. Pomeroy, p. 197.

100. Pomeroy, pp. 202-405, 424, 429-430, 440.

101. Pomeroy, p. 315.

102. Christenson, *Kinsey: a Biography,* Indiana University Press, Bloomington, Indiana, 1971, pp. 210 211. From Kinsey's speech to biology teachers entitled: "The Scientist's Responsibility in Sex Instruction." Kinsey stated in 1940, "at no time did we allow the question of morality to determine what was scientifically acceptable."

103. Jones, p. 809, f. 78.

104. Gordon Thomas, in *Journey into Madness: The True Story of the Secret CIA Mind Control and Medical Abuse,* and John Marks, in *The Search for the "Manchurian Candidate": The CIA and Mind Control, The Secret History of the Behavioral Scientists,* examine the CIA's role in human experimentation with LSD. They document that renowned scientists and academicians at accredited universities conducted unconscionable research using secret CIA funds. Thomas writes, "While political terrorism has been capturing widespread attention.... [a]lmost nothing has been made public of how doctors today use their knowledge and skills in its support. Yet they regularly medically examine political prisoners... to assess the degree of torture to be used. They attend interrogations to treat the direct physical effect of the torture they have approved so that investigation can continue. They recommend how much further torture can then be applied. Physicians... falsify autopsy reports... for persons those doctors know were tortured to death [claiming] 'cardiac failure' or 'pneumonia' on those certificates.... Psychiatry, in particular, is highly vulnerable to being used by the state to maintain power and control the thoughts and actions of its citizens."

Pomeroy adds: "Outside the boundaries of Bloomington, Kinsey's best friends were scientists like himself who, in one way or another, were a part of his grand scheme. Thus, Kinsey corresponded with an international group of gynecologists, psychiatrists, endocrinologists and such, and Kinsey 'employed a half-dozen good' scientists, pediatricians or others, 'to make experimental tests of a long series of patients.' This was in 1943, the year Kinsey said 'more hands' were needed to "push the project into high gear" (p. 93).

The prestigious American-born "Dr. E. Ewen Cameron," a "good scientist" became a fellow Rockefeller grantee. He later served as president of the American Psychiatric Association, which in 1973 changed its *Diagnostic and Statistical Manual,* largely on the basis of Kinsey's data, to say that homosexuality was no longer a disorder. Cameron was also a CIA mind-control researcher. Gordon Thomas relates in some detail his secret CIA work, and especially his preference for doing sensitive human experiments outside "the borders of the United States." Thomas writes: "[CIA Director Allen] Dulles had ordered the project as too risky to perform within the borders of the United States. Once more the director's attention focused on Dr. Cameron. Dr. Cameron's Institute... [w]as a good source for human guinea pigs.... Dulles favored the scientific approach."

Pomeroy cites Dr. Cameron's relationship with Kinsey in the same way that he cites Kinsey's ties to the pedophile jurist, Rene Guyon. A letter surfaced with a reference to Dr. Cameron as one of Kinsey's many "scientifically trained" colleagues.

In August 1947, Dr. Cameron invited Kinsey to lecture at McGill University in Montreal. Cameron at the time was head of the university's Department of Psychiatry. The topic was "Sexual Customs."

Robert Morison, the Rockefeller Foundation medical director who praised Kinsey as perhaps the Foundation's most important grantee, was also Cameron's patron: "During the past thirteen years, [Cameron] had already raised more money than any other Canadian doctor. It had begun with $40,000 in 1943 from the Rockefeller Foundation.... [Later] No one, of course, could know—Dr. Cameron had made sure—that what he had begun on that day over three and a half years ago was his first contribution to the Central Intelligence Agency's search for methods of mind control."

Marks describes Cameron's specialty as prefrontal lobotomies, which left depressed, but otherwise normal, young mothers institutionalized for the remainder of their days. Cameron also conducted sensory deprivation experiments, confining one victim alone for 35 days in a sensory deprivation chamber, followed by an additional 101 days of experimental psychological abuse. The medical staff at McGill, like the Kinsey Institute staff, appears to have remained obedient and silently loyal through it all.

Following Dr. Cameron's death, McGill's Dr. Donald Herbb asserted, "Look, Cameron was no good as a researcher .... He was eminent because of politics." A member of Dr. Cameron's team, opting to remain anonymous, said of Cameron's use of shock therapy, forced injections, mind-numbing drugs, prefrontal lobotomies, and other odious methods: "Cameron was the godfather of Canadian psychiatry.... I probably shouldn't talk about this, but Cameron—for him to do what he did—he was a very schizophrenic guy who totally detached himself from the human implications of his work.... God, we talk about concentration camps. I don't want to make this comparison, but God, you talk about we didn't know it was happening, and it was—right in our back yard."

105. William Manchester, *The Arms of Krupp,* Little Brown & Co., New York, 1964, p. 613.

106. Manchester, p. 615.

107. Manchester, p. 615.
108. Manchester, p. 614.
109. Christopher Simpson, *Science of Coercion, Communication Research & Psychological Warfare 1945-1960*, Oxford University Press, New York, 1994, p. 22.
110. Simpson, p. 21.
111. Simpson, pp. 21-22.
112. Simpson, p. 22.
113. Simpson, p. 25.
114. Simpson, p. 29.
115. Simpson, p. 29.
116. Hermann B. Wells, *Being Lucky*, Indiana University Press, Bloomington, Indiana, p. 302-311. On October 17, 1947, to May 27, 1948, Indiana University President Herman Wells took a leave of absence and went to Germany with his assistant, Peter Fraenkel. The purpose was to assist General Lucius D. Clay, who was then military governor of Germany. Wells' office was located at the former Kaiser Wilhelm Institute located at Dahlem. He had been recruited by General Clay "principally to help bring order out of considerable chaos in the cultural affairs branch... to assemble cultural activities in a single division..... Thus the Education and Cultural Relations Division was created." Strange set of coincidences, indeed.
117. Kai Bird, *The Chairman: The Making of the American Establishment*, Simon & Schuster, New York, 1992, p. 26 See also pp. 481-492.
118. Bird, p. 26.
119. Bird, p. 113. Also see William Manchester, *The Arms of Krupp*, Little Brown & Co., New York, 1964, p. 645.
120. Bird, p. 480-492, Bird, Manchester: Krupp evidence was never revealed, p. 648.
121. Manchester, p. 756, p. 652.
122. Manchester, p. 658.
123. Manchester, pp. 537-544.
124. Manchester, p. 537.
125. Manchester, pp. 537-544, p. 539.
126. Manchester, pp. 537-544.
127. Manchester, Ibid.
128. Manchester, Ibid.
129. Edward Everett Hale, "Lend a Hand," in James Dalton Morrison, Ed., *Masterpieces of Religious Verse* (1948); also, John Bartlett, *Familiar Quotations*, Emily Morison Beck, Ed., 14th Edition, Little, Brown and Company, Boston, 1968 [1855], p. 717.
130. Thomas Roder, Volker Kubillus and Anthony Burwell, *Psychiatrists: The Men Behind Hitler, The Architects of Horror*, Freedom Publishing, Los Angeles, CA, 1994, pp. 194-197. [Emphasis added.]
131. Id.
132. Id.
133. Id.
134. United States Department of Health and Human Services, FR 52880-01, report on "Protection of Human Subjects," November 23, 1982.
135. Id, p. 32.
136. Id, p. 12.
137. Id, p. 19.
138. Id, p. 26.
139. Id, p. 28.
140. Id, p. 29-30.
141. John Colapinto, *As Nature Made Him: The Boy Who Was Rasied as a Girl*, Harper Collins, New York, 2000, p. 70.
142. Id, p. 70.
143. Id, p. 76.
144. See cover story in *Brill's Comment*, "Is This What's Ahead?", addressing the Time-Warner, New Corp. Viacom/CBS, Disney and AT&T control of American Communications," January 2000.
145. The decision to include this research "Fetal Harvesting", July 1999, "Baby Parts for Sale", "A batch of eyes by UPS - 30 livers by FedEx", by J.C. Wilke, MD.
146. Life Issues Institute, 1721 W. Galbraith Rd, Cincinnati, OH, 45239.
147. Emphasis added, see Pro-Life E-News, www.Insightmag.com, editor@sunpub.com.
148. Mary Woostonecraft Shelley, *Frankenstein or The Modern Prometheus*, Bath Press, Avon, Great Britain, 1986.
149. F.M. Dostosevsky, *The Diary of a Writer*, translated by Boris Brasol, Peregrin Smith, Inc., Santa Barbara, CA, 1979.
150. Rabbi Daniel Lapin, *America's Real War*, Multnomah Publishers, Sister, OR, 1999, pp. 2-3.

ADDENDUM

The following articles appeared on Page One of every major German newspaper in May, 1957. Although Alfred Kinsey was then a household word in the United States, no American newspapers revealed that our nation's sex expert—the pioneer of our current sex education model—was writing, encouraging and guiding a German Nazi pedophile as he sexually abused innocent children. Would the public have accepted Kinsey's false claims about America's alleged promiscuous sexual life had the press published the truth—that Kinsey aided and abetted the former Nazi commandant, warning him only to "Be careful!" as he committed his brutal crimes? When the German judge declared he thought von Balluseck molested the children to "impress Kinsey and to provide him material," the pedophile proudly declared, "Kinsey himself had asked me to do so." Would the American Law Institute have changed its Model Penal Code to lighten sex offender penalties based on Kinsey's expertise, had they known von Balluseck "had close contact with the so-called American sex researcher, Kinsey, to whom he'd repeatedly and explicitly reported his perverse crimes?" Had the press revealed the truth in 1957, we might be living in a very different nation today. However, it is never too late to right a wrong.

FROM DER MORGENPOST, MAY 19, 1957

Samthandschuhe fur Kinderschander Balluseck [Velvet Gloves for Pedophile Balluseck]

...The Nazis knew and gave him the opportunity to practise his abnormal tendencies in occupied Poland on Polish children, who had to choose between Balluseck and the gas oven. After the war, the children were dead, but Balluseck lived.

...he showed himself naked to girls in his West Berlin apartment, and he seduced his own daughter to unnatural acts, and his niece who came very often from Potsdam to visit them, got the same treatment.

One of the school boys he used homosexually and who later offered his services to other men, got arrested, and related to the police how Balluseck taught him everything....even the most hardened court reporters were warned "even if you think the worst, it is still not as bad as the reality...

In a warehouse, Balluseck sexually abused a seven-year-old girl, whose father alerted the Stumm-Polizei. The investigation showed that the girl had a very vivid imagination and that poor Balluseck was merely a victim of this childish intrigue, because the Stumm-Polizei deduced that someone in his position, especially a 131er doesn't do anything like that.

...That was irresponsibility of the worst kind. Instead of protecting the Berger and his children from sexual criminals, the West Berlin Police as ever, shields the Senate from embarrassing scandal.... Today the court has got four diaries, and in these diaries, with cynicism and passion, he recorded his crimes against 100 children in the smallest detail. He sent the detail of his experiences regularly to the US sex researcher, Kinsey. The latter was very interested, and kept up a regular and lively correspondence with Balluseck, who cut out Kinsey's signature and stuck it neatly in his diary.

The expert Dr. Weiman told the court there was no evidence of mental illness in the accused, and because of that, the prosecutor (Krause) applied for 12 years top security prison and 8 years loss of civil rights, after which he should be sent to an institution. When he heard that, the accused reacted with an animal scream.

...After a break of a few hours, the verdict came, and the public protested. Instead of the justifiable proposition that Krause made, the court must be Senate friendly, decided to treat the most horrible criminal in post-war times, with kid gloves, and it used them to half the recommendations—6 years jail and 5 years loss of civil rights while in there, and then go into an institution. Balluseck breathed a sigh of relief at this incomprehensibly light sentence.

...This 100 times child molester has unquestionably deserved a much harder verdict. The law was on the side of the client, and didn't see in him a dangerous sexual criminal, but saw in him the Reigunstrat... who represented the Senate. What remains is arse-licking to the top and a hit in the face of the parents of more than 100 molested working-class children.

FROM DER MORGENPOST, MAY 15, 1957

Balluseck gab Anleitungen zur Verfurung!
[Balluseck gave instructions on how to seduce]
Perverse correspondence with the US sexual psychologist Kinsey / Deepest moral squalor (stink of infamy!)

Dr. von Balluseck reported his perverse misdeeds repeatedly and extensively to the American so-called sexual psychologist Kinsey. That was revealed during the afternoon of the first day of the trial of the sex criminal. Balluseck wrote to the American about how he abused his niece encountering "hardly any serious resistance." He reported also the seduction of 15 small girls and 5 boys between 1952 and 1954 as well as numerous "failed attempts to make contact." Despite these compromising communiques, the American Kinsey did not think it necessary to tell the police (Anzeige erstatten) about the sex criminal.

In the course of the hearings, Balluseck's abuse of his own daughter and a 14-year-old Hilfßchüler was also addressed. The criminal had first abused them separately, then coupled them with each other for his own selfish perverse ends. The presiding judge of the criminal court, Dr. Berger, commented: "You virtually gave the boy instructions on how to seduce girls!" Unmoved, the defendant justified himself with casuistic arguments and what he called a theory of purity. He said he wanted to test himself and the children. When asked by the judge if he regretted his actions, he gave an evasive answer.

After a lengthy reading from Balluseck's diaries, Dr. Berger exclaimed: "This is no longer human! What was this all for? To tell Kinsey about?"

When asked by the judge why he even abused girls of 8 and 9, Balluseck retorted, he attained his goal more quickly with the younger ones, while the older ones often repelled him. In the course of the hearing, such horrible things were revealed that the participants in the trial breathed a sigh of relief when the trial was adjourned until Wednesday morning.

FROM DER AUSSCHNITT, MAY 5, 1957
Kinderschander Balluseck vor Gericht. NZ. [Childabuser Balluseck Goes to Court]

…He [Balluseck] had close contact with the so-called American sex researcher, Kinsey, to whom he'd repeatedly & explicitly reported his perverse crimes. Balluseck had also described those in pedantic detail in his diaries.

FROM DER MORGENPOST, MAY 16, 1957
Kinsey hatte Balluseck anzeigen sollen [Kinsey ought to have reported Balluseck to the authorities]

Sharp criticism of American sex researcher by presiding judge of the "Grosse Jugendschutzkammer," Landgerichtsdirecktor Heinrich Berger. Because of the correspondence between Regierungersat Dr. FVB, accused of many counts of SKV, and Kinsey. The presiding judge exclaimed, "Instead of answering his sordid letters (Schmierigkeiten), the strange American scholar should rather have made sure that Mister von Balluseck was put behind bars…"

As reported yesterday, during his training as a religion teacher, Balluseck made the acquaintance of a vicar (Gemmeindepfarrer). The defendant complained about his quarters; the vicar subsequently got him a flat in the (Gemeindehaus) community center, but in fact it was where the vicar (Keusch) lived. Balluseck said, "As a church official I was preferable to the unchurchly previous tenant." The confidence shown him did not prevent the defendant from seducing forthwith the 11-year old son of the vicar and making him familiar with the most vile practices. The boy had to keep an exact record of his indecent activities, Ballesecuk then sent these, his victim's data to Kinsey.

> Presiding judge: "I have the impression you often only approached the children in order to be able to assert yourself [??] (auftrumpfen) vis=a=via Kinsey and to provide him material."
>
> Defendant: "Kinsey himself had asked me to do so."
>
> Presiding judge: "That would be typical of Kinsey and his work. It must be a strange scholar who relies on first-hand reports with such disgusting contents."
>
> Defendant (soothingly/appeasingly): "Well, Kinsey is dead." For Balluseck. (Lawyer)

Balluseck was proud of his correspondence with the American sex researcher; evidence is that he cut out the name Kinsey out of a letter the latter sent him and stuck it in his diary.

The discussion of other cases/counts revealed that Balluseck used any and every opportunity to make new victims submit to him. On walks, at swimming pools, in front of shop windows, in trams, even during a trip through the St. Gotthard Tunnel, he approached children under the guise of being a friendly and concerned elderly gentleman. He gave three of his students at a Hilffschüle a lesson in sex education disguised as a lesson in religion (Nachhilfuenterricht = private lessons), which ended in an indecent game of forfeits. He asked so-called madams he knew to procure him little girls. But these "ladies" had a greater sense of responsibility than the Regierungsrat. They rejected his unreasonable request.

A ten-year-old boy whom the defendant had abused in 1949 was so corrupted by this treatment that he sought the company of other men, for which he was punished.

ADDENDUM

Again yesterday, Balluseck made no serious attempt to deny his deeds. Therefore the court, fortunately, did not have to question the young witnesses. The trial continues tomorrow with the presentation of the medical (i.e. forensic) report.

FROM DER AUSSCHNITT, MAY 15, 1957
"Das ist ja Irrsinn!" rief der Vorsitzender
[That is crazy!" exclaimed the presiding judge]

Balluseck's diaries were read out yesterday–"Reports on his Successes" to Kinsey. The first day of the big sex crimes trial of 48-year-old Regierungsrat dr FvB ended yesterday with a banging of a fist.…Berger shouted, "I've had enough!" and slammed the diaries shut, in which [Balluseck] had recorded with pedantic and embarrassing accuracy all his misdeeds. Balluseck is charged with 33 counts of indecent acts (Unzucht) with minors or of having made them endure indecent acts. The trial before the JSK is scheduled to last three days.

The trial is closed to the public because of the danger to public decency. Instead… full of journalists…Expressionless and with fixed gaze his eyes wander around the room. He answers in a quiet and monotonous voice. Balluseck remains calm, even when the voice of the judge reading from the diaries becomes louder.

"Ach, no one here understands," he said at one point.

The question emerges again and again: What was going on in the mind of this person, who as lawyer and Akademiker (educated man) must have realized the import of his revolting deeds. He repeatedly quotes from the bible and Rilke. Even as a child he was already interested in questions of sex. The defendant said, "Since I was 14 I have been concerned with establishing ideals of purity." Then in a kind of scientific fervor (Forschungsdrang) he wanted to "test" himself and the children. The presiding judge asked what he as a lawyer thinks about this. Balluseck: "The juridical issue only concerned me at a theoretical level. What I could justify morally, could not be something impure. I felt obligated to help the children, to spare them a sense of guilt."

Monstrous one entry depicting his "experience" with a girl of eleven. "That is mad!" exclaimed the presiding judge–himself father of four children.

Balluseck's surprising answer: "It appears logical to me."

…The court is silent, holds its breath, as an entry from Balluseck's diary is read out in which he describes in great detail how he coupled (verkuppelte) his fourteen-year-old daughter with a Hilfßchüler (remedial school student) two years her senior. Von Balluseck sent a comprehensive report on his "successes" and the reactions of the 16-year-old to the American "sex researcher" Kinsey.

The presiding judge concluded that to read this all is not just a psychic/psychological burden but a torment, and, visibly shaken, adjourned the court. The trial continues today.

FROM NEUSS DEUTSCHLAND, (EAST BERLIN), MAY 17, 1957
Kinderschander machte Karriere "Auzch an polnischen Kindern vergangen…"
[Childabuser makes a Career]

…also during the war he was a Nazi Occupational Officer in Poland, and he abused 10-12 year old girls.…Balluseck's career catapulted because he was a fanatical member of the Nazi party.…During the war he was in the infamous civil administration of the occupation in Poland. By force they took millions of Polish nationals to Germany (for slave labor).

...After 1945, Balluseck went underground as a casual laborer, but a few years later, he was working in several West Berlin schools as a religious teacher. In 1954 he was "de-nazified". He also appears to have been employed as some sort of legal advisor to the Protestant Church Association. (evangleischen Kirche von Brandenburg).

"Ballusecks Vorbild: dte USA" (Balluseck's role model USA)

At the beginning of the trial, this horrible person sang praises to the moral and ethical collapse signs in the USA, which he followed after 1945. As a role model for his perverse actions, Balluseck named the works of the so called sexual psychologist Kinsey, who's out pourings are the highest example of the moral decay of the Imperial World and especially in the USA....In his defense speech, the accused continually used phrases such as "a holy problem" ("heliges Proglem"), and "eithical world order" ("sittliche Weltordnung") and "religious, sexual ideal purity" ("religios-sexuelles Reinheitsideal") etc.

...The presiding Judge was so shocked, that when it came to reading extracts from Balluseck's dirty diaries, he stated several times "it is painful to have to read all this" ...("Es ist eine Qual, das alles verlessen zu mussen")....Balluseck could only pursue his crimes unpunished in the last few years, because of well meaning support by the Senate who helped him again to such an prominent position, although the crimes during the war in Poland [abuse of children] had been an 'open secret'.

Already in 1955 somebody started proceedings against him for the seduction of a minor. But on the 13 August, 1955 the proceedings were stopped, after the official, came to the conclusion that she was fantasizing/had a vivid imagination. ("phantasiebegabt").

In 1954, this serial offender, along with several other prominent Nazis, moved into the "Schonenberger" Rathas (i.e. he was made an official again – the implication here is that SDP or Communist officials who were put into power by the allies because they were against the Nazis, lost their jobs and were replaced by Nazis).

But the patronage of the council for this "sittenstroich" (pervert) went even further, at the end of 1956, when his diaries were accidentally discovered and Balluseck was arrested, the Senate suspended him from his duties but carried on paying him half his salary. Not only did Balluseck make a lot of young people unhappy, but the parents 'were allowed', with their taxes, to generously support the criminal. The trial continues...

FROM DER TAGESPIEGEL, OCTOBER 1, 1957

Balluseck Korrespondierte mit Kinsey. [Balluseck Corresponds With Kinsey]

The (Vernehmugen) trial (investigation?) of the 49 year old Balluseck for the "Sittenpolizei" (Special branch of police that deals with sex crimes) ended yesterday, and all the trial papers will go to the "Staatsanwattschaft" (Public Prosecutor). The Kriminalpolizei (Dept for crime) says Balluseck is fully responsible for his crimes against children.

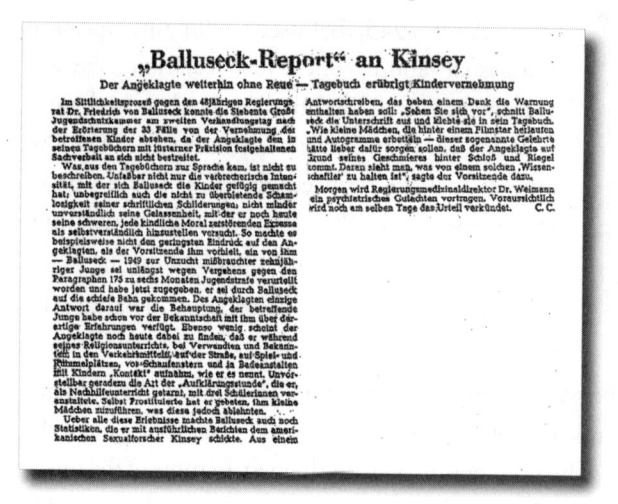

FROM DER TAGESPIEGEL, MAY 16, 1957
"Balluseck-Report" an Kinsey ["Balluseck – Report" on Kinsey]

...In 33 cases they asked the children to come and be a witness against him in court, but because the accused in hid diaries had explained things so clearly, and because he didn't deny the charges, it wasn't necessary.

...What came out of these diaries was indescribable; not only was it incomprehensible how Balluseck made the children comply with him, but what was also incomprehensible is that he had no feeling of shame–and no less comprehensive was the relaxed attitude with which he went to portray that it was nothing out of the ordinary.

...Refers to 1949–Balluseck abused a 10 year old boy. The boy was recently sent down for youth punishment, under Paragraph 175 (homosexuality). The boy admitted that it was because of Balluseck, that he had taken that path. The only reply of the accused to this, was that the boy in question had already had experience in that area before he met Balluseck.

...During his lessons, when he was with relatives, friends, on public transport, in the street, in playgrounds & fairgrounds, in front of shop windows & in swimming pools, Balluseck sought 'contact'. He had a sexual lesson 'after class' with 3 girls, and he even asked prostitutes to send little girls to him, but they refused to do it.

He made statistics of all these experiences and he sent them with comprehensive reports to the American sex research, Kinsey. In one reply, which apart from a "thank you," contained the warning "Sehen Sie sich vor"–'be careful' (or 'watch out'). Balluseck cut out the signature from this letter, and stuck it in his diary.

...Like little girls who run after film stars, and call for their autographs, this so-called expert should have made sure the accused was put behind bars because of his smutty writings.

FROM THE MEDICAL TRIBUNE, JULY 19, 1991
Kinsey's Sexreport Dubious? Misleading? Fraud?

New York–For many years puritan America was astonished over what Dr. Alfred C. Kinsey candidly stated as early as 1948: Sex is ruling the world! The people were told by Kinsey what men and women really think, how they engage in limitless sexual variations, what is really happening behind the puritan curtains. A nation in sex shock, sexual perversion as "permitted normality," and a sex- and behavior researcher on his way to worldwide fame. Until now, little has changed the almost absolute authority of Kinsey's allegations. But now it is exploding! In their recently published book: "*Kinsey, Sex and Fraud: The Indoctrination of a People,*" Dr. Judith Reisman and Edward W. Eichel substantially indict Kinsey and Co. The sex dispute is seriously on its way.

More than 40 years after the Kinsey reports achieved US and worldwide attention, the sexology dispute over Dr. Kinsey and his research methodology is raging more than ever before. The reason: Since two sexologists dissected the famous Kinsey Manifestos regarding the sexual life of "Man" and "Woman" and declared the research methodology as dubious, misleading, even fraud, Alfred Kinsey, the father of sex research and up until now a enshrined authority is in danger of being thrown from the pedestal of scientific fame.

Kinsey Institute outraged

In order to soften the crash landing of its idol and life support or to even uplift the monument, the Kinsey Institute naturally tries to counter. "Totally unfounded allegations, pure defamation, not a word true and legal actions reserved" is the insecure embittered rebuttal. But why all this excitement? Well, of course, the criticism of Dr. Reisman and her co-author Edward W. Eichel hits Kinsey & Co razor sharp and in the heart: The data from which the over spilling sex lust and obsessive desire for variation of Americans was derived were possibly altered or seriously falsified! Was there created under the name of science a sex myth which indeed influenced a society and eventually steered it into today's AIDS catastrophe without responsible and honest investigation? No wonder that from *The Washington Times* to *The [London] Times* and the medical center "*Lancet*" even honorable papers are holding their breath! And this with unusually clear language: The editorial of *The Washington Times* describes it as "Censorship Through Intimidation" and presumes considerable further wrongdoing when the Kinsey Institute shuts off public comments by Dr. Reisman in order to extinguish doubts about the public opinion about sexuality so guided by Kinsey.

Sex starts early in life expressing itself in all possible and impossible variations and does not know age- or gender borders! "Anything goes" is the Kinsey philosophy reduced to its core. According to his current critics, Dr. Kinsey based his allegations on highly unusual methods. Considerable numbers of those researched for normal sexual behavior were allegedly recruited from the milieu of prison inmates and sexual offenders. Not only scientifically unsound and unethical but indeed criminal, Dr. Kinsey allegedly conducted his studies on sex with children! Masturbation, e.g., by "technically therefore trained specialists" of more than 100 children between 2 months and 15 years of age served as a scientific basis. No wonder, according to Dr. Reisman, someone who is "researching" with such methods and making male prostitutes part of a foundation of his proclaimed "normal sexual world picture" eventually has to conclude with the ideology: Sex influences human life from cradle to grave and accordingly sexual education must reflect this "basic desire."

Sex, Lies and Kinsey

Suddenly, the scientist and research Dr. Kinsey stands in a totally new and tarnished light. His "experimentally funded" sexual revolution still endures unbroken, partially even taught in school.

One is now anxious to see what kind of material arguments the Kinsey Institute can offer to bring its hero down from the scientific "gallows."

ADDENDUM

Kinsey Report Reduces or Eliminates Common Law Sex Offenses

1989 The National Research Council Defines America as the "Pre and Post Kinsey Era"
Kinsey Begins Secret Sex Studies in 1920's; Rockefeller Funds Kinsey in 1941 and ALI Model Penal Code in 1950;
100% of Original 1955 ALI "Sex Science" Cites to Kinsey
Legislators and Judges Legalize "Recreational Sex"; Test for New Laws Becomes "Consent"

Pre - 1948 Kinsey Law 54 Sex Crimes Targeted	Post - 1948 Kinsey Law 54 Crimes/Penalties Reduced or Eliminated	1960 1st Generation Outcomes	1990 2nd Generation Outcomes
Obscenity & Pornography Language Books Letters Sex Crime Magazines Ads of certain diseases	Obscenity: words only, later pictures redefined as "Soft" or "Hard" Pornography: "Soft" = legal "Hard" = illegal "Soft" is increasingly "Hard" and "Hard" is increasingly brutalized. Post Roth 1957, America follows Kinsey "anything goes" model.	Legalize/Lighten Hetero/Homosexual Sex and Violence Media, Shift From "Words" To Images: Magazines, Film, Television, Video, Books, Pamphlets, Music, Radio, Internet, Public Libraries, Sports, School AIDS Adverts, Youth Publications. Juvenile Sexual Entitlement; School Sex Education. Legal Employment of 18+ Children In Sex Industry, Neighborhood Strip Bars, Theaters, "Adult" Bookstore, etc.	Decline of "Good Art;" Increase Of Child Abuse/Pornography Facilities Prostitution; Marital Discord/Divorce; Wife/Child Battery; Incest; Sexual Harassment: Adult/Child Rape; Impotence; Frigidity; Illegitimacy; Juvenile Sex And Violence, Homicide, "Autoerotic Fatalities," Homo- Heterosexual Promiscuity, Experiments, Sex Addictions; Covert Political/Legal Lobby Withholds Toxic Facts From Public Across All Laws Cited Here.
Fornication Adultery Cohabitation Contraception	Fornication Adultery Cohabitation Contraception	Legalize/Lighten Breach Of Promise; Seduction; Alienation Of Affection; Exhibition; Soliciation; Peeping; "No Fault" Divorce; Pornography Sex Acts. Legal Mandates Rentals To Unmarried Couples, Homosexual "Partners," Homo/bisexuals Insured; "Surrogate," (Paid) Sex Partners For "Therapy," etc.	AIDS; 25-30 New STD's, Adult And Juvenile Promiscuity, Absent Fathers; Impotence; Welfare; Povertization Of Women And Children; Illegitimacy; Child Prostitution; Female Sterility, Cervical Cancer; Unmanaged Childre Get "Ritalin," In Schools, Scholarship Declines, Sex "Science" Field Legitimized; Increases "Abstinence" Programs, etc.

Rape
  By Force
  By Statutory
Abduction
Seduction
Prostitution
	Rape
	  By Force
	  By Statutory
	Abduction
	Seduction
	Prostitution
		Reduce All Rape Laws. "Peer Sex" Play Defense, Juvenile Rapist Within 5 Years Of Child Victim Is Not Rape; Rape "Under The Influence" Not Rape; "Consent" Is Rape And "Rough Sex Death" Defense. "Privacy" Denies Rape Victim Information Of Rapist AIDS, Legal Sodomy Undermines Arrests For Public Solicitation, Publice Sex.	Drug/Alcohol/Sexual Abuse, Lawsuits Over "Consent" In Rape, Sex Harassment, "Hostile" Workplace, Sex Therapy Service Industry, Hetero/Bi/Homosexual Rape Centers, Counseling, Rape, Gang Rape, Serial Rape, Mutilation, Murder; Incest, Child Sex Abuse; Drugging Rape, AIDS Rape, etc.

Sodomy Solicitation For Sodomy Bestiality Buggery Cunnilingus Felatio	Sodomy Solicitation For Sodomy Bestiality Buggery Cunnilingus Felatio	Title X "Emancipated Minor" Subverts Parental Consent For School Instruction In Hetero/Homo/Bisexual Sodomy, Condom Distributions; Children's Genital Exams; Mandated School, State "Hate" Crimes, "Diversity" Training, etc.	Soliciting And Committing Child Sex Abuse Via Sodomy; AIDS; 25 New Venereal Diseases; Marital Discord; Prostate Disease; Street Prostitution, Youth Employment In Sex Industry; Mandated Sex Vaccines For Newborn Babies, Teen Experimentation, Reproductive Disorders, etc.
Abortion Crimes Against Infants Impairing Morals Of Minor Concealing Birth Of Child	Abortion Crimes Against Infants Impairing Morals Of Minor Concealing Birth Of Child	Contributing To Delinquency Of A Minor, "Emancipated Minor" To Avoid Pregnancy, School Sex Lessons In Masturbation/Contraception. Partial Birth Abortion And "Research" On Embryo Body Parts Partly Legal; Euthanasia Legal In Oregon, etc.	Divorce; Abandonment; Increased Breast Cancer, Sterility, Depression, Suicide, Single Moms; Gov. Sale/Experiments On Unborn Baby Body Parts To Merchants And "Scientists" For Grants, Profits. State Seizes Parental Rights, Increased Push For Elderly, Sick As In Euthanasia, etc.

Index

Symbols
10%   90, 206.
100%   27, 59, 336.
1938   16, 17, 21, 23, 24, 27, 28, 68, 78, 104, 120, 130, 151, 170, 181, 182, 306, 307, 325.
5th World Congress   180, 292.
95%   191, 210, 213, 231, 247, 248.

A
Abbey, Thelema   279.
Aberle, Sophie D.   28.
Aberrant   41, 91, 92, 95, 97, 98, 100, 196, 211.
Abnormal   31, 36, 52, 71, 106, 121, 126, 132, 148, 166, 169, 183, 189, 211, 230, 231, 236, 257, 265, 320, 328.
Abolition   232.
Abortion   107, 119, 120, 121, 158, 167, 168, 180, 184, 192, 194, 207, 209, 218, 219, 225, 242, 246, 247, 248, 249, 250, 251, 252, 253, 254, 255, 256, 267.
Academia   14, 173, 175, 182, 183, 190, 259.
Accreditation   174, 183.
Accumulative incidence   54, 92, 153.
Act up   242, 259.
Adams, Clifford   296.
Addicts   119, 252, 253, 279.
Adolescent   7, 8, 9, 60, 111, 112, 121.
Adolescent sex play   231.
Adult hysteria   215.
Adult-child sex   82, 107, 116, 121, 180, 182, 184, 215, 226, 231, 234, 235, 265, 294.
Adultery   2, 60, 87, 88, 103, 104, 107, 110, 114, 116, 184, 192, 202, 208, 209, 211, 215, 216, 217, 218, 219, 220, 221, 231, 236, 256, 263, 264, 289.
Advertising   37, 39, 178, 313.
Age of consent   82, 217, 224, 233, 234, 278.
Aggressive   10, 32, 35, 55, 96, 103, 106, 107, 120, 124, 184, 261, 293, 321.
AIDS   34, 64, 84, 104, 133, 169, 170, 174, 175, 184, 193, 209, 210, 214, 238, 239, 254, 255, 257, 260, 261, 266, 268, 289, 320, 334.
Alcohol   1, 2, 3, 119, 122, 158, 210, 253, 257, 290.
Alimony   216, 217, 219.
Allyn, David   204, 241, 262-266
American Association for the Advancement of Science   56.
American Association of Marriage and Family Counse   180.
American Bar Association   187, 188, 196, 202.
American Board of Pediatrics   147.
American Civil Liberties Union   87, 192, 193, 195, 203, 204, 232, 236, 239, 246.
American Law Institute   187, 188, 189, 195, 196, 199, 200, 202, 203, 204, 211, 215, 216, 217, 223, 224, 228, 229, 241, 242, 247, 259, 260, 261, 262, 263, 265, 267, 277, 317, 328, 336.
American Library Association   13, 14.
American Men of Science   30.
American Psychiatric Association   180, 236, 254, 256, 297, 325.
American Psychological Association   180, 255.
American Social Hygiene Association   28.
American Society of Sex Educators, Counselors and   175.
American Statistical Association   24, 37, 40, 51, 54, 55, 68, 104, 294.
Amorality   33, 294.
Andersen, Hans Christian   277.
Animal   5, 19, 31, 32, 57, 71, 72, 73, 78, 87, 88, 101, 110, 111, 112, 121, 125, 126, 137, 145, 149, 160, 162, 173, 181, 182, 207, 208, 210, 222, 225, 238, 245, 246, 257, 272, 279, 329.
Anthropology   28, 204, 305.
Around-the-clock   143.
Asexual   4, 133.
Association of Women Students   17, 25.
Attic   29, 70, 71, 73, 82, 85.
Auschwitz   305, 314, 315, 318.
Autoerotic   83, 84, 86, 123, 239, 254, 287.
Autoerotic fatalities   83.

B
Baby   61, 64, 66, 107, 125, 140, 144, 145, 147, 148, 149, 153, 169, 232, 233, 247, 263, 266, 287, 292, 318, 319, 320, 327.
Bachelor   25, 30.
Baden-Powell, Sir Robert   9, 43.
Baitsell, George A.   62.
Balluseck   132, 137, 165, 166, 167, 168, 328, 329, 330, 331, 332, 333.
Bancroft, John   17, 99, 136, 139, 140, 145, 158, 161, 162, 164, 168, 293, 322.
Bandura, Albert   133.
Barber, Bernard   128.
Barbour, John   13.
Basic Sexual Rights   81, 82, 171.
Baths   20, 42, 93, 301.
Battery   119, 120, 158, 217, 253.
Baur, Erwin   148, 303.
Beach, Frank   172, 296.
Benjamin, Harry   21, 22, 119, 131, 148, 190, 221, 231, 252, 253, 261, 296, 298, 300, 324.
Berendzen, Richard   99, 105.
Bergler, Edmund   117, 130.
Berkeley   38, 63, 110, 208, 267.
Berlin   21, 22, 23, 28, 43, 49, 95, 137, 165, 289, 292, 300, 301, 302, 303, 304, 305, 306, 307, 308, 312, 324, 325, 328, 332.
Bestiality   88, 101, 110, 111, 126, 130, 160, 174, 237, 245.
Bethany Boys' Club   7, 11.
Biblical   54, 211, 217, 262, 319, 322.
Bigamy   194, 217.
Bigotry   118, 169.
Birth   7, 12, 28, 36, 43, 102, 103, 106, 107, 121, 125, 132, 133, 148, 149, 159, 169, 202, 218, 224, 233, 246, 247, 248, 249, 251, 252, 267, 269, 288, 296, 301, 316, 320.
Birth control   28.
Bisexual   90, 94, 96, 126, 169, 205, 206, 208, 254, 288.
Bisexuality   128, 160, 172, 245, 253, 254, 258.
Black   31, 60, 110, 117, 118, 198, 251, 318, 320.
Blackmail   36, 158, 276.
Blackmun, Harry   243, 244, 247
Blindness   2.
Blueher, Hans   21.
Board of Trustees   18, 25, 27, 57.
Bok, Edward   2.
Bowdoin College   3, 5.
Bowman, Karl   232, 296.
Boy Scouts   6, 8, 9, 18.
Boyle, Patrick   8, 9, 15.
Brain   83, 86, 173, 174, 177, 184, 237, 240, 300, 302, 303, 304, 306, 308, 318, 320, 325.
Brain Institute   308.
Brandeis, Louis   193, 202, 262, 269.
Brave New World   5, 87, 236, 262, 298, 302.
Breach of promise   217, 246.
Breeding   5, 39, 202, 299, 300, 301, 310.
Breuning, Stephen   260.
Brinkman, Paul   37, 44.
British Broadcasting Corporation (BBC)   12, 35, 85, 92, 94, 102, 135, 290.
British Journal of Sexual Medicine   64, 69.
Bromley, Dorothy Dunbar   124.
Brothel   1, 2, 22, 122, 282.
Buchanan, Patrick   78, 86, 287.
Bullough, Vern   172, 174, 176.
Burden of denial   57, 59.
Burlesque   112, 114.
Buschmannshof   310, 315, 316.
Bussey School at Harvard   5, 297.

C
Caberet   21.
Calderone, Mary   149, 176, 177, 178, 179, 184, 246, 247, 251.
Calderwood, Deryck   170, 174, 175, 179.
California Legislative Assembly Subcommittee on Sex Crimes   213.
Cameron, E. Ewen   297.
Camp Winona   7.
Capacities   59, 139, 143, 149, 150, 272.
Caplan, Lester   147, 148, 181.
Carnegie   188, 196, 221, 304, 323.
Case-law   198, 204.
Castration   304.
Central Intelligence Agency   39, 297, 326.
Chamber of Horrors   279.
Chastity   169, 191.

Child abuse   158, 167.
Child molestation   138, 149, 150, 158, 233, 260.
Child pornography   79, 82, 159, 171, 172, 278.
Child prostitution   82, 171, 283.
Child rape   169.
Child sex experiments   135.
Child sexual abuse   99, 104, 107, 117, 139, 163, 164, 184, 234, 236, 245, 273.
Child sexuality   35, 36, 90, 132, 135, 139, 147, 148, 149, 150, 163, 166, 171, 180.
Childbirth   65, 106, 107.
Children   21, 34, 35, 36, 50, 57, 60, 61, 62, 63, 65, 66, 67, 70, 76, 77, 78, 82, 83, 92, 94, 99, 101, 102, 103, 106, 107, 115, 117, 118, 120, 125, 126, 128, 129, 132, 133, 134, 136, 137, 138, 139, 140, 142, 143, 144, 145, 146, 147, 148, 149, 150, 151, 152, 153, 154, 155, 156, 157, 158, 159, 160, 161, 162, 163, 164, 165, 166, 167, 168, 169, 171, 172, 174, 175, 177, 178, 179, 180, 194, 215, 232, 233, 235, 298, 301, 306.
Christenson, Cornelia   3, 23, 25.
Christian   31, 149, 197.
CIA   39.
Cinema   73, 78, 322.
Cleanliness   33.
Clinton, Bill   214, 258, 259, 269.
Clitoris   28.
Coercion   36, 38, 44, 55, 58, 59, 81, 142, 202, 262, 298, 323, 326.
Cohabitation   110, 210, 216, 218, 219, 221, 248.
Collaboration   56, 162, 167, 183, 194, 229, 292, 295, 304, 324.
Collapse   146, 241, 332.
College   1, 3, 56, 59, 64, 65, 66, 78, 79, 89, 90, 91, 97, 98, 99, 100, 101, 112, 114, 115, 117, 123, 124, 128, 218, 272, 277.
College level   90, 97, 98, 99, 100, 101, 124.
Committee for Research in Problems of Sex   28, 29, 43, 55, 68, 271, 275.
Common Law   109, 115, 117, 188, 196, 198, 200, 201, 202, 204, 206, 211, 221, 222, 228, 238, 242, 246, 249, 317, 321, 336.
Communication   37, 38, 39, 101, 134, 182, 262, 266, 271, 309, 312, 313, 323, 326, 327.
Comstock, Anthony   122, 196, 197.
Concerned Women of America   84.
Conditioning   29, 32, 33, 34, 49, 90, 129, 226, 244.
Confidence   42, 115, 191, 240, 322, 330.
Congressional   54, 104, 179, 184, 200, 203, 266, 270, 271, 274, 275, 277, 286, 316, 317, 320.
Consensual   66, 81, 82, 169, 171, 208, 230.
Consent   21, 39, 81, 82, 92, 95, 215, 218, 222, 224, 227, 230, 232, 233, 234, 246, 255, 275, 278, 295, 313, 318, 321, 336.
Consequences   2, 16, 34, 74, 83, 103, 107, 116, 119, 128, 205, 215, 219, 220, 223, 232, 236, 237, 241, 246, 248, 253, 260, 289, 298, 310.
Constitution   41, 89, 187, 198, 207, 214, 219, 236, 240, 244, 255, 262, 264, 266, 267.
Contacts   29, 39, 56, 61, 65, 66, 78, 85, 87, 88, 91, 94, 95, 111, 112, 117, 118, 134, 155, 164, 183, 193, 210, 218, 226, 227, 234, 245, 246, 256, 257, 258, 272, 292, 304.
Conventional   54, 70, 72, 90, 112, 113, 114, 115, 124, 193, 225, 229, 248.
Convulsing   147.
Corner, George W.   28, 40, 43, 275, 276.
Cover-up   59, 60.
Cowboy homosexual   9.
Cox Committee   269, 270.
Crime   2, 41, 50, 63, 65, 66, 81, 87, 88, 93, 99, 101, 102, 103, 114, 115, 116, 118, 132, 135, 138, 140, 161, 163, 166, 167, 168, 178, 179, 182, 183, 188, 192, 195, 201, 205, 206, 208, 210, 211, 212, 213, 214, 215, 216, 217, 221, 222, 223, 226, 227, 228, 229, 230, 232, 233, 234, 235, 236, 237, 240, 242, 246, 254, 255, 256, 260, 263, 264, 265, 266, 292, 310, 311, 314, 315, 328, 330, 331, 332, 333.
Crimes against nature   232, 253.
Crowley, Aleister   276, 279, 280, 281, 289, 290.
Cuba   277, 281.

D
Dachau   305.
Dallenbeck, William   72, 73, 74, 75, 76, 77, 80, 85, 137, 170, 285, 295.
Dangers   25, 30, 63, 72, 215, 270, 285.

INDEX   337

Darwin, Charles 5, 49, 144, 145, 146, 198, 211, 214, 215, 317, 321, 323, 324.
Date rape 232.
Decibels 75, 85.
Democratic National Convention 269.
Denmark 227, 263, 277, 278, 279, 281.
Department of Defense 172.
Deutsch, Albert 103, 189, 190, 191, 204, 224, 245, 261, 262, 264, 267.
Deviant 42, 66, 83, 93, 94, 97, 99, 106, 123, 169, 179, 202, 294, 301.
Diaries 8, 95, 132, 134, 158, 166, 167, 279, 280, 281, 292, 294, 323, 328, 329, 330, 331, 332, 333.
Dickinson, Robert 14, 24, 37, 164, 183, 194, 207, 209, 210, 250, 261, 296.
Direct observation 60, 71, 79, 150, 153.
Discipline 20, 67, 174, 197, 200, 215, 280.
Divorce 3, 42, 88, 102, 103, 109, 121, 128, 151, 158, 176, 207, 209, 217, 218, 219, 220, 221, 226, 249, 288.
Doctor 8, 32, 38, 79, 81, 99, 154, 168, 169, 178, 194, 229, 250, 251, 272, 291, 295, 296, 297, 303, 304, 305, 307, 319, 325, 326.
Dominance 55, 56, 68, 113, 124.
Donahue, Phil 163.
Douglas, Jack 16, 22, 71.
Douglas, William 243, 257.
Dr. Kinseys data 201.
Draft deferments 16.
Dulles, Allen 297, 325, 326.

E

Early interest 23.
Economic 34, 91, 93, 180, 205, 221, 261, 269, 270, 291, 320.
Education 3, 5, 27, 34, 41, 44, 51, 63, 81, 84, 96, 98, 99, 101, 103, 106, 108, 111, 112, 114, 117, 118, 120, 121, 128, 132, 133, 149, 169, 170, 171, 173, 174, 175, 176, 177, 178, 179, 180, 184, 187, 188, 193, 197, 198, 226, 233, 239, 244, 245, 252, 254, 256, 257, 260, 263, 266, 273, 283, 289, 293, 301, 321, 326, 328, 331, 335.
Eisenhower, President Dwight D. 39, 313.
Ejaculation 71, 79, 139, 142, 145, 146, 147, 149, 163, 181, 224, 233, 295.
Eliot, Charles William 198, 199, 211, 221.
Elite 5, 38, 62, 188, 199, 202, 203, 211, 218, 222, 255, 269, 270, 289, 293, 305, 308, 312, 313, 315, 316, 319, 321, 323.
Ellis, Havelock 22, 23, 43, 70, 175.
Emotion 16, 26, 30, 36, 42, 49, 66, 73, 103, 120, 121, 125, 144, 145, 151, 158, 159, 169, 174, 182, 183, 226, 227, 248, 272, 282, 283, 290, 314, 319.
Engineer 39.
England 5, 135, 184, 200, 263, 279, 280.
Erection 144, 145, 148, 149, 243, 282, 284.
Erikson, Eric 133.
Ernst, Morris 87, 192, 194, 197, 201, 203, 204, 219, 224, 226.
Erotic 14, 36, 70, 73, 80, 81, 83, 85, 100, 111, 122, 123, 129, 133, 134, 138, 141, 145, 149, 171, 172, 174, 179, 230, 236, 237, 241, 243, 256, 262, 266, 276, 280, 284.
Esquire 172.
Esther 78, 86, 152, 182, 183.
Estrus 121, 225.
Ethic 18, 21, 56, 60, 139, 142, 168, 181, 182, 183, 190, 194, 195, 200, 206, 208, 209, 210, 226, 231, 232, 245, 261, 263, 264, 280, 283, 293, 322, 323, 332.
Ethical Issues in Sex Therapy 134, 141, 142.
Ethics of Sex Research 168.
Eugenic 5, 12, 71, 82, 93, 129, 202, 262, 269, 277, 298, 299, 300, 301, 304, 307, 308, 310, 312, 317, 318, 319, 321, 323, 324.
Europe 2, 22, 24, 28, 29, 82, 165, 184, 204, 277, 278, 279, 280, 284, 293, 296, 311, 313, 315, 324.
Euthanasia 43, 207, 303, 305, 306, 324.
Evolutionary 39, 49, 126, 198, 199, 202, 206, 211, 214, 232, 320.
Exaggerations 32, 234.
Exhibitionism 72, 77, 78, 85, 126, 156.
Experiment 7, 25, 32, 36, 38, 58, 63, 71, 75, 76, 77, 78, 94, 95, 97, 113, 123, 132, 134, 135, 138, 141, 143, 144, 145, 149, 150, 151, 161, 164, 165, 166, 169.

Extramarital 31, 36, 88, 110, 114, 128.

F

F—korama 173.
Family 1, 2, 3, 4, 7, 9, 11, 12, 19, 21, 22, 30, 35, 73, 80, 84, 85, 87, 88, 102, 120, 122, 129, 132, 133, 150, 151, 152, 159, 162, 180, 189, 190, 197, 202, 203, 213, 214, 216, 217, 220, 221, 225, 230, 236, 247, 252, 255, 293, 298, 300, 305, 310.
Fantasy 37, 81, 174, 205, 224.
Farben, I.G. 311.
Farrell, Warren 159, 161.
Father 3, 11, 12, 13, 18, 32, 78, 87, 88, 89, 91, 95, 102, 103, 117, 130, 147, 151, 152, 157, 158, 159, 160, 162, 181, 182, 183, 196, 199, 202, 210, 216, 218, 219, 220, 226, 253, 262, 265, 270, 271, 282, 283, 300, 316, 331, 334.
FBI 137, 165, 167, 215, 223, 228, 230, 235, 264.
Fear 26, 32, 34, 49, 64, 74, 79, 84, 102, 128, 144, 145, 146, 149, 156, 157, 174, 178, 212, 217, 226, 298, 318.
Feeble Minded 92.
Felons 116, 118, 211, 215, 220.
Feminism 1, 71, 207, 208, 215, 224, 228, 290.
Film 34, 35, 70, 71, 72, 73, 74, 75, 76, 77, 78, 80, 85, 94, 115, 126, 127, 136, 164, 172, 173, 175, 244, 245, 278, 280, 285, 289, 293, 295, 301, 333.
Films 34, 70, 73, 74, 76, 77, 78, 79, 81, 82, 85, 94, 137, 171, 172, 174, 175, 182, 294.
First International Conference for Sexual Reform 49.
Fischer, Eugen 303, 304.
Focus International 172.
Force 35, 58, 61, 62, 63, 74, 77, 144, 155, 158, 167, 169, 172, 173, 174, 180, 182.
Ford 37, 172, 261, 311, 314, 323.
Forensic sexology 171.
Fornication 103, 104, 110, 184, 215, 216, 217, 218, 219, 221, 224, 246, 248, 256.
France 263, 279, 281.
Fraud 81, 104, 178, 179, 194, 195, 196, 200, 215, 221, 236, 246, 247, 248, 255, 259, 260, 264, 334.
Free love 2, 5, 83, 84, 192, 263.
Freegood, Anne G. 271.
Freud, Sigmund 1, 3, 22, 23, 59, 70, 71, 117, 133, 149, 205, 224, 231, 255, 263, 301.
Friess, Donna 157, 182.
Frigidity 117.

G

Gagnon, John 52, 63, 68, 69, 84, 92, 104, 130, 161, 170, 172, 182, 183, 225, 227, 228, 229, 264, 265.
Gajduseck, Daniel Carleton 99.
Galdston, Iago 121, 131.
Gall wasps 11, 17, 18, 19, 24, 27, 39, 49, 55, 139, 141, 162, 296.
GAP 200
Gathorne-Hardy, Jonathan 18, 34, 38, 40, 44, 61, 70, 78, 84, 91, 94, 136, 140, 143, 145, 148, 154, 157, 158, 260, 286, 296
Gay 22, 29, 43, 49, 64, 94, 117, 173, 184, 206, 209, 233, 253, 254, 256, 266, 268, 290, 301, 324.
Gebhard, Paul 13, 14, 15, 31, 32, 33, 34, 35, 44, 50, 52, 61, 63, 64, 68, 69, 70, 73, 76, 77, 78, 81, 84, 85, 89, 91, 94, 110, 115, 116, 120, 130, 131, 135, 136, 137, 141, 142, 143, 144, 148, 150, 151, 152, 158, 159, 160, 161, 164, 165, 167, 168, 170, 172, 174, 182, 213, 219, 225, 235, 246, 249, 250, 252, 263, 264, 267, 286, 293, 294, 322.
Gender and Reproductive Technology 287.
Gentleman 22, 162, 331.
George, Kenneth 170, 174, 175.
Georgetown University 269.
Germany 21, 39, 105, 165, 166, 183, 263, 273, 289, 298, 301, 302, 303, 304, 305, 306, 307, 308, 310, 312, 313, 314, 316, 317, 318, 320, 321, 324, 325, 326, 332.
Gesell, Arnold 134.
Ghetto 61, 92, 293.
Girls and Sex 111, 159, 183.
God 6, 8, 13, 20, 77, 149, 238, 261, 262, 263, 286, 315, 320, 321, 322, 326.
Gorer, Geoffrey 66, 106.

Gorney, Roderick 298, 299, 323.
Grand Inquisitor 56, 283.
Grand scheme 63, 83, 108, 189, 202, 293, 296, 300, 316, 321, 325.
Gregg, Alan 203, 229, 275, 276.
Guggenheim Foundation 303, 307.
Guttmacher, Manfred 200, 202, 203, 204, 210, 211, 216, 217, 251, 262.
Guyon, Rene 22, 119, 190, 191, 194, 221, 225, 226, 229, 231, 232, 234, 252, 261, 264, 265, 276, 280, 282, 289, 296, 298, 324, 326.

H

Haeberle, Erwin 43, 82, 170.
Haeckel, Ernst 49.
Halberstam, David 49.
Hall, Winfried Scott 2.
Hamilton, A.E. 296.
Hamon, John 296.
Happy Day v. Kentucky 172.
Hard core 243.
Harm 8, 43, 55, 70, 83, 115, 116, 128, 130, 132, 150, 151, 155, 156, 157, 158, 164, 169, 183, 184, 194, 213, 214, 215, 217, 224, 226, 227, 230, 232, 233, 236, 239, 240, 243, 246, 250, 252, 253, 254, 255, 265, 266, 272, 273, 290, 295, 318, 319.
Hartman, Carl 300.
Harvard 5, 11, 17, 56, 79, 198, 199, 200, 201, 205, 211, 244, 260, 297, 310.
Harvard Law Review 201.
Havighurst, Robert 134.
Health 2, 8, 30, 36, 49, 68, 123, 129, 133, 147, 169, 170, 174, 176, 177, 179, 180, 182, 282.
Healy, Jane 174.
Hefner, Christie 177.
Hefner, Hugh 83, 85, 102, 129, 177, 218.
Hermaphrodite 22.
Herpes 127, 128, 129, 131.
Heterosexual 81, 82, 90, 94, 96, 128, 129, 169, 172, 174, 175, 205, 206, 228, 233, 234, 235, 254, 255, 256, 258, 272, 282.
High School 1, 3, 4, 7, 11, 91, 92, 97, 98, 112, 114.
Hirschfeld, Magnus 21, 71, 161, 300.
Hitler 7, 183, 273, 280, 289, 301, 302, 303, 306, 308, 309, 310, 311, 318, 324, 326.
Hobbs, Albert 271.
Hoffecker, Pamela Hobbs 273.
Holmes, Oliver Wendell 199.
Home Sex 160.
Homosexual 3, 9, 10, 12, 19, 22, 31, 35, 42, 56, 57, 60, 68, 71, 75, 76, 77, 78, 81, 82, 87, 88, 89, 90, 91, 92, 93, 94, 95, 96, 97, 98, 99, 100, 101, 106, 111, 114, 117, 126, 129, 143, 158, 161, 169, 170, 172, 174, 175, 184, 192, 193, 196, 205, 206, 208, 209, 210, 211, 216, 218, 227, 228, 229, 231, 232, 233, 235, 236, 239, 243, 246, 253, 254, 255, 256, 257, 276, 277, 284, 285, 288, 300.
Homosexuality 8, 9, 31, 55, 56, 60, 90, 93, 94, 96, 103, 106, 118, 120, 122, 128, 160, 161, 172, 232, 253, 272, 279.
Honest 6, 7, 42, 56, 58, 60, 65, 90, 115, 133, 225, 229, 243, 260, 293, 334.
Human experiment 36, 293, 297, 305, 306, 321, 323, 325.
Human Sexuality 16, 17, 31, 32, 35, 44, 55, 65, 76, 81, 84, 86, 102, 112, 134, 148, 159, 160, 161, 170, 172, 173, 174, 175, 176, 178, 181, 204, 232, 254, 260, 263, 283, 287, 300, 316.
Husband 2, 30, 35, 77, 124, 127, 169, 182, 192, 216, 224, 249, 255, 294.
Hustler 75, 81, 82, 86, 101, 130, 131, 170, 237, 265.
Huxley, Aldous 5, 87, 298.
Huxley, Sir Julian 5.
Huxley, Sir Thomas 5.
Hygiene 20, 28, 36, 132, 133, 282, 301, 303, 324.
Hyman, Herbert 90, 112, 152, 153.
Hypocrisy 37, 285.

I

I Must Speak 2.
Illegal 35, 63, 71, 72, 78, 82, 85, 104, 130, 136, 137, 141, 148, 162, 177, 178, 179, 190, 228, 243, 247, 248, 250, 251, 255, 264, 266, 292, 319, 323.
Illegitimacy 119, 217, 218.

Illicit 50, 93, 94, 124, 126, 216, 217, 225, 245.
Impotence 76, 83, 122, 129.
Incest 79, 82, 88, 94, 99, 102, 103, 107, 116, 117, 126, 150, 151, 152, 156, 157, 158, 159, 160, 161, 165, 169, 171, 178, 179, 181, 182, 206, 210, 211, 215, 220, 224, 232, 233, 234, 235, 236, 265, 290, 295.
Indiana State Farm 50, 89.
Indiana University 4, 5, 7, 9, 14, 16, 17, 21, 24, 25, 26, 27, 29, 35, 40, 43, 44, 57, 67, 68, 70, 71, 73, 74, 78, 80, 82, 85, 90, 94, 96, 104, 106, 109, 118, 127, 130, 133, 134, 149, 152, 154, 156, 162, 163, 165, 170, 182, 183, 195, 203, 212, 213, 239, 241, 260, 261, 265, 266, 271, 286, 287, 290, 292, 293, 295, 299, 300, 305, 308, 309, 315, 316, 317, 325, 326.
Infant 63, 66, 67, 76, 78, 92, 109, 132, 133, 134, 135, 136, 139, 140, 143, 144, 148, 149, 150, 153, 163, 223, 224, 232, 290, 314, 315, 316, 319.
Inhibited 32, 117, 120, 121, 122, 126, 139, 160, 246.
Injury 107, 108, 115, 156, 201, 222, 243.
Inner circle 74, 200.
Institute for Sex Research 14, 42, 43, 68, 69, 78, 79, 81, 84, 86, 103, 120, 130, 147, 160, 180, 181, 182, 184, 229, 248, 262, 271, 290, 323.
Institute for Sexual Science 28.
Institute for the Advanced Study of Human Sexuality 32, 35, 76, 81, 86, 159, 170, 172, 176, 283.
Intent 63, 199, 201, 293.
Interview 4, 10, 12, 16, 18, 24, 25, 26, 27, 28, 29, 31, 32, 35, 41, 50, 51, 52, 53, 54, 56, 57, 58, 59, 60, 61, 62, 63, 64, 68, 71, 72, 74, 77, 88, 89, 90, 91, 92, 93, 94, 97, 98, 99, 106, 107, 109, 110, 111, 112, 113, 114, 118, 119, 120, 125, 126, 130, 135, 136, 137, 138, 140, 141, 146, 148, 149, 151, 152, 153, 154, 156, 158, 168, 182, 183, 213, 222, 230, 235, 245, 246, 253, 261, 263, 268, 273, 283, 290, 293, 294, 295, 296, 325.
Isherwood, Christopher 21.
Italy 279, 280, 281, 282, 283, 284, 285, 291, 296.

J

Jackson, Robert H. 314.
Japan 296.
Jealousy 41, 107, 158, 169.
Jewish 165, 183, 300, 303, 304, 305, 314, 319, 321.
Joe College 101, 218, 219.
Johns Hopkins 79, 263, 295, 306, 307, 319.
Joint Chiefs of Staff 259.
Jones, E. Michael 13, 275.
Jones, James 4, 7, 18, 24, 29, 35, 51, 72, 77, 80, 102, 135, 162, 163, 164, 269, 271, 275, 287, 303.
Journal of Paedophilia 79, 172, 173, 176, 184.
Journalism 39, 127, 313.
Judges 99, 118, 188, 193, 195, 198, 199, 202, 211, 216, 225, 228, 229, 244, 245, 250, 261, 279, 336.

K

Kaiser Wilhelm Brain Institute 302, 308, 325.
Karlen, Arno 52, 68.
Keller, Helen 2.
Kemeny, Margaret 174.
Kennedy, John F. 4, 314.
King, Rex 135, 136, 137, 138, 140, 143, 144, 145, 147, 148, 154, 155, 157, 162, 163, 164, 168.
Kinsey, Clara 7, 11, 12, 64, 77, 126, 127, 277.
Kinsey Era 118, 128, 217, 222, 223, 336.
Kinsey Institute 5, 8, 13, 14, 16, 17, 21, 23, 35, 43, 52, 59, 62, 63, 64, 70, 75, 76, 77, 78, 80, 81, 84, 85, 86, 102, 104, 122, 127, 130, 132, 136, 139, 142, 144, 145, 151, 152, 157, 158, 159, 160, 161, 162, 163, 164, 166, 168, 170, 176, 179, 180, 182, 183, 193, 194, 204, 228, 235, 239, 242, 245, 246, 258, 260, 263, 266, 267, 280, 285, 287, 289, 291, 292, 293, 294, 295, 315, 319, 322, 323, 326, 334, 335.
Kinsey Scale 90, 96, 205, 254, 256, 258.
Kinsey Today 84, 86.
Kirkendall, Lester 149.
Kohlberg, Lawrence 133.
Koshland, Daniel E. 260.
Kroger, William 117.
Kronhausen, Eberhard 100, 101, 105, 218, 221, 264.
Krupp, Fritz 292, 310.

L

Laboratory 36, 71, 72, 75, 79, 81, 92, 99, 133, 149, 164, 241, 262, 293, 297, 303, 306, 307, 308, 310, 317, 320, 325.
Landis, Judson 110.
Landis, William 279.
Langdell, Christopher Columbus 198, 199, 232.
Language 32, 56, 65, 66, 144, 181, 184, 194, 195, 197, 229, 250, 277, 322, 334.
Latency 70, 133, 149.
Law 1, 23, 41, 42, 50, 57, 63, 66, 82, 83, 84, 87, 88, 91, 99, 101, 102, 109, 110, 115, 116, 117, 119, 137, 154, 157, 159, 164, 168, 169, 180, 187, 188, 189, 190, 191, 192, 193, 194, 195, 196, 197, 198, 232, 277, 292.
Law of strength 174.
Lawyers 78, 99, 188, 204, 205, 216, 223, 225, 229, 246, 247.
Legal 71, 72, 92, 109, 110, 132, 187, 188, 189, 190, 191, 192, 194, 195, 196, 197, 198, 199, 200, 201, 202, 203, 204, 205, 206, 214, 216, 217, 221, 223, 224, 228, 229, 231, 232, 234, 236, 237, 239, 240, 242, 243, 244, 245, 246, 247, 248, 249, 250, 251, 254, 255, 256, 260, 261, 262, 263, 264, 265, 271, 278, 311, 314, 317, 332, 334.
Legislation 1, 88, 130, 178, 189, 195, 201, 203, 206, 209, 210, 211, 218, 238, 256, 262.
Legislative issues 215.
Legislatures 1, 195, 202, 211, 212, 223, 232.
Legman, Gershon 122, 280.
Leningrad 307.
Lenz, Fritz 303, 305.
Libido 120, 124, 125, 149, 187, 222.
Library 6, 7, 14, 16, 80, 81, 84, 122, 127, 179, 237, 261, 266, 276, 285, 312, 324.
Lightened 211, 217.
Lincoln 84, 238.
Lincoln, Abraham 84.
Loeb, Jacque 199, 297.
Love 2, 5, 6, 16, 19, 20, 31, 34, 43, 49, 65, 66, 67, 76, 87, 101, 102, 111, 121, 124, 125, 129, 137, 151, 160, 173, 176, 179, 197, 217, 219, 221, 224, 239, 241, 244, 263, 301, 302, 316, 324.
Low characters 41, 89.
Ludlow Massacre 269.
Lynch, Gary 83, 173.

M

Malinowski, Bronislow 71.
Mammalian females 121.
Mandler, George 34.
Manifesto of Nudism 6.
Marcuse, Herbert 289.
Marijuana 82, 120, 253.
Mark, Vernon 79.
Marriage 1, 2, 9, 11, 12, 16, 17, 18, 21, 23, 24, 25, 26, 27, 28, 31, 66, 67, 83, 87, 88, 101, 109, 110, 117, 120, 121, 122, 123, 124, 129, 132, 151, 158, 169, 179, 180, 187, 188, 189, 190, 196, 202, 206, 208, 216, 217, 218, 219, 220, 221, 224, 225, 226, 227, 231, 246, 248, 249, 250, 254, 255, 277, 288, 296.
Marriage Course 16, 17, 18, 23, 25, 26, 27, 28.
Married 6, 7, 9, 12, 17, 18, 30, 31, 54, 65, 66, 102, 103, 106, 109, 110, 115, 116, 117, 119, 120, 121, 125, 126, 128, 180, 184, 216, 218, 223, 226, 231, 246, 247, 248, 249, 250, 255, 264.
Marsh, Earle 296.
Martin, Clyde 19, 30, 31, 40, 51, 52, 77, 90, 164, 170, 172, 275.
Marxism 193, 307.
Maslow, Abraham 55, 112, 113, 114, 124, 125, 134, 205.
Masochism 82, 126, 180.
Mass Media 37, 38, 39, 44, 173, 237, 311, 323.
Mass sterilization 5, 269, 298.
Masters 72, 119, 134, 168, 176, 181, 182, 183, 205, 253, 322.
Masters and Johnson 72, 176, 182, 205.
Masturbation 8, 10, 24, 32, 55, 61, 65, 70, 73, 83, 103, 113, 114, 120, 123, 134, 137, 138, 146, 153, 169, 178, 179, 193, 231, 253, 254, 257, 285, 287, 288, 292, 296, 335.

Material 4, 8, 13, 17, 19, 20, 29, 31, 49, 63, 68, 70, 73, 79, 81, 90, 95, 108, 114, 116, 123, 129, 132, 136, 137, 145, 147, 148, 150, 158, 161, 162, 163, 166, 167, 168, 176, 177, 178, 179, 191, 194, 232, 236, 237, 238, 239, 240, 242, 243, 244, 245, 261, 265, 266, 304, 307.
Maudsley Hospital 279.
McCloy, John J. 313.
McIlvenna, Ted 170, 179.
McIntosh, Millicent C. 123.
Mead, Margaret 28, 71.
Measure 55, 61, 120, 121.
Media 37, 38, 39, 101, 179, 196, 212, 229, 234, 237, 241.
Medical 2, 12, 27, 28, 29, 32, 37, 38, 39, 49, 79, 213, 214, 215, 217, 226, 236, 246, 247, 250, 251, 252, 254.
Mengele, Josef 305.
Menninger, Karl Augustus 71.
Menopause 125.
Method 53, 54, 56, 59, 60, 63, 71, 161, 168, 275.
Mexico 9, 10, 13, 20, 277.
Miksche, Mike 75.
Military 16, 153, 169, 172, 258, 259, 326.
Military law 259.
Ministers 62, 169, 174, 194, 229.
Misinformation 28.
Misogynist 26, 122, 218, 225.
Model Penal Code 187, 188, 189, 196, 199, 200, 202, 203, 211, 215, 216, 218, 228, 232, 235, 242, 247, 260, 261, 267, 277, 279, 317, 328, 336.
Modern science 201.
Moe, Henry Allen 303.
Molestation 66, 89, 137, 138, 147, 149, 150, 155, 156, 158, 213, 215, 221, 235.
Money, John 79, 170, 172.
Monogamous 37.
Moore, Carl 296.
Moral 2, 4, 8, 14, 18, 29, 31, 36, 37, 42, 56, 71, 78, 83, 84, 101, 102, 123, 124, 134, 165, 168, 175, 177, 191, 193, 196, 197, 200, 201, 202, 203, 204, 205, 215, 217, 218, 221, 225, 227, 228, 231, 234, 238, 241, 242, 243, 250, 252, 255, 258, 259, 263, 264, 268, 272, 276, 280, 282, 288, 301, 310, 316, 317, 321, 322, 323, 325, 329, 331, 332.
Morison, Robert 297.
Moscow Institute for Genetics 307.
Mother 2, 3, 11, 25, 32, 66, 87, 102, 103, 106, 107, 108, 110, 125, 129, 145, 147, 154, 155, 158, 160, 216, 218, 219, 220, 234, 262, 266, 279, 300, 304, 315, 316, 326.
Mowrer, Harriet R. 55.
Mr. Man 9, 16, 17, 18, 95.
Mr. X 135, 146, 162, 163, 164.
Mr. Y 76, 126.
Mueller, Kate 26, 106, 305, 308.
Muller, Hermann J. 297.
Murder 64, 119, 120, 164, 165, 167, 168, 212, 213, 214, 215, 223, 228, 253, 294, 295, 306, 308, 310, 323.

N

Naples 282, 284, 291.
National Endowment for the Humanities 84.
National Institute for Mental Health 179, 260.
National Research Council 28, 29, 43, 55, 64, 68, 103, 105, 170, 193, 213, 227, 261, 271, 275, 299, 304, 336.
National Sex & Drug Forum 170.
National Student League 300.
Nature library 7, 127, 266, 285.
Nazi 21, 39, 43, 132, 137, 164, 165, 166, 168, 199, 273, 301, 302, 303, 304, 305, 306, 307, 308, 311, 312, 313, 314, 315, 316, 317, 318, 320, 324, 328, 332.
Nazi war criminals 199.
Negro 92, 116, 118, 119, 253, 293.
Neurochemical 83, 174, 237.
New Biology 5, 169, 170, 171, 173, 199, 296, 297, 300, 302, 310, 314.
Nightgown 61, 126.
No-Fault 209, 217, 218, 219, 220, 221, 288.
Nobile, Philip 160.

INDEX
339

Normal 23, 25, 36, 41, 42, 43, 49, 50, 56, 57, 59, 60, 65, 75, 83, 88, 89, 93, 94, 97, 99, 102, 106, 107, 108, 109, 110, 112, 115, 116, 121, 123, 124, 125, 126, 127, 133, 134, 138, 141, 145, 148, 150, 157, 159, 160, 161, 180, 181, 183, 190, 191, 196, 212, 214, 215, 221, 223, 224, 225, 226, 227, 228, 231, 232, 233, 235, 236, 239, 244, 245, 246, 248, 249, 252, 253, 254, 255, 256, 258, 265, 266, 272, 298, 320, 326, 334, 335.
Norway 263, 278, 281.
Nude 6, 7, 9, 10, 12, 19, 20, 82, 114, 124, 125, 126, 127, 155, 170, 173, 180, 226, 243, 279, 284, 301.
Nudity 7, 126, 226, 237, 242, 244.
Nuremberg 199, 310, 311, 314, 315.
Nüremberg Doctors Trial 304.
Nyiszli, Miklos 305.

O

Obedience 33, 134.
Objective 6, 10, 17, 20, 29, 35, 41, 56, 84, 134, 156, 176, 184, 191, 202, 220, 226, 243, 269, 295, 311.
Obscenity 2, 13, 79, 80, 81, 83, 84, 86, 87, 115, 119, 122, 129, 171, 184, 192, 193, 205, 208, 210, 216, 222, 228, 233, 237, 238, 239, 240, 242, 243, 244, 252, 256, 261, 266, 267, 279, 288, 289.
Observation 35, 50, 60, 62, 71, 72, 79, 92, 129, 134, 140, 141, 144, 147, 148, 150, 151, 152, 153, 198, 226, 252, 267, 282.
Observers 63, 99, 134, 139, 141, 142, 145, 147, 148, 149, 150, 181, 280, 292, 293, 294, 295, 297, 316.
Obsession 4, 6, 33, 36, 72, 84, 122, 212, 254, 266, 280, 284, 296.
Occupation 10, 51, 78, 85, 92, 93, 114, 166, 313, 314, 332.
Offender 41, 50, 52, 56, 68, 76, 89, 91, 92, 96, 97, 106, 114, 115, 116, 118, 130, 150, 156, 158, 159, 164, 189, 190, 192, 193, 194, 196, 200, 201, 202, 204, 206, 211, 212, 213, 214, 215, 219, 222, 223, 225, 226, 227, 228, 229, 230, 232, 234, 235, 245, 246, 255, 264, 265.
Offermann, Carlos 304.
Office of Research Services 177, 179.
Office of Strategic Services 39.
Office of War Information 39, 313.
Ohio State University 11, 182.
Old Testament 13, 197.
Onset of puberty 234.
Opponents 40, 42.
Opportunities 72, 81, 304, 306, 307, 318.
Orchitis 14, 282, 286, 287.
Outlaw 84, 90.
Outlets 16, 106, 123, 158, 169, 192, 199, 272, 323.

P

Parasites 190, 282.
Parents 2, 3, 12, 26, 60, 61, 62, 63, 78, 92, 102, 103, 117, 118, 154, 158, 159, 177, 194, 213, 220, 222, 226, 227, 228, 233, 241, 263, 272, 295.
Parole 118, 212, 213, 214, 215, 227, 229, 288.
Participate 38, 57, 67, 74, 78, 82, 113, 142, 170, 178, 310.
Partner 9, 15, 16, 19, 39, 65, 66, 71, 72, 75, 76, 77, 93, 96, 107, 110, 121, 147, 150, 151, 156, 157, 179, 205, 218, 246, 258, 265, 268, 313.
Passion 36, 41, 66, 80, 126, 166, 201, 328.
Pavlov, Ivan Petrovich 5, 29, 34.
Peak 122, 151, 224.
Pederast 8, 9, 19, 21, 31, 89, 137, 233, 284, 301, 310.
Pederasty 126, 233, 253, 310.
Pedophile 21, 22, 24, 31, 64, 77, 89, 101, 117, 119, 120, 122, 135, 136, 137, 141, 142, 144, 145, 149, 150, 154, 157, 163, 164, 165, 168, 172, 173, 176, 180, 184, 190, 195, 196, 211, 213, 226, 233, 236, 252, 260, 264, 278, 280, 293, 294, 295, 296, 301, 317, 320, 326, 328.
Pedophilia 57, 162, 172, 180, 184, 233, 235, 236, 237.
Penetration 235, 243, 253.
Penthouse mii, xix, xx, xvi, xxiii, 101, 130, 159, 160, 170, 175, 182, 237, 265.
Peru 14, 277, 286.
Perversion 57, 100, 110, 116, 121, 122, 126, 190, 246, 255, 279, 285, 334.

Physicians 79, 122, 143, 149, 246, 247, 250, 251, 257, 297, 305, 306, 319, 325.
Pilpel, Harriet 203.
Pimps 78, 85, 93, 97, 110.
Pioneer 9, 10, 21, 24, 44, 82, 168, 170, 175, 194, 199, 221, 230, 237, 253, 293, 296, 328.
Planned Parenthood 71, 111, 149, 176, 177, 180, 184, 192, 193, 202, 246, 247, 248, 249, 250, 251, 267, 323.
Playboy 76, 83, 84, 85, 101, 102, 117, 122, 129, 170, 176, 177, 178, 179, 180, 218, 237, 246, 258, 265, 266.
Ploscowe, Morris 88, 189, 190, 204, 210, 216, 223, 230, 235, 265.
Pneumonia 285, 287.
Polatin, Philip 296.
Pomeroy, Wardell 1, 3, 30, 64, 70, 76, 77, 78, 81, 87, 111, 134, 136, 137, 138, 139, 141, 147, 150, 156, 159, 160, 162, 163, 164, 170, 171, 172, 174, 179, 182, 257, 277.
Pornography 7, 63, 79, 81, 82, 83, 84, 85, 102, 103, 111, 129, 130, 149, 158, 159, 169, 170, 171, 175, 176, 177, 178, 180, 184, 228, 237, 239, 240, 243, 244, 245, 266, 267, 278, 301.
Portugal 285.
Positivism 198.
Posner, Richard 205.
Pound, Roscoe 198.
Power 16, 30, 35, 44, 71, 84, 165, 202, 219, 241, 262, 270, 275, 276, 297, 316, 317, 321, 325, 332.
Pre-Kinsey 103, 110, 193, 215, 218, 220, 222, 254.
Preadolescent 9, 61, 62, 65, 108, 118, 135, 146, 163, 292, 294.
Pregnancy 107, 119, 120, 121, 158, 209, 220, 247, 248, 249, 250, 251, 252, 253, 267, 290.
Premarital 31, 87, 88, 101, 103, 107, 110, 114, 121, 124, 128, 193, 219, 230, 247, 250, 252, 272, 273, 278, 288.
Primitive 28, 79, 121, 226, 261, 310, 320.
Prison 41, 45, 50, 51, 52, 60, 64, 81, 87, 89, 90, 91, 95, 96, 98, 99, 100, 101, 108, 115, 116, 118, 160, 193, 212, 215, 225, 227, 228, 234, 235, 251, 277, 279, 294, 297, 305, 307, 317, 319, 320, 325, 329, 334.
Privacy 28, 35, 74, 75, 149, 195, 209, 210, 214, 215, 241, 255.
Procreation 107, 202, 300, 317.
Prohibition 2, 14, 88, 122, 131, 194, 210, 211, 217, 225.
Prok 32, 33, 34, 73, 280.
Promiscuity 1, 55, 101, 107, 110, 158.
Promiscuous 28, 65, 107, 121, 202, 217, 218, 219, 220, 222, 241, 262, 265, 278, 282, 328.
Promotional timetable 37.
Propaganda 13, 14, 39, 66, 165, 272, 301, 309, 312, 314, 316.
Prostitutes 31, 65, 72, 77, 81, 85, 87, 89, 93, 106, 110, 114, 115, 116, 117, 119, 120, 127, 171, 176, 184, 211, 251, 252, 253, 264, 282, 284, 285, 301, 333, 335.
Prostitution 1, 2, 28, 81, 82, 88, 93, 94, 116, 117, 118, 119, 120, 122, 158, 171, 180, 210, 212, 227, 228, 229, 231, 242, 252, 253, 254, 255, 256, 262, 264, 267, 278, 282, 283, 290, 324.
Proving the answer 60.
Prudery 1, 12, 41.
Prurient 239, 242, 243, 276.
Psychiatric 117, 201, 255, 295, 300, 306, 318, 321.
Psychiatrists 62, 117, 150, 212, 216, 246, 257, 259, 272, 306, 317, 325, 326.
Psychological Warfare 39, 202, 262, 313, 323, 326.
Psychologists 7, 41, 62, 160, 174, 178, 214, 229, 257.
Psychology 5, 29, 32, 34, 43, 56, 68, 99, 101, 130, 174, 181, 201, 204, 206, 207, 261, 265, 291, 324.
Psychopathic 168, 200, 256, 257.
Public 30, 35, 36, 37, 38, 39, 41, 70, 72, 74, 84, 151, 155, 158, 163, 187, 188, 189, 197, 202, 204, 205, 206, 207, 210, 212, 214, 215, 218, 220, 229, 236, 237, 238, 240, 241, 242, 243, 245, 248, 250, 252, 259, 260, 261, 262, 263, 264, 266, 272, 289.
Public relations 35, 38, 313.
Pudor, Heinrich 7.
Puritan 224, 231, 271, 288, 290, 334.
Purity Movement 1, 2, 21, 122, 196, 197, 203, 212.

Q

Quigley, Carroll 269.

R

Ramsey, Glenn 91, 92.
Rand Study 172, 258, 259.
Random sample 27, 54, 160.
Rape 3, 50, 65, 66, 89, 96, 103, 107, 115, 116, 121, 126, 136, 169, 207, 208, 209, 212, 213, 214, 215, 220, 221, 222, 223, 224, 226, 227, 228, 229, 230, 232, 234, 235, 243, 250, 263, 264, 265, 288, 290.
Rape crisis centers 215.
Reagan, Ronald 212, 263.
Recall 59, 60, 72, 75, 80, 153, 222, 226, 229, 230, 234, 260.
Recidivism 215, 227, 230, 233, 235, 265.
Recollections 153.
Red Queen 65.
Reece, Carroll B. 269.
Reich, Wilhelm 301.
Reinisch, June 16, 52, 63, 159, 161, 162, 287, 293.
Reisman, David 31.
Reisman, Judith 64, 138, 143, 273.
Religion 13, 51, 90, 95, 106, 122, 152, 196, 197, 199, 207, 208, 210, 219, 262, 275, 298, 321, 322, 330, 331.
Remoter threats 201.
Repression 1, 3, 22, 23, 100, 192, 212, 220, 231, 252, 284.
Reputations 12, 84, 92, 94, 159, 196, 290, 293.
Resent 32, 33, 283.
Retakes 60.
Revolutionary 16, 49, 83, 93, 120, 228, 231, 236, 239, 255, 259, 273, 279, 301.
Rice, Thurman 27.
Roaring 20s 3.
Robber Barons 269.
Robinson, Paul 9, 60, 83.
Rockefeller Foundation 18, 24, 28, 29, 30, 35, 37, 38, 40, 53, 55, 80, 92, 127, 153, 156, 170, 188, 196, 200, 202, 203, 204, 210, 211, 213, 221, 229, 269, 270, 271, 273, 275, 276, 277, 293, 296, 297, 298, 299, 300, 302, 304, 307, 309, 311, 312, 313, 314, 326.
Rome 13, 284.
Rudin, Ernst 303.
Rusk, Dean 277.
Russia 165, 289, 296, 298, 307, 308, 309, 316, 318, 320, 325.

S

Sadism 75, 76, 82, 94, 126, 160, 180, 236, 237.
Sadist 76, 279.
Sakoda, James M. 113, 114.
Sample 27, 44, 45, 50, 52, 53, 55, 56, 59, 60, 64, 66, 88, 89, 90, 92, 93, 95, 96, 97, 98, 100, 101, 108, 109, 111, 112, 113, 114, 115, 116, 117, 118, 123, 125, 128, 138, 151, 152, 153, 155, 156, 157, 159, 160, 176, 234, 235, 246, 248, 250, 256, 268, 295.
Sanders, Stephanie 13.
Sanger, Margaret 71, 202.
Saunders, W.B. 39, 237.
Scandinavia 277, 278, 285.
Schwartz, Louis 171, 175, 188, 202, 203, 211, 215, 216, 217.
Science 5, 11, 13, 24, 28, 30, 36, 37, 38, 39, 41, 42, 43, 44, 49, 52, 53, 56, 63, 66, 67, 68, 69, 71, 74, 129, 131, 143, 154, 158, 161, 172, 180, 183, 184, 189, 190, 193, 194, 196, 198, 199, 201, 202, 203, 204, 205, 206, 210, 211, 224, 232, 233, 239, 248, 250, 252, 254, 260, 262, 263, 271, 273, 275, 276, 288, 289, 290, 292, 295, 305, 307, 308, 311, 312, 313, 314, 317, 321, 322, 323, 324, 325, 326, 334, 336.
Science Citation Index 205, 211, 263.
Scientific Humanitarian Committee 22, 28.
Scientifically Trained 63, 149, 150, 158, 163, 292, 294, 295, 326.
Scientomania 36, 37, 53.
Secrecy 31, 63, 70, 74, 161, 189.
Seduction 167, 192, 211, 212, 217, 221, 246, 254, 302, 329, 332.
Self-Esteem 68, 113, 124.
Sex and Drug Forum 81.

Sex behavior 29, 72.
Sex Crime 50, 63, 65, 81, 88, 93, 99, 102, 163, 195, 201, 210, 212, 214, 215, 223, 228, 230, 233, 235, 236, 263, 265, 266, 288, 292, 331, 333, 336.
Sex educators 32, 81, 178.
Sex experiment 92, 164, 263, 293, 309.
Sex Histories 12, 35, 40, 56, 88, 91, 100, 105, 119, 160, 218, 252, 264.
Sex Information and Education Council of the Unite 111, 149, 171, 176, 177, 178, 179, 180, 181, 184, 193, 239, 246, 250, 261, 266, 290.
Sex laws 23, 188, 191, 192, 196, 224, 232, 242, 245, 246, 265, 278.
Sex murder 165, 168, 213, 295.
Sex Offender 41, 50, 52, 56, 89, 91, 93, 95, 96, 104, 106, 114, 115, 118, 171, 189, 194, 196, 200, 206, 211, 212, 213, 219, 225, 226, 228, 229, 230, 232, 235, 246, 265, 277, 294, 295, 328.
Sex play 57, 60, 62, 66, 121, 143, 229, 230.
Sex Research 14, 17, 22, 23, 24, 25, 28, 30, 36, 42, 43, 52, 60, 68, 69, 70, 72, 78, 79, 81, 86, 103, 113, 120, 130, 134, 147, 160, 164, 168, 170, 174, 176, 180, 181, 182, 184, 202, 204, 205, 229, 248, 262, 267, 268, 271, 273, 277, 290, 296, 323, 333, 334.
Sex Science 52, 63, 161, 203, 233, 239, 317, 336.
Sex Therapy 79, 81, 134, 141, 142, 171, 176, 181, 183, 257, 263, 322.
Sexologists 32, 79, 82, 120, 134, 149, 151, 168, 174, 176, 236, 242, 334.
Sexology 13, 21, 23, 34, 43, 63, 67, 81, 82, 122, 139, 147, 149, 170, 173, 174, 175, 180, 184, 222, 260, 263, 264, 298, 299, 300, 319, 324, 334.
Sexual Abuse 8, 15, 78, 86, 94, 99, 104, 107, 116, 117, 118, 137, 143, 151, 156, 157, 158, 159, 182, 184, 206, 207, 208, 210, 227, 230, 235, 236, 242, 251, 263, 273, 290, 323.
Sexual activity 8, 22, 28, 33, 35, 56, 57, 70, 74, 81, 93, 95, 110, 115, 117, 121, 123, 125, 127, 132, 133, 137, 151, 162, 175, 179, 201, 202, 211, 225, 228, 233, 250, 252, 265, 276, 284, 286, 294.
Sexual Attitude Restructuring (SAR) 82, 172, 173, 174, 175.
Sexual Behavior 1, 2, 3, 13, 15, 17, 18, 27, 28, 29, 31, 36, 37, 42, 44, 49, 50, 54, 55, 56, 57, 59, 60, 62, 64, 66, 68, 69, 72, 77, 79, 81, 82, 87, 89, 92, 94, 95, 100, 103, 104, 105, 106, 109, 110, 113, 114, 116, 119, 121, 125, 128, 129, 130, 132, 150, 156, 161, 164, 175, 179, 180, 182, 183, 189, 190, 191, 192, 193, 194, 195, 200, 213, 216, 224, 240, 241, 245, 246, 247, 248, 249, 251, 253, 255, 257, 258, 261, 264, 267, 271, 272, 273, 285, 292, 322, 334.
Sexual conduct 39, 43, 102, 103, 107, 161, 169, 190, 209, 212, 223, 225, 227, 242, 262, 265, 266, 272.
Sexual contact 9, 63, 70, 155, 182, 225, 234, 245, 268, 284, 294.
Sexual ethic 226, 232.
Sexual experiments 71, 76, 78, 151, 294, 323.
Sexual Freedom 264.
Sexual freedom 24, 119, 127, 231, 264, 282, 284, 303.
Sexual from birth 7, 133, 148, 169, 224, 225, 233.
Sexual Harassment 208.
Sexual harassment 28.
Sexual history 42, 56, 60, 276.
Sexual privacy 35.
Sexual secrets 40.
Sexually transmitted diseases 119, 163, 252, 282, 285.
Sheatsley, Paul 152, 153.
Shields, Francis 296.
Shorts 3, 18, 19.
Simon, William 52, 170.
Simpson, Christopher 38, 39, 202, 311.
Skinner, B.F. 29.
Slightest penetration 235.
Smith, Linnea 79.
Social disorder 13.
Society for the Scientific Study of Sex 174.
Sodomy 60, 65, 88, 92, 94, 101, 103, 104, 114, 116, 117, 120, 126, 127, 128, 169, 172, 174, 175, 176, 179, 192, 209, 236, 237, 245, 253, 254, 255, 256, 258, 259, 283, 288, 289.
Soliciting 26, 89, 181, 224, 309, 323.
Solzhenitsyn, Alexander 307.
Soundproofing 75.

Soviet 297, 307, 308.
Spain 285.
Sperm 63, 77, 137, 145, 147, 164, 295, 298, 299, 300, 309, 323.
Spontaneous 37, 249.
Sproul, Robert 80.
Statistical 16, 24, 30, 37, 40, 51, 52, 53, 54, 55, 56, 60, 61, 62, 66, 88, 89, 93, 110, 113, 114, 116, 122, 123, 163, 180, 216, 231, 233, 236, 248, 255, 275, 294, 325.
Statutory rape 50, 89, 209, 222, 224, 230, 235.
Stevens, Christopher 6.
Stevens Institute of Technology 3.
Stone, Abraham 296.
Storm Trooper 165, 301, 325.
Stream of the Law 198.
Stream of the law 192, 195, 196, 198, 232.
Subjects 5, 9, 24, 39, 41, 50, 51, 52, 55, 56, 57, 58, 59, 60, 62, 65, 67, 70, 71, 72, 73, 77, 79, 88, 89, 90, 91, 92, 95, 96, 97, 99, 107, 108, 110, 113, 114, 117, 120, 123, 124, 126, 132, 134, 135, 140, 142, 145, 147, 150, 151, 153, 157, 158, 163, 164, 173, 192, 195, 200, 203, 212, 234, 245, 248, 292, 293, 294, 297, 315, 316, 319, 323, 326.
Surrogates 81, 171, 176.
Sweden 263, 278, 281.

T

Taboo 59, 159, 160, 161, 169, 178, 183, 184, 257.
Taboos 226.
Tappan, Paul 202, 204, 210, 211, 217
Tate, Tim 168, 183.
Tax-exempt foundations 38, 39, 203, 211, 269, 270, 274, 275, 290, 305, 323.
Teacher 229, 256.
Technically trained 99, 134, 139, 141, 280, 292, 294, 295.
Technically trained observers 142, 145, 292, 293.
Ten Commandments 197, 289.
Ten Words 197.
Terman, Lewis 58, 89.
The Advocate 75, 85, 131.
The Lancet 49, 50, 68.
The rule of law 198.
Three Wise Men 275.
Tightly knit 31.
Torture 21, 75, 213, 243, 297, 314, 325.
Tortures 308.
Trained observers 134, 141, 142, 147, 149, 150, 232, 280, 292, 293, 295, 297, 316.
Transvestite 22, 301.
Trauma 83, 105, 116, 149, 178, 234, 286, 287, 290, 301.
Trilling, Lionel 53.
Trimmer, Eric 64.
Tripp, Clarence 72, 73, 137, 138, 143, 155, 163, 164.
Truman, Harry S. 273, 309.
Trustees 275.
Tsarapkin, Sergei Rotianovich 308.
Turin girl 282, 283.

U

U.S. Congress 173, 259, 269.
U.S. population 64, 66, 89, 112, 249, 264.
U.S. v. Roth 239.
Uncle Kinsey 61, 63, 154.
Uncle Pomeroy 61.
Unconventional 56, 60, 106, 110, 113, 114, 115, 117, 124.
Underworld 58, 65, 92, 93, 97, 119, 252.
United Nations 5, 63, 264.
United States Supreme Court 169, 202, 237, 239, 242.
Unlimited 36.

V

Vatican 13, 14.
Venereal disease 2, 103, 107, 119, 122, 127, 128, 131, 132, 158, 169, 217, 218, 252, 282, 287, 288, 290, 294.
Vice 122.
Victim 33, 34, 37, 76, 83, 92, 96, 105, 115, 116, 118, 127, 136, 155, 156, 157, 158, 181, 208, 214, 215, 222, 223, 227, 229, 232, 234, 276, 308, 326, 328.
Victimized 150, 155, 158, 221, 226, 319, 321, 325.

Victimless crime 215, 217, 226, 228, 229, 264.
Victims 33, 107, 135, 140, 144, 155, 156, 157, 204, 206, 212, 213, 214, 217, 222, 227, 229, 230, 231, 232, 235, 263, 284, 290, 323, 324, 331.
Victorian 1, 12, 22, 41, 83, 192, 241, 288.
Vidal, Gore 92, 276.
Viereck, George Sylvester 165, 280.
Vigeland, Adolph Gustav 278.
Violence 81, 83, 101, 119, 130, 131, 174, 209, 215, 223, 229, 236, 237, 265, 266.
Virgin 61, 101, 102, 113, 114, 180, 217, 218.
Virginity 55, 101, 113, 180, 219, 221.
Virtuous women 1.
Volunteer 35, 50, 55, 56, 70, 74, 77, 91, 92, 96, 113, 114, 115, 124, 125, 127, 130, 210.
Von Vershuer, Freiherr 304.
Voris, Ralph 9, 17, 20, 33.
Voyeur 73.

W

Wallis, Allen 37, 51, 98, 275.
Wandervogel 21.
Wasps 5, 17, 18, 19, 24, 25, 27, 39.
Watson, J.B. 29, 34.
Weaver, Warren 24, 40, 53, 80, 89, 275.
Wechsler, Herbert 215.
Wells, Herman 18, 25, 90, 167.
Westlaw 205, 211
White, Esther 151, 157, 181, 182.
White Slave Trade 1.
Widowed 109, 249.
Wife 16, 19, 20, 26, 29, 35, 42, 71, 74, 77, 85, 124, 129, 288.
Wives 71, 74, 77, 83, 103, 106, 115, 124, 128, 158, 176.
Wolfenden Report 204, 279.
Wolfgang and Figlio 215.
Women and children 35, 83, 210, 211, 215, 217, 221, 225, 231, 254, 269, 278.
Woodward, Bob 243.
Words 54, 58, 59, 65, 66.
Workplace 74, 207, 209, 236.
World War II 38, 39, 284, 297.
Wormser, Rene A. 270.
Wylie Hall 71, 74, 286.

Y

Yale Law School 244.
Yerkes, Robert M. 28, 275.
YMCA 6, 10.
Yorkshire Television 4, 10, 24, 29, 35, 41, 72, 86, 94, 111, 135, 137, 140, 143, 144, 148, 151, 152, 154, 162, 164, 165, 166, 168, 181, 245, 250, 267.
Youths 6, 19, 21, 22, 25, 96, 104, 120, 177, 230, 233, 235, 236.
You've Changed the Combination!!! 180.

Photo Credit: Sherrie Buzby

Judith A. Reisman, Ph.D.

Dr. Judith Reisman received her Ph.D. from Case Western Reserve University. Dr. Reisman's advice and analysis is sought the world over to lecture, testify and counsel organizations, parliaments, legislatures and courts. She conducts content analysis studies of written and visual media. The special emphasis of Dr. Reisman's work has been, and continues to be, the influence of these media upon the health and well-being of children.

Dr. Reisman is a Visiting Professor of Law, Liberty University School of Law, and president of The Institute for Media Education. An author and lecturer, Dr. Reisman has been a consultant to three U.S. Departments of Justice administrations; Education; and Health and Human Services. Dr. Reisman has consulted with members of the U.S. Joint Chiefs of Staff and is listed in numerous Who's Who biographies such as; *Who's Who in Science & Engineering, International Who's Who in Education, International Who's Who in Sexology, Who's Who of American Women, The World's Who's Who of Women,* etc. Dr. Reisman's scholarly discoveries have had international legislative and scientific import, e.g., *The German Medical Tribune* and the British medical journal, *The Lancet* demanded Kinsey's reports be investigated, saying that in her previous book:

> *Dr. Judith A. Reisman and her colleagues demolish the foundations of the two reports . . . Kinsey . . . has left his former co-workers some explaining to do.*
> **The Lancet,** (Vol. 337: March 2, 1991; 547)

To schedule Dr. Reisman for speaking, consulting and to order books and research materials, please visit her website:
DrJudithReisman.com

View several documentaries on Kinsey, featuring Dr. Reisman's work at:
DrJudithReisman.com/video